Frommer's®

South Africa

My South Africa

by Pippa de Bruyn

WHEN I LIE ON THE WHITE SANDS OF CAMPS BAY BEACH, MY BACK TO the soothing murmur of the Atlantic, and gaze up at the imposing peaks of the Twelve Apostles, I experience a feeling of deep gratitude that this is home.

Years ago, having fallen for a farmer's son in England, I thought to leave, but I insisted that he first see the country of my birth, from the top of Table Mountain to the meandering rivers of the Kruger National Park. And here we are, 12 years later, happy to be surrounded by such beauty, augmented with other luxuries like affordable fine wines, world-class restaurants, and a flourishing economy.

Peace of mind, however, is a commodity that South Africans have in short supply. Crime is a concern, and—given the relative youth of our democracy—political stability is not assured. But this is Africa, not for the lily-livered. It is a place where predators roam, where rivers are swollen with hippos, and plains host enormous herds of antelope and elephants. It is a wild country, with immense poverty and pockets of unparalleled luxury. I have traveled the length and breadth of South Africa, and worked for almost a decade on the guidebook you hold in your hands. I hope the photos and the information contained here will help ignite your own grand affair with my country.

What are we waiting for?

An essential part of any Cape Town itinerary is driving (or cycling) **CHAPMAN'S PEAK DRIVE (left)**, preferably as the sun starts to sink into the Atlantic Ocean. Built between 1915 and 1922, this winding road—backdrop to hundreds of international car commercials—is the country's most spectacular, with cliffs plunging down to crashing waves, and peaks dwarfing all that passes below. Also stunning is the lesser-known coastal route to Hermanus, capital of the Whale Coast.

ARNISTON (above), a small fishing village and popular Capetonian getaway on the south coast, is characterized by huge white sand dunes, lapped by a startlingly turquoise sea. Adjacent is the Kassiesbaai community, where, by prior arrangement, you can enjoy fresh pan-fried yellowtail and green bean stew, prepared by the local fisher-women and served by candlelight in a century-old fishing cottage.

© STR/Reuters/Corbis

Get off the beaten track to experience some of the exhilarating traditions that have survived into the 21st century, like the **REED DANCES** **(above)** of the Zulu and Swazi tribes. During the most famous of these, held every September in honor of the Zulu King, some 15,000 topless virgins present their reeds (hopefully unbroken) to King Goodwill Zweliteni. The dance is best witnessed with a guide provided by Graham Chennells, whose outfit is based in Eshowe, Zululand.

Johannesburg, or "Jozi" as she's affectionately known, throbs to a relentless beat, fuelled by a heady mix of ambition and hope, and expressed in the stylish grooves of **KWAITO** **(right)**, South Africa's homegrown version of house. Look for performances of top acts Mzekezeke, Mafikizolo, Mandoza, or Zola, or pick up the soundtrack to *Tsotsi,* the Oscar-winning film that was set in the city.

© Kelvin Saunders Photography

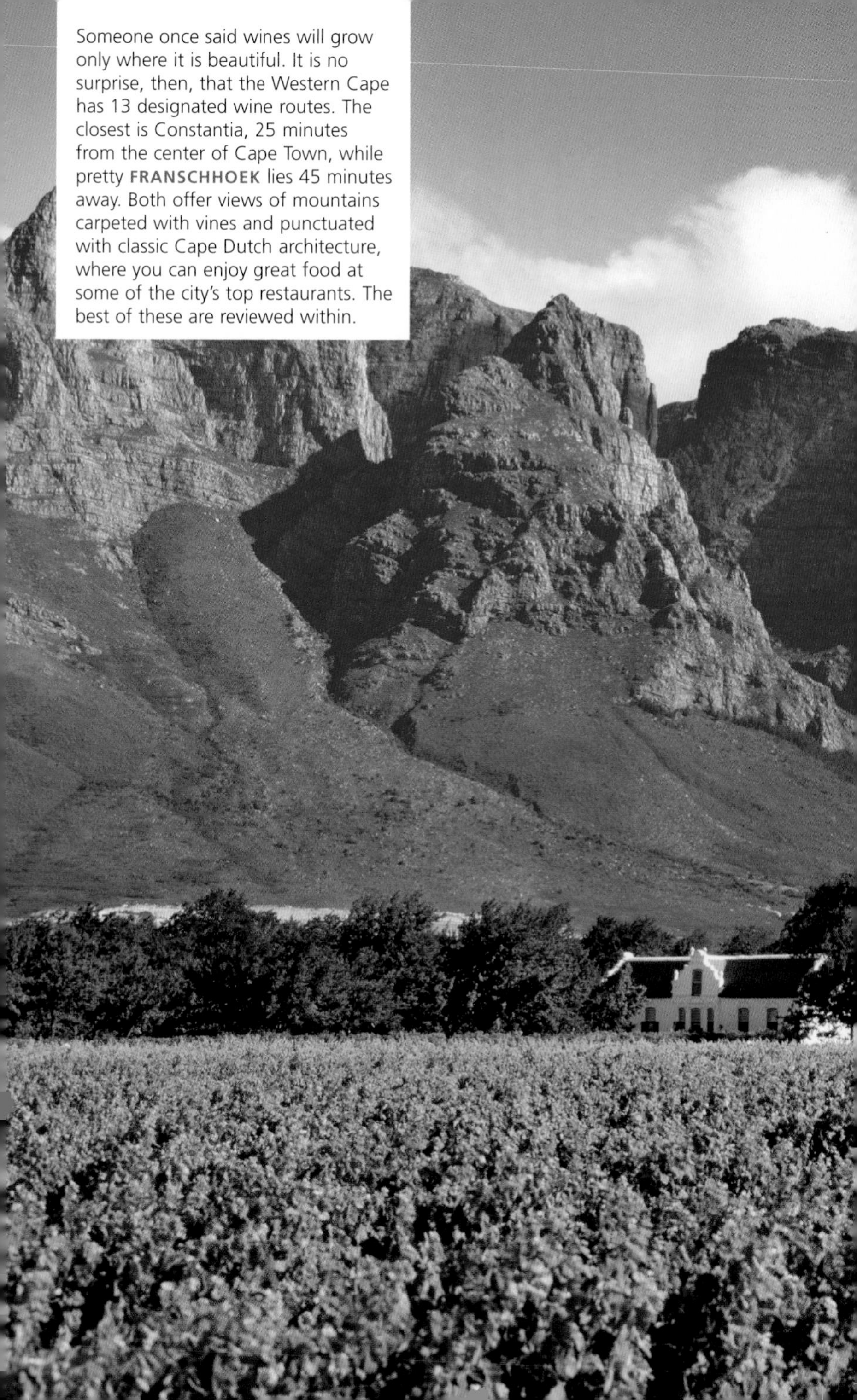

Someone once said wines will grow only where it is beautiful. It is no surprise, then, that the Western Cape has 13 designated wine routes. The closest is Constantia, 25 minutes from the center of Cape Town, while pretty **FRANSCHHOEK** lies 45 minutes away. Both offer views of mountains carpeted with vines and punctuated with classic Cape Dutch architecture, where you can enjoy great food at some of the city's top restaurants. The best of these are reviewed within.

Courtesy Singita Private Game Reserve

Southern Africa offers the best, most luxurious safari destinations on the continent, and those described in this book are worth every cent. Certainly no operator better epitomizes this experience than Singita. Staying at one of their lodges (such as **LEBOMBO, left**) doesn't come cheap, but the experience and standards are such that Singita was rated by readers of *Travel & Leisure* in 2007 as the world's best value-for-money accommodations.

The Garden Route has become known as South Africa's "golf coast," with a great selection of lush award-winning courses snaking along cliff-tops, or surrounded by majestic mountain peaks. At last count there were 14, the latest being **PINNACLE POINT (below),** carved into the cliffs above Mossel Bay, and described by Irish champ Darren Clarke as "the best golf course on the planet." If you're not up to par, sign up for lessons at the Fancourt Golf Academy.

Courtesy Pinnacle Point Beach and Golf Resort

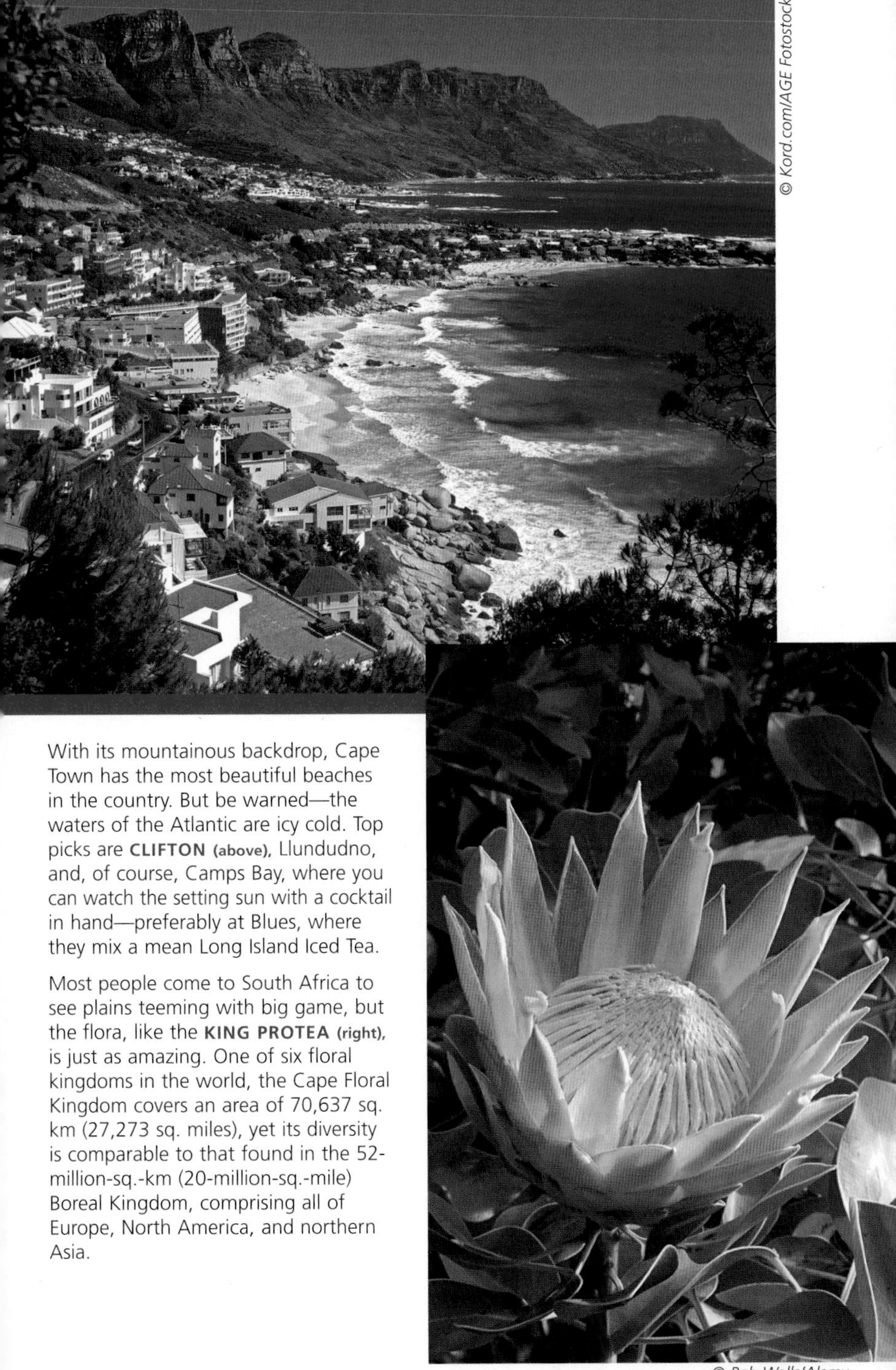

© Kord.com/AGE Fotostock

With its mountainous backdrop, Cape Town has the most beautiful beaches in the country. But be warned—the waters of the Atlantic are icy cold. Top picks are **CLIFTON (above),** Llundudno, and, of course, Camps Bay, where you can watch the setting sun with a cocktail in hand—preferably at Blues, where they mix a mean Long Island Iced Tea.

Most people come to South Africa to see plains teeming with big game, but the flora, like the **KING PROTEA (right),** is just as amazing. One of six floral kingdoms in the world, the Cape Floral Kingdom covers an area of 70,637 sq. km (27,273 sq. miles), yet its diversity is comparable to that found in the 52-million-sq.-km (20-million-sq.-mile) Boreal Kingdom, comprising all of Europe, North America, and northern Asia.

© Rob Walls/Alamy

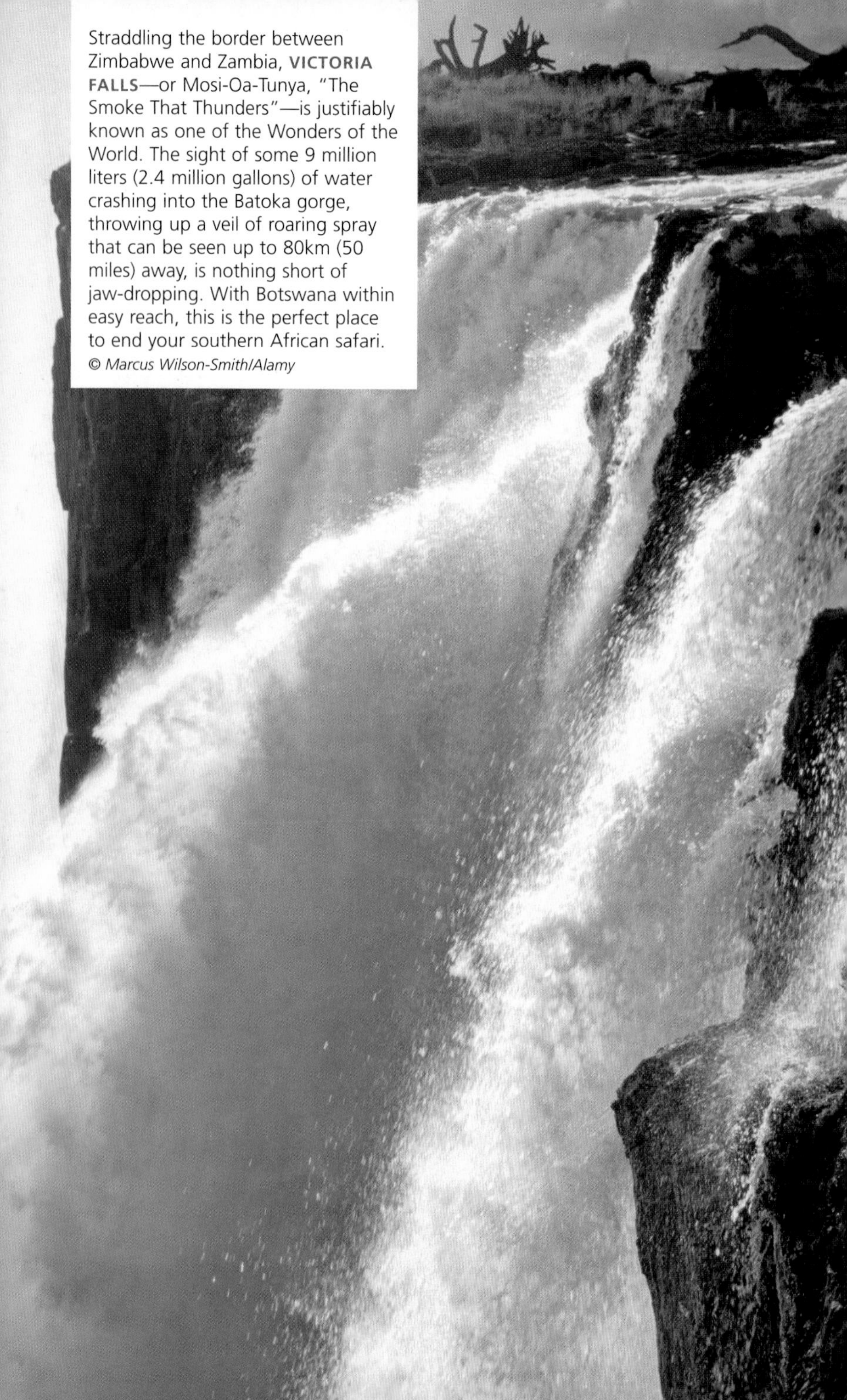

Straddling the border between Zimbabwe and Zambia, **VICTORIA FALLS**—or Mosi-Oa-Tunya, "The Smoke That Thunders"—is justifiably known as one of the Wonders of the World. The sight of some 9 million liters (2.4 million gallons) of water crashing into the Batoka gorge, throwing up a veil of roaring spray that can be seen up to 80km (50 miles) away, is nothing short of jaw-dropping. With Botswana within easy reach, this is the perfect place to end your southern African safari.

Frommer's®

South Africa

6th Edition

by Pippa de Bruyn

with Keith Bain, Janine Stephen, Philip Briggs & David Allardice

Wiley Publishing, Inc.

Published by:

WILEY PUBLISHING, INC.

111 River St.
Hoboken, NJ 07030-5774

ISBN 978-0-470-49876-7

Editor: Maureen Clarke
Production Editor: Jonathan Scott
Cartographer: Andrew Murphy
Photo Editor: Richard Fox
Production by Wiley Indianapolis Composition Services

Front cover photo: A lioness at a watering hole in Kruger National Park © Gavriel Jecan / Getty Images
Back cover photo: A vineyard in the Stellenbosch Wine region © Pictures Colour Library / Alamy Images

For information on our other products and services or to obtain technical support, please contact our Customer Care Department within the U.S. at 877/762-2974, outside the U.S. at 317/572-3993 or fax 317/572-4002.

Wiley also publishes its books in a variety of electronic formats. Some content that appears in print may not be available in electronic formats.

Manufactured in the United States of America

5 4 3 2 1

CONTENTS

4 SUGGESTED SOUTHERN AFRICAN ITINERARIES 71

5 THE MOTHER CITY: CAPE TOWN & THE WINELANDS 82

6 WILD FLOWERS, WHALE COAST & GARDEN ROUTE: THE WESTERN CAPE 203

7 UNDISCOVERED WILDERNESS: THE EASTERN CAPE 280

8 AFRICA'S BIG APPLE: JO'BURG 304

9 BIG-GAME COUNTRY: KRUGER NATIONAL PARK AND PRIVATE RESERVES & CONCESSIONS 327

10 KINGDOM OF THE ZULU: KWAZULU-NATAL 389

11 THUNDERING WORLD WONDER: VICTORIA FALLS & VICINITY 426

12 ORIGINAL EDEN: BOTSWANA 438

13 FAST FACTS 460

INDEX 463

LIST OF MAPS

ACKNOWLEDGMENTS

Our heartfelt thanks to those in the industry whose hospitality and passion turn the grueling task of painstaking research into pleasure. You know who you are.

HOW TO CONTACT US

In researching this book, we discovered many wonderful places—hotels, restaurants, shops, and more. We're sure you'll find others. Please tell us about them, so we can share the information with your fellow travelers in upcoming editions. If you were disappointed with a recommendation, we'd love to know that, too. Please write to:

Frommer's South Africa, 6th Edition

Wiley Publishing, Inc. • 111 River St. • Hoboken, NJ 07030-5774

AN ADDITIONAL NOTE

Please be advised that travel information is subject to change at any time—and this is especially true of prices. We therefore suggest that you write or call ahead for confirmation when making your travel plans. The authors, editors, and publisher cannot be held responsible for the experiences of readers while traveling. Your safety is important to us, however, so we encourage you to stay alert and be aware of your surroundings. Keep a close eye on cameras, purses, and wallets, all favorite targets of thieves and pickpockets.

ABOUT THE AUTHORS

Pippa de Bruyn was born in Durban, raised in Johannesburg, and has now settled in Cape Town. She is an award-winning journalist and is also a coauthor of *Frommer's India*. Cape–based **Keith Bain** is a coauthor of *Frommer's India, Frommer's Kenya & Tanzania, Frommer's Eastern Europe, Pauline Frommer's Italy,* and *Pauline Frommer's Ireland.* **Janine Stephen** is a freelance writer and editor working and living in Cape Town, with a deep passion for South Africa's wilderness areas. **Philip Briggs** is based in KwaZulu-Natal and travels extensively through Africa as the author of books on Tanzania, Malawi, Uganda, Ethiopia, Ghana, and Rwanda. **David Allardice** lives in Cape Town, from where he makes regular forays to the rest of the country, particularly his beloved KwaZulu-Natal, where he was born. He is also a coauthor of *Frommer's India.*

FROMMER'S STAR RATINGS, ICONS & ABBREVIATIONS

Every hotel, restaurant, and attraction listing in this guide has been ranked for quality, value, service, amenities, and special features using a **star-rating system.** In country, state, and regional guides, we also rate towns and regions to help you narrow down your choices and budget your time accordingly. Hotels and restaurants are rated on a scale of zero (recommended) to three stars (exceptional). Attractions, shopping, nightlife, towns, and regions are rated according to the following scale: zero stars (recommended), one star (highly recommended), two stars (very highly recommended), and three stars (must-see).

In addition to the star-rating system, we also use **eight feature icons** that point you to the great deals, in-the-know advice, and unique experiences that separate travelers from tourists. Throughout the book, look for:

Finds	Special finds—those places only insiders know about
Fun Facts	Fun facts—details that make travelers more informed and their trips more fun
Kids	Best bets for kids, and advice for the whole family
Moments	Special moments—those experiences that memories are made of
Overrated	Places or experiences not worth your time or money
Tips	Insider tips—great ways to save time and money
Value	Great values—where to get the best deals
Warning!	Warning—traveler's advisories are usually in effect

The following **abbreviations** are used for credit cards:

AE American Express　**DISC** Discover　**V** Visa
DC Diners Club　**MC** MasterCard

TRAVEL RESOURCES AT FROMMERS.COM

Frommer's travel resources don't end with this guide. **Frommers.com** has travel information on more than 4,000 destinations. We update features regularly, giving you access to the most current trip-planning information and the best airfare, lodging, and car-rental bargains. You can also listen to podcasts, connect with other Frommers.com members through our active-reader forums, share your travel photos, read blogs from guidebook editors and fellow travelers, and much more.

1

The Best of Southern Africa

People come to southern Africa for its natural beauty, wildlife, and sunshine, and few leave disappointed. With its immensely varied terrain supporting a rich diversity of fauna and flora, the region offers a correspondingly diverse range of experiences. Whether you're here on safari, on a self-drive tour through the vast hinterland, or simply on vacation in one of the world's most beautiful regions, this chapter will help you experience the very best southern Africa has to offer.

1 UNIQUE SOUTHERN AFRICAN MOMENTS

- **Spotting Zebra Grazing on the Mountain from the Highway** (Cape Town): Zebra, wildebeest, and various antelope graze on Table Mountain's slopes, literally minutes from the city center. Look out for them from the highway as you drive in from the airport. See chapter 5.
- **Enjoying the Sunset from Table Mountain** (Cape Town): From this great vantage point, you can watch the sun sink into the Atlantic Ocean, turning the Twelve Apostles a deep pink; then walk across the tabletop to the lip and watch the city lights start to twinkle and take in the dusky outline of the hinterland mountains under a moonlit sky. See chapter 5.
- **Feeling Humbled at Mandela's Prison Cell** (Cape Town): Tours of Robben Island are pretty restrictive, but looking into the tiny cell where Nelson Mandela spent most of his time in prison leaves few unmoved. Further insights are provided by guides, some of whom were incarcerated at the same time as Mandela, in what came to be known as the "University of Robben Island." See chapter 5.
- **Getting Caught Up in the Cape Minstrel Carnival** (Cape Town): Every new year, brightly dressed troops of "coloured" (mixed-race) men and children dance through the streets of Cape Town, singing to the quick-paced strum of banjos and the thump of drums. This tradition was inspired by American minstrels who came to the Cape in the late 1800s, but the celebration dates to 1834, when slaves took to the streets to celebrate their liberation. See chapter 5.
- **Watching Whales from White Sand Dunes** (Western Cape): At De Hoop Nature Reserve's Koppie Alleen, the massive white dunes stretch deep beneath the sea, turning its blue hue into a hypnotic turquoise. This is the perfect place to watch the Southern Right whales that come to breed off the Overberg Coast—said to offer the best land-based whale-watching in the world. See chapter 6.
- **Walking through Carpets of Flowers** (Northern Cape): In this annual miracle of almost spiritual proportions, the semi-arid and seemingly barren West Coast bursts into life after the first

spring rains. More than 2,600 species of flowers literally carpet the Namaqualand plains for a few weeks before subsiding back into the soil for another yearlong wait. See chapter 6.

- **Visiting the World's Largest Open-Air Galleries** (Western Cape and KwaZulu-Natal): The bushman (or San) paintings are one of South Africa's greatest cultural treasures and shed light on the lives, pressures, and trance experiences of Bushman shamans. Some 20,000 individual rock paintings have been recorded at 500 different cave and overhang sites between Royal Natal National Park and Bushman's Neck; one of them, Sebaayeni Cave, contains 1,146 individual paintings. Other prime sites include the main caves in Giant's Castle game reserve and Battle Cave in the Injasuti Valley. The Cederberg in the Western Cape is another treasure trove of paintings, easily accessed by overnighting at Bushmans Kloof reserve. See chapters 6 and 10.
- **Jiving with Jo'burg Jollers to the Sounds of Kwaito** (Gauteng): The best place to experience the melting pot of rainbow-nation culture, and to celebrate the emergence of a cohesive national identity, is on the dance floors, grooving to kwaito, South Africa's own homegrown version of house. Look for performances (or recordings) by Brothers of Peace (B.O.P.), Mandoza, Mafikizolo, Zola, M'Du, Mzekezeke, Kabelo, Mapaputsi, Bongo Maffin, or Mzambiya. See chapter 8.
- **Experiencing the Pure Exhilaration of Your First Early-Morning Game Drive** (Limpopo Province, the North-West, Mpumalanga, and Botswana): Winter (May–Aug) is considered to be the best time of the year to go on safari, as animals are the most visible. But be prepared: Rangers set off in their open-topped vehicles before dawn, when temperatures are barely above zero. See chapters 8, 9, and 12.
- **Seeing Virgin Maidens Dance the Zulu King's Reed Dance** (KwaZulu-Natal): Experience a centuries-old tradition as you join some 15,000 Zulus, many dressed in tribal gear, to watch the virgin maidens dance for the Zulu prince Gideon, who would traditionally pick a wife here. See chapter 10.
- **Soaking Up Victoria Falls** (Zimbabwe): You'll never forget the sight of more than 500 million liters (130 million gallons) of water a minute thundering into the Batoka Gorge, creating soaring rainbows and a mist of drenching spray. Enjoy the view with a champagne breakfast on Livingstone Island. See chapter 11.
- **Rafting the Churning Waters of the Zambezi** (Victoria Falls, Zimbabwe): There is absolutely nothing like hearing this mighty river pound past, drowning the guides' last-minute instructions as you plunge into swirling white waters, with such fitting names as The Muncher and Boiling Pot. See chapter 11.
- **Drinking the Waters of the Delta** (Okavango Delta, Botswana): As you're poled along in your *mokoro* (dugout canoe), past palm-fringed islands and aquatic game, sample the life-giving waters of the delta. Scoop up a handful (keeping an eye out for crocs!) and take a sip. See chapter 12.

2 THE WILDEST ANIMAL ENCOUNTERS

- **Staring Down a Roaring Lion** (private game reserves in Mpumalanga, Limpopo Province, the North-West, and Botswana): Tourists are notoriously hungry for shots of big cats, and if you spend 2 nights at one of the top private game reserves, you will certainly get close to lions and leopards, often on the first drive. If you're lucky, you'll get close enough that your vehicle will shudder from the noise that erupts from the king of the jungle's gut. See chapters 8, 9, and 12.

- **Waiting for a Leopard to Finish Its Dinner** (private game reserves, the North-West, Mpumalanga, and Kwa-Zulu-Natal): Holing up in your room while a leopard gnaws its dinner outside your door might happen at any of the private game-reserve lodges that are set in the bush. Animals roam freely in this environment, and if dinner happens to be on your patio, celebrate the fact that you're not it and plunder the minibar. See chapters 8, 9, and 10.
- **Stalking a Rhino on Foot** (Kruger National Park, Hluhluwe-Umfolozi Reserve): Tracking rhino is no mean feat: They can smell humans up to 800m (2,624 ft.) away. Being on foot, with only the sounds of the bush and your beating heart as you crouch just meters from an animal as large as a tank, is unbeatable. For the best rhino-tracking experience, stay at Royal Malewane lodge, in the Thornybush game reserve adjoining Kruger. You will almost definitely track white rhino on the Bushman, Wolhuter, and Napi trails run by Kruger National Park, and the Umfolozi trails run by Hluhluwe-Umfolozi. See chapters 9 and 10.
- **Swimming with Penguins** (Boulders Beach, Cape Town): This is a beautiful place to swim; large boulders create natural swimming pools shared by the only land-breeding colony of jackass penguins. Watch them waddle and dive through the crystal-clear waters, which are slightly warmer than the Atlantic seaboard side—cold comfort, given how icy that is. See chapter 5.
- **Eyeballing a Great White Shark** (Cape Town, Hermanus, and Mossel Bay, Western Cape): Forget tawdry images of razor-toothed monsters chomping at metal bars—this is a riveting, myth-dispelling opportunity to get up close and personal with one of Earth's most ancient creatures, viewing great white sharks in their natural habitat: Geyser Rock, the preferred winter breeding ground for 60,000 Cape fur seal. Most South African shark-cage diving companies adhere to a strict code of conduct, and many are involved in eco-research aimed at helping to save the endangered great white. Nowhere else on the planet can you get to the sharks with so little effort. (A tamer experience, with gentle ragged-tooth sharks at Cape Town's aquarium, lets scuba divers literally swim with the fishes.) See chapters 5 and 6.
- **Watching Rare Turtles Nest** (Zululand, KwaZulu-Natal): In November and December, the female leatherback and loggerhead turtles leave the safety of the sea at night to lay their eggs above the high-tide mark on the northern beaches of KwaZulu-Natal. Two months later, hatchlings scramble out of their nests and make a run for the ocean. Only one or two out of every thousand survive to maturity and return to the exact same beach where they were born to produce the next generation. See chapter 10.
- **Avoiding a Territorial Hippo** (Victoria Falls, Okavango Delta, Zululand, Kwa-Zulu Natal): The upper reaches of the Zambezi and the Okavango Delta's watery channels are best explored by gliding along in a canoe (for the most authentic African safari, sign up for the 3-day Kanana Mokoro Trail and camp out on islands in the Delta), but you're more than likely to meet a hippo this way. Always treat them with respect—despite a relatively docile appearance, they are Africa's most dangerous mammal and are responsible for more deaths than crocodiles or lions. See chapters 11 and 12.

3 THE BEST PRIVATE GAME LODGES & CAMPS

- **Morukuru** (Madikwe, North-West): With no schedules, no rules, and absolutely no pressure on guests to do anything other than relax, this wonderful little lodge combines the finest in safari luxury with fabulous service and really memorable game experiences. Not only can you learn to track lion and leopard with your personal Shangaan tracker, but you'll have your very own ranger, chef, and obliging butler, all on call to fulfill your every whim as you laze on your teak deck overlooking the Groot Marico River. Who's the king of the jungle? You are. See chapter 9.
- **Singita** (Sabi Sands Reserve and Kruger National Park): The much-lauded Singita offers the best game lodge experience in Africa, with a choice of styles, from plush colonial to the last word in contemporary Afro-chic, and superlative game-viewing. Elevated private viewing decks let you immerse yourself in the tranquillity of the bush without leaving your suite. Add top-notch rangers, a roving masseuse, exquisite food, and a connoisseur's selection of wines, and you're assured an unforgettable stay—the only difficulty is deciding which lodge you prefer. See chapter 9.
- **Londolozi Private Granite Suites** (Sabi Sands Reserve, Mpumalanga): Long before Singita and Royal Malewane came on the scene, Londolozi set the standard in luxury bush accommodations, and it's still a class act. Of the four camps, the Granite Suites are the most luxurious, particularly the two that are right on the river—arguably the best in the entire Kruger, with private plunge pools that drop onto the boulders that form the Sand River banks. Londolozi is justifiably famed for its leopard sightings. See chapter 9.
- **Royal Malewane** (Thornybush Reserve, Limpopo Province): With privately situated suites that offer every luxury, this is all about deep relaxation, enhanced by the recently expanded spa. If you can bear to leave your private pool and viewing deck (or in-room lounge and fireplace), you'll find the on-foot tracking is the country's best. See chapter 9.
- **Lebala and Kwara** (Kwando and Okavango Delta, Botswana): These two camps are both run by class-outfit Kwando Safaris and offer superb game-viewing, with a good mix of wet and dry-land activities. Lebala is the flagship camp, located on a massive concession shared by only one other (sister) camp, with superlative accommodations. But it's the superior game-viewing and guiding that has earned them their much-deserved reputation. See chapter 12.
- **Jao Camp** (Jao Concession, Okavango Delta, Botswana): Not only is this camp located in one of the finest concessions in the delta, but it is also one of the most gorgeous camps on the continent; if the price is too steep, operator Wilderness Safaris has 3 other options on the Jao concession, at virtually half the price. See chapter 12.
- **Mombo Camp** (Moremi, Okavango, Botswana): At the confluence of two river systems, Mombo has long been regarded as one of the best game-viewing spots in Africa, attracting large numbers of plains game and their attendant predators; for game-viewing that's much on a par, but at a much friendlier price, take a look at sister camp **Duba Plains.** See chapter 12.
- **Linyanti Bush Camp** (Chobe Enclave, Bostwana): On the edge of the Linyati marshes, bordering the Chobe National Park, this is an area that sees huge

concentrations of game in the winter months, and the only lodging option here is this intimate six-tent camp. Personally run by owners Beks and Sophia, the camp offers understated luxury, superlative guiding, and exceptional value. The couple also has a small camp in the delta and offers 3-night mobile walking safaris (see chapter 12).

- **Jack's Camp** (Makgadikgadi Pans, Botswana): Desert reserves have a very special effect on the spirit, and these classic 1940s safari camps, situated under palm trees on the fringe of the pans, offer one of the most unusual experiences in Africa. (For a more luxurious desert lodge—we're talking swimming pools and top-end service—head for Tswalu, in the Kalahari.) See chapter 12.

4 THE BEST PARKS & NATURE RESERVES

- **Table Mountain National Park** (Cape Town and Cape Peninsula, Western Cape): With so much natural, unfettered beauty so startlingly close to a major city, it's easy to forget that vast portions of the horn-shaped protruding peninsula that makes up Africa's most southwesterly point is actually a preserve, not only for an entire plant kingdom and free-roaming wild animals, but for some of the most splendid mountain and coastal scenery on the planet. You can easily see it by bike, car, or cableway—by why not hike from Table Mountain's Signal Hill all the way to Cape Point?—and discover that nature herself made Cape Town one of the world's favorite city destinations, and certainly Africa's most beautiful. See chapter 5.
- **De Hoop Nature Reserve** (Whale Coast, Western Cape): A magnificent coastal reserve featuring deserted beaches, interesting rock pools, beautiful *fynbos* (uniquely diverse shrublands), a wetland with more than 200 bird species, and a number of small game, but for many, the best reason to come here is because it offers some of the best land-based whale-watching in the world. See chapter 6.
- **Tsitsikamma National Park** (Garden Route, Western Cape): Stretching from Storms River Mouth to Nature's Valley, this coastline is best explored on foot via the 5-day Otter Trail. If the trail is full or you're pressed for time, take the 1km (½-mile) walk to the mouth, or complete the first day of the Otter Trail, which terminates at a beautiful waterfall. See chapter 6.
- **Goegap Nature Reserve** (Namaqualand, Northern Cape): This is one of the best places in Namaqualand to witness the floral transformation after the first spring rains. A recommended way to explore the reserve is to hire a bike and complete the two trails that traverse the reserve. Grazing among the flowers are zebra, springbok, and the stately gemsbok, or oryx. See chapter 6.
- **Kgalagadi (Kalahari) Transfrontier Park** (Northern Cape): This is one of the largest conservation areas in Africa—twice the size of Kruger—yet because of the long distances you need to travel to reach it, this desert reserve is seldom included in the first visitor's itinerary. Pity, for it is starkly beautiful, with red dunes, blond grasses, and sculptural camelthorn trees contrasting with cobalt-blue skies. Despite its aridity, the reserve supports a number of predators, including the famed black-maned "Kalahari" lion, hyena, wild dog, and cheetah. See chapter 6.
- **Addo Elephant National Park** (Eastern Cape): The main game-viewing area

is compact, but this is the place to see elephant by the ton—the Addo herds are famously relaxed around visitors and will pass a hair's breadth away from your car without blinking; you're also almost sure to see baggy-skinned babies up to mischief, chasing warthogs at the waterholes and whatnot. What's more, Addo extends from the edge of the Karoo to the coast—so there are whales and sharks as well as the Big 5. See chapter 7.

- **Madikwe Game Reserve** (North-West): Rapidly gathering momentum as one of the country's most sought-after getaways, this 75,000-hectare (185,250-acre) reserve offers highly diverse eco-zones (including Kalahari sandveld), allowing it to support an unusual range of species—which is why it's been dubbed the Magnificent 7 reserve (cheetahs and wild dogs in addition to the usual suspects). Best of all, it's malaria free. See chapter 9.
- **Kruger National Park** (Mpumalanga and Limpopo Province): One of Africa's greatest game parks, with probably the best-developed infrastructure, Kruger is the most cost-effective, do-it-yourself way to go on safari. Most accommodations are pretty basic but clean, functional, and affordable, and the park teems with wildlife. Good news for connoisseurs is that there are an increasing number of classy private concessions, where the finest lodgings are available—for a price. See chapter 9.
- **iSimangaliso Wetland Park** (Zululand, KwaZulu-Natal): This World Heritage Site encompasses five distinct ecosystems, includes the croc-rich estuary, swamp and dune forests, and the Mkhuze savanna and offshore coral reefs. It is also close to Hluhluwe-Umfolozi, the province's largest Big 5 reserve, which supports Africa's densest rhino population (both black and white). See chapter 10.
- **uKhahlamba-Drakensberg Park** (KwaZulu-Natal): The Drakensberg in its entirety is spectacular, but if you have time to visit only one region, head north for the Amphitheatre. One of the most magnificent rock formations in Africa, it is also the source of South Africa's major rivers: the Vaal, the Orange, and the Tugela. Rolling grasslands, breathtaking views, and crystal-clear streams can be explored only on foot or horseback. See chapter 10.
- **The Victoria Falls National Park** (Victoria Falls, Zimbabwe): This World Heritage Site offers the most stupendous views of the 1,000m-wide (3,280-ft.) falls, and the constant spray, crowned by a permanent rainbow, sustains a lush and verdant rainforest. See chapter 11.
- **Moremi Game Reserve** (Botswana): No visit to Botswana would be complete without a trip to Moremi, which makes up much of the eastern shores of the delta and offers arguably the best game-viewing in southern Africa, though the more exclusive experiences are to be had on the many concessions that border the reserve. See chapter 12.

5 THE BEST OUTDOOR ADVENTURES

- **Paragliding Off Lion's Head and Landing on Camps Bay Beach** (Cape Town): It's a breathtaking ride hovering high above Cape Town's ever-changing cityscape, the slopes of Table Mountain folded beneath your weightless feet. As you glide toward the white sands of Camps Bay, lapped by an endless expanse of ocean, you'll have time to admire the craggy cliffs of the Twelve Apostles. See chapter 5.

- **Kayaking to Cape Point** (Cape Town): Kayaking is the most impressive way to view this towering outcrop, the south-western-most point of Africa. It's also the ideal opportunity to explore the rugged cliffs that line the coastline, with numerous crevices and private coves on which to beach yourself. See chapter 5.
- **Mountain Biking through the Knysna Forests** (Garden Route, Western Cape): Starting at the Garden of Eden, the 22km (14-mile) Harkerville Red Route is considered the most challenging in the country. Its steep, single-track slip paths take you past indigenous forests, silent plantations, and magnificent coastal fynbos. See chapter 6.
- **Bungee Jumping off Bloukrans River Bridge** (Garden Route, Western Cape): The real daredevils do the highest bungee jump in the world in just their birthday suits, leaping 216m (708 ft.) and free-falling (not to mention screaming) for close to 7 seconds. See chapter 6.
- **Surfing Bruce's Beauties** (Cape St. Francis, Eastern Cape): Bruce's Beauties, the waves featured in the 1960s cult classic *Endless Summer,* form an awesome right–point break. They need a massive swell, however, and don't work very often; the same goes for *Supertubes,* hailed the perfect wave, in nearby Jeffrey's Bay. See chapter 7.
- **Surfing the Mighty Zambezi River** (Victoria Falls, Zimbabwe): Not content to merely raft down the Zambezi, adrenaline-seekers can plunge into the churning waters attached to a boogie board and ride the 2m- to 3m-high (6½–9¾-ft.) waves. See chapter 11.
- **Riding an Elephant through the African Wilderness** (Mpumalanga, Victoria Falls, and Botswana): This is a great way to explore the bush, not only because of the elevated view and the proximity with which you can approach animals, but because you can't feel any safer—no one in the jungle messes with an elephant. See chapters 9, 11, and 12.
- **Tracking Big Game on Horseback** (Mashatu and Okavango Delta, Botswana): You haven't lived until you've outraced a charging elephant on the back of your trusty steed. Experience Africa as a pioneer by taking a 3- to 10-day horse safari in the Mashatu Game Reserve, or explore the western delta bordering the Moremi Game Reserve. See chapter 12.

6 THE BEST SOUTH AFRICAN HISTORY STOPS

- **Robben Island** (Cape Town): A prison for political activists since the 17th century, including its most famous prisoner, Nelson Mandela, the island was commonly known as the Alcatraz of Africa. Today the island is a museum and a nature reserve, and a tangible symbol of South Africa's transformation. See chapter 5.
- **Bo-Kaap** (Cape Town): This Cape Malay area, replete with cobbled streets and quaint historical homes, was one of the few "nonwhite" areas to escape destruction during the apartheid era, despite its proximity to the city. Visible today only as large tracts of cleared land on the southern outskirts of town (opposite the Bo-Kaap), this once vibrant suburb was razed in the 1960s. See chapter 5.
- **Wupperthal Moravian Mission Station** (Cederberg, Western Cape): At the end of a long, dusty road in the Cederberg Mountains, Wupperthal remains

unchanged to this day and is both an architectural and cultural living legacy of the early missionaries. Other mission stations worth visiting are Elim and Genadendal, both in the Overberg. See chapter 6.

- **The Red Location Museum** (Port Elizabeth, Eastern Cape): This award-winning architectural wonder is made up of 12 individual, rusty, corrugated iron "memory boxes," filled with exhibits and narratives about local life and culture, and the community's contribution to the struggle against apartheid. See chapter 7.
- **Apartheid Museum** (Johannesburg, Gauteng): Few other museums are able to achieve the emotional impact generated by this reminder of South Africa's ugly past. The collection of images, audiovisual presentations, and intimate tales of human suffering and triumph in the face of adversity is staggering; raw and vivid, the journey from oppression to democracy is powerfully evoked here. See chapter 8.
- **Origins Centre** (Johannesburg, Gauteng): For anyone interested in understanding the great genetic strand that purportedly binds all of humanity to a common African ancestor, this new museum is filled with clues, from little bits of sharpened rock to fascinating films depicting the shamanic trance rites of the nomadic San people. While the design and layout owes much to contemporary art galleries, this new attraction is a source of fairly hard-core academic knowledge, including DNA testing (at a price) that may provide you with a better idea of where your own ancestral roots may lie. See chapter 8.
- **Cradle of Humankind** (Gauteng): Having shot to fame in 1947 with the discovery of a 2.5-million-year-old hominid skull, the region continues to produce fascinating finds about the origins of mankind. Tours with paleontologists introduce you to many intriguing aspects of human evolution, in an area that's remained unchanged for millions of years. See chapter 8.
- **Rorke's Drift and Isandlwana** (Battlefields, KwaZulu-Natal): These two Anglo-Zulu War battlefield sites, within walking distance of each other, encompass both the British Empire's most humiliating defeat and its most heroic victory in the colonies. At the Battle of Isandlwana, more than 1,300 armed men were wiped out by a "bunch of savages armed with sticks," as the mighty Zulu nation was then referred to. Hours later, 139 British soldiers (35 of them ill) warded off a force of 4,000 Zulus for 12 hours, for which an unprecedented 11 Victorian Crosses were awarded. See chapter 10.
- **The Vukani Collection** (Eshowe, KwaZulu-Natal): While most Westerners head for the cultural villages to gain some insight into Zulu tribal customs and culture, Vukani is where Zulu parents take their children. With the largest collection of Zulu artifacts in the world, this is a highly recommended excursion, particularly for those interested in crafts. Note that if you aren't venturing this far afield, the **Campbell Collection** in Durban is an alternative. See chapter 10.

7 THE MOST AUTHENTIC CULINARY EXPERIENCES

- **Preparing and Eating a Cape Malay Meal** (Cape Town): Typified by mild, sweet curries and stews, this cuisine is easy on the uninitiated palate. The most authentic restaurant is Biesmiellah, located in the Bo-Kaap in Cape Town, and many of the top restaurants in the Cape incorporate Cape Malay spicing in creative ways. While you could simply sit down to a meal, why not join an eye-opening "cooking safari," during which you cook alongside genuine Bo-Kaap families in their own homes? Learn to roll roti and fold samosas, and then tuck into a gratifying home-cooked meal, featuring the results of your own labor. Rather than leaving a tip, you'll leave having made friends with a community. See chapter 5.
- **Tucking into *Boerekos*** (Cape Town, Stellenbosch, and Tulbagh): South Africa's countryside is dotted with small-town communities where traditional Afrikaner *boerekos* (farmers' food) is still a staple, although perhaps given a contemporary update in the manner of 21st-century celebrity chefs (even Gordon Ramsey's new Cape Town venture, **maze,** plunders one or two original recipes). For the most inspired take on modern South African cuisine, try **Cognito** (✆ **021/882-8696**), in Stellenbosch. While in Tulbagh, the Wineland's darling sleeping giant, you can sample ultratraditional *waterblommetjiebredie* (water lily stew) at **Paddagang Restaurant** (✆ **023/230-0242**), on Church Street, lined with beautifully restored Cape Dutch heritage. See chapter 5.
- **Lunching in the Vineyards** (Winelands): Set aside at least one afternoon to lunch in the Winelands overlooking vine-carpeted valleys. Recommended options include the lovely terrace at **Constantia Uitsig** (✆ **021/794-4480**), on the Constantia Wine Route; a window table at **La Petite Ferme** (✆ **021/876-3016**), overlooking the lush Franschhoek Valley; or—for the most sought-after dining experience in Stellenbosch—**Overture** (✆ **021/880-2721**), with tables perched over the vineyards. See chapter 5.
- **High Tea at the Nellie** (Cape Town): Regularly voted Africa's top hotel, the Mount Nelson has been serving up the best high tea south of the equator for over a century. Luxuriate on sofas under chandeliers as plates piled high with cucumber sandwiches and cream tea are served to the strains of the tinkling pianist. A graciously colonial experience, it's a relative bargain at R150 a head. See chapter 5.
- **Braaing *Kreef* (lobster) on the Beach** (West Coast, Western Cape): The West Coast all-you-can-eat beach *braais* (barbecues) are legendary, giving you an opportunity to try a variety of local fish. Your best bet is Muisbosskerm, near Lamberts Bay, an ideal spot if you want to combine a trip to the Cederberg. See chapter 6.
- **Eating with Your Fingers:** You'll find that the African staple *pap* (maize-meal prepared as a stiff porridge that resembles polenta) is best sampled by balling a bit in one hand and dipping the edge into a sauce or stew. Try *umngqusho*—a stew made from maize kernels, sugar beans, chilies, and potatoes, said to be one of Nelson Mandela's favorites. You'll most likely sample pap on a township tour (see chapters 5, 7, and 8).
- **Dining Under the Stars to the Sounds of the Bush** (private game reserves

throughout southern Africa): There's nothing like fresh air to work up an appetite, unless it's the smell of sizzling food cooked over an open fire. Happily, dinners at private game reserves combine both more often than not. Weather permitting, meals are served in a *boma* (a reeded enclosure), or in the bush in riverbeds or under large trees. Armed rangers and massive fires keep predators at bay.

- **Chewing Biltong on a Road Trip:** Biltong, strips of game, beef, or ostrich cured with spices and dried, is sold at farm stalls and butcher shops throughout the country. This popular local tradition, dating back to the Voortrekkers, is something of an acquired taste, but it's almost addictive once you've started.

2

South Africa in Depth

South Africa is a big country. Its northeastern border, churned out by the waters of the Limpopo River, is some 2,000km (1,240 miles) from the Cape's craggy coastline, while the semi-arid West Coast, beaten by the icy waters of the Atlantic, is more than 1,600km (992 miles) from the lush East Coast. Surrounded by two oceans, it also borders some extraordinary countries to the north: Namibia, home to the ancient Namib desert; Botswana, southern Africa's premier wildlife destination; Zambia and Zimbabwe, both straddled by the world's most spectacular waterfall; and the subtropical beauty that is Mozambique. It's a region that is both vast and immensely varied, offering a correspondingly diverse array of experiences. Historically, too, the contrasts are great: Some of the world's oldest hominid remains—dating back some 4 million years—make this one of the cradles of civilization, yet it was only just over a decade ago that the country emerged from the dark shadow of an oppressive policy that made it the pariah of the modern world. Born with the dawning millennium, South Africa's peaceful transition to democracy was considered a miracle, and it boasts one of the most progressive constitutions in the world, yet almost half the population still lives in crippling poverty. Most first-time visitors are, in turn, amazed at how sophisticated the infrastructure is on the southern tip of what is still sometimes referred to as the Dark Continent, and yet appalled by the living standards of so many. This sometime unnerving combination of First and Third Worlds is also what makes it such a dynamic destination, full of unexpected contrasts and, yes, bargains. Add vast tracts of untouched wilderness, iconic natural wonders, fascinating wildlife, superb wines, world-class restaurants, and an all-year temperate climate, and it is easy to see why post-apartheid South Africa has emerged as one of the world's fastest-growing tourism destinations—which, in turn, continues spurring the economic growth needed to combat the high levels of poverty. So not least among the many reasons to visit South Africa is the very warm welcome you can expect from its citizens.

1 SOUTH AFRICA TODAY

by Richard Calland

Executive Director, Open Democracy Advice Centre and author of *Anatomy of South Africa: Who Holds the Power?*

"South Africa's is a precarious society." So says Geoff Budlender, one of the country's leading human rights lawyers, commenting on the gap between the vision of socioeconomic justice contained in one of the most modern and internationally renowned constitutions and the reality of chronic poverty endured by the majority of South Africans. For example, 8 million people, out of a population of around 50 million, do not have access to clean water. In 2007, a community in the famous Johannesburg township of Soweto challenged the lack of access by claiming that the city was infringing on the constitutional right to water. The court found that the system of prepay meters that had been installed was unlawful and ordered that

Moments Truth + Guilt + Apology = Reconciliation?

Following South Africa's first democratic elections in 1994, the **Truth and Reconciliation Commission (TRC)** was formed to investigate human rights abuses under apartheid rule. The many victims of apartheid were invited to voice their anger and pain before the commission, headed by Archbishop Desmond Tutu, and to confront directly the perpetrators of these abuses in a public forum. In return for full disclosure, aggressors, regardless of their political persuasion, could ask for forgiveness and amnesty from prosecution. Although many white South Africans went into denial, many more for the first time faced the realities of what apartheid meant. Wrenching images of keening relatives listening to killers, some coldly, others in tears, describing exactly how they had tortured and killed those once officially described as "missing persons" or "accidental deaths" were broadcast nationwide. Those whom the commission thought had not made a full disclosure were denied amnesty, as were those who could not prove that they were acting on behalf of a political cause. While some found solace in the process, many more yearned for a more equitable punishment than mere admission of wrongdoing.

Twenty-seven months of painful confessions and $25 million later, the commission concluded its investigation, handing over the report to Nelson Mandela on October 29, 1998. But the 22,000 victims of gross human rights violations had to wait until April 2003 to hear that each would receive a one-time payment of R30,000, a decision that was greeted with dismay by the victims. In contrast, big businesses (and most whites) were relieved to hear that the government had rejected the TRC's proposed tax surcharge on corporations, as well as the threatened legal action driven by New York lawyer Ed

the city provide the residents of the community with 50 liters of water per day. The government has appealed the decision, but the case shows the best and worst of modern South Africa: On the one hand, an active citizen movement is claiming its rights, backed by a strong rule of law and a decent court system. On the other, a wealthy country is still coming to terms with the socioeconomic inequalities engraved by decades of apartheid.

Surprisingly, the poor do not seem to blame the slow rate of socioeconomic change on the ruling party, the African National Congress (ANC), which has won every democratic election since 1994, when Nelson Mandela was elected as South Africa's first black president. Although the ANC's total vote dropped by 4%, their election victory in 2009—South Africa's fourth election, and again, entirely free from violence—was still decisive, with 65.9% of the popular vote. The opposition struggles to take full advantage of the failures of the government to deliver public services effectively. Even a breakaway party of former ANC cabinet ministers, led by "Terror" Lekota in late 2008, failed to make a dent in the ANC's support: The Congress of the People (COPE) secured just 7.42% at the election.

All is not lost for the opposition, however. Building on a record of stable government in Cape Town, the official opposition (16.66%), the Democratic Alliance (DA),

Fagan and others against companies that had benefited from apartheid, opting for "cooperative and voluntary partnerships." Mbeki emphasized that the TRC was not expected to bring about reconciliation, but was "an important contributor to the larger process of building a new South Africa."

While it is true that the commission affected a more accurate rendition of recent history, its focus on an individualized rather than a collective approach to human rights abuses under apartheid demanded little by way of white acknowledgement of collective guilt for the suffering their fellow citizens endured. It is against this backdrop that the **Home for All** campaign launched in 2000. Initiated, ironically, primarily by whites involved in the liberation struggle, the campaign was supposed to indicate the willingness of white South Africans to accept that they had personally benefited from apartheid, with signatories pledging to use their skills and resources to contribute to "empowering disadvantaged people, and promoting a nonracial society whose resources are used to the benefit of all its people."

But apologies come hard in South Africa: According to a *Reconciliation Barometer,* published by the Institute for Justice and Reconciliation soon after (www.ijr.org.za), only 22% of whites believed they had benefited from apartheid, and only 29% believed that they should apologize. The debate remains robust, and the pros and cons of the government's enforced "affirmative action" policies (which appear to have done little but transfer a portion of wealth into the hands of a relatively small group, while entrenching racial friction) still dominate the pages of local newspapers. Despite this, it appears that forgiveness has taken place, albeit in individual hearts. You can read some South African stories on **www.theforgivenessproject.com**.

won a historic victory in 2009 when it wrested control of the Western Cape provincial government from the ANC—the first time an opposition party has won a majority in any of the nine provinces since 1994.

The 2009 election result brought Jacob Zuma to power—a politician who has developed an international profile for all the wrong reasons. Fired by his predecessor, Thabo Mbeki, from his position as deputy president in 2005, Zuma waged a series of battles within his own party and in the courts, finally ousting Mbeki months before the election. It was a power struggle with many twists and turns, often reading like a John Le Carre novel with plenty of dodgy spies (and, yes, spawning a number of books, such as Andrew Feinstein's excellent *After the Party*). First, Zuma was charged with corruption; the charges were dismissed on a technicality. Then he was charged with the rape of a young woman who was staying with him, but he was found not guilty. Notoriously, when giving evidence in his own defense, Zuma told the court that he did have unprotected sexual intercourse even though he knew the woman was HIV positive, because in his culture it was necessary to satisfy the sexual needs of a woman, adding that he had taken a shower afterward, as a precautionary measure. (Ever since, internationally acclaimed South African cartoonist Zapiro has drawn

Zuma with a shower sticking out of his head). Throughout, Zuma, the former head of the ANC's intelligence wing during the struggle against apartheid, presented himself as a victim of the Mbeki-led new political establishment. He carefully plotted his revenge, building a coalition of enemies of Mbeki, including the leftist trade union federation (COSATU) and the S.A. Communist Party. When Zuma went on to beat Mbeki to the leadership of the ANC at a passionate and, at times, acrimonious national conference at Polokwane in December 2007, the National Prosecuting Authority simply reinstated the corruption charges. When it subsequently emerged that the senior investigator was in conversation with senior pro-Mbeki political leaders, and probably the president himself, the NPA dropped the charges just weeks before the April 2009 general election, even though it said that they still had a strong case against him on the merits of the corruption charges.

Famous for his populist tendencies and his ability to whip up a crowd with his traditional Zulu dancing and singing of his trademark song *Mashimi Wam* (Bring Me My Machine Gun), Zuma has to reconcile the urgent needs of the black, working-class poor who voted him into office with the anxieties of a corporate sector that is already under pressure from the global economic meltdown. Lucky, then, that Zuma's closest friends describe him as a "reconciler by instinct." Indeed, he has taken a strong verbal stance against cronyism, while embracing dialogue with virtually every stakeholder. As he came into office, Zuma faced an economy in retreat after 10 years of steady growth (averaging 4% per annum in the 2000s) and consequent rises in unemployment. Official estimates numbered those out of work at 23%, but discounting those in the informal economy, the figure is closer to 40%. The much anticipated soccer World Cup in 2010 has provided a much-needed boost in infrastructure and, in return, is hoped to swell the state coffers. Whether the ANC will use this opportunity and root out the systemic corruption that flourished during the Mbeki years—and fully deliver on their slogan, "A better life for all"—time alone will tell.

2 SOUTH AFRICA HISTORY 101

The history of South Africa, like any nation's, depends heavily on who is telling the tale. Under the apartheid regime, children were taught that in the 19th century, when the first pioneering Voortrekkers (predominantly Afrikaans-speaking farmers) made their way north from the Cape Peninsula, and black tribes were making their way south from central Africa, southern Africa was a vast, undiscovered wilderness. Blacks and whites thus conveniently met on land that belonged to no one, and if the natives would not move aside for the trinkets and oxen on offer, everyone simply rolled up their sleeves and had an honest fight—which the whites, who believed they enjoyed the special protection of the Lord, almost always won. Of course, for those who pursued the truth rather than a nationalistic version of it, the past was infinitely more complex—not least because so little of it was recorded.

FROM APES TO ARTISTS Some of the world's oldest hominid remains have been found in South Africa, mostly in the valley dubbed the **Cradle of Humankind,** easily accessed from Johannesburg in Gauteng (see chapter 8, "A Side Trip to the Cradle of Mankind")—ironic, really, if you think that, prior to the 1990s, evolution was a banned topic in South African schools.

These suggest that humanity's earliest relatives were born here more than 4 million years ago; if your ancestral origins are of interest, make sure you also visit the **Origins Centre** in Johannesburg, where you can apply for a DNA test to trace your origins. Much of the Centre is focused on the fascinating spiritual life of the San hunter-gatherers (or Bushmen, as they were dubbed by Europeans), the closest living relatives of Stone Age man. A few small family units of San still survive in the Kalahari Desert, but the most arresting evidence of their long sojourn in southern Africa are the many **rock paintings** they used to record events dating as far back as 30,000 years and as recently as the 19th century. The best places to see these paintings are in caves and rockfaces of the Cederberg, in the Western Cape, and the Drakensberg, in Kwazulu-Natal (see chapters 6 and 10).

From these paintings, we can deduce that Bantu-speaking Iron Age settlers were living in South Africa long before the arrival of the white colonizers. Dark-skinned and technologically more sophisticated than the San, they started crossing the Limpopo about 2,000 years ago, and over the centuries, four main groups of migrants settled in South Africa: the **Nguni**-speaking group (including the Zulu and Xhosa), followed by the **Tsonga, Sotho-Tswana,** and **Venda** speakers. Iron Age trading centers were developed around copper and iron mines, such as those in and around Phalaborwa: The remains of one such center can be seen at the **Masorini complex** in **Kruger National Park.**

By the 13th century, most of South Africa's eastern flank was occupied by these African people, while the San remained concentrated in the west. In Botswana, a small number of the latter were introduced to the concept of sheep- and cattle-keeping. These agrarian groups migrated south and called themselves the **KhoiKhoi (men of men),** to differentiate themselves from their San relatives. It was with these indigenous people that the first seafarers came into contact. The KhoiKhoi saw themselves as a superior bunch, and it must have been infuriating to be called Hottentots by the Dutch (a term sometimes used to denigrate the Cape Coloured group, and still considered degrading today).

THE COLONIZATION OF THE CAPE

When spice was as precious as gold, the bravest men in Europe were the Portuguese crew who set off with **Bartholomieu Dias** in 1487 to drop off the edge of the world and find an alternative trade route to the Indies. Dias rounded the Cape,

DATELINE

- **Circa 8000 B.C.** Southern Africa is believed by many paleontologists to be the birthplace of humanity, due to hominid remains dating back more than 4 million years. Millions of years later, the pastoral KhoiKhoi (Hottentots), joined even later by the Bantu-speaking people (blacks), arrive to displace the hunter-gatherer San (Bushmen).
- **A.D. 1488** Bartholomieu Dias is the first white settler to round the Cape, landing at Mossel Bay.
- **1497** Vasco da Gama rounds the southern African coast, discovering an alternate sea route to India.
- **1652** Jan van Riebeeck is sent to set up a supply station for the Dutch East India Company. Cape Town is born.
- **1659** The first serious armed conflict against the KhoiKhoi occurs; the first wine is pressed.
- **1667–1700** First Malay slaves arrive, followed by the French Huguenots.
- **1779** The first frontier war between the Xhosa and settlers in the Eastern Cape is fought. Eight more were to

continues

which he named **Tormentoso (Stormy Cape),** after his fleet of three tiny ships battled storms for 3 days before he tracked back to what is today known as Mossel Bay. Suffering from acute scurvy, his men forced him to turn back soon after this.

It was 10 years before another group was foolhardy enough to follow in their footsteps. **Vasco da Gama** sailed past what had been renamed the Cape of Good Hope, rounding the lush coast of what is now called the **Garden Route,** as well as the East Coast, which he named **Natal,** and sailed all the way to India.

The Portuguese opened the sea route to the East, but it was the Dutch who took advantage of the strategic port at the tip of Africa. In 1652 (30 years after the first English settled in the United States), **Jan van Riebeeck,** who had been caught cooking the books of the Dutch East India Company in Malaysia, was sent to open a refreshment station as penance. The idea was not to colonize the Cape, but simply to create a halfway house for trading ships. Van Riebeeck was given strict instructions to trade with the natives and in no way enslave them. Inevitably, relations soured—the climate and beauty of the Cape led members of the crew and soldiers to settle permanently on the land, with little recompense for the KhoiKhoi. To prevent the KhoiKhoi from seeking revenge, van Riebeeck attempted to create a boundary along the Liesbeeck River by planting a bitter-almond hedge—the remains of this hedge still grow today in **Kirstenbosch,** the national botanical gardens. This, together with the advantage of firepower and the introduction of hard liquor, reduced the KhoiKhoi to no more than a nuisance. Those who didn't toe the line were imprisoned on **Robben Island,** and by the beginning of the 18th century, the remaining KhoiKhoi were reduced to virtual slavery by disease and drink. Over the years, their genes slowly mingled with those of slaves and burghers to create a new underclass, later known as the Cape Coloureds.

In 1666, the foundation stones were laid for the **Castle of Good Hope,** the oldest surviving building in South Africa, and still more elements were added to the melting pot of Cape culture. Van Riebeeck persuaded the company to allow the import of **slaves** from the Dutch East Indies; this was followed by the arrival of the **French Huguenots** in 1668. Fleeing religious persecution, these Protestants increased the size of the colony by 15% and brought with them the ability to cultivate **wine.** The glorious results of their input are still thriving in the valley of **Franschhoek (French corner),** augmenting the efforts of Simon van der Stel, second

follow in what is now known as the Hundred Years War.

- **1795** The British occupy the Cape for 7 years and then hand it back to the Dutch.
- **1806** Britain reoccupies the Cape, this time for 155 years.
- **1815** Shaka becomes the Zulu king.
- **1820** The British settlers arrive in the Eastern Cape. In KwaZulu-Natal, Shaka starts his great expansionary war, decimating numbers of opposing tribes and leaving large areas depopulated in his wake.
- **1824** Port Natal is established by British traders.
- **1828** Shaka is murdered by his half-brother, Dingaan, who succeeds him as king.
- **1834** Slavery is abolished in the Cape, sparking off the Great Trek.
- **1835–45** More than 16,000 bitter Dutch settlers head for the uncharted hinterland in ox wagons to escape British domination.
- **1838** A party of Voortrekkers manages to vanquish Zulu forces at the Battle of Blood River.
- **1843** Natal becomes a British colony.
- **1852** Several parties of Boers move farther northeast and found the Zuid Afrikaansche Republiek (ZAR).
- **1854** The Boer Independent Republic of the Orange Free

governor to the Cape, who planted the first vines in the shadow of what is still one of the most beautiful Cape Dutch homes and wine estates, **Groot Constantia.** Van der Stel also established **Stellenbosch,** lining the village streets with oak trees and Cape Dutch buildings, making this the most historic of the Winelands towns (see chapter 5).

The British entered the picture in 1795, taking control of the Cape when the Dutch East India Company was liquidated. In 1803, they handed it back to the Dutch for 3 years, after which they were to rule the Cape for 155 years.

One of their first tasks was to silence the "savages" on the Eastern Frontier—these were the **Xhosa,** part of the Nguni-speaking people who migrated south from central Africa. Essential to the plan was the creation of a buffer zone of English settlers. Between 1820 and 1824, the British offloaded thousands of penniless artisans and out-of-work soldiers in **Port Elizabeth,** in what is now the Eastern Cape; issued them basic implements, tents, and seeds; and sent them off to farm the land (much of it totally unsuitable for agriculture) and deal with the Xhosa. English-settler towns, such as **Grahamstown,** which has some fine examples of Victorian colonial architecture, were established, but at great cost. Four frontier wars decimated numbers on both sides, but it was the extraordinary **cattle-killing incident** that crippled the Xhosa: In 1856, a young girl, Nongqawuse, prophesied that if the Xhosa killed all their cattle and destroyed their crops, their dead ancestors would rise and help vanquish the settlers. Needless to say, this did not occur, and while four more wars were to follow, the Xhosa's might was effectively broken by this mass sacrifice. Today the **Eastern Cape** is still the stronghold of the Xhosa, many of whom still live a traditional lifestyle along the Wild Coast. The province is the birthplace of their most famous son, **Nelson Mandela,** who now resides there in humble surrounds. Massive tracts of failed farmland in the Eastern Cape have, since the advent of tourism, been rehabilitated and restocked with wildlife, forming the **Eastern Cape game reserves,** popular because they are near the Garden Route and malaria free.

THE RISE OF THE ZULU & AFRIKANER CONFLICTS At the turn of the 19th century, the **Zulus,** the Nguni group that settled on the East Coast in what is now called **KwaZulu-Natal,** were growing increasingly combative, as their survival depended on absorbing neighbors to gain control of pasturage. A young warrior named **Shaka,** who took total despotic

State is founded by another party of Boers.

- **1858** The British defeat the Xhosa after the Great Cattle Killing, in which the Xhosa destroy their crops and herds in the mistaken belief that with this sacrifice their ancestors will destroy the enemy.
- **1860** The first indentured Indian workers arrive in Natal.
- **1867** Diamonds are found near Kimberley in the Orange Free State.
- **1877** The British annex the ZAR.
- **1879** Anglo-Zulu War breaks out, orchestrated by the British.
- **1880–81** First Anglo-Boer War is fought. Boers defeat British.
- **1883** Paul Kruger becomes the first president of the ZAR.
- **1886** Gold is discovered on the Witwatersrand.
- **1899–1902** The Second Anglo-Boer War is fought. British defeat Boers.
- **1910** The Union of South Africa is proclaimed. Louis Botha becomes the first premier. Blacks are excluded from the process.
- **1912** The South African Native National Congress is formed. After 1923, this

continues

control of the Zulus in 1818, raised this to an art form. In addition to arming his new regiments with the short stabbing spear, Shaka was a great military tactician and devised a strategy known as the **"horns of the bull,"** whereby highly disciplined formations of warriors outflanked and eventually engulfed the enemy. Shaka used this tactic to great effect on tribes in the region, and by the middle of the decade, the Zulus had formed a centralized military state with a 40,000-man army. In a movement called **Mfecane,** or "Forced Migrations," huge areas of the country were cleared. The Zulus either killed or absorbed people; many fled, creating new kingdoms such as **Swaziland** and **Lesotho.** In 1828, Shaka's two brothers killed him, and one, Dingaan, succeeded him as king.

On the Cape, British interference in labor relations and oppression of the "kitchen Dutch" language infuriated many of the Dutch settlers, by now referred to as *Afrikaners* (of Africa), and, later, *Boers* (farmers). The abolition of slavery in 1834 was the last straw. Afrikaners objected to "not so much their freedom," as one wrote, "as their being placed on an equal footing with Christians, contrary to the laws of God and the natural distinction of race."

Some 15,000 people (10% of the Afrikaners at the Cape) set off on what is known as the Great Trek and became known as the *Voortrekkers,* or "first movers." They found large tracts of unoccupied land that, unbeknownst to them, had been cleared by the recent Mfecane. It wasn't long before they clashed with the mighty Zulu nation, whom they defeated in 1838 at the **Battle of Blood River.** A century later, this miraculous victory was to be the greatest inspiration for Afrikaner nationalism, and a monument was built to glorify the battle. Today the **Voortrekker Monument** is a place of pilgrimage for Afrikaner nationalists and can be seen from most places in Pretoria.

The Voortrekkers' victory was, however, short lived. The British, not satisfied with the Cape's coast, annexed Natal in 1845. Once again, the Voortrekkers headed over the mountains with their ox-wagons, looking for freedom from the British. They founded two republics: the **Orange Free State** (with similar boundaries to what is now the Free State) and the **South African Republic** or **Transvaal** (now Gauteng, the North-West, Mpumalanga, and the Northern Province). This time the British left them alone, focusing their attention on places of more interest than a remote outpost with only 250,000 settlers. Needless to say, the 1867 discovery of **diamonds** in the Orange Free State and, 19 years later, **gold** in the Transvaal, was to change this attitude dramatically.

would be known as the African National Congress (ANC).

- **1913** The Native Land Act is passed, limiting land ownership for blacks.
- **1914–18** South Africa declares war on Germany.
- **1923** Natives (Urban Areas) Act imposes segregation in towns.
- **1939–45** South Africa joins the Allies in fighting World War II.
- **1948** D. F. Malan's National Party wins the election, and the era of apartheid is born. Races are classified, the passbook system is created, and interracial sex is made illegal.
- **1955** ANC adopts Freedom Charter.
- **1956** "Coloureds" lose the right to vote.
- **1958** H. F. Verwoerd, the architect of apartheid, succeeds D. F. Malan and creates the homelands—territories set aside for black tribes.
- **1959** Robert Sobukwe forms the Pan African National Congress (PAC).
- **1960** Police open fire on demonstrators at Sharpeville, killing 69 people. ANC and PAC banned. ANC ends its policy of peaceful negotiation.
- **1961** South Africa leaves the Commonwealth and

Impressions

The more of the world we inhabit, the better it is for the human race. Just fancy, those parts that are at present inhabited by the most despicable specimens of human beings, what an alteration there would be if they were brought under Anglo-Saxon influence.

—C. J. Rhodes, British imperialist and South African mining magnate of the 1800s

GETTING RICH & STAYING POOR In both the diamond and the gold fields, a step-by-step amalgamation of individual claims was finally necessitated by the expense of the mining process. In Kimberley, **Cecil John Rhodes**—an ambitious young man who was to become obsessed with the cause of British imperial expansion—masterminded the creation of **De Beers Consolidated,** the mining house that, to this day, controls the diamond-mining industry in southern Africa. (The discovery of diamonds was also the start of the labor-discrimination practices that were to set the precedent for the gold mines and the ensuing apartheid years.) The mining of gold did not result in the same monopoly, and the **Chamber of Mines,** established in 1887, went some way to regulate the competition.

Paul Kruger, president of the South African Republic, became a spoke in the wheel, however. A survivor of the Great Trek and a Calvinist preacher (his home in Pretoria, a museum today, is directly opposite his church), Kruger did not intend to make things easy for the mostly British entrepreneurs who controlled the gold mines. He created no real infrastructure to aid them, and *uitlanders* (foreigners) were not allowed to vote. Britain, in turn, wanted to amalgamate the South African colonies to consolidate their power in southern Africa. British forces had already attempted to annex the Transvaal in 1877, just after the discovery of diamonds, but they had underestimated Paul Kruger; in 1881, after losing the first Anglo-Boer war, they restored the Boer republics' independence. In 1899, when the British demanded full rights for the *uitlanders,* Kruger invaded the coastal colonies.

At first, the second **Anglo-Boer War** went well for the Boers, who used hitherto-unheard-of guerilla warfare tactics,

becomes a republic. Albert Luthuli is awarded the Nobel Peace Prize.

- **1963** Nelson Mandela and others are sentenced to life imprisonment in the Rivonia sabotage trials.
- **1970s** Worldwide economic and cultural boycotts are initiated in response to South Africa's human rights abuses.
- **1976** Police open fire on unarmed black students demonstrating against the use of Afrikaans as a teaching medium; the Soweto riots follow.
- **1977** Black-consciousness leader Steve Biko dies in police custody.
- **1980–84** President P. W. Botha attempts cosmetic reforms. Unrest escalates. Bishop Tutu, who urges worldwide sanctions, is awarded the Nobel Peace Prize.
- **1985** A state of emergency is declared, gagging the press and giving security forces absolute power.
- **1989** F. W. de Klerk succeeds P. W. Botha.
- **1990** de Klerk ends the state of emergency, lifts the ban on the ANC, and frees Mandela.

continues

Impressions

Natives will be taught from childhood to realize that equality with Europeans is not for them.

—H. Verwoerd, Afrikaans "architect" of apartheid, 1953

but the British commander **Lord Kitchener** soon found their Achilles' heel. Close to 28,000 Boer women and children died in Kitchener's concentration camps—the first of their kind—and his scorched-earth policy, whereby the Boer farms were systematically razed to the ground, broke the Boer spirit. Ultimately, Britain would pit nearly half a million men against 88,000 Boers. In 1902, the Boer republics became part of the Empire—the Afrikaner nationalism that was to sweep the country in the next century was fueled by the resentments of a nation deeply wounded and struggling to escape the yoke of British imperialism.

OPPRESSION & RESISTANCE The years following this defeat were hard on those at the bottom of the ladder. Afrikaners, many of whom had lost their farms and families, streamed to the cities, where they competed with blacks for unskilled jobs on equal terms and were derogatively referred to as the "poor whites." It is worth noting here that black South Africans had also suffered immense losses during the Anglo-Boer War (including the loss of some 14,000 in the concentration camps), but in later years, when Afrikaner fortunes turned, this was neither recognized nor compensated. With the creation of the **Union of South Africa** in 1910, the country joined the British Commonwealth of Nations and participated in World War I and World War II. Back home, loyalties were divided, and many Afrikaners were bitter about forging allegiances with a country they had so recently been at war with. In 1934, a new "purified" **National Party (NP)** was established, offering a voice for the "poor white" Afrikaners. Under the leadership of Dr. D. F. Malan, another preacher who swore he would liberate the Afrikaners from their economic oppression, the NP won the 1948 election by a narrow margin—46 years of white minority rule were to follow before internal and international pressure would finally buckle the NP's resolve.

- **1993** de Klerk and Mandela win the Nobel Peace Prize.
- **1994** The first democratic elections are held, and on May 10, Mandela is sworn in as the first black president of South Africa. de Klerk and Thabo Mbeki become joint deputy presidents.
- **1995** The Truth and Reconciliation Commission is created under Archbishop Desmond Tutu.
- **1997** South Africa's new constitution, one of the world's most progressive, comes into effect on February 3.
- **1998** The Truth and Reconciliation Commission ends. The U.S. gives Mandela the Congressional Gold Medal.
- **1999** The second democratic elections are held. The ANC gets 66.03% of the vote; Thabo Mbeki becomes president.
- **2000** UNESCO awards five sites in South Africa World Heritage status. The Kgalagadi, Africa's first Transfrontier Park, is created. UNAIDS reveals that South Africa has the largest AIDS population in the world.
- **2004** The ANC, with Thabo Mbeki at the helm, wins the country's third democratic election, with a landslide 70% victory.

Impressions

I have cherished the ideal of a democratic and free society, in which all people live together in harmony and with equal opportunities. It is an ideal which I hope to live for and achieve. But if needs be, it is an ideal for which I am prepared to die.

—Nelson Mandela at the Rivonia Trial, 1963

One of the first laws that created the segregationist policy named **apartheid** (literally, "separateness") was the **Population Registration Act,** in which everyone was slotted into an appropriate race group. This caused great division among those of mixed descent, now to become a new "race" (see "The 'Coloureds': Creation of a New 'Race,'" below). One of the most infamous classification tests was the pencil test, whereby a pencil was stuck into the hair of a person of uncertain racial heritage. If the pencil dropped, the person was "white"; if not, they were classified "coloured." In this way, entire communities and families were torn apart. This new group, dubbed the coloureds, enjoyed slightly more privileges than their black counterparts—a better standard of housing, schooling, and job opportunities—an overture to their white ancestors. Interracial sexual relations, previously illicit, were now illegal, and the Group Areas Act ensured that families would never mingle on the streets. The act required the destruction and relocation of total suburbs too, almost none of which were white.

Perhaps the most iniquitous new law was the **Bantu Education Act** that ensured that black South Africans would have a second-rate education, given that they were to be providers of semi-skilled labor, and never to challenge the better-educated white South Africans for jobs. During this time, the majority of English speakers condemned the policies of what came to be known as the Afrikaner NP (as did certain Afrikaners); but because they continued to dominate business in South Africa, the maintenance of a cheap labor pool was in their interests, and life was generally too comfortable for most to actually do anything other than engage in robust debate over dinner tables.

By the mid-20th century, blacks outnumbered whites in the urban areas but resided "unseen" in **townships** outside the cities. Their movements were restricted by

- **2005** President Mbeki fires his deputy president, Zuma, when he is implicated in the corruption trial of his financial advisor. Zuma cries foul play and sweeps up populist support.
- **2007** Tony Leon steps down as leader of the opposition (DA), and Helen Zille takes over. The ANC holds its national conference and decides on the man most likely to be voted president in 2009: Jacob Zuma, despite accusations that Zuma accepted bribes from a French arms company involved in a massive weapons deal in the late 1990s.
- **2008** The Zuma-led ANC party forces Mbeki to resign as national president in September.
- **2009** Hundreds of Zuma supporters revel in the streets after prosecutors said they would not pursue him—now or in the future. A month later, the ANC wins its fourth general election by 65.9%.

pass laws; they were barred from trade union activities, deprived of any political rights, and prohibited from procuring land outside their reserves or homelands. **Homelands** were small tracts of land, comprising a shameful 13% of the country, where the so-called ethnically distinct black South African "tribes" (at that time, 42% of the population) were forced to live. This effectively divided the black majority into tribal minorities.

The **African Nationalist Congress Party (ANC)** was formed by representatives of the major African organizations in 1912, but it was only in 1934 that it was to find the inspired leadership of **Anton Lembede, Oliver Tambo, Walter Sisulu,** and **Nelson Mandela,** who formed the **ANC Youth League** in that year. The ANC's hitherto passive resistance tactics were met with forceful suppression in 1960 when police fired on unarmed demonstrators in **Sharpeville,** killing 67 and wounding 200. It was a major turning point for South Africa, sparking violent opposition within and ostracism in world affairs.

In 1963, police captured the underground leaders of the ANC—including the Black Pimpernel, Nelson Mandela, who was by now commander-in-chief of their armed wing, **UmkhontoWe Sizwe (Spear of the Nation).** In what came to be known as the **Rivonia Trial,** Mandela and nine other leaders received life sentences for treason and were incarcerated on **Robben Island.** The imprisonment of key figures effectively silenced the opposition within the country for some time and allowed the NP to further entrench its segregationist policies. But it wasn't all clear sailing: Hendrik Verwoerd, the cabinet minister for Bantu Affairs under Malan and the man named the "architect of apartheid," was stabbed to death one morning in the House of Assembly—strangely, not for political reasons; the murderer insisted that a tapeworm had ordered him to do it. In 1966, B. J. Vorster became the new NP leader. He was to push for the independence of Verwoerd's black homelands, which would effectively deprive black people of their South African citizenship, and enforce the use of Afrikaans as a language medium in all schools. Ironically, the latter triggered the backlash that would end Afrikaner dominance.

SOUTH AFRICA GOES INTO LABOR

On June 16, 1976, thousands of black schoolchildren in **Soweto** took to the streets to demonstrate against this new law, which, for the many non-Afrikaans speakers, would render schooling incomprehensible. The police opened fire, killing, among others, 12-year-old **Hector Pieterson** (you can see the photograph that shocked the world, taken minutes after, in the **Hector Pieterson Museum** in Soweto), and chaos ensued, with unrest spreading throughout the country. The youth, disillusioned by their parents' implicit compliance with apartheid laws, burned schools, libraries, and *shebeens,* the informal liquor outlets that provided an opiate to the dispossessed. Many arrests followed, including that of black-consciousness leader **Steve Biko** in the Eastern Cape, who became the 46th political prisoner to die during police interrogation. Young activists fled the country and joined ANC military training camps. The ANC, led by Oliver Tambo, called for international sanctions—the world responded with economic, cultural, and sports boycotts, and awarded the Nobel Peace Prize to **Archbishop Desmond Tutu,** one of the strongest campaigners for sanctions. The new NP premier, **P. W. Botha,** or, as he came to be known, *die Groot Krokodil* (the Big Crocodile), simply wagged his finger and declared South Africa capable of going it alone despite increasing pressure—in the words of Allen Boesak, addressing the launch of the United Democratic Front, the students of Soweto wanted *all* their

Impressions

We have triumphed. We enter into a covenant that we shall build the society in which all South Africans will be able to walk tall, without any fear in their hearts, assured of their inalienable right to human dignity—a rainbow nation at peace with itself and the world.

—Nelson Mandela, inaugural address, 1994

rights, they wanted them *here,* and they wanted them *now.* The crocodile's bite proved as bad as his bark, and his response was to pour troops into townships. In 1986, he declared a **state of emergency,** giving his security forces power to persecute the opposition, and silencing the internal press.

The overwhelming majority of white South Africans enjoyed an excellent standard of living, a state of supreme comfort that made it difficult to challenge the status quo. Many believed the state propaganda that blacks were innately inferior, or remained blissfully ignorant of the extent of the human rights violations; still others found their compassion silenced by fear. Ignorant or numbed, most white South Africans waited for what seemed to be the inevitable civil war, until 1989, when a ministerial rebellion forced the intransigent Botha to resign, and new leader **F. W. de Klerk** stepped in. By now, the economy was in serious trouble—the cost of maintaining apartheid had bled the coffers dry, the Chase Manhattan Bank had refused to roll over its loan, and sanctions and trade-union action had brought the country's economy to a virtual standstill. Mindful of these overwhelming odds, de Klerk unbanned the ANC, the PAC, the Communist Party, and 33 other organizations in February 1990. Nelson Mandela—imprisoned for 27 years—was released soon thereafter.

BIRTH OF THE "NEW SOUTH AFRICA"

The fragile negotiations among the various political parties were to last a nerve-racking 4 years. During this time, right-wingers threatened civil war, while many in the townships lived it. **Zulu nationalists,** of the **Inkatha** party, waged a low-level war against ANC supporters that claimed the lives of thousands. Eyewitness accounts were given of security force involvement in this black-on-black violence, with training and supplies provided to Inkatha forces by the South African Defence Force. In 1993, **Chris Hani,** the popular ANC youth leader, was assassinated. South Africa held its breath as Mandela pleaded on nationwide television for peace—by this time, there was no doubt about who was leading the country.

On April 27, 1994, **Nelson Mandela** cast his first vote at the age of 76, and on May 10, he was inaugurated as South Africa's first democratically elected president. Despite 18 opposition parties, the ANC took 63% of the vote and was dominant in all but two provinces—the Western Cape voted NP, and KwaZulu-Natal went to Buthelezi's Zulu-based Inkatha (IFP) Party. Jubilation reigned, but the hangover was bad. The economy was in dire straits, with double-digit inflation, gross foreign exchange down to less than 3 weeks of imports, and a budget deficit of 6.8% of GDP. Of an estimated 38 million people, at least 6 million were unemployed and 9 million destitute. Ten million had no access to running water, and 20 million no electricity. The ANC had to launch a program of "nation-building," attempting to unify what the NP had spent a fortune dividing. Wealth had to be redistributed without hampering the ailing economy, and a government debt of almost R350 billion ($52 billion) repaid.

Still, after 300 years of white domination, South Africa entered the new millennium with what is widely regarded as the world's most progressive constitution, and its murky history was finally held up for close inspection by the Truth and Reconciliation Commission, the first of its kind in the world (see "Truth + Guilt + Apology = Reconciliation?," above). South African sports heroes, barred from competing internationally for 2 decades, added to the nation's growing pride, winning the Rugby World Cup in 1995 (a movie about the events surrounding this, directed by Clint Eastwood, will be released in 2010) and its first gold Olympic medals in 1996. Augmenting these ideological and sporting achievements were those that have happened on a grassroots level: 1999, when the ANC won the second democratic elections with a landslide victory of 66.03% of the vote, saw a change in ANC leadership style, with new president **Thabo Mbeki** centralizing power and promising to focus on delivery rather than reconciliation. The fiscal discipline the ANC pursued resulted in a robust economic outlook, and by late 2000, 6 years after the first democratic election, more than one million houses had been completed, 412 new telephone lines installed, 127 clinics built, and 917,220 hectares (2,265,533 acres) of land handed over to new black owners. Some 37,396 households had benefited from land redistribution, and water supply had increased from 62,249 recipients in 1995 to a whopping 6,495,205. Black-owned business grew, and an estimated four million blacks comprised half of the top earners in the country. But with unemployment estimated at between 30% and 40%, the concomitant rise in crime was hardly surprising. The specter of AIDS was also stalking South Africa, and by 2000, it would find itself with the highest HIV-positive population in the world. Equally distressing was the continued divide between black and white incomes, reinforcing South Africa's strange mix of first- and third-world elements, and prompting Mbeki's controversial "two nations" speech in which he stated that "the failure to achieve real nation-building was entrenching the existence of two separate nations, one white and affluent, and the other black and poor."

But the man who kick-started the concept of an African Renaissance became hamstrung by corruption (much of it shrouded in the secrecy surrounding the arms deal he oversaw in the 1990s) and political infighting. Mbeki's Oxford-don demeanor and his inner circle—members of a New Establishment of black intellectuals, industrialists, and professionals, many of them millionaires who benefited from the government's Black Economic Empowerment (BEE) policies—never sat well with the vast majority of South Africans. Into the gap marched the irrepressibly populist former deputy president, Jacob Zuma, whom Mbeki sacked in 2005 after Zuma's main business confidante and associate was convicted of corruption and sentenced to 15 years in jail. Encouraged by the ANC's two powerful alliance partners—the trade union federation, COSATU, and the South African Communist Party, which now represents the traditional social democrat wing—Zuma has doggedly pursued the ultimate prize, despite facing his own serious corruption investigation and being dragged through a rape trial in 2006.

Mbeki's favorite rhetorical question, "Will the center hold?," written by Yeats, one of Mbeki's favorite poets, was finally answered in 2008, when the ANC, having chosen Jacob Zuma as their president, effectively fired Mbeki, and the splinter party COPE was launched soon thereafter. With Zuma taking over as president in the 2009 elections, which the ANC won by a nearly 70% majority, a new era is ushered in.

3 THE RAINBOW NATION

South African stereotypes are no simple black-and-white matter. Historically, the nation was made up of a number of widely different cultural groups that under normal circumstances might have amalgamated into a singular hybrid called "the South African." But the deeply divisive policy of apartheid only further entrenched initial differences, and while "affirmative action" policies, still in place 12 years after the dismantling of apartheid, were intended to redress the balance, they have ironically further highlighted the importance of race.

At a popular level, Mandela appeared as the architect of the post-1994 "nation-building," utilizing Desmond Tutu's "rainbow nation" to capture the hearts and minds of black and white South Africans alike. But despite the ANC government's stated objective to end racial discrimination and develop a unique South African identity, this "rainbow nation" remains difficult to define, let alone unify. Broadly speaking, approximately 76% of some 38 million people are black, 12.8% are white, 2.6% are Asian, and 8.5% are "coloured" (the apartheid term for those of mixed descent; see "The 'Coloureds': Creation of a New 'Race,'" below). Beyond these are smaller but no less significant groups, descendants of Lebanese, Italian, Portuguese, Hungarian, and Greek settlers, as well as the estimated 130,000-strong Jewish community. The latter has played an enormous role in the economic and political growth of South Africa, as seen at the Jewish Museum in Cape Town.

In an attempt to recognize the cultural diversity of South Africa, the government

The "Coloureds": Creation of a New "Race"

Afrikaans-speaking people of mixed descent—grouped together as a new race called the "coloureds" during the Population Registration Act, from 1950 to 1991—were perhaps the most affected by the policies of apartheid. They were brought up to respect their white blood and deny their black roots entirely, and the apartheid state's overture to the coloureds' white forefathers was to treat them as second in line to whites, providing them with a better education, greater rights, and more government support than black people (but substantially less than "pure" whites). These policies were even evident on Robben Island, where Indian and coloured inmates were given better food and clothing than the black prisoners, despite the fact that they were mostly close political comrades. The destruction of the coloured sense of self-worth was made evident when the New Nationalist Party (NNP) won the 1994 election race in the Western Cape (where the majority of coloureds reside). Voting back into power the same racist party that had created their oppressive new identity was seemingly a result of the false sense of hierarchy that apartheid created. Fear of *die Swart Gevaar* (an NP propaganda slogan meaning "the Black Danger") is slow to dissipate, and the increasingly Africanist policies of the ANC, in which "affirmative" positions are seen as being held for blacks only, does little to dispel them. Ideally, South Africans would heed the calls of those within the coloured ranks to do away with the label entirely, but as long as the majority believe that the coloureds are in a class of their own, this remains a pipe dream.

gave official recognition to 11 languages: Zulu, Xhosa, Afrikaans, English, Sotho, Venda, Tswana, Tsona, Pedi, Shangaan, and Ndebele. Television news and sports are broadcast in the four main language groups, English, Nguni (Zulu and Xhosa), Afrikaans, and Sotho. But while languages provide some clue to the demographics of the population, particularly where a specific language user is likely to live (another apartheid legacy), they give no real idea of the complexity of attitudes within groups. For instance, urban-born Xhosa males still paint their faces white to signal the circumcision rites that mark their transition to manhood, but unlike their rural counterparts, they may choose to be circumcised by a Western doctor. A group of Sotho women may invest their *stokvel* (an informal savings scheme) in unit trusts, while their mothers will not open a bank account. And an "ethnic" white Afrikaner living in rural Northern Cape is likely to have little in common with an Afrikaans-speaking coloured living in cosmopolitan Cape Town.

While life is better than it was under apartheid, and incidences of racial prejudice are now condemned in banner headlines, poverty and crime are the new oppressors. Even among the new black elite—the so-called "black diamonds," typified by conspicuous consumption (and best observed striding through the previously whites-only shopping malls of Jozi)—there are those who feel that the New South Africa is taking too long to deliver on its promises. "There is no black in the rainbow," an embittered Winnie Madikizela-Mandela said. "Maybe there is no rainbow nation at all." Hardly surprising, really. Despite the peaceful transition, years of fragmentation have rendered much of the nation cautious, suspicious, and critical. Many are still molded by the social-engineering experiment that separated them geographically and psychologically. But when our school-age youth stand up to sing their national anthem—proudly singing the verses in three languages—those old enough to remember the dark days of apartheid feel a thrill at new beginnings. A new, shared South African identity will take time to emerge—enough, at least, for the colors to mingle.

4 THE LAY OF THE LAND

SOUTH AFRICA

Geographically, much of South Africa is situated on an interior plateau (the highveld), circled by a coastal belt which widens in the eastern hinterland to become bush savannah, or lowveld, where South Africa's most famous reserve, Kruger National Park, is situated. For the first-time visitor, there are usually three crucial stops: a trip to **Big-Game Country,** most of which is located in and around Kruger National Park, which spans **Mpumalanga** and the **Limpopo Province;** a visit to **Cape Town** and its Winelands; and, time permitting, a self-drive tour of the **Garden Route** in the Western Cape. **Kwazulu-Natal** is another area worth considering, not least for the fabulous crafts, lush game reserves, and magnificent Drakensberg mountains.

THE WESTERN & EASTERN CAPE

The least African of all the provinces, the Western Cape is also the most popular, primarily due to the legendary beauty of its capital city, **Cape Town,** the neighboring **Winelands,** and the scenic coastal belt called the **Garden Route,** which winds through South Africa's well-traveled Lakes District. It also offers some of the best beach-based whale-watching in the world on the **Overberg Coast;** the world's most spectacular spring flowers display on the West Coast, north of Cape Town; and, in

Fun Facts **Endemic: Occurring Nowhere Else**

Did you know that 15% of South Africa's mammals, 30% of its reptiles, 6% of its birds, and 80% of its plants are found nowhere else in the world?

the **Karoo,** the quaint *dorps* (small towns) that typified rural Afrikaans culture. The mountains and hills that trail the coastline are a botanist's and hiker's dream, with the Cape Floral Kingdom—an awesome array of more than 8,000 species—a treat year-round. The Eastern Cape is where you'll find the Big 5 reserves (those parks where you can spot the Big 5 animals: lion, leopard, rhino, elephant, and buffalo) closest to Cape Town (also malaria free), as well as two of the country's top trails: the **Otter Trail,** in the Tsitsikamma National Park, the exit point of the Garden Route; and the **Wild Coast,** bordering KwaZulu-Natal.

Established as a port in 1652, Cape Town was the first gateway to southern Africa from Europe and still retains more of a colonial feel than any other major city. It is cut off from the rest of the country by mountain ranges and has its own distinctive climate—cool, wet winters and hot, windy summers—ideal for the wine and deciduous fruits that further cocoon the Cape's inhabitants from the harsh realties of the hinterland. This geographic insularity and the wounds inflicted by apartheid have bred their own set of unique problems, however. Gang warfare and drug trafficking in the Cape Flats—a region created by the notoriously draconian Group Areas Act, which relocated people of color to housing projects on the outskirts of town—as well as the increased rancor of the swelling homeless (further exacerbated by the stream of economic refugees from the Eastern Cape and beyond) are serious problems. In a city this size, such problems are hardly unusual, but what is surprising is how cut off from them you'll feel as a visitor.

MPUMALANGA & THE LIMPOPO PROVINCE To the east of Gauteng and the Free State lies the **Escarpment**—the end of the Drakensberg mountain range that rises in the Eastern Cape, running up the western border of KwaZulu-Natal before dividing Mpumalanga and the Limpopo Province into the high- and lowveld. Traveling through the Escarpment to reach the lowveld's **Big-Game Country,** you will find some of the country's most gorgeous views, the continent's second-largest canyon, and the country's first gold-rush towns, one of which has been declared a living monument. Traveling east on scenic mountain passes, you will drop thousands of feet to the lowveld plains. For those who want to see Africa's wild animals on a budget, **Kruger National Park** offers the best deal on the continent—a high density of game combined with spotlessly clean, albeit spartan, accommodations. For well-heeled visitors (or those who want that once-in-a-lifetime treat), Kruger is also home to several high-end **private concessions** that combine ultraluxurious lodgings with great game-viewing (though you cannot go off-road). Along Kruger's western flank, with no fences between, lie the **private game lodges** in the **Sabi Sand, Manyeleti,** and **Timbavati reserves,** which offer a variety of experiences—from over-the-top-decadent luxury chalets with private plunge pools to rough huts with no electricity. Closer to Johannesburg, the malaria-free **Welgevonden** reserve offers a Big 5 alternative for those with limited time, while

Exploring the World's Oldest Richest Kingdom

The **Cape Floral Kingdom** (69,930 sq. km/27,000 sq. miles) covers only .04% of the world's land surface, yet it contains 24,000 plant species; the most diverse of the world's six floral kingdoms—comparable only to the Boreal Kingdom, which comprises all of northern America, Europe, and Asia (51.8 million sq. km/20 million sq. miles). This high concentration makes it as important a conservation area as the Amazon basin. Although it is by no means as threatened, the battle to control alien invasive species introduced during the past century is ongoing.

The delicate inhabitants of the Cape Floral Kingdom are referred to as *fynbos* (literally, "fine bush," pronounced "*feign*-boss")—an evergreen vegetation characterized by the ability to thrive on nutrient-poor soil and to survive the Cape's windy, baking summers and wet winters. They're thought to be the oldest floral kingdom, and they're certainly the most diverse. Three-quarters of fynbos species are found nowhere else—many are so specialized they grow only in one valley, while popular indigenous species that have found their way into gardens across the world include the gardenia, red-hot poker, arum lily, strelitzia (bird of paradise), agapanthus, gladioli, and freesia. The most well-known fynbos group is the sculptural protea (of which the King protea is S.A.'s national flower), tiny ericas (with fine, bell-shaped flowers), and restios (reeds). Appearing as a homogenous gray-green heathland from afar, the Cape Floral Kingdom has a delicacy and variety of textures best appreciated at close range. Beyond the Kirstenbosch Botanical Gardens in Cape Town, you'll find the best views at Table Mountain and the De Hoop Nature Reserve and Grootbos Private Reserve. For more information, see the Cape Town and Western Cape chapters.

Madikwe likes to market itself as a Big 7 reserve—cheetah and the rare wild dog being the additional pull. The latter two are discussed in the Gauteng chapter.

KWAZULU-NATAL Hot and humid in summer, warm and balmy in winter, the KwaZulu-Natal coast makes for an excellent beach holiday. Temperatures never drop below 61°F (16°C), and the Indian Ocean is kept warm by the Mozambique Current, which washes past its subtropical shores. Unfortunately, this is no well-kept secret, and development along much of the south and north coasts (Durban being the center) has resulted in another paradise lost and an endless string of ugly, generic vacation and timeshare beach resorts. There are exceptions, the best of which lie north, such as the **St Lucia Wetland Park,** Africa's biggest estuary and home to large populations of Nile crocodile and hippo, and within easy striking distance of **Hluhluwe-Umfolozi,** the province's largest Big 5 resort.

After Cape Town, **Durban** is the most enjoyable city in the country to visit, though it's not in the same league in terms of natural beauty. It's sultry, with that run-down charm associated with the tropics, and home to a fascinating blend of cultures—besides the Zulu, the largest indigenous group in South Africa, the biggest population of Indians outside of India resides here. Perhaps this is why Durban is a design hothouse, producing the most talented interior and fashion designers in South Africa, and it's a great place to shop for crafts. It is also well situated, should you be interested in combining a visit to a Big 5 game reserve with diving or snorkeling, taking one of the historic battlefields tours, tooling along the Midlands Meander, or hiking through the vast and majestic Drakensberg range (top choice for local hikers). With a new international airport in Durban scheduled for completion in 2009, this relatively undiscovered region is set to offer the Cape some stiff competition.

BOTSWANA

Straddling the Tropic of Capricorn in southern Africa, Botswana is truly one of the last pristine wilderness areas on the continent. Roughly the size of France, it is bordered by Namibia to the west and north, Zimbabwe to the east, and South Africa to the south.

A sparsely populated country of just over one million inhabitants, Botswana offers a varied wilderness experience, from forest to salt pan, bushveld to rolling savanna, ancient lake beds to palm-fringed islands. The waterless Kalahari covers two-thirds of its surface, so it is nothing short of incredible that it is also home to one of the world's largest inland delta systems: the **Okavango Delta,** highlight of Botswana. This 15,000-sq.-km (5,850-sq.-mile) inland flood plain fans into the northwestern corner of the country, creating a paradise of palms, papyrus, and crystal-clear channels and backwaters. The life-giving waters provide an oasis for birds and animals, and consequently unparalleled opportunities for humans to view them.

In addition to the delta, Botswana has **Chobe National Park** to the northeast, a 12,000-sq.-km (4,680-sq.-mile) park that is famed for its huge elephant herds, while to the southeast are the spectacular wide-open spaces of **Makgadikgadi** and **Nxai Pans.** Time and money allowing, visits to these areas are essential to your southern Africa itinerary.

VICTORIA FALLS

Victoria Falls is easy to reach and safe to visit, with two airports within easy striking distance. Chapter 11 deals with the best way to experience what has justifiably been described as one of the wonders of the world, from both the Zimbabwean and Zambian sides of the falls. Note that the falls are also accessible as a day trip from Chobe National Park, Botswana.

5 RECOMMENDED BOOKS

As the first South African novel, ***The Story of an African Farm*** (1883)—a beautifully rendered account of daily life in the harsh Karoo—was written at the close of the 19th century by Olive Schreiner, the literature produced in this southern tip captured the imagination of its colonizers with its evocation of a bleak landscape and tough survival. This reached its apotheosis with the advent of the "Jim-comes-to-Jo'burg novel," a phrase coined by Nadine Gordimer to describe the plot in which a naive rural African moves into the corrupt and evil urban landscape—the most famous example being Alan Paton's ***Cry the Beloved Country*** (1948). Lesser-known and more devastating is the work of Sol Plaatje, founding ANC member, who wrote ***Native Life in South Africa*** (1916), about the devastation of the Land Act in 1916. Even our best-known imports—Nadine Gordimer, whose awards have included a Booker and a Nobel Prize (read ***The Conservationist*** [1974], ***The House Gun*** [1998], or ***The Burger's Daughter*** [1979], the prolific Doris Lessing, winner of the Nobel Prize for Literature, and J. M. Coetzee, first author to win the Booker prize twice—deal with the painful issues surrounding race, usually with love across the color bar; Coetzee's novels in particular explore the painful constraints of humanity when saturated in the racist fears of the "Dark

Continent." He won the first Booker prize for ***The Life & Times of Michael K,*** in 1983, and the second, in 1999, for the book ***Disgrace,*** since made into a (not very successful) film. Both are brilliant reads, but my personal favorite remains ***Age of Iron*** (1990), in which a white woman who is dying of cancer befriends the black tramp living in her garden. Ironically it is this theme that won awards for the latest offering from the superbly talented Afrikaans writer Marlene van Niekerk: ***Agaat*** (2007; beautifully translated into English) features the relationship between a mute 67-year old woman dying of ALS motor neuron disease and her "colored" nurse, Agaat. It is political in some sense, but mostly it is a psychological analysis of a relationship that reverberates on many levels—an absolute must for any serious lover of literature. Zakes Mda is another recommended novelist in this genre; either his first book ***Ways of Dying*** (1995), which follows the adventures of a self-confessed "professional mourner," or his third book, ***The Heart of Redness*** (2002), a fictional narrative inspired by the real-life story of Nongqawuse, the Xhosa prophetess responsible for the tragic Cattle Killing of 1856 (see history above).

For a political overview of the country, packaged as rollicking read, you can't go wrong with Richard Calland and Allistair Sparkes, both eloquent, intelligent, and incisive political analysts, and a joy to read. Of course political autobiography often provides the most direct insights into the complex past of South Africa, and there is no shortage here. Mandela's ***Long Walk to Freedom*** (1995) is an obvious choice, as is—if you can stand the harrowing truth—***Country of My Skull*** (1998), Afrikaans poet Anjie Krog's account of her work as a journalist reporting on the Truth Reconciliation Commission. Head of the Commission, Archbishop Desmond Tutu, authorized a good biography (***Rabble Rouser for Peace,*** by John Allan, 2006), but look for the book by his successor, Njongonkulu Ndungane: ***A World With A Human Face: A Voice from Africa*** (2003) provides an excellent analysis of the challenges facing the country, and how the West exacerbates many of the problems. The gripping autobiography ***My Traitor's Heart*** (1989), written by the talented Rian Malan, gave eloquent voice to white South Africa's primal fears in the 1980s and is essential reading for anyone who finds it hard to understand how white people could live with themselves under apartheid. For a less intense read, but with plenty of insight, pick up a copy of ***Playing the Enemy*** (2008), in which John Carlin explores how Nelson Mandela used rugby to set South Africa on the path to reconciliation.

Other reads worth looking into are Fred Khumalo's autobiographical novels, ***Touch My Blood*** (2006) and ***Bitches Brew*** (2005), and Kopano Matlwa's ***Coconut*** (2007), a look at race and class in South Africa—the latter two are both winners of the EU Literary Awards. Equally so, ***Dog Eat Dog*** (2005), by hip newcomer Niq Mhlongo, dubbed the "voice of the *kwaito* generation," and—for comic relief—***Some of My Best Friends Are White*** (2004), by the ever-satirical Ndumiso Ngcobo. ***The Native Commissioner*** (2006), by Shaun Johnson, and ***The Good Doctor*** (2003), by Damon Galgut, are both recipients of the Commonwealth Writer's Prize. If you like poetry, Gcina Mhlope is one of the country's most beloved poets; purchase ***Love Child*** (2002) and see why. If you'd like to dip into a compendium of South Africa's best writers, ***Lovely Beyond Any Singing*** (2008) is a good choice, with snippets and excerpts from some 30 authors.

However, if all you want to do is escape with a good crime thriller that happens to be set in South Africa, pick up anything written by Deon Meyer (***Dead at Daybreak*** [2000] and ***Heart of the Hunter*** [2003] are both recommended), or Margie Orford's ***Like Clockwork*** (2007), in which her heroine, Clara Heart, tracks a serial killer in Cape Town. Also set in Cape Town is the excellent debut by Roger Smith, ***Mixed Blood*** (2009), in which four men are drawn into a web of murder and vengeance. Better still, find your favorite crime writer in ***Bad Company*** (2009), a compendium of short stories by South Africa's top thriller writers (South Africa's *real* gold mine, according to master of suspense, Lee Child, who wrote the foreword). Or opt for light humor with Alexander McCall Smith's ***The No. 1 Ladies' Detective Agency*** (1998), a series set in Botswana. The sassy ***Moxyland*** (2008) by Lauren Beukes is worth highlighting; set in a futuristic Cape Town, and tackling issues such as globalization and consumerism, it transcends South Africa's past, and the lack of baggage is refreshing. Memoirs of a haunting African childhood have become a publishing trend and produced some fine reads, among them the superbly balanced ***Don't Let's Go to the Dogs Tonight,*** by Alexandra Fuller (2001); ***Ja No Man*** (2007), by Richard Poplak; ***Stealing Water*** (2008), by Tim Ecott; and ***A Fork in the Road*** (2009), by Andre Brink, the latter of course one of South Africa's most respected writers, with a host of fictional titles worth browsing through.

6 FILM OVERVIEW

By Dr. Keith Bain
PhD, Cinema Studies

Sadly, there aren't yet many good South African-produced movies likely to give you a really coherent picture of life in the country today. That's partly because there's such huge cultural and social diversity here that it's absolutely impossible to pack everything into a single story or within a 90-minute frame. Decent local cinema that has garnered critical acclaim usually fails dismally at the box office: South Africans tend to go to movies to be entertained and escape; with so much political intrigue and real-life soap opera in our daily news, you can't really blame us. After big budget Hollywood blockbusters, South Africans consume principally stupid films about stupid South Africans making fools of themselves. Our ability to laugh at ourselves is second to none. The best known example of this type of slapstick comedy event is *The Gods Must Be Crazy,* which astonished audiences when it was first released in 1980. Deceptively, that film was about a bushman traveling to the ends of the earth to dispose of a Coca-Cola bottle dropped into the desert from a passing plane, but in more metaphoric terms, it deals with the clash of cultures that's still, even 30 years later, apparent within South African society. If you can sit through something slightly silly and potentially embarrassing, *Gods Must Be Crazy* remains a classic of South African cinema, and is not without its charms.

Since then the only South African to consistently make money-spinning films has been Leon Schuster, a pranks and pratfalls comedy man who makes fun of the contradictions and paradoxes that are so obviously a part of life in a country that still has deep underlying racial resentment and wide social imbalance. Schuster—in films like *Mr. Bones* (2001, with a sequel in 2008), *Oh Shucks It's Shuster* (1989) and *Oh Shucks I'm Gatvol* (2004), and *There's a Zulu on my Stoep* (2009)—capitalizes on his knack for hitting on a collective funny bone that is inherently connected to the confusing, catastrophic, and potentially wonderful cultural stew. Watch these at your own risk.

Cheap slapstick films aside, early post-apartheid cinema tended to focus heavily on "issue" narratives. *Forgiveness* (2004), exploring the possibilities for redemption, was ultimately a bad reminder of the worst of apartheid-era South Africa—see it if you want to learn about some of the furious tensions that exist in our society. Picking up a number of international film festival awards, *Promised Land* (2003) deals with "white identity syndromes" evident in post-apartheid South Africa, but bewildered audiences with its cartoon stereotypes and art-house posturing; however, the film will give you a vague idea of how some people in this country have grown up with socialized hatred. Two small, but very memorable, late-1990s dramas that do justice to their subject matter are *Paljas* (1998), directed by South Africa's most prolific female filmmaker, Katinka Heyns (and quite possibly the best art-house film to have come out of South Africa), and *A Reasonable Man* (1999), directed by Gavin Hood, who went on to make South Africa's first-ever Oscar winner, *Tsotsi,* in 2005. *Paljas* is a small, riveting movie about a tiny, forgotten Afrikaans village and the intricacies of family and community life there. As a drama, it's searing, tender, and deeply moving, with some of the finest-ever screen performances by South Africans. *A Reasonable Man* explores the notion of justice in an unjust world (Hood, in fact, studied law and the legal system has always played some part in his movies).

In the last few years, three South African films have achieved international recognition: The much-lauded township opera, *U-Carmen e-Khayelitsha* (2005); the Oscar-nominated AIDS movie, *Yesterday* (2004); and the aforementioned *Tsotsi,* which won the Best Foreign Language Film Academy Award, albeit for a version of the film that featured not only a different soundtrack, but an alternate ending to the one shown in South Africa. Be that as it may, *Tsotsi* blew South African audiences away with its gripping human tragedy and a story that got under the belly of some of the country's most painful realities. Another film worth seeing (this time by Darrell Roodt, director of *Yesterday*), is *Faith's Corner* (2005), starring Lelethi Khumalo, the singular talent who headlines *Yesterday.* It's a very simple tale of a homeless woman's struggle to beg for enough money to feed her hungry children; a heartbreakingly honest reflection of life for many South Africans struggling on the streets. Three more films worth looking at are *Stander* (2004), which showcases the country as it looked and felt in the '70s—it's also a very good portrayal of the only South African bank robber to have attained cult status; *Jerusalama* (2008), a gritty crime thriller that looks at one of Jo'burg's more audacious crime heists—the hijacking of entire buildings by entrepreneurial slumlords; and the gripping, stirring, and sometimes hard-hitting Hillary Swank–starring *Red Dust* (2006), which uncovers some of the horrors of the past through episodes revealed at the Truth and Reconciliation Commission (TRC). Another one worth viewing is the well-made biopic of Nelson Mandela's prison warden *Goodbye Bafana* (2007), directed by Oscar-winning director Bille August. Then there's the Clint Eastwood-directed film, *Invictus* (2009), starring Matt Damon as a South African rugby hero and Morgan Freeman as Mandela, in a recounting of the country's most memorable victory ever on the sports field: the Rugby World Cup, in 1995. The most sensational South African movie in recent years is also a 2009 release: *D*istrict 9 is a gutsy action/sci-fi film that does an interesting job of parodying the country's ongoing struggle with social geography and race politics. Although not to be taken at face value, the film is set in a highly recognizable Johannesburg but uses humanoid aliens as stand-ins for the country's economically deprived multitudes. It plays up all sorts of social stereotypes that—mercifully—you're unlikely to encounter on a visit here. With some impressive special effects, it's probably the first commercially viable film set in South Africa that steers clear of the slapstick-comedy route.

While we clearly have exciting enough material upon which to base them, we seem to lack the industry capacity to locally produce films, it seems. What we do have, though, is a massively talented film industry—for years South African crews have been honing their skills on the plethora of international commercials and films that are shot here. Hopefully, now that the finishing touches are being put on the long awaited Cape Town Film Studios, there will be a more concerted push towards establishing a thriving, consistent industry in S.A., and we can look forward to more brilliantly-written, entertaining and insightful films such as *Gums and Noses* (2004), perhaps the most underrated South African film of the last decade. A slick little comedy set in the world of contemporary advertising, it's one of the few intelligent, locally-made films that sidesteps politics and discovers a South Africa that is both unique and globally accessible.

7 CUISINE IN SOUTHERN AFRICA

Southern Africa does not have an extensively developed cuisine to call its own, but a few signature dishes, snacks, and sweet treats are worth sampling.

The most popular local cuisine is **Cape Malay,** characterized by sweet aromatic **curries.** These include *bobotie,* a delicious baked meatloaf, mildly curried and served with chutney; and *bredie,* a tomato-based stew, usually with lamb, often served with pumpkin sweetened with brown sugar. Another Cape delicacy not to be missed is *waterblommetjie bredie,* or water lily stew, also usually cooked with lamb. Many South African menus feature **Karoo lamb,** favored because the sweet and aromatic herbs and grasses of this arid region flavor the animals as they graze, and **ostrich,** a delicious red meat that tastes more like beef than anything else, though it is fat free. Game cuts such as springbok, kudu, eland, impala, and warthog are common on menus catering to tourists. Try them if you must, but be warned that they are usually less tender than ostrich, lamb, or beef. Look out for **vetkoek** (literally, "fat cake")—a deep-fried bread-dough, stuffed with curried mince; in Durban, they serve a **"bunny-chow"**—a half-loaf of white bread, the soft innards pulled out for the crust to become a receptacle for various curries.

Durban is, in fact, famed for its hot **Indian curries,** whose burn potential is usually indicated by names such as Honeymooners' Delight (hot) and Mother-in-Law Exterminator (damn hot!). **Samosas** (pastry wrapped around meat or vegetable filling and fired) are also popular as street snacks, as well as on some upmarket menus.

The coastline supplies seafood in abundance: fish, abalone, mussels, oysters, crabs, squid, langoustines, and the Cape's famous rock lobster (crayfish). For a uniquely South African–flavored seafood feast, head for one of the West Coast beach restaurants. Here, **snoek,** a firm white fish, is traditionally served with *konfyt* (fruits preserved in sugar syrup, from the French *confit,* a legacy of the French Huguenots).

Look for the spiraling smoke trailing over suburban fences and township yards each weekend, when throughout the country South Africans barbecue fresh meat over coals. The ubiquitous ***braaivleis*** (barbecues) or ***tshisanyamas*** ("burn the meat") feature anything from ostrich to ***boerewors*** (a coriander-spiced beef-and-pork sausage, arguably South Africa's staple meat). The most basic African foodstuff is corn, most popularly eaten as ***pap,*** a ground-maize polentalike porridge, or the rougher wholegrain ***samp.*** Both are served with a vegetable- or meat-based sauce.

Choice desserts are ***melktert,*** a cinnamon-flavored Dutch custard tart; ***malva pudding,*** a hot, sticky sweet Dutch pudding, served with custard or cream; or ***koeksisters,*** plaited doughnuts deep-fried and dipped in syrup.

3

Planning Your Trip to South Africa

South Africa's major cities are generally smaller than those in Europe and the United States, but they offer comparable facilities and make a comfortable starting point or base for your travels. Unless you're heading into really remote areas for an extended period of time, don't worry about packing for every eventuality: Anything you've forgotten can be bought here, credit cards are an accepted form of payment, and you're no more likely to be affected by water- or food-borne illnesses that you would be back home. You'll also find a relatively efficient tourism infrastructure, with plenty of services and facilities designed to help you make the most of your trip. Start by browsing the Web, or simply read through this chapter. For additional help in planning your trip and for more on-the-ground resources, see chapter 13 (p. 460).

1 WHEN TO GO

Roughly speaking, the summer months are December to March, autumn is April to May, winter is June to August, and spring is September to November. Because southern Africa is such a large area, and each region's offerings change with the seasons, when you go may determine where you go.

THE COAST South Africa's southwestern coast (the province known as Western Cape) tends to attract the majority of international visitors during the summer months. Fortunately, the country is big enough to absorb these increased numbers without causing the discomfort most people associate with busy seasons, though parts of Cape Town become unbearably full for locals' tastes. Be aware, however, that accommodation prices do increase in summer, some by as much as 70%; and if you dislike crowds, you should try to avoid South Africa's coast during the busiest school holidays, which—like elsewhere—take place from around mid-December to mid-January. In fact, the hot months of February and March are considered by most Northern Hemisphere dwellers to be the best times to visit; not least, to escape what by then has felt like a very long winter up north. April, too, is a great month to visit, when the light takes on a softer hue, sunsets are often spectacular, and balmy temperatures are preferable for those who dislike baking heat. Note, though, that you'll need to book early if your visit coincides with Easter weekend, when you will compete with locals on their 10-day school vacation.

Depending on your interests, winter (June–Aug) brings substantial benefits, too: July to November are the months when the Southern Right whales migrate to the Cape's southern coast, providing the best land-based whale-watching in the world (and plenty of opportunities to see them by boat). With the Cape a winter rainfall area, local tourism authorities have aptly dubbed the May-to-August period its "green season," and indeed the Cape's valleys and mountains are an ideal verdant

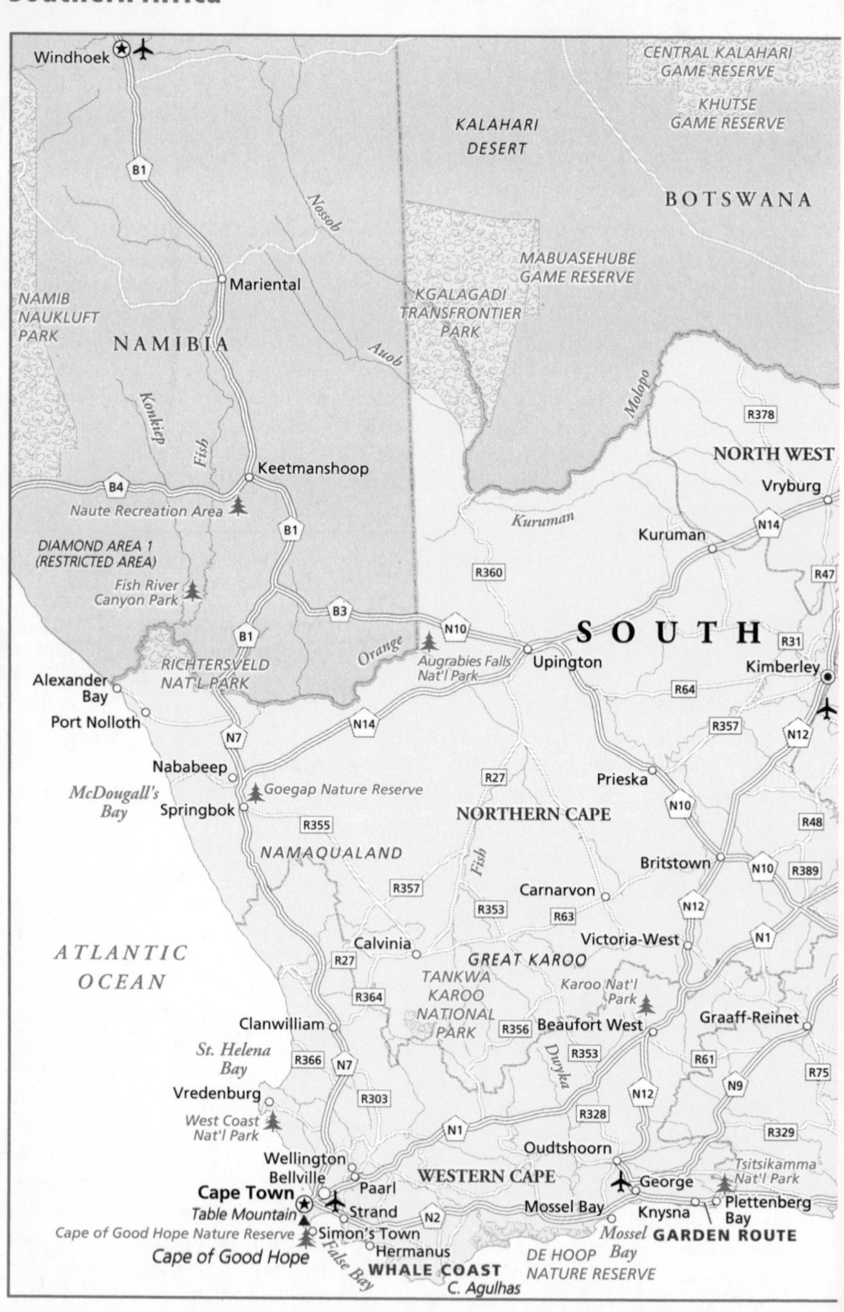
Windhoek
CENTRAL KALAHARI GAME RESERVE
KHUTSE GAME RESERVE
KALAHARI DESERT
BOTSWANA
B1
Nossob
MABUASEHUBE GAME RESERVE
Mariental
NAMIB NAUKLUFT PARK
KGALAGADI TRANSFRONTIER PARK
NAMIBIA
Auob
Molopo
Konkiep
Fish
R378
NORTH WEST
Keetmanshoop
Vryburg
B4
Naute Recreation Area
Kuruman
N14
Kuruman
DIAMOND AREA 1 (RESTRICTED AREA)
R360
R47
Fish River Canyon Park
B3
N10
SOUTH
R31
B1
Orange
Augrabies Falls Nat'l Park
Upington
Kimberley
Alexander Bay
RICHTERSVELD NAT'L PARK
R64
Port Nolloth
N14
R357
N12
N7
Nababeep
R27
Prieska
McDougall's Bay
Goegap Nature Reserve
Springbok
N10
NORTHERN CAPE
R48
R355
NAMAQUALAND
Fish
Britstown
N10
R389
R357
Carnarvon
R353
R63
N12
ATLANTIC OCEAN
Calvinia
Victoria-West
N1
R27
GREAT KAROO
TANKWA KAROO NATIONAL PARK
Karoo Nat'l Park
R364
Clanwilliam
R356
Beaufort West
Graaff-Reinet
St. Helena Bay
R366
N7
Dwyka
R353
R61
R75
Vredenburg
R303
N12
N9
West Coast Nat'l Park
R328
N1
R329
Oudtshoorn
Wellington
Bellville
WESTERN CAPE
Tsitsikamma Nat'l Park
George
Paarl
Cape Town
Table Mountain
Strand
Mossel Bay
Knysna
Plettenberg Bay
N2
Cape of Good Hope Nature Reserve
Simon's Town
Mossel Bay
GARDEN ROUTE
Hermanus
False Bay
Cape of Good Hope
DE HOOP NATURE RESERVE
WHALE COAST
C. Agulhas

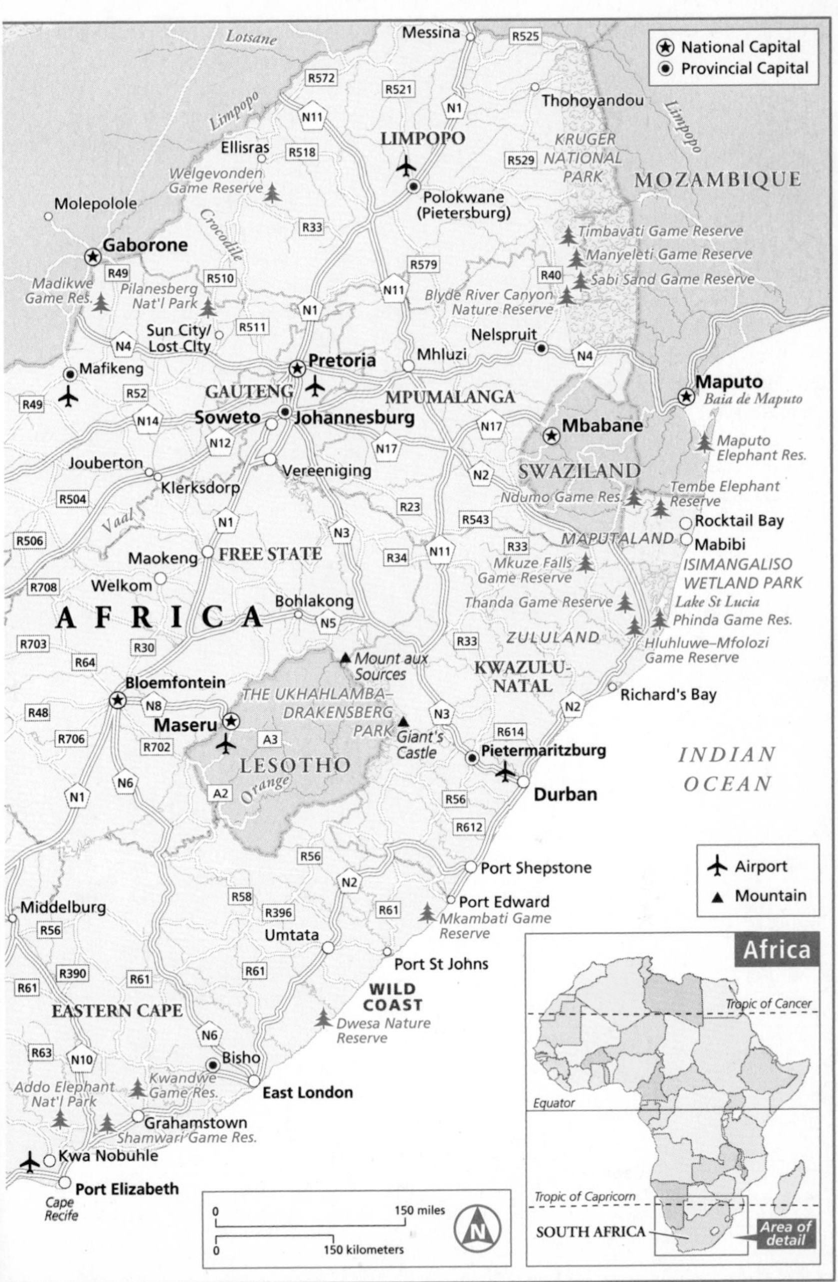
National Capital
Provincial Capital
Airport
Mountain
Messina
Thohoyandou
LIMPOPO
KRUGER NATIONAL PARK
MOZAMBIQUE
Ellisras
Welgevonden Game Reserve
Molepolole
Polokwane (Pietersburg)
Gaborone
Timbavati Game Reserve
Manyeleti Game Reserve
Sabi Sand Game Reserve
Madikwe Game Res.
Pilanesberg Nat'l Park
Blyde River Canyon Nature Reserve
Sun City/ Lost City
Nelspruit
Mafikeng
Pretoria
Mhluzi
Maputo
Baia de Maputo
GAUTENG
MPUMALANGA
Soweto
Johannesburg
Mbabane
Maputo Elephant Res.
Jouberton
Klerksdorp
Vereeniging
SWAZILAND
Ndumo Game Res.
Tembe Elephant Reserve
Rocktail Bay
Mabibi
MAPUTALAND
Maokeng
FREE STATE
ISIMANGALISO WETLAND PARK
Mkuze Falls Game Reserve
Welkom
Thanda Game Reserve
Lake St Lucia
Phinda Game Res.
Bohlakong
AFRICA
ZULULAND
Hluhluwe–Mfolozi Game Reserve
Mount aux Sources
KWAZULU-NATAL
Bloemfontein
THE UKHAHLAMBA-DRAKENSBERG PARK
Richard's Bay
Maseru
Giant's Castle
Pietermaritzburg
LESOTHO
INDIAN OCEAN
Durban
Orange
Vaal
Limpopo
Lotsane
Crocodile
Port Shepstone
Port Edward
Mkambati Game Reserve
Middelburg
Umtata
Port St Johns
WILD COAST
EASTERN CAPE
Dwesa Nature Reserve
Bisho
Kwandwe Game Res.
Addo Elephant Nat'l Park
East London
Grahamstown
Shamwari Game Res.
Kwa Nobuhle
Port Elizabeth
Cape Recife
0 150 miles
0 150 kilometers
N
Africa
Tropic of Cancer
Equator
Tropic of Capricorn
SOUTH AFRICA
Area of detail
R525
R572
R521
N1
N11
R518
R529
R33
R579
R40
R49
R510
R511
N4
R52
N14
N12
N17
N2
R504
R23
R543
R506
N3
R34
R708
R703
R30
N5
R64
N8
R48
A3
R614
R706
R702
N6
A2
R56
R612
R58
R396
R61
R390
R63
N10

backdrop to dramatic displays of *fynbos* (shrublike plant) in flower. While it can at times rain continuously, the pattern is usually broken every few days with balmy, sun-drenched days. It's a wonderful time for Capetonians, who get to air their winter coats for only these few months and reclaim the city, now virtually empty of visitors, as their own.

If you're at all hankering for the sun, plan to head to the Garden Route and Karoo, preferably along Route 62, where year-round sunshine ensures that any time of year is a great time to tackle a driving tour of this region. Winter is also the ideal time to visit the east coast of Kwazulu-Natal, which can be oppressively humid in summer.

October to November is when the Cape floral kingdom again wows her human inhabitants with a new batch of flowering species, while the beaches, still relatively empty, sparkle in the temperate sun, and guesthouses and hotels, hungry after the winter wait, offer some of the best deals of the season.

INLAND May to August are considered the best months for sighting big game in and around Kruger National Park. The foliage is less dense, malaria risk is lower, yet many of the private game reserve lodges drop their prices substantially.

June to October, however, is peak season in the Delta, Botswana; game-viewing is best at this time, thanks to the rains. Given the low-volume approach to tourism, lodges are booked months in advance, despite charging top dollar. The Delta is often combined with a visit to Victoria Falls, but the Falls are widely considered most impressive in full flood, between March and May, when some 500 million cubic liters of water cascade into the Batoka gorge every minute. The spray can obscure views, however, and prohibit riding the Batoka's Grade 5 rapids—renowned in rafting circles as one of the most exhilarating rides in the world—as they are out of bounds when the falls are in flood.

Weather Chart for Southern Africa

Cape Town, South Africa

	Jan	Feb	Mar	Apr	May	June	July	Aug	Sept	Oct	Nov	Dec
Temp. (°F)	61/79	59/79	57/77	54/73	50/68	46/64	45/63	45/64	46/66	50/70	55/75	59/77
Temp. (°C)	16/26	15/26	14/25	12/23	10/20	8/18	7/17	7/18	8/19	10/21	13/24	15/25
Rainfall (in.)	0.6	0.7	0.7	2.0	3.5	3.3	3.5	3.1	2.0	1.4	.5	.6

Johannesburg, South Africa

	Jan	Feb	Mar	Apr	May	June	July	Aug	Sept	Oct	Nov	Dec
Temp. (°F)	59/79	57/77	55/75	52/72	46/66	41/61	41/61	45/66	48/72	54/75	55/77	57/77
Temp. (°C)	15/26	14/25	13/24	11/22	8/19	5/16	5/16	7/19	9/22	12/24	13/25	14/25
Rainfall (in.)	4.5	3.8	2.9	2.5	0.9	0.3	0.3	0.2	0.1	2.7	4.6	4.3

Victoria Falls, Zimbabwe

	Jan	Feb	Mar	Apr	May	June	July	Aug	Sept	Oct	Nov	Dec
Temp. (°F)	65/85	64/85	62/85	57/84	49/81	43/76	42/77	47/82	55/89	62/91	64/90	64/86
Temp. (°C)	18/30	18/30	17/30	14/29	9/27	6/24	6/24	8/28	13/32	17/33	18/32	18/30
Rainfall (in.)	6.6	5	2.8	1.0	0.1	0	0	0	0.7	1.1	2.5	6.8

Maun, Botswana

	Jan	Feb	Mar	Apr	May	June	July	Aug	Sept	Oct	Nov	Dec
Temp. (°F)	66/90	66/88	64/88	57/88	48/82	43/77	43/77	48/82	55/91	64/95	66/93	66/90
Temp. (°C)	19/32	19/31	18/31	14/31	9/28	6/25	6/25	9/29	13/33	18/35	19/34	19/23
Rainfall (in.)	4.3	3.2	2.8	1.0	0.3	0.1	0	0	0	1.2	2.0	3.8

THE CLIMATE

Depending on where you are, average maximum temperatures can vary from 80°F (27°C; Cape Town) to 90°F (32°C; Kruger National Park) in the summer, and from an average 69°F (21°C; Cape Town) to 77°F (25°C; Durban) in winter. While summer is the most popular time, high humidity in KwaZulu-Natal can make for muggy days, and gale-force winds often occur in Cape Town and Port Elizabeth. Winter visitors would be well advised to pack warm clothes, despite higher average temperatures than in the United States or Europe. South African buildings are not geared for the cold; insulation is low on the priority list, and central heating is nonexistent. Temperatures in the interior fluctuate wildly in winter; you're best off layering.

RAINFALL

South Africa is generally considered an arid region; two-thirds of the country receives less than 500mm (20 in.) of rain a year. In the interior, rain usually falls in the summer, and spectacular thunderstorms and the smell of damp earth bring great relief from the searing heat. The Garden Route enjoys rain year-round, usually at night. In Cape Town and surrounds, the rain falls mostly in the winter, when the gray skies are a perfect foil for the burnt-orange strelitzias, pink proteas, and fields of white arum lilies—and an equally good accompaniment to crackling fires and fine South African red wines.

HOLIDAYS

If you are traveling during the South African school holidays, make sure you book your accommodations well in advance. (Check exact school holiday dates with South African Tourism, as provinces differ, but they usually run 4 weeks in Dec and Jan, 2 weeks in Apr, 3 weeks in June and July, and 1 week in Sept.) Flights can also be impossible to find, particularly over the Christmas holidays. Easter holidays (usually late Mar to mid-Apr) can also be busy, while the Kruger is almost always packed during the winter vacation (mid-June to mid-July). There's another short school break in spring, from late September to October 7. For public holidays in South Africa, see chapter 13 (p. 461).

ZIMBABWE/ZAMBIA

Zimbabwe and Zambia's climates are similar to that in South Africa's northern provinces, with a rainy season in summer, mostly between December and mid-March. Summers are warm to hot (late Oct–Dec can be uncomfortable), and winters are mild. Malaria is still a danger in many areas. There are tsetse flies in parts of the Zambezi Valley and in the southeast. And certain rivers, lakes, and dams are infected with bilharzia. Victoria Falls are often at their fullest around mid-April, at the end of the rainy season (Nov–Apr), though this is also when the mist created by the falling water may obscure the view and malaria-carrying mosquitoes are at their most prolific. Temperatures range from 90°F (32°C) in October and November to 60°F (16°C) in June and July. Many think the best time to see the falls is from August to December, when the view is clearer (though the flow of the water is at its lowest). June through December is high season for many of the upmarket lodges, which raise their prices during these months. You are unlikely to be affected by public holidays.

BOTSWANA

Botswana has a pleasant, temperate climate with low humidity, with a maximum mean temperature of 91°F (33°C) in January and a minimum mean temperature of 38°F (4°C) in June. There are effectively two seasons: summer (Sept–Apr), with frequent rains and thunderstorms, and winter (May–Aug), with cold and dry days and nights. Rainfalls make the summer months a great time to visit the delta if you're interested in birds and plants, but it can get very hot. From April to September, the days are mild to warm, but temperatures drop sharply at night and early in the morning, particularly around June and July. Most consider these 2 months the best time to visit the delta, when the rain that falls on the Angolan bushveld plains seeps down to create what is referred to as the "flood." At this time, water lilies bloom, countless aquatic creatures frolic in the water, and a huge diversity of game from the surrounding dry areas moves into the delta. You are unlikely to be affected by public holidays.

SOUTH AFRICA CALENDAR OF EVENTS

A comprehensive list of events throughout South Africa can be found at www.sa-venues.com/events—even the smallest of festivals, as well as the dates—useful to know even if you don't want to participate in festival gatherings, as parking and accommodation can become more problematic. For a more broad-based yet specialist look at the South African calendar, take a look at the official website www.southafrica.net; choose the country "South Africa," then and click on any of the themed options (green season, beach, floral, adventure activities, and so on). For an exhaustive list of events beyond those listed here, check http://events.frommers.com, where you'll find a searchable, up-to-the-minute roster of what's happening in cities all over the world.

JANUARY

Cape Minstrels Carnival, Cape Town. Festive Cape Malay or "coloured" groups compete and parade, dressed in colorful outfits, through the city's streets, singing and jiving to banjo beats. Several days in January.

Spier Arts Festival, Spier Estate, Stellenbosch, Winelands. The Western Cape's premier arts festival features local and international opera, classical music, comedy, jazz, and drama at the Spier Amphitheatre. January to March.

Shakespeare Open Air Festival, Maynardville, Wynberg, Cape Town. Pack a picnic to enjoy this annual Shakespeare play performed in the Maynardville Gardens. Mid-January.

Duzi Canoe Race, Pietermaritzburg, KwaZulu-Natal. The country's most prestigious canoeing event covers the 115km (71 miles) between Pietermaritzburg and Durban. Late January.

J&B Metropolitan Horse Race, Kenilworth Race Course, Cape Town. The Western Cape's premier horse-racing event is Cape Town's excuse to party, and it attracts many of the city's socialites. Last Saturday in January or first in February.

South Africa Open, new venue every year. South Africa's golfing greats battle it out on one of the country's premier courses. Mid- or late January.

FEBRUARY

Sangoma Khekheke's Annual Snake Dance, Zululand, KwaZulu-Natal. Some 6,000 to 8,000 Zulus gather to slaughter cattle and dance under the auspices of Sangoma Khekheke. Late February.

Dance Umbrella, various venues, Johannesburg. A platform for the best contemporary choreography and dance in South Africa. Mid-February to mid-March.

Design Indaba Cape Town, Cape Town. At South Africa's premier design event, a host of international talent addresses the main conference (usually sold out), and South Africa's most talented designers hawk their wares at the Expo. It's a must for anyone looking for retail inspiration, or simply wanting to go home with a rare one-off design piece.

MARCH

Cape Argus Cycle Tour, Cape Town. The largest of its kind in the world, this race attracts some 30,000 cyclists from around the world and covers 105km (65 miles) of Cape Town's most scenic routes. Second Sunday of March.

Cape Town International Jazz Festival, Cape Town. The best local jazz talent, joined by international greats (often including a great lineup from all over Africa), perform for enthusiastic audiences for 2 days; go to **www.capetownjazzfest.com**. Late March.

Klein Karoo National Arts Festival, Oudtshoorn, Western Cape. Showcases the country's best; many productions (often in Afrikaans) premier here. Predominantly drama, as well as excellent dance and music acts. End of March or early April.

APRIL

Two Oceans Marathon, Cape Town. This 56km (35-mile) scenic route attracts some 12,000 athletes. Easter Saturday.

MAY

Cape Times Waterfront Wine Festival, V&A Waterfront, Cape Town. Some 400 wines from 95 estates and wineries are represented, as well as a great selection of South Africa's finest cheeses—this has got to be the easiest way to sample some of the culinary wonders of the Cape. Early May.

The Gourmet Festival, Cape Town. Sample the fare of the city's best chefs, with set menus aimed at the budget-conscious gourmand; take your pick from the participating restaurants on **www.gourmetsa.com**. Mid-May.

Prince Albert Olive Festival, Prince Albert. This 2-day festival in the rural hamlet of Prince Albert is a real treat—a gathering of predominantly local people, unpretentious entertainment (care to join in the annual olive-pit-spitting championship?), and great food. May.

Franschhoek Literary Festival, Franschhoek. Thanks in part to the gorgeous surrounds—Franschhoek is the Cape's most beautiful village, and the gourmet capital of the region—this relative newcomer is already attracting some big names in literature.

JUNE

Comrades Marathon, Pietermaritzburg, KwaZulu-Natal. More than 13,000 runners participate in this 89km (55-mile) race, which started in 1921. Mid-June.

Standard Bank National Arts Festival, Grahamstown, Eastern Cape. The largest arts festival in the Southern Hemisphere features performances from cutting-edge to classical. Pack warm woolies. Late June to early July.

JULY

Knysna Oyster Festival, Knysna, Garden Route, Western Cape. The festival encompasses the Forest Marathon, a mountain-bike cycling tour, a regatta, a golf championship, and flea markets. First Friday to second Saturday of July.

S.A. Fashion Week, Sandton Convention Centre, Johannesburg. A great showcase of the abundance of new Afro-centric design talent. Late July.

Mr. Price Pro Surfing Classic, Durban beachfront. This world-class watersports- and beach-related tournament includes what is still referred to as the Gunston 500, one of the world's premier surfing events. Mid- or late July.

The Sardine Run, Eastern Cape and KwaZulu-Natal. Every year the east coast of South Africa is host to the greatest dive show in the world, when some three billion sardines, followed by hundreds of predators, move from the cold Atlantic to the subtropical waters of the Indian Ocean—a migration to rival that of the Serengeti.

August

Namaqualand Wild Flower Season, Western and Northern Cape. From mid-August on (sometimes later, depending on rain), the semiarid West Coast is transformed into a floral paradise, with more than 2,600 species in bloom. August to October.

Jomba! Contemporary Dance Experience, Durban, KwaZulu-Natal. A contemporary dance festival featuring the best of KwaZulu-Natal's considerable dance and choreography talent. Late August to early September.

September

Arts Alive International Festival, Johannesburg. This urban arts festival features local talent and international stars. Includes the Jazz on the Lake Concert held at Zoo Lake. Contact the **Gauteng Tourism Authority** (www.gauteng.net) for dates.

Whale Festival, Hermanus, Western Cape. The Whale Festival includes drama performances, an arts ramble, a crafts market, and whale-route lectures and tours. Late September to early October.

King Shaka Day Celebrations and the **Zulu Kings Reed Dance,** Zululand, KwaZulu-Natal. King Shaka Day sees all the Zulu heads, from Chief Buthelezi (leader of the IFP party) to Prince Gideon, dressed in full traditional gear, addressing their minions in a moving day celebrating Zulu traditions. Later in the month, some 15,000 Zulu maidens participate in the colorful Reed Dance, in which the king would traditionally choose a new wife. Prince Gideon, mindful of the AIDS crisis, uses the opportunity to address some of the issues affecting the nation today by abstaining from the tradition. Both events are highly recommended. Last week in September.

Out in Africa Gay & Lesbian Film Festival. A gay and lesbian film festival held each year in the major cities in South Africa covers the latest and best movies and documentaries available on the international circuit.

October

Shembe Celebrations, Zululand, KwaZulu-Natal. The prophet Shembe, the fourth successor of the first prophet, presides over a congregation of some 30,000 who gather to hear his words; Sunday, when Shembe leads the crowds into prayer-dancing, is the highlight. Last 3 weeks of October.

November

Turtle-tracking in Maputaland, Zululand, KwaZulu-Natal. Every year from November to January, the rare loggerhead and leatherback turtles return to the very beaches on which they were born, to nest and lay their eggs in the soft sands. The best place to witness this ancient ritual is at Rocktail Bay and Mabibi, both blessed with coral reefs and fabulous lodgings.

December

Mother City Queer Project, Cape Town. This masked costume ball features some 10 dance zones and costumed teams celebrating Cape Town's vibrant and creative gay culture. The best party of the year. Mid-December.

Million Dollar Golf Challenge, Sun City, North-West Province. This high-stakes tournament attracts the world's best golfers. Call Sun City at ✆ **014/557-1544** for exact dates.

Appletiser Summer Sunset Concerts, Kirstenbosch Gardens, Cape Town. Start of the new season: Pack a picnic and get there by 4:30pm to grab a choice spot on the lawn before the concert starts at 5:30pm. Program runs to March.

Vortex New Year's Eve Rave Party, Grabouw, Cape Town surrounds. An almost weeklong nonstop camp-out party, where Cape Town's hippest hippies pay homage to the beat from dusk to dawn.

2 ENTRY REQUIREMENTS

PASSPORTS

Every traveler entering South Africa, Zimbabwe, Zambia, and Botswana is required to show a passport valid for at least 6 months. Note that under South Africa's Immigration Act of 2002, the passport must also contain at least one unused page for endorsements. If you do not yet have a passport, allow plenty of time before your trip to apply for one. For information on how to get a passport, see chapter 13 (p. 462). The websites listed provide downloadable passport applications and list the current processing fees.

VISAS

South Africa Aside from a valid passport, citizens of the United States, the E.U., the U.K., Canada, Australia, and New Zealand need only a return ticket for a 90-day stay in South Africa. Upon entering, you will automatically be given a free entry permit sticker. Visitors wanting to stay for a longer period will have to apply formally for a visa, as opposed to relying on the automatic entry permit. For more information, visit the South African Home Affairs Department website, **www.home-affairs.gov.za**.

Botswana To enter Botswana, sufficient funds to finance your stay, as well as outgoing travel documents, are required. Holders of U.S., Commonwealth, and most European passports do not require visas.

Zimbabwe At press time, to enter Zimbabwe, visa fees depend on nationality. For British nationals, a single entry costs $55 ($70 for double entry). U.S. nationals must pay $45 (this is automatically a double-entry visa). Canadians pay $75. Australians and New Zealanders can purchase one for $30 (double entry $45). If you intend to purchase a visa upon arrival, double check these figures—they tend to change pretty regularly. Remember to take two passport photographs; you can print out and complete the application forms beforehand (for forms, see "Travel Document Systems," below). All visitors need tickets of return or onward travel, cash at the border to pay the visa fee, and sufficient funds to support their stay. Note that visa fees are subject to frequent changes, due to diplomatic and economic unease within Zimbabwe, and visitors are advised to check current status with a travel agent. You can, of course, obtain your visa in advance, which will reduce the amount of time you need to spend at any border post, but this will incur an additional fee ($25 and upward); consult your travel agent in this regard or use **Travel Document Systems.** (For visa applications and physical addresses in New York, San Francisco, and Washington, D.C., visit **www.traveldocs.com**.)

Zambia Regarding visa fees to Zambia, 2009 saw a return to a more equitable tourism policy. All passport holders are now charged $50 for a single-entry visa and $80 for a multiple-entry visa. Note that day visitors to the Zambian side of Victoria Falls from Zimbabwe can purchase a $20 **day visa** at the bridge (see www.zambiaimmigration.gov.zm). For additional information on entry requirements, see chapter 11, "Visitor Information," or one of the lodges or operators.

CUSTOMS

For information on what you can bring into and take out of South African countries, see South Africa Fast Facts at www.frommers.com.

What You Can Take Home from Southern Africa

For information on what you're allowed to bring home, contact one of the following agencies:

U.S. Citizens U.S. Customs & Border Protection (CBP), 1300 Pennsylvania Ave., NW, Washington, DC 20229 (© **877/287-8667;** www.cbp.gov).

Canadian Citizens Canada Border Services Agency (© **800/461-9999** in Canada, or 204/983-3500; www.cbsa-asfc.gc.ca).

U.K. Citizens HM Customs & Excise (© **0845/010-9000,** or 020/8929-0152 outside the U.K.; www.hmce.gov.uk).

Australian Citizens Australian Customs Service (© **1300/363-263** or www.customs.gov.au).

New Zealand Citizens New Zealand Customs, The Customhouse, 17–21 Whitmore St., Box 2218, Wellington (© **04/473-6099** or 0800/428-786; www.customs.govt.nz).

MEDICAL REQUIREMENTS

No inoculations are necessary, unless you're from (or traveling via) a country where yellow fever is endemic, in which case you'll need a vaccination certificate to enter. If you're a nervous traveler or are traveling off the beaten track, ask your doctor or a travel-health specialist about vaccinations for tetanus and hepatitis. It's no sweat to make sure you're immunized against polio; it's administered as drops on the tongue.

But the only real medical risk, depending on where you travel, is malaria. Parts of northern KwaZulu-Natal, Kruger National Park and surrounding reserves, Zimbabwe, and Botswana are all high-risk malaria zones, though some become low-risk areas in the dry winter months (see **www.travelclinic.co.za** for a map of malaria zones, as well as maps showing risk areas for yellow fever and hepatitis; **www.meditravel.co.za** is another useful site). Both Hluhluwe-Umfolozi (KwaZulu-Natal) and the Kruger are usually low-risk areas from May to September (generally, this means no medication is necessary, though other protective measures are advisable; see below). Do note that this depends on the rainfall during the previous summer—a very wet summer will heighten the risk in what is normally a low-risk area in the winter. Check with a travel clinic, or contact **malaria@mweb.co.za**.

For more detailed information, see "Health" and "Safety," both later in this chapter.

3 GETTING THERE & GETTING AROUND

GETTING TO SOUTH AFRICA

By Plane

Johannesburg's International Airport, now known as **OR Tambo International Airport** (JNB), and Cape Town International (CPT) are the major airport hubs in Southern Africa. While it has a vibrant energy, Jo'burg is very much a transit city, and its airport is the busiest in Africa; if you can avoid flying into Johannesburg, do so. By contrast, Cape Town, a destination city, has a far smaller airport (though it's in the process of being transformed for 2010) and a dinky, manageable size, by comparison. Both of these airports offer direct connections into regional airports adjoining Kruger National Park and surrounding private game reserves (quite a few lodges have their own airstrips); to Durban in KwaZulu-Natal (a 3-hr. drive from the Zululand reserves); and to George and Port Elizabeth, the exit or start of a Garden Route trip. Port Elizabeth is also within easy driving distance of the malaria-free Eastern Cape game reserves.

To add Botswana to a trip to South Africa, you will have to fly via Maun, gateway to the Okavango, or Kasane, gateway to Chobe, both reached from Johannesburg (or Cape Town via Johannesburg). Note that Vic Falls can be reached by road from Kasane. Alternatively, fly from Johannesburg to Livingstone, the Zambian town nearest the falls, or to Victoria Falls Airport in Zimbabwe. For more details on getting there, see "Arriving," in each chapter.

From the U.S. There are two direct flights to South Africa. Star Alliance member **South African Airways (SAA; ✆ 800/722-9675;** www.flysaa.com) departs from New York (JFK) at 11:35am and arrives in Johannesburg the next morning at 8:45am, then provides same-day connections to more business and leisure destinations throughout Africa, including Botswana. **Delta Air Lines** (**✆ 800/221-1212;** www.delta.com) launched their daily nonstop flight between Johannesburg and Atlanta in June 2009. The flight departs Atlanta at 8:05pm and arrives in Johannesburg at 5:10pm the next day. From Chicago, New York, L.A., Miami, San Francisco, or Washington, D.C., you can fly via a European capital with a European carrier such as Air France (stopping in Paris), Lufthansa (stopping in Frankfurt), KLM (stopping in Amsterdam), and so on. Do take a look at British Airways and Virgin. Both stop in London and offer a relatively smooth operation, and connection times are usually no longer than an hour before flights continue on to Johannesburg or direct to Cape Town.

From the United Kingdom This is an 11-hour (Jo'burg) to 11½-hour (Cape Town) flight, but with an hour-long time difference (2 hr. during daylight saving) and no jet lag, because the travel is north to south. **SAA** (**✆ 0171/312-5005;** www.flysaa.com), **British Airways** (**✆ 800/AIRWAYS** [247-8297] or 0181/897-4000; www.british-airways.com), and **Virgin Air** (**✆ 800/862-8621;** www.virgin-atlantic.com) offer direct flights to both Johannesburg and Cape Town. Alternatively, as above, check out any of the European carriers.

From Australia & New Zealand Contact **SAA** (**✆ 02/9223-4448**) or **Qantas** (**✆ 13-13-13;** www.qantas.com.au). Qantas offers direct flights from Sydney to Johannesburg, and South African Airways offers direct flights from Perth. Flying time is approximately 14 to 15 hours from Sydney and 10 to 11 hours from Perth.

TO ZIMBABWE

The easiest way to get to **Victoria Falls** is to fly to Livingstone (LVI), in Zambia, or Victoria Falls International airport (VFA), Zimbabwe, from Johannesburg; the flight takes under 2 hours. Contact either **SAA** (www.flysaa.com) or **British Airways/ComAir** (www.british-airways.com). Victoria Falls is not far by road from Kasane, in Botswana; Kasane is accessible via **Air Botswana** (see below).

TO BOTSWANA

To reach the Okavango Delta, you'll need to fly to Maun (MUB) via Johannesburg on **Air Botswana** (**✆ 267/395-1921;** fax 267/395-3928 in Botswana; **✆ 27/11/975-3070** in Johannesburg; www.airbotswana.co.bw). Air Botswana, still state-owned at press time, is looking for an investment partner; until such time, it is notoriously difficult to book online e-ticketing with this airline. The toll-free number in the U.S. and Canada is **✆ 800/518-7781,** where it's marketed through

Air World Incorporated. In the U.K., call **Flight Directors (© 44/845/838-7943)**. Air Botswana also flies from Johannesburg to Kasane (ideal to reach the Chobe reserve), from Maun to Kasane, and from Kasane to Victoria Falls.

In the unlikely event that you will want to visit Gaborone, the capital, **Air Botswana** also flies from Johannesburg to **Sir Seretse Khama International** (**© 267/395-1921**), as do **SAA** and **British Airways.**

From Maun, you will board a light aircraft, chartered by the camp you have booked. Note that strict luggage restrictions currently apply: 10 to 12kg (22–25 lb.), preferably packed in soft bags. Charter prices vary, so be sure to compare the following companies' prices for the best deal: **Sefofane** (**© 267/686-0778;** www.sefofane.com) is recommended; alternatively, there's **Mack Air** (**© 267/686-0675;** www.mackair.co.bw) and **Delta Air** (**© 267/686-0044;** DeltaAir@AirBotswana.com), a division of Air Botswana.

By Boat

Cape Town features on a number of luxury liner world cruise itineraries, but getting here this way takes plenty of time and money, and, naturally, your experience of Southern Africa will be somewhat limited. However, if this has always been a dream vacation, book with the best, and take a look at **www.cunard.com** or **www.crystalcruises.com**.

GETTING AROUND

How you choose to get around depends largely on the length of your vacation. Visitors with limited days at their disposal usually hop by plane between two or three key destinations, but in many ways, this is underutilizing a holiday in South Africa. With a well-maintained and well-organized road system traversing arresting landscapes, a good range of car-rental companies, relatively low fuel costs, and—outside the cities—roads that are virtually empty of traffic, a combination of flight and road travel is the way to go if you are here for 2 weeks or longer. The Western and Eastern Cape region, in particular, is a wonderful area to explore by car, with charming B&Bs, wine farms, and guest lodges wherever you choose to rest your head. There is a choice of malaria-free game reserves in the Eastern Cape, and as such, it makes logistical sense to go on safari here. If you can afford the time, though, I'd recommend you fly north, either to the Kruger area or the Delta. Or, if you've experienced these destinations on a prior trip, head east to the majestic mountains and lush subtropical game and coastal reserves of KwaZulu-Natal.

Of course, nothing beats the romance of rail, and South Africa is blessed with two trains regularly included in the top 10 train trips in the world. There can be no better way to recover from jet lag than to fly to Johannesburg on an SAA flight (arrive in the morning), arrange for a transfer to Pretoria, board your Rovos Rail carriage (see below), and spend the next 2 nights being rocked south to Cape Town. At the other end of the scale, those with a tight budget (and time to burn) can opt to travel by bus: The major intercity bus companies are reliable for long-distance hauls, and some are fairly flexible; for this, the Baz Bus, which offers a hop-on, hop-off service on interesting routes throughout the country, is unbeatable. Traveling in Zimbabwe, Zambia, and Botswana is not as straightforward—public transport is unreliable, roads can be bad (or virtually nonexistent), fuel in Zimbabwe can be scarce, and help can take a long time coming in the event of a road emergency. The safest thing to do in these countries, particularly with limited time, is to fly directly to your intended destination, with all air transfers prearranged.

By Plane

If you have limited time to cover Africa's large distances, flying is your best bet.

Tips A Home on Wheels

Britz Africa (✆ **27/11/396-1860;** fax 27/11/3961937; www.britz.co.za) offers fully equipped camper vans and four-wheel-drive vehicles, with a full listing of places to park it; they'll also pick you up in your vehicle from the airport. Britz currently charges R1,400 a day for a motor home sleeping two, R1,650 for a motor home sleeping five; minimum rental period 5 days (and the per-day rate goes down after 20 days).

You'll need your driver's license to rent a car—your home driving license is good for 6 months—and most companies in South Africa stipulate that drivers should be a minimum of 21 years old (in Botswana, you must be 25 or older). Armed with a letter of authority from the rental agency, vehicles rented in South Africa may be taken into Botswana and Zimbabwe, though this requires 72 hours' notice, and additional insurance charges are applicable. You can leave the vehicle in these countries for a fee; in South Africa, you can hire a one-way rental car to any of the major cities. All the major companies have branches in South Africa, including **Avis** (www.avis.com), **Hertz** (www.hertz.com), and **Budget** (www.budget.com). Also check out **Europcar,** voted the best rental agency in Africa in the 2007 and 2008 World Travel Awards. **Tempest Car Hire** (www.tempestcarhire.co.za) is my personal choice, offering a combination of professional service, branches throughout the country (as well as Namibia), and great rates (from R149 per day, at press time). Note that it's best to prebook your vehicle, particularly if you're traveling during the peak season (Dec–Feb).

Thankfully, as a result of pressure created by the budget airlines **Kulula.com** and **1Time** (see below), South African Airways launched its own budget airline, **Mango,** which usually offers the lowest fares on the best fleet of planes (though the corporate colors may have you grabbing a sick bag, though being assaulted by neon is marginally more comfortable than the endless puns and wisecracks that Kulula force on their passengers). If you wait for last-minute deals, SAA is also more prone to slashing its own fares for passengers booking through the Web.

Details for the domestic airlines servicing all the major cities in South Africa are as follows: **SA Express** and **SA Airlink** (both domestic subsidiaries of SAA; ✆ **27/11/978-1111;** www.flysaa.com), **BAComair** (✆ **27/11/921-0222;** www.ba.com), **Kulula.com** (✆ **086/158-5852;** www.kulula.com), **Mango** (www.flymango.com), and **1Time** (✆ **086/134-5345;** www.1time.co.za). All the lodges recommended in this book will arrange to charter a flight into the reserve (usually at a surcharged rate) if time is of the essence.

By Car

Given enough time, this is by far the best way to enjoy rural South Africa. In urban centers, drivers comfortable traveling on the left side are also better off hiring a car to get around, because public transport in the cities is generally not geared toward tourists and can be unsafe (though Cape Town rail is slowly getting its act together). Alternatively, utilize taxis while you are in the city and hire a car once you're ready to head out to the hills. All the major car-rental companies have agencies here, as do a host of local companies. All offer much the same deals, but cars are in big demand during the busiest period (Dec–Jan), so book well in advance.

CAR-RENTAL INSURANCE Before you drive off in a rental car, be sure you're adequately insured, covering such things as whether your policy extends to all persons who will be driving the rental car, how much liability is covered in case an outside party is injured in an accident, and whether the type of vehicle you are renting is included under your contract.

GASOLINE Fuel is referred to as "petrol" in South Africa and is available 24 hours a day in major centers. At press time, 1 liter cost just under R7 (4 liters is approximately 1 gal.). Gas stations are full-service, and you are expected to tip the attendant R2 to R5. ***Note:*** Credit cards are not accepted as payment.

ROAD RULES Again, South Africa has an excellent network of tarred and dirt roads, with emergency services available along the major highways; you cannot rely on this sort of backup on road conditions in Zimbabwe, Zambia, or Botswana. Driving in all three countries is on the left side of the road—repeat the mantra "drive left, look right," and wear your seat belt at all times; it's mandatory, and, in any case, driving skills on the road vary considerably. Generally, the speed limit on national highways is 120kmph (74 mph), 100kmph (62 mph) on secondary rural roads, and 60kmph (37 mph) in urban areas. The **Automobile Association of South Africa (AA)** extends privileges to members of AAA in the United States and the Automobile Association in Britain. South African road condition information, route planning, toll information, distances, and directions are available in English via telephone, fax, or e-mail from the **Travel Information Centre** (© **27/11/799-1400;** fax 27/11/799-1254; Mon–Fri 8am–5pm). For breakdowns, contact the local emergency number (© 083-843-22); however, if an international member has rented a vehicle, it is recommended that they confirm with the relevant car rental company the procedures for dealing with an emergency or vehicle breakdown, and then use the emergency number provided by the car-rental company.

By Train

If the journey is as important as the destination, splurge on a Deluxe Suite in the world-famous **Rovos Rail** ★★★ (© **27/12/315-8242;** www.rovos.co.za) or the longer-running **Blue Train** (© **27/12/334-8459;** www.bluetrain.co.za). Both are billed as luxury hotels on wheels and predominantly run between Pretoria (the capital, near Johannesburg) and Cape Town. I can't think of a better way to get to Cape Town if you must arrive in Jo'burg. Of the two, Rovos Rail has the edge: It has the largest suites on wheels, the best en-suite bathrooms, beautiful dining rooms, great butler service, and an incredible wine list (included in the price, and a great introduction to South Africa's top wines). The Pretoria–Cape Town journey is a leisurely 3-day trip. (***Tip:*** I'd skip the Kimberley tour, a scheduled stop and tour on Day 2, and stay cocooned in my suite.) Aside from the Pretoria–Cape Town run, there are a number of exciting routes, such as the 13-day journey to Tanzania or the 9-day journey to the Kruger, Durban, Garden Route, and Cape Town. It's expensive (from R22,000 double for 3-day one-way trip between Pretoria and Cape Town, all-inclusive) but relative to the other great train journeys of the world, rather good value. For a full listing of departure days for this year and the following two, as well as times, schedules, and up-to-date rates, visit the website.

Shosholoza Meyl, South Africa's long-haul rail transporter, has eight primary routes linking South Africa's cities with smaller towns along each route; ticket prices for a first-class carriage are comparable to a bus ticket to the same destination, but invariably take longer and are less comfortable. Second class is inadvisable, lacking comfort and safety.

The one option worth investigating is the **Premier Classe,** a kind of budget Blue Train, which travels between Johannesburg and Cape Town, Johannesburg and Durban, and Cape Town and Port Elizabeth (✆ **086/000-8888;** www.premierclasse.co.za). The latter could be a nice way to return to Cape Town after a self-drive exploration of the Garden Route and Eastern Cape game reserves. The most popular route remains the leg between Cape Town and Johannesburg: The Premier Classe train departs for Cape Town from Johannesburg every Thursday and Sunday, and arrives in Johannesburg from Cape Town every Tuesday and Saturday. It costs between R3,000 and R4,900 double one-way (all-inclusive); Johannesburg to Durban is R1,500 to R2,200 double one-way; Cape Town to Port Elizabeth is R2,200 to 3,500 double one-way.

By Bus

The three established intercity bus companies are **Greyhound, Intercape,** and **Translux;** all offer unbeatable value when it comes to getting around the country. My preference is for Intercape, the largest privately owned intercity passenger transport service in Southern Africa, and the most luxurious in Africa. Book a ticket on their Sleeperline so you can recline and book your seat (try for the top front for the best view). Johannesburg to Cape Town takes approximately 19 hours, which is about 8 hours less than the same trip by train.

An alternative to these is the 22-seater **Baz Bus,** which offers a flexible hop-on, hop-off scheme aimed at backpackers and covers almost the entire coastline, including some really off-the-beaten-track destinations, such as Port St Johns and Sodwana. It's a great way for budget travelers to explore the coast, areas around the Mpumalanga game reserves, Drakensberg, Swaziland, and Maputo, capital of neighboring Mozambique. You can purchase direct routes or 7-day, 14-day, and 21-day passes, which allow you to get on and hop off anywhere you wish for a fixed price.

- **Baz Bus National** (✆ **27/21/439-2323;** www.bazbus.com; central reservations)
- **Greyhound** (✆ **27/83/915-9500;** www.greyhound.co.za)
- **Intercape** (✆ **08/61/287-287,** or 27/21/380-4400 international; www.intercape.co.za)
- **Translux** (✆ **08/61/589-282** or 27/11/774-3333; www.translux.co.za)

4 MONEY & COSTS

We have included only the two strongest currencies, the South African rand and Botswanan pula. Currency conversions as quoted above were correct at press time; as rates will no doubt continue to fluctuate, consult a currency exchange website such as **www.oanda.com/convert/classic** or

Fun Facts **Worth Its Weight in Gold . . .**

The direct translation of *pula,* the official currency of Botswana, a predominantly arid country with severe water shortage, is "rain."

Tips Tipping Point

In South Africa, you should exchange enough petty cash to cover airport incidentals, tipping, and transportation to your hotel before you leave home, or withdraw money upon arrival at the airport ATM. Aside from ATMs, for the most favorable rates, change money at banks rather than hotel or exchange bureaus. If you are a U.S. visitor, bring dollars in small denominations for tips in Botswana, Zimbabwe, and Zambia; if you are a non-U.S. visitor, think about changing some money into the highly valued U.S. dollar, again in low denominations, for tips and trinkets from roadside vendors *before* you leave home, as you will otherwise be obliged to change your currency into the local currency.

www.xe.com/ucc to check up-to-the-minute rates.

The **South African currency unit** is the **rand** (ZAR or R), with 100 cents making up R1. Notes come in R10, R20, R50, R100, and R200. Minted coins come in 1-, 2-, and 5-rand denominations, and 2, 5, 10, 20, and 50 cents—small change doesn't buy much; gather and use for tips. The good news for foreign visitors is that the current climate has knocked the rand, despite the relative stability of the economy or the size of its gold reserves. To give some idea: In 2007, the rand was hovering at R7 to $1 and R14 to £1; at the start of 2009, it was fluctuating between R9 and R11 to the $1 and hit highs of R18 to the £1.

Even the **pula,** official currency of **Botswana,** the most expensive region in southern Africa, has taken a bit of a beating in recent years: At press time, it was hovering at P7.6 to $1—up from P6.15 2 years previously. It has little effect on visitors, though; lodgings and camps quote and charge in U.S. dollars almost without exception. In Zambia, lodgings do the same, quoting rates in dollars or euros; even roadside hawkers prefer foreign currency (see "Tipping Point," below). If you do pick up some local currency, you will find the **Zambian** currency unit is the **kwacha (K),** in denominations of 50, 100, 500, 1,000, 5,000, and 10,000, 20,000, and 50,000 kwacha notes.

Zimbabwe's hyperinflation—kicked off in the early 2000s by Mugabe's "land reform" policy, in which vast swathes of productive white-owned farmland were given to so-called war veterans and now lie fallow—led to a spontaneous replacement of the Zim dollar with foreign currencies. This "dollarization" process was finally legalized in late January 2009, and the Zimbabwe dollar was suspended in April (by which time a trillion note could not even buy a loaf of bread, and its value against the U.S. dollar was cut in half every 2 days). The payment of goods and services in Zimbabwe is thus now only in foreign currencies, including the U.S. dollar, euro, pound, South African Rand, and Botswana Pula.

ATMS

ATMs (or cashpoints) offering 24-hour service are located throughout South Africa, even in small towns. (Obviously, this does not apply to lodges in remote locations, such as nature reserves, with the exception of Skukuza Rest Camp in Kruger.) It is not worth drawing money from an ATM in Zimbabwe (see below). Be warned that while travelers can withdraw money (in local currency) from ATMs in Zambia, banks often lose their connections with the credit card exchanges, thus making withdrawals impossible. You will

The Value of Local Currencies vs. Other Popular Currencies

	US$	C$	UK£	Euro (€)	AU$	NZ$
R1	$0.11	C$0.14	£0.08	€0.09	A$0.16	NZ$0.20
BWP1	$0.13	C$0.16	£0.09	€0.10	A$0.19	NZ$0.24

find ATMs only in major towns in Botswana, and they accept only Visa.

Please be wary when drawing cash—don't be distracted by strangers, and make sure they keep their distance. Most ATMs in cities are guarded at night, but it's better to draw in daylight. The **Cirrus** (✆ **800/ 424-7787;** www.mastercard.com) and **PLUS** (✆ **800/843-7587;** www.visa.com) networks span the globe; look at the back of your bank card to see which network you're on, then call or check online for ATM locations at your destination. This is important, as a Visa card's PIN (personal identification number) will not apply at a MasterCard-accredited ATM, and vice versa (Visa accepts only a four-digit PIN, while MasterCard accepts a five- or six-digit PIN). Be sure you know your PIN and daily withdrawal limit before you depart. ***Note:*** Remember that many banks impose a fee every time you use a card at another bank's ATM. In addition, the bank from which you withdraw cash may charge its own fee. The exchange rate may also be unfavorable (as is the case in Zimbabwe, where the exchange rate is based on the official interbank rate, which is extremely low). If you're concerned about international withdrawal fees, ask your bank before you leave.

CREDIT CARDS

Credit cards, for use at ATMs and virtually any retailer in southern Africa, are the most convenient way to carry money in the region. They also provide a record of all your expenses and generally offer relatively good exchange rates. (Keep in mind that many banks now assess a "transaction fee" of around 1%–3% on all charges you incur abroad. And you'll pay interest from the moment of your withdrawal, even if you pay your monthly bills on time, so try to settle your account immediately on return.) With the proper precautions (see below), credit cards that require a PIN are also the safest way to carry money. Just don't let your card out of your sight, as the use of card skimmers and cloning devices, mainly employed by organized criminal syndicates, has dramatically increased in heavily touristed areas such as airport restaurants and Cape Town's Waterfront. The new generation of card skimmers are smaller than the card itself, and it takes a fraction of a second to clone a card. A server can swipe your card through a skimmer concealed in his or her hand while you are distracted by signing the authorization slip. If you are at a restaurant, always request that a tabletop portable pay point be delivered to your seat. If they don't have this facility, follow your server to the pay point. Once your card has been swiped, immediately take it back into your possession.

If you have only an American Express, MasterCard, and/or Diners Club card, it's worth opening a Visa account, as this is by far the most accepted choice in Southern Africa (many lodgings in Zimbabwe won't accept MasterCard). Camps in remote areas do not always have credit card facilities, but in all likelihood, you will be booking and paying for these all-inclusive experiences ahead of time. For the most part, you'll find credit cards to be invaluable. (Debit cards are also useful as a backup for drawing cash from ATMs.)

TRAVELER'S CHECKS

Traveler's checks are somewhat redundant in South Africa—and useless in Zimbabwe, where banks rarely accept traveler's checks for conversion to local currency. As mentioned above, credit cards are generally accepted throughout southern Africa, particularly MasterCard and Visa, and both credit and debit cards are an easy way to draw cash at ATMs everywhere but Zimbabwe, where the ATM exchange rate is based on the official interbank rate, which is extremely low.

Those who nevertheless prefer carrying traveler's checks can buy them at almost any bank. American Express offers denominations of $10, $20, $50, $100, $500, and (for cardholders only) $1,000; you can also purchase them in South African rands, though it's inadvisable, given the fluctuating exchange rate, usually in favor of the dollar. You'll pay a service charge ranging from 1% to 4%. You can also get American Express traveler's checks over the phone by calling ✆ **800/221-7282;** by using this number, Amex gold and platinum cardholders are exempt from the fee. AAA members can obtain checks without a fee at most AAA offices or by calling ✆ **866/339-3378.**

Visa offers traveler's checks at Citibank locations nationwide, as well as several other banks. The service charge ranges between 1.5% and 2%; checks come in denominations of $20, $50, $100, $500, and $1,000. Call ✆ **800/732-1322** for information. **MasterCard** also offers traveler's checks. Call ✆ **800/223-9920** for a location near you.

5 HEALTH

STAYING HEALTHY

Health Care Access

Visiting South Africa should pose no threat to your health: Private hospitals are efficient and the staff is of the highest caliber, hygiene is rarely a problem in tourist areas, tap water is safe, stomach upsets from food are rare, there are no weird tropical viruses, and medical assistance is generally always within a 10-minute to 2-hour drive. Procedures, particularly dental and plastic surgery, are so highly rated and relatively inexpensive that there is now a roaring trade in safari/surgery holidays. That said, there are a few things to watch out for, discussed below. Unless you're already covered by a health plan while you're abroad, it's probably a good idea to take out medical travel insurance, particularly if you're going to participate in adventure activities. Be sure to carry your identification card in your wallet. In the event of serious medical conditions in Botswana, Zambia, and Zimbabwe, every effort should be made to go to Johannesburg.

While you will find an excellent range of over-the-counter medicines in pharmacies, bring your own prescription medications as well as copies of your prescriptions, with the generic name, in case you lose your pills or run out. If you wear glasses or contact lenses, pack an extra pair.

Contact the **International Association for Medical Assistance to Travelers** (www.iamat.org) for up-to-date tips on travel health concerns, as well as lists of local, English-speaking doctors; of course, your local host or concierge will do same, and the reference is probably more reliable. You will find listings of clinics overseas at the **International Society of Travel Medicine** (www.istm.org), though, personally, I'd go straight to **www.netcare.co.za**, a collection of top private clinics throughout South Africa, with listings of all their specialists in every region on the website, the Netcare Hospital they practice from, and their direct telephone number. For travel-specific queries, I'd look no further than **www.travelclinic.co.za**, also with branches throughout South Africa.

If you need more reassurance, the United States **Centers for Disease Control and Prevention (© 800/311-3435;** www.cdc.gov) provides up-to-date information on health hazards by region or country and offers tips on food safety. The website **www.tripprep.com**, sponsored by a consortium of travel-medicine practitioners, offers helpful advice on traveling abroad. Alternatively, bear the following in mind:

AIDS South Africa has more people living with AIDS than any other country in the world. If you're entering into sexual relations, use a condom. If you need medical treatment during your stay, there's no real risk that you'll contract the virus in the process. Even so, it's best to err on the side of caution and insist on treatment at a private hospital, if possible.

BILHARZIA Do not swim in dams, ponds, or rivers unless they are recommended as bilharzia free. Symptoms are difficult to detect at first—tiredness followed by abdominal pain and bloody urine or stools. But they can be effectively treated with praziquantel.

BUGS, BITES & OTHER WILDLIFE CONCERNS You are unlikely to encounter snakes—they are shy, and, with the exception of puff adders, they tend to move off when they sense humans approaching. If you get bitten, stay calm—very few are fatal—and get to a hospital. Scorpions and spiders are similarly timid, and most are totally harmless. To avoid them, shake out clothing that's been lying on the ground, and be careful when gathering firewood. If you're hiking through the bush, beware of ticks; tick-bite fever is very unpleasant, though you should recover in 4 days. To remove ticks, smear Vaseline over them until they let go. Visitors to the national parks and reserves should bear in mind at all times that they are in a wilderness area: Even animals that look cute are wild and should not be approached (this includes baboons, who will sometimes vandalize cars in search of food). If you're on a self-drive safari, make sure you get out of your vehicle only at designated sites. While most rest camps in the national parks are fenced for your protection, this is not the case with lodges and camps situated in private reserves: Animals, including such dangerous ones as hippos, lions, and elephants, roam right through them. After dark, it's essential that you seek accompaniment to and from your room by a guide. Even when you're in a safari vehicle on a game drive, your ranger will caution you not to stand up, make sudden or loud noises, or otherwise draw attention to yourself. Occasionally, the ranger may leave the vehicle to track game on foot; always remain seated in the vehicle. It is probably unnecessary to point out that lions and crocodiles are dangerous; however, hippos kill more humans in Africa than any other mammal, and you should take this seriously. Hippos may look harmlessly ponderous, but they can move amazingly fast and are absolutely lethal when provoked. Even some of the smaller animals should be treated with a great deal of respect: The honey badger is the most tenacious of adversaries, and even lions keep their distance from them. And of course, the most serious bite comes from a tiny female insect, known as the Anophele (mosquito).

CHOLERA There has been a big cholera outbreak in Zimbabwe, with more than 94,000 cases reported since August 2008. This has spread to the Lusaka district (Zambia) and northeastern province of Limpopo (S.A.), which border Zimbabwe. According to the UN, risk to travelers anywhere in Southern Africa is minimal, and the cholera vaccine is recommended for aid and refugee workers only.

Malaria: Frequently Asked Questions

Parts of northern KwaZulu-Natal, Kruger National Park and surrounding reserves, Zimbabwe, and Botswana are all high-risk malaria zones (transmitted only by the female mosquito, who requires blood to develop her eggs), though some areas become low-risk in the dry winter months (see www.travelclinic.co.za for a map). Both Hluhluwe-Umfolozi (KwaZulu-Natal) and the Kruger are usually low-risk areas from May to September (generally, this means no medication is necessary, though other protective measures are advisable; see below). Please note that this depends on the rainfall during the previous summer. Always check with a travel clinic or contact **malaria@mweb.co.za**. Another useful website is **www.meditravel.co.za**. Here are some commonly asked questions about malaria:

- **Do I really need to take antimalarial drugs?** If you are entering a high-risk zone for the first time, a course of antimalarial tablets (aka prophylactic), for which you will need a prescription, is essential. What is prescribed is dependent on your health profile, but Malarone (or Malanil, as it also known) is the most effective (98%) and has the fewest side effects. You have to take it only 1 day before entering a malarial area and continue the course for only 7 days after you leave the area. The downside is that it's quite expensive. Larium is 91% effective but has strong potential side effects and should be started 2 weeks prior to entering the area, to allow you to switch, if necessary (this should happen within 3 days). Side effects may include depression, anxiety, disorientation, dizziness, insomnia, strange dreams, nausea, or headaches; the principal contraindications are a history of anxiety, psychiatric problems, or epilepsy. If you've taken Larium before and suffered no side effects, you can start the course 1 week before. If you do suffer side effects, the medication is usually changed to an antibiotic containing Doxycycline—a daily tablet taken 1 day before. Both Larium and Doxycycline need to be taken for 28 days after leaving the area—and make sure to take your full course of tablets.
- **Are Tablets Enough?** Keep in mind that no prophylactic is totally effective, so your best protection is to avoid being bitten. Sleep under a mosquito net, if possible; burn mosquito coils or plug in mosquito destroyers if you have electricity; wear loose, full-length clothing; and cover exposed skin with insect repellent.
- **How do I know if I've got it?** The flulike symptoms—fever, diarrhea, headaches, and joint pains—can take up to 6 months to develop. If they do, consult a doctor immediately—a delay in treatment can be fatal.
- **What if I'm traveling with kids or I'm pregnant?** Taking medication is inadvisable for children under the age of 5 and pregnant women. Your best bet is to choose a malaria-free Big 5 reserve: Pilanesberg and Madikwe in the North-West, Welgevonden in the Limpopo Province, and those located in the Eastern Cape. In the dry winter months, the Kruger and the Hluhluwe-Umfolozi reserve in Zululand (3 hr. from Durban) have a very low risk.

DIETARY RED FLAGS Vegetarians and others with special dietary requirements visiting game lodges and camps must let their hosts know well in advance; in fact, it is worth alerting any establishment serving dinner and/or lunch that you have dietary requirements well in advance. Note that many South Africans who describe themselves as "vegetarians" eat fish or chicken, so it's best to specify exactly what your requirements are. Outside the major cities, vegetarians may struggle to find restaurants that offer any kind of choice. Travelers with any kind of intolerance or allergy should impress upon servers the seriousness of their condition when inquiring about the ingredients in a particular dish.

SUN Remember that the sun doesn't have to be shining to burn you. Wear a broad-brimmed hat at all times, and apply a high-factor sunscreen or total block—at least initially. Wear sunglasses that reduce both UVA and UVB rays substantially, and stay out of the sun between 11am and 3pm. Children should be kept well covered at the beach; it can take as little as 15 minutes for an infant's skin to develop third-degree burns.

WHAT TO DO IF YOU GET SICK AWAY FROM HOME

South Africa has excellent doctors and specialists throughout the country; if you're not feeling well, let your host or concierge know and they will make an appointment with a reputable professional nearby. If you're unhappy with the diagnosis, get a second opinion, like elsewhere. In an emergency, you'd be better off going to a private hospital. There are plenty in urban centers (see www.netcare.co.za), facilities are excellent, and you'll avoid a lengthy wait. It doesn't come cheap, though, and many expect to see proof of medical insurance. For **emergency numbers,** see chapter 13 (p. 461).

6 SAFETY

Safety rules for travelers are the same as elsewhere in the world, though the high incidence of crime warrants extra caution in southern African cities. However, most cases occur in the townships and in areas away from the main tourist destinations. The South African authorities make it a high priority to protect tourists; tourism police are deployed in several of the large towns, and the vast majority of visitors complete their travels in South Africa without incident.

CRIME

Take care, however: Criminals operate out of the airport in Johannesburg; do not accept unsolicited assistance with transport when arriving at this airport. As a general rule, always be aware of the people around you, whether you're walking down a busy city street or driving through a deserted suburb. If you sense danger, act on your instincts. Don't flash expensive jewelry or fancy cameras or phones; wear handbag straps across the neck, and keep a good grip on items. Don't walk any of the major city-center streets after dark, especially if you're alone. Be on guard if you are alone on an empty beach or mountainside near urban areas; it's worth carrying a mobile phone on you at all times, with emergency numbers (see chapter 13, p. 461) keyed in for easy access. Avoid no-go areas, such as Hillbrow and Berea, the inner-city suburbs of Johannesburg, and find out from your hotel or host how best to get where you're going and what's been happening on the streets recently. Finally, if you're confronted by an assailant, keep calm, don't make eye contact, don't resist in any way, and cooperate. Note also that pilfering of luggage at international airports is an increasing problem: Travelers are encouraged to secure their luggage with Transportation Security Administration (TSA)–approved locks; use an airport plastic wrapping service; and avoid placing electronics, jewelry, cameras, or other valuables in checked luggage.

With such widespread poverty, you will inevitably have to deal with beggars, some of them children. Money is often spent on alcohol or drugs; should you feel the need to make a difference, donate to a relevant charity. Some beggars offer services, such as watching your car while you shop or dine. There is no need to feel intimidated, and how much you decide to tip them is entirely personal, though with unemployment running as high as 40%, this is the best way to help the many who need the dignity of employment as much as your small change.

ON THE ROAD

If you're used to civilized, law-abiding drivers, you'll find South African road manners leave a lot to be desired. Drunk driving can be a problem, so try to limit driving to daytime trips, and be extra aware of others when driving at night. When driving, keep your car doors locked, particularly in Johannesburg (it's a good idea to also lock your room, and don't open the door unless you're expecting someone or the person is known to you). Don't leave valuables in clear view in your car, even when you are in it. Do not pick up hitchhikers, and if you're on a self-drive holiday, hire or keep a cellphone with you. Call the **Automobile Association of South Africa** (see chapter 13, p. 460) should you break down. Call the police should you feel nervous and wish for an escort or company. If you are at a remote site or beach, be aware of who is there when you approach the spot, and don't leave your car if you don't feel safe. Also be aware of suspicious persons approaching you at a remote site; again, a cellphone, with the correct emergency numbers on speed dial, is recommended for peace of mind.

DISCRIMINATION

South Africa has come a long way since 1994 and, generally speaking, is home to some of the world's most politically sensitive communities. That said, you will still come across some die-hard racists and homophobes, usually (but by no means exclusively) outside of the urban areas. This should not be the case with any of our recommendations; if you encounter problems, let us know in writing and we'll take it up.

7 SPECIALIZED TRAVEL RESOURCES

In addition to the destination-specific resources listed below, please visit Frommers.com for additional specialized travel resources.

GAY & LESBIAN TRAVELERS

South Africa's constitution outlaws any discrimination on the basis of sexual orientation, making it one of the most progressive in the world. Big cities are gay friendly, and Cape Town, often called the gay capital of Africa, was voted the second-largest gay capital in the world (see chapter 5, "The Great Gay EsCape," for details on gay-friendly accommodations and nightlife). For a comprehensive listing of gay-friendly or gay-only places and events, accommodations, adventure activities, tours, and entertainment, visit www.capetown.tv. Gay Pages, a Yellow Pages of sorts, is South Africa's largest and longest-running directory for gay and lesbian people; you may also want to refer to the newcomer Pink Pages (www.gaysouth africa.org.za), though the focus in the latter is more on places to stay. For a host of up-to-the-minute news, as well as such opportunities as SMS dating, look at **www.Q.co.za**.

The Western Cape is a great area to tour by car, with gay-run and gay-friendly lodgings in myriad little villages in the Winelands, coast, and Karoo (Barrydale has even been fondly nicknamed "Marydale"). Upmarket lodges and camps in private game reserves are equally accepting. The same cannot be said of countries bordering South Africa, however. Zimbabwean President Robert Mugabe is a virulent homophobe, and homosexuality is effectively a criminal offense, so be discreet if visiting here or Zambia (though the towns adjoining the Falls are pretty international in their outlook). For more information, visit **The International Gay and Lesbian Travel Association** (www.iglta.org), the trade association for the gay and lesbian travel industry. It offers an online directory of gay- and lesbian-friendly travel businesses; go to their website and click on "Members."

TRAVELERS WITH DISABILITIES

While the legislation here is not the world's most sophisticated, it now demands that travelers with disabilities be taken into account. Great strides have been made at tourism facilities; many lodgings provide wheelchair-accessible and comfortable en-suite rooms. Plenty, however, are entirely unsuitable, and it may be easiest to join a tour provided by an operator that specializes in wheelchair travel and inspects every facility for your comfort. One such group is **www.rollingsa.co.za**, specializing in small group tours throughout South Africa; the reputable **www.flamingotours.co.za**, personally run by Jeff and Pam Taylor, offers trips tailored to clients' specific needs, interests, and budget. Adventure lovers should contact South African Bernard Goosen, who was an accountant until he climbed Kilimanjaro in a modified wheelchair, becoming the first person in the world to do so. After many requests for talks after this momentous achievement, Bernard now works full-time on motivational and team building, as well as assisting individuals, both able and disabled, to fulfill their dreams and experience the things that they never thought possible. His company, **Get Motivated,** has put together specially designed outings and is able to hire out "off-road" wheelchairs. Contact him at **bern@getmotivated.co.za**, or call ✆ **27/83/648-7770.** If you plan to travel with friends rather than join a group, Johannesburg-based **Mobility One** (✆ **27/11/892-0638;** www.mobility one.co.za) rents wheelchairs and scooters; they will deliver to the airport or hotel. For more information, contact the National Council for **Persons with Physical Disabilities in South Africa** (ncppdsa@cis.co.za).

FAMILY TRAVEL

South Africa is regarded as the most child-friendly country in Africa, with plenty of family accommodations options, well-stocked shops, sunshine, safe beaches, high hygiene standards, wild animals, baby-sitters, and burgers on tap. Hotels and guest lodges usually provide discounts for children under 12, and children under age 2 sharing with parents are usually allowed to stay for free. Ages and discounts vary considerably, however, so it's best to check beforehand. South Africa also has a large number of excellent self-catering cottages, increasingly referred to in the trade as "villas"—often the cheapest and most comfortable luxury accommodation option for families, with space and privacy (and a concierge service to arrange chef, chauffer, au pair, and so on, if you so wish). We asked a Cape-based freelance villa specialist to highlight the best villas on offer in chapter 5, "Cape Town." Bear in mind that many operators in private game reserves are loathe to accept children under 12. Because prophylactics are not recommended for those under 5, choose a malaria-free area, or visit during a dry winter (see "Malaria," above). Again, nothing beats renting your own space, be it a self-drive budget safari in the Kruger or staying and having your own vehicle and guide for a flexible safari that the entire family will enjoy.

To locate accommodations, restaurants, and attractions that are particularly kid-friendly, see the "Kids" icon throughout this guide.

SENIOR TRAVEL

South Africa is not a difficult destination for seniors to navigate. Driving on the "wrong" side of the road is probably the most intimidating prospect you'll have to face here. Admission prices to attractions are usually reduced for seniors (also known as "pensioners" in South Africa). Don't be shy about asking for discounts, and always carry some kind of identification, such as a driver's license, that shows your date of birth. Accommodations discounts are unusual; national parks, for instance, may offer special rates, but these are for South African nationals only. Note that members of **AARP,** 601 E St. NW, Washington, DC 20049 (✆ **888/687-2277;** www.aarp.org), have access to a wide range of benefits, including *AARP: The Magazine* and a monthly newsletter; anyone over 50 can join. **Elderhostel** (✆ **877/426-8056;** www.elderhostel.org) is an excellent site, arranging study programs for those ages 55 and over, to all the countries listed in this book; **ElderTreks** (✆ **800/741-7956;** www.eldertreks.com) does the same. **INTRAV** (✆ **800/456-8100;** www.intrav.com) is a high-end tour operator that caters to the mature, discerning traveler (not specifically seniors), with trips around the world that include guided safaris. In the U.K., **Saga** (www.saga.co.uk) leads the charge, offering a wide range of options for those over 50.

STUDENT TRAVEL

If you're traveling internationally, you'd be wise to arm yourself with an **International Student Identity Card (ISIC),** which may offer savings on some entrance fees and has basic health and life insurance and a 24-hour help line. The card is available from **STA Travel** (✆ **800/781-4040** in North America; www.sta.com or www.statravel.com; or www.statravel.co.uk in the U.K.), the biggest student travel agency in the world. If you're no longer a student but are still under 26, you can get an **International Youth Travel Card (IYTC)** from the same people, which entitles you to some discounts (but not on museum admissions). **Travel CUTS** (✆ **800/667-2887** or 416/614-2887; www.travelcuts.com) offers similar services for both Canadian and U.S. residents. Irish students may prefer to turn to **USIT** (✆ **01/602-1600;** www.usitnow.ie), an Ireland-based specialist in student, youth, and independent travel.

South Africa has a large number of lodges and activities catering to the backpacker market—in Cape Town, contact **Africa Travel Centre** (✆ **27/21/423-5555;** www.backpackers.co.za), a recommended backpackers' resource near the center of town, with comfortable accommodations and an excellent travel desk aimed at the budget traveler.

8 SAFARI SPECIFICS: FAQ

What are the safari options available? Wildlife viewing and interaction is the reason most set their sights on southern Africa, which has resulted in a number of ways to experience the bush. You can opt for a **self-drive safari** in a national park, fly straight to a luxurious lodge in a **private game reserve,** or—best of all—combine the two. The more adventurous take their chances on a specialist safari and go on **foot, horseback, bike, canoe,** or even the back of an **elephant.** If you're keen to walk the wilderness accompanied by an experienced, armed game ranger, consider the trails in **Umfolozi** (Imfolozi)—30,000 hectares (74,100 acres) of pristine bush and savanna (with no roads or paths other than those created by animals), rated by experienced hikers as South Africa's best. The most popular trail is the 2-night Short Wilderness Trail. Trails are run from mid-February to mid-November, afford an authentic wilderness experience, and introduce walkers to the broad diversity of fauna, flora, and ecological habitats that characterize KwaZulu-Natal. Alternatively, the walking safaris in **Kruger National Park,** which offers a choice of seven separate wilderness trails, are also highly recommended (see chapter 9). Some Eastern Cape Reserves, such as **Samara** and **Blaauwbosch,** also offer "walk and stalk" opportunities, where you can track cheetah on foot (though these are short walks, not trails). For game-spotting on horseback, book a horseback-riding trail in the Delta (see chapter 12). Families can saddle up in the malaria-free Waterberg (see chapter 9). Other Botswana highlights include cycling safaris in **Tuli,** quad-bike safaris at **Jack's Camp** in the Makgadikgadi Pans, and *mokoro* (dugout canoe) safaris in the **Okavango Delta**—the traditional way to get around its waterways, unhindered by buzzing motors or gas fumes. If you've always had a soft spot for the pachyderm, you can now mount your very own elephant and go tracking in almost all the game-viewing regions, but the best experiences are in **Abu Camp** in the delta (see chapter 7) and **Camp Jabulani** near Kruger (see chapter 12).

Which country should I focus on? South Africa has the best-managed national parks in Africa, as well as some of the most luxurious private reserves; but if you're looking for the original untamed Eden, nothing beats Botswana, particularly the Okavango Delta. This is largely due to a government policy aimed at low-density, high-cost tourism. So be warned: Little here comes cheap. Until the land grab and economic crisis is resolved in Zimbabwe, visiting there should be restricted to Victoria Falls, which is close to the Botswana/Zambian border.

How do I get around between reserves? In South Africa, most of the reserves are concentrated around **Kruger** (see chapter 9), or north of Johannesburg. You can reach them by flying directly to Johannesburg or Cape Town, then catching a connecting flight to an airport in or near the reserves, or even directly to the reserves. You can also opt for the 4- to 5-hour drive (or longer, if you include the Blyde River Canyon) from Johannesburg to the Kruger; the scenery is pleasant, and there are fabulous lodging options in the forests and farms along the way. Madikwe and Welgevonden are even closer—3- and 2½-hour drives, respectively; camps here will arrange to meet you at Johannesburg's airport and whisk you straight to the bush.

To reach **KwaZulu-Natal**'s reserves, most of which are in the northeast of the province in an area called Zululand, fly from Johannesburg or Cape Town to Durban or Richard's Bay airport. The closest reserve is 30 minutes away, while the biggest, Hluhluwe-Umfolozi, is an easy 3-hour drive from Durban airport (2 hr. from Richard's Bay).

Port Elizabeth is the airport closest to the **Eastern Cape reserves;** most are a mere 20- to 90-minutes' drive away. The best of these are comparable with the top reserves in the country, though vegetation is not as lush and trees aren't as plentiful as in the north or KZN. Best of all, they are malaria free. Visiting one is the ideal start or end point of a road trip along the Garden Route to or from Cape Town, a wonderfully scenic drive with great choices in lodgings and activities.

From South Africa, you'll have to fly via Johannesburg to get to **Botswana's reserves and camps,** most of which are accessible by charter flight from Maun or Kasane.

What should I do if I'm on a budget? By far the best budget option is to rent a car and drive yourself around the reserves, concentrating on the national parks (such as Kruger) and/or the provincial reserves (such as Hluhluwe-Umfolozi); see our recommended itinerary for this. The roads in these reserves are in good condition, so you won't need a four-wheel-drive. There are a number of advantages besides cost: You can set your own pace, take in more than one environment (many visitors, for instance, combine a trip to Kruger with a KwaZulu-Natal reserve trip), and bring the kids (many private game reserves don't accept children). Kruger accommodations are usually in semiserviced rondawels (pronounced "ron-*da*-villes")—round, thatch-roof cottages with basic en-suite bathrooms that offer excellent value for the money (R575 per night; there are also standing tents from R285 at some camps). Cheaper units won't have their own kitchen, but all feature a fridge, tea-making facilities, and a barbecue area. Linens and towels are also provided. The more expensive units will have the added advantage of better views or more privacy—take your pick from the reviews in chapter 9. Most rest camps have a shop selling supplies, including such basics as dishwashing liquid, wood, firelighters, tinned foods, frozen meat, toiletries, and aspirin; you can also purchase field guides here. Most also have a restaurant serving breakfast, lunch, and dinner. Try to combine this with at least 2 nights in a private reserve (for reasons discussed below). The best-value Big 5 options close to Kruger are **Gomo Gomo, Arasutha,** and **Umlani Bushcamps**—all charge less than R5,000 for two, including all game activities and all meals. For those prepared to "rough it," Mosetlha Bush Camp in Madikwe offers one of the most authentic safari experiences for the staggeringly good-value rate of R3,370 for two. The best-value Big 5 private reserve option in KwaZulu-Natal is currently Phinda Forest Lodge in the Phinda Private Game Reserve (R3,295–R5,985 all-inclusive), which offers luxury award-winning accommodation, a diverse ecosystem from sand forest to ilala palm veld and bush savannah, excellent game-viewing, and great cuisine. The only budget option in the delta is Oddballs, the base lodge from which *mokoro* (pole-propelled canoe) camping trips are made, but I'd plunder savings and upgrade to Xakanaxa Camp or Khwai Tented Camp—for more, see "Delta on a Budget," in chapter 12.

Do I need to visit a private reserve? The best reason to visit a private reserve is that you are guaranteed to see more animals, and you will learn more about the intricacies of the bush. Visitors are taken for game drives in an open-topped vehicle by an armed and knowledgeable ranger, usually helped by a tracker, and in radio communication with other vehicles. Sightings are excellent on game drives (at least two of the Big 5 in one drive), and it's great to have your questions answered without having to flip through a book. In certain reserves, such as **Sabi Sand, Timbavati, Thornybush,** and **Phinda,** rangers are allowed to drive off-road, taking you almost within touching distance of animals (note that this is not possible in private concessions within National Parks). A typical day starts with a 3-hour, early-morning game drive, during which eight guests (or fewer at the more expensive lodges) are accompanied by a game ranger and tracker. A large cooked breakfast follows, possibly in the bush. A guided walk generally takes place before lunch, and afternoons are spent relaxing at the pool or on a viewing deck. Night drives take place during the sunset/early-evening hours, when drinks (sundowners) are served in the bush. The last hour or so is spent driving with a spotlight. Night drives can be incredibly dull (it's pitch black) or totally exhilarating, when nocturnal predators stalk and kill prey—a rare but privileged sighting. Dinners are large, often served buffet style under the stars by firelight.

What's the difference between private reserves? Should I visit more than one? It's definitely worth combining reserves, moving to new landscapes that support different species. If this is your first time, it's worth choosing a Big 5 reserve—the presence of lion, leopard, rhino, elephant, and buffalo usually means a great concentration of other species as well. The Big 5 reserves flanking Kruger **(Sabi Sands, Manyeleti, Timbavati)** and the new **concessions inside the Kruger** are your best bet in South Africa—there are no fences between them and Kruger, creating a massive wilderness area where game moves freely. **Sabi Sands** is the private reserve that has the highest concentration of both game and luxury lodges. Another Big 5 reserve worth considering is **Madikwe** in the North-West, where a number of excellent new lodges have opened in the past couple of years. The Eastern Cape reserves are malaria free, and many offer top-quality game-viewing, though the landscape is not as arresting as the bushveld up north. Most desirable are **Kwandwe** and **Shamwari**, both an easy drive from Port Elizabeth, while less expensive options can be found in a multitude of smaller reserves. Lovely **Samara**, deep in the Karoo, and the extremely reasonable **Blaauwbosch** on its fringes are also well worth a visit, especially for those who love cheetah and would like to track them on foot (note that Samara doesn't have elephant).

The race for a genuine Big 5 safari experience in the **Western Cape** has been heating up, but none of the current options afford the authentic wilderness experience you'll get in the Eastern Cape, around Kruger, or in KwaZulu-Natal. These Western Cape "mini" reserves do have some or all of the Big 5 on the property, but the lions and/or elephants are often not free roaming and the reserves themselves are small. The accommodations can be lovely, and the experience is very satisfying for newcomers to the scene, but it's still best to travel farther, if you can. The current exception to the rule is **Sanbona,** about 3 hours from Cape Town, a 54,000-hectare (133,380-acre) reserve in the Karoo, which has the wide-open spaces and quality game-viewing expected on an authentic safari. It bears repeating, though, that this is not bushveld country. For those who can't get farther than the Garden Route, consider **Buffelsdrift,** near Oudtshoorn. They don't have big cats, but it's an excellent deal. Those desperate to see the Big 5 near Cape Town itself, no matter what, can opt for a day trip (or longer stay) at **Aquila** (it's less than 2 hr. from the city); the lions are in a separate area, but at least you can be guaranteed a sighting.

Although the reserves surrounding Kruger are typical of the African bush and savanna, the **Okavango Delta** in flood offers a lush landscape that attracts an incredible variety of bird life (not to mention a dense concentration of game). It's a must on any safari itinerary. Then there are the desert reserves such as **Tswalu, Kgaligadi Transfrontier Park,** and **Makgadigadi Pans.** With huge horizons and stark landscapes, these support species that have adapted to harsh conditions, such as cheetahs and gemsboks (oryx). By contrast, **KwaZulu-Natal**'s semitropical climate creates a more junglelike environment—it's beautiful, but spotting animals is a little more difficult in dense foliation—and visitors can combine a safari with diving and snorkeling excursions. Zululand reserves include a variety of terrain, from sand, swamp, and mangrove forests to savannah, bush, and veld. As a result, it offers a range of flora and fauna endemic to these particular ecosystems.

I've heard that malaria medication can have side effects, and I want to take my children. Are there malaria-free reserves worth visiting? The best malaria-free Big 5 reserve is Makweti, but it's also worth looking at the options in Welgevonden, a pretty reserve very close to Johannesburg with numerous lodges, as well as the reserves in the Western and Eastern Cape. Staff and programs are often geared specifically for children in malaria-free reserves (we've indicated these with the "Kids" icon, but Lalibela and River Bend are best in Eastern Cape, and Jaci's Safari Lodge is best in Makweti).

I've decided on the private reserve. How should I choose my lodge or camp? It's worth mentioning that some of the larger lodges simply feel like plush hotels. Budget permitting, select a private lodge that takes no more than 18 guests per camp—this means you'll be ensured very personal service and the peace and quiet to absorb your surroundings. Privacy is paramount—units are usually set far apart, often with such luxuries as private plunge pools. If, however, you want to get a real feel for the bush, consider tented bush camps, where such essentials as hot water and en-suite bathrooms are standard features, but canvas walls allow the sounds of the bush to connect you with the outdoors. If you don't mind living out of a suitcase, moving from camp to camp is the ideal way to see different environments as well as plentiful game. And nowhere does it get as good as Botswana. See chapter 12 for a listing of safari operators who specialize in this area, as well as for a detailed description of the type of accommodations available.

If I'm visiting a private reserve, do I still need to include a national park or provincial reserve in my itinerary? Not necessarily. A private reserve should deliver all that you expect in terms of flora and fauna interaction and experience. In a national park or provincial reserve, you are, after all, in a closed vehicle, on demarcated roads which you can't leave, and you're not trained to spot animals in the bush. These reserves can also become very crowded, especially during school holidays, when queues are known to form around game sightings. With limited time, a private reserve is the best option, but for a more extended stay, a national park, perhaps with a trail, is an excellent option. Outside school holidays, you may enjoy sightings in the Kruger in total solitude—a privilege you'll seldom have in a private reserve, where other guests are usually onboard, and another vehicle is on the way as soon as an animal is spotted.

When's the best time to go on safari? The dry winter months (June–Oct, particularly Oct) are considered best. That's when the vegetation has died back and animals are easier to see, concentrated around the diminishing sources of water. Unless it was a particularly wet summer, the malaria risk is also considerably lower. But spring and summer bring their own benefits: Many animals have young (there's nothing quite as delightful as a baby giraffe), the vegetation is lush and often flowering, and colorful migrant birds adorn the trees. It is more difficult to spot

	Jan	Feb	Mar	Apr	May	June	July	Aug	Sept	Oct	Nov	Dec
Kruger National Park	P	P	P	F	F	G	E	E	E	E	G	F
Private Game Reserves	G	G	G	G	G	E	E	E	E	E	E	G
Moremi & Okavango Delta	G	G	G	G	E	E	E	E	E	E	E	G
Chobe	F	F	F	G	G	E	E	E	E	E	E	G
Makgadikgadi & Nxai Pan	E	E	E	E	G	F	F	P	P	P	F	G
Zululand					F		F		F		E	
E E					E		E		E		G	
G F												
Reserves (Hluhluwe—Umfolozi, Phinda, Thanda)												

E = Excellent, G = Good, F = Fair, P = Poor

animals in spring and summer, however, and you'll almost definitely need to spend time in a private reserve if you want to be assured of seeing big game.

How long do I need to spend on safari? To honestly say you've experienced the bush, you'll need a minimum of 3 nights and 3 full days at one lodge—preferably 4 to 5, split over two destinations.

How safe am I on safari? You are undertaking a journey through a landscape where wild animals abound, but if you behave sensibly, the risk posed by wild animals is minimal. Malaria is also a serious threat—potentially fatal. See "Staying Healthy," p. 52, for tips on how to ensure you survive your safari.

I've heard that walking safaris are the best way to experience the bush. Is this true? In a sense, yes. Guided by an armed and knowledgeable ranger, you will see many things that people in cars blindly cruise by, and the experience of spotting a rhino just yards away on foot is unforgettable. The emphasis, however, is not on tracking game (no ranger would take you within striking distance of a big cat) as much as it is on understanding the intricacies of the relationships in the bush, communing with nature, and learning about the medicinal use of indigenous plants. The ranger is armed, so there is no real danger (though a ranger was recently trampled to death by an elephant in Hluhluwe-Umfolozi, so be aware that these seemingly gentle giants need to be treated with the utmost respect). The wilderness trails in Kruger and Hluhluwe reserves enjoy an unblemished safety record for visitors.

What should I pack? Pack light, particularly if you are taking a charter plane to Botswana, which currently allows only one soft-sided bag weighing 10kg (22 lb.). Choose colors that blend in with the bush: Gray, brown/beige, and khaki are best. Loose cotton clothing tends to be the most comfortable and protects your limbs from mosquitoes. If you intend to walk, you'll need long pants to protect you from prickly vegetation and ticks, as well as comfortable hiking boots. A warm sweater, a coat, long pants, a scarf, and gloves are recommended during evening game drives in winter (May–Aug); you'll also need warm sleepwear. A fitted broad-brimmed hat, swimwear, good sunglasses, and sunscreen are essential in summer. Though many lodges supply insect repellent, pack your own, as well as every other malaria precaution (see "Health" and "Safety," earlier in this chapter). And, of course, don't forget binoculars and a camera (ideally, with high magnification lens, zooming to 300x or more). If you're not using a digital camera, bring plenty of film, though you can usually purchase more at the camp. If you bring a video camera, pack a 12-volt adapter for charging the batteries (keep in mind, however, that electricity isn't always supplied on safaris).

9 SUSTAINABLE TOURISM

Tourism is big business. According to the World Tourism Organization, the world's largest and fastest-growing industry generated $856 billion in revenue in 2007, with 903 million international arrivals recorded—100 million more people than in 2006. By 2020, the forecast is 1.6 billion. That's a lot of people tramping around our increasingly fragile planet. Faced with the long-term costs associated with this kind of rapacious growth, "responsible tourism" has become the 21st-century tourism buzz phrase, and recent years have seen a rash of new awards recognizing properties and operators making an effort to do the right thing. Even mainstream tourism has taken elements of this on board—though one cannot help suspecting that discreetly placed signs asking you to reuse your towels are geared more toward conserving laundry costs than the environment, or wondering just how big that percentage of profits donated to local schools really is.

Ironically, the seeds of global eco-tourism were laid in Africa's "nature" tourism. During the 20th century, vast areas, such as the Kruger, were unilaterally set aside for conservation, and local inhabitants were often forcibly removed to make way for reservation areas. This left tourism regions ring-fenced by communities, unable to graze herds, hunt, or forage for building materials and food. As human developments grew, problems were exacerbated. Such forward-thinking pioneers as the Varty brothers in Londolozi and the founders of Wilderness Safaris in Botswana realized that a different approach was called for, and pioneering partnerships between the government, private business, and locals were forged. With a proportion of "safari tourism" revenue now plowed into both wildlife protection and local community development, responsible tourism was born. As revenue grew out of ground-breaking rehabilitation projects such as Phinda in KwaZulu-Natal, where degraded farmland was slowly returned to its original pristine state, others followed suit, particularly in the Eastern Cape.

In 1996, South Africa became the first in the world to adopt responsible tourism as an official policy, and the 2002 Cape Town Declaration, basis for the international World Responsible Tourism awards, was formulated in accordance with this policy, as were the Imvelo Awards, Africa's Responsible Tourism awards (for past winners, visit www.imveloawards.co.za). South Africa is also the only country in the world to have a "fair trade" label for its tourism products. To find accredited operators as well as places to stay (and various links providing tips on how to become a responsible traveler), visit www.fair

tourismsa.org.za. Note that the accreditation is stiff (and rather pricy), with stringent criteria including fair wages, working conditions, distribution of benefits, and so on. For more ideas on how to green your vacation, visit **www.icrtourismsa.org**, the website for the **International Centre for Responsible Tourism South Africa.** For volunteer opportunities in South Africa, see "Special-Interest Trips & Escorted General-Interest Tours," below.

Wilderness Safaris, Southern Africa Adding to a long string of achievements (including a highly commended recognition for their Damaraland Camp in the International Responsible Tourism Awards), Wilderness Safaris (www.wilderness-safaris.com) clinched a win at the Imvelo Awards for Responsible Tourism with their Skeleton Coast Camp in 2008, winning the category Best Overall Environmental Management System. Their Kalamu Camp, in Zambia, was also highly commended in the category Best Single Resource Management Programme—Energy.

Tswalu Kalahari Reserve, South Africa Committed to Fair Trade Tourism principles, **Tswalu** (www.tswalu.com) rehabilitated 38 overgrazed cattle farms and turned them into the largest privately owned reserve in southern Africa, restocking it with game, including the endangered wild dog, rhino, and cheetah. Hence, it receives continued international applause, including *Condé Nast Traveler's* World Savers Award and the Relais & Châteaux Global Environmental Trophy.

Madikwe Game Reserve Like Tswalu, Madikwe (www.madikwe.info) was once kilometers of overgrazed farmland until it was transformed in 1991 into a 75,000-hectare (185,250-acre) reserve, South Africa's fourth largest. Within a period of 6 years, some 10,000 animals were again roaming the plains in what was dubbed Operation Phoenix, the largest game translocation in the world. Book at Buffalo Ridge Safari Lodge, the first wholly owned community safari lodge to be developed in South Africa, or Thakadu River Camp—also owned by the local community.

&Beyond, Africa Besides rehabilitating 23,000 hectares (56,810 acres) and introducing game to severely degraded farmland in Kwazulu Natal and creating Phinda private reserve, &Beyond (née CCAfrica) has done sterling work with the Africa Foundation, an organization founded to facilitate the development of people living in or adjacent to protected areas. In 14 years of operation, it has raised and committed over $6 million to consultative community development projects and was awarded the *Condé Nast Traveler* World Savers Award in 2009.

Ant's Hill, Waterberg From waste disposal to water recycling, sourcing locally produced food and energy management, these Waterberg bush villas (www.waterberg.net) are model eco-lodges. They were awarded four stars in this year's Eco Hotels of the World competition, one of only two southern African destinations to be included (the other being the charming Hog Hollow Country Lodge in the Crags, near Plettenberg Bay).

GENERAL RESOURCES FOR GREEN TRAVEL

In addition to the resources for South Africa listed above, the following websites provide valuable wide-ranging information on sustainable travel. For a list of even more sustainable resources, as well as tips and explanations on how to travel greener, visit www.frommers.com/planning.

- **Responsible Travel** (www.responsibletravel.com) is a great source of sustainable travel ideas; the site is run by a spokesperson for ethical tourism in the travel industry, and all operators featured on the site have met the company's strict membership criteria. They also cosponsor the international Responsible Tourism Awards (nominated by tourists who recognize individuals, companies, and organizations in the travel industry who make a difference). Winners are announced every November on WTM World Responsible Tourism Day. **Sustainable Travel International** (www.sustainabletravel international.org) also promotes ethical tourism practices and manages an extensive directory of sustainable properties and tour operators around the world; Greenstop (www.greenstop.net) is another, providing an "eco-worthiness" audit for every entry.

- **Carbonfund** (www.carbonfund.org), **TerraPass** (www.terrapass.org), and **Carbon Neutral** (www.carbonneutral.org) provide information on carbon offsetting, or offsetting the greenhouse gas emitted during flights.
- **Greenhotels** (www.greenhotels.com) recommends green-rated member hotels around the world that fulfill the company's stringent environmental requirements. **Eco Hotels of the World** (www.ecohotelsoftheworld.com) is another worthwhile guide. Hotels cannot pay to be featured, nor do the editors take commission on bookings, so it is a truly independent guide, and one to which readers and visitors can contribute. **Environmentally Friendly Hotels** (www.environmentallyfriendlyhotels.com) offers more green accommodation ratings.
- For information on animal-friendly issues throughout the world, visit **Tread Lightly** (www.treadlightly.org). For information about the ethics of swimming with dolphins, visit the **Whale and Dolphin Conservation Society** (www.wdcs.org).

10 SPECIAL-INTEREST TRIPS & ESCORTED TOURS

BIRD-WATCHING TRIPS

With so many habitats, southern Africa is one of the most rewarding bird-watching destinations in the world. Birders looking for escorted tours of the bush throughout the country, with the focus primarily but not exclusively on bird-watching, contact Peter Lawson (© **27/13/741-2458;** www.lawsons.co.za). Not only is he excellent company, but he also loves what he does and puts together itineraries to suit your particular interests or needs.

CULTURAL & HISTORICAL TOURS

Another good Cape Town tour worth booking in advance is a **Cape Town Jazz Safari,** offered by **Andulela Tours** (© **021/790-2592;** www.andulela.com). The highly personal tour kicks off with a visit to the District Six Café for a drink, then heads off to the home of a well-known local musician, such as Mac McKenzie, the king of Goema (a fusion of jazz, samba, and traditional drumming), and ending at a restaurant in Landsdowne. For more tours of this nature, refer to chapter 5.

Palaeo-Tours (© **011/726-8788;** www.palaeotours.com) offers fascinating trips to some of the key sites in what has become known as the Cradle of Humankind, declared a World Heritage Site in 1999 for the significant paleoanthropological discoveries made in the area since 1966 (for more, see chapter 8). Guides are paleoanthropology scientists or Ph.D. students who will explain the history of evolution while taking you to working excavation sites. The area is some 20

Guides for Gourmets & Gourmands

Cape Town is regularly cited as one of the best-value cities in the world for serious gourmets, who rave about the fine dining to be had at a fraction of what it would cost in comparable restaurants in New York, London, Paris, or Sydney. If you're a serious gourmand or are going to be here for a while, don't miss these three restaurant guides: ***Eat Out*** (www.eatout.co.za), an annual overview of restaurants throughout the country, with an annual top 10 that is highly rated (and coveted), is very thorough, and you can find a review on the restaurant closest to you with the click of a button. More discriminating and critical, ***dine,*** published by *Wine* magazine (www.winemag.co.za), also covers the country and publishes an annual top 100. ***Rossouw's Restaurants*** (www.rossouwsrestaurants.com) is an annual guide that divides top picks according to budget, as well as useful selections under such categories as "Family" and "Romantic"; diners send in most of the review notes, so you're not being influenced by a few food critics' palates (though Rossouw does the final edit).

minutes from Johannesburg city; tours, comprising two site visits, usually last 5 hours. All Palaeo-Tours are by arrangement only, so book before you leave home.

ADVENTURE ACTIVITIES

From dropping like a stone into the Batoka ravine to walking with lions and surfing the Zambezi as it churns like a washing machine, Victoria Falls is a mecca for adrenaline junkies and outdoors enthusiasts. For a complete list of what to do in the Victoria Falls area, check out **Safari Par Excellence** (www.safpar.net), though it's worth noting here that their elephant-back safaris have been very controversial; see chapter 11 for information. For a complete directory of operators specializing in adventure pursuits in South Africa, purchase the ***Getaway Adventure Guide*** or take a look at www.getawaytoafrica.com.

FOOD & WINE TRIPS

The delightfully named **Samp and Soufflé** (www.sampsouffle.com) specializes in custom-designed luxury "food adventures," in which you can help cook your meals with some of South Africa's most well-regarded chefs; learn to cook venison, say, in a tented camp deep in Big 5 country, or take self-driven or chauffeured gourmet tours that lead from one destination restaurant to the next. Excursions can include visits to authentic produce markets and working wine estates, where you will meet some of the country's most interesting wine makers. (Of course, you could just as easily book yourself a suite in Franschhoek, justifiably known as the culinary capital of the Cape, and just work your way through the superb selection of restaurants in that lush little valley.) For a short culinary tour, consider booking one of Andula's **Cape Malay** or **African Cooking** safaris (www.andulela.com), in which you visit a home in the local community and prepare a three-course meal with your hostess. This is not haute cuisine, by any means, but the interaction with real Cape locals (rather than the Eurocentric community that runs much of the tourism industry in the city) will be a lasting memory.

There are countless wine tours on offer, but serious wine lovers would do well to book a tour with **Stephen Flesch** (© **021/705-4317** or 083/229-3581;

www.gourmetwinetours.co.za). Former chairman of the Wine Tasters Guild of S.A. and an ardent wine lover, Stephen personally knows many of the winemakers and proprietors of the top wine estates—his knowledge of South African wines spans 4 decades. He will take into account your particular interests or wine preferences, and tailor an itinerary that covers both historical estates and rustic farms off the beaten track. The day trip includes a stop at one of the Winelands' top award-winning restaurants (he is, after all, secretary of Cape Town's Slow Food Convivium). Rates for a full day are R1,500 for the first person and R700 for each additional person. Half-day is R1,000 for the first person and R450 for each additional person.

11 STAYING CONNECTED

Landlines are reliable, and cellphone reception is good for most parts of South Africa, though it's worth letting go while on safari.

To call southern Africa from another country: Dial the international access code (United States or Canada 011, United Kingdom or New Zealand 00, Australia 0011) plus the **country code** (the country code for South Africa is 27; for Zimbabwe, it is 263; for Botswana, it is 267), plus the local region code (minus the 0) and the number.

To make an international call from South Africa: Dial 00, then the country code (U.S. or Canada 1, U.K. 44, Australia 61, New Zealand 64), the area code, and the local number.

To charge international calls from South Africa: Dial AT&T Direct (© 0-800-99-0123), Sprint (© 0800-99-0001), or MCI (© 0800-99-0011).

To make a local call: If you have a number with the country code, you will need to drop the country code and add a zero (0) to the city code (except in Botswana, which has no city codes). In South Africa, you now have to dial the city or region code (for example, 012) before every Cape Town number. Note also that if you are using a mobile phone, you always need to enter the network code before the telephone number; codes 082, 083, 084, 072, 073, and 074 are mobile or cell numbers, and these codes must also not be dropped.

Looking for a number: In South Africa: Call directory assistance at © **1023** for numbers in South Africa, and © **0903** for international numbers. To track down a service, call © **10118.** Be patient, speak slowly, and check spellings with your operator. Because hotels often charge a massive markup, it's worth using a cellphone (see below) or purchasing a telephone card for international calls—these card-operated pay phones are also often the only ones working. Cards are available from post offices and most newsagents, and come in units of R20, R50, R100, and R200.

CELLPHONES

Most South Africans, regardless of race or class, carry a cellphone; reception is generally excellent. If your cellphone is on a GSM system and you have a world-capable multiband phone, simply call your wireless operator and ask for international roaming to be activated on your account. Note, though, that per-minute charges can be very high—if you plan to use your phone a lot (and incoming calls are equally expensive), it's definitely worth purchasing a local SIM card, which costs between R1 and R20, depending on where and when you buy it, and purchasing pay-as-you-go airtime (available in bundled minutes that cost upward of R20). You will find retailers selling SIM cards and airtime throughout metropolitan areas; look for signs pasted on shop windows or inquire at small general dealer shops. For many, **renting a phone** is a good idea; you can do this (as well as purchase a SIM card and airtime) at a **Vodafone** outlet at any of the international airports in South Africa. Vodacom has 24-hour desks at all major international airports, as well as desks in big malls (such as the Waterfront in Cape Town), with a range of mobile phones to purchase or rent.

INTERNET & E-MAIL

Without Your Own Computer

There are literally thousands of cybercafes throughout South Africa's urban areas—anywhere you find travelers. Aside from these, virtually all lodgings will have a computer on which you can access your mail or surf the Internet, either for free or for a small fee. The same goes for hotels, though many of them still charge for this, a real irritant (we have indicated fees where possible). Information bureaus in cities also provide Internet access, as do major airports. Internet access is less predictable while on safari and, frankly, counterproductive to the experience. For what will, after all, be a relatively limited time, we suggest you let everyone know that you will be out of reach, switch off all forms of 21st-century technology, and immerse yourself in the sights and sounds of the bush.

With Your Own Computer

Large hotels, resorts, and airports in South Africa offer Wi-Fi access, charging a small fee (you pay online, using your credit card) for usage. For free Wi-Fi access in South Africa, take a look at who has joined www.redbutton.co.za (click on "Sites"). These hotels, guest lodges, restaurants, and cafes (the vast majority of them in the Cape) all offer free Wi-Fi—unlimited or limited, from 5MB to 100MB per day. There are other establishments that offer free Wi-Fi, such as the delightful **Café Neo** in Cape Town (great food, plus a sea view; see chapter 5). Others charge a small fee, such as the **Vida e Caffe** chain (www.caffe.co.za; click on "Stores" to find one near you); though it's a franchise, the coffee is still good. You may also want to check out **www.jiwire.com**; its Hotspot Finder holds the world's largest directory of public wireless hotspots. For dial-up access, most business-class hotels offer dataports for laptop modems; if you do not have Wi-Fi capacity, remember to bring a **connection kit** of the right power, phone adapters, a spare phone cord, and a spare Ethernet network cable—or find out whether your hotel supplies them to guests.

12 TIPS ON ACCOMMODATIONS

The choice of accommodations can make or break a holiday, so we take special pride in providing you with the best recommendations. The selection in this book covers a wide variety of budgets, but all share the common ability to delight—be it because of a fabulous location, special decor, great service, or excellent views (and, of course, some cover all those criteria). For the sake of variety, I'm not keen on booking an entire holiday through one hotel chain, but sometimes you can negotiate a better deal this way. **Three Cities** (www.threecities.co.za) is probably my favorite hotel group, though it doesn't include my favorite hotels. They offer a wide variety of properties in South Africa's best locations. If you want a luxury safari with a possible beach stop, you will certainly want to contact Wilderness Safaris and &Beyond,

both in Kruger, Botswana, and Kwazulu Natal (www.wilderness-safaris.com and www.andbeyond.com). Wilderness Safaris has the best (and most) locations in Botswana; &Beyond has the edge in terms of design and such luxuries as personal butlers.

The following sites featuring property collections are highly recommended: Specializing in owner-managed establishments with real character, often in unusual locations, is the **Greenwood Guide to South Africa** (www.greenwoodguides.com). If you intend to spend a lengthy amount of time in South Africa and cover a lot of ground, and if you like self-catering options off the beaten track or intimate places where you can interact with the owners, the Greenwood team's unerring eye for unusual and personal lodgings will stand you in good stead. **Portfolio** (www.portfoliocollection.com) brings out an attractive range of free booklets profiling the full spectrum of options across the country; all the properties are online as well. The B&B Collection offers fair to excellent budget options, some in quite luxurious surroundings. If anything, you have almost too many choices—not all of them to our standard—but if you stick to the Luxury and Great Comfort options (indicated by colored shields), you're likely to be delighted with the good value. In the Retreats Collection, the focus is upmarket guesthouses where you usually can't go wrong (though a few duds creep in every year); top of the range is the Country Places Collection, which includes some of the best game lodges in the country. Each review comes with at least one photograph—with more on their website. If a safari is the primary reason you're heading south, you'd be well advised to take a look at the excellent selection in **Classic Safari Camps of Africa** (www.classicsafaricamps.com).

Note: South Africa has a great selection of self-catering options—good for families or for those wishing to prolong their stay—and, thanks to restaurant delivery services in most urban centers, you won't even have to cook. A number of companies offer what is referred to as the Villa Stay, most of them in Cape Town. **Icon Villas** (www.icape.co.za) offers a particularly good service, with a wide range of properties, from flats in the center of Cape Town to private villas on game lodges; but it is the hands-on management by proprietor Therese Botha, with her attention to detail, from quality of linen to great location, that gives them an edge. Icon also offers a full concierge service. For more information, see individual chapters for suggestions. For rural options, try to track down the excellent Budget Getaways, or go to **www.farmstay.co.za** for more off-the-beaten-track options. Last but not least, those looking at the most cost-effective way to travel should visit **www.homeexchange.com**. There are some superb South African homes listed here—many of them in the most sought-after areas in Cape Town, with views, pools, and ultra-luxurious furnishings and fittings.

Suggested Southern African Itineraries

Most people fly to southern Africa to witness Mother Nature firsthand at her most powerful—from the wonder of seeing a leopard haughtily surveying you from a branch, with her bloodied paw carelessly slung over her kill, to the haunting majesty of the white-cloud "tablecloth" billowing down Cape Town's Table Mountain. These itineraries are designed to lead you into the wild.

1 THE REAL RELAXER: CAPE TOWN IN 1 WEEK

You've chosen to stay put in one region and relax. Sensible, really: You're in one of the most beautiful cities in the world, surrounded by vineyard-carpeted valleys and a whale nursery off the coast—why rush off? This tour starts off in Cape Town then takes you out of the city—but not too far.

Day 1: Cape Town

Having arranged for an airport transfer through your lodgings (where you have booked for 4 nights; see recommendations in chapter 5), spend the first day sleeping late. Then take a stroll around the **Victoria & Alfred Waterfront** in the late afternoon before dining at a table with a view of the iconic **Table Mountain,** magically lit up at night. We recommend either **Den Anker** (for delicious Belgian-inspired cuisine) or the more flashy **Baia** (for seafood). Be sure to book ahead for either (in the summer, make your reservation even before you leave home). Alternatively, if you want to watch Capetonians at play, head for the tiny piazza at **Cape Quarter** and grab an outside table at one of the restaurants there; or, if you're a dedicated foodie (and ready for a bit of nightlife), book a table at **Jardine** in the city. If you've still got energy after your meal, stroll the sidewalk through heady **Long Street,** one of the city's key nightlife nodes, and get a glimpse of Cape Town's "real" city action.

Day 2: Table Mountain's Eastern Slopes or Cape Town's Famous Beach Scene

With any luck, at the start of your second full day, your batteries will be fully recharged. Your rental car should be delivered to you this morning. Spend the morning on the eastern slopes of Table Mountain exploring **Kirstenbosch Botanical Gardens.** From Kirstenbosch, make your way farther south to lunch at the manor house at **Constantia Uitsig,** for pastoral vineyard views and old-style elegance. Alternatively, if you're a beach lover, skip the gardens and take a book, sunscreen, and sunglasses to **Clifton Beach,** where it's a short drive to a fabulous lunch at **Rumbullion** (again, reserve well ahead), set in a forest overlooking palm-fringed

Camps Bay. Or worship the sun on Camps Bay and saunter over to **The Grand** for lunch. Weather permitting, ascend **Table Mountain** in the late afternoon to watch as the sun sinks into the western horizon and the city lights start to sparkle.

Days ❸ & ❹: Cape Peninsula

By the third day, you'll set off on the **peninsula drive** (see p. 158) to cruise the awesome **Chapman's Peak Drive** (if it's open) and get off the beaten track in the **Cape Point Nature Reserve.** (If you've not yet done Kirstenbosch Gardens, stop there in the morning.) It's also an opportunity to wander through the boho fishing town of **Kalk Bay,** where you'll get your fill of galleries and antique shops. Have lunch at **Harbor House** for the close-up views of crashing waves and seals catching fish. Rather than head back to the city, consider overnighting at *uber*-elegant **Rodwell House** in teensy **St James,** where you can kick off your shoes, hang with the local surfers, or join the old-timers in the famous tidal pool. Alternatively, book a night at cool-white **Zensa Lodge,** in idyllic Scarborough. Your first night here will make you thankful you've booked another, with time to explore the laid-back villages that surround Cape Point.

Days ❺ & ❻: Winelands: Franschhoek & Stellenbosch

The next day, set off fairly early for **Stellenbosch,** where the majority of South Africa's award-winning wines are grown. Arrange in advance for a personal wine guide (see p. 180 for recommendations) to take you to select wine estates. Lunch at **Overture** (the views are beautiful; the food is divine), then spend the late afternoon exploring Stellenbosch's bustling town on foot. The town is alive with students, except in mid-summer, and it's packed with great restaurants. For the best take on New South African cuisine, book your place at **Cognito** for dinner. Then see if you can catch a local band later in the evening, before retiring at either **River Manor** or **Asara.** Alternatively, get to **Franschhoek** by midafternoon to spend the night at the gorgeously located **Le Petite Ferme,** where you'll spend the night lording over the valley below. Next day, continue your oeno-expedition.

Day ❼: Whale-Watching in Hermanus or Village-Vibing in Tulbagh

You could easily spend another night in Stellenbosch (for the myriad restaurant options alone). But if it's whale-watching season (June–Nov), keep following the magnificent **Coastal Road** south from Gordon's Bay to **Hermanus,** whale-watching capital of the world, approximately 112km (69 miles) from Cape Town. Spend the night here (preferably at the **Marine**), and check out some of the world's biggest fish at Shark Alley (see p. 203) before returning to Cape Town. If it's not yet whale season, head from Stellenbosch in the opposite direction, passing through Paarl and stopping there for lunch if you're hungry. Then head up over the sublime **Bain's Kloof Pass** to reach unspoiled **Tulbagh,** a gem of a village, packed with charming historical houses and surrounded by vineyards. Stay in a treehouse at **Vin Doux,** or imbibe the country hospitality at the guesthouse on Church Street, where dozens of Cape Dutch houses are lined up for viewing.

Day ❽: Cape Town

Extend your stay by 1 day and celebrate with a meal at the **Roundhouse** (same venue as Rumbullion, but this time indoors); the food, service, and formidable list of South African wines and top-class spirits will put you in the mood for a party. Make sure you preorder a taxi, and if it's the right night of the week, hit a bar or club of your choice. Whether you dance or mourn on your final night, you'll forever be dreaming of your return.

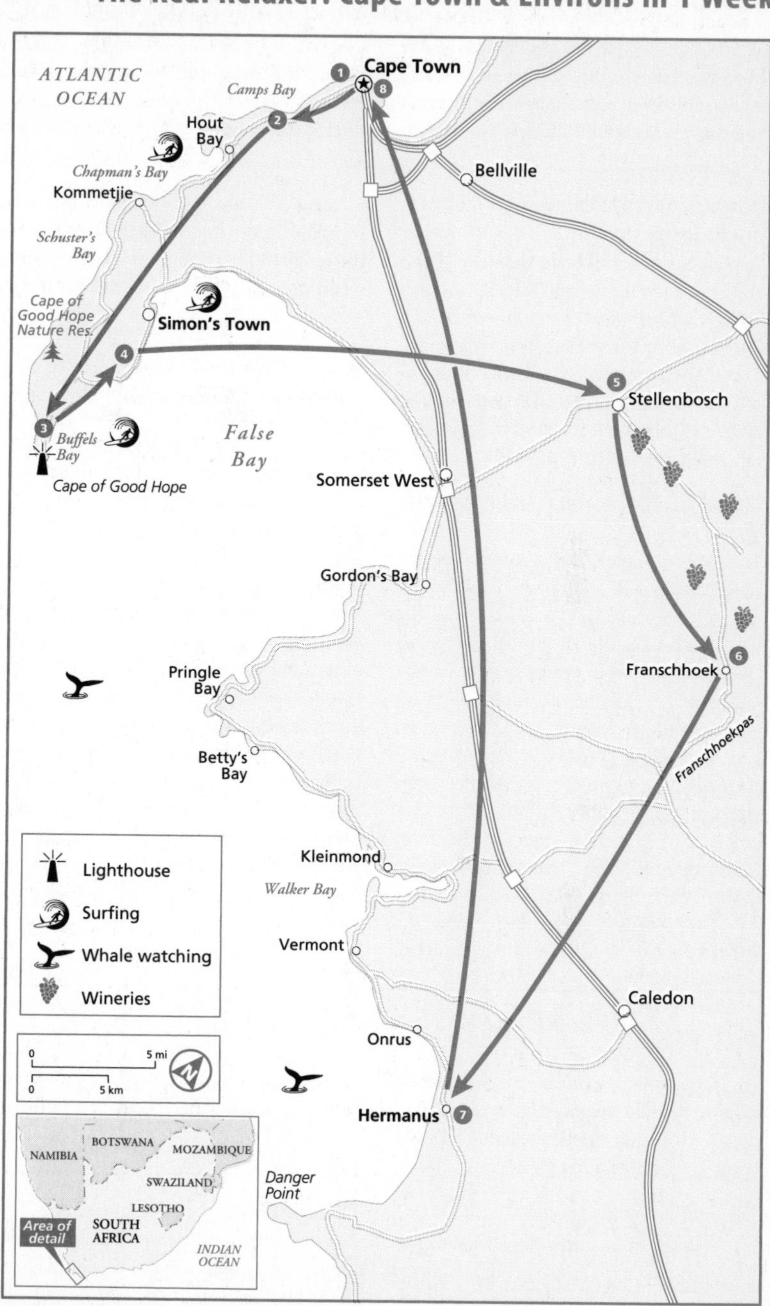
ATLANTIC OCEAN
Cape Town
Camps Bay
Hout Bay
Chapman's Bay
Kommetjie
Bellville
Schuster's Bay
Cape of Good Hope Nature Res.
Simon's Town
Stellenbosch
Buffels Bay
Cape of Good Hope
False Bay
Somerset West
Gordon's Bay
Pringle Bay
Franschhoek
Franschhoekpas
Betty's Bay
Kleinmond
Walker Bay
Vermont
Caledon
Onrus
Hermanus
Danger Point
Lighthouse
Surfing
Whale watching
Wineries
0
5 mi
0
5 km
NAMIBIA
BOTSWANA
MOZAMBIQUE
SWAZILAND
LESOTHO
SOUTH AFRICA
INDIAN OCEAN
Area of detail

2 THE QUICK FIX: THREE TOURS IN 1 WEEK

Botswana is generally considered the last untouched wilderness in Africa, Victoria Falls is a world wonder, and Cape Town is one of the most beautiful cities on Earth. A week covering these sights will leave you with unparalleled memories.

Days ❶, ❷ & ❸: Okavango Delta or Linyanti

Your priority should be to spend at least 3 nights in the **Okavango Delta,** preferably between June and October, when the abundance of game attracts a huge number of predators. A good alternative (or add-on) is in one of the **Linyanti** reserves, where a number of camps offer better value; see chapter 12 for more.

Days ❹ & ❺: Chobe National Park/ Victoria Falls

Transfer to Kasane for a couple nights' sojourn at Chobe National Park, where elephant sightings are believed to be the very best on Earth. One of the most luxurious and accessible camps here is **Chobe Chilwero.** Near the northern town of Kasane, and overlooking the Chobe River, Chilwero also organizes day trips to **Victoria Falls,** just an hour away. Alternatively, you can skip Chobe National Park altogether and charter a direct flight from Maun to Livingstone and spend 2 nights at one of the options discussed in chapter 11. For colonial pampering, book the **River Club,** on the banks of the Zambezi, or for a real adventure, book **Sindabezi,** an island in the middle of the Zambezi. If you're an adrenaline junkie, don't miss spending a day river rafting the Zambezi.

Days ❻ & ❼: Cape Town & the Winelands

Fly via Johannesburg to get to **Cape Town** the next day. There are wonderful places to stay all over town, but given that your time is limited, opt for lodging in the City Bowl (a natural amphitheater created by Table Mountain and the encircling arm of Signal Hill) or the Atlantic Seaboard, if it's summer; see chapter 5 for the top choices. If the weather is bad, book a personalized wine tour and spend the day sampling the superb red wines produced in the Stellenbosch region's tasting rooms, many of them heated with crackling fires. If the sun's out, spend the day driving the Cape Peninsula route (see chapter 158). End your last day on **Clifton** or **Camps Bay beach,** or with a bottle of champagne on **Table Mountain** as the sun sets over the Southern Hemisphere and you toast your next trip here.

3 THE SPLURGE SAFARI: IN 10 DAYS

For the southern African safari experience of a lifetime, you really need to experience Botswana's Okavango Delta or Linyanti, a desert reserve, and the abundant wildlife of South Africa's Kruger Park region.

Days ❶ to ❺: Botswana

Fly directly from either Johannesburg to Maun in Botswana, and spend 3 nights at one of our recommended **Okavango Delta** or **Linyanti** camps. Spend your first day relaxing and recovering from your long journey, watching the wildlife from the privacy of your deck. You'll wake the

The Quick Fix: Botswana, Vic Falls & Cape Town in 1 Week

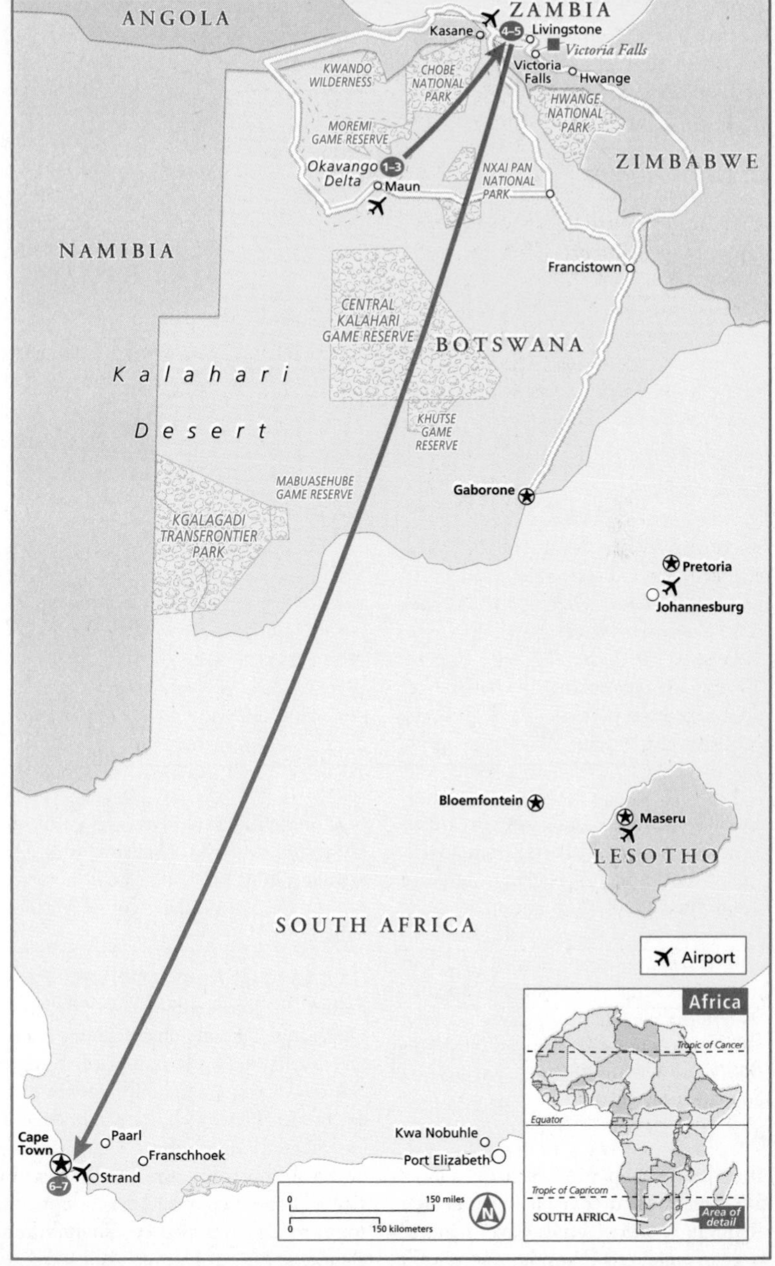

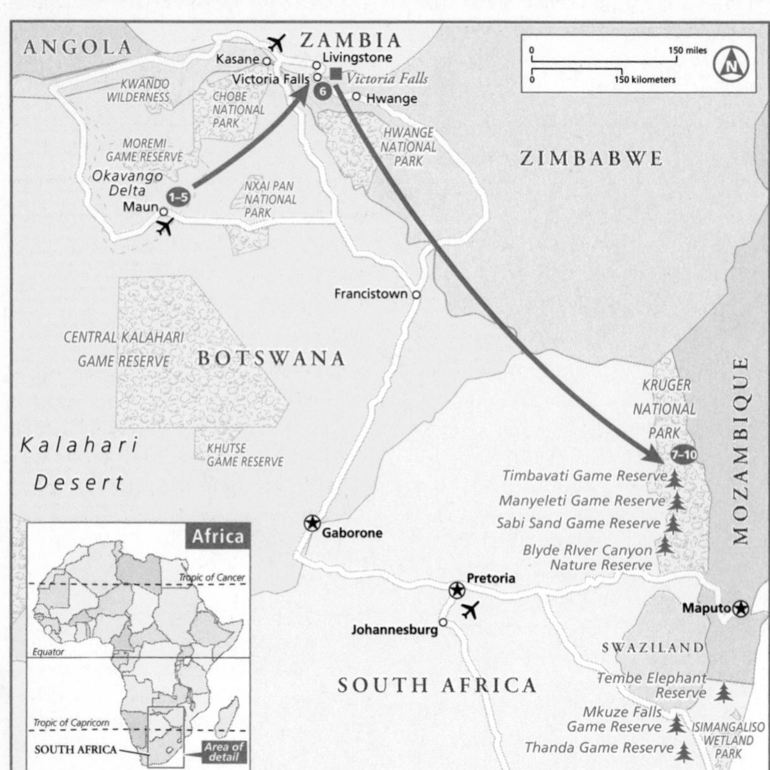

next day refreshed and ready for a day's intensive game-viewing. Alternatively, book the 3-night **Kanana mokoro (canoe) trail,** and camp out on an island with your own dedicated staff. From the pristine delta, move on to spend 2 nights at **Jack's Camp** in Botswana's Kalahari wilderness, where the desolate desert is nature at its most surreal; take a quad-bike safari to view some **Bushman rock art,** or to **Kubu Island.**

Day 6: Zambia/Victoria Falls

From Jack's Camp, you can charter a flight to Livingstone, in Zambia, and spend a night at the colonial-style **River Club** or funky **Tongabezi**—both located on the edge of the Zambezi River—or Stanley & Livingstone on the Zimbabwe side. All provide a most romantic base from which to visit the spectacular sight of **Victoria Falls.**

Days 7 to 10: Kruger National Park

Return to Johannesburg (directly from Livingstone). From Johannesburg, it's an easy flight to world-renowned **Kruger National Park,** along South Africa's eastern border. Here, a choice of ultraluxurious game lodges offer smart design, impeccable comfort, and excellent game-viewing. For the absolute best options, spend 4 nights at two of **Singita's** four luxurious camps (two in **Boulders** or

Ebony, the following two in **Lebombo** or **Sweni**), or combine Lebombo with **Londolozi** or **Royal Malewane.** The latter is the best choice if you're interested in on-foot rhino tracking. Londolozi is the ultimate for leop gita will bowl you cated design, servi game-viewing is also

4 THE BUDGET SAFARI: IN 14 D

Given the standards of the game-viewing and the public rest camps, this self-driving tour is definitely the best-value safari to be had on the continent: You will see everything you ever dreamed of, for a fraction of the third itinerary, above. You could shave off 2 days by flying direct from Jo'burg to Nelspruit, the nearest airport to southern Kruger.

Days 1 & 2: Mpumalanga Escarpment

A relaxed 4- to 5-hour drive from Gauteng brings you to the scenic escarpment, with its myriad viewpoints over the lowveld and magnificent Blyde River Canyon, where the Forever Blyde Canyon Resort makes for a wonderfully located and very affordable overnight base. If you arrive in time, stretch your legs on one of the short day trails that lead to the valley floor, and then spend the next day taking in the highlights of the Panorama Route, from God's Window and Bourke's Luck Potholes to the restored Victorian gold-rush town of Pilgrim's Rest.

Days 3 to 5: Southern Kruger

A short drive from Blyde River brings you to the southern Kruger, which is the most densely touristed part of the vast park, but also usually the best for game-viewing. Several rest camps are scattered in the south, of which Lower Sabie is a firm favorite, not only for its relaxed atmosphere, lovely riverine location, and good selection of budget-friendly accommodation options, but also as the epicenter of three of the finest game-viewing roads anywhere in the park. Three days here will give you an excellent chance to see all the Big 5: Elephant, buffalo, and, to a lesser extent, lion are almost guaranteed and might be seen driving in any direction; rhino are most common along the road to Crocodile Bridge; and leopards hang in the riparian undergrowth that follows the Sabi River toward Skukuza. If Lower Sabie is full, other good camps in the south include Skukuza and Berg-en-Dal.

Days 6 to 7: South-Central Kruger

It's worth dedicating 2 nights to the central plains around Satara, an area known for its dense lion population, high concentration of cheetahs, and seasonal herds of zebra and wildebeest. Satara is the most central base here, but it's also the second-largest rest camp in the park, with an undistinguished setting and rather impersonal atmosphere; there's a strong case for booking one of the wonderful tented units at Tamboti Camp (near Orpen Gate) instead. The best game-viewing in this area is usually along the main road connecting Satara to Tamboti, and the loop road running between Satara and the Nwanetsi picnic site.

Days 8 to 9: North-Central Kruger

Wildlife is less varied north of the Olifants River, but it's an excellent area for large elephant and buffalo herds, and it feels decidedly untrammeled by comparison to the south. Olifants Camp, on a cliff overlooking the river, has the most spectacular setting in the park, usually complete with browsing elephants and giraffe along the

udget Safari: in 14 Days

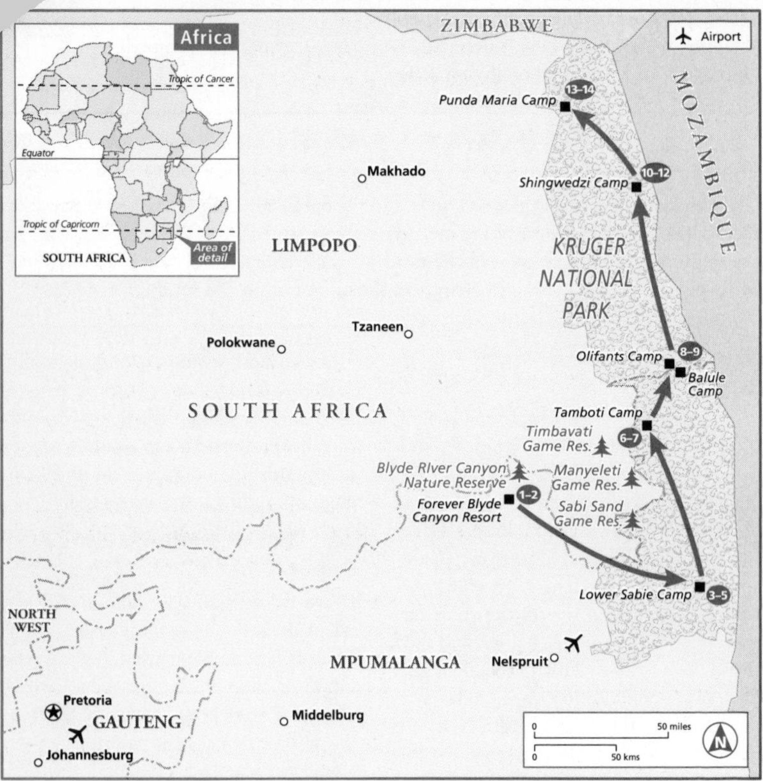

bank. Alternatively, the tiny primitive camp of Balule is ideal for those seeking a real bush experience (and the huts are the cheapest of anywhere in the park), while the more northerly Letaba Rest Camp overlooks the eponymous river and is known for its wonderful birdlife. The area around Letaba also hosts localized antelope such as roan, sable, and tsessebe.

Days ⑩ to ⑭: Northern Kruger or Private Game Reserve (Optional)

Those who reckon 7 nights of Kruger is enough of a good thing should head to the nearest airport (Hoedspruit or, farther south, Nelspruit) and fly to the reserves of subtropical KwaZulu-Natal (or, if you've had enough of wildlife, to Cape Town; see above). But to say you've really experienced the Kruger, you should continue northward for 4 nights, divided evenly between the rest camps of Shingwedzi and Punda Maria. The former is a riverside camp surrounded by a small network of great game-viewing roads; it feels strikingly remote even by comparison to Olifants or Letaba. More remote still is the hillside camp of Punda Maria, which is the best base for day trips to the lush Pafuri area, where a host of unusual birds can be seen in the vicinity of the confluence of the Levuvhu and Limpopo rivers (the three-way border with Zimbabwe and

Mozambique). The Thulamela Heritage Site protects the remains of a large stone city built in the 16th century after Great Zimbabwe was abandoned. On Day 14, we recommend an early start to get back to Gauteng in good time (or fly from Phalaborwa).

Alternatively: Days ⑩ to ⑭: KwaZulu-Natal

Days 10 to 12 Fly into Durban International Airport, hire a car, and take an easy drive north up the scenic N2 through rolling green fields of sugar cane and indigenous forests on a well-designed, well-marked toll road. Take the turn-off for Cape Vidal in the heart of the iSimangaliso (formerly St Lucia) Wetland Park, a UNESCO World Heritage site, where you have prebooked a rustic KZN Wildlife chalet a stone's throw from the beach, under the welcome shade of the casuarinas. Snorkel, dive, fish, or walk on the deserted beach and around Lake Bhangazi. Diverse wildlife in the highest vegetated dune and sand forests in the world include elephant, hippo, buffalo, and an array of birdlife.

Days 13 to 14 A short 90 minutes' drive west from Cape Vidal and the eastern shores lies the Hluluwe–Umfolozi Game Reserve, one of the oldest wildlife sanctuaries in Africa and site of the Zulu kings' ancient hunting grounds. Make reservations for the award-winning Hilltop camp there, or consider the purely self-catering Mpila Camp in the Umfolozi section—a series of comfortable canvas tents, where you really are in the bush proper. If you are feeling adventurous and need to stretch your legs, book a Wilderness Trail, the best foot safari in southern Africa.

If, on the other hand, you've had enough of wildlife, fly direct from Kruger to Cape Town, booking into **African Villa, The Fritz Hotel, Daddy Long Legs, Walden House,** or **Villa Zest**—all good value options—and spend your last few days exploring Table Mountain National Park.

5 ROAD TRIP: WESTERN CAPE IN 10 DAYS

There's nothing like a good road trip, with the freedom to stop exactly where and when you like. This drive will take you through incredible scenery from the slopes of Table Mountain to the thorny wilderness of the Eastern Cape. You could do the trip in less time, but the secret is to get off the beaten track and take it slow. See map p. 80.

Days ❶ & 2: Route 62

Choose your vehicle with care: It will become your friend and chariot. Go for fuel efficiency and comfort (A/C in summer is a must). Travel north from Cape Town on the N1; branch off at Worcester and head for Robertson on the R60, then turn onto the R62 to Montagu soon afterward. Stretch your legs at the fabulous Kogmanskloof Pass, with its incredible fold mountains. If you're a wine lover, don't miss one of the multitude of estates on the Robertson–Montagu stretch. **Les Hauts de Montagu,** just past Montagu, is worth a stopover; otherwise, press on past Barrydale (stopping for lunch at **Clarke of the Karoo,** if you have time) to **Sanbona** for your first safari experience in the arid Karoo. It's pricey but it is the top private game reserve in the Western Cape; alternatively, the **Retreat at Groenfontein,** near Calitzdorp, is another wonderfully remote stop. You'll need at least 2 nights at either. The Karoo landscape is huge, starkly

beautiful, and often empty: There are fewer towns along this stretch, so watch your gas gauge. Keep traveling along the R62 to ostrich capital **Oudsthoorn.**

Day ❸: Prince Albert

Visit the **Cango Caves**, see an **ostrich farm,** or try ostrich carpaccio or filet at one of the town's restaurants before taking the knuckle-clenching turn up the awesome **Swartberg Pass** to Prince Albert and spending the night at **Dennehof.**

Day ❹ & ❺: Wilderness/Knysna

Take the spectacular Meiringspoort Pass, Outeniqua Pass, and Kaaimansriver Pass to **Wilderness.** If you like the peaceful atmosphere of this small village, surrounded by water, spend a night at one of the excellent-value guest houses (such as **Moontide**) and enjoy the deserted beaches (beware the currents) and the lakes of Wilderness National Park, with a day trip to Knysna. Alternatively, press on to Knysna, which has plenty of accommodations; top choice is **Phantom Forest.** While in Knysna, try to fit in a **forest walk** to admire centuries-old yellowwood trees (or choose a horse-riding trail), a boat trip to the Heads, and a visit to **Noetzie** beach. Golfers may want to play a round or two at Pezula. Restaurant choices for all pockets and tastes abound, but we recommend curry at **Firefly,** and fabulous fresh bread at **Isle de Pain.**

Days ❻ & ❼: Tsitsikamma

The drive from Knysna farther east is lovely: This is forest territory. Leave time to either paddle or cruise up the **Keurbooms River** (near Plettenberg Bay); visit **Monkeyland** (or **Tenikwa,** for cat lovers), in the Crags; or spend some time on Nature Valley Beach (a wonderful diversion from the N2). End up in the glorious coastal forest of **Tsitsikamma National Park.** Give yourself a full extra day to hike, swim, and relax in this natural paradise. Accommodations aren't swish, but it's the scenery that counts; if you'd prefer creature comforts and fine dining, trade this time for a stay at polo destination **Kurland** or **Tsala Treetops Lodge**—all west of Plettenburg Bay and closer to the Crags.

Days ❽, ❾ & ❿: Port Elizabeth & Eastern Cape Reserves

Get acquainted with the struggle against apartheid at the **Red Location Museum,** or visit the beaches (if you need to stretch your legs, walk the **Donkin Heritage Trail** and take in some history). You could spend the night at one of the fine accommodation options (**Shamwari Townhouse** and **Hacklewood Hill Country House**) or push on to an Eastern Cape Reserve, most about 2 hours from the city.

You're spoiled for choice, but, budgetary concerns aside, my personal favorite in the P.E./Grahamstown region would be **Kwandwe;** Shamwari's **Eagle's Nest** or **Bayete** camps or **Gorah** come a close second. Aim to spend 3 nights at your reserve of choice—2 at the very least. Those on a strict budget could book in at **Addo Elephant National Park** and search in their own vehicle for elephant and other beasts. It's a wonderful experience, though you are unlikely to see as much as you would with trained guides. (The other option is to stay at **Elephant House** or **Hitgeheim Country Lodge** and enjoy their safari tours into Addo—more expensive, but very relaxing and at nowhere near the prices you'll pay for the top reserves.) There are a fair number of midrange game lodge options, too, such as the lovely **RiverBend Lodge.** Other excellent options, farther into the Karoo, are **Blaauwbosch** or the magic **Samara** (near Graaff-Reinet)—you can track cheetah at both of these. (If you have the time, spend 2 nights at one of the Karoo destinations—my favorite is the charming Graaff-Reinet) before heading back to P.E. and flying home via Jo'burg or Cape Town.

5

The Mother City: Cape Town & the Winelands

Cape Town, the oldest city in southern Africa, is regularly heralded as one of the most beautiful on Earth. The massive sandstone bulk of Table Mountain, often draped in a flowing "tablecloth" of clouds, forms an imposing backdrop, while minutes away, pristine sandy beaches line the cliff-hugging coast. Mountainous slopes sustaining the world's most varied botanic kingdom (some 9,000 species strong) overlook fertile valleys carpeted with vines. As you drive away from the highway, you can spot zebra and wildebeest grazing unperturbed by the hubbub below. The place has the uncanny ability to make everyone feel at home. Every year brings a slew of new awards and recognition.

Situated in the country's far-southwestern corner, Cape Town is physically separated from the rest of the continent by a barrier of mountains. It feels—and is—very different from the rest of Africa (so much so that during the 2009 national election campaign, a group calling itself the Cape Party campaigned with a call for regional independence). The hot, dry summers and cool, wet winters are Mediterranean, while the Atlantic Ocean remains icy throughout the year. It is by far the most cosmopolitan city in Southern Africa, and you're as likely to hear locals speak German and French as you are Afrikaans, English, and Xhosa. Unique, too, is the architectural heritage—a multifaceted colonial past gave us Cape Dutch homesteads, neo-Gothic churches, Muslim minarets, and Georgian and Victorian terraces that punctuate an evolving Art Deco and brutalist cityscape where cranes seem to be ever in motion.

Inevitably, colonialism has left its mark on the residents of Cape Town as well; the majority of the population is made up of the mixed-blood descendants of European settlers, Asian slaves, and indigenous people. This Afrikaans-speaking group is referred to as the "coloureds"—a divisive designation conferred during the apartheid era, when those of mixed race were relocated behind Table Mountain into the grim eastern interior plain known as the Cape Flats. Since the scrapping of influx control in 1986, this area has seen phenomenal growth, and today squatter towns form a seamless ribbon of cardboard-and-corrugated-iron housing that many visitors only glimpse on their way from or to the airport; for real insight into contemporary South African society, though, you'll want to join an eye-opening cultural tour of these townships, where you're likely to discover common ground through music, food, or humor.

Cape Town's newest residents come from the poverty-stricken Eastern Cape; others hail from as far afield as Somalia, Angola, and Mozambique, making it one of South Africa's fastest-growing cities. Unfortunately, the gangster-ridden Cape Flats have also made it one of the most violent. Although violent crime is mostly contained in these areas, visitors to Cape Town should take the same precautions they would in any large city—don't wear expensive jewelry or flash fancy cameras, and don't let your credit card out of your sight; in the buildup to the much-anticipated 2010 FIFA World Cup championships, great strides have been made in tourist security, but organized crime syndicates will be eyeing the blossoming city with avarice.

Many who come to Cape Town choose to just whip straight out from the airport to the Winelands, where you can stay amid some of the best-preserved examples of Cape Dutch architecture, sample award-winning wines, and play golf on a variety of gorgeous courses. This area makes a great base if you're looking for a relaxing, rural escape, with the bright lights of the city a mere 60-minute drive away; the coastal town of Hermanus, capital of the Whale Coast, a 70-minute drive away; and the lakes, lagoons, and forests of the Garden Route an easy 4- to 5-hour drive along the N2. Alternatively, visit the Winelands or Whale Coast as a day trip, and base yourself here, overlooking the Atlantic Ocean, where the sun sets on an unbelievably azure sea. Regardless of where you choose to stay, you will leave Cape Town wishing you had more time to explore, so plan your stay, then add at least 2 more days or a week, if possible.

1 ORIENTATION

ARRIVING

BY PLANE At press time, **Cape Town International Airport** (© **021/937-1200,** or 086/727-7888 for flight information) is undergoing a final phase of a much-anticipated expansion in preparation for unprecedented arrivals in 2010. The good news is that authorities have been listening to passenger feedback and taking complaints and suggestions seriously, so airport staff, security, and even passport control have been upgrading their systems to cope with the expected influx. The airport is 17km (11 miles) from the center of town, so it should take no longer than 20 to 30 minutes to get into the city and surrounds (set aside at least twice that amount of time if traveling toward the airport

Tips Airport Transfers

In the rare instances that a hotel offers a complimentary airport transfer, we have mentioned this. You can ask any of our recommended lodgings to arrange an airport transfer, but you will definitely save money by doing this directly with **Centurion** (© **021/934-8281;** centuriontours@telkomsa.net), a hugely reliable company that offers an efficient door-to-door service in clean minibuses. Ideally, you should book your ride 2 days in advance. From the airport to the city center, it costs R140 for the first person and R20 per person thereafter. Mail or call them, and they'll be waiting at the airport arrivals area with your name on a sign board; note that there's an early-morning (before 6:30am) and late-night (after 10:30pm) surcharge of R40. **Rikkis** (© **086/174-5547**) offers an efficient airport taxi service costing R180 (city center) or R200 (Atlantic seaboard) for the first passenger; discounts apply to each additional person. You'll also find taxis directly outside the terminals; the same trip costs upward of R300, but you can usually bargain them down if you agree on a price up front. Car-rental desks are inside the arrival terminals, and a *bureau de change* stays open for international flights; the rates aren't always the best, so use an ATM instead.

Warning! **The Early Bird . . .**

Getting *to* Cape Town's airport can be the ultimate vacation come-down; traffic jams, breakdowns, and accidents have caused many people to miss their flights home, particularly during the weekday rush hour. Don't let Cape Town's relatively small size fool you: Plan sensibly and head for the airport well ahead of schedule.

during evening rush hour, 4–6pm). ***Tip:*** If you've arrived early or are waiting for a connection, you can relax in a **Rennies Travel "Premier Club" lounge** (✆ **021/936-3014**), which offer first-class lounge facilities; entry costs R145 (international terminal) or R90 (domestic).

BY CAR If you're driving directly from Johannesburg, you will arrive on the N1, traveling past the Winelands area of Paarl. From Port Elizabeth, via the Garden Route, you'll approach the city center on the N2, passing Somerset West in the Winelands. The N2 splits into the M3 (the highway, known as De Waal Dr., that connects the southern suburbs to the city center and the City Bowl suburbs) and Eastern Boulevard, which joins the N1 as it enters the perimeter of town. The entrance to the Waterfront is clearly signposted off here, and there are signs pointing the way to the Table Mountain cableway as well as Camps Bay.

BY BUS The main intercity buses, **Greyhound, Intercape Mainliner,** and **Translux,** all terminate at the junction of Strand and Adderley streets. Note that the **Baz Bus**—a minibus service aimed at backpackers—offers a more flexible hop-on, hop-off option throughout the country. (See chapter 3 for regional numbers.)

BY TRAIN The luxurious **Blue Train** (✆ **021/449-2672;** www.bluetrain.co.za) and **Rovos Rail** (✆ **021/421-4020;** www.rovos.co.za) roll into Cape Town station (✆ **021/449-2991**) from Pretoria. A more affordable alternative is a Premier Classe coupe from Johannesburg on **Shozoloza Meyl** (✆ **086/000-8888;** www.shosholozameyl.co.za), South Africa's main-line passenger services (see chapter 3 for more). Note that the bus is quicker and much cheaper, albeit not as comfortable (the Trans-Karoo to Jo'burg takes 25 hr., and the bus takes 18 hr.).

VISITOR INFORMATION

You'll find a Cape Town tourism desk at the airport (✆ **021/935-3160;** international terminus daily 7am–5pm, domestic daily 8am–midnight), but the best place to gather information is at **Cape Town Tourism,** in the city center at the corner of Burg and Castle streets (✆ **021/487-6800;** www.capetown.travel; Mon–Fri 8am–6pm, Sat 8:30am–2pm, Sun 9am–1pm). Knowledgeable staff can assist with anything from specialized tour bookings to transport queries and general information. You'll also find a wine bar, where you can do wine tastings and arrange for exports, a foreign-exchange desk, a VAT desk (to claim back the tax on certain purchases; see chapter 3 for details), and an Internet cafe. There are hundreds of brochures, but look for the ***Footsteps to Freedom Cape Town City Guide,*** which has a good map covering the top sites, as well as the series of special-interest maps. Shuttles to the city's top attractions, the hop-on, hop-off Cape Town Explorer bus (see "Getting Around," below), and city walking tours depart regularly from here.

A satellite tourism office at the **Waterfront Clock Tower** (✆ **021/408-7600**) has similar services and longer hours (9am–9pm), and there are many more information offices scattered throughout the region, including one at the Table Mountain lower cableway station (✆ **021/422-1075**).

The **Netcare Travel Clinic,** 1107 Picbell Parkade, 58 Strand St. (✆ **021/419-3172;** www.travelclinic.co.za) offers expert advice and medical services (inoculations, malaria tablets), should you be traveling farther afield. **MTI Medi-Travel International** (✆ **021/ 419-1888;** www.meditravel.co.za) has similar services, but you may find its Waterfront Clock Tower location more convenient.

CITY LAYOUT

Cape Town lies on a narrow peninsula that curls southward into the Atlantic Ocean. Its western and eastern shores are divided by a spinal ridge of mountains, of which Table Mountain is the most dramatic landmark. On the western shore, the relatively small **city center,** together with the residential suburbs that cradle it, is known as the **City** Bowl—the "bowl" created by the table-topped massif as backdrop, flanked by jagged Devil's Peak to the east and the embracing arm of Signal Hill to the west. Upmarket family homes, small businesses, and apartments—as well as a plethora of excellent guesthouses—range along these slopes and make up the neighborhoods of Tamboerskloof, Higgovale, Oranjezicht, and Gardens. From here, views north look over the city center and harbor, where the **Victoria & Alfred Waterfront** is situated at the icy waters of Table Bay. On the slopes of Signal Hill, snuggling up close to the center, is the **Bo-Kaap** (literally, "Upper Cape"), where most of the population are the descendants of Cape Town's original Muslim slaves.

Within easy striking distance of Bo-Kaap, the city center, and the slightly isolated **Waterfront,** are the dense, built-up suburbs of tiny **De Waterkant** (arguably Cape Town's most fashionable suburb, and a must-see destination for shoppers who hate malls), and rapidly evolving Victorian-era **Green Point,** where the rise of the city's much-hyped, visually spectacular soccer stadium—planned specifically for the 2010 FIFA World Cup—has brought in untold millions for a total revamp of the area, making this Cape Town's waking giant, with numerous new hotels, restaurants, shops and places to hang out. Adjacent Green Point is the high-density coastal suburb of **Sea Point,** which has an always-busy, rather rough-and-ready Main Road, lined with shops, bars and eateries, and a generous promenade where Capetonians like to walk and jog during the summer. Between Green Point and the sea, is **Mouille Point,** which runs into the V&A Waterfront. Moving farther south from Sea Point, the western slopes of the Cape Peninsula mountain range slide almost directly into the sea, and it is here, along the dramatic coastline referred to as the **Atlantic seaboard,** that you can watch the sun sinking from Africa's most expensive real estate. Of these, the beaches of **Camps Bay** ★★ and **Clifton** ★★★ are the most conveniently located—easily reached from the City Bowl via Kloof Nek, they are a mere 10- to 15-minute drive from the city center (although in summer, traffic can seriously irk). **Bakoven** ★★ is the choice for those of you looking to escape the crowds—two relatively tiny patches of sand (one called Big Beach, the other Little Beach) are hidden betwixt massive boulders where those in the know congregate for mesmeric, uncrowded sunsets.

Traveling along the Atlantic seaboard is the most scenic route to Cape Point, but the quickest route is to travel south along the eastern flank of the mountain, via the M3, past the **southern suburbs** of **Woodstock,** Observatory, Rondebosch, Claremont, Wynberg, Kenilworth, Bishopscourt, and **Constantia** (the closest wine-producing area to the city, some 30 min. away, Constantia vies with the Atlantic seaboard as real estate gold), and then snake along the False Bay seaboard to the point. These eastern slopes, which overlook False Bay (so called by early sailors who mistook it for Table Bay), are the first to see the sun rise and have price tags way below those in places such as Camps Bay and Clifton. Cutting west across the peninsula from the False Bay seaboard will take you to more sleepy seaside villages, such as **Scarborough** and neighboring Misty Cliffs, ideal if you want to be right near the unspoiled wilderness of Cape Point and have utterly pristine beaches at your fingertips. Heading north from here, you can complete a "peninsula loop" and arrive back in the city via **Hout Bay, Llandudno,** and the Atlantic seaboard suburbs.

East of the peninsula are the **Cape Flats,** where the majority of so-called "Cape coloureds" live (see "The 'Coloureds': Creation of a New 'Race,'" in chapter 2), and the **"black townships,"** including Gugulethu, Langa, Nyanga, and Khayalitsha—proof that, sadly, despite 12 years of democracy, an unenforced geographic apartheid still keeps the Cape's communities effectively separate. These are accessed via the N2, the same highway that provides access to the airport and the Winelands, which lie north of it. **Stellenbosch,** unofficial capital of the Winelands, is just over an hour's drive from the center of town, and from here the pretty wine-growing valley of **Franschhoek,** some 85km (53 miles) northeast of Cape Town, is reached via the scenic Helshoogte Pass. A quicker route to Franschhoek is via the northern-bound N1, the highway that connects Cape Town to **Paarl,** a 40-minute drive from the center of town. Deeper into the Winelands (but no more than 90 min. away) are a number of charming villages surrounded by vineyards, such as **Riebeek Kasteel** and **Tulbagh,** the latter where some important heritage architecture competes for attention with spectacular mountain scenery and a choice of wine-tasting venues; turn to the following chapter, on the Western Cape, for information on these.

Consider investing in a detailed street atlas, such as ***Mapstudio Street Guide,*** sold at most newsagents; but if you get lost, don't despair: With Table Mountain (and relatively excellent street signage) as a visual guide, it's difficult to stay lost for long.

THE NEIGHBORHOODS IN BRIEF

City Bowl ★

Near the Waterfront, beaches, and Winelands, and in easy reach of most of the city's best restaurants, with great views, the residential suburbs that flank the **city center** are the most convenient place to stay. Opt for one of the many elegant guesthouses on the mountain slopes of the upmarket suburbs of Oranjezicht, Higgovale, and Tamboerskloof, with excellent views of the city and harbor.

Bo-Kaap (Upper Cape) ★

Stretching from the edge of the inner city and up the slopes of Signal Hill, this lively suburb of historic houses painted in a rainbow of pastels and bold colors is historically one of the most interesting parts of Cape Town. With its concentration of historic mosques, rough cobbled streets, and a distinctive sense of community and vibrant "Cape Malay" culture, this is a great place to experience Cape Town's much-vaunted "diversity," although it's slowly changing under the influence of foreign investment.

De Waterkant, Green Point, Mouille Point & Sea Point

Wedged into a strip of land between Signal Hill and the Atlantic Ocean, this area—with a mix of residential and commercial property—for some time, has been the most dynamically evolving part of Cape Town. **De Waterkant** ★★ is a tiny enclave that has evolved into a chi-chi shopping area, with cobbled streets and a fine square (Cape Quarter) surrounded by restaurants. It's world-renowned for its popularity with gay travelers, who spend a lot of their vacation time swinging through the densely concentrated bars and clubs located here and in neighboring **Green Point** ★. Closer to the water, the beachfront that stretches along the coast of Mouille Point and Sea Point has been largely ruined by the construction of dense high-rise apartments (although, come sunset, the **seaside promenade** is still a salubrious place to walk, jog, or hold hands), while pockets along Sea Point's **Main Road** are hangouts for hookers and drug dealers. This area used to be the heart of Cape Town's nightlife and is experiencing a steady comeback, especially as vibey Green Point puts on the glitz for 2010. You'll find a wide selection of restaurants on Main Road, from Green Point to the very end of Sea Point, but mind yourself after dark.

The Waterfront

The Victoria & Alfred (V&A) Waterfront is one of the most successful in the world and—for good or bad—one of Cape Town's top attractions. Hotels have glorious sea and mountain views, and many shopping, dining, and entertainment options are right at your doorstep. You'll pay for the privilege of staying here, though (the cheap options aren't worth it). And it's a little out of touch with the rest of the city; most of the locals you'll meet here are the ones working the shops.

Atlantic Seaboard ★★★

If you're looking for a beach holiday, stay on the Atlantic seaboard, where Table Mountain drops steeply into the ocean, creating a magnificent backdrop to the seaside "villages" of Bantry Bay, Clifton, Camps Bay, Bakoven, and Llandudno. The beaches are the most beautiful (Camps Bay, lined with restaurants and cocktail bars, is the most accessible), and gorgeous people strut their stuff on the pristine, fine white sands. The sunsets here are awe inspiring.

Southern Suburbs

The three worth highlighting are Woodstock, Observatory, and Constantia. **Woodstock,** with its totally unglamorous, semi-industrial feel, has been targeted for (positive) development and is seeing an injection of capital and creative energy that is transforming it into the next residential hub, already boasting the city's most fabulous Saturday market and enticing new shopping venues. **Observatory** (less than 10 min. from town), with its quaint Victorian buildings and narrow streets, has an interesting bohemian feel; its proximity to both the University of Cape Town and the huge Groote Schuur hospital makes for a particularly eclectic mix of people. Farther south (about 20 min. from town), the oak-lined streets and old, established mansions of **Constantia** ★★★ are arguably the city's most exclusive addresses, with the lush surrounds of the Cape's oldest wine-producing area attracting the rich and famous who prefer their privacy to the glare of the sun-soaked hoi polloi in Camps Bay.

False Bay

Distance from city attractions is the drawback of the suburbs of the naval base of Victorian-era **Simons Town** ★, overdeveloped Fish Hoek, **Kalk Bay** ★★, St. James, and Muizenberg, but they are definitely worth a day or two of your attention, particularly if this is not your first visit to Cape Town. Kalk Bay, in particular, has a plethora of quaint restaurants and shops—even a dinner theater. The sea is a few degrees warmer on this side of the mountain, and because this part of the coast faces east, dawn can be breathtaking, though obviously at the expense of sunsets.

Southern Peninsula & Cape Point

Surrounded by mountains, the fast-developing town of **Hout Bay** has its own harbor and marks the start of the breathtaking **Chapman's Peak Drive** ★★★, which snakes past the burgeoning town of Noordhoek, and such sweet villages as Kommetjie, Misty Cliffs, and **Scarborough** ★★, before reaching **Cape Point Nature Reserve** ★★★. Close to the shore, the best of these seaside enclaves have superbly white sandy beaches backed by magnificent cliffs, and they retain a dreamy, villagelike feel. Some, such as Noordhoek, though, have spawned huge housing developments. If you need to be near the action rather than surrounded by nature, you'll probably find these places a little too far from the city.

Cape Flats

This is where the majority of "coloureds" (the apartheid name for people of mixed descent) live, many forcibly relocated from District Six (a now-razed suburb adjacent to the city) by apartheid policies. The residents of the Cape Flats suffer from a high unemployment rate and lack of cohesive identity and hope, and the area has become a fertile breeding ground for drug-fueled gang wars. Even farther east are the "black suburbs" (historically referred to as "townships") of Gugulethu, Langa, and Nyanga, and the vast shantytowns and new residences of Khayalitsha (visible from the N2 as you drive into town from the airport). To get a balanced view of Cape Town and a real insight into South Africa's history, a visit to these areas is highly recommended; see "Getting Around," below, for township tours.

Winelands

No trip to Cape Town would be complete without at least a day spent here; indeed, many prefer to stay here for the duration of their visit—Cape Town lies no more than an hour or so away; the airport, 45 minutes. The university town of **Stellenbosch** ★★★ is the cultural epicenter of the Winelands, and its oak-lined streetscape offers the greatest sense of history; the wine produced by its terroir is also generally the best. However, **Franschhoek** ★★★—reached via either Stellenbosch or Paarl—is located in the prettiest of the wineland valleys and has a well-developed, albeit very touristy, infrastructure that includes an overwhelming concentration of award-winning restaurants; if you overnight in only one wine-producing region, make sure it's Franschhoek. Deciding where to stay is ultimately a matter of availability; places situated on wine estates with views of the vineyards and mountains are most desirable. By contrast, the town of **Paarl** is far from attractive, but it makes a convenient stop-off for lunch as you head toward the quaint winelands village of ★★ **Tulbagh.** The lack of pretense, scant traffic, and prime accommodations at a fair price make Tulbagh one of the sweetest little destinations in the country.

Northern Suburbs

With their kitsch postmodern palaces and endless "first-home" developments, these suburbs don't really warrant much attention. However, if you're heading north to see the West Coast, you should consider stopping at **Blouberg Beach** for the classic postcard view of Table Mountain across the bay; take the R27 Marine Drive, off the N1, to get here.

2 GETTING AROUND

The city center is small enough to explore on foot, and the city's ongoing makeover (destined to be ready in time for the 2010 FIFA World Cup) includes smart pedestrian walkways and cycling routes that will link the city center with Green Point. The city's upgrade includes a plan to establish a much-awaited integrated public transport system that will link the center and the Waterfront with top attractions such as the Table Mountain cableway, Camps Bay, the southern suburbs, Kirstenbosch Botanical Gardens, False Bay, Cape Point, and the Winelands (although not Tulbagh). However, to move at will and have scope to explore more thoroughly, you'll still be better off renting a car. Beyond the city, with some frustrating exceptions (especially during rush hours in such places as Stellenbosch), roads are relatively uncongested, parking is easy to find, and signs are straightforward.

BY PUBLIC & PRIVATE TRANSPORTATION

BY TRAIN Trains are not always reliable, clean, or safe; choose first-class cars with other occupants, and watch your bags. One option I recommend is the spectacular cliff-hugging route along the False Bay seaboard to Simons Town aboard **Biggsy's Restaurant Carriage & Wine Bar** ★★★ (**✆ 021/788-7760;** Tues–Sun, three trips daily), with breakfast, lunch, or snacks en route. Take the breakfast run, and alight at Kalk Bay—Cape Town's quaintest fishing "village," retaining a distinct character and worth a day exploring—then catch the lunch or sunset trip back. The return from the city station takes 2½ hours. Note that Biggsy's was closed for renovation at press time, but should be up and running again by late 2009; prior reservations are, in any case, essential, especially on weekends—only 32 diners can be accommodated.

BY BUS As mentioned, Cape Town is due to have a new integrated transport system in place by mid-2010, with a new fleet of buses operating routes daily from 4:30am to midnight, two major bus stations constructed on Adderley Street and at Hertzog Boulevard, as well as various pedestrian bridges (note that the total pedestrianization of Waterkant St., allowing safe on-foot access from the city to Green Point, is also on the cards). For maps and routes, as well as where to purchase the new prepaid smart card, contact the Cape Town tourism offices.

Until then, the most expedient way to get around the city is with a vulgarly touristy **CitySightseeing** bus. These open-top hop-on, hop-off circuit buses visit the city's top attractions, departing from the Two Oceans Aquarium between 8:30am and 4:35pm (you don't have to catch it from here; see www.citysightseeing.co.za for a detailed schedule; R200 buys you a 2-day ticket). A **V&A Waterfront bus** (**✆ 0800/65-6463**) leaves from Adderley Street (in front of the station); the trip costs R3.50. Alternatively, head for the tourist bureau, where shuttles depart regularly (maximum 10-min. wait) for the Waterfront (R60), Kirstenbosch (R150), the Table Mountain cable car (R60), and the airport (R160–R200 for one and R20–R40 per person thereafter); hotel pickups can be arranged but may cost extra. Note that around 250 new buses will begin operating soon after press time (to get commuters to Green Point Stadium), when a tourist-friendly transport system will start running; until then, it's better to hail a taxi or call for a Rikki (see below).

BY CAR Cape Town is a relatively car-friendly city, with a minimum of traffic jams and enough parking lots to warrant driving into town—all you need is to keep some change

Moments Sidecar Tours

Tim Clarke's **Cape Sidecar Adventures,** 2 Glengariff Rd., Three Anchor Bay (✆ **021/434-9855/6;** www.sidecars.co.za), offers another unusual way to see the city—you can either motor yourself and a partner around the city and beyond, or opt to travel in the road-level sidecar with a chauffer-guide. The sidecars were modeled on original 1938 German BMW sidecars and manufactured for the Chinese Red Army from as early as the mid-1950s. A full-day chauffeured excursion with two passengers costs R1,785.

handy and be prepared to pay the mobile meter-carrying attendants up front (rates start at around R3.50 for 30 min.; if you overstay, you can pay in the difference when you return). Apart from the city center and Sea Point's Main Road, there is no charge, but business- or self-appointed "parking attendants" will offer to watch your car; although you are under no obligation to reward them, it is customary to tip those who are clearly hired by local businesses (they will usually wear a bib or hand over a card) on your return; R2 to R7 is fine, but be aware of aggressive and threatening tactics by some of these freelancers.

You'll find numerous car-rental companies in Cape Town. For a cheaper deal, try **Penny K's** (✆ **072/736-6957;** www.pennyks.co.za; from R170 per day) or **Value** (✆ **021/386-7699;** www.valuerentalcar.com; from R189 per day). Both include insurance and unlimited mileage. For a one-way rental to another province, you'll have to use a company with nationwide offices, such as **Budget** (✆ **086/101-6622**) or **Hertz** (✆ **086/160-0136**)—however, I find **Avis** (✆ **021/424-1177**) the most consistently priced, and great because you can book online without inserting your credit card details (www.avis.co.za). To tool along the coast with the wind in your hair, rent a classic convertible, with or without chauffeur, from **Motor Classic** (✆ **021/461-7368** or 072/277-5022; www.motorclassic.co.za; from R1,290 per day self-drive) or **Cape Cobra Hire** (✆ **083/321-9193;** www.capecobrahire.co.za).

BY TAXI Metered taxis don't cruise the streets looking for fares; you'll have to phone. Most charge at least R10 per kilometer, but the new **Cab Co.** (✆ **082/580-9030**) charges R9 and is a small, personal operation (so call ahead). Much cheaper than a metered taxi are **Rikkis,** London-style cabs that keep prices down by continuously picking up and dropping off passengers en route. You pay according to city zones, priced from R20 to R35 (after 7pm, a R5 surcharge applies). These are operational 24/7 and will drop you off anywhere in the center, City Bowl suburbs, the Waterfront, or Camps Bay (✆ **086/174-5547;** www.rikkis.co.za). You can also contact Rikkis from dedicated telephones they have set up in locations around the city; if you'd rather not share your fare, you can pay extra for sole use of their cabs. Trips farther afield—even to Cape Point—are charged at a flat rate or by the hour. Better still, contact **The Green Cab** (✆ **086/184-3473** or 082/491-5972; www.thegreencab.co.za), which is Cape Town's first taxi company with a green agenda and an eco-friendly fleet (small seven- and four-seaters that run on liquefied petroleum gas) that operates door-to-door. Drivers are mostly women (it's also entirely woman owned) and, like Rikki's, fares are run on a share-ride system.

BY BIKE If you just want to get from the beach to the city, zip around on a sexy scooter from **La Dolce Vita Biking,** 13D Kloof Nek Rd., Gardens (✆ **083/528-0897;** www.ldvbiking.co.za; R120–R165 per day, including unlimited mileage, a helmet, and insurance)—they also rent motorbikes (R210–R280 per day). If you require more muscle, you can hire a real machine from **Motorcycle Tours** (✆ **021/794-7887;** www.sa-motorcycle-tours.com; prices vary). You can also go top-end by contacting **Harley-Davidson Cape Town** (✆ **021/446-2999;** www.harley-davidson-capetown.com). Bikes go for around R1,100 to R1,300 per day, or R3,250 to R4,400 for a weekend. The regular Sunday morning breakfast run to Stellenbosch and Franschhoek is worth joining; ask Thomas Kellerman about these routes and other rallies when you collect your bike. Alternatively, get off the road and explore the mountain on a bike from **Downhill Adventures** (✆ **021/422-0388;** R140 per day).

ORGANIZED CRUISES & TOURS

These tours concentrate on the city and immediate surroundings; for tours farther afield, see chapter 4.

ON FOOT The excellent 3-hour guided walk **Footsteps to Freedom** ★★★ (✆ **083/452-1112** or 021/671-6878; www.footstepstofreedom.co.za) departs Monday to Saturday at 10:30pm from Cape Town Tourism (Burg and Hout sts.) and covers the most fascinating parts of the city center. It's a good way to get oriented and come to grips with Cape Town's multifaceted history; your guide will take you to some secret spots—if you're lucky, you'll get to stand on the balcony where Mandela first addressed the public as a free man on February 11, 1990. The scheduled tour costs R150; personalized tours are also available (ask for Garth Angus, whose expertise is unparalleled).

BY BOAT One of the best vantages of Cape Town is undoubtedly from the sea. I highly recommend the 90-minute **sunset cruise** ★★★ from the harbor to Clifton (R200), offered by the **Waterfront Boat Company** (✆ **021/418-5806;** www.waterfrontboats.co.za). They also have two gaff-rigged schooners—the ***Spirit of Victoria*** and ***Esperance***—that cruise the Table Bay and Blouberg area, and luxury motorboats that cruise to Clifton Bay. The company has a whale-watching permit, and there's even some chance you'll spot whales while on the sunset cruise (as I did the last time I went out), a spectacle that'll leave you breathless as the disappearing sun sets the water aglow and the lights of the city effervesce in the background. ***Tigresse*** (✆ **021/421-0909;** www.tigresse.co.za), a huge luxury catamaran, is another great way to get to Clifton (R110 adults, R180 sunset cruise with bubbly). Alternatively, get your pulse racing and strap up with **Atlantic Adventures** (✆ **021/425-3785;** www.atlanticadventures.co.za), which sets off at 120kmph (74 mph) across Table Bay in a rubber duck (R350 per person per hour). In Hout Bay harbor, **Drumbeat Charters** (✆ **021/791-4441;** www.drumbeatcharters.co.za) offers 40-minute trips to see the Cape fur seals on Duiker Island (R60 adults, R25 children under 14; daily in season).

BY BUS A large number of operators offer driving tours of the city and its surrounds. While I don't usually recommend such tours because they're way out of touch with the places they're supposedly exploring, a 2-day ticket for the kitsch hop-on, hop-off **City Sightseeing bus** (✆ **021/511-6000;** www.citysightseeing.co.za; R200 per person) is admittedly a convenient way to get around and see many of the highlights at more or less your own pace. In 2 days, you can cover both available routes—one takes in the peninsula and the other covers top city sites, even trundling through glamorous Camps Bay, when the double-decker bus inevitably turns every head on every bronzed body.

African Eagle (✆ **021/464-4266;** www.daytours.co.za), **Hylton Ross** (✆ **021/511-1784;** www.hyltonross.co.za), and **Springbok Atlas** (✆ **021/460-4700;** www.springbok atlas.com) are long-standing operators offering a variety of half-day, full-day, and multi-day tours. You might want to check on the size of any tour group, and bear in mind that seeing the Cape through a bus window is hellishly frustrating.

BY AIR For an aerial tour of the city or peninsula, contact **Civair Helicopters** (✆ **021/419-5182**) or **Sport Helicopters** (✆ **021/419-5907/8;** www.sport-helicopters.co.za), which has flights from R2,700 per lift-off. **The Hopper** (✆ **021/419-8951;** www.thehopper.co.za) promises to take single bookings (from R400 per person for short scenic hops) any day of the week. Also based at the V&A Waterfront, **The Huey Helicopter Co.** (✆ **021/419-4839;** www.thehueyhelicopterco.com) offers half-hour low-flying "simulated combat" tours (R1,800 per person; seven-passenger minimum) in a retired Vietnam combat chopper, plus exhilarating scenic flights (R32,400 for a 60-minute full peninsular tour). **Aquilla** (✆ **021/712-1913**) takes to the sky in microlights, and **ThunderCity** (✆ **021/934-8007;** www.thundercity.com) caters to adrenaline junkies with expensive tastes—an hour-long ride in one of their fighter planes starts from R24,045.

TOWNSHIP TOURS For a more holistic view of the still essentially segregated Cape Town community, and an insight into the Cape Muslim culture of the Bo-Kaap, a so-called "township" tour is essential. A good option is Trail of Two Cities, run by **Cape Capers** ★★★ (✆ **021/448-3117;** www.tourcapers.co.za; R580 per person, full day)—it introduces visitors to some of the interesting entrepreneurs working in the poorer areas of the city. These include Victoria Mxenge, who has a group of previously homeless women learning house building, and Abalimi Bezekhaya, who inspires township greening efforts. Another outfit offering cultural tours of the townships is **Camissa Travel & Marketing** ★★ (✆ **021/462-6199** or 078/657-7788; www.gocamissa.co.za), whose tours, like those of Cape Capers, help you forgo the sense of being a voyeur. They also run a tour that includes a trip to Robben Island. Also offering a chance to learn and feel inspired rather than emerging guilt-ridden from a tour of the townships, is **Uthando** (✆ **021/683-8523;** www.uthandosa.org). For more possibilities, see "Cultural Sights: Cape Muslim to Khayalitsha," on p. 150.

SPECIALIST TOURS For reality-shifting cultural tours that range from interactive jazz, reggae, or hip-hop evenings (where you meet legendary musicians and even dine and possibly jam with them), to community soccer expeditions and art tours, get in touch with **Coffeebeans Routes** ★★★ (✆ **021/424-3572;** www.coffeebeansroutes.com). Within their innovative portfolio is a "spirituality route" (R550 per person), where you meet two very different spiritual leaders, perhaps a *sangoma* (traditional healer) and a Muslim Imam, in the course of a 4-hour Friday afternoon tour; and I personally love their "storytelling route," where you meet and listen to some exceptionally engaging local residents in their own homes (R495 per person; Thurs 7–11pm). **Cape Fusion Tours** (✆ **021/461-2437;** www.capefusion.co.za) runs culinary tours and cooking classes with some of the Cape's top chefs. More community-geared Cape Malay and African "cooking safaris" are offered by **Andulela Experience** ★★★ (www.andulela.com; see p. 150). This excellent outfit, which works closely with Coffeebeans, also conducts music, art and poetry, and township tours, always with a commitment to local communities. **Daytrippers** (✆ **021/511-4766;** www.daytrippers.co.za) specializes in hiking and biking trips. For specialist **wine tours,** see "The Winelands," later in this chapter.

Fast Facts Cape Town

Airport See "Arriving," earlier in this chapter.

American Express Main local offices are in the city center at Thibault Square (✆ **021/425-7991**) and at the Waterfront, Shop 11A, in Alfred Mall (✆ **021/419-3917**). City center hours are from 8:30am to 4:30pm Monday through Friday. Waterfront hours are from 9am to 7pm Monday through Friday, and from 10am to 5pm Saturday and Sunday.

Area Code The area code for Cape Town and the Winelands is **021.**

Babysitting Contact **Supersitters** (✆ **021/552-1220;** www.supersitters.net; R45 per hour 7pm–midnight; R58 per hour all other times).

Bookstores Cape Town's best is **The Book Lounge** (see p. 167). The biggest commercial outlets are **Exclusive Books** (✆ **021/419-0905**) and **Wordworth Books** (✆ **021/425-6880**), both in Victoria Wharf at the Victoria & Alfred Waterfront.

Car Rentals See "Getting Around," above.

Climate See "When to Go," in chapter 3.

Doctors & Dentists Call ✆ **021/671-3634** or 021/671-2924 for a 24-hour referral service. Or try **SAA Netcare Travel Clinic** (✆ **021/419-3172**) or **MTI Medi-Travel International,** in the Clock Tower, Waterfront (✆ **021/419-1888**).

Driving Rules See "Getting Around," above.

Embassies & Consulates **U.S.:** 2 Reddam Ave., Westlake (✆ 021/702-7300); **Canada:** 19th Floor, Reserve Bank Building, 60 St Georges Mall (✆ **021/423-5240**); **U.K.:** 15th Floor, Southern Life Centre, 8 Riebeeck St. (✆ **021/405-2400**).

Emergencies For an ambulance or general emergencies, call ✆ **10177;** for police, call ✆ **10111;** in case of fire, call ✆ **021/535-1100;** for a sea rescue, call ✆ **021/449-3500;** for Mountain Rescue Services, call ✆ **021/873-1121.**

Hospitals **Groote Schuur** (✆ **021/404-9111**), in Observatory, is the Cape's largest hospital. However, for immediate attention in more salubrious surrounds, you're best off heading for a private clinic (this is why medical insurance is recommended). **The Chris Barnard Memorial Hospital** (✆ **021/480-6111**) is in the center of town, at 181 Longmarket St., while the **Cape Town Mediclinic** (✆ **021/464-5500**) is at 21 Hof St., in Gardens. Contact **Mediclinic** (✆ **021/883-8571**) if you're in Stellenbosch.

Hot Lines **Automobile Association** (for vehicle breakdown; ✆ **082/161-11**); **Rape Crisis** (✆ **021/447-9762,** for 24-hr. advice and counseling).

Internet Access There are numerous Internet cafes all over the city (especially on Long and Kloof sts., and along Main Rd. in Sea Point). Just about every hotel and guesthouse in town offers free (or prepaid) Wi-Fi. Cape Town also has a "Free Wi-Fi Super Circuit," whereby a growing number of cafes and restaurants offer up to 20MB worth of free browsing (if you have a laptop), provided by a company called **RedButton** (✆ **0861/288-866;** www.redbutton.co.za).

Maps See "City Layout," earlier in this chapter.

Newspapers & Magazines The morning paper, *Cape Times,* and the more sensationalist afternoon and evening paper, *Argus,* are sold at most street corners. You'll find international titles at the Waterfront's bookstores (see above).

Pharmacy **Lite-Kem** (✆ **021/461-8040**), 24 Darling St., opposite the city post office, is open Monday through Saturday from 7:30am to 11pm and Sunday from 9am to 11pm. **Sunset Pharmacy** (✆ **021/434-3333**), in Sea Point Medical Centre, Kloof Road, is open daily from 8:30am to 9pm.

Post Office The best-located branch, if you want to park easily and get served relatively quickly, is the Vlaeberg branch on Loop Street (corner of Pepper; ✆ **021/424-7477**), near the center of town. There's also a branch in the Promenade center in Camps Bay. Hours are Monday through Friday from 8am to 5pm (Wed from 8:30am) and Saturday from 8am to 1pm. Note that local postal service is notoriously dodgy.

Restrooms The city's large population of homeless people means that the hygiene of public restrooms can be of varying quality. You're best off going to a coffee shop or restaurant, or visiting a gas station.

Safety The formation of the Central City Improvement District (CCID), the ongoing installation of closed-circuit cameras, a dedicated city police force, and 24-hour care centers for Cape Town's street children has resulted in a drastic reduction in crime in the city center. This is no reason to let down your guard, however. Muggings can be avoided by taking the same precautions you would in any large city—lose the jewelry and stash the wallet. Be aware of street children, many of whom beg at large intersections and along Long Street at night. Visitors are requested to give them food coupons (inquire at the CCID Kiosks in St George's Mall and Company Gardens) or make a donation to one of the child-care centers rather than giving them cash, which keeps them on the streets. Note that it is inadvisable to pull over and stop on the N2 (the airport highway), and always travel with a cellphone in case your car breaks down. For detailed advice, pick up a brochure on safety from any tourism office.

Taxis See "Getting Around," earlier in this chapter.

Weather Call ✆ **082/231-1640.**

3 WHERE TO STAY

Cape Town's popularity has produced an ever-expanding list of accommodation options, and many seasoned globetrotters contend it offers the best selection of guesthouses in the world, though over the years its reputation as a great-value destination has been somewhat tarnished by a handful of greedy operators. That is why I am delighted to report that—finally, after a decade of wallet-stripping increases—rates have finally stabilized.

The City Bowl (which denotes the residential suburbs on the slopes of Table Mountain), the V&A Waterfront, and Camps Bay remain the most popular areas to stay; most options listed here have great views and/or good access to restaurants, attractions, and beaches. If you're traveling between May and September, you'll inevitably get a fantastic low-season (or "green-season") rate. The exception will be during the FIFA World Cup

Self-Catering Options for Budgets Big & Small

Renting an apartment or home is a good-value option, particularly for families or couples looking for absolute privacy. Thanks to Mr. Delivery (see "Where to Dine," later in this chapter), you won't even have to cook. A good option is **Côté-Sud Apartments** (✆ **072/608-1889;** www.cotesud.co.za; R850–R1,600 for 4, according to season)—four neat two-bedroom apartments with separate entrances and a communal pool conveniently located on busy Kloof Street (plenty of dining options are within walking distance and it's literally a stone's throw from an excellent pizzeria and useful minimart). Proprietors Robyn and Jacques are very flexible, so it's worth dealing with them directly; book an upstairs apartment for views from a private balcony (downstairs units have gardens). These days there are plenty of online agencies where you can browse through images of potential rentals. Best of the lot is **Icon Villas** (✆ **086/184-5527;** www.icape.co.za), which deals with a broad spectrum of well-dressed apartments and luxury villas in upmarket suburbs throughout the city and as far afield as the Winelands, Hermanus, and the Garden Route—again, there's a strong Camps Bay bias, useful if you feel the pull of the Atlantic seaboard. They also offer a full concierge service to ensure your holiday is as relaxing as possible. You'll see a few similarly exquisite apartments and villas for rent at **www.campsbayapartments.com**—very chic, very exclusive; and check out **www.cliftononsea.co.za** (✆ **021/557-9132**), which actually covers places all along the Atlantic seaboard and as far inland as De Waterkant. Most places have pools and superb sea and sunset views of Africa's Côte d'Azur. **Platinum Places** specializes in modern apartments and villas across the city, but with a focus on Camps Bay (www.platinumplaces.co.za); rental prices vary considerably, as they do with the selection at **Cape Portfolios** (✆ **021/438-3416;** www.capeportfolios.com). And if push comes to shove, you may be forced to contact overextended **Village & Life** (✆ **021/438-3972;** www.villageandlife.com), which runs a bloated assortment of self-catering accommodations options, some way more exclusive than others, in popular tourist districts and as far away as the West Coast. At the absolute upper end of the rental spectrum, there's little to beat the spectacular **La Montagne** ★★★ (www.la-montagne.co.za; R56,000 per night), a sublime ivy-clad mansion in Bishopscourt, or the Atlantic Ocean–facing mansion of your dreams, **Ellerman Villa** ★★★ (see p. 110). If all this seems like a lot of work (and finding the right place does take time), contact Cape-based Michelle Snaddon, editor of **www.justtheplanet.com**. She has visited all the villas she puts forward, so she will ask all the right questions and give you information you can trust (and it doesn't cost more). Simply e-mail michelle@justtheplanet.com or call ✆ **27/83/463- 4435.**

series in mid-2010, when peak-season (or worse) rates will apply, and many places, in any case, will be sold out at press time.

Note: The airport is no more than a 20- to 30-minute drive from most hotels, so it's not necessary to move to an airport hotel for early-morning or late-night flights. All the places listed below will arrange airport transfers.

Where to Stay in Cape Town

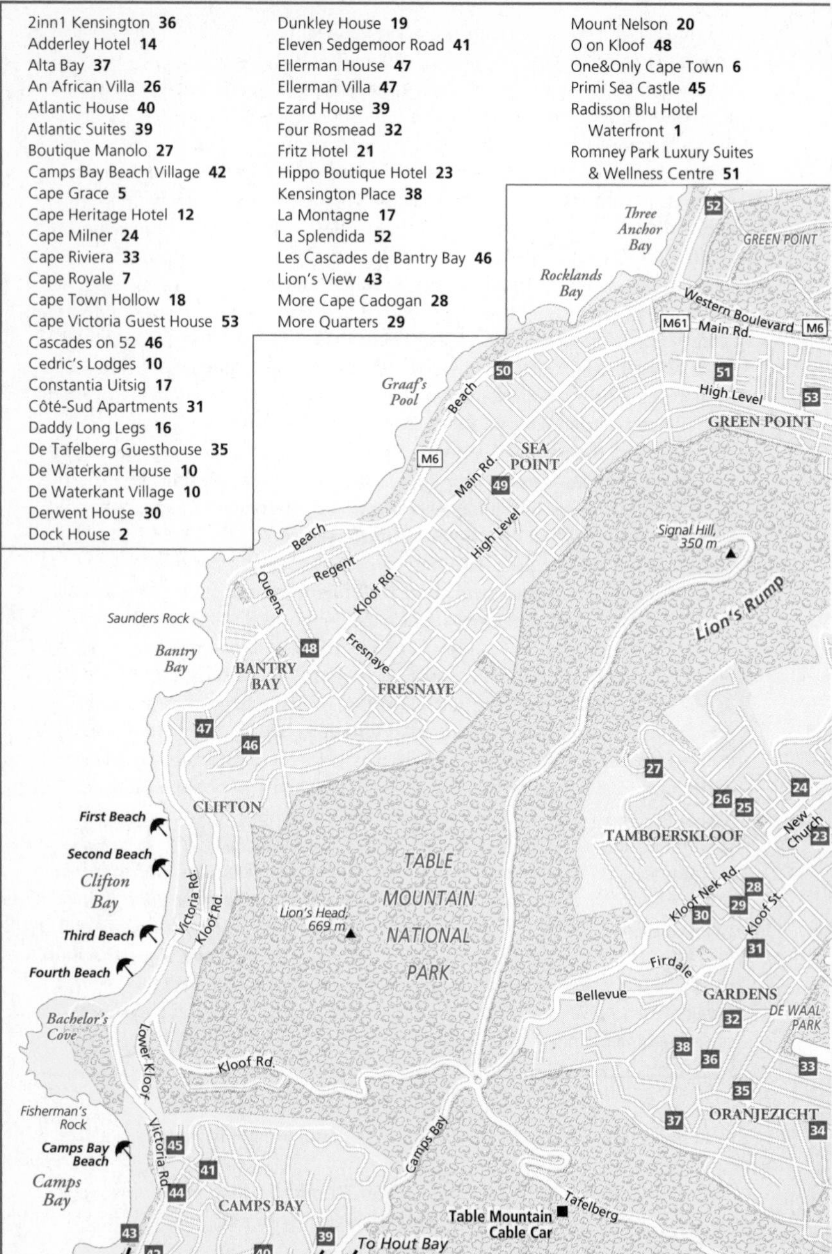

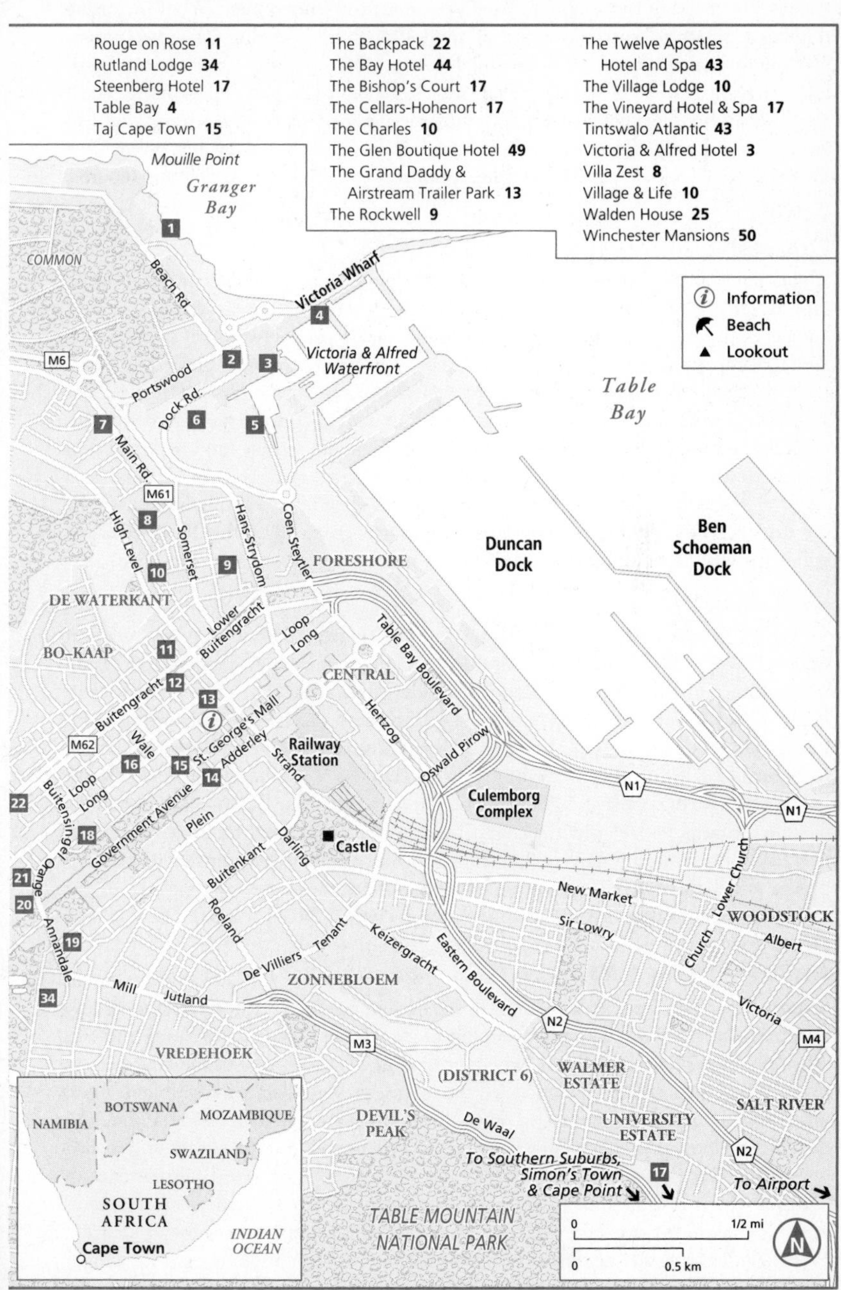
Rouge on Rose 11
Rutland Lodge 34
Steenberg Hotel 17
Table Bay 4
Taj Cape Town 15
The Backpack 22
The Bay Hotel 44
The Bishop's Court 17
The Cellars-Hohenort 17
The Charles 10
The Glen Boutique Hotel 49
The Grand Daddy & Airstream Trailer Park 13
The Rockwell 9
The Twelve Apostles Hotel and Spa 43
The Village Lodge 10
The Vineyard Hotel & Spa 17
Tintswalo Atlantic 43
Victoria & Alfred Hotel 3
Villa Zest 8
Village & Life 10
Walden House 25
Winchester Mansions 50
Information
Beach
Lookout
Mouille Point
Granger Bay
COMMON
Beach Rd.
Victoria Wharf
Victoria & Alfred Waterfront
Table Bay
M6
Portswood
Dock Rd.
Main Rd.
M61
High Level
Somerset
Hans Strydom
Coen Steytler
FORESHORE
Duncan Dock
Ben Schoeman Dock
DE WATERKANT
Lower Buitengracht
Loop
Long
Table Bay Boulevard
BO-KAAP
CENTRAL
Buitengracht
St. George's Mall
Hertzog
M62
Wale
Adderley
Railway Station
Oswald Pirow
Strand
Loop
Long
Government Avenue
Buitensingel
Plein
Culemborg Complex
N1
N1
Castle
Darling
Orange
Buitenkant
New Market
Lower Church
Annandale
Roeland
Sir Lowry
WOODSTOCK
Albert
Church
Keizergracht
Tenant
De Villiers
Eastern Boulevard
Mill
Jutland
ZONNEBLOEM
Victoria
N2
M4
M3
VREDEHOEK
(DISTRICT 6)
WALMER ESTATE
DEVIL'S PEAK
De Waal
UNIVERSITY ESTATE
SALT RIVER
N2
To Southern Suburbs, Simon's Town & Cape Point
To Airport
TABLE MOUNTAIN NATIONAL PARK
NAMIBIA
BOTSWANA
MOZAMBIQUE
SWAZILAND
LESOTHO
SOUTH AFRICA
Cape Town
INDIAN OCEAN
0
1/2 mi
0
0.5 km
N

CITY CENTER

As the **city center** tries to reinvent itself as a residential entity, there are an increasing number of smart places to stay—bear in mind, though, that bedding down here means you will inevitably forgo a full-on mountain or sea view. Also be aware that while you'll enjoy the convenience of having the city's nightlife and dining at your doorstep, you'll also have its ever more congested traffic and associated parking problems (not a problem if you like to walk). Described here are the best city-center options, but given Cape Town's geography, my money is on the options in the residential City Bowl suburbs, reviewed later.

Expensive

If you like intimate, boutique-style accommodations, the centrally located **Cape Heritage Hotel** ★★, 90 Bree St. (✆ **021/424-4646;** www.capeheritage.co.za), on Heritage Square, is the top pick, but certainly not the cheapest place in town. It is a gracious heritage property (the real McCoy—take a look at its tasteful colonial-themed interiors) that provides immediate access to one of the city's best restaurants (Savoy Cabbage) and an excellent wine bar (Caveau). Summer rates start at R2,520 for a standard double (in this category, book room no. 111), but it's worth upgrading to the more spacious (and better-dressed) luxury category (R3,120 in summer).

Note: A couple of large, posh hotels are slated to open by 2010. The biggest will be the first foray into South Africa by India's Taj Hotels group (✆ **021/426-4759;** www.tajhotels.com). Expect unbridled luxury.

Moderate

An agreeable value is the **Adderley Hotel** ★ (✆ **021/469-1900;** www.relais.co.za), on Adderley Street. Made up of three historical buildings, it has tidy, modern rooms and more character than the nearby Mandela Rhodes apartments. The rates (from R1,610 double; R1,920 for a good-size junior suite) include breakfast overlooking the early-morning bustle of one of Cape Town's most interesting streets, and are negotiable, so call to discuss. Walking distance from the Company Gardens is eclectically furnished **Dunkley House** ★ (✆ **021/462-7650;** www.dunkleyhouse.com; R850–R1,350 double, based on season), at 3B Gordon St., near Dunkley Square and not far from Parliament. The larger Bay units are modern and slick, and some of these have private patios with plunge pools and room enough to sunbathe—naturally, these ones are a tad pricier, but worth it. There's a decent communal pool, too, as well as Wi-Fi access, a DVD library, and an honor bar.

The Grand Daddy & Airstream Trailer Park ★ Value A relatively high level of luxury and a strong buzz make this one of the liveliest hotels in town (if you're not going to join in on the weekends, bring earplugs). The Grand Daddy—occupying the old, much-revamped Metropole hotel (which opened in 1870)—is one of the best deals in town. While the new owners remodeled the rooms, making them perkier, brighter, and more contemporary, they also scaled down prices. Bedrooms are smart, comfortable, and design conscious, with South African iconography stamped into the fabrics or stenciled onto walls. But the big innovation is up on the rooftop—the world's first Airstream Trailer Park—a collection of reconditioned and thematically spruced-up vintage caravans. I wouldn't recommend these for extended stays (interiors are funky but a tad overwhelming, and they get hot in summer, even with air-conditioning), but for a night of rollicking fun, it's worth checking out. Coming soon: an open-air rooftop cinema, The Pink Flamingo.

38 Long St., Cape Town 8001. ✆ **021/424-7247.** Fax 021/424-7248. www.granddaddy.co.za. Grand Daddy: 26 units. R990–R1,950 double; R1,750–R2,450 Sugar Daddy suite. Airstream Trailer Park: 7 units. R1,750–R2,450 per caravan. AE, DC, MC, V. **Amenities:** Restaurant; 2 bars; airport transfers, high-speed Internet; room service; tours and travel arrangements. *In room:* A/C, TV, hair dryer, minibar, Wi-Fi (R60 for 1 hr.; R90 for 2 hr.).

Rouge on Rose ★★ Value Finds On Bo-Kaap's burgeoning Rose Street strip, this innovative little boutique hotel offers hot accommodations within skipping distance of the city center, at rates that'll knock your socks off. Packed with style, bedrooms are a blend of modern chic (all clean lines, with fabulous white linens on extra-long king-size beds and excellent bathrooms) and Bohemian styling (antiques collected over 3 decades, chunky armchairs, hand-carved armoires, random pretty *objets,* and rainfall showers folded into curved walls); there's a mix of deluxe rooms and self-catering suites (with space for kids on a sleeper couch). Room 302 is especially fabulous. De Waterkant and the city center are within easy reach, and there are several interesting shops and Bo-Kaap's interesting cobbled roads and mosque (personally, I love the melodious call to prayer resounding through the neighborhood, but be prepared, as there's no escaping it). The on-site daytime restaurant, **Side Dish,** is good for light meals, and owner-manager Ursula is planning a revival of the original **Die Kaapse Tafel** (Cape Table) restaurant, hopefully next door.

25 Rose St., Bo-Kaap. ✆ **021/426-0298.** Fax 021/422-2355. www.capetownboutiquehotel.co.za. 9 units. High season R1,200 suite; low season R900 suite. Rates include breakfast. MC, V. **Amenities:** Cafe-restaurant; airport transfers; Wi-Fi (R0.65 per megabyte). *In room* A/C, TV/DVD, hair dryer, microwave, minibar (stocked on request).

Inexpensive

Farther up Long Street, in the direction of the never-ending throng of watering holes and late-night establishments that make this Cape Town's headiest stretch, is one of the most photographed hotels in Africa: **Daddy Long Legs** ★, 134 Long St. (✆ **021/422-3074;**

Finds More Space, More Freedom, More at Home . . .

While there's great atmosphere in and along the cobbled streets of De Waterkant, that area can be a bit of an enclave for out-of-towners, and years of construction are transforming what is already a very-overpriced neighborhood into a dedicated shopping district. For a more keen sense of Cape Town's diverse city life, I'd recommend staying in the City Bowl suburbs. Right off bustling Kloof Street (with its plethora of restaurants) is brand-new **More Quarters** ★★★ (✆ **021/480-8080;** www.morequarters.co.za), a cluster of historic semidetached cottages that have been converted into self-catering apartments, each one individually styled, shaped, and apportioned with all the conveniences of a small but spacious modern home. There's a dedicated check-in—one that doesn't feel like a tourist hub or travel agency (which is what's happened to Village & Life in De Waterkant)—with an upstairs breakfast room ('cause the morning meal is included in the good-value rate; R1,810–R2,125 for a one-bedroom, R3,190 for two bedrooms in high season; low-season rates are much lower). There's also a four-bedroom house with pool that you can take over for R6,250 per night in high season. Lodged here, you'll feel like you have Cape Town at your fingertips, and obliging staff are adept at helping out with any request.

www.daddylonglegs.co.za) is a conceptual boho hotel that, thanks to its 13 en-suite rooms decorated by 13 Capetonian artists, got the glossies and design annuals to sit up and take note of what imagination can do with an essentially small amount of living space. Rooms go for between R600 and R860 per night (no breakfast) and are probably priced well below what they're worth, which is why this place is always packed to capacity.

CITY BOWL SUBURBS

For easy access to sights, top restaurants, and beaches, you can't beat the **City Bowl,** which here includes the residential neighborhoods that tumble down the slopes of the mountain. Most enjoy fabulous views of the city center and the best take-in vistas of the mountain—of the accommodations listed below, the **Mount Nelson** is still the classiest large hotel option. **Boutique Manolo** is the top guesthouse.

Very Expensive

Mount Nelson ★★★ Kids Having opened its doors in 1899 to accommodate the passengers of the Union and Castle lines, this is the undisputed grande dame of colonial hotels. The opening of the slinky **Planet Champagne Bar** and the gorgeous new **Librisa Spa** is pulling in a sophisticated local crowd as well, alongside the celebs and film shoots. The Nellie, as this hotel is affectionately known, is a 10-minute stroll through the Company Gardens to the center of the city, yet the great pink ship is adrift in 3.6 hectares (9 acres) of mature gardens that make it feel as though it's out in the country. A regular winner of various Best Hotel in Africa titles, the Mount Nelson ensures excellent service. ***Note:*** While this place is a firm favorite, also consider the equally gracious and far more exclusive Ellerman House (see p. 110).

76 Orange St., Gardens 8001. ✆ **021/483-1000.** Fax 021/483-1001. www.mountnelson.co.za. 201 units. High season R6,754–R7,227 superior double, R7,733–R8,300 luxury double, R10,015–R17,090 suite; low season R4,714 superior double, R5,385 luxury double, R6,952–10,875 suite. Rates include breakfast. AE, DC, MC, V. **Amenities:** 2 restaurants; bar; gym; 2 pools; room service; spa; squash; 2 tennis courts. *In room:* A/C, TV/DVD, hair dryer, minibar, Wi-Fi (R100 per hour; R225 per day).

Expensive

Alta Bay ★★★ On the steep slopes of wind-free Higgovale (the City Bowl's most prestigious suburb), Alta comprises seven suites on separate levels with private courtyards or decks and a great sense of space and light throughout. This is among the most stylish operations in town, with plenty of thoughtful touches, including a self-service bar and a thoughtfully packed gym bag. It's equipped with all the modern conveniences you'd expect in this price category, and furnished with what has become the signature South African Modern style—clean, angular lines softened with suede, leather, and timber; neutral warm colors; a few ethnic touches; and high-quality fabrics (not a faux zebra skin in sight). The house also offers plenty of access to the outdoors, either through large doors that lead to the shaded garden or with gorgeous vistas of the sparkling city below.

12 Invermark Crescent, Higgovale 8001. ✆ **021/487-8800.** Fax 021/487-8822. www.altabay.com. 7 units. High season R2,500 deluxe double, R3,000 superior double; low season R1,500 deluxe double, R1,900 superior double. Rates include breakfast. AE, MC, V. Children 12 and over only. **Amenities:** Breakfast room; complimentary bar; DVD and CD library; gym access; plunge pool; spa treatments; airport transfers; yoga and Pilates (on request). *In room:* A/C, TV/DVD, CD player, hair dryer, free Wi-Fi.

Boutique Manolo ★★★ Value Finds Views from this beautiful, plush-modern, peppermint-colored guesthouse are without parallel. Magnificently located—high above the city, along Cape Town's Mulholland Drive—it ranks among the most fabulously designed and warmly hosted places to bed down. Accommodations spill over various levels, and the architectural recrafting of the original cliffside mansion is remarkable. Each room has an outdoor area with seating arrangements, and besides the luscious red pool, there's a secret garden, too. The chic interiors are immaculate white, offset by colorful artwork and bold light fittings in each room, and outfitted with books, fine linens, useful gadgets, radiant floor heating, and heated towel racks. Outside, thick vegetation helps frame jaw-dropping vistas of Table Mountain. By day the panoramas are staggering, but when the sun descends, the lights come up and the city glitters and pulsates beneath your feet. Anyone seeking sublime romance should book the top-of-the-world, two-storey Penthouse suite (a bargain, at R4,000).

33 Leeukloof Dr., Tamboerskloof 8001. ✆ **021/426-2330.** www.boutique-manolo.co.za. 5 units. High season R2,250 luxury double, R2,750 grand luxury double, R4,000 penthouse suite; low season R1,800 luxury double, R2,250 grand luxury double, R4,000 penthouse suite. Rates include breakfast; penthouse suite rates include minibar and laundry. AE, MC, V. **Amenities:** Dining area and lounge; library; pool; free Wi-Fi; wine cellar. *In room:* A/C, TV/DVD, hair dryer, iPod docking station, minibar.

Four Rosmead ★★★ (Finds) Like Cape Cadogan (below), this small, well-oiled boutique hotel provides excellent service and plenty of thoughtful touches. Decor manages to be soothingly tasteful and full of character—the entire house functions as an art gallery, so it's fascinating, too. Rooms are spacious and airy—the luxury category is just fine (with shower only), but if you decide to splash out on a deluxe room (with balcony), try for Oranjezicht or Leeuwenzicht, both with mesmeric city views. The "cottage" in the Provençal-inspired garden is a honeymooner's choice—big, without distracting views, and with an al fresco shower. A lot of thought has gone into each room, right down to the beach bag, with large towels and a Frisbee. Some rooms have fireplaces. There is also a personal restaurant guide, suggesting hot spots such as walking-distance **Liquorice & Lime,** to as far afield as Constantia; they'll even plate take-out meals from local eateries for you. Several "green" projects are running, including water recycling and a solar-heated pool.

4 Rosmead Ave., Cape Town 8001. ✆ **021/480-3810.** Fax 021/423-0044. www.fourrosmead.com. 8 units. High season R1,800–R2,150 luxury double, R2,150–R2,525 deluxe double, R2,550–R2,950 suite; low season R1,400 luxury double, R1,625 deluxe double, R1,900 suite. Rates include breakfast. AE, MC, V. Children 12 and over only. **Amenities:** Dining room; lounge; art gallery; free high-speed Internet and Wi-Fi; library; massage and spa treatments (on request); heated pool; room service. *In room:* A/C, TV/DVD, hair dryer, iPod docking station, minibar.

Kensington Place ★★★ This award-winning boutique hotel has beautiful views of the city, harbor, and mountain, and you feel surrounded by greenery (although the views and value are better at Boutique Manolo; see above). Each bedroom is the size of a minisuite, with expensive finishes, luxurious fabrics, and plush furnishings. Thoughtful touches include laptops, an "emergency box" stocked with such necessities as condoms and headache pills, ready-to-go beach kits, and a little gym-in-a-bag. The best rooms on the second floor have balconies overlooking the city—ask for nos. 1, 2, or 3. Near the pool, sultry room no. 7 is larger than most; no. 8 has a private entrance, exquisite modern decor, and gorgeous views through massive picture windows. The small, timber-decked pool is fringed by a comfortable casbah-style lounge with billowing curtains—a calm oasis that belies the proximity of bustling Kloof Street, heaving with restaurants.

38 Kensington Crescent, Higgovale 8001. ✆ **021/424-4744.** Fax 021/424-1810. www.kensingtonplace.co.za. 8 units. High season R2,860 standard double, R3,410 superior double; low season R1,850 standard double, R2,355 superior double. Rates include breakfast. AE, DC, MC, V. Children 12 and over only. **Amenities:** Dining area, bar; access to city health club; massage; pool; room service; free Wi-Fi. *In room:* A/C, TV/DVD, gym-in-a-bag, hair dryer, iPod docking station, minibar.

Moderate

Besides my favorites, fully reviewed below, Cape Town has a few more guesthouses worth considering in this price category. All are in gorgeous historic homes high up on the slopes of Oranjezicht, with great views of the city and harbor lights.

One of the slickest newcomers to the ever-burgeoning luxury guesthouse scene in Oranjezicht is **2inn1 Kensington** ★★, 21 Kensington Crescent, Oranjezicht (© **021/423-1707** or 076/452-6028; www.2inn1.com), adjacent to the pretty wooded estate of the Western Cape Premier. The two side-by-side renovated houses have undergone a chi-chi, modern makeover, with luxurious finishes and exhaustive in-room amenities, including iPod docking stations and under-floor heating. Facilities are extensive: pool, Jacuzzi, DVD library, in-room massage, and free high-speed Internet. Rates are very fair—luxury doubles go for R1,980 in summer, while standard units are even cheaper, and the suites (R2,500) sleep four.

Cape Riviera ★ (© **021/461-8535;** www.caperiviera.co.za; R900–R1,540 standard double) is also on one of Cape Town's most beautiful streets, amid grand turn-of-the-20th-century homes overlooking the Molteno reservoir. Rooms, furnished in dark wood and white, are elegantly stark (framed black-and-white photographs, pretty chandeliers, and fresh flowers add personality) and equipped with all the comforts (air-conditioning, Wi-Fi, satisfying linens). Superior rooms (R1,100–R1,800 double) have personal sitting areas. The views are best from luxury room no. 10 (R1,300–R2,270).

A wooded garden, charming home, and large pool make **Rutland Lodge,** 5 Montrose Ave., Oranjezicht (© **021/461-7062;** www.rutlandlodge.com; R1,100–R1,800 double), another tidy proposition. With its modern conveniences, tasteful decor, and hands-on owners, it doesn't get better—unless you insist on one of the three top-floor rooms, each of which has phenomenal views from a private deck. Also in Oranjezicht, **De Tafelberg Guesthouse** (© **021/424-9159;** www.detafelberg.com; from R1,300 double in summer) is yet another grand home with superb views from most rooms, as well as a great breakfast "room"—a deep covered balcony overlooking the pool, with views of the city and harbor in the distance. A few bedrooms aren't air-conditioned, and some have showers only. Finally, if you prefer to keep it anonymous and impersonal, there's always that good-value stalwart, **Cape Milner,** 2 Milner Rd., Tamboerskloof (© **021/426-1101;** www.capemilner.com), a hotel offering a fairly smooth, convenient base with modern comforts (and a recent glossy makeover); avoid the roadside rooms, though, as the windows don't silence traffic noise.

An African Villa ★★ **Value** Louis and Jimmy have skillfully reworked the spaces in several adjoining 19th-century double-story Victorian houses into a chic African-Zen boutique-style guesthouse. Using a clever mix of ethnic and modern furniture, and off-setting muted modern tones and earthy textures with playful touches of vivid color, they've created a stylish, good-value, and very warm, welcoming environment—one of Cape Town's loveliest. The cheerful public spaces all lead to an outdoor area with plunge pool and timber loungers. For privacy and views, the rooms on the second floor are marginally preferable to those on the ground—those facing Table Mountain (like no. A2) have a wonderful ambience; but the platinum units, with doors that lead to the Victorian balcony overlooking the street, are the ones to go for if you need extra space.

19 Carstens St., Tamboerskloof 8001. © **021/423-2162.** Fax 021/423-2274. www.capetowncity.co.za. 13 units. Oct 2009–Sept 2010 R990–R1,400 double; Oct 2010–Nov 2011 R1,100–R1,600. Winter discounts available. Rates include breakfast. AE, DC, MC, V. **Amenities:** Breakfast areas; honor bar; small library; pool; Wi-Fi. *In room:* A/C (in some), TV, hair dryer.

Derwent House ★★ For the sheer vivacious energy of its hosts, Jo and Carol, this slick boutique hotel deserves the numerous accolades it has received from online travel forum TripAdvisor. These ladies came from northern England and fell in love with Cape Town; still high on their transition to paradise, they'll sweep you off your feet with their hospitality, dispense insider knowledge, and make all kinds of bookings (for foodies, they're particularly resourceful). They've managed to carve 10 attractive bedrooms—designated either Fabulous or Beautiful—out of a formerly derelict property, now transformed into unfussy luxury with swish furnishings and an intelligent art collection. Despite encroaching low-rise apartments and proximity to the city hubbub, there's a mellow vibe here, as well as a sheltered pool area. Some rooms have views of Table Mountain (book no. 3). Jo and Carol use solar energy to heat water, and they're gearing up toward carbon neutrality.

14 Derwent Rd., Tamboerskloof 8001. ✆ **021/422-2763.** www.derwenthouse.co.za. 10 units. High season R1,600 Fabulous double, R1,950–R2,050 Beautiful double, R2,150–R2,250 family suite; low season R1,250 Fabulous double, R1,600 Beautiful double, R1,200 family suite. Rates include breakfast and all-day tea, coffee, and cake. AE, MC, V. **Amenities:** Breakfast room; honor bar; pool. *In room:* A/C, TV/DVD, free Wi-Fi.

Hippo Boutique Hotel ★ Value Conveniently located just off the vibrant cafe-and-dining strip of Kloof Street, this slick, good-value, no-nonsense hotel actually occupies a small modern apartment block. It's ideal if you prefer to be left to your own devices, with privacy that B&Bs and guesthouses don't always provide. Standard doubles are clean-lined and smart (and best suited to business travelers), while the five loft-style executive suites on the fourth floor have full-on views of Table Mountain; each of these has a kitchenette (with a microwave, crockery and cutlery, and a decent-sized dining area). Each one has been individually designed, but not in any intrusive manner and not as self-consciously as those at Daddy Long Legs; these rooms are also bigger, with excellent in-room technologies, such as personal computers in every room (ADSL and Wi-Fi). Downstairs are a number of sociable eateries, some of which provide meals that can be charged to your room; or you can have meals delivered. It's not the top choice if you seek character, but for functionality, it's an excellent value.

5–9 Park Rd., Tamboerskloof 8001. ✆ **021/423-2500.** Fax 021/423-2515. www.hippotique.co.za. 25 units. R1,195 double; R1,950 suite. AE, DC, MC, V. **Amenities:** 3 restaurants; room service; Wi-Fi. *In room:* A/C, TV/DVD, hair dryer, iPod docking station, minibar, free Wi-Fi.

More Cape Cadogan ★★★ Value One of the original farmhouses built on the slopes of Table Mountain, this elegant double-storied Georgian is just steps away from bustling Kloof Street, yet it's a thoroughly peaceful sanctuary. Stylish renovations have imbued it with 12 well-groomed en-suite bedrooms decorated with a mix of contemporary and antique furnishings. Lovely touches, such as a plush Victorian chair or gilt-framed mirror, offset the cool white-and-gold minimalism, meaning that even the smaller standard rooms ooze grandeur. Rooms to book are nos. 2 and 8, both huge, beautifully furnished, and airy, with vast travertine bathrooms and double-volume showers—no. 8 has an especially interesting view from a little balcony. Adjacent, the double-story Owner's Villa is a cushy home for two, with added privacy, a large personal outdoor area, and a plunge pool.

5 Upper Union St., Gardens, Cape Town 8001. Reservations ✆ **011/484-9911,** direct 021/480-8080. Fax 011/484-9916. www.capecadogan.com. 12 units. High season R2,125 standard double, R2,725 luxury double, R4,100 owner's villa; low season R1,715 standard double, R2,300 luxury double, R3,525 owner's villa. Rates include breakfast. AE, DC, MC, V. **Amenities:** Bar; free high-speed Internet; small pool; airport transfers. *In room:* A/C, TV/DVD, hair dryer, minibar, Wi-Fi (R50 per 500MB).

Walden House ★ This quiet, turn-of-the-20th-century guesthouse offers stylish rooms in one of the city's oldest residential areas. White features predominantly—from the floorboards to the linen—with many wicker touches and handsomely tiled bathrooms. The standard double rooms are compact, no-nonsense, and comfortable, with a choice of twin rooms or queen-size beds. The spacious garden suite is a personal favorite, but the most popular room is the upstairs honeymoon suite, with a door opening onto the first-floor veranda with a great view of Table Mountain. Kloof Street, with its large selection of restaurants, is within easy walking distance, and nearby there are popular bars, cafes, and a good independent cinema.

5 Burnside Rd., Tamboerskloof 8001. ✆ **021/424-4256.** Fax 021/424-0547. www.walden-house.com. 7 units. High season R1,100 standard double, R1,320 luxury garden suite, R1,700, honeymoon suite; low season R800 standard double, R920 garden suite, R1,100 honeymoon suite. Rates include breakfast. AE, DC, MC, V. Children 12 and older only. **Amenities:** Breakfast room; lounge; pool; airport transfers; free Wi-Fi. *In room:* A/C, TV, hair dryer, minibar.

Inexpensive

If you'd rather spend your money on restaurants or a high-end fling in a game reserve, take a look at the aforementioned **Daddy Long Legs,** on bustling Long Street. If rooms there have already sold out (as they do), consider booking a private room in one of the city's first-rate backpacker lodgings: **The Backpack** (✆ **021/423-4530;** www.backpackers.co.za; R550–R800 en-suite double) is one of the oldest and most popular. It's clean and convivial, with a busy courtyard, cafe, bar, good travel center, shuttle bus, and pool, and it's an easy stroll from the nightlife and restaurant options on Kloof and Long streets (walking is inadvisable late at night, though).

Fritz Hotel ★ Value Finds Fritz Hotel is within easy reach of the Kloof Street restaurant strip, right on the edge of the city center, furnished with an eclectic selection of Art Deco and 1950s antiques (collected by Swiss owner Arthur Bisig). It's more like a large colonial-style guesthouse (Edwardian, with Victorian bits) than a hotel, but it remains a bargain, with neatly maintained, individually styled bedrooms, all with knock-off designer beds. Ask for a room that opens onto the first-floor wraparound veranda; they have high ceilings and wood floors, and room nos. 6 and 14 are the biggest. Room no. 11 is small but has a great view of Table Mountain from the bed. Breakfasts and drinks are served in the relaxed, breezy courtyard.

1 Faure St., Gardens 8001. ✆ **021/480-9000.** Fax 021/480-9090. www.fritzhotel.co.za. 13 units. High season R750–R900 double; low season R500–R575 double. Rates include breakfast. AE, DC, MC, V. *In room:* TV, fax, hair dryer, minibar, free Wi-Fi.

WATERFRONT

Bear in mind that the Waterfront is very much a tourist enclave. Everywhere but the ultra-exclusive boutique hotel, Dock House (reviewed below), you're likely to find yourself surrounded by many, many fellow travelers.

Very Expensive

Competing with the Mount Nelson, Ellerman, Dock House, and Cape Grace as the preferred location for the rich and famous, the glitzy **Table Bay** (✆ **021/406-5000;** www.suninternational.com) occupies what serious shoppers consider a prime position on the Prince Alfred Breakwater—connected to the Victoria & Albert mall. It doesn't have the sense of exclusivity or privacy of its competitors, but shopaholics couldn't want for more. Public spaces have a "wow" factor, but standard rooms are small and dull (from R3,275 double); opt for a luxury room (R4,075–R5,425 double) or suite (R5,400–R10,200). Better still, check out the options below.

Cape Grace ★★★ (Kids Of the larger Waterfront hotels, the Grace remains the most elegant, and it's still the first choice for visiting VIPs, though Dock House is by far the most exclusive. The difference between this hotel and the Mount Nelson—the other top choice—is primarily one of location; the Cape Grace is on a busy marina, surrounded by apartments and the nearby V&A mall, while the Nellie is surrounded by lush, tranquil gardens at the edge of the city center. The entire hotel has been given an updated look, and in some ways the new Grace resembles a sexy museum (with polished artifacts and antiques, glass display boxes, and quirky experimental chandeliers). Bedrooms remain impeccable, all dressed up in locally printed textiles and tasteful finery. Rooms are smaller than at the more modern One&Only, across the marina, but they're truly luxurious, with French doors opening onto mountain or harbor views. It's child friendly, too—kids are welcomed with gift baskets, stories read aloud, and milk before bedtime, and the hotel rents such gear as car seats and prams.

West Quay, V&A Waterfront 8002. ✆ **021/410-7100.** Fax 021/419-7622. www.capegrace.com. 122 units. High season R5,750 luxury double, R6,150 rooftop luxury double, R6,620 superior double, R6,970 rooftop terrace double, R10,840–R15,000 suite; low season R4,810 luxury double, R5,250 rooftop luxury double, R5,850 superior double, R6,180 rooftop terrace double, R9,600–R13,000 suite. All rates include breakfast. Children under 12 stay free in parent's room. AE, DC, MC, V. **Amenities:** Restaurant; bar; babysitting; concierge; library; pool; room service; spa. *In room:* A/C, TV, minibar, free Wi-Fi.

Dock House ★★★ Originally the Harbor Master's residence, this heritage building has been transformed into one of the most perfectly intimate hotels in Cape Town. Infinitely more stylish and exclusive than any other Waterfront options, it's so discreetly situated that hardly anyone knows of its existence. Yet because of its position overlooking the V&A and its access to so many useful amenities (including its own pool and spa and a nightly sunset cruise), you'll feel yourself at the epicenter of Cape Town. Contemporary, stripped-down neobaroque interior design complements the original architecture. The six individually designed bedrooms all include modern art, pretty chandeliers, silk drapes, gigantic framed mirrors, original plasterwork and fireplaces, and epic bathrooms. Service is highly personal—there's no reception or lobby, and relaxed, gracious staff members treat you like guests in a private home. ***Note:*** Avoid the ground-floor bedrooms, as they are noisy early in the morning.

Portswood Close, Portswood Ridge, V&A Waterfront 8001. ✆ **021/421-9334.** Fax 021/419-7881. www.dockhouse.co.za. 6 units. High season R5,495–R6,875 double, R8,245 suite; low season R4,125–R5,155 double, R6,185 suite. Rates include breakfast and tea and coffee service. AE, DC, MC, V. **Amenities:** Restaurant (at V&A Hotel); bar; breakfast room; pool; room service; spa; airport transfers. *In room:* A/C, TV, hair dryer, free high-speed Internet, free minibar, free Wi-Fi.

One&Only Cape Town ★★★ Forty years after hotel magnate Sol Kerzner built the country's first five-star hotel, he has come home to establish Cape Town's most expensive resort. Lording it over a manmade channel, it's built on a massive scale: The lagoon-style pool meandering between the island villas in front of the main hotel block (Marina Rise) is the city's largest hotel pool; the spa and the humungous Island suites also win the size prize, though it feels like the middle of a concrete real estate development resort down there. The standard rooms are more attractive and seriously lavish, with the city's best beds and great mountain views (request a unit on the fifth floor); the rates below rise in conjunction with room size. Personally, I'd rather be at Dock House, which offers more class for less money.

Dock Rd., V&A Waterfront, Cape Town. ✆ **021/431-5888.** Fax 021/431-5230. www.oneandonlyresorts.com. 131 units. High season R6,900–R8,000 Marina Room, R7,900–R10,500 Island junior suite, R13,750–R35,000 suite, R31,250–R55,000 penthouse suite; low season from R5,500 Marina double, from R6,500 Island junior suite, from R11,000 suite, from R25,000 penthouse suite. Rates are per room and include breakfast for 2 at maze by Gordon Ramsey. AE, DC, MC, V. **Amenities:** 3 restaurants; 2 bars; concierge; fitness center; pool; spa; airport transfers; free Wi-Fi. *In room:* A/C, TV/DVD, hair dryer, iPod docking station, minibar.

Expensive

Radisson Blu Hotel Waterfront ★ On the outskirts of the Waterfront (500m/1,640 ft. from the mall entrance), the Radisson enjoys an exceptional setting—right on the sea, with waves spraying off the rocks just beyond the popular outdoor terrace and garden area. Behind the hotel looms the glowing hulk of the new Green Point Stadium. The price reflects the location—almost every room, furnished in dark blues and gold—has a fine sea view. There's no beach, however, and service is lackluster for the price. To be near the ocean, I'd rather stay in one of the intimate spaces on the Atlantic seaboard or around the southern part of the peninsula. This place, with its preppy nautical theme and mall-like overtones, is a throwback to anonymous hotels everywhere.

Beach Rd., Granger Bay 8002. ✆ **021/441-3000.** Fax 021/441-3520. www.radissonblu.com. 177 units. High season R3,200–R4,275 standard double, R3,640–R4,870 superior double, R4,550–R6,050 business class double, R8,200–R10,500 two-bedroom suite; low season R2,310 standard double, R2,785 superior double, R3,360 business class double, R6,300 two-bedroom suite. Children sharing stay free. AE, DC, MC, V. **Amenities:** Restaurant; bar; babysitting; fitness center; pool; room service; spa. *In room:* A/C, TV, hair dryer, minibar, free Wi-Fi.

Victoria & Alfred Hotel ★★ Value Situated alongside a working dock in what was once a warehouse (now called Alfred Mall), this was the Waterfront's first hotel, and it remains the most centrally located choice. Benefiting from a much-needed refurb when they added 26 new loft units in 2009, the hotel remains the Waterfront's best value, with gorgeous harborside views. Since the opening of the Dock House (reviewed above), a nearby sibling hotel, V&A guests have access to a superb spa and lawn-fringed pool. Bedrooms are spacious; each features a king-size bed and a warm, rich palette. You pay a small premium for rooms with Table Mountain views, but it's worthwhile to wake up to that classic vista. **OYO,** the in-house restaurant, has a great al fresco terrace, but food and service are a letdown; it's better to take the short stroll to **Den Anker** (see p. 130), one of the best Waterfront restaurants.

Pierhead, Waterfront 8002. ✆ **021/419-6677.** Fax 021/419-8955. www.vahotel.co.za. 94 units. High season R3,450 piazza-facing double; R3,950 superior loft double; R4,650 mountain-facing double; low season R2,590 piazza-facing double, R2,965 superior loft double, R3,490 mountain-facing double. Rates include breakfast. Children 2–12 stay in parent's room for R90, or R425 for extra bed. AE, DC, MC, V. **Amenities:** Restaurant; bar; babysitting; gym, pool, and spa access (at Dock House); massage; room service; shuttle to city center. *In room:* A/C, TV, hair dryer, minibar, free Wi-Fi.

DE WATERKANT, GREEN POINT, MOUILLE POINT & SEA POINT

These suburbs virtually neighbor town and the Waterfront, but despite their location at the start of the Atlantic seaboard, the mountain makes beach access a little more time-consuming than from the City Bowl. That said, the area affords sea views and is a good value, particularly when compared with accommodations in the adjacent Waterfront. Plus, it's a stone's throw from Green Point Stadium and all the exciting new shops and restaurants popping up in the surrounding precinct. If you're staying for a while and don't mind the bland anonymity of apartment-style hotel suites, look at the one- and two-bedroom options at **The Rockwell** (✆ **021/421-0015;** www.therockwellapartments.co.za); some units have full kitchens.

Very Expensive

Cape Royale ★★★ Smack-dab at the heart of the newly rejuvenated Stadium precinct, this hotel is a good alternative to the Waterfront's Cape Grace. It's not as grand, but its strengths are many: It has numerous family-sized suites, all with full kitchens; it's set in the middle of the action, as opposed to being in a tourist island at the Waterfront, and is walking distance from almost everything; and the views are spectacular—especially from the rooftop pool area. It also affords greater access to local culture; nearby are many laid-back cafes with Green Point's villagey vibe. The suites are big and beautiful, but the bedrooms feel boxy and small, and there's a dearth of public spaces. The exquisite **Equinox Spa ★★★** is my top choice for a balancing rubdown, but the steakhouse, **1800°,** has received scathing reviews. A big bonus is the hotel's complimentary transfer service to any point within a 5km (3-mile) radius.

47 Main Rd., Green Point 8005. ✆ **021/430-0500.** www.caperoyale.co.za. 92 units. High season R4,240 1-bedroom suite, R5,820 2-bedroom suite, R9,930 3-bedroom suite, R11,620 4-bedroom suite; low-season R3,030 1-bedroom suite, R3,650 2-bedroom suite, R7,400 3-bedroom suite, R9,680 4-bedroom suite. AE, DC, MC, V. **Amenities:** 2 restaurants; 2 bars; concierge; gym; pool; room service; spa; airport and city transfers. *In room:* A/C, TV/DVD, hair dryer, full kitchen, free Wi-Fi.

Expensive

O on Kloof ★★ One of *Tatler*'s Top 101 Hotels in the World, this posh urban sanctuary is a great addition to Cape Town's boutique hotel scene. Ideal if you like your lines straight and your aesthetic modern, Olaf Dambrowski's design-conscious pad is situated on busy Kloof Road, at the junction of Sea Point and Bantry Bay; and although it's wedged into a high-density residential neighborhood, it makes excellent use of space. Its best rooms—massively proportioned and superluxurious—have views over a vast swath of cityscape, and Lion's Head rears up right behind the hotel; from here, it's a gorgeous sunset walk along the promenade that stretches all the way past Clifton to Camps Bay. Guest rooms are pristine, plush, and carefully decked out. Reserve room no. 5, an exquisite, stunning space, with a large private rooftop terrace with a Jacuzzi and pair of sun-loungers.

92 Kloof Rd., Sea Point/Bantry Bay. ✆ **021/439-2081** or 082/568-2784. Fax 021/439-8832. www.oonkloof.co.za. 8 units. R2,130–R2,300 standard double; R2,700–R2,950 luxury double; R3,140-R3,400 superior double; R3,950–R4,250 suite. Rates include breakfast. AE, MC, V. **Amenities:** Restaurant; bar; DVD library; gym; library; pool; room service; spa. *In room:* AC, TV/DVD, free high-speed Internet, hair dryer, iPod docking station, minibar, free Wi-Fi.

Moderate

If none of the options below appeals to you, check out the delightful **Cape Victoria Guest House ★** (Wigtown Rd. and Torbay Rd.), Green Point (✆ **021/439-7721;** www.capevictoria.co.za); standard doubles are an excellent value (R750–R1,250), and a magnificent suite with ocean views from a private balcony goes for R1,900–R2,200 in summer. The guesthouse is run by excellent hostess Lily, whose architect son converted the building.

Village Life for Hire

In the oldest residential area of Cape Town, amid partly cobbled streets and quaint 18th-century Cape Malay architecture, De Waterkant has an almost European feel, and places you in the heart of Cape Town's most fashionable shopping district, with great restaurants and nightlife options within easy strolling distance. The city center is also easily managed on foot (by day). Unfortunately, for much of 2008 and 2009, the entire area has been a monstrous construction site as a second Cape Quarter shopping mall takes shape (obscuring views, creating noise, blocking off roads, and generally upending any form of village life. Hopes are that, by mid-2010, the cranes will have departed and the area will have returned to its fabulous self, albeit with more traffic (as there will soon be supermarkets and general-use stores). There's no telling how De Waterkant will really be affected (some hoteliers say their views may be lost forever, but they nevertheless welcome the real estate upgrade). **Village & Life** (✆ **021/409-2500;** www.dewaterkant.com) has the widest selection of properties for hire in the 'hood and will match you up with the style, size, and level of luxury you require (or can afford); rates start at R1,200 for two people in summer. For guests who don't care to self-cater, there's **De Waterkant House,** a well-placed B&B with plunge pool and lounge (www.dewaterkanthouse.com; around R1,300–R2,200 double in summer); guests here eat breakfast at **The Charles,** another Village & Life's guesthouse. Decorated in a more contemporary style, it's certainly worth considering (www.thecharles.co.za; R1,800–R2,800 double in season) and also offers a few studios and small cottages. Also take a look at **Cedric's Lodges** (✆ **021/425-7635;** www.cedricslodge.com), a pair of luxury four-bedroom guesthouses, which can be rented in their entirety for a more exclusive holiday.

Villa Zest ★★ *Finds* Small, swanky, and highly personal, this brand-new addition to Green Point's evolving accommodation scene occupies a large, four-level Bauhaus-style building with sleek, minimalist interiors, and a zen garden with a gorgeous pool. It will appeal to younger travelers looking for a space that's upbeat, fashion-conscious, and surgically clean. It's also near favorite hotspots and walking distance from De Waterkant and (by day) the Waterfront. Bedrooms, each named for a 1970s cult movie, are extremely comfortable, with spectacular beds, the best linens money can buy, and spunky retro-inspired wallpaper against an all-white palette. They're not terribly spacious, so make sure you secure Studio 54 if you need room enough to disco. San Diego–born owner Kevin Gerlach is very hands-on and committed to sustainability, evident in organic toilet paper and toiletries and eco-friendly cleaning products.

2 Braemar Rd., Green Point 8005. ✆ **021/433-1246.** Fax 021/433-1247. 7 units. High season R1,690–R1,890 deluxe double, R2,090 superior deluxe double, R2,590–R2,990 superior double; low season R1,490 deluxe double, R1,890 superior deluxe double, R2,290 superior double. Rates include breakfast. AE, DC, MC, V. **Amenities:** Dining area/lounge; heated pool. *In room:* A/C, TV/DVD, hair dryer, iPod docking station, free Wi-Fi.

Winchester Mansions ★★ Built in the 1920s in the Cape Dutch style, this gracious, low-slung hotel faces the sea, though it's separated from the ocean by a busy road and broad swath of park. Still family owned, the hotel is distinguished by its friendly service. Rooms vary by size, style, and configuration. Those in the converted loft feature classy modern interiors, earthy tones, and dark wood. The best "classic" rooms marry modern design with old-fashioned charm (a few antiques, floral artworks)—ask for no. 306. The sea-facing Winchester "suites" are the best value. From the big sea-facing Robben Island suite, guests can watch as health-conscious Capetonians jog along the promenade. The bar and restaurant is popular with locals, particularly on Sunday, when a jazz brunch is served to the strains of live music in the beautiful colonnaded central courtyard, built around a fountain and encircled with trees. Family-sized suites are available, as is secure parking (R50 per night).

221 Beach Rd., Sea Point 8001. ✆ **021/434-2351.** Fax 021/434-0215. www.winchester.co.za. 76 units. High season R2,120–R2,332 classic double, R2,380–R2,618 modern classic double, R2,760–R5,445 suite; shoulder season R1,470–R1,617 classic double, R1,650–R1,815 modern classic double, R1,930–R3,300 suite. Rates include breakfast. AE, DC, MC, V. **Amenities:** Restaurant; bar; currency exchange; pool; room service; spa. *In room:* A/C, TV/DVD, CD player (in suites), hair dryer, minibar, Wi-Fi (R250 per day; R60 per hr.).

Inexpensive

La Splendida (Value) If you want to be close to the Waterfront and the ocean, this is a fair value. The Art Deco exterior wouldn't look out of place in Miami, and the seafront promenade stretches all the way past Sea Point, so bring your in-line skates. There's a dearth of public spaces, and in-room comforts are few—the atmosphere is a little hollow and the furniture is iffy—but you have your choice of mountain- or sea-view rooms (the latter are R300 extra and sell fast). The best value is the penthouse, which sleeps four. Meals are served in the attached ground-floor restaurant, which opens onto a sidewalk terrace. In winter (June–Aug), noise from the foghorn can be bothersome, as boats approach before turning out to sea. In summer, the nonstop traffic can make you dilly.

121 Beach Rd., Mouille Point 8001. ✆ **021/439-5119.** Fax 021/439-5112. www.lasplendida.co.za. 24 units. High season R1,210–R1,540 double, R1,895 suite, R2,195 penthouse; low season R855 double, R1,125 suite, R1,375 penthouse. AE, DC, MC, V. Children allowed by prior arrangement. **Amenities:** Restaurant; bar; babysitting; massage; room service. *In room:* A/C, TV, hair dryer (on request), minibar, Wi-Fi (R60 per hr.; R120 for 24 hr.).

ATLANTIC SEABOARD

Most visitors to the Cape want to wake up to a seascape and stroll down to the beach, but you'll need to book early and shell out for the privilege. By far, **Camps Bay** has the most ocean-facing units and the city's most accessible beach, lined with dozens of bars, coffee shops, and restaurants. It's also a mere 10-minute drive from the center of town. The area has numerous B&Bs (check out www.portfoliocollection.com), but be warned: Good taste and great location seem to enjoy an inverse relationship here, and you're really paying for the sea view. There are a few exceptions, of course. If you're on a more restrictive budget, take a look at **Camps Bay Beach Village** (✆ **021/438-4972;** www.villageandlife.com): Its studio apartments, built around a heated pool, are a great value, at R1,500 to R2,000 double in summer. They're a good deal cheaper in winter (from just R850), during wet season—hardly an ideal time to be on the seaboard, though sunsets are best then. Neighboring **Clifton** is more secluded but requires you to negotiate a long stairway to the beach, below relatively steep cliff paths. And in summer, you'll deal with traffic and parking problems. It's the most beautiful bay in Cape Town but not the most convenient place to stay, so guesthouses are scarce; you're best off renting your own seaside bungalow and living like a local (see "Self-Catering Options for Budgets Big & Small," earlier in this chapter). Neighboring **Bantry Bay** has two excellent options (reviewed below).

Very Expensive

Ellerman House & Villa ★★★ On a spectacularly elevated site overlooking the Atlantic Ocean and the premier suburb of Bantry Bay, this gorgeous Edwardian mansion is in a class of its own. With only 11 extraordinary rooms, it's the most exclusive address in Cape Town. To my mind, it's also the classiest by some stretch: Views evoke comparisons with the Riviera, and the sheer grace and style of the place make you feel like royalty. Everything—from walls hung with the country's most important private art collection to the perfect flavor of the seared tuna—tells you that the prices below are a very fair reflection of the high level of luxury, refinement, and comfort on offer; prepare for the mother of all vacations.

If you're planning a big family or group getaway, neighboring **Ellerman Villa** ★★★, is another winner—a triumph of modern architecture with up to five bedrooms, a multitude of lounges and dining areas, various pools, an art gallery, and spa, all spread over large, open-plan levels affording drop-dead views that sweep off into infinity. It's particularly devastating when you lie in bed and, with your electronic drapes and wall-sized doors rolled back, feel as if you're hovering over the sea; all told, it's priced from R38,300 (for three bedrooms).

180 Kloof Rd., Bantry Bay 8005. ✆ **021/430-3200.** Fax 021/430-3215. www.ellerman.co.za. 11 units plus the villa. High season (Oct–May) R5,300–R7,000 double without balcony, R8,800–R9,900 double with balcony, R14,500 suite; low season R4,500–R6,000 double without balcony, R7,500–R8,400 double with balcony, R12,300 suite. Rates include airport transfers, breakfast, laundry, tea, coffee, beer, spirits, house wines, in-room bar, sunset cocktails, pantry snacks, Wi-Fi, and Waterfront shuttles (3 daily). AE, DC, MC, V. Children 12 and over only. **Amenities:** Restaurant; bar; art gallery; butler service; concierge; gym; library; pool; room service; sauna; spa; wine cellar. *In room:* A/C, TV, hair dryer, minibar, free Wi-Fi.

Ezard House ★★ This luxury lodging probably has the highest vantage over the Atlantic seaboard, and the views are stellar. Far below you is spread all of Camps Bay and Bakoven—a fine place to witness the sun dipping below the horizon. Behind is the mountain, and various trails lead directly up it. Arranged on different levels around a variety of sundecks, koi ponds, terraces, lounges, and dining areas, rooms are large and comfort oriented—suites even more so—try to book no. 3. It's not in the same league as Ellerman House, nor as personal as Atlantic Suites, but the bevy of fresh-faced butlering staff members will take good care of you, suggesting activities and providing detailed driving directions to some of the city's best restaurants. Although they cruise around in collar and tie, you can't help but pick up on their enthusiasm for Cape Town.

20 Theresa Ave., Camps Bay 8005. ✆ **021/438-6687.** Fax 021/438-1378. www.ezardhouse.com. 11 units. High season R4,750 luxury double, R5,250 superior luxury double, R6,000 suite; low season R4,250 luxury double, R4,750 superior luxury double, R5,500 suite. Rates include breakfast, and poolside and sunset canapés. AE, DC, MC, V (surcharge). **Amenities:** Restaurant; bar; Jacuzzi; pool; room service; free airport transfers. *In room:* A/C, TV/DVD, hair dryer, free Wi-Fi.

The Twelve Apostles Hotel and Spa ★ Kids Okay, so the isolated location (about 3km/2 miles from the edge of Camps Bay/Bakoven), smallish accommodations, and endless traffic in front of all the best rooms are drawbacks. And when the wind blasts through here, it feels as if the entire place is about to take off. But given the full-on views of the ocean (and *that* sunset), an international-class spa, and a setting that's ideal if you actually *want* to escape the crowds, the 12 Apostles is a good choice. A couple of small coves and beaches are within walking distance, and walking trails through the *fynbos* mountain reserve have been mapped out. Bedrooms are elegant enough, but the most affordable ones are very boxy, and the prices here are generally outrageous—bathrooms are tiny. Children get plenty of attention here, though—especially in the 16-seater cinema, where matinees screen daily.

Victoria Rd., Camps Bay 8005 (midway btw. Camps Bay and Llandudno). ✆ **021/437-9000.** www.12apostleshotel.co.za. 70 units. High season R5,325–R5,810 classic double, R5,890–R6,430 mountain-facing double, R6,635–R7,240 luxury double, R8,625–R9,705 superior sea-facing double, R11,195–R20,760 suite; low season R4,310 classic double, R4,765 mountain-facing double, R5,310 luxury double, R6,790 superior sea-facing double, R8,700–R14,825 suite. Children under 12 sharing with adults stay free; children 12–16 sharing pay R400 each. Rates include breakfast. AE, DC, MC, V. **Amenities:** 2 restaurants; bar; cinema; concierge; helipad; pool; room service; spa. *In room:* A/C, TV/DVD, CD player, hair dryer, minibar, free Wi-Fi.

Expensive

Besides the options reviewed below, there are some spectacular opportunities for anyone who prefers to self-cater. Sexy **Lion's View** ★★★, 4 First Crescent, Camps Bay (✆ **021/438-0046** or 083/719-5735; www.lionsview.co.za), is an architect-designed modern dream pad that's featured in a string of glossies (including *Wallpaper**). It features awesome, open-plan living areas and a wonderful heated pool that flows off into infinity. The two-bedroom Penthouse Apartment is good for families (up to four people; R3,900 in high season, 5-night minimum), while the Main House down below, with five en-suite bedrooms, is an ideal setting for memorable celebratory gatherings (R8,500 per night in high season). To view a collection of similarly exciting Camps Bay apartments and villas, which you can hire for a self-catering holiday for a relatively affordable price, visit **www.campsbayapartments.com**.

I'm also fond of the eponymous **Eleven Sedgemoor Road** ★★ (✆ **021/438-7219** or 083/628-8620; www.11sedgemoor.com), a chic, elegant, small, modern guesthouse within walking distance of the beach and Camps Bay dining strip. There are five guest rooms (R2,000–R4,000 double), the most fabulous of which is undoubtedly the penthouse suite, which offers better privacy and one of Camps Bay's best views. You can also rent the entire house as an exclusive villa from R15,000 per night.

Atlantic House ★★★ Stylishly understated decor makes this one of the best-dressed joints in Camps Bay; its good looks compete respectably with an endless ocean horizon. It's more relaxed and intimate than pricier Ezard House, even higher up the slopes. Public spaces are gorgeous—dark timber boxes frame the blue sky and sea, and elegant touches include a massive photographic mural that covers the entire double-volume stairwell. But the main attraction is the rooms—you'd be happy to cut short a day of sightseeing to luxuriate in one. The three seaview rooms on the top floor are the most popular, but my favorite is the garden room, which has a private outdoor area and alfresco shower from where you can see Table Mountain and Lion's Head. Pool level rooms are less private, *sans* views.

20 St. Fillians Rd., Camps Bay 8005. ✆ **021/437-8120** or 082/781-2145. Fax 021/437-8130. www.atlantichouse.co.za. 5 units. Peak season R3,200 double; high season R2,800 double; midseason R2,200 double; winter R1,500 double. Rates include breakfast. MC, V. **Amenities:** Breakfast room; honor bar; DVD library; free high-speed Internet and Wi-Fi; library/lounge; heated pool; spa treatments. *In room:* A/C, TV/DVD, hair dryer, minibar.

Moments Tintswalo: On the Edge of the Atlantic

For its location alone, **Tintswalo Atlantic** ★★★, Cape Town's loveliest oceanfront accommodations, deserves your attention. There's nowhere like it anywhere in Africa—a luxury safari-style lodge tucked among a grove of protected milkwood trees, and backed by the looming craggy cliffs of famous Chapman's Peak Drive (star of international car commercials and much local controversy). A chauffeured Mercedes whisks you down a steep, winding driveway culminating with the beautifully-designed, ecologically-sensitive hideaway that's completely invisible from above. Opened late-2008 (and already on *Condé Naste*'s Hot List), it has just 10 superb suite-sized rooms—all water's edge cottages with balconies on stilts, which let you feel as if you're hovering over the water. From your room, soothed by a symphony of crashing waves, you can watch southern right whales just off shore; and at night, Hout Bay twinkles on the other side of False Bay, while fishing vessels trawl the waters like fireflies on the water. Each pretty suite-sized cottage (with a predominant palette of azure and silver) features wood floors, beautiful chandeliers, Persian rugs, ceramic fireplace, and a unique design based on the island after which it's named.

One drawback, though, is that while there's a lovely pebble "beach," you can't expect to go jumping into the ocean here—it's more for voyeurs than full-on adventurers (although guided mountain walks and helicopter flips will get the blood pumping). And at night, after plundering the wine cellar for some fine local vintages, you're lulled to sleep by the cacophonous roar of waves just meters from your bed—or order a bottle or two of bubbly and stay up late toasting one of Africa's most epic locations. While Tintswalo is well-positioned for exploring the southern part of the peninsula, it takes a little more effort to get to the city (for some, this may be a strong selling point, and a shuttle service is provided).

The real downside? Tintswalo isn't in everyone's price bracket—R7,000 double gets you a matchless location with gorgeous sleeping quarters, all house drinks, airport transfers, breakfast and a luxurious afternoon tea. Dinner time dining here is a touch outrageous (R550 per head for a good, but by no means thrilling, three-course dinner). Nevertheless, this is Cape Town at its most mesmerizing and—for nature lovers at least—dynamic. Check it all out at www.tintswalo.com; or book immediately by contacting ✆ **011/300-8888** or 087/754-9300, or emailing res@tintswalo.com.

Atlantic Suites ★★★ This is a first-class act, ensuring intimate, personalized attention from your hosts. They've created a handsome guesthouse with four elegant bedrooms, each one paired with spectacular views. Each room—like the entire light-filled house—is done out in pale, neutral tones that focus your attention on the vast Atlantic seaboard soundstage that spreads out before you. Great big picture windows frame the scene, and at night you can drift off to a symphony of tirelessly crashing waves. Distinguishing features include living orchids and arum lilies rather than cut flowers; unique spa-quality toiletries; in-room home theaters (with a selection of discs); complimentary minibar; a personalized high tea that's worth dragging yourself off the beach for; and the best breakfast spread in town. The Honeymoon Suite is pretty, but I personally love the layout of Atlantique, with views from the bed, Jacuzzi, and shower.

30 Hely Hutchinson Ave., Camps Bay 8005. ✆ 021/438-9455. Fax 021/438-0960. www.atlanticsuites-campsbay.com. R3,295–R3,995 double. Rates include breakfast, snack platter, and high tea. MC, V. Amenities: Breakfast room; bar service; free laundry; library/lounge with DVD library; pool. In room: A/C, TV/DVD, CD player, hair dryer, free high-speed Internet, Jacuzzi, microwave, free minibar, free Wi-Fi.

Les Cascades de Bantry Bay ★★★ Value High on Bantry Bay's mercifully wind-free cliffs, this beautifully appointed boutique villa exudes class and comfort. It's an excellent value, considering the privileged position and attentive service. Spacious rooms and ultraexpansive suites are finished in warm, modern earth tones—with a distinctly Balinese influence—that contrast with the blue sky and sea views. Connected to the original guesthouse is the newer **Cascades on 52 ★★**, a similarly sumptuous property with two enormous suites and a mix of rooms—the two without private balconies are excellent value. Public spaces seamlessly flow onto decks with pools; snag your couch on the main terrace early, and order a bottle of bubbly at sunset. Hosts Luc and Els are always on hand to assist, and their eye for the finer things in life means that everything from the choice of wine in your minibar to the selection of cold meats at breakfast is perfect. All but standard rooms have espresso machines. Suites have computers with printer and fax; the two-bedroom suite has a private pool.

48 and 52 De Wet Rd., Bantry Bay 8005. ✆ **021/434-5209.** Fax 021/439-4206. www.lescascades.co.za. **Les Cascades:** 6 units. High season R2,950 double, R3,250 suite; other seasons R2,250–R2,750 double, R2,450–R2,950 suite. **Cascades on 52:** 7 units. High season R2,150 standard double, R2,450 deluxe double, R2,950 superior double, R3,750–R5,200 2-bedroom suite (2–5 people), R3,750 penthouse suite; other seasons R1,500–2,150 standard double, R1,800–R2,450 deluxe double, R2,250–R2,750 superior double, R2,900–R4,700 2-bedroom suite (2–5 people), R2,900–R3,750 penthouse suite. Rates include breakfast. AE, DC, MC, V. **Amenities:** Restaurant; bar service; 2 pools; room service. *In room:* A/C, TV/DVD, CD player, hair dryer, iPod docking station, minibar, free Wi-Fi.

SOUTHERN SUBURBS

If the beach isn't your scene and you prefer your landscapes with mountains and trees, you'll find blissful peace in **Constantia,** the wine-producing area closest to the city, some 20 to 30 minutes away (halfway between the city and Cape Point). A little closer to town are leafy **Bishops Court** (Cape Town's embassy district) and **Newlands.** Being home to landmark rugby games and the world's largest rugby museum, Newlands is ideal for fans of the game, but for the most part it is bland middle-class suburbia. It does have some large, gracious lodgings that may suit less adventuresome travelers who want to be pampered, notably The Vineyard Hotel & Spa, which offers a good-value alternative to the pricey hotels at the waterfront; see below. You should also check out the lavish rooms at **The Bishop's Court ★**, 18 Hillwood Ave., Bishopscourt (✆ **021/794-6561;** www.thebishopscourt.com)—particularly lovely is room no. 3, with its commanding vista (R3,900 double in summer). If you're a keen golfer, check out the swanky, good-value **Steenberg Hotel ★★** (✆ **021/713-2222;** www.steenberghotel.com), on a beautifully restored 17th-century wine farm at the foot of the mountains in Constantia. A worthy contender in this part of the peninsula, biting at the heels of The Cellars-Hohenort, Steenberg has an 18-hole championship golf course and better room decor than Uitsig. Rates start at R3,090 double (less in winter).

It's also worth browsing the guesthouses on **www.thelastword.co.za**, a collection of superluxurious guesthouses concentrated in the southern suburbs, offering chauffeurs and managers who administer advice and arrange tours.

The Cellars-Hohenort ★★★ Sometimes described as The Nellie in Constantia, this gracious historic hotel affords expansive views of the densely forested eastern slopes of Table Mountain. It's a genteel hotel, much smaller and more intimate than the Mount Nelson. An oasis of sorts, it's perfect if you're interested in a mountain retreat. Nearby are excellent trails up the back of Table Mountain, and Kirstenbosch Gardens is very close. Antique furnishings and original artworks adorn the original Hohenort manor house, where the best rooms are. Considerable pluses are the beautifully manicured 3.6-hectare (9-acre) garden and, opening onto it, a fabulously appointed bar-lounge, serving Cape Town's best martinis—*sans* sunset, alas. (False Bay sees sunrises.) The Dove Cote suite has a fireplace and Jacuzzi; the Villa has a fireplace, service kitchen, butler, and private pool.

93 Brommersvlei Rd., Constantia 7800. ✆ **021/794-2137.** Fax 021/794-2149. www.collectionmcgrath.com. 53 units. High season R4,000 double, R5,100–R6,000 luxury double, R7,000–R10,000 suite, R15,000–R17,500 villa; low season R2,250 double, R3,000–R3,500 luxury double, R4,000–R6,000 suite, R10,000–R13,000 villa. Rates include breakfast. AE, DC, MC, V. Children 12 and over only. **Amenities:** 2 restaurants; 2 bars; croquet lawn; full-scale golf green (designed by Gary Player); 2 pools (1 heated); room service; spa; tennis court. *In room:* A/C, TV/DVD, hair dryer, free Wi-Fi.

Constantia Uitsig ★★ A wine estate on the lower slopes of Table Mountain, this aptly named hotel (*uitsig* means "view") has commanding vistas of the surrounding vineyards and jagged mountains. A calm sense of rural peace prevails here, underscored by the rhythms of genuine everyday farm life. Still, it's the three tip-top restaurants that draw the crowds (see "Where to Dine," below), including **La Colombe,** South Africa's Restaurant of the Year in 2009. After dining well, it's wonderful to simply roll back to one of the well-appointed cottage suites spread around the tranquil gardens (each suite has a fireplace and kitchenette). Much of the architecture is Cape Dutch, echoing that of the 17th-century manor house, and the decor tries to reflect this influence. It's nowhere near as elegant as the guestrooms at Cellars-Hohenort, but it's generally more relaxed, with less of a hotel atmosphere. The new spa is an ideal counterpoint to the dining options.

Spaansgemacht River Rd., Constantia 7848. ✆ **021/794-6500.** Fax 021/794-7605. www.constantia-uitsig.com. 16 units. High season R3,250 garden twin, R4,100 Victorian double, R4,700 Manor suite, R6,600–R6,900 family and superior suite; low season from R1,850 double, from R2,200 suite. Children under 12 pay R700 if sharing. Rates include breakfast. AE, DC, MC, V. **Amenities:** 3 restaurants; lounge; babysitting; cricket oval; pool; room service; spa; wine shop and wine tastings. *In room:* A/C, TV, hair dryer, minibar, Wi-Fi (R100 per hr., R150 for 6 hr., R200 for 12 hr.; R350 for 24 hr.).

The Vineyard Hotel & Spa ★★ Value Although the Vineyard is a big, busy hotel (weddings, conferences, and morning business meetings happen here), it's a fine choice for responsible travelers. The hotel supports various community-improvement projects, and there's a strong green policy. The setting is extremely beautiful, too, with a conscious attempt to retain a country atmosphere despite the dense residential surrounds and nearby shopping mall. Besides **Myoga** (see p. 137), one of Cape Town's top restaurants, there's a great **Agsana Spa.** A stroll through the sylvan 15 hectare (6-acre) garden is a great pick-me-up. Given the focus on local rather than foreign guests (you see a cross-spectrum of actual South Africans using the public spaces and hanging out at breakfast), I'd rather stay here than at any of the large hotels at the Waterfront. The rates clarify why *GQ* voted it Best Value for Money Destination.

Colinton Rd., Newlands 7700. ✆ **021/657-4500.** www.vineyard.com. 175 of units. High season R2,530–R2,960 courtyard double, R2,860–R3,350 courtyard deluxe double, R3,410–R3,990 mountain double, R4,200–R4,910 mountain deluxe double, R4,850–R5,670 junior suite double, R6,260–R9,990 suite and garden cottage double; low season R2,420 courtyard double, R2,680 courtyard deluxe double, R2,930 mountain double, R3,850 mountain deluxe double, R4,610 junior suite double, R5,680–R7,060 suite and garden cottage double. Rates include breakfast. AE, DC, MC, V. **Amenities:** 2 restaurants; bar; gym; pool; room service; spa; tennis court; airport transfers. *In room* A/C, TV/DVD, hair dryer, free high-speed Internet.

FALSE BAY & THE SOUTHERN PENINSULA'S COASTAL VILLAGES

Even Capetonians look at this part of Cape Town as a totally different city experience and talk about moving here in the same dreamy tones as they would of moving "to the country." It's very laid-back, probably more suited to the older traveler or someone who's been to Cape Town before and fallen in love with the naval atmosphere and Victorian architecture of Simons Town, or the quaint fishing village atmosphere of Kalk Bay (these are the two best suburbs in which to base yourself). Staying on this side of the mountain, you are well positioned to visit major attractions like the penguins at Boulders and Cape Point (some 10–20 min. away), but it's about 40 minutes from the city center. If Kalk Bay appeals to you (and it really is delightful, with a plethora of dining options and dinky antiques shops, art galleries, and quirky clothing), the best accommodations options for you are in gracious, turn-of-the-20th-century mansions in neighboring St James: **Rodwell House** (reviewed below) and **The St James** ★★ (www.thelastword.co.za; from R3,400 double in summer) are both within walking distance of Kalk Bay's main drag. Based here, you're phenomenally central: within walking distance of Kalk Bay's numerous restaurants, 10 minutes by car from Simons Town, and 20 minutes from Cape Point. The city is a short half-hour hop, and the Constantia wine route starts 15 minutes away.

In Simons Town, families should consider the **British Hotel Apartments** (✆ **021/786-2214;** www.british-hotel.co.za)—lovely, large, old-fashioned self-catering apartments (R1,400–R2,280 for up to four people) in a Victorian-era hotel on the main road

Finds B&B Ubuntu

To experience real *ubuntu* and the warm spirit of African hospitality, you can arrange to spend a night in one of the city's "townships," or black suburbs. Portfolio has approved four guesthouses in Cape Town's townships: In Khayelitsha, there's **Kopanong** (✆ **021/361-2084;** www.kopanong-township.co.za) and **Malebo's B&B** (✆ **083/475-1125;** malebo@webmail.co.za); in Guguletu, it's **Liziwe's Guest House** (www.liziwesguesthouse.com); and **Ma'Neos** is in Langa (✆ **073/146-0370;** maneo@absamail.co.za). Expect to pay around R420 to R800 for a double, and prepare for a display of unbridled hospitality. Even if bedrooms are small and lack most of the amenities of a big hotel, the welcome and personal insight you'll get more than compensates. Ask in advance if your hosts will be willing to take you to their neighborhood restaurant, and get them to recommend the best time to come to catch local musicians in action. For an utterly authentic cultural experience, a night at one of these establishments will be a major talking point of your stay in the Cape.

with sea views. Alternatively, there's **Simons Town Quayside Hotel** (✆ **021/786-3838;** www.relais.co.za; R1,120–R1,350 double, with breakfast), right on the water, with just 26 rooms. This is part of the Simons Town Harbour development, with a number of shops and Bertha's Restaurant below. Most of the rooms are typical bland mass hotel style, but pleasant enough, with French doors opening onto beautiful views of the False Bay coast and Simons Town yacht basin. If you're looking for accommodations right on the beach, take a look at **Whale View Manor** ★ (✆ **021/786-3291;** www.whaleview manor.co.za; from R1,000 double), just above a sandy crescent on the outskirts of Simons Town; each room is heavily styled along thematic lines (the Jardine room is the least showy), but they're all comfortable and cared for. More upmarket and over on the other side of the peninsula, **The Long Beach** ★ (www.thelongbeach.com; R2,500–R5,500 double) is a luxury B&B villa with six shuttered suites leading onto the fabulous expanse of Kommetjie beach. And then, south of Kommetjie, adjacent the Cape Point Nature Reserve, is heart-warming Scarborough—where it's possible, with some luck, to spot the exceptionally shy Cape clawless otter at Schuster's Bay. If you're clever enough to seek out this idyllic village, without street lights but with quick access to a mesmeric stretch of pristine white beach, you'll probably want to stay at the sensational new **Zensa Lodge** (see below).

Rodwell House ★★★ Built—like so many of the gracious mansions on this seaboard—by a Randlord millionaire in the 1930s, Rodwell House is luxury on a grand scale, yet you're invited to kick off your shoes and let your hair down. Start your day with a refreshing dip in the famous St James tidal pool right across the road, and spend time hanging with local surfers or simply watching them from the balcony of this classically proportioned manor house. Your view across the terraced gardens stretches far across False Bay, and at your back are the looming Kalk Bay mountains. Stylish suites all have either sea or mountain views and offer privacy and peace. The house holds a dynamic collection of artworks and an exciting wine cellar: Get expert knowledge on local wines from sommelier-manager, Chris Weston, and sample a few rare vintages. Nearby Kalk Bay is flush with fine restaurants; in-house dining, however, is extraordinary. And you'll love the staff.

Rodwell Rd., St James, 7945. ✆ **021/787-9880.** Fax 021/787-9898. www.rodwellhouse.co.za. 8 units. High season R3,000–R4,000 double, R4,500–R6,500 double suite, R7,000–R10,000 family-size suite; low season R2,000 double, R3,000–R4,000 double suite, R5,5000–R6,000 family-size suite. Children under 12 pay R500 if sharing with 2 adults. Rates include breakfast. MC, V. Children 7 and older only. **Amenities:** Dining room; 2 lounges; airport transfers; art gallery; *pétanque* court; gym; library; massage; pool; free Wi-Fi; wine cellar. *In room:* A/C, TV/DVD (centralized), hair dryer, minibar, free Wi-Fi.

Zensa Lodge ★★★ Value Finds If you're after a restful, shoeless, Zen sort of seaside holiday, this sexy retreat in a dreamy village is heaven sent. A dashing Belgian couple have transformed Scarborough's original homestead into one of the most delightful guesthouses: Small, yet beautifully detailed, the informal, uncluttered lodge consists of two interconnecting houses with an assortment of pretty, all-white bedrooms, each with unique artworks and—like the entire house—designer furniture, including a museumlike chair collection. You won't find lavish luxury or an endless lineup of services. Part of Scarborough's great charm is that it's a genuine backwater, and the lodge is walking distance from one of the world's most pristine beaches. Inside, there are a variety of lounges and kitchen areas with honor bars; outside, a fabulous garden is strung with hammocks where you can laze under the trees or feast on barbecued, freshly dived crayfish beside the pool.

534 Egret St., Scarborough 7975. ✆ 021/780-1166 or 072/814-4441. www.zensalodge.com. 7 units. Double R1,200–R2,000 summer; R1,000 winter. Rates include breakfast. MC, V. Amenities: Dining area and barbecue; honor bar; lounges w/fireplaces; library; massage; pool; free Wi-Fi. In room: CD, hair dryer.

4 WHERE TO DINE

For centuries, Cape Town has set the table for a varied and increasingly discerning public. Visitors have raved about its world-class fare, augmented by historical venues and great views. For harbor settings and Table Mountain views, there's the touristy Waterfront, but you'll see few Capetonians eating there. For uninterrupted ocean views and great sunsets, the Atlantic seaboard is tops—but consider carefully if you're food focused, because the restaurant strip that lines the beachfront is too brash and overheated for my taste, however great it is for people-watching in summer. I'd stick to The Roundhouse (reviewed below) or head back over the Nek to Kloof Street, the road that runs down the slope of Table Mountain into Long Street. There the options are almost limitless, and each one has some kind of charm or quirk, or at least a handful of dashing servers. But whatever you do, enjoy at least one lunch in the Winelands, where you can drink in views of the vineyards and mountains along with a selection of fine Cape wines. If you're setting off for Cape Point, a journey that will take you most of the day, try to time lunch at one of the recommended restaurants in the Constantia area, among the vineyards, or one overlooking the False Bay coast.

Be sure to sample at least one dish inspired by the unique hybrid of Cape cultures. For traditional fare, you can't get more authentic than Biesmiellah in the Bo-Kaap, but there's more to Cape cuisine than *bobotie* and *denningvleis.* Cape Town's scenic setting and regular influx of cosmopolitan visitors has attracted some of the world's top chefs, many of whom are creating an exciting modern Cape cuisine, combining local ingredients with elements of the Portuguese, Dutch, French, German, English, Indian, and Malaysian influences that have made up the city's multicultural past.

THE CITY CENTER & THE CITY BOWL

There is simply not enough space to cover the many superb restaurants concentrated in this area, so in some cases, a simple mention will have to suffice.

Very Expensive

Haiku ★★ ASIAN Initially a side project for the couple who started neighboring **Bukhara** (still Cape Town's top North Indian restaurant), chic Haiku is where Capetonians will try to sidestep the waiting lists in order to impress out-of-town visitors. The concept—which favors dim sum, grilled and wok-fried Chinese, and tapas-style Japanese sushi and grills—has spawned a branch in London (with a more diverse menu). Locally,

Eating In

If you're self-catering, contact **Mr. Delivery** (✆ **021/423-4177** in City Bowl; ✆ **021/439-9916** in Sea Point; ✆ **021/761-0040** in Constantia) and ask them to drop off a menu. Mr. Delivery delivers meals from more than 20 restaurants and takeout joints, as well as groceries, directly to your door.

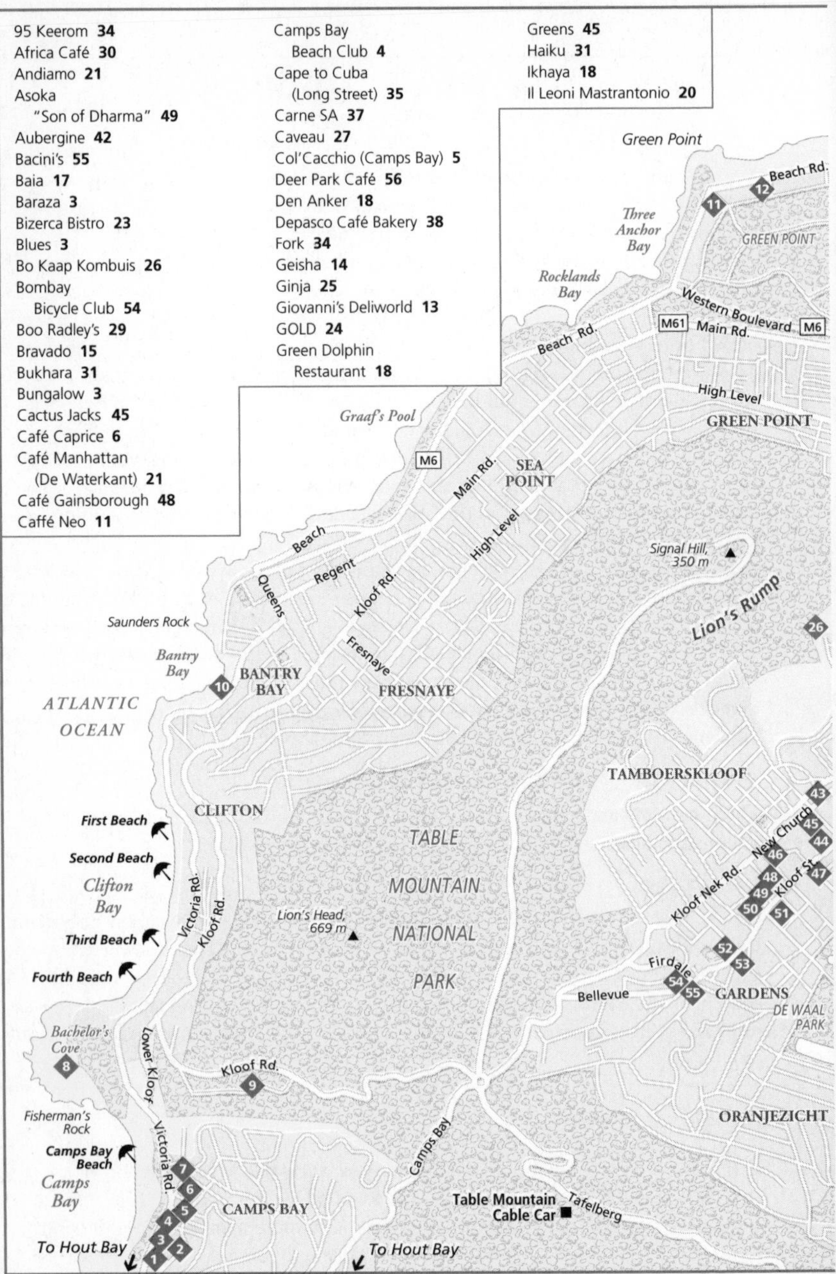
95 Keerom 34
Africa Café 30
Andiamo 21
Asoka "Son of Dharma" 49
Aubergine 42
Bacini's 55
Baia 17
Baraza 3
Bizerca Bistro 23
Blues 3
Bo Kaap Kombuis 26
Bombay Bicycle Club 54
Boo Radley's 29
Bravado 15
Bukhara 31
Bungalow 3
Cactus Jacks 45
Café Caprice 6
Café Manhattan (De Waterkant) 21
Café Gainsborough 48
Caffé Neo 11
Camps Bay Beach Club 4
Cape to Cuba (Long Street) 35
Carne SA 37
Caveau 27
Col'Cacchio (Camps Bay) 5
Deer Park Café 56
Den Anker 18
Depasco Café Bakery 38
Fork 34
Geisha 14
Ginja 25
Giovanni's Deliworld 13
GOLD 24
Green Dolphin Restaurant 18
Greens 45
Haiku 31
Ikhaya 18
Il Leoni Mastrantonio 20
Green Point
Beach Rd.
Three Anchor Bay
GREEN POINT
Rocklands Bay
Western Boulevard
M61
Main Rd.
M6
Beach Rd.
High Level
GREEN POINT
Graaf's Pool
M6
Main Rd.
SEA POINT
Beach
High Level
Regent
Queens
Kloof Rd.
Signal Hill, 350 m
Lion's Rump
Saunders Rock
Bantry Bay
Fresnaye
BANTRY BAY
FRESNAYE
ATLANTIC OCEAN
TAMBOERSKLOOF
CLIFTON
First Beach
Second Beach
Clifton Bay
Third Beach
Fourth Beach
Victoria Rd.
Kloof Rd.
TABLE MOUNTAIN NATIONAL PARK
Lion's Head, 669 m
New Church
Kloof Nek Rd.
Kloof St.
Firdale
Bellevue
GARDENS
DE WAAL PARK
Bachelor's Cove
Lower Kloof
Kloof Rd.
Fisherman's Rock
Camps Bay Beach
Camps Bay
Victoria Rd.
Camps Bay
ORANJEZICHT
CAMPS BAY
Table Mountain Cable Car
Tafelberg
To Hout Bay
To Hout Bay

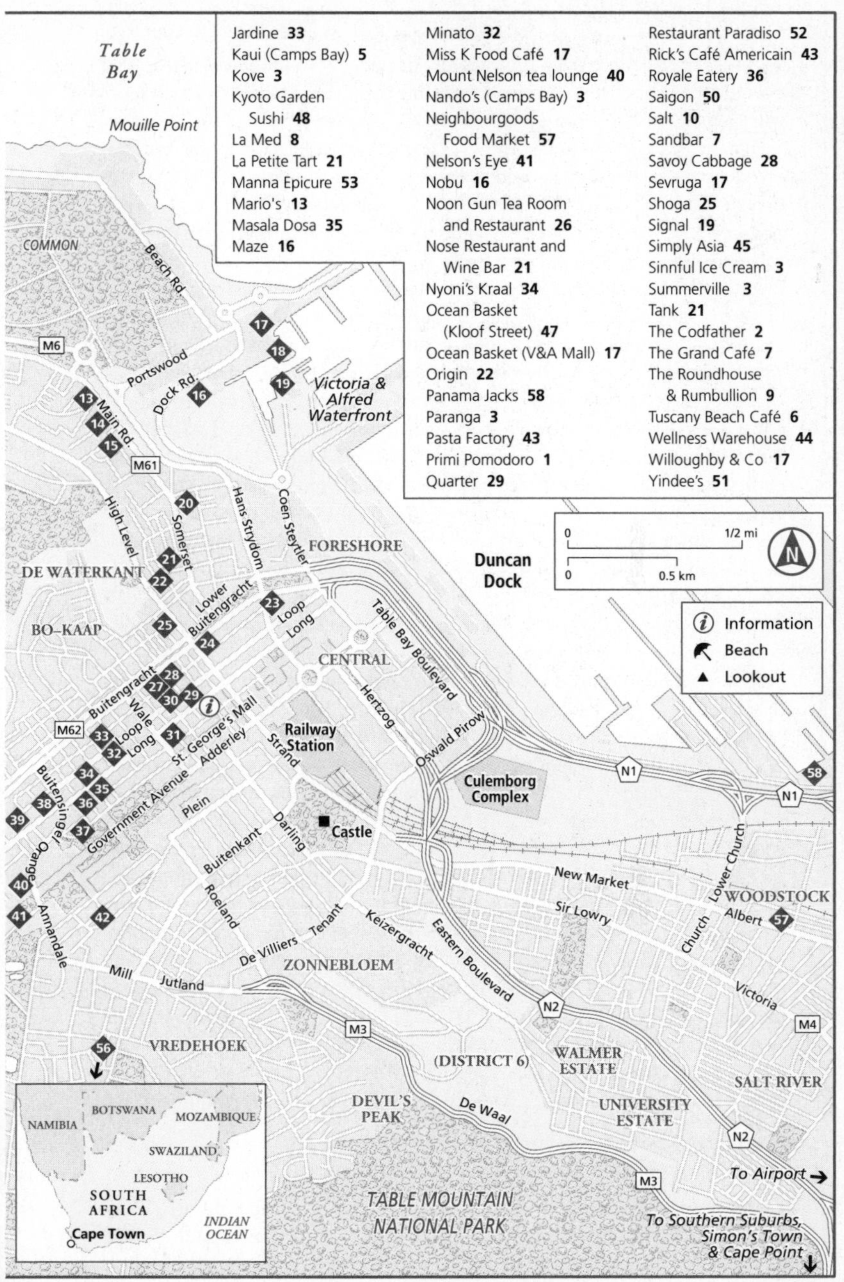
Jardine 33
Kaui (Camps Bay) 5
Kove 3
Kyoto Garden Sushi 48
La Med 8
La Petite Tart 21
Manna Epicure 53
Mario's 13
Masala Dosa 35
Maze 16
Minato 32
Miss K Food Café 17
Mount Nelson tea lounge 40
Nando's (Camps Bay) 3
Neighbourgoods Food Market 57
Nelson's Eye 41
Nobu 16
Noon Gun Tea Room and Restaurant 26
Nose Restaurant and Wine Bar 21
Nyoni's Kraal 34
Ocean Basket (Kloof Street) 47
Ocean Basket (V&A Mall) 17
Origin 22
Panama Jacks 58
Paranga 3
Pasta Factory 43
Primi Pomodoro 1
Quarter 29
Restaurant Paradiso 52
Rick's Café Americain 43
Royale Eatery 36
Saigon 50
Salt 10
Sandbar 7
Savoy Cabbage 28
Sevruga 17
Shoga 25
Signal 19
Simply Asia 45
Sinnful Ice Cream 3
Summerville 3
Tank 21
The Codfather 2
The Grand Café 7
The Roundhouse & Rumbullion 9
Tuscany Beach Café 6
Wellness Warehouse 44
Willoughby & Co 17
Yindee's 51
Table Bay
Mouille Point
COMMON
Beach Rd.
Portswood
Dock Rd.
Main Rd.
Victoria & Alfred Waterfront
Hans Strydom
Coen Steytler
High Level
Somerset
FORESHORE
Duncan Dock
0
1/2 mi
0
0.5 km
DE WATERKANT
Lower Buitengracht
BO-KAAP
Loop
Long
Table Bay Boulevard
CENTRAL
Information
Beach
Lookout
Buitengracht
Wale
Loop
Long
St. George's Mall
Adderley
Strand
Railway Station
Hertzog
Oswald Pirow
Culemborg Complex
Buitensingel
Government Avenue
Plein
Orange
Buitenkant
Darling
Castle
New Market
Lower Church
WOODSTOCK
Sir Lowry
Albert
Roeland
Annandale
Church
De Villiers
Tennant
Keizergracht
Eastern Boulevard
ZONNEBLOEM
Mill
Jutland
Victoria
VREDEHOEK
(DISTRICT 6)
WALMER ESTATE
SALT RIVER
NAMIBIA
BOTSWANA
MOZAMBIQUE
SWAZILAND
LESOTHO
SOUTH AFRICA
Cape Town
INDIAN OCEAN
DEVIL'S PEAK
De Waal
UNIVERSITY ESTATE
To Airport
TABLE MOUNTAIN NATIONAL PARK
To Southern Suburbs, Simon's Town & Cape Point

The Dining Mile

If you like to check out the options before deciding where to settle, take a stroll down Kloof Street. This is the road that runs parallel to Kloof Nek, which takes you up the saddle of the mountain and over into Camps Bay.

Start at the top, where **Bacini's** (✆ **021/423-6668;** ask for a table outside) serves pizzas in a family-oriented atmosphere. Across the road is **The Bombay Bicycle Club** ★★ (✆ **021/423-6805**), a spanking new venue that blends bohemian styling, great buzz, and a pretty eclectic menu. Start with gravalax, calamari and roast veg salad, or brandy-seared chicken livers; work through an assortment of pastas (try the spinach, butternut and ricotta lasagna); and end up with Moroccan-style bobotie, succulent Bombay ribs, or slow-roasted springbok shank. Save room for their legendary chocolate-filled cigars, served with ice-cream. It's all a bit over-the-top, and perhaps too crowded (with a too-lax policy on indoor smoking; do complain if necessary), but it's already one of Cape Town's "in" spots, meaning you'd better book ahead. Next down the hill is **Restaurant Paradiso** Kids, 110 Kloof St. (✆ **021/423-8653**), a sprawling terracotta villa with affordable Alsatian food that will delight those with children in tow. This is an ideal all-day or balmy-evening venue: Grab a table under a tree or umbrella on the terrace outside and peruse the menu, which features plenty of vegetarian options, scrumptious salads, and ultrathin, crispy Alsace-style pizzas, called *flamkuchen* (try one with salmon, cream cheese, and yogurt). Diagonally opposite is the all-white Manna (see below), attracting a more chi-chi crowd, with service by fresh-faced cherubs.

Next up is **Melissa's,** one of Kloof Street's most popular eateries (and one of the best delis in town; ✆ **021/424-5540.** www.melissas.co.za.), and a slew of variable, well-priced local eateries. **Saigon** ★★ (corner of Kloof and Camp; (✆ **021/424-7670**), an elevated venue with great views, specializes in Vietnamese cuisine (don't miss the crystal prawn spring rolls or the karma-free curry with pumpkin and sweet potato). Many locals rate this their ultimate city eatery. **Asoka "Son of Dharma"** (68 Kloof St.; ✆ **021/422-0909**), in the chocolate-colored, open-plan house next door, is a great place to imbibe drinks and light meals. Artfully renovated around a central courtyard and tree, with soothing lighting and groovy music, it's highly recommended for a pre- or postdinner drink. The vibe, fed by Cape Town's happening young crowd (mid-20s and up), is great, but you'll find much better food across the road at **Yindee's,** 22 Camp St. (✆ **021/422-1012**), another one of Cape Town's Thai restaurants.

A little farther down is **Café Gainsborough** ★★, 64 Kloof St. (✆ **021/422-1780**), a casual bistro-type restaurant built around an open-plan kitchen. Get there early (no reservations) to grab a table with a view of Table Mountain, and

it still attracts foodies and society bigwigs, though not so many since the arrival of Nobu and Maze. Multiple kitchens work on different sections of the menu, so dishes arrive in dribs and drabs, making it a bit of a culinary adventure—the cool crowd keeps things interesting as you eat one moment, and then ogle other diners as you wait for your next order the oxtail. Just a little farther down is the unbelievably good value **Ocean Basket** ★, 75 Kloof St. (✆ **021/422-0322**), with a patio-style back garden and decent waitstaff. The fish is superfresh (hardly surprising, considering the volumes they move), perfectly cooked, served in the pan, and seriously cheap.

Numerous takeout joints and casual restaurants pack all of Kloof Street. If you're health conscious, check out the **Wellness Warehouse** up the escalator in the Lifestyle Centre mall. The cafes here are fine, too, but the next good cluster of eateries occurs on Park Road, just off Kloof Street. **Greens** ★ (✆ **021/422-4415**) is one of my favorite pizza destinations, serving ultracrispy thin bases with interesting toppings. The two adjacent ethnic chains, **Cactus Jacks,** for Mexican, and **Simply Asia,** serve surprisingly good (and reasonable) fare. Across the road, **Rick's Café Americain** (✆ **021/424-1100;** www.rickscafe.co.za) is a sociable afternoon hangout where you're likely to end up staying for dinner (start by snacking on the heavenly chili poppers, stuffed with feta and cream cheese). The novel **Pasta Factory** (✆ **021/423-3003**) serves some of the city's best deals on Italian food, and the staff is helpful. If you're a vegetarian, keep heading down Kloof, stopping at the original **Vida e Caffé,** 34 Kloof St. (✆ **021/426-0627**), for a quick espresso and an eyeful of the city's hippest cats quelling their caffeine addiction. (***Note:*** For coffee quality, the top shop in town is Origin, down in De Waterkant; see. p 130). Continuing down into the city, consider stopping for a smoothie at gargantuan **Depasco Café Bakery** (✆ **021/424-7070;** daily 7am–8pm), which faces onto the hectic traffic intersection where Kloof becomes Long Street; diagonally across the road are the **Long Street Baths** (✆ **021/400-3302**), which opened a century ago and still lure locals to Turkish steam rooms and an indoor pool. Cross onto Long Street and you're in a backpacker-filled Soho, coughing up the city's most energetic nightlife (see "Cape Town After Dark," later in this chapter). The energy here is palpable, but ignore the frequent offers of cannabis, known here as "dagga," from casual dealers—it's illegal). Even carnivores should seek out vegetarian **Lola's,** 228 Long St. (✆ **021/423-0885**), where, in their words, "faggy Afro-trash meet to slip-sexy music." The people-watching is unmatched. (***Note:*** Upstairs is **Fiction,** the hottest club in town; see p. 175.) On the other side of the street, continue farther to **Masala Dosa** ★, 167 Long St. (✆ **021/424-6772**), where the decor is tongue-in-cheek Bollywood kitsch; the best way to enjoy the South Indian selection is to get a variety of dishes—a couple of curry-filled *sev puris,* and a mixed *thali* (platter)—to share. The gurana-and-wheatgrass-laced *bang lassi* isn't quite Goa-worthy, but it's a ballsy pick-me-up nonetheless.

dish. Sushi's good, but you'd best sample the eclectic range of Asian tapas that allows you to sample myriad flavors—bank on around three to five per person, and share (and pray someone else is picking up the bill). You'll probably need help choosing from your server, and you may have to put up with a stroppy tone when the place gets packed, but on good nights, things run smoothly enough.

Perusing the Wine List

Look out for these wine estates when you're choosing a selection for your table. They consistently turn out good-to-excellent products at less devastating prices than you'd imagine.

THE STALWARTS Fortunately, in South Africa as in many other wine-producing countries, some wineries consistently turn out good-to-excellent products at reasonable prices, even after sometimes steep restaurant markups. Anything from **Fairview** falls in this category. Ditto **Graham Beck Wines, Jordan Winery, Kanonkop Estate, Neil Ellis Wines, Simonsig Estate, Villiera Wines, Steenberg Vineyards, Hartenberg Estate,** and **Vergelegen,** generally acknowledged as South Africa's leading cellar. Other stalwarts that reliably deliver high quality and value across a spectrum of styles include **Beyerskloof, Glen Carlou, Mulderbosch, Rustenberg, Springfield Estate, Thelema Mountain Vineyards,** and **Boekenhoutskloof** (their alternative label, **Porcupine Ridge,** offers particularly good value). Edgier, but worth a try, is the envelope-pushing **Flagstone Winery.**

BOUTIQUE WINES Definitely worth sampling are the boutique wines of **De Trafford** and **Rudera,** both owned and run by husband-and-wife teams; **Hamilton Russell Vineyards'** minerally pinot noir and chardonnay; **De Toren**'s expressive Bordeaux-style reds; and **Le Riche Wines**' elegant cabernet-based reds. Also impressive are the handcrafted **Sadie Family/Sequillo** wines; the crystalline whites of **Cape Point Vineyards, Paul Cluver Estate,** and relative newcomer **Oak Valley Wines;** the ebullient reds of rising star **Raka;** and the personality-packed offerings of **Tulbagh Mountain Vineyards.**

PICK OF THE PINOTAGE No self-respecting local wine list would be complete without pinotage, South Africa's own variety (now also grown in other countries). The annual Pinotage Top Ten competition regularly elevates such names as **Beyerskloof, Kanonkop, Kaapzicht, Tukulu, DeWaal,** and **L'Avenir.** My own top 10 also would include **Grangehurst, Laibach, Ashbourne** (made

58 Burg St., Cape Town ✆ **021/424-7000.** Haiku entrance is on Church St. ✆ **021/424-7000.** Reservations highly recommended. Dinner main courses R140–R200. Minimum spend policy enforced. AE, DC, MC, V. Mon–Sat noon–3pm; daily 6:30–11pm.

Expensive

On the outskirts of the cobblestoned Bo-Kaap is the much vaunted **Ginja** ★, 121 Castle St. (✆ **021/426-2368**), a fine-dining stalwart that continues to earn rave reviews, but earns just as much criticism. It's a curious venue—a carefully renovated semi-dilapidated double-volume space, but many visitors grumble about such details as the toilets, despite the memorable fusion cuisine. Upstairs is Ginja's smaller, spunkier sister restaurant, **Shoga** ★★ (✆ **021/426-2369**), where prices (and atmosphere) are more relaxed, and there's a simpler menu (also with Asian influence) that doesn't skimp on quality. Start by sharing a selection of tapas, and then ask about the day's fish (the chef's "twist" usually convinces me); also worth noting is the very fine ostrich, woodfired and tandoori-marinated.

by Hamilton Russell Vineyards), **Southern Right,** and **Simonsig.** Pinotage also features, to a lesser or greater extent, as a blend partner in an evolving category called the Cape Blend. At their best, these red wines are distinctive and full of character. A tasting of **Kaapzicht**'s Steytler Vision, **Vriesenhof**'s Enthopio, **Grangehurst**'s Nikela, and **Welgemeend Estate**'s Amadé (a pioneer of this genre) will confirm this.

LOCAL ICONS Regrettably, South Africa cannot yet claim a wine as iconic as a Latour or a cult wine such as Valandraud or Screaming Eagle. Still, we do have a small but growing number of internationally recognized wines, as well as a clutch of new wines that have the potential to attain lasting international repute. For the visiting connoisseur, the established labels to look for certainly include **Kanonkop** Paul Sauer, **Meerlust** Rubicon, and **Vergelegen** Vergelegen (all Bordeaux-style reds), as well as **Klein Constantia**'s ever-superlative nectar, Vin de Constance. Vying for future icon status are a fascinating and varied field, including **Boekenhoutskloof** cabernet sauvignon, **Sadie Family** Columella (shiraz/syrah, mourvèdre) and Palladius (chenin blanc, viognier, chardonnay, grenache blanc); **Engelbrecht & Els** Ernie Els, **Capaia Wines** Capaia, and **Vilafonté** Series C and Series M (all Bordeaux-style reds); **Rudera**'s multi-awarded chenin blanc; **Tokara**'s instant-hit Red (also a Bordeaux blend) and White (wooded sauvignon blanc); and the seductive cabernet sauvignon-shiraz blend **Anwilka,** hailed by U.S. critic Robert Parker as "the finest red wine I have ever had from South Africa." All of the above could face stiff competition from a next generation of wines gestating in cellars such as **L'Ormarins,** revivified by billionaire Johann Rupert, and **Glenelly,** transformed by the redoubtable hands of May-Eliane de Lencquesaing of Bordeaux's Pichon-Longueville-Comtesse de Lalande.

—*Philip van Zyl, editor of the annual award-winning* Platter Guide to Wines, *the most respected guide to wine in South Africa*

I prefer the vibe here and perhaps because there's less pressure to perform (Shoga doesn't see the accolades thrown at Ginja), there's more chance of coming away impressed.

Africa Café ★★ PAN-AFRICAN What started as a humble enterprise in Jason and Portia's Observatory home has turned into a big tourist enterprise in the heart of the city, but it remains a good place to sample traditional dishes from all over Africa. Meals are brought to your table in bowls and you can eat as much as you want. The lineup changes seasonally (check out the menu online), but expect to taste dishes unlike anything back home: Ethiopian black-eyed bean stew; Xhosa *imifino* patties (made with spinach and *mielie* meal); *seswaa,* a game-meat masala curry from Botswana; chicken breasts in Malawian macadamian sauce; and Moroccan *chermoula* (tomato gravy served with crispy fish). They're all served with tapioca flatbread baked with cheese and yogurt, and finished with Kenyan coffee or mint tea. There's a great moment when the floorboards shake as the

Finds Where Are the Africans?

Although recommended, Africa Café, GOLD, and Moyo (near Stellenbosch) cater primarily to well-heeled foreigners, and visitors come away nonplussed at how European the Cape Town scene is. If you'd like to sample South African cuisine along with other Africans (for considerably less money), head for the balcony of the **Pan African Market,** Long Street (✆ **021/426-4478**), for lunch with the traders. Out of town, in Gugulethu (you'll need to arrange reliable transport to get here), is **Mzoli's** (✆ **021/638-1355**), where you choose your meat (vegetarians strongly cautioned), which is then barbecued al fresco. The place rocks on weekends (although it closes at 8pm), drawing local celebs and politicos, but its fame means that it, too, has become a tourist hotspot. Mzoli's neighbors are forcing the establishment to move (again) because of the noise and traffic problems generated by his venue. More touristy, but still a very unique, authentic, more intimate experience is a meal at **Lelapa** ("The Home"; 49 Harlem Ave.; ✆ **021/694-2681**), in Langa, where mother-daughter team Sheila and Monica serve traditional township cuisine to tourists (R105 per head; daily noon–11pm). It's still best to arrange this along with a township tour. In the Hout Bay township of Imizamo Yethu (home to around 14,000 mostly Xhosa-speaking people) is what is probably the most easily accessible township restaurant, **Sibanye** (✆ **082/568-7978;** www.sibanye-restaurant.com; Fri–Sun lunch only). Designed like an artist's take on a typical tin shack, the entrepreneurial project is the brainchild of two friends—one white, one black—and an inspiring tale of pioneering efforts to effect social cohesion. It's the only such eatery you can easily drive to (during the day) without fear of getting lost (check out the directions on their website). The three-course set menu costs just R60 and must be booked by the previous day. Another venue worth considering is **Ikhaya,** serving South African and central African cuisine in the Waterfront's Clock Tower Centre (✆ **021/418-3728**). Almost every element, from staff recruitment to the wine choices, is linked to an empowerment initiative, though you're still likely to find the majority of black faces doing the serving. When it comes to social transformation, Cape Town works to a uniquely African rhythm.

ululating staff dance through the restaurant with unrestrained joy. All in all, it's a very touristy experience (there's even a shop attached), but it's memorable nonetheless. ***Note:*** If you're interested in the cuisine of *southern* Africa, nearby is **Nyoni's Kraal,** 98 Long St. (✆ **021/422-0529**), where you can try delicacies like curried tripe, *amangina* (chicken feet), mopani worms, or a "smiley" (sheep's head). Or head for a real township "restaurant" (see below).

Heritage Sq., 108 Shortmarket St., Cape Town. ✆ **021/422-0221.** www.africacafe.co.za. Reservations essential. Set-price menu R200 per person. AE, DC, MC, V. Mon–Sat 6:30–11pm.

Aubergine ★★★ INTERNATIONAL/MODERN CAPE Harald Bresselschmidt is a genius, able to conjure up new magical combinations month after month, making it hard to decide what to order. There's stiff competition between the printed a la carte menu and choices on the ever-changing tasting list, recited for you by one of Aubergine's polished servers. To make matters worse, you can also mix 'n' match between the two

 (Kids) **High Tea at the Nellie**

High tea at the **Mount Nelson** (© **021/483-1850;** R150; daily 2:30–5:30pm) is a Cape Town institution. As you sink into the comfortable armchairs in the elegant chandeliered room, you'll sink your teeth into savory smoked salmon grissini and cucumber sandwiches, as well as sinful tarts, scones, cakes, and tea-themed confectionary such as forest berry tea–infused Turkish delights, green tea cake, and chamomile lemon loaf, served buffet style. Whether you stay indoors and hum along with the tinkling piano or escape to the verdant shady gardens, it's a wonderful way to experience Mount Nelson's gracious ambience and watch those who frequent the place. The experience is even more fabulous now that the loose-leaf teas are supplied by Origin, my top coffee and tea venue in the country (see p. 130); each blend comes to you DIY style with boiling water and an egg timer.

menus, creating your own degustation program of any three, four, or five courses you prefer. The signature Aubergine soufflé, filled with goat's milk cheese, is among my favorites. Meat-eaters should go for the venison medallions with apple and date confit, or the lamb-and-aubergine baked strudel. Come for a superlative dining experience and the chance to sample what is certainly Cape Town's most complex cuisine (admittedly, a little rich for some palates).

39 Barnet St. © **021/465-4909.** www.aubergine.co.za. Reservations for restaurant essential. Lunch menu R168 (2 courses) or R215 (3 courses). Dinner main courses R80–R140. Dinner degustation menu R225–R275 (3 courses) or R380–R395 with wine; R310–R330 (4 courses) or R455–R485 with wine; R355 (5 courses) or R553 with wine. A la carte main courses average R129. AE, DC, MC, V. Wed–Fri noon–2pm; Mon–Sat 7pm–10pm.

Bizerca Bistro ★★★ (Finds) FRENCH When award-winning French chef Larent Deslandes and his Afrikaans wife, Cyrillia, decided to pack up and move back to South Africa after 17 years in France and Australia, their friends called them *bizerca* (berserk). The name stuck, and their crazy relocation has paid off with instant accolades. Since opening in late 2007, it's already among the country's top 10 restaurants, with a devoted following. Located in the lackluster Foreshore end of the city center, Bizerca's popularity is proof of that the food is sensational. Memorable main courses include Larent's signature braised pig trotters with seared scallops, but he also has a way with homemade sausage, makes a mean Provençal-style stew with Karoo lamb, and does perfectly flambéed veal kidneys and rabbit fricassee. Save space for ginger *tuile millefeuille,* with fresh berries and lemon grass–coconut ice cream. Thankfully, despite the high pedigree of the food, this isn't just another fine-dining establishment aimed at euro-carrying tourists.

15 Anton Anreith Arcade, Jetty St., Foreshore. © **021/418-0001.** Reservations recommended. Main courses R98–R160. MC, V. Mon–Fri noon–3pm; Mon–Sat 6:30–10pm.

Five Flies ★★ FRENCH/INTERNATIONAL In the old Netherlands Club, adjacent Rembrandt House (built 1754), this is one of the classiest venues in the Cape. Chef Ian Bergh serves a menu that combines two to five courses for a set price. Start with venison spring rolls with apple and quince dripping sauce, and then consider coriander-crusted kingklip or grilled springbok loin with "fritz." Finish with crème brûlée, infused with vanilla pods.

14–16 Keerom St., Cape Town. ✆ **021/424-4442.** www.fiveflies.co.za. Reservations essential. 2 courses R170–R185; 3 courses R235; 4 courses R275; 5 courses R325. AE, DC, MC, V. Mon–Fri noon–3pm; daily 7–11pm.

Gold ★★ PAN-AFRICAN It's the food, more than the venue or entertainment, that's memorable here. Adapted from traditional African and Cape Malay recipes, the range of dishes, with a slightly globalized influence, gives a good feel for what the people of Africa eat; and vibrant servers, who describe the origins of each dish and explain how it's been adapted, give an even better sense of how ravishing Africa can be. To start, you'll get Mozambique-inspired peri-peri prawns; they contrast with subtle-flavored maize nut fritters, an adaptation of an ancient tribal snack called *mukhomo,* served with an apple and mint yogurt raita. One African staple that you'll learn to appreciate is *pap* and spinach (*umfino* in Zulu, or *morogo* in Setswana), and you'll finish with pumpkin fritters, dusted with cinnamon, or freshly skewered fruit. Between courses, you'll be entertained by dancers, actors brandishing tall Mali puppets, and stirring voices belting out traditional, sometimes kitschy African tunes.

Gold of Africa Museum, 96 Strand St., Cape Town. ✆ **021/421-4653.** www.goldrestaurant.co.za. Reservations highly recommended. Dinner R220. AE, DC, MC, V. Mon–Sat 10am–11pm; Sun 6:30–11pm.

Jardine ★★★ CONTEMPORARY FUSION Rated among the world's top 100 restaurants, this is a labor of love for chef George Jardine, for whom the accolades don't stop pouring in. The only way to find out what all the hype is about is to reserve a table and ask for ringside view of the Scotsman and his team making magic in their unexpectedly tiny kitchen. Jardine doesn't like his style to be labeled, but I think CNN got it right when they termed it "funky Euro–South African fusion." If the a la carte descriptions make it difficult to decide, go for the chef's menu—simple-sounding, delectable combos such as "beetroot, tongue, apple, sorrel," "yellowtail and thyme" and "blesbok and butternut." Otherwise, zoom in on the daily-changing options—aged beef stuffed with bone marrow; or seared blesbok filet with roast figs, pumpkin seeds, and foie gras sauce. ***Note:*** This is now also a local hotspot for weekday takeaways, when delicious sandwiches are served from the street-level cafe-style/bakery window; there's almost always a line at lunchtime.

185 Bree St., Cape Town. ✆ **021/424-5640.** Reservations essential. 2 courses R240, 3 courses R280. Set-price chef's menu R400 (must be ordered by the entire table), optional wine pairing R350. AE, MC, V. Tues–Sat 7–10pm, last orders 9pm.

Nelson's Eye ★ (Finds) STEAKHOUSE This vintage steakhouse doesn't promise fine dining, good looks, or commendable service, but ask local steak lovers where they get their fix, and they'll point you here. It's old-fashioned, and the prize for the steeper- than-expected prices is breathtakingly large meat cuts that remind you that South Africans are, first and foremost, carnivores. On the side are passable chips and vegetables. Service can be slow and slack, but do as the others have done for years as they wait their turn at this always-packed venue—order more wine. It's worth it.

9 Hoff St., Gardens. ✆ **021/423-2601.** R115–R160. AE, DC, MC, V. Tues–Fri 12:30–3pm; Mon–Sun 6–10:30pm.

Savoy Cabbage ★★★ INTERNATIONAL This stylish restaurant celebrates the trend toward "sophisticated peasant food." If you enjoy viscera such as sweetbreads, you'll find this one of the country's best choices. Chef Peter Pankhurst changes the menu daily to make the best of what's available, but if you haven't yet tried Karoo lamb, pray that he's included his extraordinary three-way variation—roasted rack, braised shoulder, and grilled Merguez sausage, all served with a braised fennel and red wine sauce. If you want to venture beyond the usual suspects, there's loin of warthog (fennel dusted and brined); wildebeest crusted with spice; or a delicious pork chop with smoked filet served with sautéed apple and cider jus. The classic venue remains fairly unchanged since I first dined here in 1998—a narrow double-volume L-shape with old brick walls exposed and juxtaposed with glass-and-steel fittings. But the consistently wonderful food continues to garner fresh accolades, including travel guru Andrew Harper's prestigious Restaurant of the Year Award for 2009.

101 Hout St., Heritage Sq. ✆ **021/424-2626.** www.savoycabbage.co.za. Reservations essential. Main courses R95–R165. AE, DC, MC, V. Mon–Fri noon–2:30pm; Mon–Sat 7–10:30pm.

Moderate

A favorite place to kick-start the evening (or end the day) is **Caveau** ★ (✆ **021/422-1367**), a Cape Town haunt on Heritage Square, within strolling distance of Long Street. It's a wonderful, warm, informal venue that spills out onto the street, with excellent wines by the glass to accompany a range of tapas and more filling meals. It's a hugely popular after-hours watering hole, and you'll struggle to get a table here after 5pm. Wonderful tapas plates are also in abundance at **Fork** ★★, 84 Long St. (✆ **021/424-6334**). Kick off with puff pastry stuffed with oven-roasted peppers, asparagus, and caprino; slices of tuna on cannellini beans; or slightly overdone but extremely tender lamb cutlets.

Carne SA ★★ (Value) STEAKHOUSE "When you work with good ingredients, it's impossible to mess up," says Giorgio Nava. To prove his point, he uses only organically reared Romagnola beef and Dorper lamb grown on his very own Karoo farm at this meat-centric venture—directly across the road from his popular Italian place, 95 Keerom. Nava runs both kitchens simultaneously and checks on both firsthand to be sure his customers are satisfied. How's that for hands-on? Besides insisting on the best-quality meat, game, and bird, Carne celebrates offal (the "fifth cut," according to Italians). The menu minimizes waste by expanding on the often-limited possibilities of sweetbreads, tripe, liver, kidneys, and tongue. Everything (including the stripped-down neoindustrial decor, with Starck ghost chairs) is focused on the unfettered flavor of the meat.

70 Keerom St., Cape Town. ✆ 021/424-3460. www.carne-sa.com. Reservations recommended. Main courses R70–R145. Mon–Sat 6:30–10:30pm.

Manna Epicure ★★ (Value) TAPAS/SALADS/BAKERY A wonderful all-white venue at the top of bustling Kloof Street (aka "the Dining Mile"; see above), Manna attracts an interesting and glamorous post-30 crowd—all with big sunglasses and groomed hair—and the food is just as interesting. It's probably my favorite casual lunchtime haunt. Service can be slow, but with so much to look at, who cares? Dishes worth looking for are the roasted aubergine with toasted pecan nuts and gorgonzola; the ostrich burger with pear, granadilla, and onion chutney; and a simple, zestful homemade linguine with steamed asparagus and herb and lemon butter. An array of delicious cocktails and fresh breads complete the picture; the latter are served with every meal and can be bought from the in-house bakery—if they're not sold out.

151 Kloof St. ✆ **021/426-2413.** Main courses R40–R120. AE, MC, V. Tues–Sun 8am–7pm.

95 Keerom ★★★ (Value) ITALIAN When this urbane restaurant opened in 2005, it was proof that the Cape Town dining scene had come of age. Not only because it feels good to walk through, but because the food is simple and straightforward, service is excellent, and owner Giorgio doesn't charge exorbitant prices just because he can. It's affordable glam, and Capetonians love it. The food here is also wonderfully pared down, free of the rich, sauce-heavy dishes favored by many top chefs. ("Rich sauces are what keep you awake at night," says Giorgio). The menu is extensive, but I recommend starting with one of the carpaccio choices and follow with the tuna, seared slightly "New York–style," with capers, olives, and tomatoes. If fish isn't fresh off his boat, Giorgio doesn't serve it. For meat-eaters, the slow-cooked springbok is a definite hit; a good vegetarian choice is the butternut ravioli, tossed in browned sage butter.

95 Keerom St., City Center. ✆ **021/422-0765.** www.95keerom.com. Reservations essential. Main courses R45–R130. AE, DC, MC, V. Thurs–Fri noon–2pm; Mon–Sat 7–10:30pm.

Inexpensive

&Union ★ Finds, 110 Bree St. (✆ **021/422-2770**), is a slick-casual "beer and charcuterie" venue beneath the church near Heritage Square from the entrepreneurs who started the feisty Vida e Caffé brand (now marching into London; www.caffe.co.za). Place your order at the counter (the cured meat platters and tapas are perfect accompaniment to the high-end artisanal German-style beers) and park yourself at one of the benches beneath the trees outside (or settle for a bar stool inside).

Also right in the heart of the city, and this time from Bruce Robertson, the culinary wizard who created much-hype with The Showroom (now closed), is **Quarter** ★★ (✆ **021/424-1175**), which is a bit like a slightly upmarket street food outlet specializing in a truly South African favorite called Bunny Chow. Any South African will probably be able to tell you how late night bunny chow meals—a quarter loaf of bread stuffed with any variety of fillings (in my day it was always chicken curry, but fillings can be quirkier)—rescued them from the munchies and staved off a hard-earned hangover. Bruce's slick, chic, sexy little eatery lets you sit at communal tables and jive with the locals. Definitely one worth trying, if only to say you've had something truly South African; it's next to the entrance of the Grand Daddy Hotel, at 44 Long St., and open weekdays 10am to 10pm and Saturday 4pm to 4am.

If you like the idea of pizza but could do without the cheese, head over to **Limoncello** ★★, 8 Breda St. (✆ **021/461-5100**), a tiny restaurant in Gardens frequented by locals who love the ultrathin, crispy pizza base (tomato free), topped with smoked salmon (or aubergine), lemon juice, and fresh rocket (arugula). Equally good is the tender baby squid, flash-fried with chili and garlic. Their risotto of the day is usually spot on.

Biesmiellah ★ Value CAPE MALAY A number of places offer Cape Malay fare, but none is quite as authentic as Biesmiellah. Run by two generations of the Osman family in the historic Malay quarter of Bo-Kaap, Biesmiellah has been serving the local Cape Muslim community and, increasingly, tourists for 2 decades. Start with a selection of *samoosas* or *daltjies* (chili bites), and then consider the much-recommended *denningvleis*—this sweet-sour lamb stew flavored with tamarind is so tender it practically melts in the mouth. Or try the *penang* curry, with beef, bay leaves and spices, served on rice that's boiled, then fried in olive oil, then flavored with nuts, raisins, and almonds. As a Muslim establishment, it prohibits alcohol on the premises. Order a refreshing *falooda* instead. Biesmiellah also offers takeout—try the *roti* (flatbread) stuffed with cubed mutton. ***Note:*** Another Cape Malay restaurant worth trying is the **Bo Kaap Kombuis** (Kitchen) ★, 7 August St. (✆ **021/422-5446;** Tues–Sat 8:30am–late and Sun 8am–3pm). It serves a more sophisticated menu and has great city views via wraparound glass walls (as opposed to Biesmiellah's ultra-ordinary boxed-in interior). It has been called the Bo-Kaap's first high-end restaurant, but that doesn't mean it isn't family run and infused with an appealing

Moments Boom with a View

One of Cape Town's more idiosyncratic habits is the sounding of the Noon Gun, a tradition that has informed Capetonians of their lunch break since 1806. The South African Navy fires the Signal Hill cannon, letting out a familiar rumble across the city, 6 days a week, and it's quite a thrill to experience it at close quarters. You can drive up there by following the road signs—or walk to the Gun by heading up steep Longmarket Street via the Bo-Kaap. The best place to wait for the boom (or recuperate afterward) is with a cup of tea and slice of traditional *melktert* (milk tart) at the **Noon Gun Tea Room and Restaurant** ★, 273 Longmarket St. (✆ **021/424-0529;** open Mon–Sat 10am–8pm). The tearoom affords magnificent views of the city and mountain, and serves authentic Cape Malay fare. One word: *babotie.*

sense of community. Besides the satisfying curries and Cape Malay stews, it's worth arriving in time to see the city bathed in a sunset glow, and then lit up in glittering lights.

2 Upper Wale St., Bo-Kaap. ✆ **021/423-0850.** www.biesmiellah.co.za. Reservations recommended. Main courses R46–R96; seafood platter R120. MC, V. Mon–Sat noon–10pm.

Royale Eatery ★★ Value GOURMET BURGERS A better burger you won't find anywhere—be it the lamb with mint (referred to as the "baaa baaa" burger); the fish-of-the-day burger with mango, Peppadew, and coriander salsa; the "big bird" (ostrich with beetroot relish); or the "fat bastard" (double everything). Even vegetarians will be happy: Try the "googamooly"—made from soya, lentils, sunflower seeds, and chickpeas, topped with guacamole, feta, and hummus. It's hip and trendy, and if you're lucky, you'll be served by a demure Gwyneth Paltrow look-alike. Upstairs, Royale Kitchen is a little more grown-up (no under-23s), but still with the same feisty, artful atmosphere. Royale milkshakes are second to none (ask for avocado, if available)—and not to be taken lightly. Pizzas, however, are terrible.

273 Long St., Cape Town ✆ **021/422-4536.** Main courses R42–R76. AE, DC, MC, V. Mon–Sat noon–11:30pm.

THE WATERFRONT & DOCKLANDS

There's quality at the Waterfront, sure, but nothing so fine that I make a regular pilgrimage, with the exception of Willoughby. Foodies have been queuing up to sample the goods at Gordon Ramsey's first African restaurant, **maze** ★, just off the lobby of the new One&Only hotel (✆ **021/431-5222**). Ramsey is no stranger to South Africa (he regularly runs the Comrades Marathon in Kwazulu-Natal). During his time here, he's prepared a menu inspired largely by local cultural influences and produce—roast rack of Karoo lamb, Cape Malay–style mussels, Mozambican prawns, springbok filet, ostrich, and even fish *frikkadels* (spiced meatballs) are featured. There's a fairly even split between steak (broiler grilled at 650°) and seafood; and by all accounts, a focus on simple, stripped-back cuisine, rather than overfussy, complex combinations satisfy. Imported beer-fed Aussie wagyu costs dearly. The place just opened in April 2009, so the verdict is out, but reports so far have been less than glowing, and feedback on the service quite scathing. Only time will tell if this celebrity import will rise above being another pricey hotel eatery.

If you'd rather be at the Waterfront than inside one of its hotels, then first among the recommended choices is **Den Anker** ★★★, Pierhead (✆ **021/419-0249;** ask for a map at one of the information desks in Victoria Wharf). It's worth the trip, if only to wolf down a pot of the freshest West Coast mussels, accompanied by Belgian beer, in a casual atmosphere with great harbor and mountain views. Rabbit, simmered in Belgian beer and served with applesauce and potato croquettes, is another specialty; and the steaks are out of this world.

In the Victoria Wharf shopping center proper is **Willoughby & Co.** ★★★ (✆ **021/418-6116**), arguably the best place in town for fresh, unpretentious seafood dishes, and a consistent favorite in the top sushi polls. Certainly, it doesn't get any fresher (it's the best fish market in town, too). That said, the venue is very much mall-like; those after a formal dining experience (with celebrity credentials) will probably prefer **Nobu** (✆ **021/431-5222**), within the worldly confines of the One&Only.

If eating in a mall (or hotel) in the most beautiful city in the world depresses you, head upstairs to the terrace at **Baia** ★★ (✆ **021/421-0935**), for linen tablecloths and picture-perfect harbor and mountain views; the seafood's excellent, too, but caters predominantly to a foreign market, as most rand-wielding locals think it's overpriced. Down below, with some open-air tables just a few meters from the harbor, **Sevruga** (✆ **021/421-5134**) is a relative newcomer (and sister establishment to Greenpoint's very popular Beluga). The menu is a mix of fresh sushi and meat offerings, such as slow-braised lamb. The servers' condescending attitude and inefficiency are offputting.

For a more refined atmosphere and competent service, try **Signal** ★★ (✆ **021/410-7100**). It's the Cape Grace's entirely reinvented venue for Malay-inspired dishes, prepared by local chef Malika van Reenen and served in a refined setting. Malika personally recommends the Malay curried chicken soup to start—it's mildly spicy and flavored with coconut, crispy onions, bean sprouts, and fresh coriander—followed by her very good cumin-crusted springbok loin, served with potato samoosas, sautéed spinach, and beetroot chutney.

Finally, no review of Cape Town's restaurants would be complete without a mention of **Panama Jacks** ★, Quay 500 (✆ **021/448-1080;** www.panamajacks.net), a celebrated dockside restaurant that predates the Waterfront development. It has no view or elegance, but the simple seafood dishes—steamed, grilled, or flambéed—are superb. Fresh crayfish [lobster] is the specialty. Located in the old working section of the harbor, it's beyond walking distance from the Waterfront, and it's very difficult to find. You're best off using a taxi; otherwise, head for the Royal Cape Yacht Club and take the second road left.

DE WATERKANT

This tiny enclave within Green Point has always enjoyed a reputation as a Cape Town nightlife hot spot and center of the gay scene, but in the past few years, De Waterkant has also developed into the city's most exciting shopping precinct (see "Shopping," later in this chapter). But one needs sustenance to plunder, and the restaurants and eateries in and around the recently expanded Cape Quarter don't disappoint. Start with the best coffee (or tea) in the country at **Origin** ★★★, 28 Hudson St. (✆ **021/421-1000;** www.originroasting.co.za), where the buzz is as heady as the brilliant blends served by an intensely knowledgeable crew. Tea lovers should head directly for the glass-enclosed room at the back—the fishbowl-like venue is said to heighten the experience. For dining choices, head around the central cobbled courtyard, where four fine options have tables spilling out around the central fountain: **Tank** ★★ (✆ **021/419-0007;** www.the-tank.co.za), with its oversize fish tank and massive ego, is great for sushi (they're very proud of their Japanese sushi master chef), Asian fusion, and people-watching—*if* you can get a table outside. Indoors, the acoustics can be a problem, but head right to the back room and grab the banquette seats with views of the city skyline. Equally popular but more casual is **Andiamo** (✆ **021/421-3687**), which has a small but good Italian menu and a testosterone-strong staff pumping up the action. Food is good, but when it's packed, tables are a little too close together and the vibe is frenetic. Inside the actual deli-shop, you'll find the greatest selection of edible items this side of the equator. It's a good place to stock up for a picnic or gifts for foodie friends. Across the tiny piazza is the **Nose Restaurant and Wine Bar** (✆ **021/425-2200**), which serves superb wines by the glass, with personal write-ups by the owner to ease the selection process. Food is perfectly serviceable, too, and the atmosphere is a great deal more laid-back than at Andiamo, which you can watch buzzing from your table. If it's a delicious light meal you're after, the pick of the bunch is **La Petite Tart** ★★★, on the "outside" of the Quarter, on Dixon Street (✆ **021/425-9077**). Owned and run by Jessica, a French model who has successfully re-created her own little bit of the Left Bank here, it has the longest tea list in town and the most wonderful tart selection (apricot and almond is a big favorite); if you're in the mood for savory, try a traditional croque-monsieur or quiche (such as the blue cheese, butternut, and beetroot option). These are fresh-baked daily, and you can virtually follow your nose to find this tiny restaurant.

GREEN POINT, MOUILLE POINT & SEA POINT

Even before Green Point's pre-2010 transformation, these bustling, adjoining neighborhoods experienced an explosion in growth. New restaurants and retail outlets opened monthly along their respective main roads, while the modern apartment blocks that rise above them were being built or renovated faster than for the restaurants could handle. Green Point has a number of fashionable and good-value restaurants. Besides Anatoli, reviewed below, you should check out **Il Leoni Mastrantonio** ★★★, 22 Coburn St., on the corner of Prestwich (✆ **021/421-0071**), is hailed by some as their top Italian pick. Moving farther away from the city, Mediterranean **Manos,** 39 Main Rd. (✆ **021/434-1090**), is a reliable choice with better value than most (although who can tell what Green Point's soccer-inspired upgrade will do). Inside the Cape Royale Hotel is **Geisha** ★★, 47 Main Rd. (✆ **021/439-0533**), known for its quality Asian fusion and

Finds Become a Main Road Local

Long before the arrival of Green Point Stadium and the attendant influx of cash, a couple of stalwarts have pulled devoted locals. **Giovanni's Deliworld** (✆ **021/434-6893**)—owned and run by the Esposito brothers—is a traditional Italian deli that for 2 decades has served serious espressos and a good selection of home-cooked meals. Nearby, unchanged since 1971, is **Mario's,** 89 Main Rd. (✆ **021/439-6644**), started by a pair of Italian immigrants, the Marzagallis, during the days when Green Point was near-deserted. Mario passed away back in 1986, but widow Pina is still satisfying regulars with her legendary artichokes, authentic homemade pasta, bacon-wrapped quail, and traditional veal. Pina is now assisted by daughter Marilena and taciturn son Marco-Giovanni, and her recipes still come from her ancient *La Grande Cucina* cookbook. She'll gladly take requests, too, so chat to her before you order. Mario's is closed Mondays.

Moments **Chocolate Fever**

For a hand-on approach to chocolate addiction, sign up for one of Cape Town's chocolate workshops, offered by the Lindt-endorsed **Chocolate Studio** in Green Point, at The Foundry, Cardiff Street (© **021/417-5080;** www.chocolatestudio.co.za). Cape Town–born chef Alfred Henry puts you through the paces as you learn to make luscious chocolates, decadent chocolatey desserts, Lindt cakes, truffles, and more, including ice cream and sorbet. There are multiday courses, but a 3-hour evening workshop costs R500. Early booking is essential.

tapas. Altogether more relaxed dining (plus Cape Town's prettiest cupcakes) is what you get at **Miss K Food Café,** Winston Place, 65 Main Rd. (© **021/439-9559**), where Kirtsen Zschokke is especially revered for her satisfying breakfasts (served till 1pm) and a great lunchtime buffet spread, perfect for an unhurried day on the town.

But if the idea of working up an appetite with a fresh sea breeze appeals, Mouille Point's Beach Road is the place to be. If you're looking for something really casual (and inexpensive), just grab a table on the sea-facing deck at **Caffé Neo** ★, 129 Beach Rd. (© **021/433-0849**). With its bizarre mix of modern decor peppered with family photographs, this is a daytime venue run by a charming Greek family. Wi-Fi is free, hence the many people sitting with their laptops and the central timber table. Also near the Cape Royale is brand new **Bravado** ★ (© **021/433 1496**), which is the relocated and expanded version of Bravo, an old favorite Mouille Point haunt (which has now been claimed by the hotel in which its located), with dishy owners, a vibey serving staff, plenty of Stella Artois on tap, and delicious square, thin-crust pizzas. If there's one place that's injecting the Green Point dining strip with a bit of upbeat fun, this is it.

Wakame ★★ SUSHI/ASIAN FUSION Wakame is a swish, clean-lined place with a sea view and airy modern interior where Japanese chefs skillfully slice, dice, wrap, and roll. Ceiling-length glass doors fold back entirely to reveal a postcard-perfect view of the ships sailing in and out of the nearby harbor. There's sushi and sashimi, but I'd go for hot offerings; the menu's superstar is seared tea-smoked tuna served on wasabi mash, or sesame-crusted tuna served with slivers of deep-fried sweet potato. Start the evening upstairs at Cape Town's sexiest cocktail venue, **Wafu** (open all afternoon), preferably with a bottle of bubbly, and watch as a cosmopolitan crowd schmoozes on the lounge-style wooden deck (see "Cape Town After Dark," below).

Corner of Beach Rd. and Surrey Place, Mouille Point. © **021/433-2377.** www.wakame.co.za. Dinner reservations recommended. Main courses R75–R135. AE, DC, MC, V. Mon–Thurs noon–3pm and 6–10:30pm; Fri–Sat noon–3:30pm and 6–11pm; Sun noon–3:30pm and 6–10pm.

ATLANTIC SEABOARD

The Grand Café ★★ **Moments** This is the most romantic of the water-facing options along Camps Bay's increasingly bling-oriented sunset strip. It's also currently the only semismart dining option with any sort of individual personality. This has more to do with the venue's theatrical Parisian cafe good looks—bohemian chic accented by casual collectibles, antiques, casual *tromp l'oeil* effects, and fab pieces of vintage furniture—than with the menu offerings. A bar and snack selection includes mussels with chips and a very expensive toasted crayfish mayonnaise sandwich. Keep it simple: Ask about the grilled line fish of the day, or order the steak, which is superb. The crayfish linguine is superb but pricey. Watch the sun sink from the gallery-style upstairs terrace table (it's worth reserving an upstairs table) and see how the fairy lights and flickering candles transform this place into a dreamy cocoon—often filled with an L.A.-meets–Eastern Europe type of crowd.

35 Victoria Rd., Camps Bay. ✆ **021/438-2332.** www.thegrand.co.za. Dinner reservations highly recommended. Main courses R80–R145, prawns and crayfish R200–R240, mixed seafood platter for 2 R695. AE, MC, V. Tues–Sun 12:30–11pm.

The Roundhouse & Rumbullion ★★★ **Moments** This is the most romantic dining experience in Cape Town: an 18th-century hunting lodge with extraordinary views and an enchanting location, hidden away in a little-known woodland version of Camps Bay. Lunch at Rumbullion and dinner at the Roundhouse make for two very distinctive dining experiences. At Rumbullion's al fresco bistro-style lunch, start with roasted bone marrow on toast, follow through with matured Hinkley's sirloin, and then spoil yourself with what may be the most decadent-tasting brownie on Earth (pastry chef Vanessa Quellec is some kind of chocolate sorceress). You'll fall victim to the charms of gracious, witty servers, and a laid-back ambience that is miles away from the touristy maelstrom on the beachfront down below. After lunch, book a table at the Roundhouse for dinner, and return for an extraordinary tasting menu turned out by chef P. J. Vadas (who worked under Gordon Ramsay in New York) and some of the country's best wines and world's finest spirits. Choices are sublime—foie gras ballotine with plums, candied popcorn, and toasted brioche; smoked trout risotto; roasted eland filet; slow-braised pork belly—each dish perfectly prepared and served with gusto. If only they'd open for breakfast!

The Glen on Kloof Rd., Camps Bay. ✆ **021/438-4347.** www.theroundhouserestaurant.com. Reservations essential. Roundhouse: 3 courses R330, R480 with wine, R780 with reserve wine; 4 courses R440, R640 with wine, R1,040 with reserve wine; 5 courses R550, R800 with wine, R1,300 with reserve wine. Rumbullion: Main courses R85–R120. AE, MC, V. Roundhouse: Tues–Sun 6:30–9pm, but open for drinks 5pm–late. Rumbullion: Tues–Sun noon–3pm.

Salt ★ **Moments** SOUTH AFRICAN FUSION After revamping the bar and restaurant with floor-to-ceiling windows in 2006, the Ambassador once again became *the* place to meet for cocktails and enjoy excellent food by well-known local chef Peter Goffe-Wood. Perched over boulders into which the Atlantic Ocean crashes with rhythmic regularity, Salt is optimally located, but the food doesn't rate with the glorious setting, though it is unpretentious and served in large portions. Service is polished, and the winelist is extraordinarily good (and available by the glass). Arrive presunset, sip a glass at the bar, and toast the scene.

Ambassador Hotel, 34 Victoria Rd., Bantry Bay. ✆ **021/439-7258.** www.ambassador.co.za. Reservations essential for dinner. Main courses R85–R130. AE, DC, MC, V. Daily 12:30–3pm, 6:30–10pm. Tapas menu 3–10pm.

SOUTHERN SUBURBS & THE CONSTANTIA WINE ROUTE

The Constantia wine estate, **Uitsig,** is fortunate enough to house three fabulous dining options: The first, Constantia Uitsig, is reviewed in full below because the setting is the best, in an old Cape Dutch farm. But in 2009, all the accolades went to ultrapricey sister establishment **La Colombe** ★★★ (✆ **021/794-2390**), when chef Luke Dale Roberts took the *Eat Out* Chef of the Year Award. Roberts's seven-course tasting menu is a once-in-a-lifetime experience for most (especially at R800 per head, including wine; a la carte

The Sunset Strip: Wining, Dining & Posing in Camps Bay

When the summer sun starts its slow descent into the ocean, most Capetonians feel compelled to head over to the Atlantic seaboard to soak up the last of its pink rays and watch the kaleidoscope unfold. Toasting nature's miracle with fast-flowing refreshment is usually part of the deal, and Victoria Road—the street that hugs Camps Bay's palm-fringed beachfront—is where you'll find a swath of tightly packed refreshment stations, all posing as luxury restaurants, and all boasting good-to-glorious views of the ocean, white-sand beach, and some of the most ravishing examples of humanity to grace the insides of a bikini or pair of board shorts.

Warning: In summer, the atmosphere on this strip gets frenzied, and any genuine desire to service individuals' needs or produce noteworthy food takes a backseat to turning tables as fast as possible (Blues, Grand Café, and Sandbar being notable exceptions); if you're looking for a more laid-back seaside alternative, where views are not tainted by brash or low-level aggressive staff, head for **The Roundhouse** (high above the sea; reviewed below) or **Wakame,** on Mouille Point's Beach Road (despite the name, there is no real beach), or escape altogether to one of the sleepy village-size towns in the southern part of the peninsula.

Starting on the northern edge of Camps Bay beach is **La Med,** part of the Glen Country Club, clearly signposted off Victoria (✆ **021/438-5600**). It's a rather tacky indoor/outdoor bar in a sublime location, with lawns that run into the ocean. The summer buzz (with excellent music, especially on Sun nights—in 2008–09, world-class electro-jazz duo Goldfish turned this into a throbbing mini-Ibiza every week through the season) and sheer size (it packs in well over 500) can attract a rowdy, quite young crowd—but it's definitely an iconic Cape Town experience (sunglasses optional). For slightly more staid drinking partners, stay south, down Victoria Road, in Camps Bay proper. First up is the revamped **Sandbar** (✆ **021/438-8336**): One of Camps Bay's oldest sidewalk bistros, this is right on the edge of the strip, so it's usually more laid-back and friendly and still serves a mean daiquiri. Great salads, too, but people don't come here for the food. Next door, the flavor of the moment hereabouts is **The Grand Café** (reviewed below), while two other long-running stalwarts of this strip are nearby: **Tuscany Beach Café** (✆ **021/438-1213**) and **Café Caprice** (✆ **021/438-8315**), both of which also recently underwent plastic surgery (emphasis on *plastic*). You're welcome to enjoy just a drink at these venues while you (pretend to) peruse the menu. If you don't like what's on offer, simply move along. **Vida e Caffé** is where I get my morning fix of caffeine, but the sloppy table arrangement is hardly conducive to people-watching. Unless it's for a fruitful smoothie, avoid next-door **Kaui,** where food has become hideously bland. If you have children, try to bag a window table at **Col'Cacchio** (✆ **021/438-2171**) upstairs.

Farther along the main drag, beyond the sports field, for the price of a steak elsewhere, you can snack on a sandwich at **Camps Bay Beach Club,** tucked beside the entrance to The Bay hotel, like some neon-lit modernist cave.

Even better views are had from the elevated options housed farther south, in the mall-like Promenade Centre beyond The Bay hotel. Here you'll find the greatest concentration of eateries on the Atlantic seaboard, though few can be recommended for their food, and outlandish rent means venues are extremely schizophrenic. First up is well-dressed **Paranga** (✆ **021/438-0404**), on the first floor, with great cushy banquette seating along the walls (book terrace seats for the best views); food is nothing to write home about and quite pricey, but for watching the beach scene (sunglasses essential), the venue is pretty unbeatable. Above is **Summerville** (✆ **021/438-3174**), which relies on its view to draw customers. Sit outside, and it can be a great place to crack open an icy Heineken and imbibe the landscape—soon you might be hungry enough to attempt one of their salads. Alongside is **Blues** (✆ **021/438-2040**), also with great views and, having just celebrated its 22nd birthday, the most old-fashioned (read: grownup) establishment on the Promenade. You often need to book a dinner table days before, proof that with a sublime location, you can get away with inconsistent cuisine resulting from an ever-changing lineup of chefs. Adjacent is **Baraza** (✆ **021/438-1758**), finished in muted earth tones and furnished with comfortable sofas, with counters that run the length of the windows to frame the elevated views of the sunset strip; you can order from the Blues menu here, and there's often cool DJ-spun music. Below Blues and Baraza, there's a massive lineup of glitzy venues purpose-made for a see-and-be-seen crowd that's typically primped up after a day on the beach: **Kove** and **Bungalow** are both from the man (Paul Kovensky) who brought us Paranga—and it shows. They're elegant and *a la mode,* but I wouldn't want to eat in either. The other eateries in this neck of the (concrete) woods are too sad to contemplate, although the *peri-peri* chicken at **Nando's** is a celebrated South African export (and served here in a licensed restaurant). If you want a taste to remember Camps Bay by, though, cruise into the back part of the Promenade and seek out **Sinnfull** ★★★, Britta Sinn's heaven-sent ice cream emporium (✆ **021/438-3541**). There's no view or space to pose here, but you'll be back.

Farther along the strip, you'll find **Primi Pomodoro** (✆ **021/438-2923**); like its sister establishment in the Waterfront, this casual eatery offers quick-fix Italian dining known primarily for its fast-as-lightening service—an extensive menu of pizzas and pastas has become increasingly variable, quality wise, over the years, but low prices and filling portions help it maintain a strong following.

Finally, no round-up of Camps Bay's generally mediocre dining scene would be complete without mention of **The Codfather** ★, 37 The Drive (✆ **021/438-0782**), which may not be as near the water as the modish, well-dressed joints already discussed. Despite the tattiness of the exterior, it will satisfy any craving for fresh seafood. You choose your fresh fish from a formidable display that's barely off the boat, and it's up to you to ask about the price (besides the color-coded conveyor-belt sushi, it's sold by weight). There's no guarantee that the chef won't botch the job, but this is one place Capetonians generally rave about.

Tips Sushi? The Best Raw Deals in Town

If you love your sushi, welcome. Cape Town is heaving with sushi joints. Most locals vote **Willoughby's** ★★★ (in the V&A Mall; see "Where to Dine, Waterfront"; open daily) as the top choice for the freshest fish and most delectable combos—don't leave without ordering a portion of rainbow rolls. But if you don't like dining in a mall, **Kyoto Garden Sushi** ★★★, 11 Lower Kloofnek Rd. (✆ **021/422-2001**), is the place to go. Tucked away next to a florist at the intersection at the bottom of Kloofnek Road, interiors are styled with near-surgical precision. Proactively owner-managed by an American import named Scott, who takes his Japanese food and cocktails very seriously, Kyoto serves ultrafresh, classic sushi (try sashimi made with local specialty fish, like kabeljou), as well as delicious cooked noodle broths and delicate vegetable and seafood sautées. Addicted to detail, Scott imports real wasabi root (rather than the ready-mix paste) and doesn't skimp on finery. He also offers an exacting bar service, including shots of *shochu*. At the opposite end of this *a la mode* sushi joint is **Minato** ★★, a no-nonsense windowless venue, and the only one filled with Japanese customers. It's hidden away (4 Buiten St., off Long St.), and you have to ring the doorbell to gain access (heaven forbid you've neglected to book, turned up late, or arrived with the wrong number of guests). Arrive early so you have time to choose thoughtfully from the elaborate menu, which goes well beyond the obvious fare. The service, with only two servers, is about as charming as the setting, with bright lights and plastic chairs. But the food is great, at the right price (✆ **021/423-4712;** reservations essential; Mon–Fri noon–2pm, Mon–Sat 6:30–10:30pm).

main courses cost R120–R260). The menu includes his extremely popular fricassee of quail and langoustine, and smoked tomato gazpacho with Alaskan crab. But you should consider his duo of lamb (lamb shouler with two lamb kidneys, plus rack of Karoo lamb) and the decadent springbok with foie gras. We highly recommend it, though we've recently received a scathing report about dire service from an irate reader (unforgivable, given the prices charged here). You can avoid any such controversy by trying the casual fare for friendlier prices at Constantia Uitsig's **River Café** (✆ **021/794-3010**), where a fine cafe-style menu is complemented by items such as Karoo-lamb burger. Breakfasts are tops, too.

Resting less overtly on its laurels, though, and increasingly making waves in Cape Town's culinary ocean, is Steenberg Hotel's delectable **Catharina's** ★★★ (✆ **021/713-2222**), where chef Garth Almazan's contemporary take on South African cuisine satisfies a regular bevy of rich local housewives but also manages to lure many city slickers from the center of Cape Town. Lunches, accompanied by amazing views, are lighter, but you miss out on the chance to sample utterly memorable combinations, like warthog loin served with a grilled tiger prawn, butternut ginger tortellini, avocado salsa, oyster mushrooms, poached quail egg, and honey star anise jus. Also recommended is the springbok loin, prepared differently according to the time of day.

The biggest tourism drawing card in this area—with a gracious manor house museum and lovely grounds—is **Groot Constantia.** The relaxed **Jonkershuis Restaurant** ★

(✆ **021/794-6255**), also in a historic building, is another wonderful venue. On a fine day, it's worth grabbing a table under the oaks; bookings are essential.

Another Constantia option worth considering, with a lovely garden setting but a great deal more formal, is **The Greenhouse** ★★ (✆ **021/794-2137**), at the Cellars-Hohenort hotel, where chef Peter Tempelhoff offers a seasonal menu, using herbs from the hotel garden; he does especially notable things with duck. On the same property is the **Cape Malay Kitchen,** now with stiff competition from Signal, at the Waterfront's Cape Grace. If you want an exceptional, innovative menu in a lively, fun environment, book your place at **Myoga** (no dress code, dashing service), reviewed below.

Buitenverwachting ★★★ INTERNATIONAL/MODERN CAPE Like Uitsig, Buitenverwachting (meaning "Above Expectation") is situated on one of the historic Constantia wine farms, with lovely views and an exceptional reputation. It's perhaps more formal and more expensive, but the food is also better—it wows almost everyone who eats here. A rising star, Austrian chef Edgar Osojnik combines local ingredients with international techniques and flavors to turn out inspired dishes, such as pumpkin-encrusted ostrich, served with its own tartare; beef crusted in marrow; grilled springbok loin flavored with hanepoot chutney; and quail saltimbocca. No need to make choices, however—there's a great tasting menu, with as many courses as you can handle.

Klein Constantia Rd., Constantia. ✆ **021/794-3522.** www.buitenverwachting.co.za. Reservations essential. Main courses R150–R355. AE, DC, MC, V. Tues–Fri noon–1:30pm; Tues–Sat 7–8:30pm.

Constantia Uitsig ★★★ **Moments** INTERNATIONAL/ITALIAN If you're here for lunch, Uitsig (literally, "Views") combines perfect mountain and vineyard vistas with a predominantly Italian menu. Chef Clayton Bell is filling the shoes of the late-maestro, Frank Swainston, and still serves the inspired dishes that have long been favorites here, some with his unique spin. His paper-thin fish carpaccio comes with a ginger-seaweed dressing, the grilled springbok loin with a caramelized honey and lemon sauce remains a confirmed favorite, and the legendary *trippa alla Florentina* (a tomato-based tripe with carrots, celery, and onions) is, well, legendary. Finish up with the most sinful dessert ever: Marquise au Chocolat. Sadly, consistency has become a bit of a problem, and some dishes are simply not up to par; but the servers give excellent and frank advice, and the overall experience is still tops.

Spaanschemat River Rd. ✆ **021/794-4480.** www.uitsig.co.za. Reservations essential. Main courses R75–R150; prawns R220. AE, DC, MC, V. Daily 12:30–2pm and 7:30–9pm, but open till late. Closed for 1 month in winter.

Myoga ★★★ INNOVATIVE/FUSION If you like highly experimental food, Myoga is hard to beat. Take, for example, the sashimi scallops, partially deconstructed; served with soft-shell crab and both tempura and smoked lobster; and finished with squid ink (for visual effect as well as taste). It's a labor of love and hard work by restaurateur Mike Bassett. He just started Myoga ("Ginger Blossom" in Japanese) in late 2007, hot on the trail of his successful cityside ventures, Ginja and Shoga, and it quickly shot onto Conde Naste's Hot List of Top 100 New Restaurants in the World. The staff is fabulously talented, including a sommelier who's keen to talk intimately about his clever wine list (with bottles from R95) and ready to recommend a decent mixed drink for teetotalers. And the appreciative, mostly local clientele makes for a *lekker* (great) buzz. For so many reasons, I love it here.

Vineyard Hotel, Colinton Rd., Newlands. ✆ **021/657-4545.** Reservations highly recommended. R115 1-course meal; R199 2-course meal; R245 3-course meal; R265 4-course meal. AE, DC, MC, V. Mon–Sat 11:30am–3pm year-round, 7–10:30pm summer, 6:30–10:30pm winter.

Family-Friendly Restaurants

Most city restaurants have limited space, but **Deer Park Café** ★★★ (✆ **021/462-6311**) opens onto a shady children's park in Vredehoek, Cape Town, open for breakfast, lunch, and early dinners. Great cappuccinos, too. At 75 Kloof St., **Ocean Basket** (✆ **021/422-0322**) has a lovely terraced back garden and kiddy portions of perfectly cooked fish in minipans. Farther up the street, outdoor seating and a wooden jungle gym at **Restaurant Paradiso,** 110 Kloof St. (✆ **021/423-8653**), make it a popular, good-value venue for parents. If the kids are clamoring for pizzas, check out nearby **Bacini's** (✆ **021/423-6668**), or head into Camps Bay to **Col'Cacchio** (✆ **021/438-2171**)—ask for a bit of dough to make 'n' bake in the pizza oven. Moving south, **Jonkershuis,** on the Groot Constantia Estate (see above), doesn't have a play area, but it's a fine child-friendly venue, with a children's menu and an outdoor area in which to run around. Over in Hout Bay, at **Dunes Bar & Restaurant** (✆ **021/790-1876**), you can relax at a table with your feet in the sand and watch Junior play on the swings and climbing frame—just don't forget the sun block. If you're heading toward Cape Point, consider stopping at the Noordhoek Farm Village for brunch at the totally unpretentious **Café Roux** (✆ **021/789-2538;** www.caferoux.co.za; open daily 8am–5pm). It's extremely child friendly, with a supervised, fenced off playground and special kiddies menu, as well as ultrahealthful items such as salads made with organic quinoa and adzuki beans. In the Winelands, Franschhoek's **Bread & Wine** (see p. 196) has plenty of open space for kids to roam. Stellenbosch's **Bodega** (see p. 188) on the Dornier wine farm has a large play area where children can go crazy throughout the afternoon.

THE SOUTHERN PENINSULA: TRAVELING TO CAPE POINT

There's a string of memorable, often unpretentious and sociable places in which to eat on a tour of the southern peninsula. Below are some of the best. Note that you may not always find the same kind of snappy service and cosmopolitan crowd that you might expect in the city, but a mellow vibe best suits this corner of the world.

FROM HOUT BAY TO CAPE POINT The family-run restaurant at the **Chapman's Peak Hotel,** Chapman's Peak Drive, at the base of the Peak on the Hout Bay side (✆ **021/790-1036**), is famous for its fresh calamari and fish—served still sizzling in the pan with fat fries—and wide veranda with views of the small fishing harbor. It's a jolly, unpretentious place that long predates Cape Town's burgeoning restaurant scene, yet it still pulls in the punters from all over the city. On the southern side of Chapman's Peak Drive, the place that has everyone talking is **The Foodbarn** ★★★ (✆ **021/789-1390**), in Noordhoek Farm Village. It is co-owned by Franck Dangereux, the celebrated French chef who, after putting La Colombe on the map (it was Restaurant of Year six times under his watch; see p. 133), opted for a more laid-back lifestyle (and cuisine style) and relocated here in 2007. The food is simple and exquisitely presented, ingredients are predominantly organic, and the ambience, after a recent shabby chic makeover by

Finds Fish & Chips with Real Cape Locals

Diagonally across from Harbour House is **Kalky's ★** (© **021/788-1726**), the most unpretentious restaurant in Cape Town, attracting a diverse cross-section—from flat-capped and tattooed roughnecks with foul-mouthed wives to Constantia types twirling their wine glasses and tittering at the large ladies who dispense plates with a great running commentary on patrons. There's a substantial seafood menu, but everyone is here for the succulent fish and chips—superbly battered, absurdly large—for a paltry R31 per portion. Order at the till and wait for your number to be screamed out. There's no corkage if you bring your own, so pick up some chilled vino or beer beforehand.

Franck's wife, is superb. It's comfortable and family friendly, and Franck is succeeding in his dream to bring fine dining to the people.

KALK BAY You'll find the most atmospheric False Bay restaurants in the charming and increasingly trendy fishing village of Kalk Bay. In the small fishing harbor, where fishermen still hawk their hand-caught fish directly to the public and surrounding restaurants, three options are right on the water. For looks and views of the crashing waves, the best venue is the breezy **Harbour House ★** (© **021/788-4133**)—book a table by the window, and you can sit with the ocean crashing on the rocks just below. Linefish are listed in chalk on the board and scratched off as they disappear down the hungry maws of patrons. Downstairs, **Live Bait** (© **021/788-5755**) is a more casual affair, with mosaic tables, mismatched chairs, and a similarly dramatic full frontal assault of waves. Prepare for worryingly casual service, though, as you wait, and wait, and wait for your sushi, fresh mussels, or beer-battered line fish. If you can make do without the in-your-face seafront theater, consider **F SH ★★** (pronounced "fish"), at The Quays on Main Road (© **021/788-1869**); choose a few cuts of different types of fish, and they're weighed, priced, and grilled either Cajun style or with the homemade spice mix. The sushi is straight out of False Bay, too.

If you have a yen for something besides seafood, **Olympia Cafe & Deli ★★★**, Main Road, diagonally opposite the turnoff to the harbor (© **021/788-6396**), is an excellent deli-restaurant serving light meals to the hippies and trendy bohemians who venture over to this side of the mountain to join the locals who've made this their haunt of choice. The casual dining is almost as sexy as the crowd, but you may need to fight off competition for a table. Beware, too, that house rules strictly forbid "smoking, split bills, self discipline, bull shit . . . ever. . . ." so you're advised to keep it real. Also rather sexy is **Cape to Cuba,** Main Road (© **021/788-1566**), a fabulous place to pop into for a cocktail—eclectically decorated with mismatched chairs, numerous chandeliers, and Catholic kitsch on rich, saturated-color walls. It's extremely comfortable, and the mojitos are drop-dead delicious; pity the food isn't up to snuff. For real home-style dining, go to **Theresa's ★★**, at the corner of Harbour Road and Boye's Drive (© **021/788-8051**), for the absolute bottom line in old-fashioned grub, prepared with love and care in a take-it-or-leave-it atmosphere.

SIMONS TOWN I love **The Meeting Place** (© **021/786-5678**), located on the main road, a casual cafe-deli-bistro with fresh, delicious produce and light meals. Upstairs is where you'll head at night, where the menu gets more serious; I've never had a bad meal

Picnic Fare

Table Mountain is one big garden, and its "tabletop" makes a great picnic venue, as do the slopes—particularly at Kirstenbosch Gardens, where sunset concerts are held every Sunday from December to March. You can put together a picnic at the self-service restaurant near the main entrance, but the food is mass produced. For a real feast, take your pick at **Melissa's,** Kloof Street (✆ **021/424-5540;** or see www.melissas.co.za for the closest outlet to you); **Giovanni's,** 103 Main Rd., Green Point (✆ **021/434-6893**); or **Andiamo,** at Cape Quarter, De Waterkant (✆ **021/421-3687**). The latter two are Italian delis with mouthwatering prepared meals and sandwiches. To picnic on one of Cape Point's deserted beaches, check out the fare at Kalk Bay's **Olympia Café** (✆ **021/788-6396**) on the way there. Or order a picnic hamper from the **Picnic Company,** to be delivered to your door (✆ **021/706-8470;** www.picnics.co.za; R55–R165 per person, depending on your choices, plus R100 delivery to city center).

Great Winelands options are **Le Pique Nique** (✆ **021/870-4274**), at the gorgeous Boschendal Estate (near Franschhoek), where you can buy a hamper filled with local delicacies and spread out on their oak-shaded lawns. Advance booking is essential (see p. 190). An even more beautiful wine estate is **Vergelegen,** in Somerset West, where picnicking at the tables in the camphor forest is a sublime way to spend a summer afternoon; advance booking is advisable (✆ **021/847-1346;** R150 per head; noon–2pm Nov–Apr). Back nearer the city, **Jonkershuis,** at Groot Constantia, offers a similar service (✆ **021/794-6255**).

at either venue (female shoppers should pop into Mauve, a great little clothing boutique just around the corner). On the way out of Simons Town, heading for Cape Point, you'll see the **Black Marlin,** Main Road (✆ **021/786-1621**), a venue that enjoys one of the best sea views in the Cape, making it a popular tourist spot (arrive early to avoid the tour buses); seafood is the specialty, so order the line fish—and ask for all three butters (lemon, garlic, and chili) on the side.

5 EXPLORING CAPE TOWN

From ascending its famous flat-topped mountain to indulging in the sybaritic pleasures of the Winelands, Cape Town has much to offer sightseers. You could cover the top attractions in 3 days, but to really get a sense of how much the city and surrounds have to offer, you'll need to stay at least a week.

TABLE MOUNTAIN NATIONAL PARK

Nowhere else in the world does a wilderness with such startling biodiversity survive within a dense metropolis; a city housing some 3½ million people effectively surrounds a national park, clinging to a mountainous spine that stretches southward from Table Mountain's Signal Hill massif to the jagged edges of Cape Point at the tip of the Peninsula. Hardly surprising, then, that the city's best attractions are encompassed by Table Mountain National Park (formerly Cape Peninsula National Park): world-famous **Table Mountain,** also known as Hoerikwaggo (Mountain of the Sea); the dramatic **Cape**

Fun Facts **A Devil of a Wind**

Legend has it that the "tablecloth," the white cloud that tumbles over Table Mountain, is the work of retired pirate Van Hunks, who liked nothing more than to climb Devil's Peak and smoke his pipe while overlooking Cape Town. One day the devil, not happy that someone was puffing on his patch, challenged him to a smoking contest. Needless to say, the competition continues to rage unabated, particularly in the summer months. The downside of this magnificent spectacle is that hurricane-force winds will simultaneously whip around Devil's Peak and rip into the city at speeds of up to 150kmph (93mph). The Cape Doctor, as the southeaster is often called, is said to clear the city of pollution, germs, and litter; but most just wish Van Hunks would give it up and stop infuriating the devil. For sanity's sake, head for the Atlantic seaboard, where the most protected beach is Clifton. Alternatively, escape to the Winelands, or visit in March and April, when the wind usually dies away completely.

Point, most southwesterly tip of Africa; the unparalleled **Kirstenbosch Botanical Gardens,** showcase for the region's ancient and incredibly varied floral kingdom; and **Boulders,** home to a colony of rare African penguins. Ascending Table Mountain warrants half a day, as does a visit to Kirstenbosch—though you could include it as part of a (rather rushed) daylong peninsula driving tour, which encompasses Boulders and Cape Point; for details, see "Exploring Farther Afield: Southern Suburbs & Constantia," later in this chapter.

Table Mountain ★★★ This huge, time-sculpted slab of shale, sandstone, and granite that rose from the ocean some 250 million years ago is Cape Town's most instantly recognizable feature. A candidate for selection as one of the New 7 Wonders of Nature (www.n7w.com), the flat-topped mountain dominates the landscape, climate, and development of the city at its feet, and provides Cape Town with a 6,000-hectare (14,820-acre) wilderness at its center.

The best view of the mountain is from Table Bay (another good reason to take a sunset cruise; see p. 91), from where you can get some idea of the relative size of the mountain—while the city shrinks to nothing, the "Mountain of the Sea" is visible some 150km (93 miles) from shore. Other views of the mountain are no less beautiful, particularly from the wooded eastern flanks of **Constantiaberg,** which greet the sun every morning, and the bare buttresses of a series of peaks named the **Twelve Apostles,** kissed by its last rays. The mountain is thought to be the most climbed peak in the world, with some 350 paths to the summit and more plant varieties (some 1,470 species) than the entire British Isles.

You can ascend the mountain on foot or via cable car and, once there, spend a few hours or an entire day exploring. The narrow table is 3km (1¾ miles) long and 1,086m (3,562 ft.) high. **Maclear's Beacon** is its highest point, and really suitable only for serious hikers. From Maclear's, it's another hour's trek to the upper cable station and restaurant, which are on the mountain's western edge, from where you can view the Twelve Apostles towering over Camps Bay. (Walk eastward and you'll have a view of the southern suburbs.) The back table, with its forests, *fynbos* (shrublike vegetation), and the reservoirs that supply Cape Town with its water, is a wonderful place to hike, but much of it is off-limits.

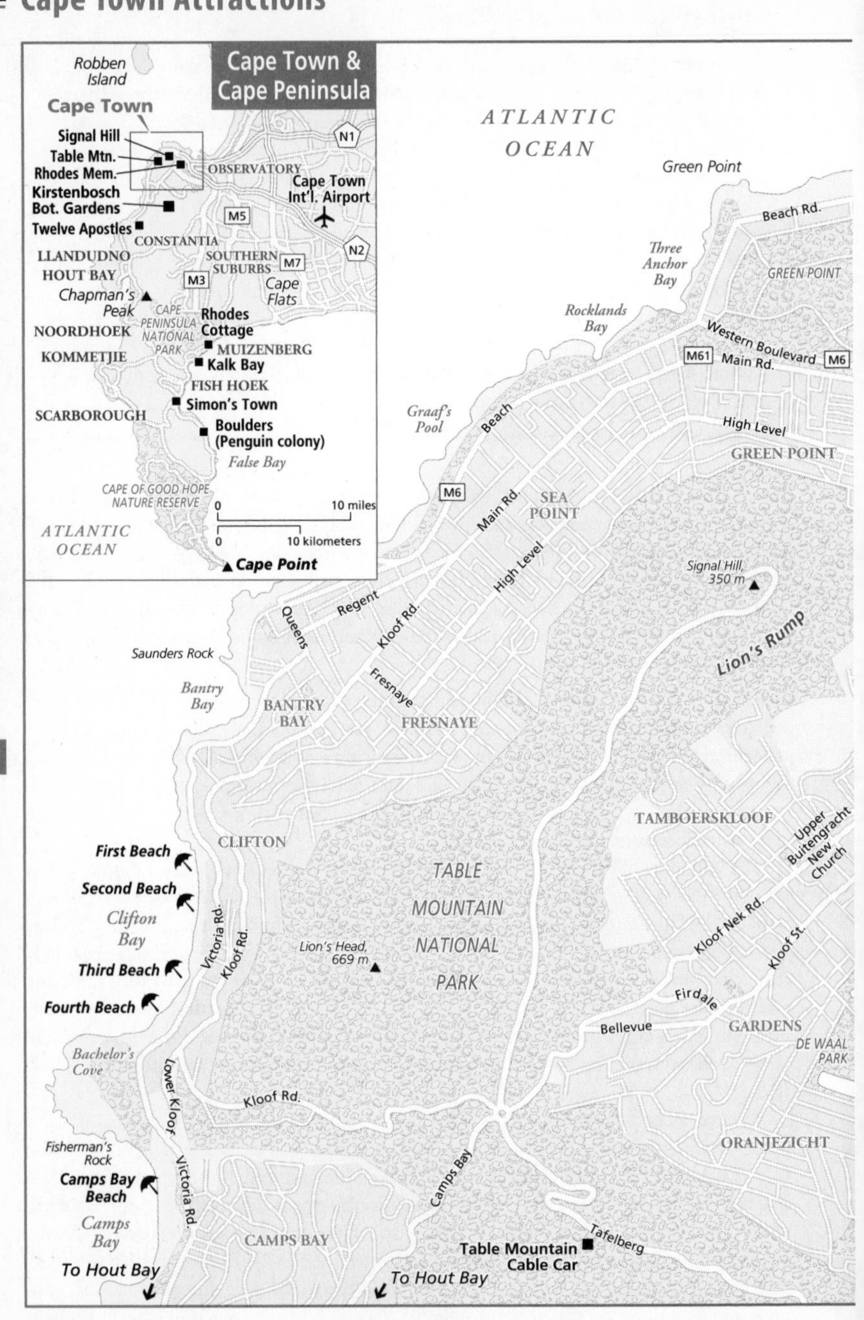
Cape Town & Cape Peninsula
Robben Island
Cape Town
Signal Hill
Table Mtn.
Rhodes Mem.
Kirstenbosch Bot. Gardens
Twelve Apostles
CONSTANTIA
LLANDUDNO
HOUT BAY
Chapman's Peak
CAPE PENINSULA NATIONAL PARK
NOORDHOEK
KOMMETJIE
SCARBOROUGH
OBSERVATORY
Cape Town Int'l. Airport
SOUTHERN SUBURBS
Cape Flats
Rhodes Cottage
MUIZENBERG
Kalk Bay
FISH HOEK
Simon's Town
Boulders (Penguin colony)
False Bay
CAPE OF GOOD HOPE NATURE RESERVE
ATLANTIC OCEAN
Cape Point
0 10 miles
0 10 kilometers
ATLANTIC OCEAN
Green Point
Beach Rd.
Three Anchor Bay
GREEN POINT
Rocklands Bay
Western Boulevard
Main Rd.
High Level
GREEN POINT
Graaf's Pool
Beach
Main Rd.
SEA POINT
High Level
Signal Hill, 350 m
Lion's Rump
Regent
Queens
Kloof Rd.
Fresnaye
Saunders Rock
Bantry Bay
BANTRY BAY
FRESNAYE
TAMBOERSKLOOF
Upper Buitengracht
New Church
CLIFTON
First Beach
Second Beach
Clifton Bay
Third Beach
Fourth Beach
Victoria Rd.
Kloof Rd.
TABLE MOUNTAIN NATIONAL PARK
Lion's Head, 669 m
Kloof Nek Rd.
Kloof St.
Firdale
Bellevue
GARDENS
DE WAAL PARK
Bachelor's Cove
Lower Kloof
Kloof Rd.
Fisherman's Rock
Camps Bay Beach
Camps Bay
Victoria Rd.
Camps Bay
ORANJEZICHT
CAMPS BAY
Tafelberg
Table Mountain Cable Car
To Hout Bay
To Hout Bay

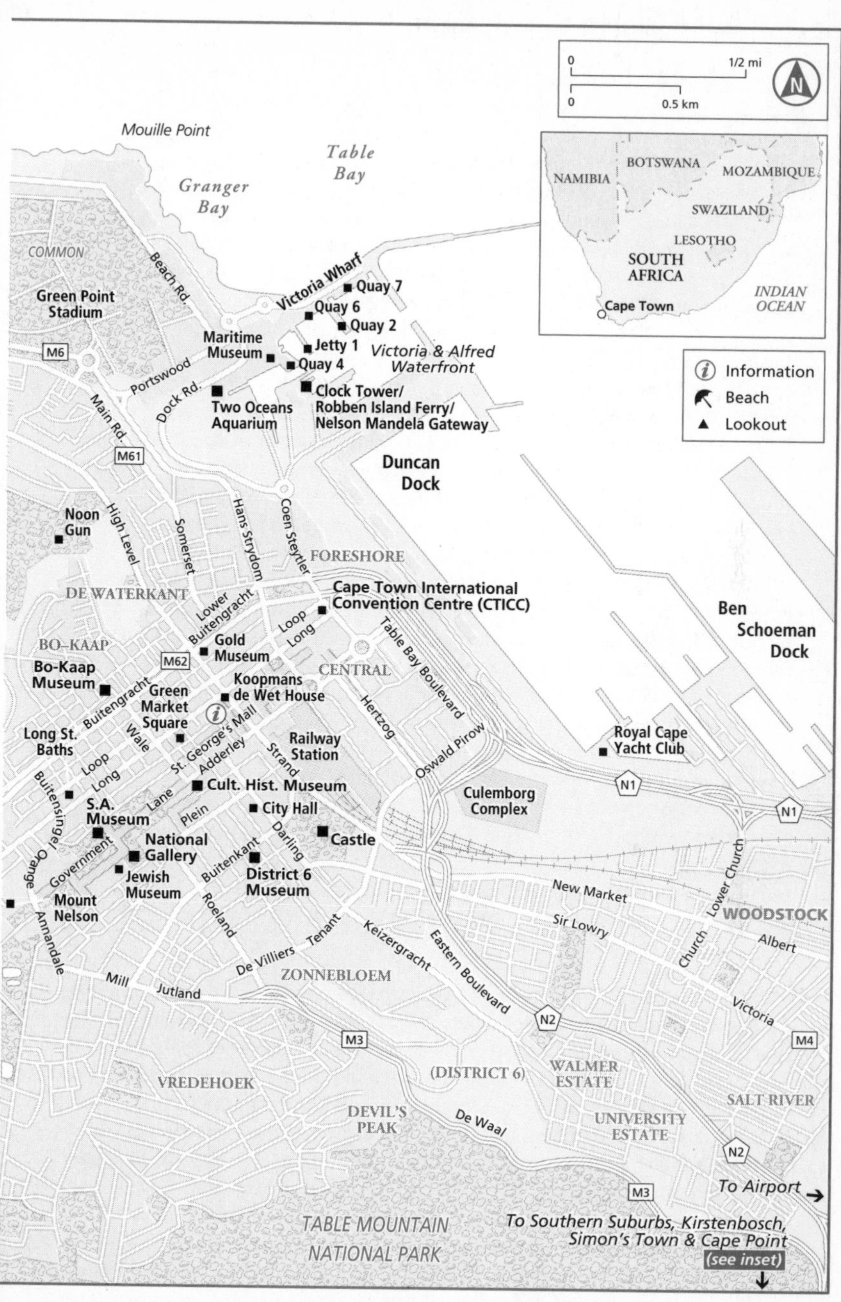
0
1/2 mi
0
0.5 km
N
NAMIBIA
BOTSWANA
MOZAMBIQUE
SWAZILAND
LESOTHO
SOUTH AFRICA
INDIAN OCEAN
Cape Town
Information
Beach
Lookout
Mouille Point
Table Bay
Granger Bay
COMMON
Beach Rd.
Green Point Stadium
Victoria Wharf
Quay 7
Quay 6
Quay 2
Maritime Museum
Jetty 1
Quay 4
Victoria & Alfred Waterfront
M6
Portswood
Dock Rd.
Two Oceans Aquarium
Clock Tower/ Robben Island Ferry/ Nelson Mandela Gateway
Main Rd.
M61
Duncan Dock
Noon Gun
High Level
Somerset
Hans Strydom
Coen Steytler
FORESHORE
DE WATERKANT
Lower Buitengracht
Cape Town International Convention Centre (CTICC)
Loop
Long
Table Bay Boulevard
BO-KAAP
M62
Gold Museum
Ben Schoeman Dock
Bo-Kaap Museum
Koopmans de Wet House
CENTRAL
Buitengracht
Green Market Square
Hertzog
Long St. Baths
Wale
St. George's Mall
Railway Station
Royal Cape Yacht Club
Loop
Adderley
Strand
Oswald Pirow
Buitensingel
Long
Cult. Hist. Museum
N1
Lane
Culemborg Complex
S.A. Museum
Plein
City Hall
N1
National Gallery
Darling
Castle
Government
Buitenkant
Lower Church
Orange
Jewish Museum
District 6 Museum
New Market
Mount Nelson
WOODSTOCK
Roeland
Sir Lowry
Annandale
Tenant
Keizergracht
Albert
Church
De Villiers
Eastern Boulevard
Mill
ZONNEBLOEM
Jutland
Victoria
N2
M3
M4
(DISTRICT 6)
WALMER ESTATE
VREDEHOEK
SALT RIVER
DEVIL'S PEAK
De Waal
UNIVERSITY ESTATE
N2
M3
To Airport
TABLE MOUNTAIN NATIONAL PARK
To Southern Suburbs, Kirstenbosch, Simon's Town & Cape Point
(see inset)

The 2010 World Cup in Cape Town

The year 2010 has been much anticipated by South Africans, bringing with it the coveted FIFA World Cup Soccer Championships. Some 500,000 additional visitors are expected, welcomed by a host of impressive new infrastructure developments—from the total overhaul of the nation's international airports to the implementation of long-awaited rapid transport systems linking airports with host cities. The world's most widely played and televised sport will bring South Africa massive global media exposure, the likes of which have never been witnessed in this part of the world. More eyes will be trained on South Africa from June 11 to July 11, 2010, than during Nelson Mandela's release from prison almost 2 decades earlier. All things being equal, a growth spurt in an already burgeoning tourism industry is pretty much a foregone conclusion.

Nowhere is this optimism and energy more evident than in Cape Town, where numerous developers, restaurateurs, and tour operators have been focusing their entrepreneurial spirit. Impervious to the flurry of development at its feet, Table Mountain National Park still dominates the city, and I challenge you to find another urban destination with quite so much diversity packed into such a compact and genuinely beautiful area. Be prepared to regret that you cannot double whatever length of time you plan to spend here.

The lynchpin to these developments is, of course, the newly finished **Green Point Stadium,** glowing like a luminescent sculpture on a vast, freshly landscaped urban park near the Waterfront (see p. 154). This area, which includes the cobblestone De Waterkant enclave, is set to become ground zero for pedestrians on the prowl for great shopping, dining, and entertainment diversions. Visitors can sample it now along the newly constructed Fan Walk, stretching from Grand Parade in the city center to the stadium. At the heart of it all, **Cape Royale** (p. 107)—a smart new all-suites hotel with one of the city's best spas and a rooftop pool—is practically across the road from the stadium. The Waterfront, which is within walking distance, has also been expanded and now incorporates a bevy of designer stores, as well as two new hotels: the resort-atmosphere **One&Only** (p. 105) and the fabulously intimate and luxurious

By aerial cable car: Cars depart every 15 minutes from the lower station at Tafelberg Road (✆ **021/424-8181;** www.tablemountain.net) daily from 8:30am until between 7:30 and 8:30pm, depending on the season—and always weather permitting. A round-trip ticket costs R145 for adults, R98 for students, and R76 for children, depending on the season (free for children under 4). Operating since 1929 but upgraded in 1997, the Swiss-designed cable car has a floor that rotates 360 degrees, giving everyone a chance to gape at the breathtaking views during the 4-minute journey up. The upgrade has meant that lines are now much shorter—even during the busiest months from November to April, the longest you'll wait is 15 minutes. Afternoons are generally less crowded.

On foot: The most commonly used route to the top is via **Platteklip Gorge**—the gap is visible from the front, or north face, of the mountain. The route starts just east of the lower cable station (see below) and will take 2 to 3 strenuous hours. Be sure to bring

Dock House, the finest place to stay in this touristy quarter. The city's best-looking new guesthouse is **Boutique Manolo** (p. 100), a chic and fabulous hideaway on Tamboerkloof's very own "Mulholland Drive," with 'round-the-clock views of Table Mountain and the city of Cape Town. Manolo is a good value, given the standards of accommodation, but if you're looking for a real bargain, look no further than the new **Rouge on Rose,** in Bo-Kaap, just above the city, and **Grand Daddy,** in the center of town; the chapter also has some great self-catering options, ideal if you're traveling as a family. We've also extended accommodation coverage on the False Bay coast, with its selection of delightful seaside towns that lead to Cape Point: If a dreamy setting with the sound of the ocean lulling you to sleep sounds like it's just the ticket, pack your bags for a seaside sojourn at **Zensa Lodge,** one of the most beautiful and laid-back shabby-chic B&Bs in the country (see p. 116).

Wherever you decide to base yourself, make sure you plan to have at least one meal at **The Roundhouse,** tucked into a forest on the grounds of an old hunting lodge, with distant views of Camps Bay's palm-lined beach. Finally reopened after many years, the latest addition to Cape Town's fine dining scene enjoys by far the best location in the city; prepare to be bowled over by the views, food, discreet service, and wine selection (see p. 133). After immersing yourself in the city's natural splendors, do make time to visit the so-called black and "coloured" townships, where a number of novel tours and experiences enable you to get under the skin of various local cultures—whether through dining, listening to personal stories and parables, or making music, visitors can get up close and personal with the people of Cape Town in ways once never imagined possible (see p. 92 and p. 150). Other new experiences are visits to our headline-grabbing democratic **parliament** (see p. 148), or touring the operating theater where the world's first heart transplant took place, now called the **Heart of Cape Town Museum** (see p. 158).

water. A more scenic route starts at the Kirstenbosch Botanical Gardens and climbs up the back via **Skeleton Gorge.** It's steep, requiring reasonable fitness, but should take approximately 2 hours to the summit; your efforts will be rewarded with fine views of False Bay and the Constantia Valley. Rather than walk another hour to the upper cable station, most return by walking down via **Nursery Ravine.** Those who take their hiking seriously, though, continue to Maclear's Beacon, and then head for the cableway. Be aware that the mountain's mercurial weather can surprise even seasoned Capetonians—more people have died on Table Mountain than on Mount Everest. Don't climb alone, stick to the paths, and take water and warm clothes. For guided hikes, you can contact **Table Mountain Walks** (© **021/715-6136**), or call **Riaan Vorster** ★★★ (© **021/438-6073** or 083/683-1876), a qualified and highly experienced mountain guide (and rock-climber) who will take you up the mountain—on any of more than 20 routes—armed

Warning! Don't Feed the Monkeys

Be aware that the peninsula's baboons, which have become habituated to humans, can be dangerous; don't approach them, keep your car windows closed, and never feed them. Recent newspaper articles have been plastered with pictures of these crafty fellows opening car doors vandalizing them.

with an extensive knowledge of its geology, flora, fauna, and history. Rates start at R300 per person for a half-day, and R500 for a full-day hike. The **Mountain Rescue** number is ✆ **10177** or 021/948-9900. Targeted to launch by June 2010, the proposed 97km (60 mile) **Table Mountain Hoerikwaggo Trail** is a 5-night, 6-day hiking route from Cape Town to Cape Point. At press time, three of the five overnight tented camps were already operational, and hikers can book 3-, 2-, and 1-night hikes covering those sections of the trail that are already complete. The Trail includes comfortable lodgings, catering, and baggage portering at R420 for 2 full days, plus R350 to overnight; a minimum of six hikers are required. You can book through the South African National Parks website (www.sanparks.org; hoerikwaggobookings@sanparks.org), or call ✆ **021/465-8515.**

Boulders ★★ Kids A few minutes from the center of Simons Town, on the way to Cape Point, is the turnoff to pretty Boulders (signposted PENGUIN VIEWING), named after a cluster of large granite boulders that form a number of small sheltered bays, providing sanctuary for a breeding colony of African penguins (colloquially known as jackass penguins because of their braying). You can swim at either Seaforth Beach or Boulders Beach, which the penguins visit, but the best place to view them is from the raised boardwalk overlooking Foxy Beach (accessed via the cashier kiosk); they are a treat to watch and almost human in their interactions. A monogamous species, the penguins mate in January and nest from February to August.

Boulders Beach (off M4), Simons Town. ✆ **021/786-2329.** R30 adults, R10 children. Dec–Jan daily 7am–7:30pm; Feb–Mar daily 8am–6:30pm; Apr–Sept daily 8am–5pm; Oct–Nov daily 8am–6:30pm.

Cape of Good Hope Nature Reserve ★★★ Kids Best known for **Cape Point,** the farthest tip of the Cape Peninsula, this is an unequivocally striking slither of protected reserve that horns its way into the ocean. Various scenic drives and picnic sites put you in the midst of a fabulous terrain that's home to baboons, zebras, elands, red hartebeests, ostriches, and the pretty bontebok. The usually windswept reserve can be pretty bleak, but the coastal views are arresting, and the beaches are almost always deserted. The walks from **Gifkommetjie** and **Platboom Beach,** on the western coast (good for windsurfing), are recommended, or follow the turnoff to Bordjiesdrif or **Buffelsbaai** on the east coast, where you can swim in protected tidal pools or even *braai* (barbecue); at the latter, you can see the remains of one of the more than 20 ships that have wrecked on this coast.

Most head straight for Cape Point, taking the **Flying Dutchman funicular** (R44 round-trip; 9am–6pm summer, 9am–5pm winter) to the viewing platforms surrounding the old lighthouse (built too high, it was often obscured by mists) and walking to the "new" lighthouse—it's the most powerful on the South African coast, built after yet another liner wrecked here in 1911. From these cliffs, towering more than 180m (600 ft.) above the lashing ocean, the view is truly "bird's-eye"—hundreds of seagulls wheel below. ***Note:*** Despite the T-shirt slogans and the name of the Two Oceans Restaurant, most experts agree that this is not the meeting place of two oceans; that would be Cape Agulhus, southeast of here.

Entrance off M4 and M65. ✆ **021/780-9204.** www.capepoint.co.za. R65 adults, discounted for children under 12. Oct–Mar daily 6am–6pm, Apr–Sept daily 7am–5pm.

Kirstenbosch Botanical Gardens ★★★ Kids Situated on the eastern slopes of Table Mountain, Kirstenbosch is the third-most-visited attraction in Cape Town and is without a doubt one of the most beautiful gardens in the world. Its shaded lawns and gurgling streams are the perfect antidote to the searing summer heat, and they're equally glorious in winter, when the rain coaxes out some of the best blooms. With the cultivated sections seamlessly blending into the adjoining Table Mountain nature reserve, some 8,000 of South Africa's 22,000 plant species (including a giant baobab tree) grow here. There are a number of themed walks and areas; as an introduction to the indigenous flora, the *fynbos* walk is recommended. Of historic interest are the remains of the wild almond hedge that Jan Van Riebeeck planted in 1660 to demarcate the colony from the indigenous Khoi. Easiest is to hire an audio guide, or avail yourself of the free guided garden walks that take place on Tuesday, Wednesday, and Saturday (or take a golf cart tour—see below). **Summer sunset concerts** ★★★ are held every Sunday at 5:30pm from late-November to mid-April and feature an eclectic mix of mediocre-to-brilliant bands, orchestras, and solo artists. It's usually worth attending simply to check out the crowd (seating is on the lawn—bring a blanket, food, and drinks, and arrive very early if you want a spot near the stage). At the main entrance there are two restaurants (✆ **021/762-9585**): the self-service **Fynbos** (9am–5pm) and adjacent **Silver Tree,** serving a la carte lunches and dinners. The venue and views are lovely, but the food is pricey and unremarkable. Locals and visitors in the know avoid these tourist traps and opt to enter through Gate 2 to eat breakfast or lunch at the small, thatched **Tea House** (✆ **021/797-4883**), with tables outside and a well-priced menu.

Rhodes Dr., Newlands, 13km (8 miles) from the city center. Take De Waal Dr. (M3) toward Muizenberg, at the first traffic light intersection turn right (southward) into Rhodes Dr. (M63), and follow the signs. ✆ **021/799-8899** or 021/799-8783. www.nbi.ac.za. R32 adults, R10 children 6–17. Sept–Mar daily 8am–7pm; Apr–Aug daily 8am–6pm. Free guided garden walks Mon–Sat at 10am and Tues also at 11am. Audio guides R35. Golf-cart tours (R35) depart every hour 9am–3pm. Summer sunset concerts R50 adults, R15 children. Call for other events.

Rhodes Memorial Designed by Herbert Baker and Francis Macey, this monument—inspired by a Greek temple—was erected in honor of Cecil John Rhodes, the man who, incidentally, donated the land for Kirstenbosch Gardens in 1902. Rhodes made his fortune in the Kimberley diamond mines and became prime minister of the Cape in 1890. A true British imperialist, he "owned" Zimbabwe (previously known as Rhodesia), and it was his lifelong dream to see a Cape-to-Cairo railway line built so that the "sun would never set on the British Empire." A bust of Rhodes is at the top of an imposing lion-flanked granite staircase flanked by lions and overlooking the Cape Flats and Table Bay. In one of the Cape's most bizarre juxtapositions, herds of wildebeests and zebras graze on the slopes around the memorial, oblivious to rubberneckers driving the M3 below.

Groote Schuur Estate (from the M3/De Waal Dr., follow the signposted turnoff just after the University of Cape Town). ✆ **021/689-9151.** Free admission. Daily 9am–5pm.

ATTRACTIONS IN THE CITY CENTER

Cape Town is South Africa's oldest and most pleasant city center, featuring a combination of Cape Dutch, Georgian, Victorian, and 20th-century architecture, all framed by the backdrop of Table Mountain. Hardly surprising, then, that Cape Town is also the only South African city that, with the efforts of the Cape Town Partnership, is slowly transforming itself into a residential enclave, with many of the city's period buildings being redeveloped into apartments and hotels, and retail and restaurant outlets planned to service these new city dwellers.

The prettiest axis, **Adderley Street,** runs past the railway station, cutting the city in half. East of Adderley is the **Castle of Good Hope, Grand Parade,** and **City Hall.** West are the more charming shopping areas, the best of which, **Long Street** and, to a lesser extent, **St George's Mall** (a pedestrian street), run parallel to Adderley. **Greenmarket Square,** a lively flea market surrounded by coffee shops, lies between these two streets and Longmarket and Shortmarket streets. South of Adderley Street (where it takes a right turn at The Slave Lodge and melds with Wale St.) is the **Company Gardens,** Cape Town's very own central park, and the green lung where most of the museums are situated. These Gardens started out as the vegetable patch to supply the Dutch East India Company, which first established Cape Town as a refreshment station for passing ships in the 17th century. From the Gardens, you can also get a clear view of **Tuinhuis,** the official Cape Town residence of the President, where world dignitaries are received. Also adjacent to the Gardens and Tuinhuis is **Parliament,** scheduled for expansion in the next few years. To arrange a free **tour** through the halls of one of the world's most intriguing, controversial and hard-fought-for democratic parliaments, call © **021/403-3341,** and ask to speak to Ms. Zelda or Mr. Govender. You'll need to bring your passport along for security purposes—the entrance to Parliament is from the other side of town, at the junction of Roeland and Plein streets.

The city is small, so the best way to get to know it is on foot (or by carriage—see Castle review below); you can either take a 3-hour guided walking tour, which departs from the tourism office at 10:30am (offered by knowledgeable guides, these are highly recommended) or enjoy your own pace: Start at the Castle, then head down Darling Street to Adderley Street. Either turn right to look at the brilliant blooms trading at Trafalgar flower market before continuing up Darling to browse the markets and shops at Greenmarket Square, Church Street, and Long Street, or turn left onto Adderley to complete a loop that takes in The Slave Lodge, the Company Gardens, the National Gallery, and/or the South African Museum before returning down Queen Victoria Street or Long Street to Greenmarket Square. Besides the recommended museums and galleries below, you might want to take a look at **Koopmans–De Wet House,** 35 Strand St. (© **021/481-3935;** R10 adults; Tues–Thurs 10am–5pm), which is the country's oldest house museum, from 1914, and a repository for some of the finest Cape furniture and silverware to survive the 18th and 19th centuries; there's also a priceless ceramics collection. Originally built in the 18th century, the facade of this urban mansion really stands out among some of the city's towering modern structures, and the gracious interiors provide insight into a world of privileged circumstance and social entitlement. Another even grander example of 18th-century townhouse architecture is **Rust en Vreugd** ★, 78 Buitenkant St. (© **021/464-3280;** free admission, donations appreciated; Tues–Thurs 10am–5pm), built in 1778 and sporting a remodeled period garden. Housed here is part of the eye-opening **William Fehr Collection,** donated by the super-conservationist, Dr. Fehr (1892–1968); his collected historical paintings, etchings, and lithographs provide amazing insight into the early colonists and how they were to change the face of the Cape completely. The collection's painted works are housed at the Castle of Good Hope (see below).

Castle of Good Hope ★★ Built between 1666 and 1679, the castle—really a pentagonal fortress typical of the Dutch defense system adopted in the early 17th century—is the oldest surviving building in South Africa and marks the original shoreline. Once the hub of civilian and administrative life, the long-serving castle is still the regional headquarters of the South African Defence Force, though the most invasive force it's ever dealt with are the tourists ambling through its ramparts (and, in a wonderful exorcism of the ghosts of the past, more than 5,000 camp brides and other gay revelers at "The Wedding," a costume ball that MCQP hosted here in 2002). The fort combined local materials with European imports—note the slate paving stones, taken from Robben Island in the 17th century, and the bell at the entrance, cast in Amsterdam in 1697. It still looks much as it has for centuries.

Get here at 10am or noon sharp if you want to see the Key Ceremony, a kind of changing of the guard (Mon–Fri only). There are also 30-minute tours departing at 11am, noon, and 2pm (ask about the many ghosts that wander the ramparts), or you can explore on your own. Unless you're fascinated with colonial military might, you can skip the **Military Museum,** but don't pass on the paintings that form part of the **William Fehr Collection**—an ideal way to brush up on your colonial history. Witness the crazy scene, for example, in Thomas Baines's spectacular painting *The Greatest Hunt in Africa,* which depicts the mindless slaughter of 30,000 animals in honor of the visiting Prince Alfred.

Note that, at press time, the quality of food at the central courtyard restaurant at the Castle is suspect. Tenders are being sought for a new dining enterprise, but until the right people move in, don't eat here. Alongside the Castle in front of the old **City Hall** (from whose balcony Mandela made his first public address after release from prison), the so-called Grand Parade is being rejuvenated for the 2010 FIFA World Cup, when it will serve as a Fan Park for soccer enthusiasts without match tickets.

Corner of Buitenkant and Strand sts., opposite the Grand Parade. ✆ **021/464-1260/4.** R20 adults (R10 on Sun), R10 children 5–16 (R5 on Sun). Mon–Sun 9:30am–4pm.

Gold of Africa Museum ★★ The blingiest addition to Cape Town's list of indoor diversions, this museum houses a collection of African gold artifacts purchased from the Barbier-Mueller Museum in Geneva for R11 million. Created in Mali, Senegal, Ghana, and Cote d'Ivoire during the 19th and 20th centuries, the pieces here represent a refreshing change from the chiefly Eurocentric designs available commercially, and the intention is to foster an appreciation for and pride in African design. The museum is housed in the historic **Martin Melck House,** constructed in 1781 as the parsonage for the pretty Lutheran church, located next to the house. If you're truly interested, you can even sign up for one of their weekly courses, such as a Byzantine jewelry-making workshop where you'll make a gem-studded chain out of brass or copper (3hr.; R400 per person). Targeting tourists, the Gold restaurant (see p. 126) here turns out tasty pan-African flavors and presents drumming lessons as part of the predinner entertainment.

Martin Melck House, 96 Strand St. ✆ **021/405-1540.** www.goldofafrica.com. R25 adults, R20 students and seniors, R15 children. Mon–Sat 9:30am–5pm.

The Slave Lodge Built in 1679 to house the Dutch East India Company's slaves, this building is just meters away from the very spot where people were once inspected by

Cultural Sights: Cape Muslim to Khayalitsha

On the slopes of Signal Hill—the arm that stretches out of Table Mountain to overlook the city and harbor—is the suburb of **Bo-Kaap.** Home to a section of the Cape's Muslim community (often referred to as the Cape Malays, despite the fact that only 1% of their forefathers, skilled slaves imported by the Dutch, were born in Malaysia), this is one of the city's oldest and most interesting areas. Its character is somewhat under threat, though, from property speculators and foreign investors keen to own a piece of the city's quaintest suburb. Narrow cobbled streets lead past colorful 19th-century Dutch and Georgian terraces and tiny mosques; try to visit at sunrise and sunset when the air is filled with the song of the muezzins in their minarets, calling the community to prayer.

The protected historic core of the Bo-Kaap ranges from Dorp to Strand streets, and between Buitengracht and Pentz streets. The best way to visit is on foot, with a local guide and, preferably, one who will expose you to more intimate aspects of the community and its culture, such as you'll experience with **Andulela Tours** ★★★ (✆ **021/790-2592;** www.andulela.com), on their half-day **Cape Malay Cooking Safari.** It's a great way to take in the entire area, with a detailed, lively account of its history, culture, architecture, and, of course, cuisine. Rather than observing everything from the outside, you'll finish up by visiting with a Bo-Kaap family in their home, where you'll get a brief hands-on cooking lesson. I learned to roll *rotis* and also fold and stuff *samosas.* Best of all, you finish up by enjoying the three-course fruits of your labor (with a few more complicated dishes prepared by your delightful hostess).

Andulela's tour start at the **Bo-Kaap Museum,** 71 Wale St. (✆ **021/481-3939;** Mon–Sat 10am–5pm; R10 adults, children under 16 free), set in a house dating back to the 1760s, and set out to give a basic idea of how a relatively wealthy 19th-century Cape Muslim family lived. Curatorship is lackluster, though, and proper explanation lacking, so it's best seen as part of a guided tour (such as one offered by Andulela). One block south of the museum, at Dorp Street, is **Auwal,** South Africa's oldest mosque, dating back to 1795 and said to be where Afrikaans was first taught.

The charm of the Bo-Kaap provides some measure of what was lost when **District Six** was razed; across town from the Bo-Kaap, and clearly visible from any raised point, this vacant land is located on the city's southern border. When bulldozers moved in to flatten the suburb in 1966, an estimated 60,000 Cape Muslims (referred to as "coloureds") and other "nonwhites" were living in what was condemned as a ghetto by the apartheid hardliners. Much like Sophiatown in Johannesburg, District Six housed people from every walk of life—musicians, traders, teachers, craftsmen, *skollies* (petty criminals), hookers, and pimps—and was one of South Africa's most inspired and creative communities, producing potent poets, jazz musicians, and writers. When the bulldozers finally moved out, all that was left were a few churches and mosques (in a weird attempt at morality, religious buildings were exempt from the demolition order). The community was relocated piecemeal to the Cape Flats—a name that accurately describes both the geography and psychology of the area. Many argue sensibly that Cape Town's ongoing gangster problems, spawned in the fragmented, angered, and powerless Cape Flats communities, resulted from the demise of District Six.

Renamed Zonnebloem (Sunflower), the so-called white area of District Six remained largely vacant, as even hardened capitalists spurned development in protest, and only the state-funded Cape Technicon was ever built on the land (purchased, incidentally, for R1). Restitution is underway, with a "homecoming ceremony" held in November 2000 and construction of 1,700 homes for some of the wrongly evicted resumed in April 2003. It's still weighed down by bureaucracy and in-fighting, and life will never be the same here again, but it's hoped that by returning the land to the original families, the damage to the national psyche can be reversed. Until then, the scar on the cityscape is a constant reminder.

Most organized tours of District Six are part of a trip to **Gugulethu** and **Langa,** two of Cape Town's oldest "townships," as black suburbs are still referred to, and the shantytowns of **Khayalitsha.** While you can self-drive to such crafts centers as Sivuyile Tourism Centre in Gugulethu, to get an in-depth understanding of how "the other half" of Cape Town lives, a tour is definitely recommended. Most tours kick off from either the Bo-Kaap or District Six museums, then head for a short visit to the townships to visit a crafts center, an "informal" home, a *shebeen* (traditional drinking house), and a housing project; both can extend the tour to include Robben Island, though this really isn't recommended. You could book your tour with **Grassroots** (✆ **021/706-1006**) or **IliosTours** (✆ **021/697-4056**), but a more specialized and personalized approach is offered by **Camissa** (www.gocamissa.co.za), as well as the aforementioned **Andulela Tours** and the excellent **Coffeebeans Routes** (www.coffeebeansroutes.com). These cooperate to offer a wide variety of eye-opening experiences, such as the innovative **Urban Futures** tour, where you visit urban planners, township revival zones, and major transformation projects in order to get at look at the vision for Cape Town, circa 2030. The extremely successful, interactive **Jazz Safari** is a fantastic nighttime trip into the heart of the pioneering music scene, much of which happens in the Cape Flats suburbs. You'll meet legends such as Mac McKenzie, the "king of Goema" (a fusion of jazz, samba, and traditional drumming), and engage with musicians in casual living room conversations, listening to impromptu recitals and even getting a chance to jam along.

Kids Especially for Kids

Many of the Waterfront activities have been designed with children in mind, making it Cape Town's foremost family destination. The top attraction here is the **Two Oceans Aquarium.** Face painting, drawing, and puzzles are on offer in the aquarium's Alpha Activity center, and staff often arranges sleepovers and excursions to interesting and educational locations for ages 8 to 12. Call © **021/418-3823** to find out what special kids' entertainment will be available when you're in town. On the way, stop at the **Scratch Patch,** where kids literally scratch through mounds of semiprecious stones, selecting their own "jewels," after which they can play a round of crazy golf.

Catch the kiddies' **Blue Train** in Mouille Point (© **021/434-8537;** Mon–Fri 3–5pm, Sat–Sun 11–5pm); next door is a maze and an outdoor putt-putt (crazy golf) course. In town, the noon **Planetarium** show is held every Saturday and Sunday, where they attempt to answer such simple astronomy questions as "Why is the sky blue?" and "Is the sun round?" To get there, take a stroll along Government Avenue (enter from Orange St., opposite Mount Nelson), armed with a bag of nuts to feed the almost-tame squirrels. Afterward, take high tea in the **Mount Nelson gardens,** or head for **Deer Park Café.** It's the city's most child-friendly restaurant, with a great kids' menu, and it opens onto a large public play park shaded by stately trees. End the day by ascending **Table Mountain** in the rotating cable car—a thrill for kids, with rewarding views for adults. Pack a picnic as well as sun block, hats, and a jacket, in case the weather turns.

potential buyers before sold off to the highest bidders. Slated to become a world-class memory bank that honors the slaves who have featured in the colony's history, this museum's curators have been slow to develop a consistent body of work such as you'll find at Johannesburg's Apartheid Museum (see p. 321), but big things are in the offing. Ongoing, changing exhibitions—such as the Iziko Freedom Project, marking the bicentennial of the abolition of the slave trade in the British Empire in 1807—draw attention to the legacy of slavery at the Cape (and beyond), as well as related issues such as human trafficking, forced labor, and other infringements of basic human rights that are so much a part of South Africa's turbulent history.

Corner of Adderley and Wale sts. © **021/460-8242.** R15 adults, R5 students and seniors, children under 16 free. Mon–Sat 10am–5pm.

South African Jewish Museum ★ Opened by Nelson Mandela in 2000, this architecturally astonishing museum—like the nearby District Six Museum—celebrates the history of a particular South African community. A contemporary arena gallery was grafted onto Cape Town's original Old Synagogue (South Africa's first, consecrated in 1863), where various cultural items are kept. Creatively curated, there are a few stirring moments—a film in which Mandela talks respectfully about the Jewish community is particularly poignant, as are sound bites by Jews discussing their views on apartheid.

A gentler experience is to chill out with a picnic next to a burbling stream at **Kirstenbosch Gardens,** or—if you don't want the hassle of shopping at a deli—head for the shady oaks at **Le Pique Nique,** Boschendal, near Franschhoek (or **Groot Constantia,** where Jonkershuis restaurant supplies the goodies). In the Paarl area, visit **Butterfly World** (✆ **021/875-5628**), where 22 different species of butterfly flit about a tropical garden; **Drakenstein Lion Park** (✆ **021/863-3290**), a sanctuary for captive-born lions; or the **Le Bonheur Croc Farm** (✆ **021/863-1142**). Better still, head to **Spier** ★★★, near Stellenbosch, a one-stop wonder for kids. Here they can get up close to cheetahs and other predators, watch a fantastic bird show at Eagle Encounters Raptor Rehabilitation Centre (this is really tops), ride horses, or feed ducks and play in the parks (www.spier.co.za). For Eagle Encounter bookings, call ✆ **021/858-1826.** If this wets the appetite, consider a day safari at Aquila (see box).

Closer to town is a walk through the **World of Birds Sanctuary,** Valley Road (✆ **021/790-2730**), in Hout Bay (though it's looking a little down-at-the-heel currently, due to lack of funding). Then take one of the cruises to **Seal Island,** departing from Hout Bay Harbour. **Imhoff Farm** (✆ **021/783-4545**), in Kommetjie, offers country-style refreshments, camel rides, horseback riding, crafts shops for kids, and a snake and nature park to entertain.

When all else fails, there's always the beach. Try **Boulders,** where the temperature is slightly warmer, tidal pools are safe, and the penguins are genuinely entertaining. Visit the **Warrior Toy Museum** (✆ **021/786-1395**), on Georges Street, in Simons Town, on your way.

Downstairs, reached via a fantastic spiral staircase, is a digital repository of Jewish identity and family trees—useful if you'd like to trace your own roots or connections here. Although the earliest records of Jewish settlers are dated to 1669, most of South Africa's Jewish immigrant community arrived after 1880 from the Baltic region, especially Lithuania; their roots are memorialized through a miniature version of a *shtetl* (Lithuanian village), reproduced here in exacting detail. It won't appeal to everyone, but this is the city's most meticulously curated museum.

88 Hatfield St., Gardens. ✆ **021/465-1546.** www.sajewishmuseum.co.za. R50 adults, R15 scholars under 21. Sun–Thurs 10am–5pm; Fri 10am–2pm. Closed on Jewish holidays.

South African Museum & Planetarium Founded in 1825, South Africa's oldest museum is showing its age and, in many respects, still resembles a Victorian collection of ghoulishly stuffed animals, many of which have little or nothing to do with South Africa. In addition to the vast, oftentimes macabre, taxidermy project, there's a fairly extensive shark and whale section, which includes a four-story whale well, hung with two massive whale skeletons. Given the abundance of tribal and indigenous culture that makes up the local social fabric, the ethnographic displays are wearisome and compare extremely poorly with the engaging work being done at the contemporary Origins Centre in Johannesburg.

25 Queen Victoria St. Museum: ✆ **021/481-3800.** R15 adults, children under 16 free. Daily 10am–5pm. Planetarium: ✆ **021/481-3900.** Planetarium show: R20 adults, R6 children. Mon–Fri 2pm, Tues 8pm; Sat–Sun noon, 1pm, and 2pm.

South African National Gallery ★★★ This small gallery, started with an initial donation by Victorian landlord Sir Thomas Butterworth Bayley, has room to exhibit only a fraction of its collection of more than 8,000 artworks. Despite this, and despite a lack of funding, it is considered by many to be the country's premier art museum, with many artworks reflecting South Africa's turbulent and painful history. Clever curatorship in recent years saw the gallery collecting works neglected by other South African institutions, including rare examples of what used to be considered crafts, such as Ndebele beadwork and *knobkierries* (fighting sticks). The gallery also often hosts excellent traveling exhibitions—look out for anything by William Kentridge, South Africa's biggest name working today.

Government Ave., Company's Gardens. ✆ **021/467-4660.** R15 adults, children under 16 free. Tues–Sun 10am–5pm.

ATTRACTIONS IN & AROUND THE WATERFRONT

Redevelopment of this historic core started in the early 1990s, and within a few years, the Victoria & Alfred Waterfront (www.waterfront.co.za) had been rated as the best of its kind, successfully integrating a top tourist attraction with southern Africa's principal passenger-and-freight harbor. Views of Table Mountain and the working harbor, as well as numerous restored national monuments and a wide array of entertainment options, attract an estimated 20 million visitors a year. The smells of diesel and fish mingle with the aromas wafting from pavement bistros, tugboats mingle with catamarans, and tourists mingle with, well, tourists. (If you're seeking tattooed sailors and ladies of dubious repute, you'd be better off taking a drive down to Duncan Dock, where the large working ships dock.)

In 2006, the V&A Waterfront was sold for R7.04 billion, and developments have been overwhelming—if you've been here before, expect to see profound change, including massive new blocks packed with very exclusive chi-chi shops and almost disgusting displays of wealth. A rather sanitized place, the shopping precinct is concentrated in the Victoria Wharf Mall, which on its own contains over **500 stores** (open until 9pm daily), an indoor crafts market, a wellness center, and a choice of more than **30 restaurants,** as well as **mainstream-movie screens** (Nu Metro; ✆ **021/419-9700**) and a smaller **art-movie cinema complex** (Cinema Nouveau; ✆ **0861/300-444**). While Victoria Wharf has some lovely views in places, it feels like any other mall in a large city. Try to avoid getting stuck inside the V&A buildings—the waterside action between Quay 5 and Pierhead Jetty is far more appealing, and you get some splendid Table Mountain vistas, to boot.

If you do only two things on the Waterfront, you should book a **boat trip,** preferably to Robben Island, and visit the **Two Oceans Aquarium** (see below). Most cruises (see "Organized Cruises & Tours," earlier in this chapter) take off from Quay 5. **Steamboat Vicky** (✆ **083/411-3310;** R45 for 30 min, R80 for 1 hr.), which tools around the harbor, takes off from North Quay. From June to November, you can also book a **whale-watching** cruise with the **Waterfront Boat Company,** at Quay 5 (✆ **021/418-5806;** R400 adults, R200 children under 12). You may also want to keep at the back of your head that the Waterfront is also the starting point for Cape Town's popular **helicopter flips,** operated by four different companies, most based at Quay 5.

Tips Big 5 in 1 Day

Those unable to go on a proper safari can still see the Big 5 on a day-long safari (or longer stay) at **Aquila Private Game Reserve** (✆ **021/431-8400;** www.aquila safari.com; near Touws River), which is less than 2 hours from the city. The lions are in a separate area, so this is not comparable with safaris east and north, but at least you're guaranteed to see them. There are game drives (or horseback safaris), and the 4,500-hectare (11,120-acre) reserve does have some attractive, thatched premier chalets. They're not cheap, starting at R6,080 for a double, but there are standard cottages available for half that price. Day trips cost from R1,220 per person.

Beer lovers seeking more down-to-earth fun should make the detour to **Mitchell's** (✆ **021/425-9462**) to sample the ales from the family-run microbrewery (try a pint of Bosun's Bitter, South Africa's first "real ale"), while boat spotters may be interested in the **Maritime Centre**—a museum with one important floating exhibit, the **SAS** ***Somerset*** (the only surviving boom-defense vessel in the world), now berthed in front of the One&Only hotel.

Robben Island ★ To limit access to the delicate ecosystem of this legendary island, only government-run tours managed under the banner of Robben Island Museum (encompassing the entire island) are allowed to land on this World Heritage Site, for many years a source of controversy and mismanagement (including scandals of disappearing funds). Visitors are transported via a large catamaran that takes approximately 25 minutes. (The views of Table Mountain and Cape Town as you pull out of the harbor are fantastic—arrive first to ensure you have a top-deck, open-air seat.) Unfortunately, the tour of the island itself is quite underwhelming; passengers are packed like sardines in a bus, and chances are, you'll be on the receiving end of fairly neglectful, unexciting narrative that hardly welcomes any sort of interaction. The 45-minute bus tours of the island provide passing glimpses of the **lepers' church and graveyard;** PAC leader **Robert Sobukwe's house,** where he was imprisoned; the **"warden's village,"** a collection of houses and a school that seem stuck in some lifeless period movie; the **lighthouse; World War II fortifications;** and Robben Island's **wildlife** (keep your eyes peeled for colonies of African penguins). At one point, you'll be stationed (seemingly endlessly) beside the **lime quarry,** once worked by political prisoners (take sunglasses—the brightness ruined many inmates' and wardens' eyes). Mercifully, at one point you're let off the bus to admire the view of Cape Town across the water—this is by far the best part of the bus ride. The tour's real highlight, though, comes right at the end, when an ex–political prisoner takes you through the "maximum security" prison, where you can view the tiny cell in which Mandela slept for 18 of his 27 years of imprisonment. Unfortunately, none of this provides a very fitting or poignant account of what it was like to live here; the prison has been sanitized, and the walk through the buildings seldom evokes much pathos. Tours take 3½ hours (including boat trip) and are terribly cloying and formulaic. Many visitors leave feeling thoroughly ripped off, and you'd do well to consider that feedback you might have heard from celebrities and VIPs almost certainly refers to a totally different tour experience.

Tickets and departure from the Nelson Mandela Gateway at the Clock Tower terminal on Quay 5. ✆ **021/413-4220.** Advance bookings: www.robben-island.org.za. R180 adults, R90 children under 18. Ferries depart daily every hour 8am–5pm. Tours may be increased to include sunset tours in summer, and decreased in winter or because of inclement weather—please call ahead. Advance bookings (✆ 021/413-4233) are highly recommended and essential during the busy summer months; you can book online through the website, but be sure to do this well in advance, and note that ticket dates and times are not transferable. ***Note:*** Reports of ticket sales irregularities continue, with bribes being paid to secure tickets for tours that are apparently sold out.

Two Oceans Aquarium ★★★ Kids This is by far the most exciting attraction at the Waterfront itself. From the brightly hued fish found on coral reefs to exhilarating encounters with ragged tooth sharks, more than 3,000 live specimens are literally inches from your nose. Besides the Indian and Atlantic underwater tanks displaying the bizarre and beautiful, there are a number of well-simulated environments, including tidal pools, a river ecosystem, and the magnificent Kelp Forest tank. The walk through the aquarium (30–90 min., depending on how long you linger) ends with an awesome display on deep-sea predators. There are child-height window benches throughout and a "touch pool" where kids can touch kelp, shells, and anemones. On weekends, kids are entertained in the Alpha Activity center with face painting and puppet shows. Predators are fed at 3pm daily (the sharks on Sun), but if you have a diving license, you won't want to mss the chance to jump in the tank and swim with the shark—no cage, no need to fear, as the raggies are considered nonaggressive creatures (although you might not think so, judging by the bite marks on some of the smaller fish).

Btw. New Basin and Dock Rd. ✆ **021/418-3823.** www.aquarium.co.za. R85 adults, R40 children 4–13, R65 children 14–17. Daily 9:30am–6pm.

EXPLORING FARTHER AFIELD: SOUTHERN SUBURBS & CONSTANTIA

Groot Constantia is a good place to start your exploration of the Cape's oldest and closest Winelands, an area that comprises eight wineries, the most famous being **Groot Constantia, Klein Constantia, Buitenverwachting, Uitsig,** and **Steenberg.** All feature Cape Dutch homesteads, oaks, and acres of vineyards, and because they're about 30 minutes from town, spending time here is definitely recommended, particularly if you aren't venturing into the surrounding Winelands. If you're looking for an ideal luncheon venue, look no farther than Buitenverwachting or Uitsig—both are on the eastern slopes of the Constantiaberg, with views of vineyards and the sea, and both are renowned for their cuisine (see "Where to Dine," earlier in this chapter).

Groot Constantia ★★ Groot Constantia was established in 1685 by Simon van der Stel, then governor of the Cape, who reputedly named it after his daughter Constancia and planted the Cape's first vines. A century later, the Cloete family put Constantia on the international map with a dessert wine that became the favored tipple of the likes of Napoleon, Bismarck, King Louis Philippe of France, and Jane Austen. An outbreak of phylloxera in the 1860s bankrupted the family, however, and the land lay fallow until 1975, when substantial replanting began. Today Groot Constantia is known for its reds, particularly the Gouverneurs Reserve. In addition to tasting the wines in the modern cellars here, you can visit a small museum showing the history of the manor, as well as the beautiful Cape Dutch house itself, furnished in beautiful late-18th-century Cape Dutch furniture. Behind the house are the old cellars, originally designed by French architect Louis Thibault; note the celebrated pediment sculpted by Anton Anreith in

Island of Tears

The remarkably varied history of Robben Island goes back some 400 years. It has served variously as a post office, a fishing base, a whaling station, a hospital, a mental asylum, a military base, and—most infamously—a penal colony, for which it was dubbed "South Africa's Alcatraz." The banished have included Angolan and West African slaves, princes from the East, South African chiefs, lepers, the mentally insane, French Vichy POWs, and, most recently, opponents of the apartheid regime. But all that changed on September 24, 1997, when the Robben Island Museum was officially opened by its most famous political prisoner, Nelson Mandela.

The island, once the symbol of political oppression and enforced division, was to be transformed into a symbol of reconciliation. In Mandela's words, "Few occasions could illuminate so sharply the changes of recent years; fewer still could bring to sharp focus the challenges ahead." Rising to this challenge is an eclectic complement of staff—artists, historians, environmentalists, ex–political prisoners, and ex-wardens. It's hard to imagine how a group of people with such diverse backgrounds and ideologies could work together, but it seems anything is possible once you've established common ground—in this case, the 586 hectares (1,447 acres) of Robben Island.

Patrick Matanjana, one of the prison tour guides, spent 20 years behind bars on the island. Now he spends time at Robben Island's bar, fraternizing with the very people who upheld the system he was trying to sabotage. "They know me; they respect me," he says when asked what it's like to sit and drink with former enemies. "We are trying to correct a great wrong. They also buy the drinks," he grins. The island's ironies don't end here. Even the bar, the Alpha 1 Officers' Club, has historic significance: This is where Patrick's latrine bucket would have been emptied in the 1960s and 1970s, before the prisoners had access to toilets (not to mention beds, hot water, or adequate nutrition).

Despite the radical changes, the remaining ex-wardens, some of whom remained in charge of island security, did not want to leave. "You cry twice on Robben Island," explained skipper Jan Moolman, who first stepped onto the island in 1963 as one of PAC leader Robert Subukwe's personal wardens, "the day you arrive, and the day you have to leave."

For the many day-trippers, all it takes is the sight of Mandela's cell.

1791. The cellars also contain an interesting **wine museum.** A cozy, pleasant restaurant, **Jonkershuis** (✆ **021/794-6255**), serves traditional Cape Malay dishes, and **Simons** (✆ **021/794-1143**)—surrounded by vineyards and lawns—is where the locals can be found quaffing from the extensive wine list and marveling at the pinkness of the seared tuna or lamb.

Groot Constantia Rd., Constantia (from the M3, take the Constantia turnoff; follow the GROOT CONSTANTIA signs). ✆ **021/795-5128.** www.grootconstantia.co.za. Museum R15 adults, children under 16 free. Wine tasting and cellar tour R60. Tour only R30 adults, R5 students. Daily 10am–5pm.

Heart of Cape Town Museum ★★ The site of the world's first heart transplant, performed on December 3, 1967, by a dashing surgeon named Christiaan Barnard, has recently been transformed into one of the country's most compelling specialist museums, and a fascinating 2-hour experience. Although there's a distinctly clinical ambience in the museum "galleries" (it is, after all, a hospital building—now part of UCT's medical school), there's a lot of heart in the way the story of the operation unfolds, with sharp focus on the various players—including the unfortunate female car accident victim who became the world's first heart donor. There's an excellent documentary on Barnard himself, and the highlight is when you enter the pair of side-by-side operating theaters where the startling procedure took place. Latex sculptures produced by film industry specialists simulate all the characters who were present, and the excitement of the operation comes to life through a gripping account by a very knowledgeable guide. A hugely inspiring museum, although not for younger kids.

Groote Schuur Hospital, Main Rd., Observatory. ✆ **021/404-1967.** www.heartofcapetown.co.za. R200 adults. Daily 8am–7pm; visits by guided tour only, at 9 and 11am, and 1, 3, and 5pm.

DRIVING TOUR A PENINSULA DRIVE

START: **Take the M3 out of town; this follows the eastern flank of the mountain, providing access to the southern suburbs.**

FINISH: **Kloof Nek roundabout in town.**

TIME: **The full tour will take at least 1 full day.**

Not all the sites listed below are must-sees; personal interest should shape your itinerary. That said, get an early start, and make an effort to fit Kirstenbosch and Groot Constantia into the morning, leaving Cape Point for the afternoon and Chapman's Peak Drive for the evening. Because this is a circular route, it can also be done in reverse, but the idea is to be back on the Atlantic seaboard at sunset, or stay out on the False Bay coast and wait for sunrise. Should Chapman's Peak be closed, return from Cape Point via Ou Kaapse Weg and Silvermine Nature Reserve, rejoining the M4 north. Head through Constantia (past the Alphen Hotel) over Constantia Neck and descend into Hout Bay. Drive the Atlantic seaboard back to Cape Town, passing the coastal suburbs of Llundudno, Bakoven, and Camps Bay as the sun sets.

As you approach the Groote Schuur Hospital on your left, scene of the world's first heart transplant (see Heart of Cape Town Museum review, above), look for the wildebeest (gnu) and mountain zebras grazing on the slopes of the mountain. Art lovers should consider taking the Mowbray turnoff to the:

1 Irma Stern Museum

Stern, a follower of the German expressionist movement—and acknowledged as one of South Africa's best 20th-century artists—was also an avid collector of Iberian, African, and Oriental artifacts. The museum, on Cecil Road (✆ **021/685-5686;** Tues–Sat 10am–5pm; R10), also exhibits new talents.

Back on the M3, still traveling south, you will pass Mostert's Mill on your left, another reminder of the Cape's Dutch past, and look out for left-hand turn to:

2 Rhodes Memorial

You can see the imposing memorial high up on the slopes on your right (see "Table Mountain National Park," earlier in this chapter); the restaurant behind the memorial has awesome views, so break here for tea or breakfast if you have the time, or return another day. Back on the M3, you will pass a series of imposing ivy-clad buildings, which comprise the **University of Cape Town,** built on land donated by

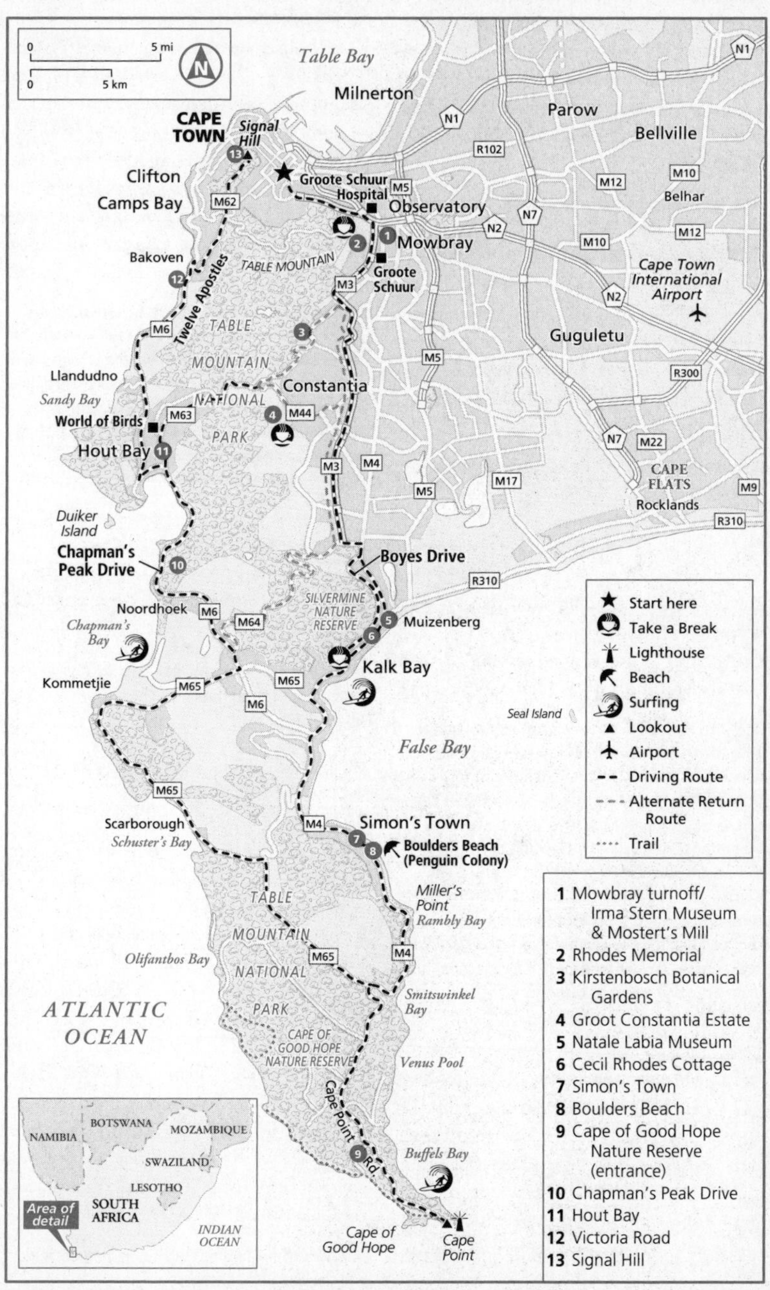
Table Bay
Milnerton
Parow
Bellville
CAPE TOWN
Signal Hill
Clifton
Camps Bay
Groote Schuur Hospital
Observatory
Mowbray
Groote Schuur
Bakoven
TABLE MOUNTAIN
Twelve Apostles
Cape Town International Airport
Guguletu
Llandudno
Sandy Bay
Constantia
TABLE MOUNTAIN NATIONAL PARK
World of Birds
Hout Bay
CAPE FLATS
Rocklands
Duiker Island
Chapman's Peak Drive
Boyes Drive
Noordhoek
Chapman's Bay
SILVERMINE NATURE RESERVE
Muizenberg
Kalk Bay
Kommetjie
Seal Island
False Bay
Scarborough
Schuster's Bay
Simon's Town
Boulders Beach (Penguin Colony)
Miller's Point
Rambly Bay
Olifantbos Bay
Smitswinkel Bay
ATLANTIC OCEAN
CAPE OF GOOD HOPE NATURE RESERVE
Venus Pool
Cape Point Rd.
Buffels Bay
Cape of Good Hope
Cape Point
NAMIBIA
BOTSWANA
MOZAMBIQUE
SWAZILAND
LESOTHO
SOUTH AFRICA
INDIAN OCEAN
Area of detail
Start here
Take a Break
Lighthouse
Beach
Surfing
Lookout
Airport
Driving Route
Alternate Return Route
Trail
1 Mowbray turnoff/ Irma Stern Museum & Mostert's Mill
2 Rhodes Memorial
3 Kirstenbosch Botanical Gardens
4 Groot Constantia Estate
5 Natale Labia Museum
6 Cecil Rhodes Cottage
7 Simon's Town
8 Boulders Beach
9 Cape of Good Hope Nature Reserve (entrance)
10 Chapman's Peak Drive
11 Hout Bay
12 Victoria Road
13 Signal Hill

Rhodes. If you're interested in colonial architecture, you can make an appointment to visit **Groote Schuur,** also donated by Rhodes, and designed by Herbert Baker, "the architect of the Empire," and up until the end of Mandela's term, the official government residence; call ✆ **021/686-9100.**

From here, the suburbs become increasingly upmarket. Take the turnoff to:

❸ Kirstenbosch Botanical Gardens

Consider visiting Kirstenbosch (you'll need at least an hour, preferably more) before heading through the suburbs of Bishop's Court and Wynberg for Constantia. See "Table Mountain National Park," earlier in this chapter.

If you've decided against Kirstenbosch, you may have time along the way to visit the:

❹ Groot Constantia Estate

You can visit the 17th-century manor house and wine museum, and possibly try a wine tasting (see above). Alternatively, set aside a full afternoon to travel the full Constantia Wine Route, visiting at least three estates (don't miss Klein Constantia).

Keep traveling south on the M3 until it runs into a T-junction, then turn left to the next T-junction, where you join the M4; turn right and look for Boyes Drive and the gorgeous elevated views of False Bay. This short detour of the coastal route is often less congested than the narrow road that runs through the coastal suburbs of Muizenberg, St James, and Kalk Bay, though you'll miss much of the interesting turn-of-the-20th-century architecture which spawned the title Millionaire's Mile. If this history interests you, try to time your visit for a Monday and make an appointment to view the:

❺ Natale Labia Museum

Built in the Venetian style, the **Natale Labia Museum,** Main Road, Muizenberg (✆ **021/788-4106** or 021/481-3800; by appointment only), was the sumptuous home of the Count and Countess Labia, and is a fabulous example of the holiday homes built by Cape Town's glam society in the last century, when False Bay was the favored seaboard of wealthy randlords.

Another attraction on Muizenberg's Main Road (also called the Historical Mile) is:

❻ Cecil Rhodes Cottage

This house, on the main road (✆ **021/788-1816;** Mon–Fri 9:30am–4:30pm, Sat–Sun 10am; donations welcome), is where Rhodes purportedly died—a remarkably humble abode for a man who shaped much of southern Africa's history. If you enjoy this area and want more information, contact **Cape Point Route** (✆ **021/782-9356**).

Another popular stop along this tight coastal road cutting between Muizenberg and Kalk Bay, is the St James tidal pool beach (right near the St James train station; look for the sign), with its trademark bathing boxes painted in different colors. Continue on Main Road to the quaint fishing village of Kalk Bay, which has a number of good places to eat and junk shops to explore.

> **TAKE A BREAK**
>
> Whether you've taken Muizenberg's main road or Boyes Drive, stop in at quaint **Kalk Bay** to browse the antiques shops, galleries, junk shops, and retro-modern boutiques. See "Where to Dine," earlier in this chapter.

The drive then resumes south along the M4 to Fish Hoek and the naval village of:

❼ Simon's Town

This vies with Kalk Bay as the most charming of the False Bay towns, lined with double-story Victorian buildings, which is why many regular visitors to the Cape choose to stay here. If you feel like lingering, visit the **Simon's Town Museum,** Court Road (✆ **021/786-3046;** R4 adults, R1 children; Mon–Fri 9am–4pm, Sat 10am–1pm, Sun 11am–3pm), or take a 40-minute cruise around the bay (✆ **021/786-2136**). For more details on what the town has to offer, visit the **Simon's Town Tourism Bureau,** also on Court Road (✆ **021/786-8440**).

If you're hot and bothered, don a bathing suit and join the penguins at nearby:

8 Boulders Beach

View the large breeding colony of jackass (African) penguins that settled here in the early 1980s—to the horror of residents, who now have to deal with the attendant coachloads of tourists.

From Simons Town, it's 15 minutes to the entrance of the:

9 Cape of Good Hope Nature Reserve

Once inside, take Circular Drive to spot game, or head for one of the usually deserted beaches; if you're pressed for time, head straight for Cape Point (see "Table Mountain National Park," earlier in this chapter). From the nature reserve, it's a relatively straightforward and spectacular drive back to town (if Chapman's Peak is open; if not, see tip above). Take the M65 left out of the reserve past the **Cape Point Ostrich Farm** (✆ **021/780-9294;** daily 9:30am–5:30pm; tours are R30 and include coffee), and travel through the pretty coastal town of **Scarborough** (a gorgeously peaceable place to stay overnight, by the way; see p. 116), the aptly named **Misty Cliffs,** and **Kommetjie** (you can opt to bypass Kommetjie, but note that this, too, has some fabulous beachfront accommodations options) to **Noordhoek.**

Noordhoek has a famously beautiful beach, the aptly named Long Beach (make sure you don't walk it with valuables), but if you're pressed for time, follow the signs and head north to ascend the exhilarating:

10 Chapman's Peak Drive

Built between 1915 and 1922, this winding 10km (6¼-mile) drive must rate as one of the world's best, with cliffs plunging straight into the ocean, dwarfing the vehicles snaking along its side. Not surprisingly, hundreds of international car commercials have been shot here. Note that this opened as a toll road in 2003 (count on paying around R30), but these days, it's frequently and controversially closed to all traffic; look for signs alerting you to any closure, or ask your host to find out before you set off.

From Chapman's Peak, you descend into:

11 Hout Bay

Here you could either stop for the most delicious calamari, on the veranda at the **Chapman's Peak Hotel,** or head for the harbor and book a cruise to view the seal colony and seabird sanctuary on **Duiker Island** (see "Organized Cruises & Tours," earlier in this chapter), or visit the **World of Birds Sanctuary** (Kids) on Valley Road (✆ **021/790-2730;** www.worldofbirds.org.za; daily 9am–5pm; R59 adults, R37 children), home to more than 400 species of birds and small animals; it's Africa's largest bird park and includes a monkey jungle.

From Hout Bay, you can now take the coast-hugging:

12 Victoria Road (or M6)

Take this road to Camps Bay—with any luck, it will coincide with sunset, or you'll have a moon to guide you.

Follow the M6 through Camps Bay and turn right at the KLOOF NEK ROUNDHOUSE sign to snake up the mountain to the Kloof Nek roundabout and take the turnoff to:

13 Signal Hill

The views from the hill are breathtaking, particularly at night, when the twinkling city lies spread before you.

6 STAYING ACTIVE

For one-stop adrenaline activity shopping, contact **Downhill Adventures** (✆ **021/422-0388;** www.downhilladventures.com), which offers everything from its own surf school (see below) to helicopter rides.

ABSEILING ★★★ **Abseil Africa** (✆ **021/424-4760;** www.abseilafrica.co.za) will throw you 100m (328 ft.) off Table Mountain—attached to a rope, of course (R495, excluding cable car fees; R650 hike and abseil combo). But their best trip is **Kamikaze Kanyon** ★, a day's *kloofing* (scrambling down a river gorge) in a nature reserve, ending with a 65m (213-ft.) waterfall abseil (R695).

BALLOONING Board a balloon in the early morning and glide over the Paarl Winelands—the 1-hour flight (R2,350 per person) takes off every morning from November to April and includes a champagne breakfast at the Grande Roche. Contact **Wineland Ballooning** (✆ **021/863-3192**).

BIRD-WATCHING The peninsula attracts nearly 400 species of birds; Kirstenbosch Botanical Gardens, Cape Point, and Rondevlei Nature Reserve are some of the best areas for sightings. For guided tours of the area and farther afield, contact **BirdWatch Cape** (✆ **021/762-5059;** www.birdwatch.co.za). A half-day tour costs R1,800 (for up to three people), and includes pick-up and drop-off but not reserve entrance fees; full-day trips cost R2,800.

BOATING An exhilarating boating experience, ocean rafting reaches speeds of up to 130kmph (81 mph) across Table Bay or around Robben Island in an 11-passenger inflatable (✆ **021/425-3785;** www.atlanticadventures.co.za; R350 per person for 1 hr.). For more options, see "Organized Cruises & Tours," earlier in this chapter.

CANOEING/KAYAKING **Real Cape Adventures** (✆ **021/790-5611;** www.seakayak.co.za) covers almost every sea-kayaking route on the western and southern coasts and caters to all levels of ability—request a trip to the rugged coastline of Cape Point.

DIVING Wreck diving is popular here, and the coral-covered wrecks at Smitswinkel Bay are particularly worth exploring, as are Maori Bay, Oak Burn, and Bnos 400. Call **Dive Action** (✆ **021/511-0815;** www.diveaction.co.za).

FISHING **Big Game Fishing Safaris** (✆ **021/674-2203**) operates out of Simons Town on a 12m (39-ft.) catamaran and offers bottom/reef fishing (as well as crayfish lunches, sundowner cruises, and onboard skeet shooting). You can also go online and charter a deep-sea fishing trip with **Cape Sea Safaris** (www.capeseasafaris.com). **Trout fishing** is popular in the crystal-clear streams found in the Du Toits Kloof Mountains near Paarl and in Franschhoek, where salmon trout is a specialty on every menu. For guided trips, call Tim (✆ **083/626-0467**). For general advice, tuition, and permits in Franschhoek, contact **Dewdale Fly Fishery** (✆ **021/876-2755**).

GOLFING The **Royal Cape** (✆ **021/761-6551**) has hosted the South African Open many times. **Milnerton Golf Club** ★ (✆ **021/552-1047;** www.milnertongolf.co.za) is the only true links course in the Cape, with magnificent views of Table Mountain, but is best avoided when the wind is blowing. **Rondebosch** (✆ **021/689-4176;** www.rondeboschgolfclub.com) and **Mowbray** (✆ **021/685-3018**)—both off the N2—have lovely views of Devil's Peak (the latter course is the more demanding). **Clovelly** (✆ **021/782-1118**), in Fish Hoek, is a tight course requiring some precision. **Steenberg** (✆ **021/713-2233**) is *the* course in Constantia.

In the Winelands, the Gary Player–designed **Erinvale** ★, Lourensford Road (✆ **021/847-1144**), in Somerset West, is considered the best, but **Stellenbosch** (✆ **021/880-0103**), on Strand Road, is another worthwhile course, with a particularly challenging tree-lined fairway. Nestled in the Franschhoek valley, Jack Nicklaus's **Pearl Valley Golf Estate** ★★ (✆ **021/867-8000;** www.pearlvalleygolfestates.com) will host the South African Open in 2010 (for the third time since opening in 2003); the 13th hole is legendary, and views provide a great distraction throughout.

HIKING Most hikers start by climbing Table Mountain, for which there are a number of options (see "Table Mountain," earlier in this chapter); call the **Mountain Club** (✆ **021/465-3412**). For hikes farther afield, contact Ross at **High Adventure** (✆ **021/447-8036**)—as a trained climbing instructor, Ross can spice up your walk with some exhilarating ascents. If you're staying in Stellenbosch, the trails (5.3km–18km/3.25–11 miles) in the mountainous **Jonkershoek Nature Reserve** are recommended. Recommended reading for hikers: *Day Walks in and Around Cape Town,* by Tim Anderson (Struik), and Mike Lundy's *Best Walks in the Peninsula* (Struik).

HORSEBACK RIDING Take an early-morning or sunset ride on spectacular Long Beach, Noordhoek, by contacting **Sleepy Hollow** (✆ **021/789-2341**). To ride among the vineyards on horseback stopping for wine tastings, see "Getting Around" and "Guided Tours" in the "Franschhoek" and "Stellenbosch" sections, later in this chapter, or contact **Wine Valley Horse Trails** (✆ 083/226-8735; www.horsetrails-sa.co.za) for a range of rides commencing on Rhebokskloof Wine Estate.

KITE-SURFING ★★★ Cape Town is considered one of the world's best kite-surfing destinations. Big Bay, at Blouberg (take R27, Marine Dr., off the N1), provides consistent wind, good waves, and a classic picture-postcard view of Table Mountain. Other popular spots include Milnerton Lagoon, and Platboom, off the Cape Point Nature Reserve. For lessons and rentals, contact the **Cabrinha Kiteboarding School** (✆ **021/556-7910;** www.cabrinha.co.za; R495 per 2-hr. lesson), or visit their shop at Marine Promenade, Porterfield Road, in Table View, right at Blouberg's renowned Kitebeach. Or head north to Langebaan Lagoon.

MOUNTAIN BIKING There are a number of trails on Table Mountain, Cape Point, and the Winelands, but the Tokai Forest network and Constantiaberg trails are the best. Contact **Day Trippers** (✆ **021/511-4766;** R495) for guided rides on Constantiaberg and around Cape Point; or **Downhill Adventures** (✆ **021/422-0388;** www.downhill adventures.com; R655) for a full-day Cape Point and Winelands tour.

PARAGLIDING ★★★ An unparalleled way to see Cape Town is while hanging weightlessly on the thermals above the city. Soar off Lion's Head for a jaw-dropping view of mountains and sea, and land at Camps Bay Beach or La Med bar for cocktails at sunset. Another rated flight is over the Franschhoek valley, but there are jump points all over the Peninsula and as far away as Hermanus. The most reliable starting point is Signal Hill, but bear in mind that if the wind doesn't cooperate, you can't fly, so it's best to call at the start of your holiday and provide a mobile number where you can be reached on short notice when conditions are right. This is an exhilarating trip; no prior experience is necessary for the carefree tandem session (R950; 10–25 min.), but the brief taste of the remarkably cool sensation of effortless flight might inspire you to sign up for a full course. Either way, contact Barry or Candice at **Birdmen** (✆ **082/658-6710;** www.birdmen.co.za).

SANDBOARDING South Africa's answer to snowboarding takes place on the tallest dunes all around the Cape. Contact **Downhill Adventures** (see above) for trips and tuition (✆ **021/422-0388;** R655 full-day).

SHARK-CAGE DIVING ★★★ You don't have to stay in Hermanus to have a riveting up-close and personal experience with one of Earth's most ancient creatures in its natural habitat. Most South African shark-cage diving companies will do Cape Town hotel pick-ups, though some commence as early as 3:45am (if you're based in Camps Bay). If you're at all fascinated by creatures of the deep, the excursion is worth it. The boat trip is usually

Surf & Sand: Cape Town's Best Beaches

You'll find Cape Town's most beautiful beaches along the Atlantic seaboard, with Clifton, Camps Bay, and Llandudno the most popular. A combination of four beaches semiseparated by large granite boulders, gorgeous **Clifton** ★★★ has Blue-Flag status, is often the only place where the wind isn't blowing, and is good for swimming (albeit freezing), but it's a long walk back through the cliff-hugging village to your car. Oft-crowded **Camps Bay** ★★ offers easy access, a few rock pools, and numerous bars and cafes within strolling distance. You can also hire loungers and umbrellas on the beach (in season), even summon a personal masseuse, and get takeaway pizza delivered from Col'Cacchio across the way. For better privacy, gigantic boulders, and a family-friendly vibe, move along to the tucked-away miniature beaches of **Bakoven** ★★. Laid-back **Llandudno** ★★ is one of the city's prettiest beaches, though parking can be a real problem during high season. **Sandy Bay,** adjacent to Llandudno, is the Cape's only nudist beach. Reached via a narrow footpath, it is secluded and popular with gay men and wankers—this is not a great spot for women, unless you're in a group. The pristine, empty 8km (5-mile) stretch of **Long Beach** ★, featured in a thousand television commercials, is best traversed on horseback; farther south, the white sands of **Scarborough** ★★ have serious allure. On the False Bay side, where the water is warmer, the best place to swim is with the penguins at **Boulders** (although on a bad day you may have to contend with gawking tourists as well). The tidal pool at **St James** is where old-timers start the day in the warmer-than-Clifton waters, backed by much-photographed colorful beach huts.

the undoing of most divers—unless you're regularly at sea, you should consider taking sea-sickness medication (ask your doctor), which must be administered in advance. Take warm clothing along (the water is icy and the onboard breeze gets very fresh). Other than this, you're supplied with everything you need for the experience. See chapter 6, under "Hermanus," for operators.

SKYDIVING ★★★ Free-fall for up to 30 seconds, attached to an experienced instructor. **Skydive Cape Town** (✆ **082/800-6290;** www.skydivecapetown.za.net) offers tandem dives (R1,450) off the West Coast, some 3,600m (11,808 ft.) above Melkbosstrand. You can also jump solo by undertaking a basic static line course; R900 includes the theoretical and practical training, as well as the first exhilarating jump. Licensed skydivers can rent gear and get on jump craft at good rates.

SURFING ★★★ For the daily surf report, call ✆ **082/234-6340.** The beaches off Kalk Bay reef and Noordhoek are considered hot spots, but Muizenberg and Big Bay, at Blouberg (take R27, Marine Dr., off the N1), are good for beginners. **Downhill Adventures** (✆ **021/422-0388;** www.downhilladventures.com) has a surf school with all equipment provided (R655 full day, with lunch and transfers). If all you need is equipment or advice, call **Matthew Moir** (✆ **083/444-9442**).

WHALE-WATCHING Hermanus, just over an hour's drive on the N2, is one of the world's best land-based spots. Call the **Whale Hot Line** (✆ **083/910-1028**). For the city's best whale-watching, drive along the False Bay coast, or contact Evan at **Atlantic Adventures** (✆ **083/680-2768**), which operates trips out of the V&A Waterfront. Contact the **Waterfront Boat Company** (✆ **021/418-5806;** www.waterfrontboats.co.za) for trips in Table Bay, departing from the Waterfront.

7 SHOPPING

You'll find a large selection of shops and hundreds of street hawkers catering to the African arts-and-crafts market, but because very little of it is produced locally, you will pay a slight premium. The better the gallery, the larger the premium. Beadwork, however, is a local tradition; a variety of beaded items is for sale at the tourism bureau, also the place to pick up an *Arts & Crafts Map.* But Cape Town shopping now offers a great deal more than naive wooden carvings and beaded trinkets. Sophisticated Eurocentric products with superb local twists are finding their way into design-savvy shops all over the world; and, from minimalist handbags made with richly patterned Nguni hides to gorgeous lamps made with polished horn or porcupine quills, you'll find them here, particularly in the De Waterkant area, for far less. For more listings, page through the annual *Time Out Cape Town for Visitors,* available in the city's bookstores. Remember that you are entitled to a 14% VAT refund before you leave.

If you take your shopping seriously and want the lowdown on the city's hottest consumer venues, contact Sandra Fairfax of **Blue Bayou** ★★★ (✆ **083/293-6555** or 021/762-5689; www.bluebuyou.co.za) for one of her highly personalized **shopping tours.** She'll pick you up and put together a shopping and browsing itinerary that takes into account your tastes and interests. She has helped some of Cape Town's most prestigious visitors shop and led them to the front door of top designers, world-renowned artists, and splurge-worthy outlets where you'll meet the owners and get to know the history or background of *objets* that might otherwise mean nothing to you.

GREAT SHOPPING AREAS

City Center

Sadly, in the heart of the city center, historical **Greenmarket Square** (Mon–Sat 9am–4pm)—surrounded by some of the loveliest buildings in Cape Town—has devolved into a tourist trap (most of the stalls are owned by the same wholesaler, and goods here seldom inspire excitement). Do browse here, however, just for the atmosphere (it's an interesting cultural crossroads) and then check out the surrounding architecture. More serious shopping starts along nearby **Church Street,** where the pedestrianized cobbled walkway that links to Long Street attracts casual traders dealing in antiques, hand-fashioned leather jewelry, and T-shirts emblazoned with logo-style township names. Don't miss **African Image,** on the corner of Church and Burg (see below); the **Cape Gallery,** 60 Church St. (✆ **021/423-5309**), for fine artworks with an emphasis on plant, animal, and birdlife; and the **Association for Visual Arts,** 35 Church St. (✆ **021/424-7436**), an important nonprofit art gallery. The **Collector,** 52 Church St. (✆ **021/423-1483**), trades in the expensive end of what they term "tribal" artifacts and antiques, while **Imagenius** (see below) is the heavyweight specialist in desirable modern African *objets,* and plenty else besides.

Take a Break

Even if you haven't yet handed over your credit card, the sheer intensity of browsing through Cape Town's multifangled stores should earn you a pit stop. To sample Afro-chic hospitality, pop into beautiful **Nzolo Brand Café,** 48 Church St. (✆ **021/426-1857** or 083/353-3724; Mon–Sat 8am–5pm), where the colors and distinctive logos of Africa's most iconic products form a slick backdrop to quality teas (try the homegrown rooibos mixed with elderflower and rose), local-blend coffees, fresh cakes, and delectable dishes from the African continent. Beautifully packaged, the take-home tinned teas make great gifts.

Where Church meets Long, turn right and head for the **Pan African Market,** probably the best place to pick up African crafts in Cape Town (see "Best Buys," below). It's a total contrast to the swanky interior of **Tribal Trends,** 72–74 Long St. (✆ **021/423-8008**), which showcases an audacious (but pricey) selection of great African-inspired design.

If you double back down Church Street, you can continue all the way to **St George's Mall,** a pedestrian street that runs the length of town. Buskers and street dancers perform here, and a few street hawkers peddle masks and sculptures. For more options, head 1 block down to **Adderley Street,** cross via the Golden Acre, and browse the station surroundings, where the streets are paved with wood and soapstone carvings. It's also paved with pickpockets, so don't carry valuables here. By now you'll have had your fill of African crafts, so head back up to **Long Street** and walk toward the mountain. This is the city's most interesting street—lined with Victorian buildings, Long Street houses, antiques shops, galleries, gun shops, porn outlets, hostels, cafes, bars, a church or two, and eventually a Turkish bathhouse. Be on the lookout for **210Long,** a small, sustainable shopping "mall" at 210 Long St., where you'll find a small selection of good South African stores; **Gravy** sells T-shirts by local designer Craig Native (under the Electric Zulu label), which make perfect gifts for younger friends back home. On the other side of the road is **Still Life,** stocked with cool homeware items and beautiful *objets.* If you continue up Long and cross onto **Kloof Street,** it's definitely worth looking at the intriguing local homeware and design parody items displayed at all-white **O.live** (next to the Chinese eatery), where you'll fall under the spell of the dreamlike soundtrack (and dreamy-eyed shop assistant). Next door is **laLesso,** a boutique selling ladies' exotic garments made from Kenyan fabrics—the Swahili logos on the dresses are good wishes; the innovative label has already found its way to Tokyo, London, Paris, Barcelona, and New York.

Finally, it's worth noting that life in the East City—stretching from Parliament toward the dodgy end of town where District Six was once razed to the ground, is on the up and up, and rapidly filling up with some unique shopping stops. On Roeland Street, in particular, intriguing little stores are opening and a cafe culture is flaring. Witness the utterly local homeware and kitchen products on display in **Dorp** (Afrikaans for "Town;" ✆ **082/829-7176**), at 76 Roeland St., where the layout is reminiscent of quintessential small-town South African naïveté and you can buy homemade baked treats (ask for some *hertzoggies* and *koeksisters*). Just down the drag is Cape Town's finest bookstore (see box below).

De Waterkant

Created in 2001, this area has developed into one of the most exciting shopping precincts in town, with lovely cobbled streets, a lively dining square (good protection when the wind is up), and a mob of excellent shops and cafes. With its 15 stores about to be bolstered (for better or worse) by the arrival of a new mall-like center, it won't take you long to find your favorites. You could start anywhere, but Jarvis and Waterkant streets and, of course, the Cape Quarter's inner sanctum are proven stomping grounds. Whatever you do, don't miss **Africa Nova** or **Fibre Designs** (details below). If you're interested in art, check out **VEO Gallery,** 8 Jarvis St. (✆ **021/421-3278**), and **Lisa King Gallery,** Shop B14, Cape Quarter (✆ **021/421-3738**). The great thing about Lisa is that she combines an excellent eye with an unpretentious approach. Already referred to as the South African Abercrombie & Finch, the brilliant new **Kingsley Heath,** 117 Waterkant St. (✆ **021/421-0881**) has a stylish look inspired by adventures in the African bush. The sophisticated clothing and fashion accessories, including leather jewelry and cowhide shoes, prove that you needn't go in for obvious and unflattering khaki wear just because you're heading out on safari. There's even a Kingsley Heath men's fragrance.

Waterfront

Shopping here is a far less satisfying experience than in the bustling streets of town or the gentrified cobbled streets of De Waterkant; at the end of the day, Victoria Wharf is simply a glam mall with a famous and fabulous location (which is totally wasted on what has become an almost exclusively indoor shopping experience). There are, however, a few gems, such as **Out of Africa** (adjacent to **Exclusive Books**), for a fantastic, albeit pricey, range of items from all over the continent. And if you're looking for a dress or shirt that will really make heads turn—we're talking proper African designer wear—head straight upstairs for **Sun Goddess** (✆ **021/421-7620**). Outside the shopping center, in the old offices of the Port Captain (on the way to the Clock Tower), is the truly excellent selection of sculptures, jewelry, tableware, textiles, ceramics, and furniture at the **African Trading Post,** Pierhead, Dock Road (✆ **021/419-5364**); spread over three stories, this is worth a visit even if you're not buying.

Woodstock & Southern Suburbs

Every Saturday morning, a selection of the city's hippest congregate at **The Old Biscuit Mill** ★★★, 375 Albert Rd., Woodstock, a warehouse space that's been cleverly transformed to make way for the weekly **Neighbourgoods Market** ★★★

Bibliophiles Browse Here

Although there are several well-stocked bookstores on Long Street (Clarke's is an institution), the best place to browse for quality reads (no rubbish stocked), fabulous coffee table tomes, and the best in South African writing is **The Book Lounge,** 71 Roeland St. (✆ **021/462-2425**), with seating for bookworms and a cafe on the downstairs level. It's also where you can catch regular literary events (held almost every Tues, Wed, and Thurs, but occasionally on other nights, too, usually commencing 5:30 or 6pm); these include book launches and discussions involving some of the biggest names in South African literature and publishing. Pick up a program of forthcoming events in-store.

(✆ **021/462-6361;** Sat), now a defining Cape Town event with packed tables groaning under organic produce and great on-site prepared meals. There are a few stalls selling collectible T-shirts or jewelry, but most are here for the food (don't miss the Lebanese pies, cured meats from Bread & Wine, or addictive tarts from Queen of Tarts), with upcoming artisans waiting patiently in the wings as they move up the impossibly long waiting list for a stand here. While you're here (or on any weekday, too), it's worth your while to check out some of the permanent shops opposite the market. **Imiso** is owned by three young black ceramicists whose work is among the most exciting, even revolutionary, I've ever seen. **Clementina Ceramics** (✆ **021/447-1398**) showcases a range of wonderful talent in glass, jewelry, and other materials, and the Clementina van der Walt tableware is stunning. Farther south, in Newlands, there's plenty of creative flair (as well as opportunities to join pottery workshops, watch ironmongers, and grab a bite at the farm stall) at the **Montebello Design Centre** ★★★, 31 Newlands Ave. (✆ **021/685-6445**), where you could spend anywhere between an hour and an afternoon browsing the myriad shops.

BEST BUYS

Souvenirs, Gifts & Memorabilia from Africa

African Image This store offers a well-chosen selection of authentic crafts and tribal art ranging from headrests and baskets to beadwork and cloth. 52 Burg St. ✆ **021/423-8385.**

Africa Nova ★★★ Arguably the best of its kind, this large selection of contemporary handmade African goods has been chosen by someone with a keen eye; it's where craft meets art. Best of all, it's on the cobbled Cape Quarter Square (right next to Andiamo deli). 72 Waterkant St. ✆ **021/425-5123.**

Amulet Goldsmiths Add value to the world's safest investment by commissioning Gerika and Elizabeth to make a contemporary jewelry item (or simply pick one up at their studio). 14 Kloof Nek Rd., Tamboerskloof. ✆ **021/426-1149.**

A.R.T. Gallery This gallery sells brightly hued African-motif tableware, created by popular ceramicist Clementina van der Walt, as well as a selection of textiles, woodwork, baskets, and ceramics created by up-and-coming local artists. Main Rd., Kalk Bay. ✆ **021/788-8718.**

Heartworks It's more of a crafts showcase, but items here are chosen with a modern design slant; look for beautiful ceramics and bead- and wirework. Gardens Centre, Mill St. (satellite store on Kloof St.). ✆ **021/465-3289.**

Imagenius ★★★ Three floors of a refurbished turn-of-the-20th-century building are jampacked with great gear, from Shirley Fintz's ceramic hunting trophies to interesting furniture pieces by Haldane Martin (www.haldanemartin.co.za) and Gerard Back. They even carry CDs by Goldfish, a Cape Town–based electro-jazz duo that has been wowing audiences around the world (www.goldfishlive.com). 117 Long St. ✆ **021/423-7870.** www.imagenius.co.za.

Imiso Ceramics ★★ There's work of pure genius here; Andile Ayalvane is but one of the seriously talented kiln operators turning out fine items you can use or display. Either way, your home will never be the same again. The Old Biscuit Mill, 375 Albert Rd., Woodstock. ✆ **021/447-7668.** www.imisoceramics.co.za.

Pan African Market Three stories of rooms overflow with goods from all over Africa, from tin picture frames to large, intricate carvings and beautiful pieces of beadwork.

There's also a small cafe with traditional food on the first-floor balcony. 76 Long St. ✆ **021/426-4478.** www.panafrican.co.za.

Sophisticated African Interior Design

Colonial House Design Another interior shop producing wonderful furniture and accessories with a unique African twist, it's a one-stop shop if you're looking to furnish an upmarket game lodge. Shop A17 Cape Quarter, De Waterkant. ✆ **021/421-1467.** www.colonialhouse.co.za.

Fibre Designs The best carpet shop on the continent, with the most exciting designs, in wonderful color combinations. You'd be hard-pressed to find any of the items anywhere else in the world. This is a perfect global match, with carpets designed in Africa and woven by master weavers in the East. 3 Jarvis St., De Waterkant. ✆ **021/418-1054.** www.fibredesigns.co.za.

LIM This tiny shop produces some of the city's best examples of homegrown, simple, modern furniture and accessories—be it an asymmetrical Mozambican vase, a paper-thin Shapiro bowl, or a leather cube foot rest. 86a Kloof St. ✆ **021/423-1200.**

Maya Prass Known for her floral-print designs and vibrant, vivid colors, Maya Prass has a distinctive and quirky style—her fabrics are fresh and contemporary, yet have a vintage feel; her handmade garments and homeware items, from wallpaper to patchwork bedspreads and scatter cushions, are good bets. Constantia Courtyard, Constantia Village. ✆ **021/794-8805.** www.mayaprass.com.

T&Co This smart, ethical lifestyle store has a perfect little cafe attached, and there are many beautiful objects to take home. 78 Victoria Junction, Ebenezer Rd., Green Point. ✆ **021/421-3112.**

Fine Art

South Africa has a vibrant art scene, best experienced at the annual **Art Fair** ★★★ held in Johannesburg every April, but the following galleries offer a good taste of what's out there. One of Cape Town's most successful exports, Paul du Toit's (www.pauldutoit.com) paintings have drawn comparisons with the work of Matisse and Picasso, and his recent creation of a bronze version of Madiba's hand is a permanent installation in one of the penthouse suites at the new One&Only hotel at the Waterfront. Paul works from his studio at his home in Hout Bay and welcomes interested art enthusiasts and potential buyers who'd like to meet with him or browse the limited work available for sale (his output is usually gobbled up by collectors before his exhibitions even open). E-mail him if you'd like to visit him, or make arrangements with **Sandra Fairfax** (✆ **083/293-6555**), who can also lead you to a number of galleries and artist workshops, where you'll enjoy a warm introduction to the local art scene.

The Bell-Roberts Gallery Host to regular, interesting exhibitions by up-and-coming artists. 89 Bree St. ✆ **021/422-1100.**

Erdmann Contemporary Heidi Erdmann has a knack for unearthing new talent—she also handles work by brilliant talents such as Varenka Paschke, whose beautiful canvases are well worth snapping up. 63 Shortmarket St. ✆ **021/422-2762.** www.erdmanncontemporary.co.za.

Everard Read Gallery For one of the best selections of South African art, particularly African landscapes and wildlife paintings, this is your best bet—be warned, though:

The Great Gay EsCape

Like sister cities San Francisco, Sydney, and Miami, Cape Town is a sexy seaside spot with a variety of gay things to do. Promoted as "The Gay Capital of Africa" (South Africa's constitution was the first in the world to expressly protect the rights of homosexuals), Cape Town's queer tribes are increasingly rich and varied, with an excellent rapport between straights and gays, and plenty of boundary-crossing to keep the scene interesting. Traditionally associated with its late-night hedonism and tony designer neighborhoods, Cape Town's gay scene is also becoming a more multicultural environment. In April 2009, the annual **Miss Gay Cape Town** event included a special section for competitors from the myriad African states where homosexuality is still outlawed. It's also striking to witness the coming-out of many of the city's gay Muslims, some of whom took part in the Pride parade for the first time in 2009.

Most gay-friendly venues are situated in and around the City Bowl, particularly in Green Point's "De Waterkant Queer Quarter," Sea Point's Main Road, and the mountain end of Long Street. Centered on Somerset Road and up the slopes of Signal Hill to Loader Street, De Waterkant's Gay Village is where you'll find the best selection of clubs, bars, bathhouses, cafes, and guesthouses. Check the local press or the annually produced *The Pink Map* (available from tourism bureaus), or visit www.cape-town.org for more information. **Wanderwomen** (✆ **021/788-9988;** www.wanderwomen.co.za) is a personalized women's-only travel agent; for events and parties for women who love women, go to www.lushcapetown.co.za.

GAY EVENTS Africa's biggest gay circuit party is the annual **MCQP** (Mother City Queer Project) costume party, an extraordinary themed dress-up spectacular, held at great venues and attended by thousands of queers and straights of all ages and persuasions—expect a red carpet arrival, numerous DJ-controlled dance floors, and riotous entertainments. For details of this mid-December event, go to www.mcqp.co.za. **Cape Town Pride** is a 10-day festival in late February (www.capetownpride.co.za); there are new cultural and entertainment events each year, but the highlight is the Pride Parade through the center of Cape Town. Held in September, **Out in Africa** (www.oia.co.za; ✆ **044/382-1610**) is the continent's most important gay and lesbian film festival, with something to satisfy all celluloid tastes. Also worth planning around is the **Pink Loerie Mardi Gras,** held at the end of May, when some 5,000 camp revelers take to the streets of Knysna ("Africa's gayest town"), on the Garden Route—a welcome extension to a trip to Cape Town, with plenty of gay-friendly places to stay along the way.

RECOMMENDED GUESTHOUSES & TOURS A variety of options can be had in **De Waterkant Village** (see "Where to Stay," earlier in this chapter), which is in the heart of the "Queer Quarter," within easy walking distance of clubs and bars. The most tasteful men-only choice, though, is the **Glen Boutique Hotel** ★★ (✆ **021/439-0086;** www.glenhotel.co.za), in Sea Point, which has good facilities and very, er, well-equipped rooms. The Glen is known for its regular all-male gatherings—especially around the pool—that are a great place to meet new friends. Standard rooms go for R1,200 to R1,950 double, in the summer months, and just R600, in winter. But for genuine luxury, book one of the lavish suites (from R1,350, in winter). And if you feel the need to clear your head and get out of town, the men-only **Shisa Guest Farm** (www.shisafarm.com; from R780 double), in the fabulous Winelands town of Tulbagh, is just 80 minutes away. Franschhoek is also known as a gay-friendly town; if you spend the night, check out **Ashbourne House** (© **021/876-2146;** www.ashbourne.co.za; from R880 double). If you're heading farther afield and want to search for gay-friendly accommodations, visit www.pink.co.za, or pick up a free copy of the **Pink South Africa Guide.** There are plenty of competent tour operators in Cape Town, but if you want to make friends, book with **Friends of Dorothy Tours** (© **021/465-1871;** www.friendsofdorothy tours.co.za). They cover pretty much everything in Cape Town, as well as the multiday tours of the Garden Route and whale-watching excursions. **Cape Classic Tours** (© **021/686-0013** or 083/251-7274; www.classiccape.co.za) is a gay-owned operator specializing in Cape Town and the Garden Route (but also handling safaris), and will provide you with a gay guide wherever possible.

BEST BEACHES Clifton's **Third Beach** is where you'll find international male models parading in garments so tight you can tell what religion they are. **Sandy Bay** is Llandudno's famous nudist spot, with discreet cruising at the far end of the beach. ***Beware:*** The freezing ocean will bring you down to size.

A GAY NIGHT OUT Kicking off with a bit of culture in town, you'll find **On Broadway,** 88 Shortmarket St. (© **021/424-1194**), a great cabaret and theater restaurant with excellent shows. Moving to Long Street, **Lola's,** corner of Long and Buiten (© **021/423-0885**), is the queerest vegetarian joint in town, with a delectable crowd. Traveling from town to the Queer Quarter, the first stop worth considering is buzzy **Café Manhattan,** 74 Waterkant St. (© **021/421-6666**), a friendly, chatty bar with a good-value restaurant, which gets busy after 9pm nightly. You can walk from here to Somerset Road, where you'll find **Bronx** ★★ (© **021/419-9216;** www.bronx.co.za), a very popular late-night bar on the corner of Napier Street; the upstairs nightclub, **Navigaytion** (www.navigaytion.co.za), gets a dedicated dance crowd pulsating and sweating to house every Wednesday, Friday, and Saturday from 11pm until late. To get you in the mood with a few civilized drinks before the night turns sweaty, stop by the **Loft Lounge** ★★, 24 Napier St. (© **021/425-2647;** www.loftlounge.co.za), where topless barmen provide great eye candy along with, ahem, cocktails. Occasionally, the venue stages strip shows and other events. **Crew,** wedged between Bronx and Loft, tends to fill up a little later, and entertainment includes beefy dancers. Around the corner, **Beaulah Bar** (named for the local gay-speak term meaning "beautiful"; © **021/421-6798**) is a favorite lesbian hangout where boys needn't feel left out. Cape Town's leathermen and uniform-fetishists hang out at **Bar Code,** 18 Cobern St., off Somerset (© **021/421-5305;** www.leatherbar.co.za), a men-only cruise bar with slings, dark rooms, a maze, and more—ask at the bar about the underwear parties and naked nights, when a strict (un)dress code applies. Nearby, but even steamier, the **Hot House,** 18 Jarvis St. (© **021/418-3888**), is a European-style men-only leisure club, with sauna, steam room, and outdoor sun deck with spectacular views over the city and the harbor.

 You won't find a bargain here. 3 Portswood Rd., Waterfront. ✆ **021/418-4527.** www.everard-read-capetown.co.za.

iART Upstairs, you'll find heftier price tags attached to some of the country's exemplary, well-established artists' pieces; downstairs is the terrain of up-and-coming and less-mainstream canvases and sculptures. Serious collectors should not pass this by. 71 Loop St. ✆ **021/424-5150.** www.iart.co.za.

João Ferreira Gallery Also a good bet for contemporary works by such artists as William Kentridge—whose video work *History of the Main Complaint* has a room all to its own in the Tate Modern in London—which João both exhibits and sources. 70 Loop St. ✆ **021/423-5403.** www.jaoaferreiragallery.com.

Rose Korber Art One of the city's most distinguished art dealers, Rose Korber is a former art critic; some of the top names in the business have canvases in her collection, which are kept in her Camps Bay home. Call to arrange a visit. 48 Sedgemoor Rd. ✆ **021/438-9152.** www.rosekorberart.com.

Salon91 Probably the coolest art gallery in town, owner Monique du Preez has envisaged this intimate new space as an affordable showroom for emerging talent. Investors with lighter wallets and vision should browse here first. 91 Kloof St. ✆ **082/679-3906.** www.salon91art.co.za.

Whatiftheworld/Gallery Selected in 2007 by *Contemporary Magazine* (London) as one of the Top 50 Emerging Galleries from Around the World, Whatiftheworld/Gallery is a platform for a new generation of emerging South African contemporary artists. This fast-rising young gallery has become a destination point for curators and collectors to experience innovative work and to become acquainted with some new names. By giving voice to new talents, the gallery intends to grow public dialogue within the local contemporary art community and provide an alternative to the traditional art structures and institutions. The first gallery to move to the now art-centric Woodstock precinct of Cape Town, Whatiftheworld has been firmly behind the careers of several rising stars on the local contemporary art scene. 208 Albert Rd., 1st floor, Woodstock. ✆ **021/448-1438.**

Food & Wine

Andiamo The best deli in town, with a huge selection of imported goodies but plenty of local produce, too. Cape Quarter. ✆ **021/421-3687.**

Atlas Trading Co. (Finds) Re-create the mild, slightly sweet curry flavors of Cape Malay dishes back home by purchasing a bag of mixed spices from the Ahmed family, proprietors of Atlas, who've been trading here for over a century. 94 Wale St. ✆ **021/423-4361.**

by nature (Finds) Although it's without any outlet to call its own just yet, it's worth tracking down Peter Owen's organic and totally natural produce, including the purest honey. He makes an appearance at the weekly farmers' market in Stellenbosch (Sat), but has stalls at other markets, too. ✆ **083/658-3998.** www.bynature.co.za.

Caroline's Fine Wine Cellar Caroline has an exceptional nose for finding those out-of-the-way gems most Capetonians, let alone visitors, simply don't have the time or know-how to track down. Arguably the best wine shop in Cape Town. V&A Waterfront. ✆ **021/425-5701.** Also at 15 Long St. ✆ **021/419-8984.**

Joubert & Monty This is one of the best places to sample good biltong; try a bit of kudu and beef—ask for the latter to be slightly moist and sliced. Waterfront. ✆ **021/418-0640.**

Steven Rom This liquor merchant (with two other branches) has a large selection in stock but will also track down and order anything you request (even once you're home) and arrange shipping. Galleria Centre, 76 Regent Rd., Sea Point. ✆ **021/439-6043.** www.stevenrom.co.za.

8 CAPE TOWN AFTER DARK

Pick up a copy of the monthly *Cape etc.* or the annual *Time Out Cape Town.* Alternatively, the weekly *Mail & Guardian* covers all major events, as does the *Argus,* a local daily—look in the "Tonight" section—or consult Friday's "Top of the Times" insert in the *Cape Times.* You can book tickets to theaters and movies and most major music/party events by calling **Computicket** (✆ **083/915-8000;** www.computicket.com) and supplying your credit card details.

THE PERFORMING ARTS

Critics in the Mother City can be appallingly sycophantic, so take whatever you read in the press with a pinch of salt (reviews in the *Mail & Guardian* tend to be more reliable). Anything directed by Martinus Basson, Jaco Bouwer, or Fred Abrahamse is not to be missed. In summer, take in one of the outdoor concerts (see below). Take a look at what's on at either of the city's main venues: **ARTscape** (✆ **021/421-7839**) puts on everything from top-end Broadway musicals (*Cats* returns Dec 2009) to important new South African theater, while the **Baxter Theatre,** Main Road, Rondebosch (✆ **021/685-7880**), is a vibrant hub for culture hounds. There's a mixed line-up at **The New Space,** 44 Long St. (✆ **074/134-6636**), which opened in late 2008 and plans a second, edgier stage in the near future. If you like your entertainment light, Camps Bay's **Theatre on the Bay** (✆ **021/438-3301**) hosts a mix of frothy comedies, musicals, and farces; **On Broadway,** Shortmarket Street (✆ **021/4241194**), is the city's best cabaret venue.

Established by adored local funny man Kurt Schoonraad, the city's best dedicated comedy venue is **Jou Ma se Comedy Club** (literally "Your Mother's Comedy Club"), Albert Hall, Albert Road, Woodstock (✆ **021/447-7237;** www.joumasecomedy.co.za). Sensational stand-up performances happen each Thursday (arrive at 7:30 for the 8:30pm show) and cost R70; you may battle with some of the Afrikaans jokes, but this is a top spot to get a sense of what tickles the South African funny bone.

OUTDOOR PERFORMANCES

Summer brings a wealth of fantastic outdoor concerts; tops for venue are the Sunday **Kirstenbosch Summer Concerts** (✆ **021/799-8783;** www.sanbi.org): Bring a picnic and relax to great music, from jazz bands to Cape Minstrel troupes, popular acoustic groups to the Philharmonic Orchestra, while the sun sets behind the mountain. Concerts start at around 5pm, but get there early in order to secure your patch of lawn. Early each year, **Maynardville Open-Air Theatre** in Wynberg (www.maynardville.co.za) hosts a Shakespearean play against a lush forested backdrop. Performances vary from year to year but invariably put a contemporary (or local) spin on the Bard. Arrive early with a picnic basket and bottle or two of wine, and join Cape Town's culture-loving crowd on the lawns. Summer (Feb–Mar) is when the city's public spaces become venues for the recently inaugurated **Infecting the City** festival (www.infectingthecity.com), which draws together some exciting talent in a week of site-specific performances designed to get Capetonians talking about relevant issues. Don't be surprised if buildings, monuments, and fountains become part of the production. Free concerts are held at the **V&A Waterfront Amphitheatre** (✆ **021/408-7600**); acts range from winners of school talent contests to good jazz. It's worth taking the half-hour drive to Stellenbosch, where you can picnic on the lawns before catching a show at the **Oude Libertas Amphitheatre,** Adam Tas Road (✆ **021/809-7473;** www.oudelibertas.co.za), just outside the town. Even better talent is usually on the program of the Summer Season at **Spier Wine Estate** (✆ **021/809-1158;** www.spier.co.za), which has financial pulling power that brings in great local and international opera, theater, and music acts. Note that you can make a night of it by dining at Moyo, Spier's Pan-African restaurant.

THE CLUB, BAR & MUSIC SCENE

During the summer season, Cape Town becomes one big party venue, despite the fact that die-hard dance animals rue the end of a proper club scene. Get into the mood with sundowners at a trendy bar in Camps Bay (see "The Sunset Strip: Wining, Dining & Posing in Camps Bay" in the "Where to Dine" section, earlier in this chapter) or with a bottle of bubbly on a well-situated beach (though, strictly speaking, this is illegal, so be discreet) or the top of Table Mountain. You will want to pace yourself, however—getting to *any* party before 11pm will see you counting barstools. Listings below were hip at press time, but as in most cities, sell-by dates are unpredictable. To play it safe, expect good nights out from Wednesday onward, and head for one of the following two areas: **Long Street,** particularly the mountain end (near the Turkish baths), is the central city's hot party area. Here there's a multitude of quite grungy bars—most notable is **Jo'burg** (✆ **021/422-0142**), where the heady crowd is often entertained by live local music, but the better sections are more intimate bars hidden behind discreetly located doors—make the effort to look for them. Across the road, single-malt devotees frequent the plush leather settees of **The Dubliner @ Kennedy's** (✆ **021/424-1212**). Far cozier is the cigar bar hidden in the back of **Cape to Cuba** (✆ **021/424-2330**), a prettily designed upstairs restaurant (above similarly themed **Che Bar**) that also has a lovely terrace for early-evening cocktails. On this side of the road, all the better watering holes are in upstairs venues (seek out **Neighbourhood Bar**) or hidden down side streets (ask for **Julep**), and my rule is that those that spill out onto the sidewalk are a little dodgy. The other big party strip, catering to (generally speaking) an older, more sophisticated audience, is in Green Point, which incorporates Cape Town's "Gay Quarter," centered on De Waterkant.

Alternative **Lower Main Road,** in Observatory, Cape Town's bohemian suburb, is a good place to hang out if you're into a grungier atmosphere—from **Café Ganesh** (✆ **021/448-3435**) to over-the-top baroque **Touch of Madness** (✆ **021/448-2266**).

And, finally, if you're into edgier electronic music (such as psytrance) in a '60s-revivalist idiom, you'll want to read about the "love parties," below.

Live Music

The best venue for live bands, some of them set to take the world by storm, is **Assembly** ★★★, a massive converted warehouse space on Harrington Street that kicked off the revival of Cape Town's once-deserted-after-dark east. There are masses of varied, interesting places to air out or to dance, and the owners have thoughtfully included foozball machines and arcade games so you don't get bored while waiting for the bands to start rocking the house; great bar service, too. Expect to see many students, but the grownups of the music fraternity come here to see the next step in the South African music evolution (© **021/**465-7286**;** www.theassembly.co.za). Back in the center, **Zula Sound Bar** (© **021/424-2442**), on cosmopolitan Long Street, is a much smaller but no less vibey music venue with eclectic live music, featuring something for everyone depending on the day of the week (or hour of the night) you arrive. Across the road, a less crowded venue where you can catch intimate performances, often by emerging bands and solo artists, is the **Waiting Room,** where you feel like you're watching a show in someone's lounge. In Zonnebloem (near District Six), **Mercury Live & Lounge,** 43 de Villiers St. (© **021/465-2106;** www.mercuryl.co.za), is hardly the most slick or sophisticated venue, but it's still the only place in the city where you'll find a regular lineup of original South African bands. Downstairs in the broom-closet-size lounge, catch a cutting-edge selection of up-and-coming local acts. In a totally different league, though, will be the international-caliber concerts hosted at the new **Green Point Stadium.**

It's off the beaten tourist track, but it's worth the effort to catch regular Cape jazz sessions featuring hot artists at **West End,** College Road, Athlone (© **021/637-9132**). The **Green Dolphin Restaurant,** at the V&A Waterfront (© **021/421-7471**), caters to the supper-club jazz enthusiast, attracting a good lineup of local and international performers (the food is pretty mediocre and pricey). **Manenberg's Jazz Café,** at the Clock Tower Precinct, V&A Waterfront (© **021/421-5639**), serves up an array of jazz geared toward tourists.

Clubs

Bronx ★★ Two levels of dance floor and all the characters you'd expect at Cape Town's most established gay club. Very straight friendly, this is undoubtedly still one of the better parties on a Friday or Saturday night. Green Point. © **021/419-9216.**

Chevelle ★★ Situated on steadily rejuvenating Harrington Street, in the once-scary-after-dark part of town, this is Cape Town's priciest club experience, and on weekends it gets packed with models, glam-bots, and wannabe celebrities (real ones, too). There are plenty of elegant nooks and balconies to watch the action, but the pouting and posturing may eventually have you running out the door. Or maybe not . . . 84 Harrington St. www.chevelle.co.za. Cover R100.

Decodance ★ A new hangout for the 30-something crowd—who would have thought the '80s and '90s could be so cheerfully revived? And they've got even older tracks up their sleeve, too. Old Biscuit Mill, 375 Albert Rd, Woodstock. © **084/330-1162.** www.decodance.co.za.

Fiction ★★★ Space may be at a premium at this immaculately styled DJ-centric club in the heart of the city's party zone, but the music lineup is the stuff of legend. Find a spot on the matchbox dance floor early, mark your territory, and prepare to sweat among an electric mob of musically educated party enthusiasts. The Killer Robot events are, well, killer. 227 Long St. © **021/424-5709.** www.fictionbar.com.

Galaxy ★★★ (Finds) Home to parties hosted by the local radio station's Goodhope FM and packed with a local "coloured" crowd, this is off the tourist track but the place to see real Cape Town get down. Expect to sweat a lot, unless it's a famous Galaxy foam party. A great place to party, with a lot of grinding to the sounds of house, R&B, hip-hop, and live music. College Rd., Rylands Estate, Athlone. © **021/637-9132.**

Hemisphere ★★ On the 31st floor of the Absa building in the Cape Town CBD, this club has fantastic views of the Mother City and Table Mountain. Lounges lead into dance floors, which lead into bars, but the excellent soul and funk music will keep you under the glitter ball all night. Riebeeck St. ✆ **021/421-0581.**

Jade ★★★ This attractively attired club attracts perhaps the most varied, most astonishingly beautiful, and most unpretentious crowd in Cape Town. What really leaves me gobsmacked is that, despite often-dire music (from messy hip-hop to kitsch commercial tracks spun by a DJ who refuses to let up), the crowd always appears to be having the most spectacular time. It's a fabulously civilized, unhinged spot to let down your hair, lounge on antique-style sofas, pose, stare, boogie, and meet gorgeous people from all over the world. The entrance is unmarked, just around the corner from Manos Restaurant on Green Point's main drag. 39 Main Rd., Green Point. ✆ **021/439-4108.**

Kink ★ The jury's still out on this bar pretending to be a club, perhaps because the venue also doubles as a slinky lingerie store (upstairs) during the day. But you may just find your kink here. Park Rd., Tamboerskloof. ✆ **021/424-0757.**

Bars

Alba.Lounge ★★ The classiest lounge-bar in the Waterfront, this waterside venue is unpretentious and comfortable; even children are welcome here. It's the perfect place to unwind after a full day's shopping or before wandering to a Waterfront restaurant. Pierhead, V&A Waterfront. ✆ **021/425-3385.** www.albalounge.co.za.

Asoka Son of Dharma ★★★ A favorite with the inner city's smart punters, this intimate Balinese-style venue, with comfy seating in a courtyard centered on an old tree, is apparently steeped in feng shui. Whatever the reason, it attracts a cool mix. 68 Kloof St., Tamboerskloof. ✆ **021/422-0909.** www.asokabar.co.za.

Baraza ★★ Elevated views of Camps Bay's palm-fringed beach still pull in a vivacious crowd of cocktail-sipping and beer-swilling Capetonians who can't get enough of the setting sun. Cool tunes are *de rigeur,* too. The Promenade, Victoria Rd., Camps Bay. ✆ **021/438-1758.** www.blues.co.za.

Belthezar ★ This V&A Waterfront wine bar claims to offer the largest selection of wines by the glass in the world—just the place to work your way through the winelands. (If whiskey is your poison, head for tiny **Bascule,** the itty-bitty bar situated on the edge of the yacht marina in the Cape Grace hotel; ✆ **021/410-7100**). Victoria & Albert Waterfront. ✆ **021/421-3753.**

Boo Radley's ★★ (Finds) Classic cocktails—made according to authentic, original recipes—are signature at this slick New York–style bistro with a long, sociable, polished bar counter. It's an ideal spot for pre- *and* post-theater drinks if you've got tickets for shows at either the New Space, upstairs, or On Broadway, nearby; order a perfectly mixed sazerac, made to original specifications, with rye bourbon and aged brandy. The bouillabaisse is worthwhile, too. 62 Hout St. ✆ **021/424-3040.** www.booradleys.co.za.

Cape to Cuba ★★ After dark, come to this restaurant and head straight for the clubby, library-style cigar bar in the back. The chocolate tequila is sublime. Follow it up with a delicious daiquiri or mojito—or ask the engaging barmen to make more suggestions. 227 Long St. ✆ **021/424-2330.**

Julep ★★★ (Finds) This is a favorite among Capetonians and a well-kept secret where you'll find a buzzing crowd clamoring for what many consider the best cocktails in town.

If you can't find the discreet, unpublicized entrance, just ask—it's down a little lane that runs off Long Street, more or less opposite Lola's. Vredenburg Lane. ✆ **021/423-4276.**

Karma ★ Cape Town's sexy air-kissing party crowd packs this "beach bar lounge" to capacity. Slick decor and abundant sofas make it good for schmoozing in the company of okay-to-hot DJs (expect hip hop, commercial house, and even live bands). Arrive in time to check out the seaboard's famous sunset, and use the website to get your name on the guest list (it gets busy). Predictably, sushi is served alongside Moët and Dom Perignon. The Promenade, Victoria Rd., Camps Bay. ✆ **021/438-7773.** www.karmalounge.co.za.

Loft Lounge ★★ If you prefer your cocktails served with a hint of navel, then this slick, straight-friendly bar in Cape Town's buzziest gay quarter will appeal. Occasional entertainments include strip shows headlined by a beefy exhibitionist from Minsk, but for dancing, head a few doors up the road, to Bronx. 24 Napier St. ✆ **021/425-2647.** www.loftlounge.co.za.

The Martini ★★★ Finds Take the plunge and head into the Southern Suburbs green belt, where you'll discover a most elegantly designed lounge-bar looking out at the gardens of the impeccable Cellars-Hohenort hotel. The dazzling selection of martinis will leave you stumped for choice, so put aside plenty of time, and be sure to arrange a taxi. 93 Brommersvlei Rd., Constantia. ✆ **021/794-2137.**

Neighbourhood Bar ★★ Finds Even if you make it up the steep, narrow steps to this cozy, subdued bar, don't forget that you'll still need to descend after a round or two of drinks, typically on your way to Fiction (see "Clubs," above), which is almost directly across the road. 163 Long St. ✆ **021/424-7260.** www.goodinthehood.co.za.

Perseverance Tavern ★ Finds There's nothing cool about this traditional pub—it's Cape Town's oldest licensed establishment, serving sailors and citizens since 1836, and a fine spot for a session of beer-fuelled conversation with unpretentious locals. 83 Buitenkant St., Gardens. ✆ **021/461-2440.** www.perseverancetavern.co.za.

Planet Champagne Bar ★★ If you haven't been to the gracious Mount Nelson hotel for tea, then come for its sexy bar. The decor is chic, the gardens are wonderful, and the crowd is predominantly local. 76 Orange St. ✆ **021/483-1000.**

Tobago's ★★ Not as trendy as Wafu, this is another great summer sundowner spot, with plenty of space on the sea-facing terrace to soak up the locals, who outnumber hotel residents on Friday evenings, when the sun sinks low and spirits run high. Radisson Blu Hotel, Beach Rd., Granger Bay ✆ **021/441-3000.**

Wafu ★★★ This indoor-outdoor bar (above Wakame restaurant) features great views, stylish decor, and good tapas—but the real reason to come here is to schmooze with Cape Town's beautiful people, who pile in just as soon as they leave the office or the fashion shoot comes to an end. Beach Rd., Mouille Point. ✆ **021/433-2377.**

Events

Cape Town Jazz Festival ★★★ Local and international artists combine in S.A.'s premier jazz event, held toward the end of summer. Celebrating its first decade in 2010, the festival attracts thousands of music fans for a huge variety of preeminent jazz performances, including many a legend. www.capetownjazzfest.com.

J&B Met ★ It's a horse race, but no one really watches the ponies. As one of the biggest events of the Cape Town social calendar, the J&B Met attracts the cream of S.A.'s best-dressed celebrities (and a few clots, too). www.jbmet.co.za.

Moments The Love Parties

Anyone visiting the Cape and looking to tune into the future of dance music should make a point of lining up at least one **outdoor trance party** ★★★ as part of their sojourn in and around the Mother City. It's probably the best place to catch Capetonians at their unabashed, sweaty, unpretentious best—they'll be dressed down, barefoot, and up to all kinds of mischief, but united in their heady pursuit of the most intoxicating beats and tunes, spun by world-class DJs. Parties—in some of the most luscious locations you'll ever lay eyes on—can go for 1 night or up to 4 days, and many dedicated pups set up camp, or just keep stomping for hours on end. While there's music day and night, the scene is more sociable while the sun is out, and there's no better way to witness sunrise than with a crowd of fresh-faced party animals. Bars, food stalls, and hippies selling healing crystals are plentiful, but you're welcome to bring all your own supplies (a cooler box with plenty of ice is a good idea)—just remember to take everything, except your ego, home with you. This may be an attempt at a '60s revival, but there's a strong mix of old, young, and in between—the youngsters tend to fizzle out and leave early, leaving the best part of the party to a more "mature" crowd. By far the best parties are organized by **Vortex Trance Adventures** ★★★ (✆ **021/531-2173;** www.intothevortex.co.za). It's also worth asking to be on **Alien Safari's** (info@aliensafari.net) mailing list. Or just keep your ear to the ground, as there's always someone who knows someone who knows what's going down and when.

MCQP ★★★ More than just an excuse to party in various states of undress, Cape Town's Mother City Queer Project costume party has mushroomed into Africa's quintessential gay (but very straight-friendly) extravaganza, held each December. A new venue and theme are revealed every year. www.mcqp.co.za.

Taste of Cape Town ★ A food and wine fest with music, cooking demonstrations, lots of networking, and a fair dollop of schmoozing, this is your best chance to sample a few signature tastes from the best restaurants in the city and Winelands without breaking the bank. It happens over 4 days in early April. www.tasteofcapetown.com.

9 THE WINELANDS

South Africa has over a dozen designated wine routes. The most popular—comprising the routes of Helderberg (Somerset West), Stellenbosch, Paarl, and Franschhoek—are contained within the area known as the Winelands. While the towns are all within easy driving distance, there are hundreds of estates and farms to choose from, and first-time visitors are advised to concentrate on those that offer a combination of historic architecture, excellent wines, and/or views of the vineyard-clad mountains. True oenophiles should spend the day with an expert who can tailor a tour to suit their specific interests (see "Exploring the Winelands," below). You can treat the Winelands as an excursion from Cape Town or base yourself here—no more than 30 to 75 minutes from the bright lights of the city, this is a great area if you want to immerse yourself in rural peace, superb cuisine, and fine wines. Accommodations are generally superb, and some offer better

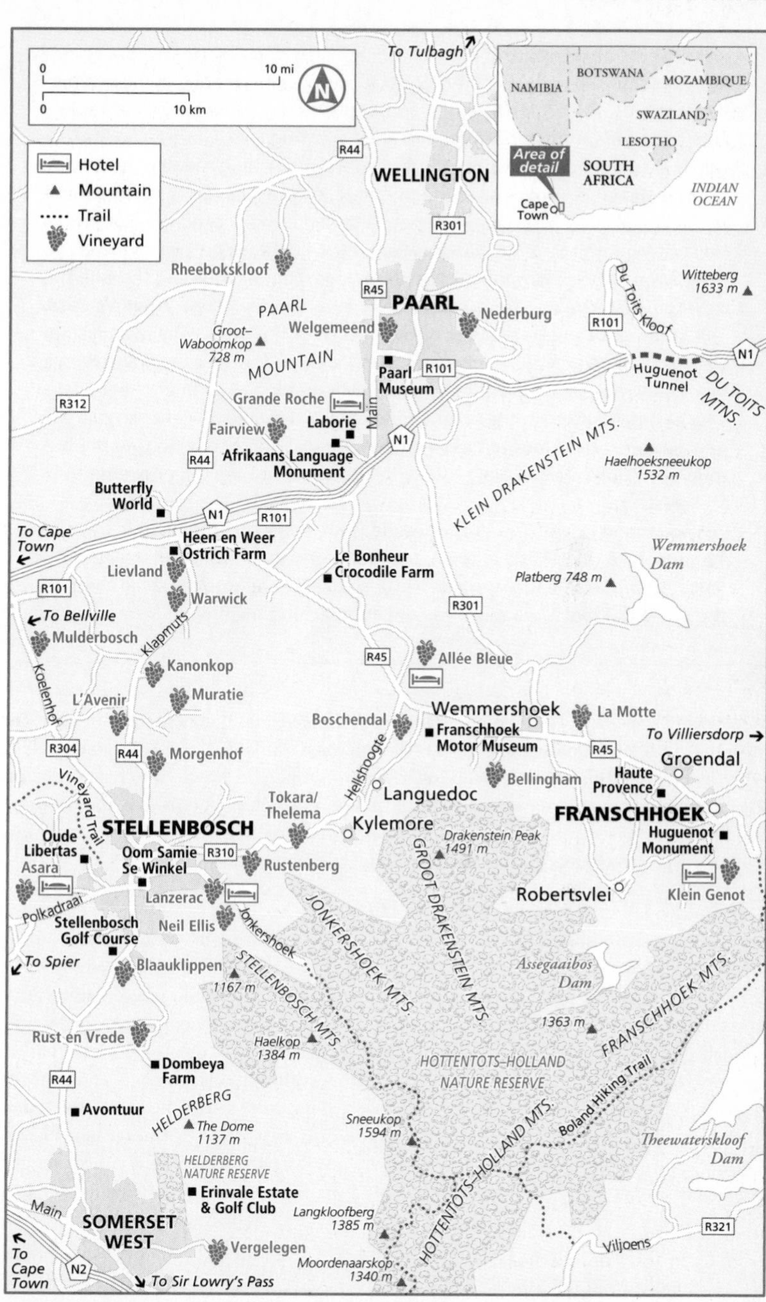

0
10 mi
0
10 km
N
Hotel
Mountain
Trail
Vineyard
To Tulbagh
NAMIBIA
BOTSWANA
MOZAMBIQUE
SWAZILAND
LESOTHO
Area of detail
SOUTH AFRICA
INDIAN OCEAN
Cape Town
R44
WELLINGTON
R301
Rheebokskloof
R45
PAARL
PAARL
Welgemeend
Nederburg
Groot-Waboomkop 728 m
MOUNTAIN
Paarl Museum
R101
Grande Roche
R312
Fairview
Laborie
Main
N1
R44
Afrikaans Language Monument
Butterfly World
R101
To Cape Town
Heen en Weer Ostrich Farm
Lievland
Le Bonheur Crocodile Farm
R101
Warwick
To Bellville
Mulderbosch
Klapmuts
Kanonkop
Koelenhof
L'Avenir
Muratie
R304
R44
Morgenhof
Vineyard Trail
STELLENBOSCH
Oude Libertas
Asara
Oom Samie Se Winkel
R310
Lanzerac
Polkadraai
Stellenbosch Golf Course
Neil Ellis
To Spier
Blaauklippen
Rust en Vrede
Dombeya Farm
R44
Avontuur
HELDERBERG
The Dome 1137 m
HELDERBERG NATURE RESERVE
Erinvale Estate & Golf Club
Main
SOMERSET WEST
Vergelegen
To Cape Town
N2
To Sir Lowry's Pass
Witteberg 1633 m
Du Toits Kloof
R101
N1
Huguenot Tunnel
DU TOITS MTNS.
KLEIN DRAKENSTEIN MTS.
Haelhoeksneeukop 1532 m
Wemmershoek Dam
Platberg 748 m
R301
R45
Allée Bleue
Wemmershoek
La Motte
Boschendal
Franschhoek Motor Museum
To Villiersdorp
R45
Groendal
Hellshoogte
Bellingham
Haute Provence
Languedoc
Tokara/ Thelema
Kylemore
FRANSCHHOEK
Drakenstein Peak 1491 m
Huguenot Monument
Rustenberg
GROOT DRAKENSTEIN MTS.
Robertsvlei
Klein Genot
JONKERSHOEK MTS.
Jonkershoek
STELLENBOSCH MTS.
1167 m
Assegaaibos Dam
FRANSCHHOEK MTS.
1363 m
Haelkop 1384 m
HOTTENTOTS-HOLLAND NATURE RESERVE
Boland Hiking Trail
Sneeukop 1594 m
HOTTENTOTS-HOLLAND MTS.
Theewaterskloof Dam
Langkloofberg 1385 m
R321
Viljoens
Moordenaarskop 1340 m

Three Dramatic Winelands Drives

If you want to see as much of the landscape as possible, try one of these **Winelands drives** ★★★ for a terrific and breathtaking overview of the region. Traversing four mountain ranges and encompassing Franschhoek and Stellenbosch, the **Four Passes Route** will take a full day, including a few stops for wine tastings and lunch. Head out of the city center on the N2, bypassing the turnoff for Stellenbosch (R310) and Somerset West (R44), and ascend the Hottentots Holland Mountains via **Sir Lowry's Pass,** with breathtaking views of the entire False Bay. Take the Franschhoek and Villiersdorp turnoff, traveling through the town of Grabouw, and traverse the Groenland Mountains via **Viljoen's Pass.** This takes you through fruit-producing valleys and past the Theewaterskloof Dam. Look for a right turn marked Franschhoek, and ascend the Franschhoek Mountains via the **Franschhoek Pass** ★★, stopping at La Petite Ferme (see later in this chapter) for tea or lunch with a view. Drive to Stellenbosch via the equally scenic **Helshoogte Pass** ★★, stopping at Boschendal to tour the historic Cape Dutch Manor House. Take the R310 back to the N2, or overnight in Stellenbosch.

The second drive takes in the Breede River Valley and the historic town of Tulbagh. Take the N1 out of town, past Paarl, and then tackle the majestic **Du Toit's Kloof Pass** (if you've made a late start, take the tunnel). Once through the Du Toit's Kloof Mountains, you are approaching the Breede River Valley, a

value than their Cape Town counterparts. If you have time to concentrate on only one area, make it Franschhoek, the prettiest (though most touristy) of the Winelands valleys, with the best selection of award-winning restaurants; or Stellenbosch, which has a charming historic center and the densest concentration of estates. This is also the area that produces the highest concentration of great wines, particularly reds. Both are within easy driving distance of one another, via the scenic Helshoogte Pass.

EXPLORING THE WINELANDS

This is a large, mountainous area, and you're best off exploring it by car so that you can choose your own estates and pace. Don't try to cover the entire Winelands in a day; tackle no more than four to six estates a day, and don't forget to book a luncheon table with a vineyard view. If you're serious about your wine, take a personalized guided tour with a specialist (tours offered by large companies or prearranged by the Wine Desk tend to focus on large producers and give no sense of the wealth of environments and tastes to be had). For tailor-made trips to a carefully selected group of cellars, including the lesser-known or those that require appointments, you can't beat a tour with **Stephen Flesch.** Former chairman of the Wine Tasters Guild of S.A., Stephen is an ardent wine lover and personally knows many of the winemakers and proprietors of the top wine estates, and his knowledge of South African wines spans 4 decades. He will take into account your particular interests or wine preferences, and create an itinerary that covers both flash estates and the rustic farms, including lunch at one of the Winelands' top restaurants. Rates are R1,500 per day for the first person, R700 extra for each additional person (a less publicized wine-producing region, no less attractive than the more famous Winelands areas; wines produced here have a distinctive berry flavor. Keep an eye out for the turnoff to the right marked RAWSONVILLE, then follow the signs north (left) to Goudini Spa and **Slanghoek** ★★; stop here to taste the award-winning Noble Late Harvest. This scenic back road meets the R43 in a T-junction—turn left and follow the signs to the small town of Wolseley before taking the R46 to Tulbagh. Once there, you'll probably want to stay, so consider leaving your options open, or book a room in advance. After lunch you might want to sample one of the Tulbagh Estate's wines before overnighting (see "Tulbagh: Where to Stay," later in this chapter). Alternatively, head back to Wolseley, this time taking the R303 to Wellington via **Bain's Kloof Pass** ★★★, a spectacular pass created by the father of the celebrated master engineer responsible for the Swartberg Pass outside Oudtshoorn. From Wellington, follow the signs to Paarl or Franschhoek and spend the night, or head for the N1 and back to Cape Town.

The third drive, another full day, takes you along the dramatic **Coastal Route** ★★★ to Hermanus, snaking along cliffs that plunge into the ocean, before turning off to sample the wines growing in the Hemel en Aarde (Heaven and Earth) valley. For more details on this drive, see "The Coastal Route: Gordon's Bay to Hermanus," in chapter 6.

half-day starts at R1,000). You can contact him at © **021/705-4317** or 083/229-3581, but book well in advance by e-mailing him at sflesch@iafrica.com; or check out his website at www.gourmetwinetours.co.za.

Espousing the principles of "slow tourism," **Bikes 'n' Wines** (www.bikesnwines.com) is a great new company, with tours that start in Cape Town (you meet on Long St.), and then take you to Stellenbosch by train before handing over bikes for an excursion through the winelands, stopping at four farms to taste a whole lot of wine (R290–R350 per person). Then it's back on the train to the city.

If you prefer the idea of a self-drive tour, then purchase a copy of ***John Platter's South African Wines*** (www.platteronline.com)—updated annually and now in its 31st printing, it's still the best in the business. The definitive guide to wine in South Africa, it not only lists all the producers, but provides ratings to all their wines (some 6,000 tasted annually). ***Note:*** Even though the majority of wine estates accept credit cards for wine purchases, you should keep some cash on hand—most estates charge a fee (R10–R40 per person) for a wine-tasting session, though this may be offset against purchases.

STELLENBOSCH

46km (29 miles) E of Cape Town

The charming town of Stellenbosch was founded in 1679 by Gov. Simon van der Stel, who, among other achievements, built Groot Constantia and planted hundreds of oak trees throughout the Cape. Today Stellenbosch is known informally as Eikestad, or "City of Oaks." The beautifully restored and oak-lined streetscapes of **Dorp, Church,** and

Drosdty make Stellenbosch the most historic of the Winelands towns (it has the largest number of Cape Dutch houses in the region), but outside the historic center, much is suburban sprawl. But this is also a university town, site of the country's most prestigious Afrikaans university, with attendant coffee shops and student bars, and it also promotes itself as the cultural center of the Cape, with a number of great theater options. Contact the Tourism Bureau to find out what's on at the open-air amphitheaters at **Oude Libertas** and **Spier.**

Essentials

VISITOR INFORMATION **Stellenbosch Tourism Bureau,** 36 Market St. (✆ **021/883-3584;** www.stellenboschtourism.co.za; summer Mon–Fri 8am–6pm, Sat 9am–5pm, Sun 10am–4pm; winter Mon–Fri 9am–5pm, Sat 9:30am–2pm, Sun 10am–2pm), is by far the most helpful in the Winelands, so head to their office as soon as you arrive. They'll provide expert advice on where to stay and what to do, and they distribute a *Discover Stellenbosch on Foot* leaflet, describing more than 60 historical sites with accompanying text. Adjacent is the **Adventure Centre** (✆ **021/882-8112;** www.adventureshop.co.za), offering a huge variety of activities in the region.

GUIDED TOURS **In Town** Guided **walking tours** (R90 per person; 90 min.) led by **Sandra Krige** (✆ **021/887-9150** or 083/218-1310; hkrige@iafrica.com) depart the tourist bureau every weekday at 10am and 3pm (Sat–Sun by appointment). Contact Sandra for private early-morning and twilight history walks. The town center is small enough to explore on foot, but you can also rent a bicycle from **Piet se Fiets** (✆ **021/887-3042;** R20 per hour, R80 per day).

To Wine Estates See "Exploring the Winelands," above, for specialist tours and self-drive tips. Note that if you don't want to drive, you can visit five Stellenbosch wine estates by using the hop-on, hop-off **Vinehopper bus** (✆ **021/882-8112;** www.vinehopper.co.za; R150 per person, excluding tasting fees).

En Route to Stellenbosch from Cape Town

From the city, the N2 takes you past the airport and straight to Somerset West, a town with the country's priciest real estate and one of its most handsome wine estates. (There's very little else of value, though, and the town itself must rank as one of the dullest on the planet.) **Vergelegen** ★★★ ("Far Location"; ✆ **021/847-1334;** daily 9:30am–4pm; call for tour times) is a must-see, marred only by the fact that you need to drive all the way across sprawled-out Somerset West to get there. Built by reprobate Willem Adriaan van der Stel (who took over from his father as governor of the Cape in 1699), the project was a serious abuse of his power, as he built it on land that did not actually belong to him and used Dutch East India Company slaves and resources to compete with local farmers. He was sacked in 1707, and the farm was demolished and divided. Today this beautifully restored wine estate, surrounded by gorgeous gardens, is known to be Mandela's favorite, as well as the only one to host Queen Elizabeth II and the Clintons during their respective state visits. The estate restaurant, the **Lady Phillips** (✆ **021/847-1346**), serves excellent meals in a wonderful atmosphere; in summer, the **Rose Terrace,** an alfresco venue, is glorious.

Another gorgeous estate en route to Stellenbosch is **Vergenoegd** ★★★, which opened the doors of its old Cape Dutch homestead to the public at the end of 2003—great news for red-wine lovers. In fact, the combination of superbly smooth red wines and the gorgeous setting makes it a firm favorite, so don't miss it (✆ **021/843-3248;** Mon–Fri 9am–5pm, Sat 9:30am–1:30pm). Good news, too, is that you needn't hit Somerset West to visit. Off the N2, take exit 33 (Baden Powel Dr.) toward Stellenbosch, and look for nearby signs on your right. From here, you can either cut across to Somerset West using the R102 to visit Vergelegen, or continue on the R310 for Stellenbosch. Consider stopping at both Warwick and Spier for lunch en route.

To get to Stellenbosch from Vergelegen (some 30 min. away), head back to the R44 and turn right (at the Lord Charles Hotel; from here, it's just 20 min.). Red-wine lovers should look for the sign to **Rust en Vrede (Rest and Peace)** ★★★ along the way—turn right onto Annandale Road to sample these raunchy reds (✆ **021/881-3881;** Mon–Fri 8am–5pm, Sat 8:30am–4pm in season); the estate also hosts the most decadently priced restaurant in the region—if you have the cash and feel the urge to splurge, it'll be a memorable lunch. Families should turn left and head for **Spier** (✆ **021/809-1100;** daily 9am–5pm; you can assemble your own picnic at their deli). Among the many activities on offer at Spier are scenic horseback rides through the estate's vineyards, as well as an outdoor activity center; their Cheetah Conservancy, where you can see these slinky creatures up close, is also very popular. A little farther along the R44 is the turnoff for **Blaauwklippen** (✆ **021/880-0133;** Mon–Fri 9am–4:45pm, Sat 9am–4pm), where from October 1 to April 30 you can take a coach ride through the vineyards (call ahead to book). It's definitely worth making a detour for the delightful **Waterford**—a wonderful example of the Cape's love affair with Tuscany (✆ **021/880-0496**)—where you can sample chocolate and wine to discover just how perfectly the two complement one another.

What to See & Do in Town

If you have time for only one historic stop in town, make it the **Village Museum** ★★, 18 Ryneveld St. (✆ **021/887-2902;** Mon–Sat 9am–5pm, Sun 10am–4pm; admission R20), which comprises the Schreuderhuis Cottage (1709), the Cape Dutch Blettermanhuis (1789), the Georgian Grosvenor House (1803), and the Victorian-era home of O. M. Bergh (1850). Each house has a guide in period dress, and the artful styling of the furniture, combined with the accessible explanations on the architecture and fashion of these eras, make these the best house museums in the country. Just around the corner from the museum is the Neo-Gothic **Moeder Kerk,** or "Mother Church," which is the only monument of its kind in the region, harking back to the early days of the town's development and still a part of community life.

From here, head south along Drosdty Street, turn right onto Dorp Street, and then stroll down the oak-dappled street to see the legendary dusty shelves at **Oom Samie Se Winkel** (✆ **021/887-2612;** 9:30am–6pm Mon–Fri, 9am–5:30pm Sat–Sun, till 6pm in summer), a Victorian-style general dealer (literally, "Uncle Sam's Shop") bursting at the seams with knickknacks. It's a great place to pick up kitschy souvenirs, such as step-by-step *bobotie* spice packs, dried-fruit rolls, and dirt-cheap enamel plates. Do browse, although you probably won't want to shop here; far better places to pick up a variety of gifts (from homeware to local music CDs) are housed in the **Black Horse Centre** ★★ a little way up the street, on the corner of Dorp and Mark streets.

If your interest is in art, then don't miss the collection of 20th-century South African art at the **Rupert Museum** ★★★ (✆ **021/888-3344;** R20 adults; Mon–Fri 9:30am–1pm and 2–4pm, Sat 10am–1pm)

The Stellenbosch Wine Route

This is the most established route, with well over 100 estates and farms to choose from, almost all of which are reached via the three major roads radiating from the town center. Note that it's worth double-checking opening times if you're traveling over the weekend. If you head southwest on the R306, you should consider visiting the 300-year-old **Neethlingshof** (© **021/883-8988;** Mon–Fri 9am–5pm, Sat–Sun 10am–4pm; summer closing times 2 hr. later) just for the pleasure of driving up its gracious pine-lined avenue and tasting the Noble Late Harvest. Once there, however, you may find the experience relatively commercial. To reach **Zevenwacht** (© **021/903-5123;** Mon–Fri 8:30am–5pm, Sat–Sun 9:30am–5pm)—one of the prettiest wine estates in the country, with a manor house on the edge of a tranquil lake and views all the way to the ocean—take the M12 to Kuilsriver.

Most of the loveliest wine estates are off the R44 north to Paarl. Your first stop should be the beautiful **Morgenhof** to sample the merlot and chardonnay (© **021/889-5510;** Mon–Fri 9am–5pm, Sat–Sun 10am–5pm, earlier closings in winter), followed by **L'Avenir** (© **021/889-5001;** Mon–Sat 10am–5pm) to try the Pinotage. The turnoff for tiny **Muratie** ★★★ (© **021/865-2330;** daily 9am–5pm), one of the most authentic and least commercial estates, is next. It's a must not only for its port and berry-rich red wines, but for the satisfying ambience of the estate. Next is **Kanonkop** (© **021/884-4656**), famous for its reds; the equally acclaimed **Warwick** ★★ (© **021/884-4410**); and **Le Bonheur** (© **021/875-5478**)—all on the road to Paarl.

Some of the best estates on the Stellenbosch wine route are on the Helshoogte Pass, which links Stellenbosch with Franschhoek; see "Stellenbosch to Franschhoek: The Helshoogte Pass," below, for recommendations.

Finally, if you're tired of tasting wine, take the 10km (6¼-mile) circular drive through the **Jonkershoek Nature Reserve,** stopping for lunch at **Lanzerac**—ask for a map from the tourism bureau. This is also where you'll find **Neil Ellis** (© **021/887-0649;** Mon–Fri 9:30am–4:30pm, Sat 10am–2pm), another superb wine estate.

Where to Stay

With the exception of River Manor, all of the places reviewed below are outside the main town. Also worth considering are a number of spots close to the historic center—attractions and a great selection of restaurants and coffee shops are only a short stroll away along the oak-lined streets. Given this, the best option is River Manor (see below), but you may also want to investigate the following: **Roosenwijn Guest House** ★ (© **021/883-3338;** www.stellenguest.co.za) offers comfortable rooms tastefully decorated in Afrikaans-Afro chic for between R990 and R1,390 double, depending on the season and room size. Given its location (a 2-min. walk from the center) and the attractive decor, this is one of the best deals in town, but it doesn't have a great pool or any real garden to speak of. Opposite is Victorian-era **Bonne Esperance** (© **021/887-0225;** www.bonneesperance.com; R590 double), worth considering only if you can get an upstairs room, specifically nos. 5, 14, or 15. Even more central, but not as good value, are **Eendracht** (© **021/883-8843;** www.eendracht-hotel.com; R930–R1,870), which has bright but impersonal rooms and no real public spaces (other than around the pool), right in the center of historic Dorp Street; and **D'Ouwe Werf**—the oldest inn in South Africa, popular for its old-fashioned hospitality, with some increasingly tattered rooms in the original building that make me want to go elsewhere.

Much, much better (but perhaps not such a quick walk to town) is **Summerwood ★** (✆ **021/887-4112;** www.summerwood.co.za; R1,500–R2,250 double), a top-caliber guesthouse on the Jonkershoek Road. Your hosts, Ann and Christian Baret, offer an intimate atmosphere (only nine rooms, of which I recommend no. 8 for the best views), large rooms, and a great pool and garden. If you find guesthouses too claustrophobic and Asara too pricey, I'd opt for **Devon Valley Hotel ★** (✆ **021/865-2012;** www.devonvalleyhotel.com): Situated a few kilometers outside of town, amid rolling hills carpeted with vines, it's popular with conference groups, but the location is great and the sunsets memorable. Rates range from R1,350 to R2,150 double, depending on the season and room type; ask for one in the Manor House, as they're more private and have more character. Managing around two dozen apartments, the rental agency **Life and Leisure** (✆ **021/886-6955;** www.lifeandleisure.co.za) has some very stylishly decorated self-catering options, all within the historical center and restaurant district; the studio apartments, located in a house with a pool, are a steal, at R780 double.

Asara ★★★ Stellenbosch's first Relais & Châteaux hotel benefits from probably the most fantastic location and unfettered views in this part of the Winelands—surrounded by 180 hectares of farmland, two-thirds dedicated to vines. Most guestrooms—and both restaurants—enjoy sweeping vistas across a sloped vineyard and distant Stellenbosch and Helderberg Mountains. Sunset, best enjoyed on your private terrace overlooking the dam, is magical. Another obvious highlight here is the huge, immaculate, unfussy bedrooms—ask for a deluxe room in the main building (those in the annex wing feel a little cut off)—and the access they afford to a vast, elegant estate. Asara suffers slightly *because* it is so new and is still easing into its skin.

Polkadraai Rd. (M12), 4km (2½ miles) from Stellenbosch. P.O. Box 882, Stellenbosch 7599. ✆ **021/888-8000.** Fax: 021/888-8001. www.asara.co.za. 34 units. Summer season R3,500 courtyard double, R3,800 classic deluxe double, R4,200 deluxe double, R5,600–R6,800 suite; green season R2,500 courtyard double, R2,800 classic deluxe double, R3,200 deluxe double, R4,600–R5,800 suite. Rates include breakfast. AE, DC, MC, V. **Amenities:** 2 restaurants; cigar and whiskey bar; babysitting; mountain bikes; deli; luxury kitchen supply store; pool; room service; steam room; wine-tasting facility and wine shop. *In room:* A/C, TV, hair dryer, minibar, free Wi-Fi.

Hawksmoor House ★★★ Value An old Cape Dutch manor house has been meticulously restored and decorated with an eclectic mix of contemporary classic and antique furniture, lending a gracious, sensuous boho texture to the grand-scale spaces. Fabulously, you're invited to treat it as your own country home—a down-to-earth atmosphere where you can make yourself totally at home and forgive some of the vagaries of farm living (such as occasional power and water outages or relaxed service). Bedrooms are so appealing and cosseting that you may not want to emerge (some have fireplaces). But do roam the 220-hectare (544-acre) wine estate and take in a spectacular array of scenes—the views stretch as far as Table Mountain. Lunch and dinner aren't served, but your hosts provide the lowdown on the local dining scene and could probably plan your entire holiday for you. ***Note:*** Hawksmoor is right near the N1, an easy 25-minute drive from Cape Town's city center, making this a most convenient base for exploring the entire region.

Majieskuil Farm, off the R304 near Klipheuwel, around 20km (12 miles) from Stellenbosch; turn left off the N1 and look for the tiny sign. ✆ **021/884-4815** or 072/367-4788. Fax 021/884-4816. www.hawksmoorhouse.co.za. 8 units. Summer R1,750 double; winter R1,250 double. Rates include breakfast and afternoon tea. MC, V. **Amenities:** Honor bar; mountain bike rental; free high-speed Internet; airport transfers and car hire. *In room:* A/C, TV and DVD (on request), iPod docking station.

Lanzerac Hotel & Winery ★★ Kids Considered one of the top spots in the Winelands, this remains a gracious historic manor, with outlying rooms and suites situated amid rolling vineyards and soaring peaks of heaven-sent Jonkershoek Valley. Recently upgraded, the entry-level "classic" rooms come with antique facsimiles and plenty of comfortable touches, but for real privacy, opt for a huge suite out in the gardens (some have a pool). Laid-back, child-friendly, and sporting vast, rollicking lawns; a newly upgraded spa; and (slightly lackluster) old-fashioned service, the Lanzerac is the classic model against which to compare the more up-to-date sense of *luxe* at brand-new Asara (reviewed above). Prices are pretty much on a par, so your choice will ultimately come down to taste. For my money, I prefer the casual embrace of Hawksmoor's shabby-chic good looks and authentic hospitality (reviewed above).

Lanzerac Rd., Stellenbosch 7599. ✆ **021/887-1132.** Fax 021/887-2310. www.lanzerac.co.za. 48 units. Peak season R3,100 classic double, R3,770 luxury double, R5,260 junior suite, R7,510 suite; value season R2,120 classic double, R2,660 luxury double, R3,710 junior suite, R5,260 suite. Rates include breakfast. Children under 4 stay free, children 5–11 pay 50% if sharing, children 12–16 pay 75% if sharing. AE, DC, MC, V. **Amenities:** 2 restaurants; bar; cigar lounge; babysitting; pool; spa; room service; wine tasting and cellar tours. *In room:* A/C, TV, hair dryer, minibar, Wi-Fi (R90 per hr.; R180 per day).

Majeka House ★★ Something of a suburban sanctuary, Majeka is an expansion of a private home on a large property with lawns, lounging areas, different accommodations wings, and a large indoor pool area. The boutique hotel doesn't rely on views to attract guests, but instead focuses on in-room comforts, cushy amenities, and a professional little spa with excellent therapists. Bedrooms are luxurious contemporary, all with little terraces and decadent bathrooms; while the standard premier rooms are just fine, the more privately located superior units are extralarge, with double-volume showers, a lounge area with two armchairs, and doors that open to a terrace with access to a second, more private plunge pool. The lounge and dining room are done out in pretty, modern Afrikaans baroque style: Rich, textured fabrics, patterned wallpaper, and a mix of vibrant and neutral shades set a romantic tone. There are also self-catering villas, sized for families.

26–32 Houtkapper St., Paradyskloof, Stellenbosch 7600. ✆ **021/880-1512/49.** Fax 021/880-1550. www.majekahouse.co.za. 18 units. Summer R1,820 premier double, R2,080 superior double, R3,900–R5,980 2- or 3-bedroom villa; winter R1,200 premier double, R1,400 superior double, R3,300–R5,080 2- or 3-bedroom villa. Rates include breakfast. AE, DC, MC, V. **Amenities:** Restaurant; bar; babysitting (on request); DVD library; gym; library; pool; spa. *In room:* A/C, TV/DVD, hair dryer, minibar, free Wi-Fi.

River Manor Boutique Hotel & Spa ★★ A few minutes' stroll from the heart of historic Stellenbosch, this guesthouse, comprising two interlinked properties with a pair of pools, ultracozy lounges, a spa, and a deli-style eatery, is on an oak-lined road that follows the course of the Eerste River. Colonial-themed rooms are comfortable and graciously outfitted (historical prints, turn-of-the-20th-century trunks, and chunky antique wardrobes are offset by bold-colored fabrics). Two pools are surrounded by table- and lounge-dotted lawns, and for those who want to escape the sun, deep verandas have comfortable chairs and striped awnings; fragrant with the scent of ripening guavas, the garden twinkles at night with fairy lights. You're best off booking a superior room (no. 16 is a personal favorite—spacious, with a large bathroom with Victorian tub). Restaurants are within walking distance, and your hosts have great ideas to make your days here all the more interesting—they run tours to Kayamandi township and have the best guides on speed dial.

No. 6, The Avenue, Stellenbosch 7600. ✆ **021/887-9944.** Fax 021/887-9940. www.rivermanorguesthouse.co.za. 18 units. High season R1,200 petit double, R1,800 standard double, R2,600 superior double; green season R860 petit double, R1,210 standard double, R2,125 superior double. Rates include breakfast. Children by prior permission only. MC, V. **Amenities:** Deli; 2 pools; room service; spa. *In room:* A/C (in most), TV, hair dryer; minibar, Wi-Fi (R60 per hr.; R285 for 12 hr.).

Where to Dine

In the last 2 years, Stellenbosch has emerged as *the* Winelands dining destination—although you'll still hear fierce arguments according that honor to Franschhoek. Stellenbosch, however, does offer greater variety and better value. Because there's a year-round buzz, which has a lot to do with the huge seasonal student population, you never want for ambience, which Franschhoek lacks come nightfall. Stellenbosch's dining scene also isn't quite so focused on tourist trade, meaning there's a better chance to get a feel for the local cuisine culture. Between meals, head for **Stellenbosch Hills,** a wine estate in Vlottenburg, for a tasting of five wines paired with different varieties of biltong (jerky)—from kudu to springbok—individually chosen by the winemaker (✆ **021/881-3828;** www.stellenboschhills.co.za; R35; Mon–Fri 8am–5pm, Sat 10am–3pm; reservations essential). If meat isn't your thing, make for **Waterford,** another fine Stellenbosch estate (✆ **021/880-0496;** www.waterfordestate.co.za), where Von Gesau chocolates are matched to appropriate wines. For substantial fare, book early at any of the places reviewed below—they're all out of town, smack dab amid the vineyard, and most offer sublime views by day.

If you want to dine in the historic center, the top two choices are both on Dorp Street. Occupying one of Stellenbosch's most beautiful heritage buildings, La Gratitude, **The Big Easy** ★★, 95 Dorp St. (✆ **021/887-3462**), is co-owned by Ernie Els and, thus, beholden to golf fans. Both a wine bar and the most stylish restaurant in town, it offers tastings most days and a great selection of vintages to pair with dishes from a small, ever-evolving menu, with something for all tastes—including impeccable salads. After a rocky start, new chef Ronan O'Dwyer has found his balance. Tee off with a dozen West Coast oysters with cabernet dressing, or sample his wonderful pan-fried soft-shell crab. Then try the venison loin with grilled polenta and rhubarb confit, or roast pork neck with mustard jus. The restaurant comprises a warren of elegant dining spaces, cozy lounge nooks, slick bars, and a 10-seat private golf-themed dining room, all serviced by primped and coiffed stud muffins.

While The Big Easy certainly has the looks, the most exciting food in town is actually being served at **Cognito** ★★, 137 Dorp St. (✆ **021/882-8696;** www.cognitorestaurant.co.za), which has foodies abuzz with its quirky menu and bold approach to contemporary African fusion fare. At lunch you can get lighter fare, such as an *inkuku* (chicken burger served on rosemary-encrusted panini, with sweet potato chips), but the self-proclaimed "showstoppers" include meat cuts and line fish, each day prepared with a different flavor or sauce (your server will fill you in), and the prawn-and-chicken Cape Malay-style curry. Don't forget to try the slightly quirky cocktail menu—a good option is the African *dawa.*

For a decent, laid-back lunch experience, there's an endless array of possibilities within walking distance of the historic center. The **Greek Kitchen,** 42 Ryneveld St. (✆ **021/887-7703**), is a small, laid-back place with outdoor seating, great *mezze,* and excellent slow-roasted lamb. Neighboring **Greengate** (✆ **021/886-6111**), a deli-cafe popular with locals, offers a daily selection of fresh quiches, salads, stews, and pies sold by weight.

Flavors are fresh, prices decent, and service almost laughable (brace yourself). Oenophiles should head for **Wijnhuis** (✆ **021/887-5844**), in the Dorpsmeent Complex on Andringa Street, where you can dine on average Mediterranean-type fare with a tasting of the region's best wines (R35 to sample six).

Finally, no overview of Stellenbosch eateries would be complete without a mention of the Pan-African buffet (R225; drinks and 10% service charge extra), served by the face-painted staff at **Moyo** (✆ **021/809-1133**), on the Spier Estate (a sprawling Disneyesque tourist mecca with hotel, amphitheater, and other entertainment): This is a great summer-night option, when the treetops are lit up, the drummers and dancers are writhing in the candlelight, and the Bedouin-tented lounge areas abutting the dining area look their most romantic and inviting. Combining the theatrical with interesting dishes from across the continent, Moyo is a recommended, albeit touristy, night out, particularly if there's something good showing at the open-air theater (see "Cape Town After Dark," earlier in this chapter).

Bodega ★★★ Value Kids MODERN FARM CUISINE Housed in carefully renovated Cape Dutch barn, this is a mellow spot for a languid lunch, conversation fuelled by wines, and unpretentious cooking. Best of all, the Winelands' tourist hype hasn't stretched to this beautiful corner of Stellenbosch. Grab a table on the terrace and linger over the views of the ultramodern wave-design winery against a stunning *fynbos*-clad mountain backdrop. Chef Naas Pienaar sources wonderful ingredients—some of which he grows himself, others that grow wild on the Dornier Estate. Then, in the tiniest of kitchens, he prepares everything to perfection and serves nourishing comfort food that's uncomplicated and delicious. There are so many great starters that you may want to make a meal of them. A glass of Donatus white goes exceptionally well with most everything (as does the homemade sparkling lemonade). Welcome during the day, kids have a roaring good time in the large, dedicated play area.

Dornier Wine Estate, Blaauwklippen Rd., Stellenbosch. ✆ **021/880-0557.** www.bodega.co.za. Reservations highly recommended. Main courses R65–R140; abalone *(perlemoen)* R200 starter, R300 main course. AE, DC, MC, V. Daily noon–5pm, Thurs–Sat 6–9:30pm. Closed late May to mid-Jun.

96 Winery Road ★★ Finds MODERN SOUTH AFRICAN/STEAK This is one of the most unassuming and unpretentious restaurants in the Winelands, yet it has a loyal following of locals—wine magazine editors and wine farmers included—who appreciate the informal atmosphere; unfussy, delicious food; great wine list; and excellent service (this is one place where waiters really know their wines). The menu changes every 6 months (with fresh and seasonal menu changes daily), but established favorites include the "famous" duck and cherry pie (with meat roasted in a rich port and black cherry sauce) and the succulent 96 beef burger (topped with brie and sautéed black mushrooms). The dry-aged steaks are legendary—a favorite being the "Hollandse" pepper filet. Or ask for a rare rump with chili and garlic butter on the side. In season, you'd better book way in advance.

Zandberg Farm, Winery Rd., btw. Stellenbosch and Somerset West. ✆ **021/842-2020.** www.96wineryroad.co.za. Reservations recommended. Main courses R80–R120. AE, DC, MC, V. Daily noon–3pm; Mon–Sat 7–10pm.

Overture ★★★ Value FRENCH At press time, this magnificently situated winery restaurant is probably the most sought-after place to eat anywhere in Africa. Or so it should be. After picking up a coveted spot in the *Eat Out* Top 10 restaurants list after its first year, the word is out, and you need to book your table weeks in advance. Keeping it real is part of the ethos that drives chef Bertus Basson, barely 30 and an astute businessman; energetic, trouper mouthed, and strongly focused on delivering food that's beyond expectation, he keeps a testosterone-fueled kitchen: "We cook like men," he says; rather than messing with anything "new and experimental," he focuses on using the freshest local ingredients to create sensational food that tastes every bit as good as it looks. By adapting the menu daily and eliminating waste—so no part of any animal or vegetable is thrown away—Bertus promises creative, always exciting menu choices, and excellent value, too. Service is polished, slick, and experiential. There is no telling what'll be served (that depends on what the market, local farmers, and fishmonger supply), and there's no signature dish here. There'll be around seven options and just a couple of desserts, each paired with a perfectly delicious wine.

Hidden Valley Estate, Annandale Rd. ✆ **021/880-2721.** www.dineatoverture.co.za. Reservations essential. 3 courses R195, or R240 with wine; 4 courses R235, or R300 with wine; 5 courses R275, or R350 with wine. AE, DC, MC, V. Tues–Sun noon–3pm; Thurs–Fri 7–9pm.

Terroir ★★★ INTERNATIONAL Chalked-up menus are *de rigeur* in the Winelands and, at this classy establishment, you find them packed with intriguingly simple-sounding, exquisitely executed dishes, courtesy of Michael Broughton, presently considered to be one of the top three chefs in the country. You have to drive through a bland housing estate to get to what is—given the status of its cuisine—a surprisingly rustic venue. Once you're seated (try to book outside), you have lovely views of the Kleine Zalze vineyards, gardens, and golf course. But it's the food, particularly the sauces it comes with, that makes the trip out here worthwhile. Much is prepared using the wood-burning oven, so you'll pick up a sensuous smokiness on items such as the braised pork. Predictably, the superior wine list features vintages from the estate and are available by the glass.

Kleine Zalze Wine Estate, Techno Park turnoff, Strand Rd. (R44). ✆ **021/880-8167.** Reservations essential. Main courses R109–R149. AE, MC, V. Mon–Sun 12:30–2:30pm; Mon–Sat 6:45–9:30pm.

Tokara ★★ MODERN SOUTH AFRICAN You'll find a few good options on the Helshoogte Pass (which links Stellenbosch to Franschhoek), but if you like your meals enhanced by stunning views, Tokara is the place to stop. And when you're not eyeing the vistas, you can admire the architecture. Effortlessly floating over the mountain slope, with plenty of space, no clutter, and great artworks, this is easily the best looking of the handful of ultramodern wine-tasting venues in the Western Cape. Of course, the menu produced by experimental, French-influenced chef Etienne Bonthuys is worth the stop, too, though everyone may not thrill to his penchant for mixing his meats (calamari and oxtail?) and rich sauces (grilled springbok is served with lobster sauce, poached mussels prepared with banana and orange cream). That said, simpler fare is always on offer, and as far as lunch venues are concerned, this is a class act (by nightfall, the views are gone).

Tokara Winery, Helshoogte Pass. ✆ **021/808-5959.** Reservations recommended. Main courses R95–R145. AE, DC, MC, V. Tues–Sat noon–3pm and 7:30–10pm.

FRANSCHHOEK

33km (20 miles) E of Stellenbosch; 79km (49 miles) E of Cape Town via Stellenbosch; 85km (53 miles) SE of Cape Town via Paarl (33km/20 miles)

If you plan to spend the night in the Winelands, the prettiest valley by far is Franschhoek (literally, "French Corner"), the land Simon van der Stel gave the French Huguenots fleeing religious persecution in 1688. Surrounded by soaring mountains, Franschhoek is so lush a local once compared it to "living in a lettuce." The genuine sense of being ensconced in a valley here, with snow on the surrounding mountains in winter, has always made it feel worlds apart from anywhere else in the country. Besides its scenic advantages, it boasts the highest concentration of fine-dining restaurants in Africa and some truly excellent accommodations options. It's very faux French, however, and some complain that it's become too touristy—at times you can set your watch by the lunchtime arrival of tour buses, and the rivalry between establishments is palpable. While it's much busier and more developed than Tulbagh (see below), relative to Stellenbosch, it's very easy to navigate and offers a comparatively rural atmosphere, with dirt tracks a few blocks from the main road, and glorious views wherever you look. Incidentally, the prison just outside Franschhoek on the road to Paarl and Wellington is the one from which Nelson Mandela was released and made his first appearance on television as he finally walked to freedom in 1990.

Essentials

VISITOR INFORMATION Pick up one of the helpful maps and a great regional brochure at the **Franschhoek Tourism Bureau,** on the main road through town (**© 021/876-3603;** www.franschhoek.org.za; Mon–Fri 9am–6pm, Sat–Sun 9am–4pm).

GETTING AROUND The town is small enough to traverse on foot, but to visit the wine farms, you may need to hire a car, taxi, or specialist guide. For the latter, see "Exploring the Winelands," earlier in this chapter; for shuttle services, transfers, and general tours, contact **Franschhoek Experience** (**© 083/234-4038**) or **Winelands Tours** (**© 082/774-2790**), or use the **Vineyard Hopper** (**© 083/301-6774;** R175 per person) to get to four different wine farms. For wine-tasting expeditions on purebred Arab horses, contact **Paradise Stables** (**© 021/876-2160;** www.paradisestables.co.za; R450 includes wine tasting). A great way to get around is by bike; rent one from **Manic Cycles** (**© 021/876-4956;** www.maniccycles.co.za).

The Franschhoek Wine Route

From Stellenbosch, the R310 heads over the scenic Helshoogte Pass, linking it with Franschhoek and Paarl, both of which lie some 30 minutes from the center of Stellenbosch. If you're heading to Franschhoek from Stellenbosch, follow the R310 for 2km (1¼ miles) before turning left into Ida's Valley and heading for **Rustenberg** (**© 021/809-1200;** Mon–Fri 9am–4:30pm, Sat 10am–1:30pm). This gorgeous estate is renowned for its red wines, as well as its peaceful and beautiful setting, with a historic manor house contrasting with a tasting center and state-of-the-art milking parlor. Stop for lunch at **Tokara** for the fine views (see review above), or push on to visit the beautifully maintained Cape Dutch estate of **Boschendal** ★★★ (**© 021/870-4200;** open from around 8:30 or 9:30am to 4:30 or 5pm; wine tastings on Sun only in season [Nov–Apr]). Together with Vergelegen and Constantia, Boschendal is one of the Winelands' most photographed estates, combining an excellent **manor house museum** (admission R10) with beautiful grounds and great wines. Boschendal also offers three different dining experiences: The luncheon buffet (**© 021/870-4272;** R240) is served in the original wine cellar, with a huge buffet table covered from end to end with tasty traditional Cape Malay and South African dishes, as well as lighter treats with a weekly-changing menu that includes such tasty treats as venison carpaccio with Satsuma preserve, watercress with local goat's cheese and walnuts, and Franschhoek specialties such as smoked salmon trout (a type of trout with salmon-hued flesh). If you're not that hungry, head for the wrought-iron tables under the oaks at **Le Café** and order one of the delicious quiches (the delicious traditional *bobotie* is recommended). From October to April, you can buy a **picnic hamper** (R135 per person, food only) and lunch on the lawns shaded by more ancient oaks. Ask about the full-moon picnics (Dec–Mar only). Prebooking is essential on weekends.

Millionaire Johann Rupert has several wine farms under his belt, including the superb L'Ormorins estate near Franschhoek, on the R45 soon after the turnoff from the Helshoogte Pass. You can enjoy a luxurious **wine-tasting** experience here (**© 021/874-9045;** Mon–Fri 9am–4:30pm, Sat 10am–3pm); you're whisked to the cellar by golf cart and then sit amid an important art collection while hearing about the vintages. There's a standard tasting (R30) with six wines and a port, but I recommend the more extensive R70 tasting that includes superior vintages, especially if you're into full-bodied wines. Also at L'Ormorins is Rupert's one-of-a-kind **Franschhoek Motor Museum** ★★★ (**© 021/874-9000;** www.fmm.co.za; R60 adults, R50 seniors and car club members, R30 children 3–12; hourly tours Tues–Fri 10am–4pm; Sat–Sun 10am–3pm self-guided tour only), where you can view and learn about some of the sexiest, or otherwise intriguing, motorized vehicles ever produced, including many rare models, all in spectacular condition. The 340-strong collection spans a century of cars, although, in fact, the oldest exhibit is an 1898 motorized Beston tricycle. You can't possibly see every car in Rupert's collection (it's so large it has to be rotated; 80 are seen per tour), but if you're lucky, you'll see one of very few examples of a "Protea Protea," a local car manufactured in 1957, and only the second model of any indigenous car ever to be made here (the first were Cycle 3 cars built in 1913); only 20 were built, and the Protea (which could reach 136kmph/84 mph) won the Pietermaritzburg Six Hours Endurance Race but wasn't financially viable. Weekday guided tours last only an hour, but on weekends, you can explore at will sans guidance.

The following estates, all clearly signposted off the Main Road (from Cape Town, Paarl, and Stellenbosch) and its extension, Huguenot Road, are recommended. **La Motte** (**© 021/876-3119;** Mon–Fri 9am–4:30pm, Sat 10am–3pm), which has been producing wines for 3 centuries, is worth visiting in order to sample its red wines; the same is true of **Rupert & Rothschild** (**© 021/874-1648;** by appointment only). If you're hungry, head for **Moreson** (**© 021/876-3055;** Mon–Sun 11am–5pm). The sauvignon blanc is a good choice for lunch at the estate's delightfully relaxed restaurant, **Bread & Wine** (reviewed below), worth visiting for the oven-fresh focaccia alone, served with Mediterranean-style dips. Pop into **Grande Provence Estate** (**© 021/876-8600;** daily 10am–6pm) to sample the semisweet Angels Tears wine (cellar tours are at 11am and 3pm), and **Mont Rochelle Mountain Vineyards** (**© 021/876-3000;** daily 10am–6pm), still owned by a descendant of the French Huguenots, for its glorious setting. If it's setting you're after, backtrack onto the dirt track to **GlenWood** (**© 021/876-2044;** Mon–Fri 11am–4pm, Sat–Sun 11am–3pm in summer) for a beautiful drive and a taste of the estate's fine chardonnays.

Huguenot Road meets a T-junction at the base of the Franschhoek Mountains. Directly opposite is the **French Huguenot Monument,** erected in honor of the French Protestant refugees who settled here between 1688 and 1700. Its three arches symbolize the Holy Trinity. Turn left to drive the Franschhoek Pass for lunch at **La Petite Ferme**—a must, if you can get a table (see below). Also on the road heading up to the Pass, **Cabrière** (**© 021/876-8500;** tastings R30, Mon–Fri 9am–5pm, Sat 10am–4pm, Sun 11am–4pm) is recommended—and not just for the excellent Pierre Jourdan bubbly. Cellar tours (R40 per person) run weekdays at 11am and 3pm, and on Saturday at 11am you can usually witness winemaker Achim von Arnim uncork his bottles by slicing the neck off with a saber; an in-depth tasting and tour follows.

Finds A Convenient Base

Award-winning wines, gallons of olive oil, fruit orchards, and herb gardens are all part of life on the up-and-coming **Allée Bleue** estate situated near Boschendal at the junction between Helshoogte Pass Road and the road to Franschhoek. Here, on a massive acreage surrounded by stunning views of the Groot Drakenstein, Simonsig, and Franschhoek mountains, you have the chance to experience genuine farm life while living it up in cosseted luxury in a convenient yet untouristed location. It's just about equidistant to Franschhoek, Stellenbosch, and Paarl, putting many excellent wine estates and country kitchen restaurants within reach. The owners are pumping a fortune into the property to set up a variety of accommodations (all in restored farm buildings) and, in addition to the roadside cafe, will soon have an atmospheric restaurant in the heart of the farm. For now, stay in the modernized but still thatched **Kendall Cottage** ★★★, the farm's original manor home, filled with idiosyncratic contemporary art and lots of modern comforts, especially in the chic, spectacular bathrooms (they're about the same size as the bedrooms), and loads of technology. You can rent it as a one- or two-bedroom cottage, and take meals in your large private lounge or dine on your terrace beneath the old oaks. Ask for a tour of the cellars, taste the wines (your stocked bar will feature several bottles), and sample the oil—and definitely set out on foot to explore the estate just before sunset. Rates are R3,700 per night for one bedroom, or R5,900 for two (✆ **021/874-1021,** -1022, or -1023; www.alleebleue.com).

If instead you turn right to the monument, you'll see many more options as you feel yourself disappearing into the countryside: The boutique-style **Boekenhoutskloof** (✆ **021/876-3320)** produces internationally acclaimed wines, particularly reds; tastings are Monday to Friday 9am to 5pm. Another boutique-style winery is **Stony Brook,** where tastings are held Monday to Friday 10am to 3pm and Saturday 10am to 1pm; outside these hours, make an appointment for a more informal and personal tasting with owners Nigel and Joy in their home (✆ **021/876-2182**). On the same Green Valley Road, **Klein Genot** (✆ **021/876-2729**) is a young estate with a chic new cellar restaurant definitely worth visiting to eat lunch, accompanied by sublime decadent vineyard views, or to taste their steadily maturing reds (✆ **021/876-2738**).

Where to Stay

Franschhoek's property boards have prices quoted in rands, euros, and dollars—proof of its popularity with visitors from all over the world who fall in love with the valley and want to own a piece of it. This tribe—commonly known as Swallows—spend the summers in Franschhoek and then head back to Europe during the miserable cold and sodden rain of winter. They've pumped serious capital into the valley, and as a result, there has been a mushrooming in accommodations options. But frankly, you'd be hard pressed to beat the following recommendations. Were it not for the mammoth price, these full reviews might include the gorgeously decorated **La Residence** ★★★, sumptuous summer residence of the owner of Domaine des Anges, a vineyard on the outskirts of Franschhoek village. Its 11 suites are by far the best dressed in the valley, and it's utterly exclusive—set on a 12-hectare (30-acre) working farm—so it's well worth considering if money's no object (© **021/876-4100;** www.laresidence.co.za; doubles from R8,200). Also take a gander at **The Owner's Cottage** ★★, at Grande Provence, which *Harper's Bazaar* recently named among its 10 Most Fabulous Villas in the World. Lodged in a sumptuously decorated Cape Dutch manor, you'll have every luxury you can imagine, as well as the run of one of Franschhoek's most exquisite wine estates. It's rented on an exclusive basis, with a maximum of five couples allowed to share; rates start at R12,000 for one room, or R14,000 for two. Check it out at www.grandeprovence.co.za.

Auberge Clermont ★★ On a working wine, plum, and olive farm, in an old wine cellar, painted cream and offset with baby blue shutters, this auberge is inspired by the tastes and colors of Provence—the gardens, redolent with the scent of lavender and roses, are an integral part of this theme. Rooms are large and comfortably decorated, yet none of the bedrooms compares with the beautiful and spacious honeymoon suite, which is as eye-catching as it is elegant. The two loft rooms are also a good choice if you require a greater sense of privacy. Breakfast is served in the breakfast room or in the courtyard under 140-year-old oak trees. A spacious three-bedroom, two-bathroom self-catering villa occupies the 150-year-old farmhouse in a formal French garden.

Robertsvlei Rd., Franschhoek 7690. © **021/876-3700.** Fax 021/876-3701. www.clermont.co.za. 6 units. R1,450 double; R1,700 honeymoon suite; R2,500 villa. Rates include breakfast, except for villa. Ask about winter (May–Sept) discounts. AE, DC, MC, V. **Amenities:** Dining room/bar; small pool; room service; tennis court. *In room:* A/C (in some), TV, hair dryer, minibar, free Wi-Fi.

Klein Genot ★★ Built near the confluence of two seasonal rivers and surrounded by vineyards on one side and 365 fruit trees on the other, this stylish, wonderfully spacious, and light-filled guesthouse was created according to the principles of feng shui. Whether or not that means anything to you, the result is a magically peaceable venture. With a superb new restaurant on the estate, and what is to my mind the best little spa in the Winelands, Klein Genot (literally, "Little Indulgence,") is plush with homey lounging areas, a small library, a help-yourself bar, and a lovely garden pool. Six large suites are attached to an open-plan courtyard with koi ponds (and the most curious fish you'll ever meet). You should definitely ask for the larger Pink suite upstairs for top views. Besides the scene-stealing mountain panorama, there's a magic little lake fancied by the estate's signature black swans, and rescued orphan marmoset monkeys—rare curiosities—are sheltered nearby, too.

Green Valley Rd. © **021/876-2738.** Fax 021/876-4624. www.kleingenot.com. 7 units. High season R2,756–R3,096 double; low season R1,956 double. Rates include breakfast, afternoon tea, soft drinks, and beer. AE, DC, MC, V. **Amenities:** Restaurant; bar; CD and DVD library; free high-speed Internet; library; pool; spa. *In room:* A/C, TV/DVD, CD player, hair dryer, free Wi-Fi.

La Cabriere Country House ★ Value A good choice if you want to be within walking distance of the village, yet surrounded by views and vineyards, this Tuscan-style house has only six guest rooms, luxuriously and individually decorated with a blend of ethnic African, colonial, and Provençal fabrics, furniture, and *objets.* The debonair Londoner in charge has redecorated the compact bedrooms but retained an attention to detail that's unusual for this price range. Three "deluxe" rooms have fireplaces as well as French doors that lead out into the olive tree-filled garden, with its koi pond, inviting swimming pool, and gorgeous mountain and vineyard vistas. The two bedrooms in the owner's house are a better value; the one standard room may lack views, but it's double the size of the deluxe units and suitable for a family.

Middagkrans Rd., Franschhoek 7690. ✆ **021/876-4780.** Fax 021/876-3852. www.lacabriere.co.za. 5 units. Summer R2,100 deluxe double, R1,750 garden double, R1,300 standard double; winter R1,600 deluxe double, R1,300 garden double, R1,000 standard double. Children 2 and up pay R400 if sharing. Children under 2 free. Rates include breakfast. MC, V. **Amenities:** Dining room; pool. *In room:* A/C, TV, hair dryer, minibar, free Wi-Fi.

La Petite Ferme ★★★ As un-hotel-like as one could possibly imagine, these five large B&B suites, located in separate cottages below the Franschhoek Pass, are a personal top Winelands choice, particularly the aptly named Vista suite, which is the most private. The estate's vineyards are within touching distance, and beyond are sweeping valley and mountain views, enjoyable from your king-size bed or private terrace with plunge pool. Rooms are spacious and graciously decorated, with all the creature comforts needed for a magical stay. Luncheons take place at the adjacent restaurant or at nearby Haute Cabriere; alternatively, staff will arrange for transfers into the village at night, or day tours of the wineries. Some may find the suites a little cut off from the action—at 5pm, the restaurant closes, and staff is now a phone call away—but I consider this level of privacy, in this kind of location, priceless.

Pass Rd., Franschhoek 7690. ✆ **021/876-3016/8.** Fax 021/876-3624. lapetite@iafrica.com. 5 units. High season R1,700 luxury suite, R2,250 vista suite, R3,200 deluxe suite; low season R1,600 luxury suite; R2,100 vista suite, R3,000 deluxe suite. Rates include breakfast. AE, DC, MC, V. No children under 16. **Amenities:** Restaurant and bar (daytime); room service. *In room:* A/C, TV/DVD (in Vista and Deluxe), fireplace, hair dryer, minibar, plunge pool.

Le Franschhoek Hotel & Spa ★★ Another hotel with fabulous views, this time looking up at a majestic mountain range, Le Franschhoek has been playing to packed houses since it opened after a kick-ass restoration of the run-down old Swiss Excelsior Hotel. Decor is clean and crisp, with colonial flair: white four-poster beds dressed in Egyptian cotton, slick marble bathrooms, and one-off furniture pieces that give the monochromatic rooms—all cream and beige—a little character. There are also self-catering chalets with kitchenettes and an on-site deli (sadly understocked during my last stay) in the bistro-style **Verger Restaurant,** where you dine in glass-walled conservatories affording views across the valley. While you're a minute's drive from Franschhoek's main street (there's a free shuttle), the views from every angle here are pure country getaway. Staff will also organize more active pursuits—from horseback riding to helicopter flips, golf, fly-fishing, and more.

Minor Rd. 16, Franschhoek 7690 ✆ **021/876-8900.** Fax 021 876-4384. www.lefranschhoek.co.za. 79 units. High season R2,740–R3,020 standard double, R3,460–R3,810 chalet double R4,420–R4,860 suite double; low season R2,070 standard double, R2,640 chalet double, R3,390 suite double. AE, MC, V. **Amenities:** 3 restaurants; deli; bar; babysitting; boule court; concierge; pool; room service; spa; tennis court. In room: A/C, TV, hair dryer, minibar (not self-catering units), Wi-Fi (R20–R500 for 10MB–500MB).

Le Quartier Français ★★★ This auberge, voted best Small Hotel in the World by *Tatler* in 2005, is the most exuberant, exciting option in the valley, with audaciously designed rooms and all sorts of clever details to make your stay extra blissful. Besides laying claim to two of the most sought-after restaurants in the winelands, the hotel offers complimentary transport within Franschhoek, so you can really relax without worrying about taxis or how much wine you sample. Ultimately, without valley views, it's the rooms that cinch it; most encircle a central courtyard with verdant gardens and a large oval pool, and are huge, comfortable, and stylish, with decor that cleverly marries classic and modern, with accents in bright, vivid fabrics. Of the standard rooms, no. 16 is best (there's a private garden seating area). If you can splurge, look at the phenomenal Four

Quarters suites in the modern wing: Extravagant extras include a private butler and an additional heated pool (ask for no. 3, for the loveliest views). Le Quartier even has a Screening Room, which serves up mainstream and art-house movies along with gourmet popcorn to guests and locals. Suites have a minibar, iPod docking station, and Wii; Pool and House suites have a plunge pool.

16 Huguenot Rd., Franchhoek 7690 ✆ **021/876-2151.** Fax 021/876-3105. www.lequartier.co.za. 21 units. R3,950 double; R7,400 auberge suite; R8,900 Four Quarters suite; R6,980 2-bedroom cottage. Rates include breakfast. Children 12 and under stay in Pool and House suite loft rooms free of charge. AE, DC, MC, V. **Amenities:** 2 restaurants; bar; cinema; library (CDs, DVDs, and books); 2 pools; room service; wellness center. *In room:* A/C, TV/DVD, CD player, hair dryer, free Wi-Fi.

Mont Rochelle ★★ Perched on a hill overlooking the valley, this vineyard hotel enjoys one of the most beautiful settings in Franschhoek; views from every window are marvelous (although not as sweeping as the La Petite Ferme suites across the valley). Offering guests full-blown luxury with all the bells and whistles one expects from a five-star establishment, Mont Rochelle's elegantly appointed bedrooms and suites are classed and priced like wines (Shiraz units look a little lackluster compared to the roomier, better-dressed Merlots and Cabernets—the latter have private terraces *and* dramatic vistas). The most expensive suites—individually decorated, with private lounge, generous bathroom, and high-tech gadgets—are in an excavated underground chamber that's completely private from the rest of the hotel. While it's lavishly put together and affords grand views, it is decidedly hotel-like (making it the antithesis of the more intimate places). **Mange Tout** serves up world-class French-inspired dishes, but I'd rather order a picnic platter from the **Country Kitchen Restaurant** (✆ **021/876-3000;** R280 feeds two) and feast under trees beside the dam.

Dassenberg Rd., Franschhoek 7690 (follow signs off the main road into Franschhoek before entering the village). ✆ **021/876-2770.** Fax 021/876-3788. www.montrochelle.co.za. 22 units. Summer R3,540–R4,230 double, R4,490–R7,800 suite; winter R1,980–R2,940 double, R3,210–R6,240 suite. Rates include breakfast. AE, DC, MC, V. **Amenities:** 2 restaurants; cigar bar; babysitting; trout fishing; gym; helipad; pool; room service; spa; free airport transfers; wine cellar & winery; Wi-Fi (free in business center; R1 per minute in bar area). *In room:* A/C (in some), TV, hair dryer.

Résidence Klein Oliphants Hoek ★★ Value The "Little Elephant's Corner" is the best place to stay in the heart of Franschhoek village—a warm, sociable, good-value guesthouse within easy walking distance of the main road, but set at the edge of a classic ornamental garden in the town's old Mission House. An Italian lady with a keen sense of style and infinite charm as a hostess, Renata is another European who came to Franschhoek, fell in love, and stayed. This is her second guesthouse here; as she cut her teeth on a smaller project, she's given all the rooms a beautiful overhaul and turned the entire place into a classy boutique guesthouse using original antiques, select artworks, and immaculate bedrooms. Standard "comfort" and courtyard rooms are just fine, but there are a couple of special spaces, such as the Sundeck Jacuzzi suite, that are really worth spending a little extra on. With its healthful-but-decadent high tea, small-but-excellent restaurant showcasing one of Franschhoek's blossoming culinary talents, and all-around understanding of what traditional hospitality is all about, I cannot recommend this budget-sensitive residence highly enough.

14 Akademie St., Franschhoek 7690. ✆ **021/876-2566.** Fax 021/876-2766. www.kleinoliphantshoek.co.za. 8 units. High season R1,100–R2,100 double, R2,320–R2,700 suite; low season R780–R1,260 double, R1,540–R1,640 suite. AE, MC, V. **Amenities:** Restaurant, bar; free high-speed Internet; library; lounge; pool. *In room:* A/C, TV, hair dryer.

Tips Booking Etiquette

During the summer months, Franschhoek's top restaurants are in constant demand, and getting a table without a reservation is practically impossible. A few may even require you to book several weeks or months in advance, and there are accounts of pig-headed tourists wandering the main road searching for nourishment only to end up at the local pizzeria, **Col'Cacchio** (© **021/876-4222**)—not a terrible choice, but hardly the reason you're here. It's in your interest to ask your host to make dinner reservations on your behalf. They have their fingers on the pulse of the local dining scene; use their suggestions to supplement this book, and don't dally.

Where to Dine

Franschhoek may not have collected quite as many restaurant accolades in 2009 as it usually does, but it clings doggedly to its self-proclaimed title as the gourmet capital of South Africa. There's an astounding amount of choice, given the relatively miniscule size of the village. Several restaurants are now fixtures on the global foodie map, and Franschhoek is renowned for its produce, particularly its rainbow trout, olives, and even handcrafted Belgian-style chocolates; chocoholics should book The Chocolate Experience at **Huguenot Fine Chocolates** (© **021/876-4096**), a national institution where you can choose from 45 chocolate varieties. Franschhoek also hosts the annual South Africa Cheese Festival, but the nearest decent cheese-tasting venue is quite far away, at the tasting room at **Anura Vineyards,** on Simondium Road, Klapmuts (© **021/875-5360;** www.anura.co.za; Mon–Sun 9am–5pm). Back in the village, **La Brasserie** (© **021/876-3420**) is where you will find the locals on Friday evenings during the summer months, when it hosts jazz evenings from 5 to 8pm. Besides the restaurants reviewed below, **Klein Oliphants Hoek** (© **021/876-2566**) is worth considering—Italian owner Renata Gaggio and local chef Thurston David have come up with a small but effective menu that suits the intimate surrounds of this homey guesthouse (reviewed above). Take your cue from the locals and order the lamb shank, and finish off with a baked chocolate pudding. If all the fine dining is too much, opt for **French Connection** (© **021/876-4056**). The brainchild of Matthew Gordon of Haute Cabriere, this informal pavement-style bistro on the main road is a favorite with the Franschhoek locals.

Bread & Wine ★★★ Kids MEDITERRANEAN With a conscious attempt to keep meals at prices even South Africans can afford, this is a hugely popular vineyard luncheon spot. Locals drive all the way from Cape Town not only for the great food, but for the relaxing courtyard venue—if you're here in summer, book an outside table. The menu changes regularly, updated on the website, so take a look to see if it suits; with luck, the risotto of Italian summer truffle, asparagus, and auricchio cheese, made with a generous dash of the wine estate's bubbly, will be back; also look out for the heavenly oven-roasted tuna, served with porcini mushrooms and bone marrow. The bread basket is exceptional—you can purchase more at the estate's "farm grocer," along with the cured meats the estate is famous for.

Moreson Wine Farm, Happy Valley Rd., Franschhoek. © **021/876-3692.** www.moreson.co.za. Main courses R80–R120. AE, DC, MC, V. Daily noon–3pm.

La Petite Ferme ★★★ COUNTRY If you are spending only 1 day in Franschhoek, make sure you lunch here: Book a table on the all-weather veranda, order the signature deboned oak-smoked salmon trout served with asparagus and sweet potato pie, and allow plenty of time to drink in both the view and one of the farm's great wines. Even the locals can't resist dining here—situated on the Franschhoek Pass with a breathtaking view of the entire valley, this family-run restaurant has arguably the best setting in South Africa. The food is refreshingly simple—if the trout doesn't appeal, try the marinated ostrich, or lighten up with a surprisingly delectable pork and fig burger. End with La Petite Ferme's own plums, transformed into a tangy meringue and served with plum and cinnamon ice cream. Better still, order at least one rooibos-flavored crème brûleé you will never forget it.

Pass Rd. ✆ **021/876-3016.** Reservations essential. Main courses R74–R135. AE, DC, MC, V. Daily noon–4pm.

Le Quartier Français ★★★ INNOVATIVE/BISTRO For years, this has been considered by many to be the best restaurant in Franschhoek—and in this haute cuisine environment, that takes some doing. To focus more exclusively on her innovative flavor combinations, executive chef Margo Janse has separated the restaurant into two sections: The bistro-style **iCi** may be more laid-back, but I adore the great tastes here. The seared Franschhoek salmon (famously tea-smoked at Môreson) with fennel and olives, served with tomato and anchovy, is a great follow-on from the wood-baked goat cheese soufflé. Then comes an irresistible bitter chocolate and geranium fondant with frozen buffalo yogurt. Chicken cooked in a wood-burning pizza oven is a huge hit with locals. Adjacent, **The Tasting Room** is one of the world's great multi-award-winning restaurants, and you need to reserve months in advance (or stay at the hotel) and really starve yourself before sitting down to dine; it will blow you away.

Corner of Berg and Wilhelmina sts. ✆ **021/876-2151.** iCi main courses R95–R110; crayfish R119. Tasting Room 4 courses R490, or R670 with wine; 6 courses R610, or R870 with wine; 8 courses R760, or R1,150 with wine. AE, DC, MC, V. iCi daily noon–3:30pm and 9–9pm. Tasting Room daily 7–9pm.

Reuben's ★★ ECLECTIC Although it's been several years since Reuben, the star of Franschhoek's favorite rags-to-riches success story, was voted Chef of the Year (and Reuben's itself, Restaurant of the Year) by the *Eat Out* team, the young culinary hero still draws a crowd, prompting the expansion of his bistro and the inevitable upping of prices. Some locals mourn the earlier days of his rising stardom; other rue the slightly cold ambience of the restaurant. Still, it's the food that won him the spotlight, and this is still the reason his restaurant is full. His menu changes constantly, but expect innovative use of the freshest ingredients to produce interesting comfort food options such as grilled quail saltimbocca, mustard-glazed ostrich filet, or pan-roasted veal liver.

Oude Stallen Centre, 19 Huguenot Rd. ✆ **021/876-3772.** Main courses R75–R155. AE, DC, MC, V. Mon–Sun 8–10:30am, noon–3pm, and 6–9pm.

TULBAGH

130km (81 miles) N of Cape Town; 80km (50 miles) NW of Stellenbosch; 45km (28 miles) E of Riebeek Kasteel

It may be a mere blip on most tourist maps, but historic Tulbagh—surrounded by the wrinkled peaks of the gorgeous Witzenberg Mountains—is a hot pick as the rising star of the Cape Winelands. Europeans first discovered the valley in 1658, and the first farmers settled here in 1699; the town's Dutch heritage is still celebrated with a Cape Dutch

Pit-stop in Paarl

Paarl, 56km (35 miles) east of Cape Town, is named after the great granite rocks that loom above the town. The first European party to visit the area in 1657 watched the dawn sun reflecting off the glistening boulders after a night of rain and named it Peerlbergh (Pearl Mountain). These 500-million-year-old domes are one of the world's largest granite outcrops, second only to Ayers Rock in Australia. The town's size and overdeveloped scruffiness makes it a far less attractive stop than the chi-chi village of Franschhoek, the oak-lined avenues of Stellenbosch, or the sleepy hamlet of Tulbagh. Still, there are a number of highly respected wine estates to visit; get a map from the **Paarl Information Bureau** (✆ **021/863-4937;** www.paarlonline.com; Mon–Fri 8am–5pm, Sat 9am–2pm, Sun 10am–2pm), on Main Road, with its 2km (1¼-mile) stretch of preserved buildings, difficult to observe because of the incessant traffic. Most visitors find a visit to the **Taal Monument** (or Afrikaans Language Monument, the large phallic sculpture visible on the slopes of Paarl Mountain) worthwhile—the views of the valley and False Bay are excellent. To get here, drive down Main Road, passing the KWV headquarters on your left, and look for the signs to your right. Cheese lovers should head for touristy **Fairview** wine estate, where goat's milk cheeses can be sampled in the popular **Goats Shed** restaurant (✆ **021/863-2450**), one of the busiest tourist stops in the Winelands. Dedicated foodies generally arrive in Paarl having reserved for the three-course lunch at **Bosman's Restaurant** ★★★ (✆ **021/863-5100;** closed mid-May to July 31), the first hotel restaurant in Africa to achieve Relais Gourmand status. Unfortunately, fabulous cuisine is marred by service that confuses sophistication with cloying formality, and a request for a glass of tap water is likely to be met with an upturned nose (not to mention scandalous reports of guests being conned into ordering ultraexpensive bottles of wine). Fortunately, there are more relaxed places to dine hereabouts. With its large windows affording views of the Klein Drakenstein mountains and massive old-fashioned skylights letting in plenty of natural light or a view of the night sky, it's fortunate that new kid on the Paarl block **Die Eethuis** (literally, "The Eating House"), Pastorie St. (✆ **021/871-1432**), doesn't rely solely on its looks. Chef Wesley Muller prepares fine starters (like duck and wild mushroom ravioli with walnut foam) and delectable grilled meats, but also offers unexpected dishes, like sheep's tails and sweetbreads. You can also try **The Restaurant at Pontac** (✆ **021/872-0445**), where chef Tiaan presides over wholesome hearty

Food and Wine Festival each March or April. Apart from its historical ambience, a good reason to visit is simply to get away from the hordes jamming up the streets in Franchhoek and Stellenbosch, and linger under the oak trees. There are 36 listed monuments in this tiny town, many of them fine examples of Cape Dutch architecture, most evident in the facades of the restored houses lining Church Street—every one was restored to its original condition after a freak earthquake measuring 6.4 on the Richter scale flattened the town in 1969, and the effect is that of an open-air museum. Stroll the street to study fare; or grab a table in the big courtyard garden at **Marc's,** 129 Main Rd. (✆ **021/863-3980**). Besides a great wine list, there's a wide array of Mediterranean-inspired dishes. A truly fabulous dining experience is **The Victorian Restaurant and Terrace** ★★, at the Rhebokskloof Private Cellar (✆ **021/869-8606;** www.rhebokskloof.co.za), where innovative South African fare, like crocodile carpaccio served with rocket (arugula) leaves, toasted pumpkin seeds, and chevin goat's cheese; or springbok Wellington, wrapped in mushroom and spinach, is served overlooking the estate's manicured lawns and lake.

While I'm not for one moment suggesting that you bed down in Paarl, you may be tempted by the beautifully restored 18th-century Cape Dutch estate in which Bosman's is located: World-famous **Grande Roche** ★★★, Plantasie St. (✆ **021/863-5100;** www.granderoche.co.za) lures the well-heeled golfing crowd to its large and luxurious rooms, surrounded by lush gardens with the Drakenstein Mountains as dramatic backdrop. It's not cheap for a town with little to hold your attention (from R2,800 double in summer), but it has all the amenities you'd expect from a classy hotel, including a spa. Too rich for your blood? Then consider **Roggeland** ★ (✆ **021/868-2501;** www.roggeland.co.za), another gracious 300-year-old Cape Dutch estate homestead in the Klein Drakenstein Valley, this time a good-value pad (from R1,040 double, *including* a four-course dinner with wine) regularly raved about by travel writers and foodies.

Alternatively, if you decide to skip lunch in Paarl, you may want to stop at Diemersfontein, a boutique winery in the Wellington area. Here, **Seasons** (✆ **021/873-2671**) serves up very reasonably priced contemporary country-style meals. The gorgeous views make it an ideal luncheon stop—and you might like to stock up with a case or two of their famously chocolatey Pintotage. In fact, if you decide you like the wines too much, you might just consider overnighting here; ask for the romantic **Manor House Suite No. 1** ★★ (✆ **021/864-5050;** www.diemersfontein.co.za; around R1,110 double).

Getting There: From Cape Town, Paarl is a straight drive along the N1; turnoffs into town are posted. To reach Paarl from Franschhoek (some 33km/20 miles northwest), simply retrace your steps down Huguenot Road and take the R303 off the main road (after the turnoff to La Motte). In town, look for the first traffic circle and turn left onto Market; keep going until Market meets Main Street.

the buildings—some of them Victorian—more closely; panels outside each monument explain the style and origin of the houses, and some of them, converted by residents into boutiques, restaurants, and guesthouses, can be seen from the inside. Within minutes of the town center are some impressive wine estates. Established in 1710, **Twee Jonge Gezellen** ★★ (✆ **023/230-0680;** www.houseofkrone.co.za; Mon–Fri 11am and 3pm, Sat 11pm) is one of the oldest estates in the country. If you find yourself here in January or February, try and book a seat at their Night Harvest dinners: for R300, you will enjoy a three-course dinner paired with the estate's wines, a cellar tour, and a visit to the vineyards to see the grapes being picked. **Tulbagh Mountain Vineyards** (© **023/231-1118**) has the connoisseurs' noses twitching in approval for not only its white (the *Platter* guide rates the 2007 blend as "silkily rich, gorgeous"), but also the Swartland Syrah and a number of others. But it's newcomer **Saronsberg** ★★★ (© **023/230-0707;** www.saronsberg.co.za; tastings Mon–Fri 8am–5pm, Sat 10am–2pm) that's been pulling in fistsful of awards; the shiraz and Full Circle blend are probably the most lauded, but the sauvignon blanc, too, demands attention. The modern tasting room has a wonderful outlook and a selection of contemporary South African art. Lastly, an essential stop for shiraz, cabernet sauvignon, and chenin blanc fans is **Rijk's Private Cellar** (© **023/230-1622;** www.rijks.co.za; tastings Mon–Fri 10am–4pm, Sat 10am–2pm, call to check on public holidays)—you can also stay the night (see below).

Essentials

GETTING THERE There are a number of less straightforward ways to get there, and they're all spectacularly scenic, especially if you approach via the jaw-dropping Bainskloof Pass (see "Three Dramatic Winelands Drives," on p. 180), but here's the straightforward route: From Cape Town, take the N1 toward Paarl (around 30 min.) and exit left at the KLAPMUTS/WELLINGTON R44 turnoff (the exit before Paarl). Take the left turn and continue to Wellington (15 min.). On entering Wellington, turn left at the traffic lights (with the R44). The sign reads DISTILLERY ROAD-HERMON/CERES. Continue for 30 minutes through the Nuwekloof Pass, and follow the Tulbagh signs.

VISITOR INFORMATION Stop by the local **tourism office** (© **023/230-1348**) for maps and brochures; before traveling, visit www.tulbaghtourism.org.za.

Where to Stay

Besides the diverse selection of places reviewed below, consider first contacting Jayson Clark—his **Cape Dutch Quarter** (www.cdq.co.za) is essentially a central booking service for several lovely self-catering properties, as well as B&Bs in historical homes (including the delightful one he runs with his mom; reviewed below). Jayson's passion for Tulbagh is part of the renaissance spirit so evident in this quiet village, and he'll set you up with accommodations, dining tips, sightseeing suggestions, and even the local drinking hole.

Bartholomeus Klip ★★★ Near the tiny hamlet of Hermon, about 30 minutes from Tulbagh, this luxury country lodge is on a working wheat and sheep farm, and proves a wonderful base from where you can combine a bit of wildlife-viewing (the vast nature reserve is stocked with buffalo, zebras, wildebeest, gemsbok, eland, springbok, bontebok, and hartebeest, and is the last habitat of the endangered geometric tortoise, one of the world's rarest reptiles) with wine tastings (in Tulbagh or Paarl). Accommodations are in a restored Victorian homestead, elegantly furnished in period style. There are only five bedrooms; the best option by far is the beautiful suite, which has its own entrance and a private veranda with great views. Alternatively, stay in a small farmhouse called Wild Olive House. It's a peaceful place, with little to do but enjoy exceptional food (included in the rate), laze around on loungers—the large, deep, farm-style pool is wonderful—and walk, cycle, or drive through the reserve.

Elandskloof Mountains, P.O. Box 36, Hermon 7308. © **022/448-1820** or 082/829-4131. Fax 022/448-1829. www.bartholomeus.com. 5 units. High season R4,070–R4,418 double, R4,444–R4,888 suite; mid-season R3,026 double, R3,714 suite. Rates include brunch, dinner, high tea, all game-viewing, and sports activities. AE, DC, MC, V. **Amenities:** Dining room; bar; mountain biking; canoeing; game drives and game walks; fly-fishing; pool; shop; wind-surfing (on dam). *In room:* A/C, hair dryer.

Tulbagh Country Guest House ★ Value A 200-year-old house oozing real character, this small, well-established B&B enjoys a prime setting among the historic monuments on Church Street. The cozy, homey atmosphere is only partly a result of the assemblage of original fittings and finishes, antiques, and artworks; even more important is the attitude of enthusiastic hosts Ginny and Jayson, who will do just about anything to enhance your stay (babysit, work out itineraries, even haul you down to the town's bush pub). The recent addition of a Mediterranean-style pool and outdoor schmoozing area has allowed for an even more potentially sociable vibe, and breakfasts at the communal kitchen table, complete with vintage china and cutlery, are legendary. Reserve the massive honeymoon suite at the front of the house—the look and furnishings are pure vintage.

24 Church St., Tulbagh 6820. ✆ **023/230-1171** or 082/416-6576. Fax 023/230-0721. www.cdq.co.za. 5 units. R600–R800 double. Rates include breakfast. AE, MC, V. **Amenities:** Dining room; babysitting; pool. *In room* A/C, TV, hair dryer, minibar, free Wi-Fi.

Vindoux ★★ Value With the only luxury treehouses in the Cape, this family-run guest farm affords novelty and comfort. With the jagged peaks of the Witzenberg Mountains surrounding you on three sides, you're ensconced here on a vast olive farm with about 70,000 trees; and while you're several meters off the ground, you still have queen beds, duck-feather duvets, and a properly amenitied bathroom (with spa tub), not to mention the option of a romantic champagne and rose petal turndown. When you're done exploring the gorgeous Tulbagh wine estates, head back here for one of their signature *fynbos* body wraps at the fine little day spa, and then climb back up to your treehouse and laze at the edge of your terrace watching the birds winging it between the branches. Later, if you can tear yourself away, sample the steak at the treehouse restaurant, with its popular bush pub, good for a totally unpretentious look at small-town South African life. More basic self-catering cottages on the ground are available, including two-bedroom units suitable for families.

Vindoux Farm, Twee Jonge Gezellen Rd., Tulbagh 6820. ✆ **023/230-0635** or 082/404-7778. Fax 023/230-0635. www.vindoux.com. 4 luxury treehouses and 4 self-catering cottages. Treehouse: R850–R900 double, discounts for stays of 2 nights or more; romantic turndown R150. Rates include breakfast. Cottage: R400–R500 double, R175–R200 per extra person (maximum 6), R100 per child under 12. MC, V. **Amenities:** Restaurant; bush pub; barbecue picnic area; bike rental; children's play area and petting zoo; fishing; gym; pool and plunge pool; day spa; free Wi-Fi. *In room:* Minibar (unstocked), spa tub.

Where to Dine

Sure, Tulbagh is not yet on the culinary map, and it doesn't have any restaurants even remotely approaching the level of sophistication and variety available in Stellenbosch, Franschhoek, or even Paarl. What you will find here, though, are a handful of charming, relaxed eateries. The most famous stop in town is **Paddagang Restaurant,** Church Street (✆ **023/230-0242**), where "boerekos" (farmers' food) is served according to time-honored recipes, making it one of those famous country stops. While quality isn't all that consistent, and the kitchen lacks innovation, it's a good place to sample a few authentic South African recipes: The Kaapse Bord ("Cape Platter") features traditional *babotie,* waterlily stew, and roast chicken. **Pielow's Restaurant** (✆ **023/230-0432**), also on Church Street, is the number-one fine-dining choice in town, and is said to have the best wine list in the valley. For home-cooked meals with a slight experimental edge, head instead to **Readers Restaurant** ★, in a mid-18th-cenury house on the other side of Church Street (✆ **023/230-0087**), where Carol Collins has been turning out satisfying country dishes in her little kitchen for over 12 years. Try the chicken breast stuffed with chocolate, spinach, and feta; ostrich with gooseberry and amarula sauce; deep-fried whole onion; or exceptional lamb strudel. If you've got a sweet tooth, stop at Schoonderzicht Farm and sample Niki de Wolf's Belgian-style **Moniki Chocolates** (✆ **023/230-0673**)—or you can even get a crash course in making your own. At **Kimilili** (✆ **023/231-1503;** www.kimililifarm.co.za), you can taste award-winning cheeses. Finally, cool cats looking for a sexier vibe—hanging chairs, schmoozy ottomans, and an open-air lounge deck—should try the new **B-Lounge** on the De Heuvel Wine and Olive Estate a few miles from town; dim sum and hot canapés are served with ever-improving cocktails, but of course, you'll opt for a bottle of locally produced vino (✆ **023/231-0350**).

Wild Flowers, Whale Coast & Garden Route: The Western Cape

The Western Cape, Africa's south-western-most tip, is the most popular tourist destination in South Africa, and with good reason. Besides the sybaritic pleasures of Cape Town and its winelands (see chapter 5), numerous treasures lie just an hour or two's drive from the Mother City. Along what is known as the West Coast, you'll find salty lagoons and laid-back beach restaurants, quaint villages surrounded by vineyards or rolling wheat fields, and the bewitching Cederberg Mountains, its craggy weathered walls adorned in ancient rock art. And after the first rains fall, usually in August, the annual miracle of spring sees the seemingly barren plains abloom with spectacular flower displays.

Then there's the vast Southern Right whale nursery that stretches along the Cape's southern coast. Some of the best land-based whale-watching sites in the world are in the Overberg, with whales migrating to its shallow coastal basin to mate and calve from mid-July to November. The Whale Coast, of which the coastal town of Hermanus is the unofficial capital, is an easy and beautiful 90-minute coast-hugging drive from Cape Town, but there's plenty to do and lovely places to stay, should you choose to spend a few days here or use this as a springboard to the hinterland.

East of the Overberg are the coastal lakes and forests of the Garden Route, fringed by the majestic mountains that separate it from the ostrich farms and vineyards of the Klein Karoo, and the distinctive architecture of the small settlements dotted in the vast arid plains of the Great Karoo. It's a great place to do nothing but unwind—but this scenic coastal belt, which encompasses South Africa's Lakes District, also takes pride of place on

Fun Facts Diving with Sharks

One of the world's greatest concentrations of **great white sharks** is found in South African waters—in particular, around Dyer and Geyser Islands, near Gansbaai, where the presence of breeding jackass penguin and seal colonies have resulted in the channel between these islands being dubbed Shark Alley. Recent studies have shown that this impressive predator (it can reach lengths of up to 6m/20 ft., although 4m/13 ft. is more usual) is a very particular hunter, and most of the (extremely rare) attacks on humans are thought to be mistakes. In Cape Town, shark spotters placed on mountain slopes keep a sharp lookout for sharks and warn bathers. But many visitors actually choose a close encounter with the creatures: Cage diving with great whites is wildly popular (see "Staying Active").

the itinerary for adrenaline junkies, with a rush of activities ranging from the highest bungee jump in the world to riding elephants and cage-diving with great white sharks. The region also boasts an increasing number of private game reserves, but none compares in terms of size with the vast reserves in the bordering Eastern Cape province. However you devise your itinerary (and this chapter is here to help you do just that), the best way to explore this part of the world is by car. You can drive the entire Garden Route from Cape Town in 5 to 6 hours, reaching Port Elizabeth in 7, but you should spend at least 3 nights en route—preferably 5—to discover the beauty off the beaten track (the N2).

1 STAYING ACTIVE

ABSEILING Take a 45m (148-ft.) abseil (rappel) next to a waterfall in the Kaaimans River Gorge in Wilderness, then canoe out (R345 per person). Call **Eden Adventures** (✆ **044/877-0179;** www.eden.co.za). They also offer a range of pure canoeing trips for those who don't fancy clinging to a cliff. Or swim, float, jump, and abseil down Kruis River Gorge with **Tstitsikamma Falls Adventure** (✆ **044/280-3770;** www.tsitsikammaadventure.co.za).

BOARDSAILING & KITE-SURFING Langebaan Lagoon, north of Cape Town on the West Coast, is considered one of the best sites in South Africa for those who get a rush from the combined power of water and air—particularly in the early afternoon, when the wind picks up (wind speeds average 20–30 knots). Book lessons and rent equipment from the **Cape Sports Centre** in Langebaan (✆ **022/772-1114;** www.capesport.co.za).

BOATING You can cruise the ocean all along the coast; recommendations can be found under each section.

BUNGEE-/BRIDGE-JUMPING The **Bloukrans River bridge-jump** (✆ **042/281-1458;** R620 per person), 40km (25 miles) east of Plettenberg Bay, is the highest bridge-jump in the world: a stomach-churning 7-second, 216m (708-ft.) free fall. Open daily from 8:30am to 5pm.

CANOEING Naturally, one of the best ways to explore South Africa's Lakes District is via its many waterways. Canoes can be rented throughout the area—contact the local tourism bureau wherever you are. The 2-day Keurbooms River Canoe Trail ★★★, near Plettenberg Bay, is unguided and takes you 7km (4¼ miles) upstream through totally untouched vegetation, to an overnight hut, where you're assured of total privacy. The trail was temporarily closed due to flooding but should be open by September 2009. The hut houses four people; you may need to self-cater. For bookings, call **Eden Adventures** (✆ **044/877-0179;** www.eden.co.za). For sea-kayaking tours of the marine-rich ocean around Plettenberg Bay, contact **Dolphin Adventures** (✆ **083/590-3405;** www.dolphinadventures.co.za). Tours start at R250 per person.

DIVING There are snorkeling and diving routes in **Tsitsikamma National Park** (✆ **042/281-1607**). Gear and guides can be rented from the **Dive Hut** (✆ **073/130-0689**) at Storms River Mouth rest camp, or from **Pro Dive** (✆ **044/533-1158**) in Plettenberg Bay; ask about Jacob's Reef, another good spot off the Plett coast. **Hippo Dive Campus** (✆ **044/384-0831**) offers equipment and dives in the Knysna area, where there are a number of wrecks to explore. The **Mossel Bay Diving Academy** (✆ **082/896-5649**) specializes in dives west of Knysna.

GOLFING You're really spoiled for choice on the Garden Route, which has supplanted KwaZulu-Natal as South Africa's Golf Coast. The almost unrestricted (and unpoliced) development of new courses in the past 8 years, however, has produced a groundswell of opposition from locals, who fear that the environmental impact of these thirsty lawns for the well-heeled is still to be felt.

In Hermanus The top choice here is the Peter Matkovich–designed course at **Arabella Country Estate** ★★★, 20 minutes from Hermanus, voted the top course in the Western Cape (no mean feat) and home to the Nelson Mandela Invitational. Like Pezula and Fancourt, it has a luxury hotel (www.westerncapehotelandspa.co.za) with a spa. Call ✆ **028/284-0000** (greens fees R720 for day visitors or R650 for hotel guests; club rental R295; golf cart R250; caddie R120).

In George The original **George Golf Club course** ★★ (✆ **044/873-6116**) is a scenic walk that will run you R440, while the much-vaunted **Fancourt** ★★★, South Africa's premier golf resort, offers visitors a chance to play on their Bramble Hill course (✆ **044/804-0000;** R290). If you're not up to par, sign up with the Fancourt Golf Academy, said to be one of the best in the world; it will cost from R240 per 30-minute lesson, or R1,200 for an 18-hole individual on-course playing lesson. Fancourt has three other Gary Player–designed championship courses, including two fine 18-hole parkland layouts that are always in the top 10 in South Africa, but you have to stay at Fancourt to play these. Near George (on the outskirts of Mossel Bay) is **Pinnacle Point Beach & Golf Resort** ★★★ (✆ **044/693-3438;** www.pinnaclepoint.co.za), a multimillion-rand leisure and residential development carved above the cliffs overlooking the Indian Ocean (a hotel is set to open in December 2009). While most courses boast 1 signature hole, the 18-hole, par-72 Pinnacle, another Matkovich creation, has no less than 7, each on a cliff edge (greens fees R400 for hotel guests, R750 for visitors; includes cart). ***Note:*** Only those who stay at the hotel or the nearby Garden Route Hotel have access to the course.

In Knysna **Pezula** ★★ (✆ **044/384-1222**), designed by Ronald Fream and David Dale, enjoys another glorious location perched atop the Knysna East Head cliffs. Along with great views, the course boasts a luxury hotel and spa (greens fees R525–R775). Deeper inland, on undulating hills that overlook the Knysna river and lagoon, is the perfectly groomed Jack Nicklaus Signature Golf Course at **Simola** (✆ **044/302-9677;** www.simolaestate.co.za), named the best new golf course in the country in 2005. The course has an interesting configuration: five par-3s and five par-5s (greens fees R550–R720; includes cart and halfway house). The estate is also home to an ultramodern luxury hotel with 40 units and a spa.

In Plettenberg Bay If you've worked your way through George and Knysna, you can now choose between the challenging 18-hole course in evergreen surrounds at the **Plett Country Club** (✆ **044/533-2132;** greens fees R335) and the Gary Player–designed **Goose Valley** ★ (✆ **044/533-5082;** R300).

HIKING **Overberg** There are plenty of walks in the undulating hills and mountains of the Overberg region, but my favorite is the **Whale Trail** ★★★ (✆ **021/659-3500;** www.capenature.org.za) in the De Hoop Nature Reserve, a 5-day walk in *fynbos* (a beautiful and diverse floral kingdom) paradise, with the last 3 days hugging the coast, with whales (in season) constantly within view and earshot. The first day is the hardest (15km), but it gets much easier after that (day 3 is only 8km)—and besides, luggage is portaged.

Garden Route This is a walker's paradise. One of the best ways to experience this is with the **Garden Route Trail** ★★, an easy 5-day coastal walk (all luggage portaged) that takes you from the forests of the Wilderness National Park to Brenton-on-Sea outside Knysna (www.gardenroutetrail.co.za). For serious hikers, the following are worth noting: the 108km (67-mile), 7-day **Outeniqua Trail** ★ (✆ **044/302-5606**), which takes you through plantations and indigenous forests (shorter versions available); the 60km (37-mile), 6-day **Tsitsikamma Trail** ★★ (✆ **044/281-1712**), an inland version of the more famous Otter Trail, which includes long stretches of fynbos, as well as forests and rivers; and the 27km (17-mile), 2-day **Harkerville Trail** ★★ (also called the Mini Otter Trail, and a good alternative), which features forest and coastal scenery (✆ **044/302-5606**). Best of all is the 42km (26-mile), 5-day **Otter Trail** ★★★, South Africa's most popular trail. It's a tough coastal walk, taking you through the **Tsitsikamma National Park,** past rivers and through indigenous forests, with magnificent views of the coast; its popularity means it must be booked at least a year in advance (✆ **012/426-5111;** www.sanparks.org). The 3-night **Dolphin Trail** is a luxury trail in the Tsitsikamma, with all luggage portaged; comfortable, fully catered accommodations; plenty of time for lolling in tidal pools; and trained field guides accompanying walkers (✆ **042/280-3588;** www.dolphintrail.co.za). For those who don't have the time (or energy) for overnight trails, the 10km (6.25-mile) **Pied Kingfisher Trail,** in Wilderness National Park, follows the river through lush indigenous forest to a waterfall; the 9.5km (5.6-mile) **Kranshoek Walk,** in the Harkerville Forest, is another great forest environment; and the 9km (5.5-mile) **Robberg Trail,** in Plettenberg Bay, is definitely worth exploring for its wild coastline and whale-watching opportunities.

West Coast Avid hikers are advised to find out more about the **Cederberg Wilderness Area,** some 3 hours north of Cape Town. With its strange twisted rock formations and tea-colored streams, this is a hiker and climber's paradise, plus it's off the beaten track (✆ **021/659-3500**).

HORSEBACK RIDING **In Hermanus** Contact **Klein Paradys Equestrian Centre** (✆ **028/284-9422** or 083/240-6448). The **African Horse Company** (✆ **082/667-9232;** www.africanhorseco.com) offers both shorter rides and longer overnight trails. Note that both are based in villages outside Hermanus.

In Swellendam Short or full-day excursions in the Langeberg Mountains are offered by **Two Feathers Horse Trails** (✆ **082/494-8279**).

In Knysna **Cherie's Riding Centre** (✆ **082/962-3223**) offers scenic trails along the Swartvlei Lake and forests, as well as a beach ride that includes a light lunch. **Forest Horse Rides** (✆ **044/388-4764**) takes small groups through the Knysna forests.

In Plettenberg Bay Contact **Equitrailing** (✆ **044/533-0599** or 082/955-0373) to explore fynbos and forests in this area.

MOUNTAIN BIKING **In and Around Prince Albert** Cycle the mighty Swartberg Pass—thankfully, downhill. Contact **Lindsay** (✆ **082/456-8848**), who also organizes the popular Three Passes Tour that takes in Meiringspoort and the Montagu Pass, as well as the Swartberg.

In & Around Wilderness To tour the foothills of the Outeniqua Mountains (close to George), contact **Eden Adventures** (✆ **044/877-0179;** www.eden.co.za); the half-day tour also involves some canoeing.

In Knysna All three of the Diepwalle State Forest trails are ideal for mountain biking, particularly Harkerville, which has four color-coded routes: The Harkerville red route, which includes forest, fynbos, and the craggy coastline, is considered one of the best in South Africa—book early. For more information on trails in the **Knysna State Forests,** contact Mrs. van Rooyen (✆ **044/302-5606**) or Jacques at **Knysna Cycle Works** (✆ **044/382-5153;** www.knysnacycles.co.za). For bike rentals, contact **Outeniqua Biking Trails** (✆ **044/532-7644**). For half- to 8-day mountain-biking tours of the region (including the Swartberg pass), or the option to cycle with the Big 5 in Botswana, contact **Mountain Biking Africa** (✆ **082/783-8392;** www.mountainbikingafrica.co.za).

PARAGLIDING Wilderness is considered South Africa's best site for coastal flying, particularly from August to May. A basic license paragliding course lasts 7 to 10 days, weather permitting—or you can do a 1-day introductory course, or take a one-off tandem flight with a qualified instructor. Experienced pilots can rent equipment. Contact **Cloud Base** (✆ **082/777-8474;** www.cloudbase.co.za).

QUAD BIKING Traverse a 14km (8.7-mile) trail between Wilderness and George on four wheels. Call **Quad Garden Route** (✆ **072/303-9011;** R400 per person). They also offer a nocturnal drive and 2- to 3-day adventures—although you'll have to camp.

SANDBOARDING It's like snowboarding, but on sand. Contact **Downhill Adventures** (✆ **021/422-0388;** www.downhilladventures.co.za) to surf the dunes around Betty's Bay or near Atlantis.

SHARK-CAGE DIVING **In Hermanus** This has become a hugely popular activity, with eight licensed operators offering a similar service for more or less the same price; for more, see "Exploring the Overberg & Whale Coast," below.

In Mossel Bay **Shark Africa** ★★★ (✆ **082/455-2438** or 044/691-3796) is the only operator in Mossel Bay, so your close-up encounter with a great white is likely to be less crowded than in Gansbaai. Cost is R1,200 per adult and R600 for children for a 4-hour trip, including the shark-cage dive, breakfast, and a light lunch; the same rate applies for viewing from boat only (closed Dec school holidays). If it's any consolation, you'll get a 25% reduction in the unlikely event that you don't see a great white.

SKYDIVING/PARACHUTING Try dropping from a height of 900m (2,952 ft.) with **Skydive Ceres** (✆ **021/462-5666** or 083/462-5666; www.skydive.co.za), based in the citrus-growing area 90 minutes outside of Cape Town. With 1-day training for the novice costing R970, including the first jump, and additional jumps costing R225, this is one of the cheapest drops from a plane in South Africa.

SURFING Top spots in the Western Cape include **Inner and Outer Pool and Ding Dangs** at Mossel Bay, **Jeffrey's Bay** (see "The Home of the Perfect Wave," p. 295), **Vic Bay** (a good right point break), and, north of Cape Town, **Elands Bay** ★, the best spot on the West Coast. Call **Surf Shop** (✆ **044/533-3253**) for rentals in Plett (board R100; wetsuit R50); see chapter 5 for rentals in Cape Town.

TREETOP CANOPY SLIDES Much like abseiling, this popular adventure activity in the Tsitsikamma forest is loads of fun. Attached to a rope on a pulley system, one glides (sometimes not so elegantly) through the indigenous forests from tree to tree, experiencing mostly what only the local monkeys are lucky enough to enjoy. Breathtaking views, albeit from a slightly hair-raising angle. Contact **Stormsriver Adventures** (✆ **042/281-1836;** www.stormsriver.com). Incidentally, Stormsriver Adventures came highly commended in the 2008 International Responsible Tourism Awards.

WHALE-WATCHING Some of the best land-based whale-watching in the world is on the Overberg coast, particularly Hermanus (see "Exploring the Overberg & Whale Coast," below), and the Garden Route from June to October or November. For boat-based encounters, note that only 13 to 20 boat-based whale-watching permits are issued for the entire South African coast—so make sure your operator has a permit. Boats are allowed to approach no closer than 50m (164 ft.), but the curious whales will often swim right up to the boat. See below for recommended companies.

WHITE-WATER RAFTING **Felix Unite** (✆ **021/670-1300;** www.felixunite.com) runs rafting trips on the Breede River near Swellendam, but it's pretty tame when compared with the Doring River, considered the best in the Western Cape and running from mid-July to mid-September. **River Rafters** (✆ **021/975-9727;** www.riverrafters.co.za) organizes all-inclusive weekend trips for R1,195 per person. Base camp is 4 hours from Cape Town, in the Cederberg area. They also run 4-day year-round trips on the Orange River, on the border with Namibia.

2 THE WEST COAST

For many, the West Coast is an acquired taste—kilometers of empty, often windswept beaches and hardy coastal scrub, low horizons and big skies, lonely tree-lined dirt roads, and distant mountains behind which lie lush pockets carpeted in vineyards make this a truly off-the-beaten-track experience. Most visitors venture up here to catch the spring flower displays that occur in West Coast National Park anytime from the end of July to early September (the park is also a world-famous birding site). But there are plenty more gems to uncover—such as eating fresh crayfish, with your feet in the sand; living like the lauded gentry at the Melck homestead at Kersefontein; or visiting some charming rural villages such as Riebeek Kasteel and Darling. If you like your windswept beaches pounded by magnificent turquoise seas, it's worth spending a night in the tiny fishing village of Paternoster: quiet and unspoiled but crammed with small-town character, it's bound to grow rapidly—visit now before it changes. Inland and parallel to the coast, the spectacular sandstone Cederberg mountains, home to citrus and rooibos farmers, march north, affording fabulous hiking among weathered crags.

ESSENTIALS

VISITOR INFORMATION The very helpful **West Coast Peninsula Tourism** (✆ **022/714-2088**) is in **Saldanha,** on Van Riebeeck Street. There's very little reason to visit this industrialized town. **Langebaan,** the closest town to West Coast National Park, may be more convenient. **Tourist Information** (✆ **022/772-1515**) is at the corner of Oostewal (the road in from the R27) and Bree streets. Farther north, the **Paternoster Village Tourism** office (✆ **022/752-2323;** Mon noon–5pm, Tues–Fri 9am–5pm, Sat 9am–6pm) is as informative; find them as you enter town, on the right side of the road before the four-way stop. For up-to-date information on the best places to view flowers at any given time, contact the **Flower Line** at ✆ **083/910-1028** (daily Aug–Oct).

GETTING THERE From Cape Town, take the N1, then turn north onto the R27. If you intend to travel farther north, say, to Cederberg, and want to get there quickly, take the N7 off the N1; this is the main road north to Namaqualand (the flower region) and Namibia.

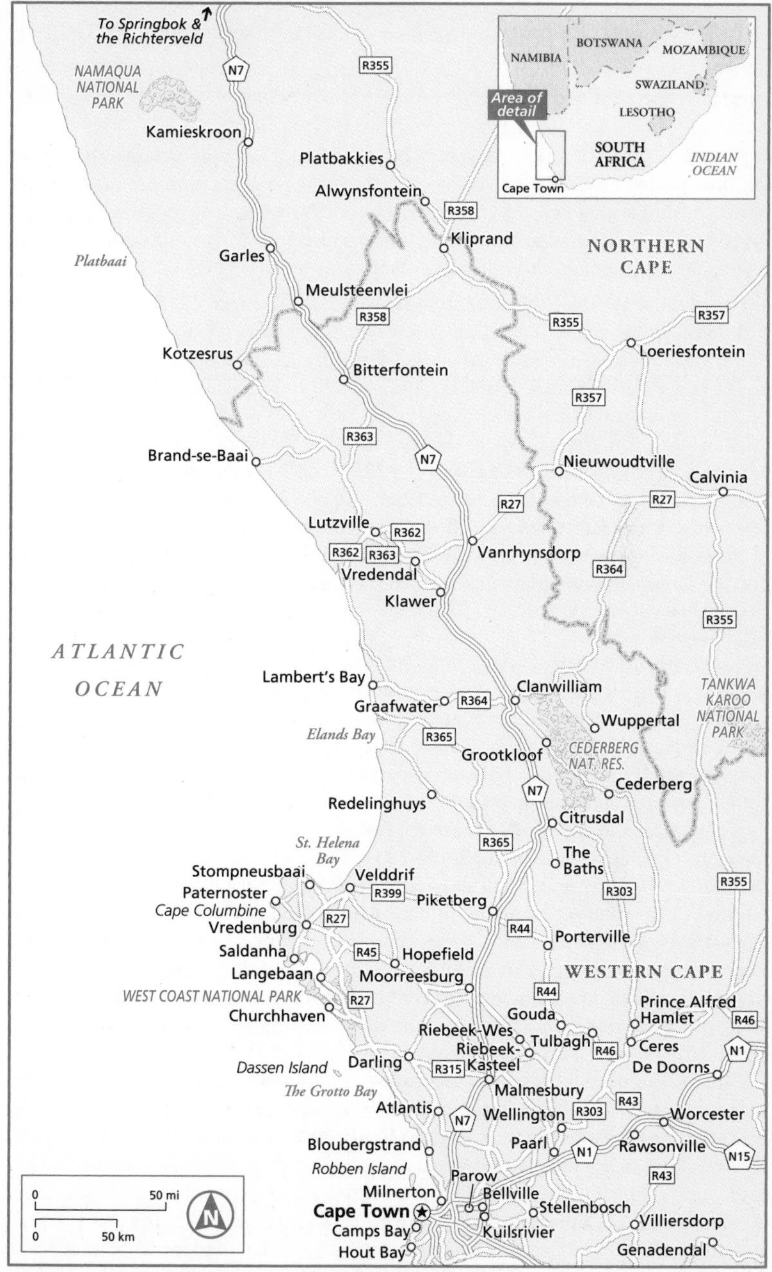
To Springbok & the Richtersveld
NAMAQUA NATIONAL PARK
Kamieskroon
Platbakkies
Alwynsfontein
Kliprand
Platbaai
Garles
Meulsteenvlei
Kotzesrus
Bitterfontein
Brand-se-Baai
NORTHERN CAPE
Loeriesfontein
Nieuwoudtville
Calvinia
Lutzville
Vredendal
Klawer
Vanrhynsdorp
ATLANTIC OCEAN
Lambert's Bay
Graafwater
Clanwilliam
Wuppertal
Elands Bay
Grootkloof
CEDERBERG NAT. RES.
Cederberg
TANKWA KAROO NATIONAL PARK
Redelinghuys
Citrusdal
The Baths
St. Helena Bay
Stompneusbaai
Velddrif
Paternoster
Cape Columbine
Piketberg
Vredenburg
Porterville
Saldanha
Hopefield
Langebaan
Moorreesburg
WESTERN CAPE
WEST COAST NATIONAL PARK
Churchhaven
Gouda
Prince Alfred Hamlet
Riebeek-Wes
Riebeek-Kasteel
Tulbagh
Ceres
Dassen Island
Darling
De Doorns
The Grotto Bay
Malmesbury
Atlantis
Wellington
Worcester
Bloubergstrand
Paarl
Rawsonville
Robben Island
Parow
Milnerton
Bellville
Cape Town
Stellenbosch
Camps Bay
Kuilsrivier
Villiersdorp
Hout Bay
Genadendal
NAMIBIA
BOTSWANA
MOZAMBIQUE
SWAZILAND
LESOTHO
SOUTH AFRICA
INDIAN OCEAN
Area of detail
0 50 mi
0 50 km

Flower Viewing

To find out where the best flower displays are, call the **Flower Line** (© **083/910-1028**).

GETTING AROUND The only way to explore the area is by car or with a tour operator. **Sun Tours** (© **021/797-4646** or 083/270-5617; www.suntourssa.co.za) offers tailor-made tours with a network of guides in vehicles ranging from Harley-Davidsons to luxury sedans. They charge per vehicle, not per person, which means good value for families or larger groups. From R330 per hour.

GUIDED TOURS In Langebaan, 62-year-old **André Kruger** (© **022/772-2412** or 073/664-0506) is one of the area's most experienced birders and guides. He offers tours of the internationally recognized Important Bird Areas of West Coast National Park and Lower Berg River Wetlands, as well as more general nature and cultural excursions, from R1,000 per day (excluding vehicle costs).

For a look at San culture and history (the San, called Bushmen in the past, are Southern Africa's First People), visit **!Khwa ttu** (© **022/492-2998;** www.khwattu.org; Tues–Sun 8:30am–5pm; tours are set for 10am and 2pm and cost R175 per person), an educational center run by the San themselves, off the R27 en route to Langebaan. San-guided tours include a game-viewing drive and nature walk, a visit to a traditional village, and an introduction to the clicks and tones that are such a characteristic part of San speech.

DARLING

A small town a mere hour's drive from Cape Town, Darling attracts its fair share of visitors, particularly in September when its **annual wild flower and orchid show** is on—usually held during the third weekend in September. Another big draw is **Voorkamerfest,** a 3-day event held toward the beginning of the month, in which visitors go from house to house to view a musical or theatrical performance, staged in the "front room" (aka sitting rooms) of the town's local participants.

A good reason to visit at any time of the year is Pieter Dirk Uys's informal theater and restaurant, **Evita se Perron** (© **022/492-2831;** closed Mon), on Arcadia Street. Famous for creating the marvelous character of Evita—the grey-haired *tannie* (auntie) who held sway over the imaginary homeland of Bapetikosweti and is now the First Lady of Darling—Uys is one of South Africa's most accomplished satirists. He has managed to make even the most conservative South Africans laugh at the country's tragic ironies (not an easy task for a man dressed in women's clothing). Evita entered the 2009 election race to help with voter education (and no doubt would have raked in votes if she'd actually registered).

Evita se Perron has cabaret shows most weekends—check the program and don't forget to book (© **022/492-3930**). You can also sample some of Tannie Evita's traditional fare at her **Station Café** after the show. **Evita se Dagkombuis** (literally, "Day Kitchen") serves breakfasts and light meals throughout the day: gay muffins, affirmative tarts, and *koeksisters* (twisted, fried dough plaits doused in syrup). To view pure Afrikaans kitsch, take a wander through her **Boerassic Park,** where garden gnomes keep an eye on plastic flowers and art students have created a monumental Gravy Train, filled with some of South Africa's most loved (and despised) politicians.

If you can't face the thought of driving back to Cape Town after dinner, stagger down to the **Darling Lodge** (✆ **022/492-3062;** www.darlinglodge.co.za; from R700 double), a charming Victorian building with six en-suite rooms, local art on the walls, and a resident wolfhound.

A popular recent addition to the annual calendar is the **Rocking the Daisies** music festival (www.rockingthedaisies.com), a weekend of the very best local bands, usually held in October, on Cloof Wine Estate. It's billed as the country's greenest festival; organizers offset carbon emissions by planting trees. To get to Darling, take the R27 (or West Coast Rd., as it's known) and turn off toward Mamre and Atlantis. From Mamre, the road to Darling cuts through fields of wheat and vineyards, and before you know it, you've arrived in town. In Darling, the local **Tourism Information** office (✆ **022/492-3361;** Mon–Fri 9am–1pm and 2–4pm, Sat–Sun 10am–3pm) staff will happily dispense various maps, details of nearby flower reserves (at their best from around July to early Oct—one of the nicest is the **Tienie Versveld Wild Flower Reserve**), and any other information needed.

RIEBEEK KASTEEL ★★

While growing slowly more chi chi, **Riebeek Kasteel** ★★, to the east of Darling on the R315 (in fact, it's even quicker to take the N7 from Cape Town, after which you could head west to reach the R27), is still delightfully rural (yes, those are sheep grazing in that garden), and the streets have retained much of their historical character (the first farms in the area were granted to farmers back in 1704). It's my favorite Winelands village in the Western Cape; locals talk about it as the new Franschhoek because of its exceptionally quaint atmosphere, quirky ex–Cape Town community, and the sweeping vineyards and olive grove surroundings—although the architecture is not nearly as twee as in Franschhoek itself. The current population is still under 3,000 people, and on a quiet day, you can perform cartwheels in the empty streets. This all changes during the annual **Olive Festival,** held at the beginning of May, when thousands of visitors drop by to sample the Valley's produce. This can also be done all year round at the **Olive Boutique,** 49 Church St. (✆ **022/448-1368**), or on the **Kloovenburg Wine Estate** (✆ **022/448-1635;** www.kloovenburg.com), which, according to *Wine* magazine, makes the best olive oil in the country—and award-winning wines, of course. Also justifiably famous for deep, fruity reds is **Allesverloren** (✆ **022/461-2320**), the oldest estate in the Swartland area. Riebeek Kasteel is a wonderful example of a small South African town, yet with enough bohemian-style cafes-cum-restaurants and galleries to satisfy any urban cravings.

Where to Stay

Bartholomeus Klip ★★★ This luxury country lodge on a working wheat and sheep farm is actually closer to Hermon, so it's about 25 minutes from Riebeek Kasteel but still in the Valley. It's a perfect base from which you can combine a bit of wildlife viewing (spot bat-eared foxes, blue cranes, a variety of antelope, or the super-rare geometric tortoise on the 4,000-hectare/10,000-acre nature reserve) with wine tastings or a day trip to Cape Town. Accommodations are in a restored Victorian homestead, elegantly furnished in period style. There are five bedrooms; the best option by far is the recently refurbished Orchid suite, which has its own entrance and a private veranda with great views. Families have the option of renting the separate, self-catering Wild Olive House (adults can arrange to eat at the main house). It's a truly peaceful place, with little to do but enjoy the exceptional food, laze around on loungers—the deep, farm-style pool is wonderful—and walk, cycle, or drive through the reserve.

Elandskloof Mountains, Hermon. ✆ **022/448-1820.** Fax 022/448-1829. www.bartholomeusklip.com. 5 units. High season R4,070 double, R4,444 suite; low season R2,750 double, R3,376 suite. Rates include brunch, high tea, 3-course dinner, and game activities. AE, DC, MC, V. No children under 16 in main house. **Amenities:** Dining room; canoeing; deckhouse; game drives and walks; mountain biking; pool; 3 sitting rooms; windsurfing. *In room:* A/C, hair dryer.

Old Oak Manor ★★ Finds It's not particularly manorlike, but this lovely guesthouse is crammed with character (and characters). It owes its good looks to Cape Town–based interior designer Salomé Gunther; its lived-in French Provençal–inspired decor has attracted the lenses of local and international style magazines. Persian carpets are well worn, colors muted, and wood weathered, all adding to the cozy, lavender-scented atmosphere. Of the four rooms in the house, Tara and Julius have the edge, as they have bathtubs and open onto the delicious pool. A simple garden cottage basks in a corner of the property, but first prize goes to the Loft (R1,600 double; can sleep four), perched above Café Felix (see below). This huge, open-plan space is littered with antique furniture and contemporary paintings and has a cloud of a double bed, two singles, and an enormous bathroom that smells gloriously of Savon de Marseille.

7 Church St., Riebeek Kasteel. ✆ **022/448-1170.** www.cafefelix.co.za. 6 units, including Loft and cottage. R750–R1,600 double. Rates include breakfast at Café Felix. MC, V. **Amenities:** Restaurant; lounge; Internet (on request); pool; room service. *In room:* TV, hair dryer, minibar.

The Royal Hotel ★ The 19th-century **Royal Hotel,** with its gracious facade, huge *stoep* (veranda), and back lawns with wonderful views of the Kasteelberg mountains, is a longtime favorite. Locals were a little disgruntled when it was gutted and revamped, claiming that all the character was stripped out and replaced with elegant but bland decor (some areas are now a study in beige); however, it's comfortable, it retains its country hotel feel, and huge displays of ostrich feathers and pink orchids lighten the atmosphere. The garden rooms (nos. 1–5) are lighter and nicer than the smaller rooms (nos. 10–14). Room nos. 1 and 2 have the least passing traffic. The colonial era bar, surrounded by pictures of long-gone South Africans, is a lovely spot to read the paper and contemplate life. For dinner, you can dine amid spotless linen with a mounted wildebeest keeping a (glassy) eye on you.

33 Main St., Riebeek Kasteel, 7307. ✆ **022/448-1378.** Fax 022/448-1073. www.royalinriebeek.com. 10 units. R1,200 double. Rates include breakfast. AE, MC, V. **Amenities:** 2 restaurants (1 smoking); bar; lounges; pool; room service; terraces; free Wi-Fi in lounge. *In room:* A/C, TV/DVD, hair dryer, minibar.

Where to Dine

This is a town where good food is reason enough to stay a while. A plethora of small cafes, boutiques, wine farms, and restaurants offer excellent country cuisine in what is generally a casual and unpretentious way. The **Kasteelburg Country Inn & Bistro,** 13 Fontein St. (✆ **022/448-1110;** lunch Wed–Mon; dinner Mon, Wed–Sat), feels ridiculously French, with its shady veranda lined with geraniums in window boxes and a cooling mist spray in summer. Situated on the town square, you can watch life passing by (slowly) while you dine on such pleasures as gnocchi and gammon with blue cheese sauce, or black-fig-and-venison carpaccio. And you must sample the fabulous bread and tapenade. Owners Julien and Allan describe the food as home cooking with country flair, and locals say it is consistently excellent. Also recommended is **Travellers Rest** (✆ **022/448-1383**), which offers rich country food in a lavishly decorated dining area. In summer, don't miss their reasonable—and varied—tapas selection. (***Note:*** Both Travellers Rest and Kasteelburg offer excellent-value B&B accommodations besides fine dining.) New kid on the dining block is the young and energetic **Bar Bar Black Sheep** (✆ **022/448-1031;** lunch Wed–Sun, dinner Wed–Sat). Furnished with bright plastic tablecloths and quirky bric-a-brac, it's tucked away amid the colorful boutiques and stores on Short Street. Even on a quiet midweek night, the place is buzzing. This is another menu that changes regularly, but expect South African favorites such as roasted marrow bones, *waterblommetjiebredie,* and *skilpadjies* (lamb's liver wrapped in kidney fat).

Café Felix ★★ COUNTRY Once an old tobacco barn, this uncluttered, airy eatery with a pretty courtyard shaded by oaks has become a bit of a Church Street landmark. And when one of South Africa's top chefs chooses to get married here (Reuben Riffel, of Franschhoek's Reuben's), you know the food should be good. Initially inspired by the popular Olympia Café and Deli in Kalk Bay, the menu's emphasis is on simple but hearty French–Italian country cuisine, while the wine list offers choice staples (and one or two special finds) from local cellars. The house special, a slow-roasted lamb shank, flies off the menu, but there are plenty of alternatives (such as the seared tuna), and the menu is always changing. Note that the popular Sunday lunch Harvest Table (a spread of pies, bakes, salads, breads, and pâtés) is on hold for the moment.

7 Church St., Riebeek Kasteel. ✆ **022/448-1170.** Reservations recommended. Main courses R80–R100. MC, V. Open Tues, Wed, Fri 8am–3pm, 6pm–9pm; Sat 8am–9pm; Sun 8am–3pm.

WEST COAST NATIONAL PARK ★★

West Coast National Park encompasses almost 30,000 hectares (74,100 acres) of wilderness, as well as a 16× 4.5km (10×2¾-mile) marine lagoon, on which the coastal town of Langebaan is situated. Pack a picnic and head for one of the picture-perfect coves near Preekstoel and Kraalbaai, where the strikingly azure waters gently lap white sands bordered by brilliant green succulents. Pack a camera and bathing suit. You also have a good chance of spotting whales from July to early November from points overlooking the Atlantic Ocean. The **Postberg** section, which contains zebra, wildebeest, and gemsbok, is open only in August and September from 9am to 5pm, when the flowers are most spectacular. The community at **Churchhaven** (marked by the Anglican church of St. Peter), which was founded in 1863 by George Lloyd, a deserter from an American merchant vessel, has now closed the road running past it; the only way to gain access is to rent one of its basic self-catering cottages (✆ **022/772-2799**). The hamlet enjoys a unique setting on one of the world's greatest wetlands. Overlooking a blindingly white beach and surrounded by salt marshes, the settlement is visited by more than 140 bird species (including the greater flamingo).

There are two entrances to the park: one off the R27, some 100km (62 miles) north of Cape Town, and the other just south of Langebaan. You can see a good deal of it by entering the one and leaving by way of the other, but make sure you visit the **Information Center** at **Geelbek** (✆ **022/772-2799**), on the southern tip of the lagoon. Meals such as slow-cooked lamb, smoked snoek salad, or ostrich carpaccio are served in the **Geelbek Restaurant** (make a reservation during the busy holiday season at ✆ **022/772-2134**). It's housed in a Cape Dutch homestead built in 1744—but it's unlikely that you'll see flamingos while eating your meal, as suggested on the website. For that, you need to take one of a number of short trails to the bird hides overlooking the lagoon—this is particularly rewarding in summer, when the hides can provide views of thousands of migrant waders and flocks of pelican, flamingo, curlew, and sandpipers. Admission to the

Fun Facts Out of Africa

In one of two leading paleoanthropological theories regarding the origin of man, it is believed that Homo sapiens evolved in Africa about 200,000 years ago, migrating north in successive waves during the Pleistocene ice ages, displacing Homo erectus and Neanderthal man in Europe and Asia. Part of the body of evidence supporting this theory resides in Langebaan Lagoon: The world's oldest fossilized tracks of Homo sapiens—dating back 117,000 years—were discovered here in 1997. Eve's Footprints, as the imprints were dubbed, were later moved to the Iziko Museum in Cape Town for safekeeping.

park is from R32 to R88 per person, depending on the season (locals pay less). The park is open daily from April 1 to August 31 from 7am to 6pm, and from September 1 to March 31 from 7am to 7pm. For more information, contact © **022/772-2144.**

Where to Stay & Dine

Langebaan has grown exponentially over the years: This is no quaint fishing village, but a sprawling town, hugely popular with watersports fans and South Africans during the summer holidays. If you'd rather be based in utter tranquillity, book a rustic cottage at Churchhaven, a cluster of cottages right on the aquamarine lagoon; bookings are through **www.perfecthideaways.co.za** (ask for Whaler's Way Cottage).

The only South African–graded five-star accommodations in Langebaan itself is **Harrison's House** (© **022/772-0727** or 084/806-6322; R950–R1,100 double), a compact boutique guesthouse with a splash pool, small gym, and some great views (the upstairs luxury lagoon room is the one to ask for). No children under 12 are permitted, and if you like your space and want to be closer to the beach, you'd be better off at **The Farmhouse** (see below). If you're on a budget, a good alternative is **Friday's Island** (© **022/772-2506;** www.fridayisland.co.za; sea-front-facing units R760–R960). The simple white-washed units are right on Langebaan beach, there's a young and very friendly vibe, and tanned locals frequent the restaurant for calamari steaks and light fare. The northern side of town is estate territory (developments are fenced off and gated for security), and apartment blocks line private beaches. If you don't mind the brasher vibe, try **Crystal Lagoon Lodge** (© **022/772-0550;** R780–R1,280). Opened in April 2009, room nos. 1 and 4 look large and comfortable; the beach is just a few meters away, and swimming is safe.

If you're not dining at The Farmhouse, **Boesmanland** (© **022/772-1564**) offers buffet-style dining from bubbling *potjies* (iron pots) and fish grilled on open fires. If fish stews and roast lamb don't fill you up in a hurry, the sourdough bread and milk tart will. But the prize for the best location goes to **Geelbek Restaurant,** right within West Coast National Park (© **022/772-2134**).

The Farmhouse ★ With West Coast National Park right at your doorstep, the azure Langebaan Lagoon (visible from almost every room), and unpretentious service, this is the best place to stay in Langebaan. The comfortable guest suites, of which 10 have their own fireplace, are very spacious, although some of the bathrooms could do with a revamp. It's worth booking a superior with a sweeping view of the lagoon—ask for room nos. 9 or 10. In the cheaper category, room nos. 2 and 4 have the best views. The Farmstead (from R2,250, plus R250 per extra person) is ideal for families—a two-bedroom unit with a king-size bed and three singles, as well as a lounge area. The restaurant, pub, and terrace all enjoy the same beautiful view of the lagoon. A la carte meals include such traditional choices as oxtail and chicken pie and, of course, seafood.

5 Egret St., Langebaan 7357. ✆ **022/772-2062.** Fax 022/772-1980. www.thefarmhousehotel.com. 18 units. High season R1,620–R2,300 double; low season R1,400–R2,250 double. Rates include breakfast. AE, DC, MC, V. **Amenities:** Restaurant; bar; babysitting (arrange in advance); access to Langebaan's Country Club facilities, including golf, tennis, and *pétanque;* spa. *In room:* TV/DVD, hair dryer, minibar.

Kersefontein ★★ Finds This is one of the most authentic, unusual experiences to be had in the country—being hosted by Julian, the eighth-generation Melck, in his beautiful Cape Dutch farmstead, an 18th-century national monument on the banks of the Berg River. This is still a 7,000-hectare (17,290-acre) working wheat and cattle farm, and the sense of history is palpable—on the way to the grand dining room, you will pass, for instance, the skull of the last Berg River hippo, shot by Martin Melck in 1876 after it bit his servant. Accommodations are separate from the main house: in one of the two "African" rooms (top choice, with doors opening onto a small private veranda and sweeping lawns), the Victorian suites (with a communal lounge and a kitchen), the self-catering cottage (situated a short drive away and blissfully tranquil), or a new bedsit room (or single room occupancy, created in a farmyard building, with its own fireplace and oodles of space). All have been masterfully decorated by Graham Viney (who did the Orient Express hotels). West Coast National Park lies less than an hour away.

Box 15, Hopefield 7355. 90-min. drive from Cape Town. ✆ **022/783-0850** or 013/454-1025. www.kersefontein.co.za. 5 units. R860–R1,100 double. Rates include breakfast. AE, MC, V. Follow signs off R45 btw. Velddrif and Hopefield. **Amenities:** Dining room; pub (located in what used to be the old Kersefontein farm bakery); mountain bikes; boats; ranch riding; private air trips (Julian is also a pilot).

PATERNOSTER & COLUMBINE NATURE RESERVE ★★★

To reach these West Coast gems, stay on the R27 past West Coast National Park and Langebaan, and then take the R45 west to Vredenburg. Drive straight through this ugly town and take the 16km (10-mile) road to **Paternoster,** a tiny fishing village that—due to strict development guidelines—retains a classic West Coast feel, with almost all of the 2,000-odd residents living in picturesque whitewashed fisherman-style cottages. Paternoster, which means "Our Father" in Latin, is suddenly the place to stay on the West Coast, with new B&Bs and guesthouses cropping up every year, most within easy walking distance of dazzling white beaches, dotted with colorful fishing boats. Paternoster also boasts a handful of surprisingly good restaurants and a growing community of artists, designers, and chefs from up-country who, having sampled the village's delights, promptly packed up and moved in. But there are more than enough salty long-term locals to keep things real (to meet some, brave a visit to the bar at the **Paternoster Hotel;** you'll be deep in conversation within minutes). Decor consists of undergarments collected from honeymooners over the years.

The 263-hectare (650-acre) **Cape Columbine Nature Reserve** (✆ **022/752-2718;** daily 7am–7pm; day visitors R10) is home to a wide variety of flowers; the best time to visit is obviously spring, but the reserve's superb location is a relief from the coastline's degradation by developers. The campsites (R87) are right on the sea, and the hikes are beautiful. Try to avoid visiting during school holidays and weekends.

Where to Stay

If after a day trip you can't bear to leave (and, believe me, it's hard), you are spoiled for choice. Budget self-catering options abound: Options include **Hocus Pocus** (✆ **022/752-2660** or 083/988-4645; R850–R950, sleeps 2–4) with its eclectic, cottagey decor, and **Die Hoekie** (✆ **022/752-2077;** from R650 double), which is right across the road from the beach and the much-loved Voorstrandt restaurant (see below). Also rather fabulous is the homey, colorful **ah! guesthouse** ★ (✆ **082/464-5898;** from R800 double, breakfast included). Even if you don't stay here, book a meal: Three-course dinners at former Jo'burg chef Arnold's communal table could feature such treats as crayfish bisque and calamari tubes with oxtail. From R190; book before noon.

The Oystercatcher's Haven ★★ Step into this beautifully furnished guesthouse studded with orchids, artworks, and antiques, and you'll quickly understand why their most famous guest, Nelson Mandela, reportedly didn't want to leave. Right on the edge of Paternoster (for now, anyway—new streets are already being laid out nearby), it overlooks massive, sea-swept black boulders and a deserted beach with views down the coast to Columbine Nature Reserve. With just three spacious rooms with separate entrances, privacy is assured—and all the showers have a view. The breakfast room is a sheltered sanctuary, as are the sun-drenched courtyards and patio. The closure of the on-site restaurant is a loss, but now guests have the place to themselves.

48 Sonkwas St., Paternoster, 7381. ✆ **022/752-2193** or 082/414-6705. Fax 022/752-2192. www.oystercatchershaven.com. 3 units. R1,250 double. Rates include breakfast. Picnic lunches on request. MC, V. **Amenities:** Lounge; plunge pool. *In room:* TV, hair dryer, minibar; heated towel racks.

Paternoster Dunes Guest House ★★ Paternoster smells of cold seas, kelp, and fynbos—a heady scent that fills this airy, contemporary guesthouse (unless Deon is preparing something delicious, such as oxtail, for dinner). You'll want one of the three rooms that face the beach: From Rose, Aqua, or Vanilla (my favorite), it's a quick skip from your private patio down a dune into the waves. Rooms open from an inner courtyard with a compact pool—lounging here is a little public for my taste, but the young or sociable will love it. Rooms are super, but the upstairs lounge, bar, and deck have such wonderful views, you'll want to spend time here, too. Look for whales while sipping a crisp glass of wine. Interior designers Gavin and Deon decorated the Dunes, and they provide great advice on where to eat and what to do.

18 Sonkwas St., Paternoster, 7381. ✆ **022/752-2217** or 083/560-5600. Fax 022/752-2217. www.paternosterdunes.co.za. 5 units. R800–1,700. Rates include breakfast. MC, V, AE. **Amenities:** Bar; lounge area w/small library; plunge pool. *In room:* A/C, TV, hair dryer, minibar.

Where to Dine

If you're just here on a day trip, time your visit to stop for lunch at **Voorstrandt** ★★★ (✆ **022/752-2038;** daily 10am–10pm). This rustic shack of a restaurant is right on the beach—when the sun sparkles off the crescent-shaped beach and ocean, the sense of contentment is almost surreal. For once there's no insipid background music, just the sound of the waves. There's a small, simple menu, but if you're here during November to April, there's only one thing to order: succulent whole crayfish (R210–R255, depending on size), served with garlic or lemon butter. Other popular dishes include the Malaysian seafood curry (R80) and the "three-fish dish," linefish caught off this coast. The **Noisy Oyster** ★★ (✆ **022/752-2196;** lunch and dinner Wed–Sat, lunch Sun; booking essential), with its rapidly changing menu, also comes highly recommended; items such as

Moments The West Coast Beach Barbecue

For dining, a meal at one of the West Coast alfresco restaurants is an unforgettable experience: Sitting on the beach breathing in the aroma of seafood on hot coals and the fresh sea breeze, you drink in the sun and the sound of seagulls, sink deeper in the sand as course after course keeps flowing, and lick your fingers clean (scrubbed mussel shells are often the only cutlery provided). Your only worry will be how you're ever going to manage to save enough space for the crayfish still to come. These eateries are so informal they're hardly restaurants, but if you like casual dining and don't mind sharing your space with strangers, they're well worth trying out. The food, prepared in the manner of a huge beach barbecue, is excellent and usually consists of several kinds of fish cooked in various ways (sometimes with jam, a West Coast specialty); *bokkoms* (salted, dried harders, or small fish), with grapes, mussels, calamari, paella, *waterblommetjiebredie* (water lily stew); and crayfish. There's also piping-hot white bread baked on the beach and served with fresh farm butter and a number of fruit preserves—this is the killer; you'll want to devour an entire loaf, much to the detriment of the remaining courses. The huge 3-hour meal will cost in the region of R175 per person; crayfish will add R35 (a half) to R70 to the bill.

Of the West Coast alfresco restaurants, **Muisbosskerm** ★★★ (✆ **027/432-1017;** www.muisbosskerm.co.za) is still the best. On the beach 5km (3 miles) south of Lambert's Bay on the Eland's Bay Road (3 hr. from Cape Town), this is where the open-air West Coast restaurant concept was born—for years Edward and Elmien Turner had simply shared their favorite food with friends on the beach, and in 1986 they decided to broaden their guest list. Tertius and Ian are now in charge, but the food is still delicious, and you can usually count on a selection of fresh linefish, grilled and baked; fresh green mealies in season; local potatoes and sweet potatoes; pots of stew (in winter season, *waterblommetjiebredie* often features); crayfish (in season); mussels; and the legendary West Coast breads and preserves. It's a long drive home after a meal like this, so head for Paternoster. Booking ahead is essential—especially as it's not open every night and seating is at set times.

wok-tossed baby calamari with a North African flavor and the Thai green fish curry keep Cape Town foodies coming back for more.

Suzi's Fine Food Eatery ★★ Finds SOUTH AFRICAN The location may not be promising—a tiny room of a restaurant next to a real estate agent—but there's a good reason why this unassuming kitchen made *Dine*'s top 100 restaurants list. That's Chef Suzi Holtzhausen, who has brought her own version of deconstructed food to Paternoster. She's big on seasonal, locally available ingredients and changes her menus regularly—you could find anything from crisp pork belly with a fresh pear salad to creamy avo and pea pasta and pan-fried yellowtail on offer. The Eatery is a breakfast and lunch venue and has no alcohol license—pack a bottle for no extra charge—but if you book in advance and there are enough takers, you may be able to persuade Suzi to cook you dinner, too. ***Note:*** If you don't mind that "there's no one around to love you," as Suzi puts it (she's often off cooking), then book in at her **Salt Coast Inn** (Mosselbank St.; ✆ **083/375-4929;** R600 double). Of the two quirky, comfortable units on offer, the Red room is more spacious and desirable—but you'll have to head around the corner to the Eatery for breakfast, and there's no access to the lounge or kitchen while Suzi is out.

Off St Augustine Rd., next to Pam Golding. ✆ **083/375-4929.** Reservations essential. Main courses R80–R100. No credit cards. Breakfast and lunch Thurs–Mon. Dinner on request (sufficient bookings are needed for 8 or more people). Occasional events Sat nights at the Eatery; call for info.

LAMBERT'S BAY

This fishing port, the last bastion of "civilization" on the coast, lies 100km (62 miles) north of Velddrif and 62km (38 miles) west of Clanwilliam. There are two main reasons to visit: to view the colony of birds on Bird Island and to feast at one of the coast's best outdoor restaurants. Accommodations options are better in Paternoster or Clanwilliam, so see this very much as a side trip.

Bird Island is accessed via a stone breakwater in the Lambert's Bay Harbour. This island houses a colony of Cape gannets and cormorants—to be amid the cacophony of a 25,000-strong community, all jostling for position on the island, is a rare privilege. Alternatively, book a sunset cruise that takes you out to see the marine life of the bay from **Eco Boat Trips** (✆ **082/922-4334**).

3 CEDERBERG

Around 200km (124 miles) north of Cape Town lies the Cederberg Wilderness Area. This hikers' paradise features majestic jagged sandstone mountains that glow an unearthly deep red at sunset; strange-shaped rock formations that dominate the horizon; ancient San (Bushmen) rock-painting sites; burbling streams in which to cool off; a variety of animals, such as baboon, small antelope, leopards and lynx; and rare mountain fynbos such as the delicate snow protea and gnarled Clanwilliam cedar. You can drive to a number of spots, but the best way to explore this area is on foot.

In keeping with its "wilderness" designation, there are no laid-out trails, though maps indicating how to reach the main rock features—the huge Wolfberg Arch and the 30m-high (98-ft.) Maltese Cross, as well as to the two main Cederberg peaks—are available. Covering 710 sq. km (277 sq. miles), the Cederberg Wilderness Area is reached via a dirt road that lies halfway between the towns of Citrusdal and Clanwilliam. Of the two, the pretty town of Clanwilliam is the more attractive base, with a few attractions of its own, including the country's main Rooibos tea-processing factory (see "Sampling the 'Erb," below), the Ramskop Wildflower Reserve, and a spectacular drive to the nearby Moravian mission station of **Wupperthal** ★★. You can camp in the Cederberg or book a self-catering chalet through Cape Nature Conservation (hikers be warned: visitor numbers are strictly limited, so book early); but if you don't want to rough it and are interested in rock art, look no further than the ultraluxurious Bushmans Kloof, northeast of Clanwilliam (see below).

ESSENTIALS

VISITOR INFORMATION The excellent **Clanwilliam Information Centre** (✆ **027/482-2024;** www.clanwilliam.info; Mon–Fri 8:30am–5pm, Sat 8:30am–12:30pm) is

Fun Facts Sampling the 'Erb

Rooibos (literally, "red bush," pronounced "*roy*-boss") is a type of fynbos that occurs only in Clanwilliam and the surrounding area. Its leaves have been used to brew a refreshing, healthful drink for centuries, but they were first exported during World War II, when the Ceylon variety was scarce. Since then it has become popular in the Japanese, German, and Dutch markets, and research shows some amazing health properties. Rooibos is caffeine free; is rich in vitamin C; and contains antioxidants, iron, potassium, copper, fluoride, zinc, magnesium, and alpha-hydroxy acid. Drinking it "neat" is an acquired taste; try it with honey, ginger, lemon, or milk and sugar, like the locals. You can try it at the **Rooibos Ltd factory,** Rooibos Avenue, Clanwilliam (✆ **027/482-2155**), or order it just about anywhere in South Africa. Also recommended is the aptly named Honeybush Tea, another local fynbos.

opposite the old church hall on Main Street. To camp or walk in the Cederberg Wilderness Area, you will need a permit from **Cape Nature Conservation,** in Cape Town, before you travel (✆ **021/659-3500;** www.capenature.org.za)—although day walkers can get permits from the local Information Centre, too.

GETTING THERE **By Car** Clanwilliam lies about 2½ hours' drive from Cape Town. Head north up the N7; after approximately 160km (99 miles), you'll pass the town of Citrusdal to your left. About 28km (17 miles) farther north on the N7 is the turnoff for Cederberg Wilderness Area (marked Algeria); 26km (16 miles) farther is Clanwilliam, also on your left.

By Bus **Intercape** (see chapter 3 for local numbers) travels the N7 to Namibia. Note, however, that unless you have someone to pick you up, you'll be left stranded on the highway.

WUPPERTHAL ★★★

It's worth visiting this isolated rural community just to travel the 90-minute dirt-road trip from Clanwilliam, with its breathtaking views of the twisted shapes and isolated tranquillity of the northern Cederberg. An interesting stop along the way is the **Sevilla Rock Art Trail** ★★★, a wonderful self-guided 2km-long trail that visits 10 fine rock-art sites and is an easy, magical introduction to the genre (you'll need a permit and map from nearby **Traveller's Rest** (✆ **027/482-1824**). Once in Wupperthal, you'll feel lost in time: It looks pretty much the way it did when it was established as a Moravian mission station in the 1830s. In fact, some Wupperthal farmers still use sickles to reap, donkeys to thresh, and the wind to sift their grain.

You can't miss the **Tourism Bureau** (✆ **027/492-3410;** www.wupperthal.co.za; Mon–Fri 8am–4:30pm), on Church Square, next to Leipoldt House. This, the oldest building in the village, also houses the **Lekkerbekkie** (Little Sweet Mouth), which serves refreshments. To get to Wupperthal, drive east of Clanwilliam via the Pakhuis Pass on the road to Soetwater. Take the road south some 40km (25 miles) off the Pakhuis Pass Road at the appropriate sign to the Biedouw Valley. From here, you have to travel some 30km (19 miles) via the Uitkyk and Kouberg passes.

There are four basic self-catering cottages in the village of Wupperthal (✆ **027/492-3410;** R120 per person). Contact **Cape Nature Conservation** for camping and self-catering information in the Cederberg reserve (✆ **021/659-3500;** www.capenature.co.za). At the time of writing, the reserve had been hit by fire and the accommodations were closed; once they're open again, ask for **Rietdak,** a self-catering cottage 400m (1,312 ft.) from the river. Recommended options in Clanwilliam itself are the gracious Victorian **Ndedema Lodge** ★ (✆ **027/482-1314;** R820–R1,020 double); of the two doubles, no. 2 is the most desirable, with its canopied king-size bed and marvelous bathroom. There are also two family units, one in the main house and a separate cottage set a little way back in the gardens. Wilma, the owner, used to head up the Pretoria tourist office and has been collecting antiques all her life—many of which now grace the bedrooms and communal areas of the lodge. The rate includes breakfast, and this is a wonderfully peaceful base for exploring the area. Less luxurious but comfortable is **Saint Du Barry's Country Lodge** (✆/fax **027/482-1537**), a relaxed B&B with five simple en-suite units (R880 double). But for all-out luxury, with excellent guided tours of San rock art, you can't beat Bushmans Kloof.

Bushmans Kloof Wilderness Reserve and Retreat ★★★ This Relais & Châteaux lodge, which made the *Condé Naste Traveler* USA gold list in 2009, is by far the most luxurious option in the Cederberg, with accommodations on par with the best game lodges near Kruger. Located on 8,000 hectares (19,760 acres) that are stocked with game and filled with flowers in spring, the reserve has over 130 rock-art sites and a resident rock-art specialist to explain anything from the mythology to the technique behind this ancient art. Declared a South African Heritage Site, Bushmanskloof is dedicated to preserving the biodiversity of the region, as well as San history. Early-morning rock-art tours are followed by botanical walks, mountain biking, or simply lazing about in the crystal-clear rock pools. Sunset brings game drives in open Land Rovers. Ultraluxurious bedrooms overlook the rolling lawns and river—of the deluxe options, Rock Pools 1 and 2, with their extravagant bathrooms and sublime views over the river, are wonderful, as are luxury River Reeds and Water's Edge units.

Past Clanwilliam, turn due east for 34km (21 miles) on Pakhuis Pass. Driving takes at least 3 hr. from Cape Town; charter flights are available. Lodge ✆ **027/482-8200;** reservations **021/685-2598.** Fax 021/685-5210. www.bushmanskloof.co.za. 16 units. R3,500–R5,800 luxury double; R4,200–R7,000 deluxe double; R5,200–R8,800 suite; R6,200–R9,800 superior suite. Ask about specials. Rates include all meals, guided rock-art walks, and game drives. AE, DC, MC, V. No children under 10 in main lodge; families can be accommodated at the Koro villa. **Amenities:** 3 dining areas; bar; mountain bikes; canoes; exercise room; heritage center; 4 swimming pools; room service; spa. *In room:* A/C, TV/DVD players, minibar, MP3 docking stations (in some), free Wi-Fi.

4 EXPLORING THE OVERBERG & WHALE COAST

During the 17th century, the Dutch settlers saw the jagged Hottentots Holland mountain range as the Cape Colony's natural border, beyond which lay what they called Overberg (literally, "Over the Mountain"). Today this coastal area—wedged between the Cape Peninsula and the Garden Route, with mountains lining its northern border and the ocean on its south—encompasses a vast patchwork of grain fields, fruit orchards, and fynbos-covered hills.

There are two main routes through it: the **N2,** which traverses its northern half and is the quickest way to reach the Garden Route; and the slightly more circuitous and scenic **Coastal Route,** which is highly recommended, particularly during the whale-watching months.

Known as "the graveyard of ships," this rugged coastline is pounded by both the Atlantic and Indian oceans, which meet at L'Agulhus, Africa's most southerly point. East of this point is Arniston (Waenhuiskrans, to locals), a bleak fishing village overlooking a magnificent turquoise bay; and De Hoop Nature Reserve, which vies with the Garden Route's Tsitsikamma as the most beautiful coastal reserve in South Africa. The Overberg gives visitors the opportunity to view a wealth of rare fynbos (see "Africa's Floral Kingdom," earlier in the chapter), as well as sightings of South Africa's national bird, the endangered blue crane.

Another sanctuary-seeker is the Southern Right whale; these return in increasing numbers every spring to mate and nurse their young off the Whale Coast. The towns of Hermanus and De Kelders, which overlook Walker Bay and Koppie Alleen in De Hoop Nature Reserve, are considered the best locations for viewing these oddly elegant 60-ton, callus-encrusted cetaceans.

THE COASTAL ROUTE: GORDON'S BAY TO HERMANUS

You can reach Hermanus in about 80 minutes via the N2, but the coastal route, which adds another 20 to 30 minutes to the journey and snakes along the sheer cliffs of the Hottentots Holland Mountains as they plunge down to the oceans below, is the recommended route. To take it, head for **Gordon's Bay,** an easy 40-minute drive from Cape Town on the N2, and take the coastal route (R44) out of town. Keep an eye out for **whales** and **dolphins** in **False Bay** as you descend the cliffs and bypass the Steenbras River mouth and Koeelbaai (pronounced "*cool*-buy"), a beautiful beach and break favored by surfers. Between rocky outcrops along this stretch of coast, you'll find small sandy coves shaded by ancient milkwood trees and grassy sunbathing areas.

Having crossed the Rooiels River (named for the red alder trees that grow in the riverine bush up the gorge, and twisting through another beautiful and usually deserted beach), you head through fynbos-covered hills passing the Buffels River and the sprawling holiday village of **Pringle Bay.** While Pringle isn't in itself a beautiful town, the coastline and mountain views are lovely, and it's in a UNESCO World Nature Reserve, which makes a relaxing stopover for nature lovers. Your best bet is probably the swish **Moonstruck** (**© 028/273-8162;** www.moonstruck.co.za; R990–R1,650 double, breakfast included), a good-looking contemporary guesthouse with just four rooms (ask for the honeymoon suite, which has an impressive four-poster bed, fireplace, and large balcony from where you can stare across the bay to Cape Town's Devil's Peak). If you're just looking for a comfortable bolt-hole, try the Cottage at the basic but reasonable **Barnacle B&B** (**© 028/273-8343;** R600–R1,000 double). It's child-friendly, offers specials for longer stays, and lies right next to both river and beach. Even if you don't stay over, Pringle Bay is a good spot for lunch: If you're in the mood for seafood, **Hook, Line and Sinker** ★★ (**© 028/273-8688**) is a thoroughly unpretentious locale, with newspaper-covered tables and fresh, fresh seafood—you'll find it at 382 Crescent Rd. Or pick up some treats from **Lemon and Lime Deli** (**© 028/273-8895**), such as smoked snoek pâté and a loaf of their famous bread, and press on.

Just past Pringle Bay, where the R44 cuts inland past the Grootvlei marshlands, is a less traveled detour to **Cape Hangklip,** pronounced "*hung*-clip"—literally, "Hanging Rock" (just check that the road is open before you leave Pringle Bay). This 460m-high

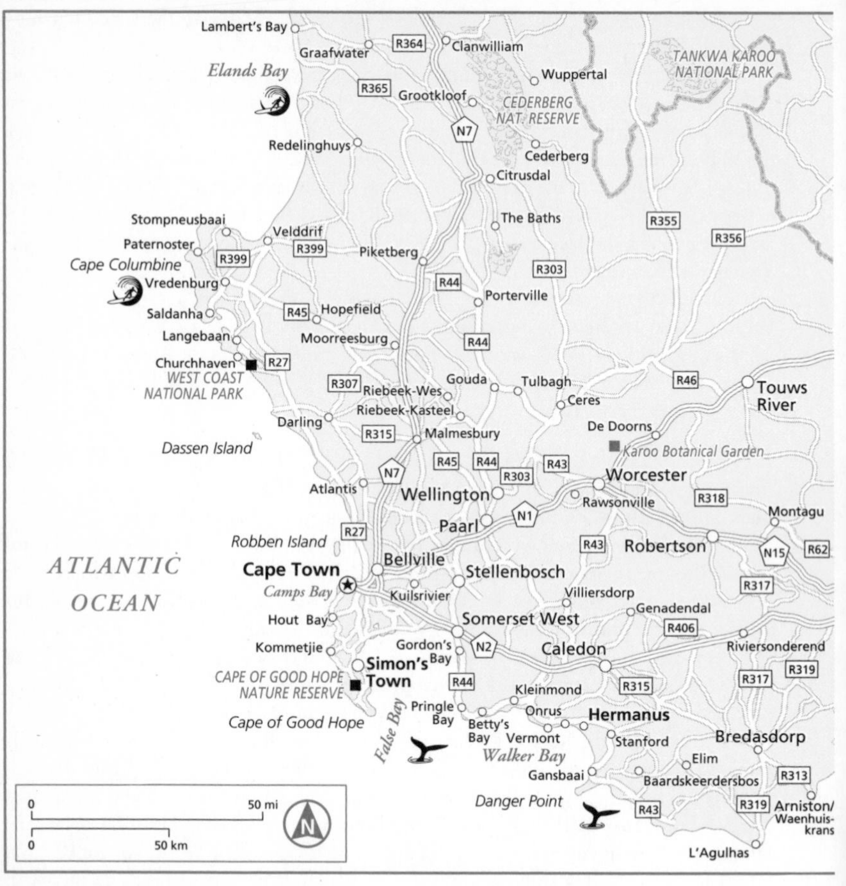

(1,509-ft.) wedge of rock was often mistaken for Cape Point, which, incidentally, is how False Bay came by its name. After skirting three lagoon-type lakes—estuaries blocked by coastal dunes—you reach **Betty's Bay,** home to a remarkable number of ugly holiday cottages, one of only two land-based colonies of jackass penguins (the other is in Cape Town), and the beautiful **Harold Porter Botanical Gardens** (✆ **028/272-9311;** Mon–Fri 8am–4:30pm, Sat–Sun 8am–5pm; R15). Take one of four trails up the mountain to the **Disa Kloof Waterfall** (duration 1–3 hr.) to appreciate the beauty of the Cape's coastal fynbos.

If you need to stop for lunch or want a five-star hotel experience attached to one of the country's best 18-hole golf courses (with one of our favorite spas), stop at the **Western Cape Hotel & Spa,** situated on **Arabella Country Estate.** The estate's lawns run into the Bot River lagoon, which provides lovely views, and the hotel offers every comfort under the sun and is particularly child-friendly. Call ✆ **028/284-0000** or visit

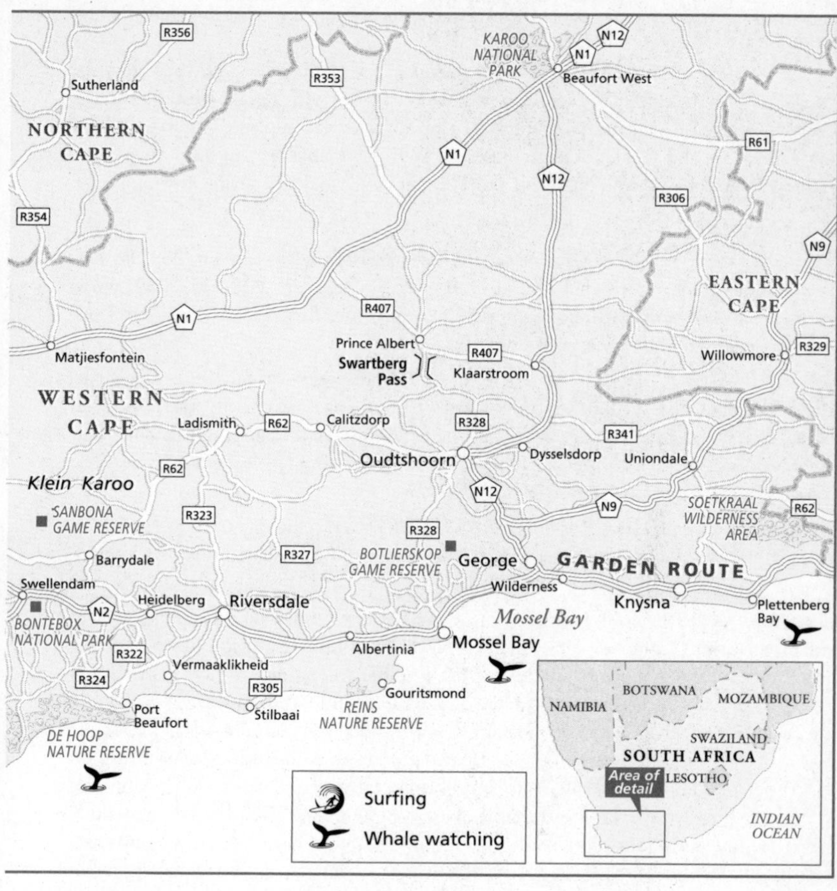

www.westerncapehotelandspa.co.za; deluxe room rates range from R1,700 to R5,400, depending on the season—ask about specials.

The R44 now heads northeastward in the direction of Caledon, while the road to Hermanus branches eastward from the inland side of the Palmiet Lagoon. This is called the R43; take it and keep an eye out for the R320 turnoff, which will take you past the vineyards of the **Hemel-en-Aarde** (Heaven and Earth) Valley. Here you can go on wine tastings at the small but excellent selection of farms that make up the **Hermanus Wine Route** (see "What to See & Do," below), stopping for lunch along the way (see "Where to Dine," below).

HERMANUS

With a backdrop of mountains, a large lagoon and long white beach, deep rock pools, and a wealth of coastal fynbos, **Hermanus** was destined to develop into one of South

Africa's premier holiday resorts. The best times to visit Hermanus are autumn and spring, when aficionados come from afar to view the whales in **Walker Bay.** Humpback, Brydes, and Minke whales make occasional appearances, but the bay is essentially frequented by Southern Right whales.

Whales aside, there are numerous **wine farms** in the Hemel-en-Aarde Valley to visit; you'll also find the chance to experience a **close encounter with a great white shark** (see "Staying Active," earlier in this chapter), **long beaches,** and a number of **good trails** in the Walker Bay and Fernkloof nature reserves. With Hermanus as your base, the **picturesque villages** of Arniston, Stanford, and Elim are only a day's excursion away.

Essentials

VISITOR INFORMATION The excellent **Hermanus Tourism Bureau,** the Old Station Building, corner of Mitchell and Lord Roberts Street (✆ **028/312-2629;** www.hermanus.co.za), is open Monday through Saturday from 8am to 5 or 6pm, and from August to April on Sunday as well from 10am to 2pm.

GETTING THERE **By Car** To rent a car, see "Cape Town: Getting Around," in chapter 5. Hermanus lies 112km (69 miles) east of Cape Town via the N2 (just under an hour). The N2 route is a pretty drive, but the winding coastal route from Gordon's Bay, at times snaking along cliffs that plunge into the sea, is simply breathtaking (see "The Coastal Route: Gordon's Bay to Hermanus," above).

By Bus Contact **Hylton Ross** (✆ **021/511-1784**) for scenic day trips to Hermanus from July 1 to November 31 via the coastal route on Wednesday, Friday, or Sunday. Expect to pay about R630.

GUIDED TOURS For an insight into the greater community, take a walking tour of the Hermanus township Zwelihle, the first black township established in the Overberg, with Wilson Salukazana, a registered SATOUR guide and proprietor of **Ubuntu Tours** (✆ **073/214-6949**). **Walker Bay Adventures** (✆ **082/739-0159**) runs kayaking trips in the Walker Bay whale sanctuary for R300 per person; you can also kayak across the lagoon for a wine-tasting session under milkwood trees on the beautiful Mosaic Farm for R400 per person. (See "Whale-Watching," below, for boat operators with permits for whale-watching.) Call **Fernkloof Nature Reserve** (✆ **028/313-8100;** www.fernkloof.com) to find out about specialized fynbos tours. Contact **Klein Paradys Equestrian Centre** (✆ **028/284-9422**) for Overberg outings on horseback. They're based in Bot River, about 33km (20 miles) inland from Hermanus. Wine lovers will enjoy an introduction to the Hemel-en-Aarde Valley's many wine farms and tasting rooms: contact Cape Wine Academy–accredited **Percy Tours** (✆ **072/062-8500;** www.percytours.com) for details. Tours start at R350 per person.

What to See & Do

Surf & Sand

The sweeping 30km (19-mile) curve of **Grotto Beach** can be seen from most vantage points of Walker Bay. This is a great family beach, made for long walks and swimming. Closer to town, **Voëlklip** is a popular swimming beach where the hip youth hang out; the closest beach, **Langbaai** (pronounced "*lung*-buy," meaning "Long Bay"), offers the best bodysurfing, though currents can render it hazardous.

Wildflowers

The **Fernkloof Nature Reserve** (✆ **028/313-8100**), which overlooks the town, offers more than 50km (31 miles) of hiking trails and great views of Walker Bay. If you're around on a Saturday, pop by the weekly **farmers' market** (8am–noon) for live music, pancakes, jaffles (a toasted sandwich), preserves, olives, and other treats.

Wine Tasting

The wineries that comprise the **Hermanus/Walker Bay Wine Route** are almost all located on the R320, known as Hemel-en-Aarde Valley; see "The Coastal Route: Gordon's Bay to Hermanus," above. (The exceptions are Mauroma and Erica, both near the picturesque village of Stanford.) The oldest and most respected of the Walker Bay wines are **Bouchard Finlayson** (✆ **028/312-3515;** tastings Mon–Fri 9am–5pm, Sat 9:30am–12:30pm) and **Hamilton Russell** ★★★ (✆ **028/312-3595**). The latter had for many years the dubious distinction of producing South Africa's most expensive wines—a chardonnay and a pinot noir—but, admittedly, they are absolutely delicious. Even a committed sauvignon blanc drinker like myself can understand why it was voted as one of the top 20 in the world. You can sample them for free, but you will be hard-pressed to walk away without a purchase. Tastings are held in a beautiful setting, Monday to Friday 9am to 5pm and Saturday 9am to 1pm. You can settle for just a tasting (daily 10am–3pm) or a picnic (Tues–Sun), arranged by calling ahead (✆ **028/312-1706**)—though you'll find a wonderful restaurant, Mogg's Country Cookhouse, nearby (see below). For an expert introduction to the Valley's wines, contact **Percy Tours** (see "Guided Tours," above).

Whale-Watching

The once-threatened Southern Right whale (a protected species since 1946) is enjoying a major comeback, with the population on the South African coastline nearly doubling every decade for the past 30 years. In recent years, as many as 2,000 whales have followed the annual migration from Antarctica to flirt, mate, and calve in the warmer waters off the southern Cape coast.

One can clearly view these playful, gentle giants—sometimes at a distance of only 10m (33 ft.)—from the craggy cliffs that run along the Hermanus shoreline. For the best sightings, take the 12km (7½-mile) cliff path from New Harbour east to Grotto Beach and the lagoon. Beware of the waves—a visitor was swept off the rocks in 2000 and drowned. Also recommended are the terraces above the Old Harbour, where a telescope and a plaque provide basic information about the bay and its whales.

Hermanus is very proud of the fact that it is the only town in the world to have a "whale crier": During whaling season, Pasika Noboba walks the town streets from 10am to 4pm, blowing a kelp horn in a sort of Morse code to alert the town's inhabitants to the presence and whereabouts of whales. If you don't understand the code, never mind; Pasika also wears a sandwich board and carries a mobile phone (✆ **079/854-0684**). Contact him directly for reports of the latest whale sightings, or call the museum (✆ **028/312-1475**).

For assured up-close encounters, consider boarding a boat with a license to approach the whales (up to 50m/164 ft.). Bank on paying between R550 and R720 per adult, children under 5 travel free, while older children are eligible for discounted rates. Some of the longest-running operators are **Ivanhoe Sea Safaris** (✆ **082/926-7977**), boasting some 8,000 close approaches to Southern Right whales over the years, and **Southern Right Charters** (✆ **082/353-0550**), who have 10 years of experience.

Note: The limestone cliffs of De Kelders, southeast along the R43, provide a superb view of Walker Bay and the whales, and are never as crowded as Hermanus in season.

Shark-Cage Diving

Fancy coming face to face with a great white? Since the likes of Nicolas Cage, Ruby Wax, Richard E. Grant, and Andie MacDowell have (the latter trio for a reality-TV program called *Celebrity Shark Bait*), cage diving has become almost as mainstream as whale-watching. Boats leave from Gansbaai (a coastal town some 30km/19 miles east of Hermanus) and head out to Dyer Island Nature Reserve. This and nearby Geyser Island are favorites of the jackass penguin and seal breeding colonies, whose pups are an all-time favorite great white shark snack—so much so that they call the channel between the islands Shark Alley. The sharks are baited (highly contentious, I might add), and you stand an excellent chance of seeing one from the cage (or the boat, if you prefer to keep your distance)—the best time of the year is April to mid-June and July.

Eight licensed operators offer a similar service for more or less the same price: The rate is R1,500 per person and includes pickup from hotel or guesthouse (in Cape Town or Hermanus), a full buffet breakfast, a day at sea on a customized catamaran, dive equipment, a White Shark Lecture (given on board), lunch, tea, and return transfer. Note that you don't need to be a certified diver to descend in the cage.

Operators with the best eco-credentials are **White Shark Projects** (**© 021/405-4537;** www.whitesharkprojects.co.za), one of the longest-running and most respected (the company was instrumental in getting the white shark protected under South African law and was the recipient of the 2004 SKAL International Ecotourism Award), and **Marine Dynamics** (www.sharkwatchsa.com), also internationally recognized for responsible tourism; the latter also offers excellent whale-watching trips in which a marine biologist will take you within 50m (164 ft) of the Southern Right whales migrating along this coastline. The third operator worth noting is **Sharklady** (**© 028/312-3287;** www.sharklady.co.za). Equally committed to conservation and education, hers is the only commercial, hands-on, women-only operator in the industry—and she doesn't feed the fish.

Where to Stay

Hermanus itself is not a particularly attractive town—walking along the streetscape away from the sea, it resembles any other sprawling suburb—but its position as the whale-watching capital has meant an unprecedented increase in new places to stay, the best of which afford grand sea views. Budget options abound, especially if you're prepared to go the self-catering route (and with the number and variety of restaurants in town, this is no great hardship). **House on Westcliff** (**© 028/313-2388;** R600–R800 double) offers cheery, cheap-as-chips garden rooms. Plusses are the shady garden, sheltered pool, and location (just across the street from the coastal path and near the new harbor). On the other side of town in Voelklip, a stroll away from a tiny, sheltered swimming beach, you may be lucky enough to bag a few nights at **Hartford Cottage** ★ (**© 028/314-0102;** R900–R1,200 double, R200 per extra person; self-catering only). An immaculate thatched wonder that Wendy and Gys Hofmeyr originally built for their children, the cottage contains everything you could possibly need, plus a good dose of charm. But they don't take people for just 1 night—in fact, regulars often book the place out for weeks at a time—and it's closed from mid-December to mid-January. Right in the center of town is the relaxed **Auberge Burgandy** ★ (**© 028/313-1201**), where standard rooms start at R1,180 double. Those with balconies and ocean views are probably your best bet—although the garden options aren't half bad, either. There are a few larger rooms, as well as a penthouse with three double rooms, for R2,950. Breakfast is just across the road at the Burgandy restaurant (see "Where to Dine," below). Also reasonable is **Harbour House** (**© 028/312-1799;** R755–R1,095 double): I'd skip the slick new hotel and ask for the Ilona room in the lovely old house; a balcony overlooks cool green gardens, and you'll be able to watch spouting whales from your room. If money is no object, more luxurious accommodations options for you are listed below.

Finds Stanford: A Gem of a Village

If you'd prefer a more rural option with an architecturally charming streetscape (from this point of view, Hermanus is horribly bland), and you don't mind being on a lagoon rather than the sea, base yourself in the village of Stanford, a 15- to 20-minute drive beyond Hermanus. Thanks to planning strictures, the village has retained its historical integrity and, popular with Cape Town's creative types, now boasts a number of lovely places to eat and stay; best of all is the secluded retreat, 12km (7½ miles) outside Stanford, called **Mosaic Farm** ★★ (✆ **028/313-2814;** www.mosaicfarm.net). There are two self-catering cottages on the reserve; one sleeps up to eight, the other just two (and, at R700 a night, is good value), but the 10 comfortable East African–style en-suite tents (due to be enclosed by glass by Sept 2009), set under whispering milkwood trees and overlooking the Hermanus lagoon and Overberg mountains, are the ones to book. Here it's so quiet, you can hear yourself breathe. Rates start at R1,920 to R2,540 double and include dinner and breakfast. You can breakfast, dine, and sample award-winning wines at the adjoining solid stone Spookhuis (Ghost House), and activities include kayaking and guided bird and nature walks. For more Stanford dining options, see below.

Auberge Provence ★★ Set on the cliffs overlooking Walker Bay, just meters from the whale-watching path that meanders above it, this Provençal-style guesthouse is planned around a central courtyard pool. Interiors are stylish, with large stone fireplaces for winter; the exterior features a rustic stone facade, heavy wooden shutters, and wrought-iron balconies. All five rooms are extremely spacious, tastefully furnished, and very comfortable: You can luxuriate in bed while watching the whales, snug under goose-down duvets. Go all out and book the Lavender Suite if you want your own private plunge pool, or the huge Overberg Suite—a double-story suite with a private lounge, courtyard, and Jacuzzi. You'll be close to the village, with its good restaurants and shops, but you'll have to get in your car to hit the beach.

25 Westcliff Dr., Hermanus 7200. ✆ **028/312-1413.** Fax 028/312-1423. www.aubergeprovence.co.za. 5 units. R1,190–R1,990 double; R1,790–R2,590 suite. Rates include breakfast; ask about winter specials. AE, DC, MC, V. **Amenities:** Library; pool. *In room:* TV, hair dryer, minibar, heated towel racks, under-floor heating.

Birkenhead House ★★★ A glam boutique hotel decorated in the Ian Schrager tradition, this exclusive guesthouse, owned by the same couple who brought us Royal Malewane (one of the most beautiful game lodges flanking the Kruger), is aimed at a slightly younger market. Decor is eclectic—French baroque meets 21st-century modern, with a touch of kitsch thrown in—with white and cream the predominant colors throughout. The public spaces are wonderfully over-the-top (massive gilded mirrors, French antiques, chandeliers), but not all bedrooms are created equal. The top choices are nos. 1 (superior) and 2 (luxury), built right at the front, with the only unobstructed sea views. No. 6 also has the most wonderful wraparound balcony. None of the pools is big enough for my liking, but Hermanus's best swimming beaches flank the rocky outcrop on which the hotel is built. Right next door is the child-friendly Birkenhead Villa;

design wise, it's a little heavy on the concrete, but the five rooms (all with ocean views; nos. 1 and 4 have the best vistas) radiate class and comfort.

7th Ave., Voelklip, Hermanus 7200. ✆ **028/314-8000.** Fax 028/314-1208. www.birkenheadhouse.com. 11 units plus Birkenhead Villa (5 units). R4,400–R7,500 double. Rates include all meals, local beverages (excellent wines), and laundry. AE, DC, MC, V. Call for extended-stay rates. **Amenities:** Gourmet dining; gym; 2 pools; spa; all excursions arranged. *In room:* TV/DVD, hair dryer, complimentary minibar, free Wi-Fi.

Grootbos Private Nature Reserve ★★★ Kids Surrounded by 1,700 hectares (4,200 acres) of fynbos, a 1,000-year-old milkwood forest, and indigenous gardens and only about 25 minutes' drive from Hermanus, this is the best place to learn about the eccentricities of the Cape floral kingdom (and bring the kids; besides numerous environmental accolades, Grootbos won the *Tatler* Best Family Hotel Award in the World in 2006). Guests stay in either the original **Garden Lodge,** in 11 privately situated stone-and-timber cottages—each a fully equipped open-plan "house" with large fireplace, multilevel sun decks, and views of Walker Bay; or **Forest Lodge.** Rebuilt after a bush fire a few years ago, the 16 private suites are strung along a ridge; each clean-lined unit has unobtrusive decor and great views. You can take a fynbos drive in the reserve every morning with a resident botanist; take evening walks or boat tours with a marine biologist; or walk, ride, or bike through the reserve. Picnic on a nearby beach or dine out on a five-course meal at the restaurants.

Off the R43, 33km (20 miles) east of Hermanus. ✆ **028/384-8000.** Fax 028/384-8040. www.grootbos.com. 27 units. High season R7,500 suite; low season R5,000 suite. Rates include meals and activities but exclude drinks; minimum 2-night stay. Children's rates on request. AE, DC, MC, V. **Amenities:** Dining room; bar; babysitting; children's programs; horseback riding; pool; guided walks and drives. *In room:* A/C, TV, fireplace, hair dryer, minibar.

Marine Hotel ★★★ Situated on the craggy cliffs close to the town center and Old Harbour, this grand dame of Hermanus (built in 1902) has wonderful views of Walker Bay and its whales. Rooms face either the sea or the courtyard (with pool); others have distant mountain views. Some rooms are a little floral and "done" for my taste, others are more blandly contemporary; but even if you're not here to see the whales, it's worth spending a little more for a luxury room with a gorgeous ocean view (note that you do need to specify "with sea view"). Guests can relax in the cool lemon and cream lounge or the comfortable wicker-furnished sea-facing bar—or head for an invigorating swim in the tidal pool below the cliffs. This Relais & Châteaux establishment offers a choice of excellent restaurants: No prizes for guessing what the critically acclaimed **Seafood at the Marine** specializes in, but it's the recently spruced up **Pavilion** (serving a larger variety of meals, see below) that has the view.

Marine Dr., Hermanus 7200. ✆ **028/313-1000.** Fax 028/313-0160. www.collectionmcgrath.com. 42 units. R2,000–3,600 double, depending on season; R2,500–4,700 luxury double; R3,400–R7,150 suite, depending on type and season. AE, DC, MC, V. No children under 12. **Amenities:** 2 restaurants; bar; concierge; high-speed Internet; pool; room service; spa. *In room:* A/C, TV/DVD player, hair dryer, ISDN, minibar, heated towel racks, under-floor heating.

Mosselberg on Grotto ★ Kids A relative newcomer to the Hermanus scene, this sleek guesthouse, designed by a stone-loving (and award-winning) South African architect, has five fine rooms situated around a courtyard with a fair-sized pool. On the border of the fynbos coastal reserve and with direct access to the famous cliff path that leads you to the nearby expanse of Grotto beach, this is one of the few upmarket options in Hermanus to welcome children. While the (heated) pool is not fenced off, a playroom stuffed with board games and a pool table will keep youngsters occupied if the weather turns. The best room is the spacious Southern Right suite, with its perfect sea views, balcony, fireplace, polished sandstone bathroom, and dressing area (pity about that whale painting). Sugarbird is a tad smaller but also desirable.

253a 10th St., Voelklip, Hermanus. ✆ **028/314-0055.** www.mosselberg.co.za. 5 units. R1,700–R2,600 double. Breakfast included. MC, V. **Amenities:** Lounge; babysitting; game room; pool. *In room:* TV, hair dryer, kitchenette, minibar, heated towel racks, under-floor heating, free Wi-Fi.

Where to Dine

For a relatively small coastal town, Hermanus offers a plethora of dining options, and not only in town. Foodies in search of superfresh organic ingredients, innovatively combined and presented with unpretentious home-style flair, should head into the glorious countryside. East lies the quaint village of **Stanford,** where Mariana and husband Peter tend to their vegetable garden as carefully as to their guests in **Mariana's Home Deli & Bistro** ★★ (✆ **028/341-0272;** lunch Thurs–Sun; no children under 10; no credit cards). If Mariana's is full (it is sometimes booked up over a month in advance), another gem to root out is **Hovercraft's** ★ (✆ **028/341-0603;** Fri–Sat from 7pm, Sun lunch from 12:30pm; no credit cards). It's just a handful of tables in a tiny ramshackle cottage surrounded by rambling moonflowers and wayward irises, and the menu is tiny and eclectic—but a decadent Sunday lunch roast is just about assured. If neither of these has a table, turn to Stanford stalwart **Paprika** (✆ **028/341-0662;** Wed–Sun dinner, Sun lunch; open more regularly in season), where new owner-chef Dolla Bruce chalks up daily specials on the blackboard outside the cottage. Alternatively, head west, turning into the sublime Hemel-en-Aarde Valley, where the burgeoning wine community has begun to capitalize on its 360° superb vistas (and dire global wine trading conditions) by diversifying into restaurants—best of these is **Heaven** ★★ (✆ **072/905-3947;** Tues–Sun noon–3pm), on the Newton Johnson Winery. The view is, okay, heavenly; and the menu, changing almost daily depending on what's available, is excellent. Signature dishes include the deep-fried onion with tandoori chicken filling, and the steak, cooked to perfection by Bruce (originally of B's Steakhouse, which you'll pass on the way here), served with a béarnaise sauce. There is also the swanky, see-and-be-seen **La Vierge** (✆ **028/313-2007;** open daily for lunch and dinner), where you can quaff the estate's fine, steely-green sauvignon blancs and enjoy French-country meals in a glass-fronted bubble with dramatic views. (Try the honey, artichoke, pickled mushroom, and tomato jelly salad with Parmesan crisps.) Deeper into the countryside is laid-back **Mogg's Country Cookhouse** ★★ (✆ **028/312-4321;** lunch Wed–Sun). Having passed all (and hopefully sampled a few) of the Hemel-en-Aarde wineries along the way, you'll find a colorful cottage at the end of a bumpy dirt track—a thoroughly rustic venue (a reincarnated laborer's hut) where mother-and-daughter team Julia and Jenny serve up a small a-la-carte menu that changes weekly; expect such delicious combinations as roasted tomato and pepper soup, or kassler chops with goat's cheese and figs. It's warm and friendly, and you can bring your own bottle of wine at no extra charge. If the presence of the ocean helps to work up an appetite, try **Milkwood** (✆ **028/316-1516**), a casual seafood restaurant located just above the Onrus beach (a short drive west of Hermanus), which scores top ratings for location and views. The food's not bad, either—you can't go wrong with a plate of oysters, followed by linefish and washed down with the region's delicious Birkenhead beer.

Back in town, you'll almost certainly want a sea view while imbibing its bounty: Few restaurants in the world can beat the location at **Bientang's Cave** ★ (✆ **028/312-3454;** daily 11:30–4pm; Fri–Sat 7–9pm; reservations essential)—a cave in the rocks literally just above the sea, with whales sometimes breaching at what feels like touching distance. You can eyeball the behemoths as you sample fresh linefish or bouillabaisse, but the food is pretty basic and the service can be slack. Also casual is **Burgundy** (✆ **028/312-2800**), opposite the old harbor. The oldest building in town (the stone-and-clay cottage was built by a Swedish boat builder in 1875), it has a large terrace overlooking the bay and offers simple, perhaps slightly overpriced fare. For lunch, expect offerings such as a seafood salad with snoek, mackerel, and marinated calamari; the dinner menu is more comprehensive. Or follow ex-head-chef Deon to his new eatery, **Joubert** (✆ **028/312-4983;** lunch and dinner Mon–Sat), tucked away in the high street. Here the slow-roasted duck is a favorite.

If you want a fine-dining atmosphere and attentive service, book a seaview table at the **Pavilion** or **Seafood at the Marine** (both at the Marine Hotel, see below), or specify the same at **Meditterea Seafood Restaurant** ★ (✆ **028/313-1685;** www.meditterea.co.za; dinner daily 6–9:30pm and Sun noon–3pm). Generally considered the best nonhotel restaurant in Hermanus, Meditterea has a great seafood selection (the seared tuna is signature but only occasionally available, as is the seafood trio of linefish, prawns, and grilled calamari). If you're stuffed with seafood, try the tender lamb cutlets with fresh mint risotto or anchovy mashed potatoes. Book well in advance, particularly if you want a window seat.

Quayside Cabin ★★ Kids SEAFOOD Grab a table in this rustic, part-converted shipping container overlooking the fishing boats and bustle of the new harbor, and you'll be surrounded by content locals digging into the freshest, most succulent seafood in town (it's off-loaded right next to you, after all). As owner-chef Mike says, they must be doing something right—Quayside scooped a 2009 *Wine* magazine award as one of S.A.'s coolest seaside restaurants, has been lauded for its wine list, and was voted one of the most popular restaurants in the country by locals. They're famous for deep-fried calamari, but such dishes as the creamy *perlemoen* (abalone) casserole with a dash of sherry or the magnificent curry "hotpot" will tempt you to branch out. Service is attentive; the decor is a casual tangle of fishing nets, puppets, and stiletto heels dangling from the ceiling.

New Harbour slipway. ✆ **028/313-0752.** Reservations recommended. Main courses around R90. MC, V. Summer daily noon–4pm and 7pm until late. Winter (May–Aug) closed Sun–Tues nights.

Seafood at the Marine & The Pavilion at the Marine ★★★ SEAFOOD/FUSION Considered the best seafood restaurant in the entire Overberg region, Seafood at the Marine has lost few fans since Peter Tempelhoff (of Grande Provance, Franschhoek, and Automat, London fame) took control. Many old favorites still feature on the menu, which injects continental creativity into the local bounty—unpretentious staples such as fishcakes and a seafood bunny chow (curry in bread), as well as Rich Man's Fish and Chips, served in the *Financial Mail.* The biggest drawback is that the restaurant has no sea view—unlike its sister, the Pavilion, which, since its refurbishment, has rather stolen Seafood's thunder. With its checkered black-and-white floor and 1920s tropical feel, it's a gorgeous place to eat. The food combines unexpected flavors, such as the duck with seared prawns on a sesame salad with green tea coconut sauce, or the Gruyere cheese soufflé with artichokes, asparagus, and a pine-nut vinaigrette.

The Marine Hotel. ✆ **028/313-1000.** Reservations recommended. Dress smart casual. Seafood at the Marine is nonsmoking. Seafood: 2 courses R180; 3 courses R215; open daily for lunch and dinner. Pavilion: Appetizers R65–R90; main courses R110–R140. Open daily for breakfast and Tues–Sat for dinner. Closed for dinner in winter. AE, DC, MC, V.

After some 20 dusty, corrugated kilometers (12 miles) on dirt roads, soon after Gansbaai, the shark-cage diving capital, you will reach a minute speck on the map called **Baardskeerdersbos,** where the most frequented building is probably the Strandveld pub. The real attraction is en route: an unassuming retreat by the name of **Farm 215** ★★ (✆ **028/388-0920;** www.farm215.co.za; suites from R2,400 double, minimum 2 nights, no children under 12). It floats in a sea of fynbos amid empty skies and blissful silence (at night, watch for the occasional flash from a far-off lighthouse at Danger Point). There are three rooms available in or around the main house and a stylish restaurant, bar, and lounge area, but what you really want is one of the three free-standing fynbos suites, powered by solar electricity and warmed by fireplaces. It's the ultimate romantic getaway for independent nature lovers.

Two coastal destinations east of Hermanus well worth visiting are the village of **Arniston** and, better still, **De Hoop Nature Reserve** ★★★. To reach either, head east to Stanford on R43 (stop at Marianna's for lunch, if you can—see above), then turn northeast on R326 before turning right and heading south for Bredasdorp. (***Tip:*** Should you find yourself driving through Bredasdorp hungry, consider **Julian's,** 22 All Saints St. [✆ **028/425-1201**], which serves a top chocolate cheesecake.) From Bredasdorp, you can go either immediately south on R316 toward Arniston, or north on R319 for De Hoop. Time allowing, you may want to take a side trip south to Africa's southernmost tip, **L'Aghulus,** which is where the Indian and Atlantic oceans meet. Barring the interesting facts of its location, the place itself is pretty unremarkable, unless you wish to view the wreck of the freighter *Meisho Maru 38* or visit the oldest lighthouse on the coast. Built in 1848, the **Lighthouse Museum** (✆ **028/435-7185**) is now a satellite of the Shipwreck Museum in Bredasdorp and keeps the same hours. (Incidentally, the museum also houses a coffee shop and restaurant, but for superb views of the oceans and their clandestine meeting, book a table at nearby **Agulhas Country Lodge** ✆ **028/435-7650**].)

A highly recommended detour, if you do decide to take the R319 south, is the tiny town of **Elim** ★★, which is clearly signposted off the R319. Established as a Moravian mission station in 1824, the town remains relatively unchanged architecturally and is still inhabited by descendents of the original Moravian church members, who make their living from harvesting fynbos, and now, tourism. (Incidentally, Elim soil produces gorgeous flinty dry sauvignons, so sauvignon blanc lovers would do well to look for wineries such as First Sightings.)

Arniston, a combination of the small fishing village of Kassiesbaai and a collection of weekend getaway homes for Capetonians, is lapped by a startling turquoise sea and surrounded by blindingly white sand dunes. If you see signs for WAENHUISKRANS, don't panic—Arniston, named after a British ship that wrecked here in 1815, is also officially known by its Afrikaans name, Waenhuiskrans, which refers to the limestone cave that is big enough to house *(huis)* a wagon *(waen)*. For centuries, the local fishermen have been setting out at first light to cast their lines and returning at night to the quaint limewashed, thatched cottages clustered on the dunes overlooking the sea. These dwellings, some of which date back 200 years, have collectively been declared a national monument and are picture-postcard pretty, though doubtless less romantic to live in. You can wander through the sandy streets of the **Kassiesbaai community** ★ on your own or visit with the local community guide (✆ **073/590-2027**).

Moments **Fish Stew by Candlelight**

One of the most authentic experiences in the Overberg has to be dining in the heart of the Kassiesbaai community. On a prearranged night, you can delight in pan-fried fish, caught by the local fishermen, and green bean stew, prepared by their wives, and served by candlelight in one of the century-old fishing cottages. The meal costs R120 per person; to book, call Lillian Newman (✆ **028/445-9760** or 073/590-2027), a resident of Kassiesbaai who can also arrange for a guided tour.

The gorgeous **De Hoop Nature Reserve** ★★★ (✆ **028/425-5020;** entry R25 per person) has what many consider to be the best whale-watching spot on the entire coast, a huge beach dune appropriately called Koppie Alleen (Head Alone). But most visitors are here to explore one of the most beautiful coastal reserves in the world—51km (30 miles) of pristine white beach dunes, limestone cliffs, rock pools, wetlands, coastal fynbos, and no one to disturb the peace but zebras, several species of antelopes, and more than 260 species of birds. Inside the reserve, there are limited routes (you can drive to the beach or accommodations), so the reserve is best explored on foot (there are four trails; make sure you do part of the Coastal Trail, as well as the Coot or Heron Vlei Trail). Do note the reserve hours (7am–6pm); visitors intending to overnight should report to the reserve office no later than 4pm on the day of arrival, or call ahead if you are running late. There is a small penalty if you arrive after the reserve gates close at 6pm.

Where to Stay & Dine

The Arniston Spa Hotel ★ This is the best hotel in Arniston, with a great location opposite the exquisitely colored sea. Come here for a real sense of escaping the rat race, and for the spa—with one of the few Rasul chambers in the country (a detox treatment involving mud and heat). The luxury sea-facing rooms are a vast improvement over the standard sea-facing rooms, and while the pool-facing rooms are less windy (the wind often blows here), it's a shame to miss out on the surreal view. Dining is good, particularly the linefish, but for a really interesting experience, book a meal with the Kassiesbaai fishing community (see "Fish Stew by Candlelight," above).

P.O. Box 126, Bredasdorp 7280. ✆ **028/445-9000.** Fax 021/445-9633. www.arnistonhotel.com. 63 units. R1,450 standard sea-facing rooms; R1,850 for recommended luxury sea-facing units. Ask about winter specials. Rates include breakfast. AE, DC, MC, V. **Amenities:** 2 restaurants; bar; babysitting; boating; cycling; pool; room service. *In room:* A/C (in some), TV, hair dryer.

De Hoop Nature Collection ★★ **Kids** This is still a wonderfully peaceful 36,000-hectare (88,920-acre) slice of nature, although it has changed dramatically since CapeNature's 2008 private partnership with Madikwe. When development of the Collection is complete, there will be accommodation for between 250 and 300 people—up from just 10 cottages in the past. The existing accommodations have been spruced up; all are comfortable (note that you'll have to share ablutions at some of the rondawels at the Opstal, and the Melkkamer cottages have no electricity). All cottages—and there are a good few new additions—have bathrooms (some just with shower) and offer bedding and towels, and many are divinely located. Try for Koppie Alleen, all alone near towering dunes, or the lovely Opstal Vlei Cottages, which are perfect for birders. At the time of writing, luxury rooms adjacent to the old manor house were still being completed. Most options are self-catering, but there is a shop, and the new Fig Tree Restaurant offers breakfast, lunch, and dinner, so you don't have to pack (although do consider bringing something to barbecue; each cottage has its own outdoor barbecue site). Those accommodated in the stone Melkkamer Vlei and Foreman's cottages (across the vlei from the Opstal) can request meals at the Melkkamer Manor House. De Hoop is ideal for young children—it has a game trail, a wetlands trail, and endless sand dunes and interesting coves to romp in.

Bookings and inquiries © **021/659-3601** or 086/133-4667. Reserve © 028/542-1253. www.dehoopcollection.co.za. 30 units, of which 5 are rondawels sleeping 2; cottages sleep 4–8. Rondawels from R500 double; cottages R400–R750 per person. Campsites from R50 per person. AE, MC, V. **Amenities:** Restaurant, *pétanque,* hiking trails; tennis courts (own racket required).

5 SWELLENDAM & ROUTE R62

Swellendam is 220km (136 miles) E of Cape Town

Most people who choose to drive through the Overberg interior (as opposed to edging along its Whale Coast) are in a hurry to get to the Garden Route and may rush through and completely bypass the excellent pit stops and side trips along the way. Most important, try to set aside enough time to take the **Route 62,** which means veering north from Swellendam and traveling through the small towns of Barrydale, Ladismith, Calitzdorp, Oudtshoorn, and Prince Albert. This makes for a great road trip, and the empty, arid spaces are a great contrast to the later lushness of the Garden Route. An additional night will do, but you could stretch it to two, or even do the entire detour in a day; see "Route 62: The Best Road Trip in South Africa," below.

Leaving Cape Town, you will ascend **Sir Lowry's Pass** ★★ to reach the fruit-growing areas of Grabouw and Elgin (incidentally, the area produces around 65% of South Africa's apple export crop) and the first of many farm stalls dotted along the way. **Peregrine** ★★★ (opposite the Grabouw turnoff) is one of the oldest and still one of the best—stop here for fresh farm produce and various traditional road trip treats (see chapter 13), such as *biltong* (air-dried meat strips) and *droëwors* (air-dried sausage). The adjacent bakery is also excellent—the pies (try the springbok), *melktert* (thick custard tart) and *koeksisters* (deep-fried dough soaked in syrup) are not to be missed.

The first detour you might consider is the **R406,** which loops past the villages of **Genadendal** and **Greyton.** Genadendal is the oldest Moravian mission village in Africa, with buildings dating back to 1738. The **Genadendal Mission and Museum Complex** documents the activities of the missionaries and their flock. It offers an authentic glimpse into the past but is rather run down and not always open; call ahead and request a guided tours: © **028/251-8582** or 028/251-8220 (Mon–Thurs 9am–1pm and 2–5pm, Fri 9am–3:30pm, Sat morning).

Greyton, a few minutes farther east on the R406, was developed much later by a more affluent community. Set at the foot of the Riviersonderend Mountains, with many beautifully restored Victorian and Georgian buildings, it's a great place to stop for lunch. Grab a table on the stoop at the **Oak & Vigne** (© **028/254-9037;** open daily, lunch only). If you feel like spending the night (and this is a great village to do so in), a good-value B&B is **Acorns on Oak** (© **028/254-9567;** R850 double), a country-style house next to the river with lush gardens crammed with roses and a fair-sized heated pool. Also make sure

Route 62: The Best Road Trip in South Africa

To reach the Garden Route from Cape Town, it's worth considering an alternative route, highly recommended for its empty roads, spectacular mountain scenery, vineyard valleys, small-town architecture, and wide-open plains. With no detours or stops, this scenic route will take approximately 90 minutes longer than traveling directly to the Garden Route along the N2, but, ideally, you should plan to overnight 1 to 3 nights along the way. Suggested route is as follows:

Travel north from Cape Town on the N1, on the toll road that takes you through the **Du Toitskloof Tunnel.** Time allowing, bypass the tunnel and traverse the **Du Toitskloof Pass**—the soaring mountain and valley views from the 1:9 gradient road are well worth the extra 15 minutes.

At Worcester, capital of the Breede River region, the **Karoo Desert Botanical Gardens** ★ (✆ **023/347-0785;** daily 7am–7pm; free except Aug–Oct, when it costs R16), off Roux Road, are definitely worth viewing, particularly in spring. The gardens showcase the weird and wonderful plants from the country's semiarid regions. From here, head southeast on the R60 to Robertson, keeping an eye out for **Graham Beck**'s cellar (✆ **023/626-1214;** Mon–Fri 9am–5pm, Sat 10am–3pm), worth a stop if you like sparkling wine—the award-winning nonvintage brut has been used at presidential inaugurations and for Barack Obama's acceptance speech, and many consider the vintage brut (made from 100% chardonnay grapes) the best *méthode champenoise* in the country.

Once in Robertson, take the R317, a scenic route that passes most of the Robertson wineries, including **Springfield** (✆ **023/626-3661**)—a wine-tasting stop here is an absolute must for the sauvignon blanc lover (particularly if you like it bone dry and grassy). If you don't want to drive farther, consider swanking it up at an old ostrich feather palace: These days, **Excelsior** (✆ **023/615-2050;** R800–R1,500 double) makes wine, but only the cabernet sauvignon reserve has been highly rated. If you have the energy, it's worth pushing on: Follow the signposts to Swellendam, but double-back at the final T-junction, turning left (toward Ashton) to rejoin the R60 and overnight at the atmospheric Cape Dutch **Jan Harmsgat Country House** (✆ **023/616-3407;** www.jhghouse.com; high season R1,080–R2,060 double, low season R880–R1,320 double, including breakfast; closed June). Don't miss the four-course dinner (R275, reservations essential). Right next door is the swish **Mardouw Country House** (✆ **023/616-2999;** www.mardouw.com; R2,236–R3,622 double DBB—dinner, bed, and breakfast), a very luxurious guesthouse on a 1,000-hectare (2,471-acre) working olive-and-wine farm. Or instead of heading toward Swellendam from Ashton, take the R62 through the 10km (6¼-mile) **Cogmanskloof Pass** ★, leading you into the pretty town of **Montagu** ★, where there are a number of B&Bs. Book one of the three garden units at **Aasvöelkrans** (✆ **023/614-1228;** www.aasvoelkrans.co.za; R800 double), a delightful guesthouse on a stud farm at the foot of the Langeberg Mountains; then take an evening stroll down to town and admire the Victorian architecture and soaring brick-red mountains, or enjoy a therapeutic dip in the nearby hot springs. (Note that, from an aesthetic point of view, however, these have been ruined by the resort that's sprung up around them; they were being renovated in early 2009.) The **springs** (© **023/614-1150**) are a constant 109°F (43°C) and are open daily from 8am to 11pm, for R60 per person. If you'd like the chance to mingle with locals and listen to golden hits played on a baby grand piano, chose a room in the Carrington Villa at the Art Deco **Montagu Country Hotel** (© **023/614-3125;** R1,280 double, including breakfast). But the nicest Montagu option is the stunning **Les Hauts de Montagu** (© **023/614-2514;** www.leshautsdemontagu.co.za; high season R1,600 double, low season R1,000 double, including breakfast), 3km (1¾ miles) outside of town (off R62) toward Barrydale. The guesthouse offers six Provençal-styled bedrooms (by 2010, there will be 10 units) in cottages on the grounds of a 19th-century Cape Dutch homestead, with commanding vineyard and mountain views and a tiny chapel.

From Montagu, take the road east to Barrydale (if you need a pit stop, you'll pass the unassuming but reputable **Clarke of the Karoo** on your left [© **028/572-1017**]). From here, follow the signs to Calitzdorp; along the way, you'll pass a turnoff for **Sanbona Wildlife Reserve** ★★ (© **028/572-1365** or 041/407-1000 for reservations; www.sanbona.com; high season from R9,000 double, low season from R7,000 double, all-inclusive). By far, the best Big 5 reserve in the Western Cape (a few others may claim Big 5 status, but the lions are in separate enclosures), this is a very beautiful (if you like arid landscapes) and large (54,000-hectare/133,380-acre) reserve, with luxurious accommodations (it's part of the Mantis Collection, the same people who manage Shamwari in the Eastern Cape). There are now three camps to choose from: the secluded Dwyka Tented Lodge, which has 9 units, each with a deck and private plunge pool; Tilney Manor, with 6 units (closed for renovations at the time of writing); and Gondwana Lodge, which welcomes children and has 12 suites. Time allowing, make this your next overnight stop—the Klein Karoo scenery makes for a very different safari experience from the Eastern Cape reserves, and is more conveniently situated if you're not traveling that far east.

Next up is the small village of **Calitzdorp;** leave enough time for a short stop to taste some of the Cape's best fortified wines at **Boplaas** (© **044/213-3326**) and **Die Krans** (© **044/213-3314**), or have a meal at **Rose of the Karoo,** 21 Voortrekker Rd. (© **044/213-3133**), the best local restaurant in the village, with a lovely vine-covered terrace. If you haven't spent the night at Sanbona, proceed to do so at **The Retreat at Groenfontein** ★★★ (© **044/213-3880;** www.groenfontein.com). This aptly named Victorian farmhouse is 20km (12 miles) northeast of Calitzdorp, reached via dirt roads that meander through beautiful countryside, in a small, remote valley with breathtaking views of the Swartberg mountains (see p. 245). By overnighting here, you also ensure that you arrive in Oudtshoorn before dark to tackle the Swartberg Pass—one of the most spectacular drives in the country. Spend your last night at Prince Albert, another highly recommended village (see "Where to Stay," later in this chapter), before continuing south to Wilderness via George, and the pleasures of the Garden Route.

you book a table at **254 Restaurant** on a Friday or Saturday night; you'll have good, solid country food and a chance to meet the locals. Other than strolling the streets, Greyton's main attraction is the 14km (8.5-mile) **Boesmanskloof Trail,** which traverses the mountains to the town of McGregor, another charming village. If you're not a dedicated hiker, a good alternative is the 9km (5.5-mile) walk to **Oak Falls**—the highlight of the route—instead. Note that from Greyton you can proceed along a back road direct to Montagu, or return to the N2 along a well-graded dirt road, so there's no need to retrace your footsteps. For information on this and more, call ✆ **028/254-9414.**

SWELLENDAM

Swellendam, a pretty town at the foot of the Langeberg Mountains and appropriately billed as the historic heart of the Overberg, is the perfect halfway stop (for lunch or the night) for visitors driving from Cape Town to the Garden Route directly via the N2.

Essentials

VISITOR INFORMATION **The Swellendam Tourism Bureau** is in the Oefeningshuis at 36 Voortrek St. (✆ **028/514-2770;** Mon–Fri 9am–5pm, Sat–Sun 9am–1pm).

GETTING THERE **By Car** The quickest way to get to Swellendam is via the N2, as described above. Alternatively, you can travel the more attractive mountain and semidesert routes (see "Route 62: The Best Road Trip in South Africa," above).

By Bus **Intercape, Translux, Greyhound,** and **Baz Bus** pass through daily on their way to the Garden Route. See chapter 3 for contact details.

GETTING AROUND **On Foot** This is the best way to explore the small village and Drostdy Museum complex. Hiking trails in the nearby Marloth Nature Reserve lead into the Langeberg Mountains; for permits and maps of hikes, including the popular but tough 5-day Swellendam Trail, contact the reserve office (✆ **028/514-1410**).

On Horseback Short or full-day excursions in the Langeberg Mountains are offered by **Two Feathers Horse Trails** (✆ **082/494-8279**) for about R200 per person per hour.

What to See & Do

Bontebok National Park ★ (✆ **028/514-2735,** or 012/428-9111 for reservations; www.sanparks.org; summer daily 7am–7pm, winter daily 7am–6pm) lies 7km (4¼ miles) out of town to the north and is accessible by car or mountain bike. South Africa's smallest reserve, it's dedicated to saving the once near-extinct chocolate and cream-colored bontebok antelope, plus the rare coastal renosterveld fynbos it grazes on. There are no large predators in the park, but it is a peaceful place to spend a day, with some easy walking trails along the Breede River. The self-catering chalets (R705 double) have been upgraded and offer good-value (if not plush) accommodation.

Historic Swellendam

Back in the early 1700s, the Dutch East India Company was perturbed by the number of men deserting the Cape Colony to find freedom and fortune in the hinterland. Swellendam was consequently declared a magisterial district in 1743, making it the third-oldest white settlement in South Africa and bringing its reprobate tax evaders once again under the Company fold. In 1795, the burghers finally revolted against this unwanted interference and declared Swellendam a republic, but the Cape's occupation by British troops later that year made their independence rather short lived. Swellendam continued to flourish under British rule, but a devastating fire in 1865 razed much of the town. Almost a century later, transport planners ruined the main road, Voortrek Street, by ripping out the oaks that lined it, ostensibly to widen it. Two important historical sites to have survived on this road are, at no. 36, the **Oefeningshuis** (where the tourism bureau is located), built in 1838, and, at no. 11, the over-the-top baroque **Dutch Reformed Church,** built in 1901.

The **Drostdy Museum complex** ★★ (✆ **028/514-1138;** Mon–Fri 9am–4:45pm; Sat–Sun 10am–3:45pm) comprises the Drostdy, the Old Goal and Ambagswerf (Trade's Yard), Mayville House, and Zanddrift, now an excellent daytime restaurant. The Drostdy was built by the Dutch East India Company in 1747 to serve as residence for the *landdrost* (magistrate), and features many of the building traditions of the time: yellowwood from the once abundant forests, cow-dung and peach-pit floors, elegant fireplaces, and, of course, Cape Dutch gables. The Drostdy also houses an excellent collection of late-18th-century and early-19th-century Cape furniture in the baroque, neoclassical, and Regency styles.

Where to Stay & Dine

Swellendam's small-town rural ambience is changing fast as a number of young entrepreneurs, both local and foreign, have opted to drop out and live the rural life. **Bloomestate** (✆ **028/514-2984;** www.bloomestate.com; R900–R1,500 double) will suit travelers who prefer contemporary design—even the banana trees sprouting outside make a change from the ubiquitous oaks everywhere else. The two sets of rooms—modern, with furniture by some interesting designers and MP3 docking stations—open onto landscaped gardens, a heated saltwater pool and a Jacuzzi perched above a pond thick with lily pads. Sip drinks in an extremely stylish lemon, lime, and gray lounge. Neighbor **Rothman Manor** (✆ **028/514-2771;** R820–R1,750 double) has similar grounds (down to the Jacuzzi and pond, although they do also have a couple of springbok and zebra), but their six rooms (not all have tubs) are more private. Inside, contemporary decor with an African edge contrasts with the whitewashed Cape Dutch exterior. If you don't mind stairs, go for the extralarge suite.

If you'd prefer to stay in a more traditional homestead atmosphere, a good-value option, with suites and cottages scattered in the abundant gardens of a historic Cape Dutch National Monument, is **Augusta De Mist Country House** ★ (✆ **028/514-2425;** www.augustademist.com; R900–R1,500 double, including breakfast; ask about winter and low-season rates). The rooms all look good, but the tastefully furnished Arum and Varkoor cottages, with reed ceilings and fireplaces, are particularly nicely situated at the top of the garden. You can easily walk to some of the town's best restaurants. This is also true of **Schoone Oordt** (see review below). For old-world luxury, **Klippe Rivier Country House** ★★ (✆ **028/514-3341;** www.klipperivier.com; R1,100–R2,400 double; R3,000 cottage), built in the 1820s, is still a premium address, although the location on the outskirts of town means you'll have to do some driving. Rooms are elegant and spacious, strewn with antiques, reading matter, orchids, and art; the downstairs rooms all have fireplaces for winter nights, and there's a honeymoon cottage for those who want to be quite alone. Even if you don't stay (it is pricey and service can be a tad snooty), consider treating yourself to a three-course dinner here (from R195 per person; reservations essential).

Although Swellendam's newcomers have been giving the country retreats a run for their money, it's still worthwhile to head farther afield: A lovely 30-minute drive from Swellendam along the R60 (see "Route 62: The Best Road Trip in South Africa," above), **Jan Harmsgat Country House** ★★ (✆ **023/616-3407** or 072/279-3138; www.jhghouse.com; R1,100–R2,060 double including breakfast) is a 1723 working fruit, olive, and nut farm with a wonderful mountain backdrop—possibly the most serene setting in the Overberg—and justifiably famous for fine country meals. Next-door neighbor **Mardouw Country House** (✆ **023/616-2999;** www.mardouw.com; R1,430–R2,140 double; R1,950–R2,714 suite), more glam boutique hotel than 1,000-hectare (2,471-acre) working farm, has upped the ante in the country house category. Last, if you're watching your budget, or simply crave real privacy, Tersia and Jeremy at **Eenuurkop Getaway Cottage** have done a wonderful job of renovating two self-catering cottages on their farm, both enjoying an idyllic setting just outside of Swellendam, and offering peace, privacy, and excellent value (✆ **082/956-9461;** www.eenuurkop.co.za; R600 (sleeps 2)–R800 (sleeps 8).

There are plenty of places to eat in Swellendam, although few of the options will blow you away. The **Old Gaol** ★★ (✆ **028/514-3847;** daily 8:30am–5pm, dinner Tues–Sat from 6:30pm, summer only) in the Drostdy Museum has long topped the lunch lists, and locals are delighted it's now open for dinner 5 nights a week in summer, too. Lunch features staples such as *bobotie,* oxtail and homemade chicken pie, but dinner is where it gets interesting: Favorites include the chicken roulade with bree and fig, wrapped in bacon (R85), and the slow-roasted rack of lamb. Locals also love **Koornlands** (✆ **082/430-8188**), housed in a cozy thatched cottage on Voortrek Street, where you can enjoy game dishes such as a crocodile sashibi starter (served with a wasabi sweet soy sauce; R55), springbok or kudu filets, or ostrich lasagna (R75–R125). At the other end of town, Cristiana and Gianni (from Milan) serve up ravioli and gnocchi at the unassuming **La Sosta** (✆ **028/514-1470;** main courses around R100); the Italian dishes incorporate some South African flavors such as game.

Alternatively, just before (or after, if traveling from George) reaching Swellendam on the N2, take the Stormsvlei/Bonnievale turnoff and you'll find **Zanddrift Restaurant** (✆ **028/261-1167;** Sun–Fri 9am–5pm) signposted (also the Breede River Wine Shoppe). Edwina Kohler is somewhat brusque (how else to describe someone who has a sign up reading TODAY'S MENU: TAKE IT OR LEAVE IT), but she prepares wonderful home-cooked food in a garden setting. The most convivial place to dine at night is still **Herberg Roosje** (review below); for finer dining, try the dining room at the **Klippe Rivier Country House** (see above).

De Kloof Luxury Estate ★★ It's one of many national monuments in town, but behind De Kloof's whitewashed walls are some seriously modern rooms, bursting with Asian and African artifacts (collected by Marjolein when she worked in West Africa and China). Set in spacious grounds complete with golf putting green and driving range, it's still walking distance to top attractions in the center of town—that's if you don't get too side-tracked by the complimentary wine tasting (from the rated Springfield and Viljoensdrift estates, among others) or the inviting pool. Some of the luxury rooms are so beautifully situated that I preferred them to the deluxe options, though they lack bathtubs and have a little less space. Those on a luxury treasure hunt should opt for the double-story honeymoon suite, with a waterbed and vast fireplace.

8 Weltevrede St., Swellendam 6740. ✆ **028/514-1303.** Fax 028/514-1304. www.dekloof.co.za. 6 units, 1 family cottage. R1,200–R1,500 luxury double; R1,300–R1,700 deluxe double; R1,900–R2,500 suite. Rates include champagne breakfast and wine tasting. AE, DC, MC, V. **Amenities:** Mountain bikes; cigar lounge in winter; exercise room; golf driving range and putting green; pool; free Wi-Fi. In room: A/C, TV, movie library, minibar, heated towel racks, under-floor heating.

Herberg Roosje Van De Kaap ★ Value Opposite the Drostdy Museum, this quaint country inn is the best value in town. Some of the rooms are quite small, but the tasteful furnishings and welcoming ambience make up for this—for more space, book one of the six garden rooms or the honeymoon room (or take a look at Augusta De Mist; see intro above). The inn has no lounge, but guests gather around the pool and at the equally charming restaurant, **Roosje Van De Kaap,** which serves traditional a-la-carte meals in an informal, candlelit atmosphere—definitely consider eating here even if you don't stay. Pizzas are popular, as is the Cape Trio (*bobotie,* a Cape casserole, and an ostrich filet) and the all-time favorite filet Roosje, tender beef medallions prepared in garlic butter and herbs. The only concern is that long-time owner Ilzebete is selling, but she assures us that few changes are expected.

5 Drostdy St., Swellendam 6740. ✆/fax **028/514-3001.** www.roosjevandekaap.com. 10 units. R580–R700 double. Rates include breakfast; picnic baskets on request. AE, DC, MC, V. **Amenities:** Restaurant (closed Mon); pool. *In room:* Hair dryer (on request).

Schoone Oordt ★ Just a stroll away from the best restaurants and museums, this carefully restored Georgian-fronted country house with the tongue-twisting name offers accommodation in eight spacious adjoining garden rooms with separate entrances. This means a chunk of the garden has been sacrificed, and the four newest rooms form a block that overlooks the others—but protected patios and beautifully landscaped rose gardens mean you won't feel crowded. If you have the funds to spare, opt for the more private honeymoon suite, with its outlook onto wilder gardens and a stream. Inside the rooms, antiques carefully restored by the owner add character to the immaculate furnishings and quality fixtures. Service is sincere and spot-on; you'll have breakfast in a vast conservatory up at the main house—drenched in sunshine and strewn with potted plants and family photos.

1 Swellengrebel St., Swellendam 6740. ✆ **028/514-1248.** Fax 028/514-1249. www.schooneoordt.co.za. 9 units. R1,400–1,650 luxury double; R1,700–R2,050 honeymoon suite. Breakfast included. AE, DC, MC, V. **Amenities:** Pool; free Wi-Fi. *In room:* A/C, TV/DVD, fireplace, fridge, hair dryer, heated towel racks, underfloor heating in bathrooms.

6 THE KLEIN KAROO & THE GARDEN ROUTE

The Garden Route and Klein Karoo have become the country's most popular tourist destination after Cape Town, drawing visitors year-round to indigenous forests, freshwater lakes, hidden coves, and long beaches, while the mountains that range along the Garden Route's northern border beckon with a series of spectacular passes that cut through to the Afrikaans hinterland of the Klein Karoo. Besides providing a stark contrast to the lush coast, the dusty *dorpies* (little towns) dotted throughout this arid area have developed a distinctive architectural style, the best-preserved examples being found in the tiny hamlet of **Prince Albert** ★★★.

The narrow coastal strip that forms the Garden Route stretches from the rural town of Heidelberg in the west to Storms River Mouth in the east; and from the shore of the Indian Ocean to the peaks of the Outeniqua and Tsitsikamma coastal mountain ranges. This is the official boundary description, but for many, Mossel Bay or George marks the entry point in the west, and Port Elizabeth the eastern point. (See chapter 7 for details to and from Port Elizabeth and the nearby hamlet of Jeffrey's Bay.)

Highlights of this region include the Wilderness National Parks Lakes District, with some of the Garden Route's loveliest coastline; Knysna's lagoon- and forest-based activities; and Plettenberg Bay, which combines some of South Africa's best swimming beaches with beautiful fynbos and forest surrounds in such areas as the Crags. The real garden of the Garden Route, however, is the Tsitsikamma National Park, where dense indigenous forests, interrupted only by streams and tumbling waterfalls, drop off to a beautiful coastline.

Time allowing, the best way to reach the Garden Route is via the Klein Karoo's Route 62; see box above.

OUDTSHOORN, PRINCE ALBERT & THE KLEIN KAROO

The Klein (Little) Karoo—a sun-drenched area about 250km (155 miles) long and 70km (43 miles) wide—is wedged between the coastal mountains that separate it from the Garden Route and the impressive Swartberg mountain range—part of the Cape Flora World Heritage Site—in the north. To reach it from any angle, you have to traverse precipitous mountain passes, the most spectacular of which is the Swartberg Pass, connecting the Klein Karoo with its big brother, the Great Karoo. Unlike this vast dry land that stretches well into the Northern Cape and Free State, the "little" Karoo is watered by a number of streams that flow down from the mountains to join the Olifants River. Grapes grow here (Calitzdorp produces some of the country's best port), as does lucerne (alfalfa), which is why farmers in the region were able to successfully introduce the ostrich—lucerne is a favorite food of the ostrich.

Today the **ostrich farms,** together with the **Cango Caves,** a series of subterranean chambers some 30km (19 miles) from Oudtshoorn—unofficial center of the Klein Karoo—are the main draws of the region, but it is the **Swartberg Pass,** rated one of the most spectacular drives in Africa, the **unique sandstone architecture,** and the **small-town Afrikaans ambience** of places such as Prince Albert and Calitzdorp that make no Garden Route itinerary complete without a sojourn in the Klein Karoo.

Essentials

VISITOR INFORMATION You'll find the **Oudtshoorn Tourism Information Bureau** (✆ **044/279-2532;** www.oudtshoorn.com; Mon–Fri 8am–5:30pm, Sat 9am–1pm) on Baron van Rheede Street. **Prince Albert's Tourism Information** is clearly signposted at 109 Church St. (✆ **023/541-1366;** Mon–Fri 9am–6:30pm, Sat 9am–1pm); or contact Lindsay, at **Dennehof** (✆ **023/541-1227** or 082/456-8848; lindsay@dennehof.co.za).

GETTING THERE **By Plane** There are no scheduled flights here.

By Car Whichever way you approach it, you'll have to traverse a mountain pass to get to Oudtshoorn. Via the N1 from Cape Town, you'll head south on the R407 to Prince Albert before tackling the majestic Swartberg Pass. Alternatively (and, time allowing, preferably), you can come via Calitzdorp (see "Route 62: The Best Road Trip in South Africa," earlier in this chapter). The quickest way to get here is to travel along the N2 to Mossel Bay before heading north over the Robinson Pass on the R328, or to George before heading north over the Outeniqua Pass (N12). Oudtshoorn is an hour (88km/55 miles) from Mossel Bay and 45 minutes (55km/34 miles) from George.

By Bus **Intercape** and **Translux**'s no-frills **City to City** service travels from Johannesburg daily. Intercape travels to Oudsthoorn from Cape Town on Monday, Wednesday, Friday, and Sunday. Translux travels from Cape Town to Mossel Bay, where you can catch a bus to Oudsthoorn. See chapter 3 for regional phone numbers.

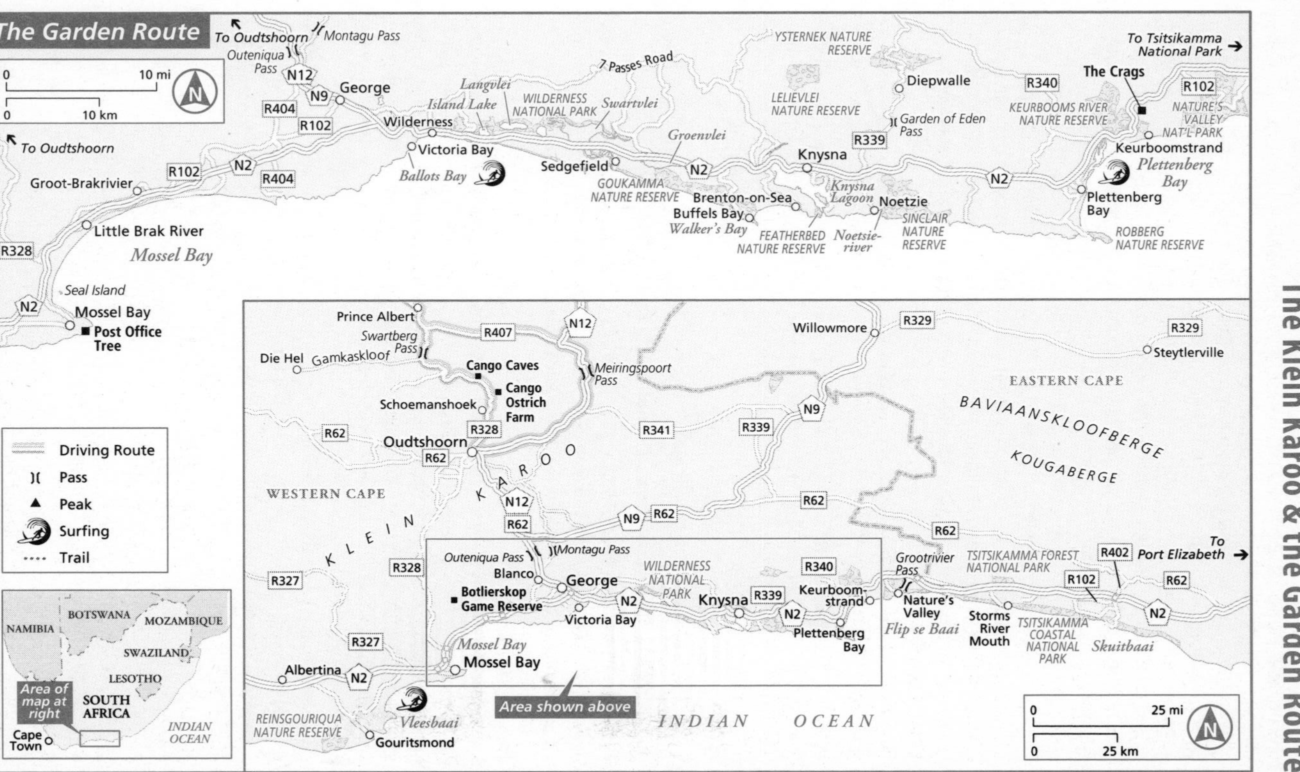
The Garden Route
0 10 mi
0 10 km
To Oudtshoorn
Montagu Pass
Outeniqua Pass
George
To Oudtshoorn
Groot-Brakrivier
Wilderness
Victoria Bay
Ballots Bay
Langvlei
Island Lake
WILDERNESS NATIONAL PARK
Swartvlei
7 Passes Road
Groenvlei
Sedgefield
GOUKAMMA NATURE RESERVE
Brenton-on-Sea
Buffels Bay
Walker's Bay
FEATHERBED NATURE RESERVE
Knysna
Knysna Lagoon
Noetzie
Noetsie-river
SINCLAIR NATURE RESERVE
YSTERNEK NATURE RESERVE
LELIEVLEI NATURE RESERVE
Diepwalle
Garden of Eden Pass
KEURBOOMS RIVER NATURE RESERVE
The Crags
To Tsitsikamma National Park
NATURE'S VALLEY NAT'L PARK
Keurboomstrand
Plettenberg Bay
Plettenberg Bay
ROBBERG NATURE RESERVE
Little Brak River
Mossel Bay
Seal Island
Mossel Bay
Post Office Tree
Driving Route
Pass
Peak
Surfing
Trail
NAMIBIA
BOTSWANA
MOZAMBIQUE
SWAZILAND
LESOTHO
SOUTH AFRICA
INDIAN OCEAN
Area of map at right
Cape Town
Prince Albert
Swartberg Pass
Die Hel
Gamkaskloof
Cango Caves
Cango Ostrich Farm
Schoemanshoek
Oudtshoorn
Meiringspoort Pass
Willowmore
Steytlerville
EASTERN CAPE
BAVIAANSKLOOFBERGE
KOUGABERGE
WESTERN CAPE
K L E I N K A R O O
Outeniqua Pass
Montagu Pass
Blanco
George
WILDERNESS NATIONAL PARK
Knysna
Keurboom-strand
Botlierskop Game Reserve
Victoria Bay
Plettenberg Bay
Mossel Bay
Mossel Bay
Albertina
Vleesbaai
Gouritsmond
REINSGOURIQUA NATURE RESERVE
Area shown above
INDIAN OCEAN
Grootrivier Pass
Nature's Valley
Flip se Baai
Storms River Mouth
TSITSIKAMMA FOREST NATIONAL PARK
TSITSIKAMMA COASTAL NATIONAL PARK
Skuitbaai
To Port Elizabeth
0 25 mi
0 25 km

Fun Facts Feather Barons & Ostrich Palaces

It was the ostrich that put the Klein Karoo on the map: During the late 19th and early 20th centuries, when the world decided that ostrich feathers were simply the hautest of haute, Oudtshoorn, where the first ostriches were farmed, found itself crowned the feather capital of the world. Local ostrich farmers, known then as "feather barons," became millionaires overnight, building themselves luxurious "ostrich palaces," clearly identifiable by their sandstone turrets and other baroque touches. Sadly, the boom went bang in 1914, with the sobering outbreak of World War I. The profitable trade in feathers never really recovered, with fickle Dame Fashion seeking her postwar inspiration elsewhere, but with the current health scares surrounding red meat, the ostrich is again enjoying a surge in popularity—it's a delicious and low-fat alternative to beef, and bears absolutely no resemblance to chicken.

By Train The **Blue Train** stops at Oudtshoorn on its Garden Route Tour (see chapters 3 and 4). The **Shosholoza Meyl** from Cape Town to East London stops at Prince Albert Road station, but you'll need someone to pick you up (it's still a couple of dozen kilometers from town). A Sunday-only economy service that takes over 7 hours, it's only for the hardy.

GETTING AROUND **Avis** (✆ **044/272-4727**) has an office on Baron van Rheede Street. If you need shuttle service, call **Boulder's Lodge** (✆ **044/272-5559**).

SPECIAL EVENTS Every March and April, Oudtshoorn hosts the **Klein Karoo National Arts Festival (KunsteFees)** ★★★, one of the biggest and best cultural festivals in South Africa. Contact the Tourism Bureau for more information.

What to See & Do

With the introduction of wire fencing and sweet lucerne, the large-scale domestication of the ostrich first became possible in the 1800s. But it was only when Victorian fashion victims developed an insatiable appetite for ostrich feathers around 1880 that it became a reality, and land values in the Oudtshoorn area shot up overnight. At the height of the feather boom, the so-called feather barons built lavish town houses where they would occasionally overnight before returning to their marble-floored farmhouses.

The best preserved of these "ostrich palaces" (albeit not the grandest) is the **Le Roux Town House,** a satellite of the CP Nel Museum, where you can peruse photographs of other houses that didn't survive the 20th century. Fortunately, more of these magnificent sandstone buildings survived than were knocked down; though most are closed to the public, they're worth walking or driving past (you can pick up a map from the tourism office). Note, particularly, **Pinehurst,** on Jan van Riebeeck Street, now part of a teachers' training college, and the elegant **Mimosa,** on Baron van Reede Street. The latter street becomes the R328, which leads out of town to the ostrich farms (see below), the **Rust-en-Vrede waterfall** (a 74m/243-ft. drop under which you can cool off in summer), and the Cango Caves, Oudtshoorn's biggest attraction after the ostrich. Animal lovers who don't object to animals in enclosures can caress cheetahs—or have close encounters with crocodiles—at the Cango Wildlife Ranch, while early risers can meet the tiny stars from the Meerkat Magic Conservation Project.

For a tiny Karoo *dorpie,* nearby Prince Albert also has a surprising number of things to do. Besides the restaurants and galleries, two experiences come highly recommended: a dusk **Ghost Tour** that winds through town (with Ailsa Tudhope; ✆ **023/541-1211**) and an adrenalin-charged **cycle down the mighty Swartberg pass** (Lindsay will provide the bikes and drive you to the top; [✆ **082/456-8848**]). Cheese lovers should also stop at **Gay's Dairy** (✆ **023/541-1703**) to taste the produce from Gay's lovely herd of Guernseys, while those with a sweet tooth must make a point of stopping at **SoetKaroo** (56 Church St; ✆ **023/5411768**), a small vineyard in the center of town, where Herman and Susan Perold produce a Red Muscat d'Alexandrie, a traditional dessert wine, bottled in gorgeous decanters.

Arbeidsgenot ★★ Arbeidsgenot (meaning "The Pleasure of Work") is not a feather palace, but the humble abode of C. J. Langenhoven, author of South Africa's first national anthem, and his family from 1901 to 1950. It's a delightfully authentic house museum, not least because everything has been left as it was when the man penned his noteworthy novels and poems. It's a tranquil place to spend a half-hour.

217 Jan van Riebeeck Rd. ✆ **044/272-2968.** R15 adults, R10 children. Mon–Fri 9am–noon and 2–4pm.

The Cango Caves ★★ Kids The **Cango Caves** were first explored in 1780 by a local farmer who was lowered into the dark, bat-filled chamber, which is now named in his honor. The **Van Zyl Hall,** 107m (351 ft.) across and 16m (52 ft.) high, has some incredible million-year-old limestone formations, including the Organ Pipes. A second chamber was discovered in 1792, and a century later the caves opened as a tourist attraction. Regrettably, they were damaged in the 1960s and 1970s, when the floors were evened out with concrete; ladders, colored lights, and music were installed; and a separate entrance was opened for "nonwhites" (who had tours at different times).

Today the caves enjoy a slightly more respectful treatment, with wardens fighting an ongoing battle to keep the limestone formations from discoloring from exposure to lights and human breath (although their running commentary is a tad irritating). There are two tours to choose from: the hour-long standard tour, which departs every hour and visits six chambers; and the 90-minute adventure tour, which covers just more than 1km (a little over a half-mile), some of which must be crawled (under no circumstances tackle this if you're overweight or claustrophobic; have heart, knee, or breathing problems; or are not wearing sensible shoes and trousers).

Approximately 30km (19 miles) from town on the R328. ✆ **044/272-7410.** www.cangocaves.co.za. Standard tour R55; Adventure tour R70. Daily 9am–4pm; last tour departs 3:30pm. Closed Dec 25.

Cango Wildlife Ranch ★ Kids Animal lovers of all ages will enjoy this well-regarded animal park (the animals may be on show, but the ranch is involved in breeding programs to help build up cheetah, Bengal tiger, and pigmy hippo numbers). Entrance fees allow you to wander on wooden walkways through the Valley of the Ancients past various tropical species, plus crocodiles, lemurs, and a pigmy hippo "village." Besides the opportunity for those over 16 to stroke cheetah (and kids over 12 to pet baby lion, tiger, or cheetah cubs, if available), the ranch's key claim to fame is the world's only crocodile cage diving facility on the planet (children from 12 years can participate with an adult). You'll be lowered into a clear, heated pool that contains five full-grown crocs—they promise you'll get close enough to see their toenails.

Off the R328, en route to the Cango Caves. ✆ **044/272-5593.** www.cango.co.za. R95 adults, R60 children 4–15; children under 4 free. Big cat/crocodile encounters R145–R300 extra per person. Booking required for groups of 10 or more. Daily 8am–4:30pm.

CP Nel Museum ★ Located in a handsome sandstone building opposite the Tourist Information Bureau, this old-fashioned museum has many exhibits relating to Oudtshoorn's boom period, as well as photographs of some of the ostrich palaces that never made it past the 1950s. It also houses a synagogue and exhibits relating to Oudtshoorn's once-large Jewish community—in fact, Oudtshoorn was often derisively referred to as Little Jerusalem by those envious of the success of the feather merchants, most of whom were Jewish. Admission includes entry to the **Le Roux Town House,** a mini feather palace on High Street. Built in 1909, the interior features some original pieces dating back to the Le Roux family's heyday, but the majority of the furnishings—imported from Europe between 1900 and 1920—have been bought and placed *in situ* by the museum.

Corner of Baron van Rheede St. and Voortrekker Rd. ✆ **044/272-7306.** R12 adults, R3 children under 13. Mon–Fri 8am–5pm; Sat 9am–1pm.

Meerkat Magic ★★★ The Oudtshoorn meerkats (also known as suricates) have starred in *National Geographic,* BBC, and Discovery Channel documentaries, but meeting them in person is far more satisfying. Grant Mc Ilrath, a.k.a. The Meerkat Man (he has been researching these fascinating creatures for over 15 years), will take you on a sunrise walking tour to a meerkat den and explain their habits and social interactions. The only problem, as with all wild animals, is that the meerkats may not be around when you want them to be—so it's essential to confirm your booking with Grant by 3pm the evening before, and then wait for confirmation that the tour will take place. This is not the kind of tour to try and organize if you're staying in the area only overnight. ***Note:*** Getting hold of Grant can take time: SMS messages are the best form of communication; alternatively, ask your guesthouse if they can help.

✆ **044/272-3077** or 082/413-6895. www.meerkatmagic.com. Price depends on a number of variables, but tours start at R1,200 per person; SMS or e-mail Grant at gmmcilrath@mweb.co.za for details. The fee helps fund conservation work. Bring sunscreen and hats. Advance reservations essential.

Visiting an Ostrich Farm

The ostrich remains the primary source of income for Oudtshoorn, with thousands flocking to see, touch, eat, and (yes) even ride the giant birds. There are some 400 ostrich farms. Highgate (incidentally, the biggest ostrich farm in the world), Safari, Oudtshoorn, and Cango all vie for the tourist buck—R50 to R60, to be exact—offering more or less the same 45- to 80-minute tour. These include an explanation of ostrich farming (from incubation to tanning), guided tours of the farm, the opportunity to sit on an ostrich and stand on its eggs, and an ostrich derby. All offer meals with ostrich on the menu (you usually need to prebook).

Of the farms, **Cango Ostrich Farm** ★★ (✆ **044/272-4623**) is considered by many to be the best, not least because of its location overlooking the beautiful Schoemanshoek Valley. Individuals are not tagged onto large tour groups, and visitors take a brief walk from one process to the next rather than being driven around a large farm. Finally, while you can sit on an ostrich, they are not raced here, saving you the embarrassment of this circus display (if you'd like to see this for anthropological reasons, opt for **Highgate** (✆ **044/272-7115;** www.highgate.co.za), the world's oldest and largest show farm. The 45-minute tours (R56) take place daily from 9am to 5pm; reserve ahead and enjoy a lunch or dinner served in restored laborers' cottages with great views overlooking the valley, where you get a wine tasting with your meal and sample the distinctive flavors of the Klein Karoo.

A Breathtaking Drive ★★★

For many, the greatest highlight of visiting the Klein Karoo is traversing the Swartberg Mountains to Prince Albert, a charming 18th-century Groot Karoo town that lies 100km (62 miles) north.

To reach the **Swartberg Pass** ★★★, a 27km (17-mile) gravel road built more than 100 years ago by master engineer Thomas Bain, take the R328 (also known as Cango Valley Rd.) north from Oudtshoorn. About 1km (a little more than a half-mile) before the road terminates at the Cango Caves, you'll find a turnoff to the west, signposted PRINCE ALBERT. This marks the start of the pass, which soon begins its steep ascent. By the time you reach the summit, you will have enjoyed stupendous views of the Klein Karoo, which lies some 1,220m (4,002 ft.) below. Stop to gird your loins, for the journey has only just begun. The northern descent is hair-raising—10km (6¼ miles) of zigzags, serpentines, twists, and steep gradients on a narrow dirt road with nothing between you and the abyss but a good grip on the wheel. You'll note a turnoff to the west that will take you to **Die Hell (Gamkaskloof)** ★★★. This is another magnificent drive, particularly popular with fynbos lovers, but unless you overnight in one of the rudimentary Cape Nature Conservation cottages, you'll have to return the way you came. Set aside most of the day for this detour.

The road continues to twist and turn before finally winding its way out of the Swartberg. At this point, you can either go to Prince Albert or turn back into the mountains and return to Oudtshoorn via Meiringspoort. Opt for **Prince Albert** ★★★; the town is an architectural gem, with almost all the buildings preserved and maintained in their original 19th-century form. If you're in need of tranquillity or wish to wander the streets at sunset to view the mix of architectural styles, consider spending the night (see below) or contact **Prince Albert's Tourism Information,** Church Street (✆ **023/541-1366;** Mon–Fri 9am–6:30pm, Sat 9am–1pm).

To return to Oudtshoorn, take the road back to the Swartberg Pass, keeping an eye out for the R407, which takes you east through Meiringspoort. This is another spectacular drive, though this time the views are up.

In prehistoric times, the Great Karoo was a swamp that apparently broke through to the sea at Meiringspoort. The majestic **Meiringspoort Pass** ★, a natural ravine created by the course of what came to be known as the Groot River, features soaring cliffs and spectacular rock formations. The 25km (16-mile) tarred road follows and crosses the river several times as it winds along the floor of the gorge.

To explore the area on foot, Erika Calitz and **CapeNature** (✆ **083/628-9394;** www.donkeytrail.com) offer a guided 4-day, 26km (16-mile) hiking trail from Calitzdorp over the Swartberg and to Die Hel; your gear is transported by rescued, rehabilitated donkeys.

Where to Stay & Dine In & Around Oudtshoorn

With the exception of Rosenhof Country House, most options described in detail below are located outside Oudtshoorn. One in-town option in Oudsthoorn is the new, chi-chi **Pictures** (✆ **044/272-6751;** www.picturesoudtshoorn.co.za; doubles range R975–R1,600), good value for the money. You should be prepared to do a bit of driving to stay at **Die Ou Pastorie** (✆ **044/272-2493;** www.pastorie-de-hoop.com; R720–R1,820 double), if you'd like to stay in a lavishly decorated old parsonage dripping with bold color, gilt, and character. (It's 12km/7½ out of town on the R62, to be exact.) First prize here is the Studio, an enormous cavern of open-plan space with a self-catering kitchen, lounge, and countless antiques. This is an incredible interior to return to after the dusty outdoors; the only downside is that you'll have to cook or drive to find dinner. ***Note:***

Check that the room you book is en suite. Closer to town is **La Plume** (✆ **044/**272-7516**;** www.laplume.co.za; R1,100–R1,820 double), a Victorian guesthouse on a working ostrich and cattle farm with some tasteful and comfortable accommodations, particularly the four honeymoon and one superior suites, and good Karoo cuisine and service. Lastly, nature lovers who don't mind being on their own may like the compact two-bedroom timber cabins on a bird-filled dam at **De Zeekoe** (✆ **044/272-6721;** www.dezeekoe.co.za; R800–R1,140 double). These are self-catering, but 5 minutes down the road is the restaurant, a wonderful pool, and more modern accommodations (note that the luxury rooms aren't huge but probably offer better value than the superiors, which are close to twice the price, at R2,400 double). De Zeekoe also has strong links with Grant McIlrath of Meerkat Magic (see above)—the meerkats sometimes live on the property's reserve.

Buffelsdrift Game Lodge ★ Sanbona (see "Route 62: The Best Road Trip in South Africa" sidebar, above) is the best Big 5 reserve in the Western Cape; the others are mini reserves, all offering a tiny taste of what it is to be on a real safari. Of these, Buffelsdrift is the best. (Other contenders are **Buffalo Hills,** just outside Plettenberg Bay [www.buffalohills.co.za], and **Botlierskop,** near Mossel Bay [www.botlierskop.co.za]; see below). Malaria-free Buffelsdrift has three of the Big 5 on its 3,000 hectares (7,413 acres) and the best-dressed accommodations of the bunch: spacious en-suite tents, tastefully furnished and built on the edge of a dam. Book a "superior"—nine tents ranged along the edge, so you're likely to see game ambling down for a drink while you're doing the same on your deck (nos. 7, 8, and 9 are closest to the game area). The lodge offers the de rigueur morning and evening bush safari drive, where the focus is on plants and the environment as well as animals, but you should see buffalo, rhino, giraffe, and zebra, as well as plenty of antelope. If you miss the elephants in the wild, you can still walk or feed tame rescued youngsters. Buffelsdrift is conveniently situated if you can't include a safari in the Eastern Cape or Kruger. It's so tranquil it's hard to believe you're only 7km (4¼ miles) from Oudtshoorn. Day visitors are also welcome.

Off R328, on the way to Cango Caves. ✆ **044/272-0106.** Fax 044/272-0108. www.buffelsdrift.com. 25 units. From R1,960–R3,980 double, depending on season; ask about specials. Rates include breakfast, dinner, and game drives. Longer stays include other activities. AE, DC, MC, V. **Amenities:** Restaurant, bar; chapel; game drives; helipad; horse trails and walks; high-speed Internet (R20 per 15 minutes); pool; room service; spa treatments. *In room:* A/C, minibar.

Jemima's ★★★ SOUTH AFRICAN INNOVATIVE Long rated the best restaurant in the Klein Karoo, this Oudtshoorn restaurant is still in the capable hands of Pierre and Debbie Malherbe, although (like most places) prices have jumped over the past few years. You'll still find good traditional South African fare with innovative twists, such as snoek samosas with curried peach salad, a Karoo lamb platter with a "drunken apricot" in muscatel jus, and the ostrich tango: a combination of filet tartare and carpaccio shavings. Pierre calls himself a "locavore": All fresh produce comes directly from farms nearby.

94 Baron van Reede St. ✆ **044/272-0808.** www.jemimas.com. Main courses R90–R175 dinner. AE, DC MC, V. Lunch Mon–Fri 11am–3pm; dinner daily from 6pm.

Kalinka ★★ SOUTH AFRICAN CONTEMPORARY Snapping at Jemima's heels for the title of best restaurant in town is this cozy, stylish restaurant located in a sandstone house on the main road. Russian-born Olga and her mom dish up innovative meals with flair and charm; besides a reputable Vodka selection and—on occasion—caviar pancakes, the menu has a strong South African focus, featuring venison.

93 Baron van Reede St. ✆ **044/279-2596.** www.kalinka.co.za. Main courses R80–R160 dinner. MC, V. Daily from 6pm.

Retreat at Groenfontein ★★ If you believe that real luxury is a star-spangled sky, with no noise or light pollution and crystal-clear air, then the Retreat must be part of your itinerary. Book one of the garden suites (nos. 8 or 9), and all you'll want to do is relax on your veranda and gaze at the sublime Swartberg mountains that surround you. The Retreat is literally that—a long, bumpy, satisfying drive along scenic dirt roads that end in this secluded valley, with nothing in it but a Victorian farmhouse, floating above pretty gardens, and a warm welcome from your hosts, Marie and Grant. If you crave solitude and walks to pristine streams or peaks—yes, you really are the only outpost for miles—this is the perfect place. Dinners, served communally, are wonderfully convivial, and the conversation flows as freely as the wine. There isn't a plethora of servants, and the decor isn't anything you'll find in a design magazine, but the atmosphere is homey and warm, with such considerate touches as early morning tea or coffee served in a flask and left outside your door.

Follow signs from R62 btw. Oudtshoorn and Calitzdorp. ✆/fax **044/213-3880.** www.groenfontein.com. 8 units. High season R1,340–R1,740 double; low season R1,300–R1,700 double. Rates include breakfast and dinner. DC, MC, V. **Amenities:** Dining room; free high-speed Internet; lounge/library; pool; room service; marked trails. *In room:* Fireplace (in some), no phone reception.

Rosenhof Country House ★★ This is the most upscale place to stay in Oudtshoorn itself: a calm, gracious oasis beautifully furnished with selected works by famous (white) South African artists, and in springtime, a rose-filled garden that saturates the air. Rooms are built around a courtyard, each with its own entrance. Though each has a different theme, they share the most important characteristics: space, beautiful linens, well-sprung beds, and elegant, traditional taste. The courtyard contains a large pool—a necessity during the searing summer heat (book one of two vast suites for your own private pool and fireplace). The staff is eager to please, especially at mealtimes: Dinners are a five-course affair (R270) served in the original 1852 homestead, with local ingredients and herbs picked fresh from the garden.

264 Baron van Reede St., Oudtshoorn 6620. ✆ **044/272-2232.** Fax 044/272-3021. www.rosenhof.co.za. 14 units. R1,980–R2,800 double; R2,750–R3,800 suite. Rates include breakfast. AE, DC, MC, V. Children by prior arrangement only. **Amenities:** Dining room; bar; lounge; exercise room, gallery; pool; room service; spa and sauna. *In room:* A/C, TV, minibar, free Wi-Fi.

PRINCE ALBERT ★★★

This is arguably the Cape's most charming Karoo *dorpie* (little village), with wonderfully preserved Cape frontier architecture; it can be reached as a day trip from Oudtshoorn (or even Wilderness), but I'd opt to overnight here rather than in Oudtshoorn. That said, it's perhaps not as authentic as Oudtshoorn; the village is very much "discovered," and the vast majority of its community is transplanted here—people who fell in love with the low-key atmosphere and irrigation canal-lined streets, and saw the tourism potential. As a result, there are numerous places to stay, most of them good. My top choice is **Dennehof Guesthouse ★★** (✆ **023/541-1227;** www.dennehof.co.za), a tranquil oasis in an 1835 farmstead on the outskirts of the village that is said to be the oldest surviving building in town; try to book the gorgeously renovated Wagon Shed (R700–R860 double, including breakfast; other room prices vary). Ria and Lindsay are not only very good at running their "Karoo chic" guesthouse, but they act as an informal tourism bureau for the area.

If you'd prefer to be in the heart of the village, a good option is **Saxe-Coburg Lodge** (✆ **023/541-1267;** www.saxecoburg.co.za; R720–R820 double), particularly the Victoria or Albert garden rooms. **Onse Rus** (✆ **023/541-1380;** www.onserus.co.za; R820 double) is far more basic but has character, a fascinating history (one of the rooms once housed the town newspaper's printing press), and a super hostess; just be aware some bathrooms are extremely small and basic. But probably the best deal in town is the gorgeous, three-bed cottage **Vergeet-My-Niet** ★, 8 De Beer St. (✆ **023/541-1069** or 083/316-4015; R500—R560 double). Tucked away on a quiet street but within walking distance of restaurants and museums, it's filled with lovely furniture and has a great fireplace, a garden, and a dam with geese. If you like your luxuries, head straight for **De Bergkant Lodge and Cottages** ★★, 5 Church St., Prince Albert (✆ **023/541-1088;** www.debergkant.co.za; R1,000–R2,000 double, depending on season; no children under 12). In a Cape Dutch national monument (with a few rooms in the new Georgian-style extension), with lovely antiques, two large saltwater swimming pools, two outdoor "star baths," and a wellness center, De Bergkant is the most upmarket guesthouse in the village. It's delightful, but I'm not sure it's worth the price (double what you'll pay elsewhere).

If you are overnighting, try to make sure it's on one of the nights that the **Olive Branch** is open (bookings depend on reservation numbers, so call **023/541-1821** and beg). This is a real family-run country-kitchen restaurant with unlikely chef Bakkie Botha at the helm. At around R190 for five courses, it's an exceptional value. Alternatively, dine on real Karoo fare (traditional *bobotie*—lightly curried ground beef cooked in a savory egg custard and served with yellow rice, Karoo lamb pie, chicken pie, or Karoo leg of lamb, followed by sticky malva pudding or steamed lemon pudding) in the wonderfully camp, over-the-top atmosphere of **Karoo Kombuis.** Be warned, you may be asked to don a hat from the selection on hand (✆ **023/541-1110;** dinner Mon–Sat; main courses R65; no credit cards; BYOB). With its wider menu, emphasis on fresh local ingredients, and convivial setting, newcomer **Gallery Café** (✆ **082/749-2128;** dinner only) is pulling in both punters and compliments (if it's warm, book a table on the veranda overlooking Church St.). The butternut and sage soup is a favorite; you will also always find poultry, venison, and lamb (a rack crusted with almonds, feta, and oregano was on offer the day I stopped by) and—scarce in the Karoo—a number of vegetarian options. Plus delectable homemade ice cream.

ENTERING THE GARDEN ROUTE—MOSSEL BAY

Traveling east on the N2, the first sign of the fast-approaching town of Mossel Bay, unofficial entry point of the Garden Route (officially, it starts at Heidelberg), is the sci-fi spectacle of the MossGas oil plant on your left. Although it has a few interesting attractions, the town does not really improve on closer inspection, so don't go out of your way if you're pressed for time. Mossel Bay is approximately 4 hours from Cape Town on the N2, and 20 minutes from George.

What to See & Do

Mossel Bay was the site of the first European landing on the South African coast, when Bartholomieu Dias, having battled a fearsome storm, tacked in for water and safety in 1488. **The Bartholomieu Dias Museum Complex** (✆ **044/691-1067**) comprises a collection of historic buildings, of which the **Maritime Museum** is excellent. It relates the early Portuguese-seafaring history (which is a bit text heavy) and houses a life-size replica of the caravel in which Dias set sail in 1487—it's hard to imagine going where no

Fun Facts The Original Snail Mail

Outside the Maritime Museum is the **Post Office Tree,** South Africa's first post office. In 1501, the first of many sailors sent his mail by leaving a letter stuffed in an old boot and tied to what the city fathers claim is this particular milkwood tree. Soon this became an informal postal system, with letters picked up by passing ships and distributed accordingly. Today you can post a letter in a boot-shaped post box and it will be stamped with a special postmark.

man has gone before in something that looks like a large toy. The ship on display was built in Portugal and sailed from Lisbon to Mossel Bay in 1987 to commemorate the 500th anniversary of Dias's arrival on southern Cape soil. The museum, located on Market Street, is open Monday through Friday from 8:15am to 5pm, and Saturday and Sunday from 9am to 4pm. Admission is R10, or R25 including access to the ship.

Mossel Bay is also one of the best places along the coast to get up close and personal with a great white shark (see "Staying Active," earlier in this chapter). If you'd prefer your ocean interlude with a little less adrenaline, contact **Seven Seas** (© **044/691-3371**) or **Romanza** (© **044/690-3101**) for whale-watching cruises or trips to Seal Island; a 60-minute cruise is about R100. For more information, contact the **Tourism Bureau** (© **044/691-2202;** www.visitmosselbay.co.za; Mon–Fri 8am–6pm, Sat–Sun 9am–4pm), in the historical center, at the corner of Church and Market streets.

If you're hungry, the newly refurbished **Cafe Gannet** (© **044/691-1885;** open daily), across the road from the main museums and the Tourism Bureau, is a good choice for seafood fans. For a finer dining experience, head 6km (3¾ miles) out of town to **Stonehill** (© **044/696-6501;** daily 7am–10pm), just a few hundred meters to your left after you've taken the Little Brak River turnoff from the N2 toward George. The Provençal/Mediterranean-inspired menu earned Stonehill a mention in *Dine* magazine's top 100 Restaurants in South Africa, and the beef Wellington with wild mushroom ragout is particularly recommended.

Where to Stay

Mossel Bay is far from pretty, and you'd be better off pushing on to Wilderness, with one possible exception: nearby Little Brak River. First-time safari-goers with no time to go farther north could stop at **Botlierskop** (© **044/696-6055;** www.botlierskop.co.za; R4,214–R7,040 double, including meals and local beverages; ask about specials). Accommodations are in 15 tents (units 11, 12, and 13 are right on the river), and the lodge itself is a good-looking thatch-and-stone structure with views. Games drives are included, but the lions and elephants are not free roaming, and getting to the main game-viewing area can take a while. Certainly don't bother if you've experienced true wilderness or you can get to the Eastern Cape or Kruger areas. Game-viewing aside, it's an attractive, if pricey, option (note that Buffelsdrift, near Oudtshoorn, offers a better-value "tame" safari). Day visitors are also welcomed with game drives, horseback safaris, helicopter flights, and elephant rides.

GEORGE & WILDERNESS

Halfway between Cape Town and Port Elizabeth, the sprawling city of George won't win any beauty competitions, but it has a majestic mountain backdrop and is the commercial heart of the Garden Route, with the most transport connections and a large choice of restaurants. It's not worth overnighting in this inland town, however, as its attractions are few and far from scintillating, and the coastal town of Wilderness, with a number of lovely lodging options, is just a 10-minute drive away. From Wilderness, Knysna lies 20 minutes east, while Plettenberg Bay is just under an hour away. Given its proximity to Oudtshoorn, it makes a good base if you'd prefer to unpack for a few days and explore, rather than hop from place to place.

Essentials

VISITOR INFORMATION **The George Tourism Bureau** (**✆ 044/801-9295;** www.visitgeorge.co.za; Mon–Fri 8am–5pm, Sat 9am–1pm) is at 124 York St. ***Note:*** It's not essential to stop here; Knysna has an excellent tourism bureau.

GETTING THERE **By Air** You can fly to **George Airport** (**✆ 044/876-9310**) daily from the major centers (including Cape Town, Johannesburg, and Durban) with **SAA** (**✆ 044/801-8434**) and its subsidiaries. Budget airlines servicing George are **1Time** and **Kulula.com.**

By Train Spoornet Shosholoza has just introduced a **Premier Classe** train (**✆ 021/449-2252;** www.premierclasse.co.za) from Cape Town to Port Elizabeth, which leaves every Friday at 3pm and will deposit you in George at around 5am the next morning; fares for this distance cost between R800 and R1,050. If you've got money to burn, board the beautiful Edwardian **Rovos Rail** (**✆ 012/315-8242;** www.rovos.co.za), which does the 24-hour run from Cape Town to George—a beautiful route, with a wine- or brandy-tasting stop—but it runs only four times a year, in October, November, February, and March. Tickets are from R6,000 to R12,000 per person, sharing; the top rate is for the 16-sq.-m (172-sq.-ft.) Royal Suite.

By Bus The intercity buses (**Intercape, Greyhound, Translux,** and **Baz Bus**) travel from Cape Town along the Garden Route to Port Elizabeth. See chapter 3 for regional numbers.

GETTING AROUND **By Car** Choose from one of six companies offering rental cars at the airport, including **Avis** (**✆ 044/876-9314**), **Budget** (**✆ 044/876-9204**), and **Hertz** (**✆ 044/801-4700**).

GUIDED TOURS **By Bus** **Eco Afrika** (**✆ 082/558-9104;** www.eco-afrika-tours.co.za) offers a large variety of tours, from township visits and golf tours to photographic safaris and adventure tours.

By Train You can travel between Mossel Bay and George on the **Choo-Tjoe steam train;** for details, see below. Another fun option is to trundle to the top of the scenic Montagu Pass in an **Outeniqua Power Van** (**✆ 044/801-8239**)—a little motorized trolley used for rail inspections; the trip takes 3 hours (with a 45-min. stop on the mountain for a BYO picnic).

By Air **On Air Helicopter Tours** (**✆ 072/842-5241** or 044/874-5432; www.onairtours.co.za) offers helicopter charters covering a range of attractions, from the ostrich farms and Cango Caves of Oudtshoorn, to flights over the coast to Knysna, Noetzie, and Plettenberg Bay.

What to See & Do

The best reason to be in George itself is to board the **Choo-Tjoe steam train** (**✆ 044/801-8288**). It used to run between George and Knysna, but after extensive flood damage to this line in 2006, only the George-to–Mossel Bay line remains up and running. If you don't wish to do the return journey, you can board in George (it runs Mon–Sat, leaving at 10am), then do the return journey by road with **Kontours** (✆ **082/569-8997;** www.kontours.co.za). ***Note:*** Train spotters and vintage-car lovers could probably spend the better part of the day examining the locomotives and cars in the **Outeniqua Transport Museum** (✆ **044/801-8202**), adjacent to the platform where the Choo-Tjoe and Outeniqua Power Vans depart and arrive.

You are spoiled for choice when it comes to the number of **excellent drives** leading out of George (or nearby Wilderness). To do a circular route to Oudtshoorn, take the **Outeniqua Pass** (or R29) to Oudtshoorn, and then return via the **Montagu Pass,** a gravel road dating back to 1843. If you're heading to Wilderness or Knysna, consider taking the **Seven Passes Road** ★★. This, the original road linking George and Knysna, lacks the great sea views of the N2, but it takes you through dense indigenous forests, crosses streams via a number of quaint Edwardian bridges, and finally traverses the **Homtini Pass,** another engineering feat by the famous Thomas Baines. Alternatively, head down the N2 for the most direct route to the pretty town of Wilderness—15km (9¼ miles) away via the lush **Kaaimans River Pass.**

Wilderness is anything but, with a residential development creeping up the forested hills that overlook the Touw River estuary, and a string of ugly mansions lining the beach; yet it is effectively an island within the national park, and still the smallest and by far most tranquil of the coastal towns along the Garden Route—hence the proliferation of B&Bs over the years. Set around the mouth of the Touw River, it marks the western end of a chain of lakes that stretches some 40km (25 miles) east, most of which are under the control of **Wilderness National Park.** Although the beaches along this stretch are magnificent, strong currents regularly claim unsuspecting and inexperienced swimmers. You're better off floating in the waters of the **Serpentine,** the waterway that links Island Lake, Langvlei, and Rondevlei to the Wilderness lagoon. Don't be put off by the tea-colored water or frothy bubbles; these are caused by plant oxides and oxygenation, and the water is perfectly clean.

You can explore the area on foot on a number of trails that take from 1 to 4 hours to walk, or cover some 15km (9¼ miles) of inland waterways in a canoe. **Wilderness National Park** (✆ **044/877-1197**) issues trail maps (for guided canoe trips; see "Staying Active," earlier in the chapter). To reach the park, follow signs off the N2, 2km (1¼ miles) east of Wilderness; should you wish to overnight in the park, see review below. For details, contact the helpful **Wilderness Tourism Information Bureau** (✆ **044/877-0045;** www.wildernessinfo.co.za; Mon–Fri 8am–5 or 6pm, Sat 9am–1pm).

Where to Stay

In George

Fancourt Hotel and Country Club Estate ★★★ Kids This is without a doubt the best address in George (though Pezula in Knysna has stolen much of its thunder), and a key destination for golfers. Host of the 2003 President's Cup, Fancourt boasts four excellent golf courses. Three designed by Gary Player (two of them consistently rated among the top in South Africa) are open only to guests. Besides the golf academy, rated the best in the country, there is a fabulous health spa. You don't have to be a golfer to appreciate the luxurious atmosphere, lovely setting, and helpful staff. Rooms are either in the original manor house or set in the beautifully landscaped gardens. Not much differentiates them, other than price; rooms are smaller in the manor house, but they are closer to all amenities. ***Note:*** Land's End Guest House (see below) has purchased a two-bedroom garden suite on the 18th fairway of the Montagu course, about 250m (820 ft.) from the hotel. The lodge costs about R1,500 a night for two people, representing great savings.

Montagu St., Blanco, George. ✆ **044/804-0000.** Fax 044/804-0700. www.fancourt.co.za. 100-plus units. R3,940 standard double; R5,550 1-bedroom garden suite; R9,490 2-bedroom garden suite; R12,625 presidential suite. Ask about discounted winter rates. AE, DC, MC, V. **Amenities:** 4 restaurants; 4 bars; babysitting; mountain bikes and 6km (3¾-mile) trail; children's programs; 4 golf courses; 4 (2 heated) swimming pools; room service; spa; 4 tennis courts. *In room:* A/C, TV, minibar, hair dryer, Wi-Fi (R50 for 30 minutes).

In Victoria Bay

Land's End Guest House ★ Finds "The Closest B&B to the Sea in Africa," it trumpets, and at 6m (20 ft.) from the high-water mark, this is no doubt true. Land's End is the last house on the only residential road in Vic Bay (a tiny bay with a sandy beach that lies btw. George and Wilderness); beyond lie the rocks and the ocean, and beside you is the safest swimming bay for miles around. The guesthouse is run in a very laid-back manner (the proprietor is a surfer) and furnished in a homey fashion, with such lovely touches as complimentary sherry. The views from the two self-catering units, each with private deck, are fantastic; try to book these rather than the downstairs rooms. ***Note:*** Land's End also owns a two-bedroom garden suite, Lodge 743, at Fancourt (see above), and other self-catering accommodations in Vic Bay.

Beach Rd., Victoria Bay. ✆ **044/889-0123.** Fax 044/889-0141. www.vicbay.com. 4 units. Rates average about R1,100 per room, ask about low-season specials. Half-price for children under 12. AE, MC, V. At the end of Beach Rd., Victoria Bay. **Amenities:** Dining room/bar; watersports equipment rental. *In room:* TV, hair dryer, minibar.

In Wilderness

Wilderness is always peaceful—even in peak season—and conveniently situated within striking distance of the Klein Karoo and day trips to Knysna and surrounds. But nothing good stays secret in an area this popular, and as a result there's been an explosion in accommodations options, particularly on the beach. In addition to the two reviewed below, consider the ocean-facing rooms at **Whales Way** (✆ **044/877-0482;** www.whalesway.co.za; high season R1,000–R2,400; low season R950–2,000). Note that a small avenue separates you from the beach. Another heavily decorated but luxurious beach option is **Xanadu** (✆ **044/877-0022;** www.xanadu-wilderness.co.za; R1,000–R3,000 double). Lashings of gilt, heavy drapes, and padded headboards are offset by the sumptuous location right on the beach (and the presidential suite really is outrageously outfitted). Just down the road, the **Great White Beach House** (✆ **044/877-1084;** www.greatwhitebb.co.za; high season R1,100–R1,360 double; no children under 16) takes the decor to the other extreme: This is a sharply sterile, tiled offering with extreme views and direct beach access; the Musselcracker and Oyster Catcher suites are the most appealing.

The Dune Guest House ★★ You know you're on holiday when you wake up and hear, smell, and see the ocean from your bed, then slide open your doors, step out onto your private patio, and pad down a short boardwalk onto an almost solitary beach that stretches as far as the eye can see. One of the few B&Bs on the entire coast that is literally right on the beach, The Dune comprises four comfortable en-suite bedrooms, each with semiprivate decks furnished with teak deck chairs, as well as a self-catering apartment for groups or families. Architecturally, the building is rather charmless, so if you're not set on a sea view or are traveling here in winter, you're better off at Moontide.

31 Die Duin, Wilderness 6560. ✆/fax **044/877-0298.** www.thedune.co.za. 5 units. R800–R1,700 double, depending on season. Rates include breakfast. MC, V. Children by prior arrangement only. **Amenities:** Lounge; pool. *In room:* Fans, TV, minibar, under-floor heating, free Wi-Fi.

Ichibi Lakeside Lodge ★★ A few kilometers' drive from the beach, town, or restaurants, Ichibi is aimed at style-conscious travelers who want to escape from the crowds. Escape you will: The quiet guesthouse is perched on 12 hectares (30 acres) overlooking Langvlei Lake, a protected natural area that is home to otters, monkeys, and fish eagles, and offers two enormous suites and one smaller room. The look is clean and minimal, but softened with rich fabrics and ancient oriental artifacts, and there are some beautiful lounges and a heated pool to drift in. As a beautiful retreat and base from which to explore the area, it can't be faulted (it was named one of the Best 100 ultimate chic collection retreats in Africa), but this is not for those who like a bit of a buzz. Marcus also offers personal safaris to such areas as the Eastern Cape and can arrange for you to play golf at Pezula or Simola.

Signposted off the N2 toward Knysna, 10 min. from Wilderness. ✆/fax **044/882-1252.** www.ichibi.co.za. 3 units. R1,320–R2,090 double, depending on room size. Rates include continental breakfast; dinner on request. MC, V. No children under 12. **Amenities:** Bar; lounges; exercise room; heated pool; free Wi-Fi. *In room:* A/C, TV/DVD, CD player, hair dryer, minibar, MP3 docking station, no phone.

Moontide Guest Lodge ★★ Finds On the banks of the Touw River, this lovely guesthouse is one of the best values on the Garden Route. The thatched homestead, with separate suites in a bird-filled garden, is set among 400-year-old milkwood trees, and all rooms have entrances that lead out into semiprivate or private seating areas. Built on stilts among the trees with glorious views, the aptly named Treetops is the most private and special option, if not the largest. Milkwood, which has a charming private alfresco seating area and very spacious bedroom (with another in the thatch) and bathroom, is another favorite. So is the luxurious Moon River, which opens onto the newly extended viewing deck and plunge pool. The cozy Boat House, a few steps from the lagoon, is small, but private and romantic. The beach is 5 minutes away.

Southside Rd. (at the end of the cul-de-sac), Wilderness. ✆ **044/877-0361.** Fax 044/877-0124. www.moontide.co.za. 9 units. High season R1,190–R1,650; low season R800–R1,020. Rates include breakfast. AE, MC, V. **Amenities:** Boat; dining room/lounge; pool. *In room:* TV, hair dryer, minibar.

Peacehaven on Sea ★ Finds This beach house, divided into four self-catering units, has been a big hit—no surprise, considering that it's on the best part of Wilderness beach, surrounded by old-style, hand-me-down family bungalows, set amid dense dune vegetation that creates a low shoreline pretty much unchanged in 40 years. Owner Deon's large house is a brash contrast, but for now it means you can wake up in your own comfortably outfitted apartment, slide open the doors, pad over the lawns past the pool, and go straight onto the (almost) deserted beach. Return to sunbathe in one of the many deck chairs on the lawns overlooking the beach.

33 Sands Rd., Wilderness. ✆ **044/877-0829** or 082/563-4885. Fax 011/894-2868. www.peacehavenonsea.co.za. 4 units R1,700–2,400 double, depending on season. Dec 10-night minimum. MC, V. **Amenities:** Airport transfers; barbecue/pizza oven; car rental; pool; housekeeping at additional cost. *In room:* TV/DVD w/surround sound, fireplace, kitchen, sitting room, free Wi-Fi.

Wilderness National Park/Ebb & Flow Value As some of the rondawels in Ebb & Flow North are very rudimentary and share washing facilities, your best options are in Ebb & Flow South, particularly the timber "forest cabins." These are slightly raised and right on the Touw River—you can almost cast for fish from your front door. All cabins now have en-suite showers, tiny kitchenettes, and barbecue areas. Of the four-bed log cottages (fully equipped if you prefer to self-cater), nos. 8 to 13 enjoy the best location, on the Serpentine River. All units are serviced daily, but you'll have to bring in your own supplies (a well-stocked Woolworth's is situated in the mall just off the N2 on the outskirts of George) or dine out. ***Note:*** Ask about the honeymoon cottages, which offer a few more creature comforts (such as DSTV).

Off N2, 2km (1¼ miles) east of Wilderness; follow signs. Bookings ✆ **012/428-9111;** direct ✆ **044/877-1197.** Fax 021/343-0905. www.sanparks.org. 49 units comprising 4-bed cottages and forest huts, and 2-bed rondawels, not all with private bathrooms. R460–R915 per unit. Camping R140–R220 double. AE, DC, MC, V.

Where to Dine

In the center of Wilderness, **The Girls** ★★ (✆ **044/877-1648;** dinner Tues–Sun), referring to owners Roxanne and Cheri, serve up a great menu, including vast numbers of fresh prawns and good seafood (order the Cajun calamari steak). The location is less than spectacular—right next to a filling station in the shadow of the N2—but this doesn't deter regulars, because the delicious food is such a great value. For more average fare, the pizzas at **Pomodoro** (✆ **044/877-1403;** daily breakfast, lunch, and dinner) aren't bad, as the full tables and constant buzz attest. It's certainly better than any of the other casual places to eat in the village.

For a finer dining experience, try **Cinnamon** (see above) or the **Serendipity** (below). For die-hard carnivores, there's **Joplin's** ★, a shack-bar (part of Pirate's Creek; look for the turnoff from the N2, just after the Wilderness turnoff; ✆ **072/292-4247**). Joplin's serves up only one dish: steak (rump, T-bone, or sirloin) topped with a fried egg (a Portuguese tradition) and served with a side order of chips.

Serendipity ★★★ **Value** INTERNATIONAL/MODERN CAPE This fine-dining spot, tucked away on a residential street, has made *Wine* magazine's top 100 restaurants list for 6 years in a row. Despite these haute credentials, it's very much a family affair: Lizelle is the young ex–Prue Leith chef; husband Rudolf is front-of-house; and the venue, a house on the banks of the lagoon, is Lizelle's parents' guesthouse. Lizelle changes the five-course set menu regularly, but expect fresh locally procured ingredients, combined with creativity and skill: Spring rolls are stuffed with ostrich *bobotie* and served with a cucumber and coriander sambal; springbok shank is braised in milk stout and accompanied by a maize risotto; and the roasted courgette and samp risotto arrives on a bed of creamy spinach. Even the crème brûlée has a twist—it's sometimes made with Amarula (a local version of Baileys Irish Cream).

Freesia Ave. (off Waterside Rd.), Wilderness ✆ **044/877-0433.** www.serendipitywilderness.com. Set menu R300. MC, V. Mon–Sat 7pm–late (closed for a month in winter).

SEDGEFIELD & GOUKAMMA RESERVE

The drive from Wilderness to Sedgefield on the N2 is very pleasant, with a series of lakes on the left and occasional glimpses of the ocean on your right. Sedgefield looks very unattractive from the road—a motley collection of shops, estate agents, and service stations—but it's worth turning off and heading for the beach, which is one of the nicest along this stretch (mostly because the houses are set back behind the sand dunes). One of the best Garden Route beach walks starts here: During low tide, walk westward to **Gericke's Point,** a hillock of sandstone where locals pick fresh mussels.

Next stop is the 2,230-hectare (5,508-acre) **Goukamma Nature Reserve,** which encompasses forests, an estuary, beaches, reputedly the highest vegetated dune in southern Africa, and Groenvlei, a freshwater lake fed by underground water sources. The reserve has a few rudimentary self-catering accommodations options (the best is probably Mvubu Bush Lodge) and several hiking trails that cover various habitats in the reserve, including a 4-hour beach walk and a short circular walk through a milkwood forest. Admission to the Goukamma Reserve is R25. Gate hours are daily 8am to 6pm. Access is through the Buffalo Bay turnoff or near Sedgefield. For more information and bookings, contact ✆ **044/383-0042** or visit **www.capenature.co.za**.

7 KNYSNA & PLETTENBERG BAY

KNYSNA

The founder of Knysna (pronounced "*nize*-na") was one George Rex. In 1802, at the age of 39—having shocked the Cape community by shacking up with a woman "of color"—he purchased the farm, which included the whole basin containing the Knysna lagoon. By the time of his death in 1839, he had engaged in a number of enterprises, the most profitable of which was timber, and had persuaded the Cape authorities to develop Knysna as a port. Knysna's development and the decimation of its forests were well underway. That any forests escaped the devastation of the 19th century is thanks to far-sighted conservation policies introduced in the 1880s, and today Knysna has the largest areas of indigenous forests left in South Africa. The Knysna elephants have fared less well—attempts to augment their numbers by relocating three young cows from Kruger National Park failed miserably when it was discovered that the last remaining Knysna elephant was also a female. The surviving cows have subsequently been relocated to the Shamwari game reserve in the Eastern Cape. Detractors believed that the forest pachyderms were extinct and that the only free-roaming elephants left in Knysna were those painted on road markers warning drivers to "beware." Then in October 2000, a 20-year-old elephant bull was spotted and photographed deep in the forest, making headlines throughout the Western Cape. A few years later, author and environmentalist Gareth Patterson set about collecting dung for Lori Eggbert, a scientist from the Smithsonian Institute, to perform DNA tests and hopefully prove his theory that at least 9 or 10 elephants remain at large. The jury is still out on the findings, however; besides the rare appearance of the older surviving female (plus one good photo), you're most likely to spot one by overindulging in the local beer.

Knysna used to be a sleepy village inhabited only by a handful of hippies and wealthy retirees, but the last decade has seen a tourist boom that has augmented numbers substantially—nowhere is this more evident than on the congested main road that runs through town. Still, Knysna has retained a great deal more of its original village charm than either George or Plettenberg Bay, and remains the emotional heart of the region, with a resident population who actually live here year-round (unlike Plett, which turns into a ghost town in winter). Its raison d'être is the large tidal lagoon, around which the town has grown, and the towering sandstone cliffs (called the heads) that guard the lagoon's narrow access to the sea. The eastern buttress has unfortunately been developed, but this means you can now overnight and play golf surrounded by a spectacular sea and fynbos environment, and the western side remains untouched—a visit to the Featherbed Nature Reserve should be high on your list of priorities.

VISITOR INFORMATION The **Tourism Information Bureau** (✆ **044/382-5510;** www.visitknysna.com; Mon–Fri 8am–5pm, Sat 8:30am–1pm; hours are extended Dec–Jan) is at 40 Main St. In the same building is the booking service, **Knysna Reservations** (✆ **044/382-6960;** bookings@knysna-info.co.za), which will help you make accommodations and other bookings. You can also visit the independent **Central Reservations** (✆ **044/382-5878** or 082/558-1661; daily 9am–6pm) for advice and bookings.

GETTING THERE & AROUND The closest airports are at **George** (see "George & Wilderness: Getting There," earlier in this chapter) and **Plettenberg Bay;** both are about an hour's drive away. Contact **Budget** (✆ **044/876-9204**) or **Economic Car Hire** (✆ **082/800-4258**). For a fun way to get around (not to mention avoid Knysna's seasonal traffic congestion), rent a mountain bike (see "Staying Active," earlier in this chapter). For a taxi, call **Benwill Shuttle** (✆ **083/728-5181**).

GUIDED TOURS For customized nature walks and tours, contact Howard Butcher (✆ **072/018-1333** or 044/388-4761; www.walkwild.co.za; howard@walkwild.co.za), a FGASA-registered guide in his 40s who covers everything from birding and fungi, to entomology, musical township tours, and unraveling complex ecosystems. He is also an accomplished bush pilot and can put together itineraries that cover the country when time rather than money is your primary consideration. All excursions, from half-day walks to full itineraries, are planned to suit your time and pocket; prices start at R100 per person per hour for short outings; the longer your itinerary, the more cost-effective it becomes.

BOAT TOURS The **Featherbed Company** (✆ **044/382-1693**) runs trips to the nature reserve of the same name (see "The Top Attractions," below). With comfortable seating and a restaurant/bar on board, the floating double-decker **John Benn Ferry** (✆ **044/382-1693**) offers a 90-minute trip on the lagoon that costs R120 for adults, meals and drinks extra. R250 buys you a ticket on the **Heads Explorer**—the only ferry licensed to go through the Heads. Featherbed also offers a range of other cruises on its paddle cruiser and Three Legs ferry. For sailing trips, contact **Springtide Charters** (✆ **082/470-6022;** www.springtide.co.za; prices on application) to charter the hand-built luxury yacht ***Outiniqua*** for one of various exclusive cruises, including breakfast, all-day, sunset, dinner, or overnight cruises (you can request your own gourmet chef).

ACTIVITIES The **Hippo Dive Campus** can organize snorkeling and scuba diving experiences. Contact ✆ **044/384-0831.**

SPECIAL EVENTS Knysna gets very busy during the annual **Knysna Loerie Festival,** a gay pride event held for a few days every May, even more so during the **Knysna Oyster Festival** held every July. **Gastronomica,** a culinary festival, is a hot new addition to the calendar, held annually in September. For information, contact the Tourism Bureau.

What to See & Do in Knysna

Besides the top attractions listed below, one of the first things first-time visitors are usually encouraged to do is take a drive to the **Knysna Heads** ★, where you can walk right up to the lagoon mouth and watch skippers gingerly navigate the treacherous surf. Stop for tea at the East Head Café, and then view the rare Knysna seahorse at the small NSRI aquarium, endangered by the ongoing development in and around the lagoon.

Exploring the forests is another major drawing card (see below), as are **lagoon-based activities;** several companies run boat trips on the lagoon, home to 200 species of fish and a major supplier of oysters—expect to see these on almost every Knysna menu. (For ferry and sailing options, see "Boat Tours," above.)

Another local product worth trying is the beer. **Mitchell's Brewery,** Arend Street (✆ **044/382-4685**), produces four types of unpasteurized "live" ales, the best of which are Bosun's Bitter and Forrester's Draught. You can either take a 10-minute tour and tasting (Mon–Fri 10:30am or 3pm; tastings only 9:30am–4:30pm) or sample them with your meal at any of the Knysna eateries. Ask for directions or a list of outlets from the Tourism Bureau, or combine oyster- and beer-tasting with a lagoon trip by boarding the **John Benn Ferry** (✆ **044/382-1693**) and heading for the bar. To reach the closest sandy shore, you'll need to head west to **Brenton-on-Sea,** an endless stretch of sand 16km (10 miles) from Knysna, or, better still, east for **Noetzie Beach** ★★★, some 11km (6¾ miles) from town. It's a steep walk down to this beautiful little beach, but a small, very swimmable estuary spilling out into the ocean and five over-the-top crenellated castles overlooking the beach make it more than worthwhile. Knysna lagoon's **Bollard Bay,** accessed from Leisure Isle, is an excellent family beach, with safe swimming in the shallow waters of the lagoon.

Last but not least, Knysna offers some of the best shopping this side of Cape Town, though much of it is very hippie-inspired and artsy. The exception to this, with its super-sophisticated take on African-influenced housewares and local crafts, is **Am-Wa,** corner of Waenhout and Vigilance Drive, Knysna Industria (✆ **044/382-3186**). The buyer has an exceptionally good eye for what is described as "original functional art," on par with anything you'd find in the best of Cape Town's design shops.

The Top Attractions

One of the top attractions on the Garden Route, the **Choo-Tjoe train** has for many years been the region's prized icon, its 1948 locomotives photographed chugging across the Knysna lagoon into the verdant valleys and lakeside settings to traverse the Kaaimans River gorge and Victoria Bay to George. However, due to the extensive flood damage that occurred in 2006, the Knysna–George route has been suspended and replaced with the less spectacular George–Mossel Bay route. Sadly, there's no sign of the Knysna route being reintroduced. If you're interested in the George–Mossel Bay route, book through **Kontours** (✆ **082/569-8997;** www.kontours.co.za); they provide a map with points of interest as seen from the train, and will pick you up, take you to George to board, and then transfer you to Knysna from the Mossel Bay station.

Featherbed Nature Reserve ★★ This privately owned nature reserve on the western head of Knysna is a Natural Heritage Site and home to the endangered blue duiker antelope. Guests are ferried over and then ascend the head in a large open-topped vehicle to enjoy magnificent views of the lagoon, town, and ocean. Qualified guides then lead the visitors down through milkwood forests and coastal flora onto the cliffs and coastal caves on the 2km (1¼-mile) **Bushbuck Trail** (you can also choose to drive down). Meals are served at the **Tavern;** the buffet is included in your ticket price. ***Note:*** The reserve's peace is seriously compromised during Knysna's busiest season, when additional trips are made.

Ferry leaves from Municipal Jetty, Remembrance Ave., off Waterfront Dr. ✆ **044/382-1693.** Morning tour admission R375 adults, R160 children 3–10, R180 children 11–15 (depart daily at 10am, with more scheduled, depending on demand; phone ahead), duration approx. 4 hr.; afternoon tour admission (depart 2:30pm) R260 adults, R100 children (no food included), duration approximately 3 hr.

Knysna Elephant Park Kids This "safari," undertaken in 4WD vehicles that depart from reception every half-hour, is a little better than viewing elephants in a zoo, as you are at least guaranteed an opportunity to touch the elephants that roam the 80-hectare (198-acre) "reserve." The park now has 14 elephants, most of which were born in Kruger and have been returned—according to the park's promoters—to "the home of their ancestors." For a hefty R1,078, you can take an exclusive sunrise or sunset walk with them through the forests with just a guide for company (a meal is included); children will no doubt enjoy the cheaper (R145), shorter 45- to 60-minute tour more. Elephant-back rides or walks are R682 for adults and R330 for children. Another option is **Botlierskip Private Game Reserve** (✆ **044/696-6055**), near Mossel Bay, in which you can go on an elephant-back safari, either as a day visitor or overnight; riders must be 6 or older—don't forget to wear thick trousers. Cost is R600 adults, R300 children.

Off N2, 22km (14 miles) east of Knysna. ✆ **044/532-7732.** 45- to 60-min. tour R145 adults, R75 kids 3 and under; R385 sundowner walk; R1,078 adults for exclusive safari; R539 kids. You'll need to book the sunrise and sunset elephant safari in advance. Tours daily 8:30am–4:30pm.

Knysna Forests ★★ These last pockets of indigenous forest, now part of the new Garden Route National Park, are some distance from town: **Goudveld State Forest** is 30km (19 miles) northwest of Knysna, while **Diepwalle** is some 20km (12 miles) north-east. Goudveld is a mixture of plantation and indigenous forest, making Diepwalle, with its ancient yellowwoods, the better option for the purist. Look out for the emerald Knysna Loerie and the brightly hued Narina Trogon in the branches. Diepwalle has three excellent color-coded circular trails, all 7 to 9km (4¼–5½ miles) long (the red route is recommended because it features the most water).

Diepwalle: Take the N2 east; after 7km (4¼ miles), turn left onto the R339 for 16km (10 miles) before taking turnoff to Diepwalle. Goudveld: Take the N2 west, turn right into Rheenendal Rd. ✆ **044/302-5606.** R12 to walk; R25 to cycle. Daily 7:30am–4pm.

Where to Stay

If The Lofts (see below) is full or you're traveling as a family or group and would like to stay on Knysna's most chi-chi island, with the lagoon at your doorstep and some of the best restaurants within walking distance, look into renting an apartment, cottage, or villa on **Thesen Island**—Thesen Islands Destinations (✆ **044/382-7550;** www.theislands.co.za) is the official short-term rental agent. Although locals are very unhappy at the rate of development on Knysna's previously pristine eastern head, there's no reason you should be. Take a look at **Head Over Hills** (✆ **044/384-0949;** www.headoverhills.co.za; R2,260–R4,390, depending on room and season). Perched high above the town and ocean, it has eight rooms, all with glass "walls" that fold back to cantilevered decks that provide one of the most dramatic sea views on the Garden Route. Not far away is **The Alexander** (✆ **044/384-1111;** www.alexanderhouse.co.za; R1,800–R4,000 double). It's won the odd award, but the best rooms are pricey, and you should be aware that not all have unimpeded views. The decor is wildly extravagant, but if you have a liking for lush atmospheres of "unashamed opulence," as they put it, this may be right for you. I preferred the look of **Stilty Bird House** (✆ **072/679-7473;** www.cape-venues.co.za), with its dramatic views of the Heads, but this is a self-catering, sole-use villa (it has four en-suite rooms, sleeping 8; R4,000–R7,000 a night).

If you don't want to spend a lot of money, but staying in the center of town at Inyathi Guest Village doesn't appeal, **Peace of Eden** (✆ **044/388-4671** or 072/528-5859; www.peaceofeden.co.za; high season R695–R950 double, low season R450–R650 double) offers a cottage and five cabins at the edge of the forest, 15 minutes away from town off Rheenendal Road. Owned by nature lovers Jen and Howard, the cabins—often booked by South African bands here to utilize Howard's recording studio—are comfortable and cozy, and ideal if you prefer the countryside or love riding horses (they keep some for guests' use). A quirky option, also off Rheenendal Road, is **Portland Manor** (© **044/388-4604;** www.portlandmanor.com; R900–R1,450 double). Lawnwood Lodge has some comfortable rooms (nos. 2, 7, 11, and 17 have good views), but if you want something different, stay in the slightly spooky Manor House. Mod it's not: The dining room looks like the original inhabitants have quietly stepped out for a while (and will soon be back); antiques date back to when the manor was built in the 1850s, and some rooms are slightly fusty (Kate's Place and the Sun Room are good options). It's certainly full of character, and the property boasts a restaurant, a wonderful pub, a hippo, and some antelope.

Golfers who find Pezula out of their league should consider newcomer **Simola** (© **044/302-9600;** www.simolaestate.co.za; R2,250–R2,550 one-bed double). Situated high on a hill behind Knysna with sweeping views, a Jack Nicklaus Signature golf course, and a spa, Simola offers comfortable rooms at reasonable prices. The one-bed units (not to be confused with the tiny standard rooms) have their own fully equipped kitchens, so guests can cut costs by self-catering rather than dining at the on-site restaurant, the Orchid Room. Accommodations at Pezula may be more luxurious, but Simola's golf course is more highly rated.

Also on a hill just out of town, overlooking the Knysna lagoon, is the friendly **Elephant Hide Lodge** (© **044/382-0426;** www.elephanthide.co.za; R1,320—R1,640 double)—seven standalone stone and timber cottages, most with views and decks, and a main lodge area. The rooms are delightful, but you'll have to drive to town—or ask the owners about their tailor-made tours to local attractions. To experience a different side of Knysna, look into a Knysna home stay and spend the night in the local township with a warm and welcoming family (call **Glendyrr,** at © **044/382-5510,** for more information). For more long-stay options (of up to 2 weeks or so), contact **Knysna Booking Services** (© **044/382-5510;** bookings@knysna-info.co.za). Prices vary depending on season; most specify low, mid, and peak seasons. Low season is usually from May 1 to August 31, with peak season usually from mid-December to mid-January.

Belvidere Manor ★ In the picture-postcard-cute suburb of Belvidere (at least for now; big developments pending), these detached cottages on lawns that sweep down to the water's edge are the most upscale places to stay on the actual lagoon (but they're nowhere near as nice as Phantom Forest). The best units are the original lagoon suites. Unfortunately, the addition of the cheaper garden suites in the manor's back garden turned what used to be an exclusive retreat into a more run-of-the-mill hotel experience. Even so, the suites, which are, in effect, small cottages, are spacious, tastefully decorated, and fully equipped for self-catering. Meals are served either on the veranda of the historic Belvidere House, a national monument, or in the charming pub.

Duthie Dr., Belvidere Estate, Knysna 6570. © **044/387-1055.** Fax 044/387-1059. www.belvidere.co.za. 30 units. High season R2,000–R2,600 double; low season R1,400–R1,820 double. Rates include breakfast. AE, DC, MC, V. Children 10 and over are welcome. **Amenities:** Restaurant; bar; free high-speed Internet in lounge; pool; room service; free Wi-Fi in pub. *In room:* Fans, TV, hair dryer, heated towel rack.

Falcon's View Manor ★★ Set high up on Thesen Hill, overlooking the lagoon and surrounded by peaceful gardens, this guesthouse offers a gracious retreat from the hustle and bustle of town. The 1899 Manor House features a wraparound veranda and elegant sitting room, as well as garden- or lagoon-view rooms on the upper level. Since their much-needed refurbishment in 2005, these have a more contemporary look (room no. 4 gets my vote for decor, size, and views). If you're here for a few days, opt for one of the luxurious **garden suites,** where the generously sized en-suite bedrooms, each comfortably furnished in muted modern colors, lead out onto private terraces overlooking the gardens and pool. A Mediterranean-styled dinner is usually available in the Manor House—or enjoy tea on the terrace while looking down on the village.

2 Thesen Hill, Knysna 6570. ✆ **044/382-6767.** Fax 044/382-6430. www.falconsview.com. 9 units. Standard rooms from R1,090 double; garden suites R1,610–R2,370. AE, DC, MC, V. **Amenities:** Dining room; bar; pool; room service; free Wi-Fi. *In room:* A/C, TV, hair dryer, minibar (in some); heated towel rack.

Inyathi Guest Village Value Kids In the heart of Knysna, Inyathi attracts a younger visitor with a great combination of value and inoffensive taste. Despite its location just off the busy main road, with tourist information and dining options within close walking distance, Inyathi maintains a sense of privacy. Innovatively laid out around a courtyard, many of the double-bedded timber cabins feature beautiful stained-glass windows, and most have a luxurious slipper bathtub. While the rooms are charming and decorated with charm and creativity, they are relatively small—not the sort to lounge around in all day—and some have steps that won't suit older visitors.

52 Main Rd., Knysna 6570. ✆/fax **044/382-7768.** www.inyathi-sa.com. 11 units. R620–R720 double, depending on season. Rates include breakfast. DC, MC, V. **Amenities:** Bar; babysitting; Wi-Fi (pay per byte, credit card required). *In room:* Fans, TV, hair dryer, heaters.

Kanonkop House ★★ For attentive service and one of the best views in town, book the aptly named Paradise Room. This haven of sumptuous comfort floats loftily above a forested slope, with vistas that stretch across the lagoon to the Heads—to be enjoyed from the balcony, your bed, and even the elevated tub. This room was in such demand (don't bother with the back rooms overlooking the pool) that owner Chris Conyers added two more below it: Sunbird and Forest also offer fresh, individual decor, a plethora of personal touches, and more magnificent views. Chris, his son Mark, and his family will ply you with sundowners and advice. They offer activities such as mountain biking, water-skiing, and sunset cruises, and can arrange for golfing fans to play Pezula and Simola.

6 Cuthbert St., Kanonkop, Knysna. ✆/fax **044/382-2374.** Fax 044/382-2148. www.kanonkoptours.com. 5 units. High season R2,200–R3,060 double; low season R1,420–R1,860 double. Rates include breakfast. AE, DC, MC, V. **Amenities:** Bar; pool; lounge. *In room:* A/C, TV, hair dryer, heated towel rack, free Wi-Fi.

Lightley's Holiday Houseboats ★ Kids Escape the seasonally congested streets of Knysna: Hire a houseboat and cruise the lagoon. You need no experience to skipper—just switch on and "drive" (navigational video, charts, maps, and instructions are supplied). You can fish for dinner from your boat or simply chug along to Thesen Island. Houseboats come equipped with everything: stove, fridge, hot and cold water, chemical toilet, CD players, a mobile phone if you don't have one, electric lights, crockery and cutlery, and barbecues—just remember to pack towels, and don't run out of fuel. Rates quoted are for **Leisure Liners,** which sleep four; **Aqua Chalets** sleep six, are larger, and look better. ***Note:*** The houseboats are far from posh. If you'd prefer a more luxurious boat, complete with your own skipper and chef, charter the three-bed, 15m (50-ft.) luxury yacht ***Outiniqua*** (✆ **082/470-6022;** www.springtide.co.za).

Phantom Pass, Knysna 6570. ✆ **044/386-0007.** Fax 044/386-0018. www.houseboats.co.za. 14 houseboats. Low season R985–R1,425 per day; high season R1,895–R2,695 per day. Ask about specials or packages. MC, V.

The Lofts ★★ With good shopping options within walking distance, an in-house spa and timber-surround pool, and a laid-back marina-harbor atmosphere, this is one of the best places to stay in Knysna. Six years ago, this island was a derelict sawmill and timber yard; now it's the trendiest address in Knysna, crammed with Cape Cod–style townhouses, many with private moorings, and a great little retail heart. The Lofts is diagonally above **Il de Pain,** Knysna's most celebrated bakery-cum-casual-restaurant (effectively your dining room), and a few feet from the lagoon (the three new lagoon suites have great views). Decor is comfortable, though mostly bland and mediocre, but your eyes will likely be fixed on the shimmering waters of the Knysna lagoon anyway.

The Boatshed, Thesen Island, Knysna. ✆ **044/302-5710.** Fax 044/302-5711. www.thelofts.co.za. 15 units. R950–R1,750 double. R50 breakfast voucher included. AE, MC, V. **Amenities:** Pool; spa. *In room:* A/C, TV, hair dryer, minibar, Wi-Fi (credit card required).

Pezula Resort & Spa ★★★ Atop the Knysna East Head cliffs on a links course designed by Ronald Fream and David Dale, this idyllic retreat is not only recommended for golfers, but is the most luxurious choice in Knysna (Phantom is as special, but in a totally different way—see below). It offers superb service levels and tip-top accommodations matched only by the majestic location (including access to the beautiful semiprivate Noetzie beach)—all reasons why it made the *Condé Nast Traveler*'s 2007 Gold List, and why the Robb Report crowned it one of the top 100 Ultimate Escapes in the World in 2008. It's modern, with plenty of the currently de rigueur stone and dark slate, and adorned with lots of South African art. The restaurant, **Zachary's** (see below), is yet another reason why golfers aren't the only ones heading up the hill. Suites are in free-standing units in the grounds (four per block), and there are three room categories—the entry-level studio suite is the best value, offering the same fittings and furnishings, and only slightly smaller. ***Note:*** For that special occasion, take a look at Pezula Private Castle, perched above a near-private crescent of sea and sand (see "A Castle of Your Own," below).

Pezula Estate, East Head Cliffs, Knysna. ✆ **044/302-3333.** www.pezularesorthotel.com. 78 units, 2 castles. Suites R4,395–R13,190 double, depending on season. Rates include breakfast and access to the spa. AE, DC, MC, V. **Amenities:** Restaurant; archery; mountain bikes; canoes; golf; gym; horseback riding; library and games room; pool; spa; tennis; walking trails. *In room:* A/C, TV/DVD, hair dryer, minibar, free Wi-Fi.

The Phantom Forest Eco-Reserve ★★★ If you prefer a more back-to-nature "safari" experience, look no further. Perched amid an indigenous forest on a hill overlooking the Knysna River, Phantom is a genuine eco-friendly retreat; meandering boardwalks connect the public spaces to the privately located suites, which are more like luxurious treehouses tucked into the forest canopy. Each Classic Suite comprises a double-volume bedroom with stupendous view of the Knysna lagoon, a sitting area leading out to a small elevated deck, and a large bathroom. The newer Upper Tree Suites have additional luxuries such as bathtubs on the deck; Moroccan Suites are the biggest. The food is incredible (see "Where to Dine," below). Service is not always instantly available (you have to leave your car at the foot of the hill and wait for a vehicle to traverse the steep road; the secluded privacy of the suites and public areas means there is not always someone immediately on hand), but the setting, architecture, and views more than make up for this. (If you're looking for stellar service or a host of activities, you're better off at Pezula.)

Off Phantom Pass, 7km (4¼ miles) from Knysna. ✆ **044/386-0046.** Fax 044/387-1944. www.phantomforest.com. 14 units. Suites R2,800–R3,700; ask about winter specials. Rates include breakfast; dinner is R250 per person (advance notice needed for vegetarians/vegans). AE, DC, MC, V. Children over 12 only. **Amenities:** 2 restaurants; bar; mountain bikes; canoes; massage; pools (w/incredible views); sauna; walking trails; free Wi-Fi in lodge. *In room:* Fans, hair dryer, minibar.

A Castle of Your Own ★★★

In the 1930s, in a secluded, unspoiled cove outside Knysna called Noetzie, one Herbert Stephen Henderson set about building a holiday home using local stone. When a neighbor reportedly joked that all the house needed to become a castle was a turret or two, Henderson promptly added a few. That was the beginning of the Noetzie castles; over the next 30 years, five more were built by various people and these still line one of the most beautiful beaches on the Garden Route, accessible to all but the infirm (there's quite a steep walk up and down from the car park). One of the castles, now owned by Pezula Hotel & Spa, has been converted into remarkable accommodation options (the **Pezula Private Castle** was recently named one of the Top 101 Suites in the World by *Elite Traveler*). It is suitably palatial, with a total of five enormous luxury suites, walk-in wardrobes, gracious living areas, a 10-seat dining room, and a heated pool. A personal chef and butler cater to your every whim. All Pezula activities are included in the rate—from R54,370 a night for the main castle, with three suites, or from R74,870 for the entire complex (www.pezulaprivatecastle.com); rates includes all meals and resort activities.

If this makes you splutter, consider a room in **Lindsay Castle** (✆ **044/384-1849;** www.knysnacastles.com; R1,200–R2,400 double). Situated at the western end of Noetzie beach, it enjoys the same sublime views and privacy—and, yes, it too has turrets (don't book these; book the Honeymoon Suite, with gorgeous sea views). Even accessing Lindsay Castle can be quite an adventure; there are times that this can be done only on foot, and the journey requires some scrambling over rocks. It's charming, dinners are provided on request (but I'd head into Knysna), and you will be able to spend blissful days hiking, swimming in the estuary, and watching for otters or dolphins. You can also rent the entire castle, if you prefer—it sleeps eight.

Noetzie was declared a conservancy in 1999 and remains unspoiled (thanks to the fact that there is no public road to the beach). Locals aren't all happy at Pezula's rapacious water needs, but for now, it retains its otherworldly beauty.

The Rex ★ Right in the center of town and within waking distance of the Waterfront, this new hotel offers convenient, stylish accommodations, but without the natural beauty enjoyed by lodgings on the Eastern Head or the Phantom Pass. The feel is more exclusive apartment block than hotel. There's a lot of concrete, steel, and glass on the outside; the interior is all hushed contemporary tones, with the odd charming quirk (like a wall of carved, caged birds). The rooms are modern, escaping bland, thanks to such touches as handmade blankets and original photographs. Book a one-bed room; the standard rooms are just too small. If you don't want to cook, **Dish,** just downstairs, offers bistro-style dining with South African twists. Next door is **Mon Petit Pain,** baby sister to the famous Ile de Pain.

8 Gray St., Knysna. ✆ **044/302-5900.** Fax 044/302-5910. www.rexhotel.co.za. 30 units. R1,440–R2,060 1-bed double; R2,600–R3,730 2-bed apartment (sleeps 4). Breakfast included. AE, DC, MC, V. **Amenities:** Restaurant; limited room service. *In room:* A/C, TV/DVD, CD player, hair dryer, kitchen, minibar (on request), heated towel rack, Wi-Fi (credit card required).

Tips Oysters by the Dozen

Knysna is renowned for the oysters its estuary produces, and the **Knysna Oyster Company** (Thesen Island; ✆ **044/382-6941;** www.knysnaoysters.co.za), founded in 1949, is still the most unpretentious place to order them (R78–R183 for 12).

Rockery Nook ★★★ Finds Tucked away on the Knysna Heads, neighboring some enormous holiday houses on the water's edge in Millionaires Row, the modest but gorgeous Rockery Nook is the best-kept secret on the Garden Route. Behind the walls of this stucco-and-stone beach house, with sash windows framed by blue shutters, you'll find an eclectic, super-chic interior with an arty mix of local paintings, crystal chandeliers, and antique armoires. For families booking a long-stay holiday, the Main House is ideal, with a fully equipped kitchen, a dining area with a huge table, as well as an airy, sea-facing lounge. Two sea-facing bedrooms (main en suite) are on the upper ground floor, and a loft upstairs has two bedrooms and a bathroom. Fisherman's and Lover's Nook, two lovely apartments just a few steps away from the lagoon, are decorated with the same unique character and flair. Booking procedures can be quite casual: Reconfirm details before arrival.

George Rex Dr., The Eastern Heads, Knysna. ✆ **082/820-9246.** Fax 011/646-9278. www.rockerynook.co.za. Main House (sleeps 13) R3,300–R5,500 per day; Fishermans Nook (sleeps 2) and Lover's Nook (sleeps 2) R800–R1,400 double (self-catering). R60 breakfast vouchers available. No credit cards. **Amenities:** Varies per unit.

Under Milkwood ★★ Kids This timber "village," set under centuries-old milkwood trees, with cobbled streets running past quaint higgledy-piggledy bungalows to a sandy beach and the lagoon, is charming. It's also convenient, with the Knysna Heads and restaurants within walking distance. Each two-bedroom chalet (double bed in main bedroom and two single beds in second bedroom) has a fully equipped kitchen and an open-plan lounge, a sun deck, and barbecue facilities. If you want to be right on the beach, ask for a front chalet: Sailor's Arms, Sinbad, Manchester, or Bottom. Skylark, Bayview, Curlew, and Schooner, all hillside chalets, offer the best value for the money but require climbing stairs. Note that the middle chalets have the least privacy. Unless you're traveling with kids, peak-season prices are not a good value.

13 George Rex Dr., The Heads, Knysna. ✆ **044/384-0745.** Fax 044/384-0156. www.milkwood.co.za. 14 units. High season R2,420–R3,500 double or 4 persons; low season R860–R1,400 double, depending on location. DC, MC, V. **Amenities:** Babysitting; canoes; paddle-skis; free Wi-Fi at reception. *In room:* Fan, TV, barbecue area, hair dryer.

Where to Dine

You're spoiled for choice in Knysna, cuisine capital of the Garden Route. Besides the following recommendations, which tend toward fine dining, take a look at "Dining with a Local," below, by former restaurateur and local foodie Jacqui Mansfield.

Firefly ★★★ Value ASIAN This is one of my favorite restaurants in Knysna. It's not just the venue—a tiny dining room with rich red walls and a small outside garden patio lit up with fairy lights—or the fiery, delicious food, but the sense that you have stumbled onto something fragile. Self-taught cook Sanchia persuaded her mom (Dell, who will, in all likelihood, take your order) that it was time for them to escape the Jo'burg rat race and open a restaurant so intimate that it seemed impossible that turnover could warrant the hours a restaurant demands. But for Sanchia and Dell, it's a passion, and just 4 years later they're taking reservations months in advance. The new Pomegranate Room provides much-needed extra seating. Whatever else you order, make sure you have the *bobotie* spring rolls; for the rest, take your advice from Dell.

152A Old Cape Rd. ✆ **044/382-1490.** Main courses R62–R74. No credit or debit cards. Tues–Sun 6–10pm.

Ile de Pain Bread & Café ★★★ BREAKFAST/LIGHT LUNCHEONS Atkins dieters, be warned: When Austrian chef-patron Markus Farbinger bakes, bread is all you'll want to eat. Whether it's his potato bread, fluffy croissants, fragrant focaccia, crispy ciabattas, or signature *companion* (half-wheat, half-rye sourdough made with a 300-year-old starter dough), Markus makes you realize that there is something seriously wrong with the bland stuff in supermarkets. You sit at long wooden tables under the trees or inside the bakery, from where you can choose from daily sandwiches (in season, don't miss the toasted baguette with figs, Gorgonzola, rocket, and balsamic reduction), salads, soups, light grills, and sweet treats. ***Note:*** Can't get to Thesen Island? Drop by baby sister **Mon Petit Pain,** at Gray and Gordon streets (✆ **044/302-5767**), and pick up a sandwich or savory tart, as good as anything prepared at the mother ship.

10 The Boatshed, Thesen Island. ✆ **044/302-5707.** Lunch fare R30–R85. Tues–Sat 8am–3pm; Sun 9am–1:30pm.

Pembrey's ★★ MEDITERRANEAN BISTRO Just about every restaurant these days seems to talk up how fresh and local their ingredients are, but Peter and son (who has survived time with Gordon Ramsay) go that extra mile to make everything (including pasta and ice cream) by hand. Dishes display innovation (Peter Junior has a thing for offal) but reflect Peter Senior's Cordon Bleu training and avoid fussiness, so you'll find intriguing combinations such as roasted marrowbones with oxtail marmalade, or lamb's tongues in a caper-anchovy sauce. The roast duck on apple Waldorf salad comes with duck liver confit, and there's an award-wining wine list. And in a world seemingly addicted to chrome and glass sleekness, the laid-back, wooden-floored, fairy-lighted, and stained-glass dining room makes a nice change.

Brenton Rd., Belvidere, Knysna. ✆ **044/386-0005.** pembreys@telkomsa.net. Reservations advisable. Main courses R50–R110. Dinner Wed–Sun from 6:30pm; Sun lunch only. Closed around July/Aug.

The Phantom Forest ★★★ PAN-AFRICAN It's worth dining here just for the primal forest atmosphere and views in this stunning eco-reserve (see "Where to Stay," above). Residents enjoy first dibs on tables, though, so book in advance. Get here early enough to order a predinner drink, and grab a chair next to the pool to watch as the enormous sky changes into its sunset hues, reflected in the lagoon waters below. There are two venues: a six-course table d'hôte dinner served in the **Boma,** featuring a soup, a choice of four starters, sorbet, a choice of four main dishes, cheeses, and a choice of desserts. An African-blend coffee is served around the bonfire. With demand outstripping chair space, the team opened **Moroccan Chutzpah,** an intimate North African–themed venue, where colorful cushions, sunken lounges, and hookah pipes set the tone. Here the menu is made up of five-course platters rather than plated dishes; all spices are mixed in-house, and the variety of flavors is exceptional. Both venues afford a romantic experience and are worth the wait for the lift up from the base of the hill.

Phantom Pass Rd. ✆ **044/386-0046.** Reservations essential in high season. Set dinner R250. AE, DC, MC, V. Daily 6pm. Latest arrivals 8pm. Ask about Chutzpah's seasonal closing times.

Dining with a Local

There are many light lunch and coffee spots in Knysna. If you want to see and be seen, go to **Isle de Pain** (✆ **044/302-5707**), on Thesens Island, or its little brother, **Mon Petit Pain** (✆ **044/302-5767**), on Grey Street (see above/below). They have very good coffee, superb bread and pastries, and innovative food, but watch the wine prices, which are rather high. Another place with fantastic pastries is **Gabrielle's** (✆ **076/845-6409**), on Tide Street. They have a lovely quiet garden in the back and the food is fresh and interesting, such as a phyllo basket with roast vegetables and couscous. Stuck in town? Then stop at **Gino's** (✆ **044/382-3667**), in the Millwood Centre. Gino, who hails from Belgium, often has Belgian specialties on the menu, such as croquettes and excellent pancakes.

A popular restaurant with locals is **Caffe Mario** (✆ **044/382-7250**), at the Knysna Quays. It's best to sit outside near the water, and it offers excellent pizza, pasta, fish, and veal dishes—plus, the wine prices are very reasonable. There's a nice atmosphere and good service. **Zest** (✆ **044/382-0456**), a restaurant in Pledge Square, still offers good fusion food, atmosphere, and service. If we're in the mood for classic country cooking, we book at **Pembrey's** (✆ **044/386-0005**), on Belvidere Road, which is always full; Peter cooks while wife Viv does front-of-the-house duties, offering lots of varied and different choices on a blackboard. Service is excellent, and a huge wine menu caters to all tastes and pockets. Also in Belvidere Estate is **Belvidere Manor** (✆ **044/387-1055**), where you can either eat in the Old Manor House, with its beautiful terrace and lagoon view, or go to **The Bell,** a lovely old pub where they serve good, wholesome pub meals. I also like to work up an appetite by walking along the beautiful stretch of beach at Brenton-on-Sea, followed by a sundowner at **Nauticus** (✆ **044/381-0106**). They serve very good pizzas and seafood at reasonable prices. On the Waterfront, at the Featherbed jetty, is **Cruise Café** (✆ **044/382-1693**)—their tempura prawns are a must. In the evenings, this is a popular sundowner venue, with a great deck and lagoon views to match, and the kind of rural sophisticates that typify much of the Knysna community.

—Local foodie Jacqui Mansfield spent 25 years in the kitchens of her own restaurants before retiring to Knysna.

Sirocco ★★ FUSION/SEAFOOD In the mood for a pared-down, modern-chic atmosphere with wonderful views and natural light streaming in? Minimalist Sirocco, which offers largely Mediterranean seafood with an Asian twist (plus roasts, filets, poultry, and one or two vegetarian options), reflects its chi-chi Thesen Harbour Town location. There's a good deal of glass, all the better to maximize the lagoon setting, and colorful cocktails to sip while you're watching the sun set. Sirocco is best known for its prawns (you can try three varieties of ginger and spring onion rice), but they also produce a mean bouillabaisse, and a tender free-range petit poussin marinated in coriander, garlic, and lemon. The small lunch menu, served in addition to the main menu from noon to 4pm, offers lighter, less-exciting fare.

 Thesen Harbour Town. ✆ **044/382-7196.** www.sirocco.co.za. Main courses R69–R190, crayfish from R250, seafood platter (serves 2) R650. AE, DC, DISC, MC, V. Daily noon–10pm.

Zachary's ★★ SOUTH AFRICAN CONTEMPORARY New York–born chef Geoffrey Murray remains at the helm of Pezula's fine-dining destination. The main restaurant itself is luscious, but there are views to be had from the terrace. Murray is a devotee of the Slow Food movement, and dishes invariably celebrate the freshest seasonal fare he can find (much of the organic produce is grown in a huge on-site garden). He aims to honor "the integrity of the ingredients," which translates into nonfussy use of traditional and more unusual items (such as quinoa or flowers). Winners on the recent summer menu included the quail (sweetened with a date and sherry purée and pomegranate syrup) and the grilled impala with blueberries and cocoa. It's not cheap (the Wagyu beef rump steak will run you close to R400), but it's obvious why it scooped a 2008 Dine Award for the Top 10 Deluxe Eateries in South Africa.

Pezula Resort & Spa, Lagoonview Dr., Knysna. ✆ **044/302-3364.** www.zacharys.co.za. Reservations essential. Main courses R125–R395. AE, DC, MC, V. Open daily for breakfast, lunch, and dinner.

PLETTENBERG BAY & SURROUNDS

Several miles of white sands, backed by the blue-gray outline of the Tsitsikamma Mountains and lapped by an endless succession of gentle waves, curve languidly to create **Bahia Formosa** (Beautiful Bay), as the Portuguese sailors who first set eyes on it named it. Over the years, its beauty has inevitably drawn an ever-increasing string of admirers; some 50,000 of Jo'burg's wealthiest individuals descend on the seaside town of **Plettenberg Bay** every December, augmented by British socialites here to play the Kurland International Polo Match. But in the off-season, when most of the holiday homes stand empty, a far more laid-back atmosphere prevails. Though some find the ghost town unsettling, the empty beaches certainly make up for it.

There's not much to do in town itself but laze on the beach (though The Crags, to the east of Plett, offers a wide range of activities, from wine tasting to a variety of animal sanctuaries and craft stores). **Lookout** beach is on the eastern side and was the most popular, where bathers relished in its Blue Flag status, but most of it has been washed away in some of the fiercest storms to pound this otherwise genteel coast. The much smaller **Central Beach,** dominated by the timeshare hotel Beacon Isle, is the area from which most of the boats launch, leaving **Robberg,** on the west, as the current favorite, or **Keurbooms,** to the far east. Sadly, money and taste seem to enjoy an inverse relationship in Plettenberg Bay; huge monstrosities line most of the beachfront, particularly Robberg Beach, with the exception being the less-developed far-western edge, bordering the reserve. **Robberg Nature Reserve** ★★★ (✆ **044/533-2125**), the rocky peninsula on

Moments 3, 2, 1, Aaaaaaa!

If Plett's views aren't enough to take your breath away, remember that the world's highest bungee jump is only a 15-minute drive east on the N2. For R620, you can have the rare privilege of free-falling for 216m (708 ft.) off the Bloukrans Bridge, and then watch yourself doing it all over again on video (see "Staying Active," at the beginning of the chapter). Booking for this and other adventure activities in the region can be made through **Face Adrenalin** (✆ **042/281-1458**).

the western side of the bay, offers fantastic whale-watching opportunities during the course of a 9km (5.5-mile) trail. The going gets very rocky, so wear sun protection and good shoes, and try not to time your visit with high tide. There are shorter 2½-hour versions; pick up a map from the reserve gate when you pay your R25 to get in. To find it, follow signs off airport road; the gate is 8km (5 miles) southeast of town. The reserve is open from 7am to 8pm daily.

Plettenberg Bay (or Plett, as the locals call it) is blessed with two estuaries, with the Keurbooms River in the east by far the larger and least spoiled. You can access the **Keurbooms River Nature Reserve** ★★ (✆ **044/533-2125;** daily 6am–7:30pm in summer, 7:30am–5:30pm in winter; R25 picnic fee) only by water—it's definitely worth paddling upstream to view the lush vegetated banks and bird life; keep an eye out for Knysna loeries, kingfishers, and fish eagles. A canoe and permit will run you R60 (R90 for a double canoe); both are available at the gate kiosk at the slipway. There is also a highly recommended overnight canoe trail in the reserve—see "Staying Active," at the beginning of the chapter. For R110 per adult (R50 children under 12), you can head upstream without lifting a finger by boarding the **Keurbooms River Ferry** (✆ **044/532-7876;** departs from slipway). Daily scheduled trips, which last approximately 2½ hours, take place at 11am, 2pm, and 5pm, and include an optional 30-minute walk or picnic (bring your own food or preorder and pack a bathing suit). Beach lovers who find Plett's urbanization depressing should consider spending a day on the relatively unspoiled **Keurbooms Beach** (follow signs off N2). This wide beach shares the same bay and has rock arches and pools to explore, but the swimming is not quite as safe, so take care.

The inland area from Keurbooms River to the Bloukrans River is known as **the Crags.** If you don't mind not being on the beach, you may appreciate its lovely lodgings options, as well as **Monkeyland** ★ (signposted off N2, 16km/10 miles east of Plett; ✆ **044/534-8906;** daily 8am–5pm), a primate sanctuary situated in an indigenous forest that houses 13 different species. Saved from laboratories or the illegal pet trade, the majority of these free-roaming primates are either endangered or critically vulnerable. Basic admission is free, while foot safaris, guided by knowledgeable rangers cost R120 adults, R60 children. Next door is **Birds of Eden** ★★ (✆ **044/534-8906;** www.birdsofeden.co.za; R120 adults, R60 children under 12; daily 8am–5pm), a 2-hectare (5-acre) enclosed dome full of birds and marmosets, with its own canopy walk. The largest free-flight bird sanctuary in the world, it can simulate thunderstorms, and you can wander through without a guide. As the two sanctuaries are sister organizations, tickets to visit both for a reduced fee are available (R184 adults, R92 kids 3–12).

If you'd really like to make a day of it, drive a little farther down Forest Hall Road to reach **Tenikwa** ★★ (✆ **044/534-8174;** www.tenikwa.co.za; daily 9am–4:30pm). Len and Mandy Freeman's wildlife awareness center offers a rare opportunity to meet South Africa's seldom-seen smaller cats, from caracal and black-footed cats to cheetah. A tour takes you into enclosures where the animals live, and if they are in the mood, you can interact with them. The guides' respect for the animals is palpable, and this helps the encounters feel really special; tours (R130 adults, R60 children) pay for the rehabilitation side of the project. Cheetah sunrise and sunset walks are also available (R300 adults). Another Crags local is **Bramon Wine Estate** (✆ **044/534-8007;** www.bramonwines.co.za). Despite its distance from the traditional grape-growing areas, Bramon has produced an interesting sauvignon blanc Cap Classique sparkling wine. You can try this (and down fresh oysters) at the on-site restaurant.

Sea and Air Safaris

One of the top things to do in Plettenberg Bay is a **marine safari** ★★★ in the mammal-rich bay; you'll be provided with plenty of excellent photo ops, as well as new insights into the various species' behavior and characteristics. Apart from the Bryde whale, the Indo-Pacific humpback, and the bottlenose and common dolphins who feed in the bay year-round, Plett enjoys seasonal visits from southern right, humpback, and killer whales during their annual migration (July–Oct). It's worth booking a close encounter trip with a boat licensed to approach the whales up to 50m (164 ft.). Coastal and pelagic bird life and the historical and geological makeup of the bay are also discussed. Tours last approximately 2 hours and cost R300 to R650; proceeds benefit whale and dolphin research and conservation. The longest-running operators are **Ocean Blue Adventures** (✆ **044/533-5083;** www.oceanadventures.co.za) and **Ocean Safaris** (✆ **044/533-4963;** www.oceansafaris.co.za). A noisier way to view Plett's marine mammals—at least, for those on the water and ground—is by air. **African Ramble Air Safaris** (✆ **044/533-9006;** www.aframble.co.za) offers scenic flights in the area from R1,600; note that you can also charter their 5- to 18-seater planes to any of the private game lodges in the Eastern Cape.

Farther east lies **Nature's Valley,** a tiny hamlet on a wide, deserted sweep of beach, and beyond this **Storms River Mouth,** both in the **Tsitsikamma National Park** ★★★—a must on any Garden Route itinerary (see below).

For more information, you could visit Plett's **Tourism Bureau,** located in Melville's Corner Shopping Centre (✆ **044/533-4065;** www.plettenbergbay.co.za; Mon–Fri 9am–5 or 6pm, Sat 9am–2pm, Sun 9am–1pm); staff members, however, are well meaning but not very switched on, and service can be poor.

Where to Stay

As in Knysna, Plett prices vary considerably, depending on the summer or winter season (Dec and Jan generally considered high season). Our top choice remains The Grand, but for those who like the service, fine dining, and facilities one expects from a Relais & Châteaux hotel, book at **The Plettenberg** ★★★ (✆ **044/533-2074;** www.plettenberg.com; standard rooms R2,250–R4,000, luxury sea-facing doubles R3,500–R6,000, suites from R4,000 and up). Situated on a hill overlooking Lookout Beach with views to Keurbooms and the blue-gray mountains beyond, this hotel has an incredible vantage point, but not all rooms take advantage of this (yet can still be pretty pricey). The hotel is also split up on two sides of the road—personally, I'd specify a Lookout Beach view—but it does have the best restaurant in town (**Sand,** see "Where to Dine," below). Travelers looking for a more modern retreat could try the very chi-chi **Bay Lodge** ★ (✆ **044/533-4977;** www.baylodge.net; R2,600–R3,800 double). While the rooms in this boutique guesthouse are not enormous, and privacy is not absolute (balconies are semiprivate), it oozes great style (barring some of the oil paintings), with a marble bar and a rooftop Jacuzzi—which is no doubt what earned it a nomination for the 2008 *Tatler* 101 Best Hotels of the World Award. Make sure your room has a view of Central Beach, within walking distance.

Lastly, those looking for a reasonable option with a beach focus may like to try **Anlin Beach House** (© **044/533-3694;** www.anlinbeachhouse.co.za). It's not right on Robberg beach (100m/33 ft. away), but priced from R850 to R1,530 double per night, breakfast included, it's an affordable option. It's a fairly standard, modern converted home, though, so don't expect loads of privacy, and not all rooms are equal: The Seaview Suite is probably the most desirable.

In Plettenberg Bay

The Grand Rooms ★★★ As stylish, quirky, and classy as ever, the Grand provides a modern take on the boardinghouse and is by far the most interesting accommodations option in Plett. On the high street (close to everything, and walking distance to the beach), it's all about easy living. An extra three rooms now face the pool courtyard in addition to the original four huge suites, with their impressive views; each is very individually decorated. All lean toward a witty, bohemian feel, including king-size beds that are extrahigh (with footstools) and extralong; in room no. 6, the free-standing tub is placed, altarlike, in front of shuttered doors that open onto views of Lookout Beach. For a little extra romance—and your own pool—book the Bath House, which has twin Victorian bathtubs nestled side by side. Head downstairs to be plied with drinks around the pool or in the comfortable, wryly decorated lounge areas, and be sure to book a table at the restaurant.

27 Main Rd., Plettenberg Bay. © **044/533-3301.** Fax 044/533-4247. www.thegrand.co.za. 7 units. R1,900–R2,700 double. Rates include continental breakfast. MC, V. **Amenities:** Restaurant; lounges; pool; room service; free Wi-Fi. *In room:* TV/DVD, CD players.

Milkwood Manor ★ Value A modest, dignified guesthouse with a great location, Milkwood Manor was once tucked away amid dense trees, but massive floods changed the course of the Keurbooms River, and now the Manor is drenched in light and sunshine and perched literally meters from the river mouth; you can watch fresh water meet the sea from your bed. The Georgian-style building is decorated with a subtle Eastern flavor, and rooms are comfortable, if not huge (beds are queen-sized or twins; specify if you want a bathtub). Be sure to claim a room with a view of the sea and lagoon; no. 2 is a winner. Out back is a gate onto the river, a terrace, and on-site restaurant **Lemon Grass** (which serves fresh seafood and grills with few bells and whistles). This owner-run establishment is not flashy, but has a quiet charm.

Salmack Rd., Keurbooms River Mouth, Plettenberg Bay. © **044/533-0420.** Fax 044/533-0921. www.milkwoodmanor.co.za. 12 units. Lagoon- and sea-facing units R960–R1,800 double, depending on season. Rates include breakfast. MC, V. Children over 8 are welcome. **Amenities:** Restaurant; bar; lounge; canoes; tidal pool; free Wi-Fi. *In room:* Fan, TV, hair dryer, no phone.

Plettenberg Park ★★ Situated a few minutes from town on the cliffs overlooking the Indian Ocean and surrounded by a private nature reserve, this is a most exclusive retreat. Once a holiday home, its northern aspect overlooks a tranquil lake, and the southern views are of pounding ocean. A path winds from the elevated timber decks down the cliff to a tidal pool and private beach, but it's a stiff walk. Both the older rooms and the newer, hotel-like wing have been refurbished; while certainly airy, some might find the overall feel bland, even with the contemporary art adorning the walls. But it's the views that are king here—specify which you'd prefer (sea or lake) when making reservations. Service is attentive and personal; the chef will even create the daily menu around your preferences (a four-course dinner is R275). If you're looking for a romantic retreat with little disturbance from the outside world, this is perfect—the only drawback is that you have to share it.

Robberg Rd., Plettenberg Bay. ✆ **044/533-9067.** Fax 044/533-9092. www.plettenbergpark.co.za. 10 units. High season R4,380–R6,040 double; low season R3,260–R4,520 double. Rates include breakfast. AE, DC, MC, V. Children 12 and over are welcome. **Amenities:** Dining room; bar; Jacuzzi; pool; room service; sauna; free Wi-Fi access in library (own laptop required). *In room:* TV/DVD, fireplace, hair dryer, minibar.

Singing Kettle Beach Lodge ★ Value Finds There's nothing fancy about this beachfront hotel, but that's exactly what I like about it. Besides the fact that it really is right on the beach, and appropriately casual for a family hotel, it's small—only two spacious deluxe suites (able to accommodate four) with equipped kitchenette, and four standard double rooms with small overtures to self-sufficiency (toaster, fridge, microwave, that sort of thing). Decor is of the pine-and-laminate-floor variety, but very comfortable, and each room has a balcony with deck furniture to enjoy the lovely sea and beach views. The restaurant, **Enrico,** is a popular hangout for locals—besides the food, it's the timber deck with beach and sunset views that pulls 'em in. Rates are very affordable—it's pitched at the local market, so book well in advance.

Main St., Keurboomstrand Beach, Plett. ✆ **044/535-9477.** Fax 044/535-9478. www.singingkettle.co.za. 6 units. High season (Dec–Apr) R1,200–R1,900 double; low season R920–R1,380 double. Rates include basic health breakfast. AE, MC, V. **Amenities:** Lounge; babysitting. *In room:* TV, fridge, hair dryer.

Southern Cross Guest House ★ Value This pale-pink-and-white timber beach house is one of the most beautiful homes in concrete-dominated Plettenberg—an American Colonial seaboard-style home. It's also Plett's only guesthouse built right on the beach; a timber boardwalk leads through the vegetated dunes to the sand. Located on the western side of Robberg Beach, close to the reserve, the beach is pretty deserted and provides an excellent sense of escape. Rooms are tasteful—like the rest of the house, they are decorated predominantly in cool whites with an occasional touch of black or natural wood. The owners (who live upstairs) have definitely bagged the best views—all the guest rooms are built around a grassy courtyard, so none enjoys a sea view, and unless you close your doors and curtains, they lack privacy.

2 Capricorn Lane, Plettenberg Bay 6600. ✆ **044/533-3868.** Fax 044/533-3866. www.southerncross beach.co.za. 5 units. High season R1,560–R1,950 double; low season R1,320–R1,660 double. Rates include breakfast. AE, DC, MC, V. **Amenities:** Lounge. *In room:* TV, hair dryer.

Around Plettenberg Bay

Besides the above, Plett's best accommodations are outside of town, surrounded by indigenous bush and forests and beautiful gardens, with cliff- or riverside settings. The only drawback is that you'll have to drive to the beach. Besides these reviewed below, there are two options worth looking at, both a few miles before the Plett turnoff. **Fynbos Ridge** ★ (✆ **044/532-7862;** www.fynbosridge.co.za; rooms R1,200–R2,000 double, including breakfast; cottages R1,200–R1,600) is a small, private floral reserve with enthusiastic new owners. It offers five rooms in the Cape Dutch–style manor house, a studio apartment, and three newly refurbished freestanding cottages. **Laird's Lodge** (✆ **044/532-7721;** www.lairdslodge.co.za; R1,400–R2,200 double, including breakfast) is more like a small (15 rooms), stylish hotel.

Emily Moon River Lodge ★★ Built among milkwood trees and overlooking a wetland valley ringed by distant mountains, Emily Moon River Lodge combines an unbeatable location with Indo-Afro-chic styling. Set on the Bitou River just outside Plettenberg Bay, this is the perfect romantic getaway, a quiet sanctuary that's great for honeymooners and birders. Each secluded lodge, individually decorated with real flair and with a strong focus on comfort, has a private living area and fireplace leading onto a private deck, which overlooks the wetland below. This is the kind of room you can easily spend the whole day in. In-house restaurant **Emily's** (daily, lunch, and dinner) is also very good; it's worth booking into the lodge just to make sure you get a table, as it's now a favorite with locals.

Bitou River, Plettenberg Bay ✆ **044/533-2982.** Fax 044/533-0687. www.emilymoon.co.za. 7 units (also 1 family unit, sleeps 4). R1,070–R2,210 depending on season. Rates include breakfast. AE, DISC, MC, V. **Amenities:** Restaurant; bar; adventure bookings; canoes; mountain bikes; pool; free Wi-Fi in reception. *In room:* TV, hair dryer, minibar, under-floor heating.

Fairview ★★ Finds Fairview lives up to its name: a gracious Cape Dutch–styled family home set above a forested valley, which you can book either by the room or as one gorgeous entity. The mood is one of out-of-time elegance: Bird-and-floral wallpaper adorns the master bedroom, and a sitting room and dining area are furnished with antiques, good reading matter, a piano, and crystal decanters, plus the views of the Outeniqua Mountains from the patio. The gardens were created by owner Gillian, who wrote her book *In a Country Garden* here. The house offers a romantic retreat for couples wanting to get away from it all; it (and the nearby cottage) is also perfect for family holidays. ***Note:*** It is isolated, and you will have to drive or self-cater for meals other than breakfast.

12km (7.4 miles) drive east of Plett on the N2, signposted to the left. ✆ **034/642-1843.** Fax 034/271-8053. www.fugitives-drift-lodge.com. 3 bedrooms in main house and separate 3-bed cottage. Main bedroom R1,180–R1,600 depending on season; other rooms R640—R1,400 double. Rate includes breakfast (except Dec 15–Jan 15). AE, DC, MC, V. **Amenities:** Lounge; TV/DVD; barbecue facilities; kitchen; pool. *In room:* Hair dryer, under-floor heating.

Hog Hollow Country Lodge ★★ Overlooking the dense indigenous forests that drop away below the lodge and carpet the Tsitsikamma Mountains beyond, Hog Hollow offers charm, comfort, and privacy. Both duplex and simplex suites—all have private lounges and extended decks—are recommended: French doors lead out onto private balconies or decks with hammocks and chairs to soak in the views of the gorge. The six "forest" luxury suites are slightly bigger, but two of these are a fair walk to the main house. One of the most charming units is the "round house"; the master bedroom with wooden balcony is upstairs, and the lounge with fireplace is downstairs. Hog Hollow is renowned for its food—dinner is a set affair that will run you R240. Meals are served around the large dining room table, turning the event into an informal dinner party (although you're also welcome to dine alone). Service is excellent.

Askop Rd., The Crags, Plettenberg Bay 6600 (16km/10 miles east of Plett, signposted off the N2). ✆/fax **044/534-8879.** www.hog-hollow.com. 16 units. R2,900 double. Rates include breakfast. AE, DC, MC, V. Closed for a month in winter. Children by prior arrangement only. **Amenities:** Dining room; bar; babysitting; pool; sauna; free Wi-Fi in lodge. *In room:* CD player, fireplace, hair dryer, minibar, no phone.

Hunter's Country House/Tsala Treetops Lodge ★★★ Kids Hunter's property comprises two entirely separate lodges: Country House has charming cottages set in beautifully manicured gardens, each individually furnished with antiques, and with its own fireplace and private patio. This section is child friendly, with an informal dining area, a Teen Scene room complete with darts and pool table, and a preschool teacher to keep the little ones occupied. Meals are excellent (both Hunter's and Tsala are Relais & Châteaux members), and the personal, warm, discreet service has earned this luxurious hotel its many accolades. Hunter's biggest drawback? No views, which is one reason to head for sister lodge, **Tsala Treetops.** In the style of the luxurious safari camp, Tsala features a large double-volume open-plan public space surrounded by generous decking, off which elevated boardwalks connect 10 private glass and timber "treehouses" and 6 new stone-and-timber two-bed villas (the latter with kitchenettes). Tsala's rooms are huge, with fabulous views of the forested surrounds from every vantage, including the lounge (with fireplace) and deck, with a private plunge pool.

10km (6¼ miles) west of Plett, off the N2. ✆ **044/533-5533.** Fax 044/533-5973. www.hunterhotels.com. Tsala 16 units. Hunter's 21 units. Tsala suites high season R7,220 double, R9,580 villa (4 persons); low season suite R3,970 double, villa R5,260 (4 persons). Hunter's Garden cottage high season R3,620 double; Premier suites R4,240; Classic and Forest suites R6,100–R7,650; children sharing R710 extra. All rates include breakfast; call for low-season rates. AE, DC, MC, V. No children under 10 at Tsala. **Amenities:** Dining rooms; bar; lounges; children's facilities at Hunter's; concierge; library; massage; pool; room service; free Wi-Fi in lodge. *In room:* A/C, TV, fireplace, hair dryer, minibar, pool (in Classic, Forest, and all Tsala suites).

Kurland ★★★ Kids Surrounded by paddocks and polo fields, this gracious country house of note is the country's premier polo destination (in fact, Kurland International Day is considered one of the world's top polo matches). It's better than Hunter's (more intimate, with only 12 rooms), and despite its grand air (it's been a Relais & Châteaux member since 2006), it's not at all stuffy and has always gone all out to make kids happy, which gives it a winning edge for parents. Rooms are huge (each with a living area, some with private plunge pools) and filled with character; decorated in authentic English country-manor style, with antiques, book cases, oil paintings, and blousy bouquets. Ten suites have loft rooms, with pint-size furnishings for children—there are also two extra pools for the kids and a dedicated playroom. You have to drive to the beach, but there's plenty of other things to do—like get a massage, lounge around the library, or mount a polo pony or quad bike to explore the 700-hectare (1,700 acre) estate. Unless you need a sea view, it's the best option on the Garden Route.

19km (12 miles) east of Plett, off N2. ✆ **044/534-8082.** Fax 044/534-8699. www.kurland.co.za. High season R6,460–R9,760 double; low season R3,500–R6,460. Rates include breakfast (and dinner in high season). Ask about low-season specials. AE, DC, MC, V. **Amenities:** Dining room; bar; babysitting; mountain bikes; horseback riding; library; 2 pools; room service; spa; tennis; free Wi-Fi in library. *In room:* Fans, TV, fireplace, hair dryer, minibar.

Where to Dine

It's the location rather than the food that draws people to **Lookout Deck** (✆ **044/533-1379**). Right on the beach, with awesome views across the ocean to the Tsitsikamma Mountains stretching beyond, this is probably the best-placed restaurant on the Garden Route. Enjoy a sunrise breakfast on the upstairs deck, or get here for sundown and try the Lookout's famous wild oysters, picked off the Plett coast. Sipping sundowners at Lookout Deck is a hard act to follow, but if you tire of the semi-attired *Baywatch*-type babes and bums tossing back Mermaid's Orgasms and Beach Affairs, there's room to move on.

For sparkling wine and gourmet pizzas, head for **Cornutti Al Mare** ★ (✆ **044/533-1277**). You can't miss it—it's to the left of the hill you have to drive down to get to Central/Robberg beach. The facade and balcony are covered in hand-painted tiles and mosaics, and the views are great across the bay from the outdoor tables (book a table indoors next to the fire if you're traveling in winter). **Enrico** ★ (✆ **044/535-9818;** open daily), located below the rooms of the **Singing Kettle Beach Lodge** (p. 270), is a great beachfront option, on Keurbooms beach (a few minutes' drive east of Plett center). The predominantly Italian menu is not adventurous, but it's good (better than Lookout Deck), and the beach and ocean views really are wonderful. Also highly recommended is **Emily's** (p. 271), now routinely named by locals as their favorite place to eat: Expect hearty, contemporary fare served in a relaxed atmosphere. **Nguni** ★, at 6 Crescent St. (✆ **044/533-6710**), is named after a South African cattle breed, and, yes, you'll find beef on the menu in this black-and-white-styled restaurant with slate floors and thick white walls (it was once a fisherman's cottage). The owners also have a strong focus on fresh and local produce, "and that means fish." Also in the center of town is **The Old Post Office** (✆ **076/953-6888**), a casually stylish new venue, unfortunately placed in a mall on the main road into town. Lunch is a buffet table, while dinner offers a la carte delicacies such as truffle-infused butter bean ravioli or basil-roasted chicken supreme with orange salad. Just upstairs is the stylish Plett set's current favorite, **Fu.shi** ★★ (✆ **044/533-6497**), one of our favorite restaurants on the Garden Route (it's cracked the nod from *Wine* magazine, too). Expect consistently fine Asian fusion meals and delectable sushi in sleek surroundings. Those who want to star- or sea-gaze while eating also have the choice of the adjoining champagne bar, **BoMa.**

If you're after a fine-dining experience with exceptional sea views, you'd be hard-pressed to beat a table at the refurbished **Sand at The Plettenberg** ★★★ (✆ **044/533-2030**). Their summer tasting menu, a seven-course feast that showcases the best of the kitchen's summer dishes, can be enjoyed with wines chosen to complement each item (it'll run you R350, or R610 with wine). Or opt for forest surrounds and a more cozy candlelit atmosphere at **Tsala Treetops Lodge** (✆ **044/532-8228**), where the excellent pan-African fusion *table d'hôte* menu will run you R325. Tslala now also boasts the new African-styled **Zinzi** (✆ **044/532-8226**). The fusion menu specializes in large themed platters, from Cape to Mediterranean, Moroccan, or Pan-African; you will eat on oversize furniture (ottomans, wingbacks, cushions) surrounded by an eclectic mix of artifacts from Ethiopia to Tonga.

TSITSIKAMMA NATIONAL PARK & STORMS RIVER MOUTH

Starting from just beyond Keurboomstrand in the west, this narrow coastal belt extends 80km (50 miles) along one of the most beautiful sections of the southern Cape coastline, and includes a marine reserve that stretches 5.5km (3½ miles) out to sea. The craggy, lichen-flecked coastline is cut through with spectacular river gorges, and the cliff surrounds are carpeted in fynbos and dense forest. The fact that the Otter Trail, which takes in the entire coastline, is South Africa's most popular trail gives some indication of its beauty (see "Staying Active," earlier in this chapter).

Tsitsikamma is roughly divided into two sections: De Vasselot (which incorporates the lovely **Nature's Valley**) in the west, and Storms River Mouth in the east. There is no direct road linking them, but it's well worth taking the detour off the N2 and visiting both, though Storms River Mouth is the more awesome sight of the two. To reach Nature's Valley, the only settlement in the park, take the scenic R102 or Groot River Pass. Visit the ever-helpful Beefy and Tish, who run a local information center from the **Nature's Valley Restaurant, Pub and Trading Store** (✆ **044/531-6835;** beefy@xnets.co.za) and can help with anything from a weather report to local B&B or self-catering accommodations options.

To visit **Storms River Mouth,** take the marked turnoff, some 60km (37 miles) from Plettenberg Bay, and travel 10km (6¼ miles) toward the coast. (***Note:*** Do not confuse

Storms River Mouth with Storms River Village, which is just off the N2 and has nothing much to recommend it.) The gate is open 24 hours, and the entry fee is R88 per adult, and R44 for kids from 2 to 16. You can eat at **Tsitsikamma Restaurant** (✆ **042/281-1190**). At the beginning of the walk to the Storms River Mouth, it has one of the best locations on the entire Garden Route, right on the sea, but features pretty standard fare: a variety of linefish, steak, spareribs, and the like. A better option is to look for the sign just off the N2 (at Tsitsikamma Lodge) for **Fynboshoek Cheese** ★★ (✆ **042/280-3879**), where you can enjoy wonderful fixed-menu lunches made and grown by resident cheese maker Alje. There are only 20 seats, and reservations are essential (food is prepared for the number of people expected).

Exploring on Foot

With no roads connecting sites of interest, this is, for most, the only way to explore the park. (There is also a snorkeling and scuba-diving trail, however; for equipment and a guide, contact the **Dive Hut** [✆ **073/130-0689**] at Storms River Mouth rest camp.) **Stormsriver Adventures** (✆ **042/281-1836**) also offers activities in and around the park, including **canopy tours** ★★★, where you slide along steel cables 30m (98 ft.) above the forest floor—a delightful experience and, judging by the surrounding grins, one enjoyed by both the very young and fairly old. The easiest and most popular walking trail is the 1km (just over ½ mile) boardwalk, which starts at the visitor's office, and winds its way along the mountainside, providing beautiful glimpses of the sea and forest, and finally descending to the narrow mouth where the dark waters of the Storms River surge into the foaming sea. This walk also takes you past the appropriately named **Mooi (Pretty) Beach,** a tiny cove where the swimming is safe, though the water can be very cold. Once at the mouth, don't miss the excavated cave, with its displays relating to the Khoi *strandlopers* (beachcombers) who frequented the area more than 2,000 years ago. You can cross the suspension bridge that fords the mouth and climb the cliff for excellent ocean views, though it's steep going. To explore the otherwise inaccessible gorge, catch the ***Spirit of the Tsitsikamma*** ★, a boat that departs from the Tsitsikamma restaurant from 9:30am to 3:45pm every 45 minutes for a half-hour journey upstream. The trip costs R60 per person. To find out more about the various trails, pick up a map from the visitor's office (✆ **042/281-1607**) at the rest camp. Hours are from 7am to 6pm daily.

Where to Stay & Dine

Storms River Mouth Restcamp ★ Value The South African Parks Board is not about to win any architectural awards, but Storms River is their best attempt. Almost all the units enjoy good sea views, particularly the "oceanettes." Try to book a ground-floor apartment; in front is a narrow strip of lawn with your own barbecue, and beyond lie the rocks and the pounding surf. You can head off into the forest or walk the rocks; at low tide, the rock pools reveal a treasure trove of shapes and colors. The only drawback to the oceanettes is that they are the farthest units from the restaurant, though the short drive, which snakes along the coast, is hardly unpleasant. If you're going to have all your meals at the restaurant, consider staying in the forest huts, particularly nos. 1 and 2, which overlook a burbling stream, but keep in mind that the cabins are sweltering hot in peak summer and you share ablutions (although all units should have their own bath and shower by 2010). Better still is to book one of the following: nos. 8a, 8b, 16a, 16b, or 17 (all honeymoon suites; R900), and 9 and 10 (family cottages) are right on the ocean. Also, two spacious new guest cottages with a few more luxuries (such as TV/DVDs and nicer decor) are now available: They are a short, steep walk up from the restaurant and sea, but beautifully located and able to sleep eight people apiece.

Reserve through National Parks Board. ✆ **012/428-9111.** Direct inquiries ✆ **042/281-1607.** www.sanparks.org. 84 units, consisting of 8-bed, 7-bed, 4-bed, and 2-bed log chalets; 3- and 4-bed oceanettes; and 2-bed forest huts. Rates start at R340 for forest huts; R660 double for log cabin/chalet; R1,095 for family cottage; R620–R1,095 for oceanette; from R2,155 for guest cottage (1–4 people). 10% discount May–Aug. AE, DC, MC, V. **Amenities:** Restaurant; pool; shop.

8 SIDE TRIPS TO THE NORTHERN CAPE

A DRIVING TOUR OF NAMAQUALANDA

Most of the year, the sandveld region north of the Olifants River, a vast semiarid area known as Namaqualand, sees very few visitors. But come the rains in August or September, the seeds that lie dormant under these dusky plains explode into vivid bloom, and 4,000 species deck the ground in a magnificent, multicolored carpet. Because of the huge distances to cover to get to Namaqualand (Springbok is some 544km/337 miles from Cape Town), you might want to make sure that the season has begun before you set off on a driving tour (though you'll struggle to find accommodations if you haven't booked well in advance). Note that the season starts on the coast and moves inland. Getting there is pretty straightforward: The area is reached via the N7 highway, which connects Cape Town with Namibia. If you find the distances daunting, note that **Signature Flight Support** (✆ **021/934-0350**) will fly you by private charter to **Springbok Airport** or other Northern Cape destinations.

The seasonal flower displays start quite close to Cape Town (see "Darling," "Riebeek Kasteel," "West Coast National Park," and "Paternoster & Columbine Nature Reserve," earlier in this chapter), but you enter the more remote and more spectacular flower region soon after the N7 bypasses Vanrhynsdorp, 283km (175 miles) north of Cape Town. This marks the halfway point between Cape Town and Namaqualand's "capital," Springbok, and while it's strictly still part of the Western Cape, it's well worth planning an overnight stop in the region. To do this, ascend the African plateau by taking the R27 via Van Rhyn's Pass to charming **Nieuwoudtville** ★★, touted as the bulb capital of the world and famed for its white sandstone architecture, or travel farther east to **Calvinia.** If you're traveling in late August, note that the biggest *braai* (barbecue) in the country—the annual **Hantam Meat Festival**—is held in Calvinia at this time, offering rare tastings of such native delicacies as *kaiings* (salted crackling) and *skilpadjies* (liver in caul fat). To overnight in Nieuwoudtville during flower season, you'll have to reserve long in advance: Try booking the stone-and-thatch cottages De Hoop and Gert Boom at **Papkuilsfontien** (✆ **027/218-1246;** www.papkuilsfontein.com; dinner on request), or contact the **Nieuwoudtville Publicity Association** (✆ **027/218-1336**) for more accommodations options. A wonderful place to see the vast variety of flowering bulbs and annuals is the new 6,200-hectare (15,320-acre) **Hantam National Botanical Garden** (✆ **027/218-1200;** Mon–Fri 7:30am–4:30pm; also Sat–Sun during 3-month flower season; R10 per adult). Over 1,350 species (80 endemic) have been recorded here; a staggering 40% of which are bulbs. To find out about possible tours of the area, write to **hantam@sanbi.org**.

Having traversed the **Knersvlakte** (literally, "Plains of Grinding Teeth"), the first important stop north of Vanrhynsdorp is **Kamieskroon** (174km/109 miles farther on the N7), the last town before Springbok, which lies some 67km (42 miles) farther north on the N7. Kamieskroon is literally a one-horse town, but its claim to fame is the nearby **Skilpad (Tortoise) Wildflower Reserve** ★★★ (✆ **027/672-1948;** daily 8am–5pm in season only, entrance fee R35). Created by the World Wildlife Fund, and part of the Namaqua National Park, the reserve (18km/11 miles west of town on Wolwepoort Rd.) catches what little rain blows in off the sea and is always magnificent during the flower season. The other reason to stop here is the **Kamieskroon Hotel** (✆ **027/672-1614;** kamieshotel@kingsley.co.za). The hotel charges R335 per person during the flower season (including breakfast) and also cohosts the annual **Namaqualand Photographic Workshops** (www.kamieskroonhotel.com). Cofounded by local photographer Colla Swart and the internationally renowned Canadian photographer Freeman Patterson (the latter was involved in the 2006 workshop; for 2009, Frank Krummacher and Hansie Oosthuizen will be leading the groups), the spring workshop usually runs for 7 days and costs around R8,400 per person; look at the website for exact dates and prices (and do it soon; there is usually a waiting list). ***Note:*** Try to get your hands on a copy of *Freeman Patterson's Garden of the Gods* (Human & Rousseau), which features the beauty of Namaqualand in full bloom, to whet your appetite for a trip north.

The best place to stay (and eat) in Springbok is the **Springbok Lodge & Restaurant,** on the corner of Voortrekker and Keerom roads (✆ **027/712-1321;** www.springbok lodge.com; R300 double without air-conditioning and fridge, or R325 double with air-conditioning and fridge; family units are also available). The lodge is clean, but it's far from luxurious. Owner Jopie Kotze, who calls his lodge "a living museum," is a mine of information, and his restaurant walls are lined with photographs and artifacts relating to the area. The lodge also sponsors the Nababeep Mining Museum (found in the small town of the same name 22km/14 miles from Springbok); neighboring O'Kiep also has fascinating, if rusty, reminders of when it was a copper-mining town. You can also overnight in self-catering chalets at Springbok's top attraction, the **Goegap Nature Reserve** ★★ (✆ **027/718-9906**), 15km (9¼ miles) southeast of Springbok. It's open daily from 8am to 4pm. Admission is R15.

THE RICHTERSVELD & KALAHARI DESERT

Adventurers who appreciate spectacular, rocky mountain landscapes, almost lunar in their desolation and emptiness (except, once again, for the few weeks when spring rains turn the dusty expanses into never-ending gardens), may like to venture farther north still (about 4½-hr. drive from Springbok) to the **Richtersveld National Park,** created in 1991. Home to the Nama people (descendents of the Khoi-Khoi), this vast swathe of land, with its fascinating plant life, was recently returned to the community in one of the country's largest land restitution agreements. Now declared a UNESCO World Heritage site, the area is largely dedicated to conservation, but you will need a tough 4WD to explore it; what lodgings there are to be had are very basic and far-flung. The easiest way to access the area is probably with a guide such as Jaco (see below), although if you have a 4x4 (and a spare tire or two), you could self-drive. The National Park has 10 air-conditioned chalets at Sendelingsdrift (www.sanparks.org), but make no mistake: This is no-frills territory and you need to come properly equipped.

Equally breathtaking and more accessible (in the sense that you don't always need a 4WD), is the Kalahari Desert. The sandveld environment alone is stunning—rust-red

Kalahari sand dunes and wispy blonde grasses contrast starkly with huge cobalt-blue skies—yet this harsh and arid landscape supports a surprisingly varied and rich amount of game. Besides the big-maned "Kalahari" lion, you will find cheetahs, hyenas, elephants, jackals, and the gemsbok (oryx). Travelers on a budget should book at the **Kgalagadi Transfrontier Park.** Kgalagadi (literally, "Place Without Water") is one of Africa's biggest reserves, covering an area of more than 38,000 sq. km (14,672 sq. miles). **Twee Rivieren** is the most developed rest camp, and **Nossob,** on the dry riverbed that creates a natural unfenced boundary between South Africa and Botswana, is the most isolated; but the tented camps should be your final destination (see below).

A vastly more luxurious destination in the interior semideserts of the Northern Cape—one you would be best off flying to—is the Oppenheimer family's **Tswalu Kalahari Reserve.** At more than 1,000 sq. km, it's the largest privately owned reserve in the country (© **011/274-2299** reservations; 053/781-9211 lodge; R11,800 double; ask about specials). Located near the blips on the map that are Sishen and Kuruman (and not that far from the aptly named Hotazhel), Tswalu offers a luxurious safari-style experience in a very different setting. Initially developed by the late Steve Boler, an ardent hunter who imported 9,000 head of game, including lions, black rhinos, cheetahs, leopards, and buffalo, the Oppenheimers have received expert help in ensuring the suitability of animals to this arid terrain. Although the vegetation type does not support elephant, you could see such rarities as sable antelope, cheetah, and wild dogs; sightings are excellent, as there's no thick vegetation to conceal animals. It is also one of the most luxurious safari lodges on the continent (interiors are by the same decorators who created the much lauded Singita camps). **Motse,** the main camp found below the Korannaberg mountains, offers eight individual stone, clay, and thatch lodges with private decks overlooking a waterhole, two of which are large enough for families (**Tarkuni Lodge,** where friends or family groups of up to 10 can enjoy complete privacy in a remote valley inside the reserve, is also available when the Oppenheimers are not in residence). As a Relais & Châteaux member, expect quality food; activities include hot-air ballooning, horseback-riding, and archery, as well as game-drives. Tswalu offer direct transfer flights from Cape Town; these cost R3,050 one-way.

Essentials

GETTING THERE & AROUND Unless you really like road trips and have plenty of time, it's probably best to fly into the region. **SA Airlink** (© **054/332-2161**) flies from Johannesburg and Cape Town to **Upington Airport** (© **054/337-7900**), the closest transport hub. From here, you can contact Newton Walker of **Walker Flying Service** (© **082/820-5394**) and charter a flight, if you wish. If he takes you into the park's Twee Rivieren camp, you can pick up a prearranged car here (see below); alternatively, pick up a car at the airport. **Avis** has a desk (© **054/332-4746**) at the Upington Airport and will also drop a car off at the park. Unless you intend to enter Botswana or venture to the remote Bitterpan Wilderness Camp, you won't need a four-wheel-drive, but to get the most out of your trip here, it's worth considering. For the best game-viewing opportunities, make sure you rise early (see "Better Wildlife-Viewing for the Self-Guide Safari" on p. 352 for more game-viewing tips), take plenty of extra water, and be prepared to travel long distances—the shortest circular drive is 100km (62 miles) long. Ask at Twee Rivieren about evening game drives with experienced rangers—these are recommended.

GUIDED TOURS **Jaco Powell** ★ (© **082/572-0065;** www.jacelstours.com), an honorary ranger for South African National Parks (SANParks) and a rich source of information on the Kalahari fauna and flora, offers fully catered specialist tours in Kgalagadi and Richtersveld, as well as guided trips to Tswalu. Contact Jaco at **info@jacelstours.com**. Pieter Hanekom's **Kalahari Safaris** ★★ (✆ **054/332-5653** or 082/435-0007; www.kalaharisafaris.co.za) organizes a variety of options in Kgalagadi, designed to satisfy different budgets.

VISITOR INFORMATION For both **Kgalagadi** and **Richtersveld** inquiries, contact **SANParks** (✆ **012/428-9111;** fax 012/343-0905; www.sanparks.org). The **Kgalagadi** park is quite popular, particularly the tented camps, so book well in advance. The **Visitors Centre** (✆ **054/561-2000**) is at Twee Rivieren, the park's headquarters. There is a daily conservation fee: R140 adults, R70 children.

WHEN TO GO Rain falls mainly between January and April. The best time to visit is between March and May (autumn), when it's neither too hot nor too dry. In summer, temperatures may exceed 104°F (40°C). In winter, temperatures at night are often below zero. Note that the park's gate hours vary considerably, depending on the season, and are strictly adhered to—if you aren't going to arrive between 7:30am and 6pm, call ahead to find out exactly what time the gates close.

Where to Stay in the Kgalagadi

Given the distances, self-drivers will almost certainly have to book their first night at **Twee Rivieren,** which is run by South African National Parks (see "Visitor Information," above, for booking information). Twee Rivieren is just beyond the entrance to the park; this is also the only camp with a restaurant, a pool, and air-conditioned units. Each of the self-catering two-, three-, four-, and six-bed chalets (all en suite) has a fully equipped kitchen and a *braai* (barbecue) area. Each two-bed cottage costs R450 a night for two people; the six-bed cottages cost R760. Besides the basic restaurant, there is a takeout shop, fuel station, and grocery shop; you can buy supplies such as milk, bread, wood, frozen meat, eggs, and tinned food here, but it's best to stock up on a few extras in Upington. Better still, head northwest to **!Xaus Lodge** ★★ (www.xauslodge.co.za; R5,000 double, all-inclusive; activities include game walks with San, night drives, and more). Opening in July 2007, this small (12 units) thatched lodge is the first fully catered lodge in the Kgalagadi, overlooking an enormous salt pan where you can observe the animals drinking at the waterhole below. It's owned by the Khomani San and Mier communities, who reached a land settlement agreement with the government and South African National Parks in May 2002, taking transfer of 50,000 hectares (123,500 acres) of land, which the two communities then leased back to SANParks in one of the most successful community initiatives to date.

If, however, you are of an adventurous ilk, the reason you are here is to spend a few nights in one or more of the park's five very remote and semiprivate wilderness camps—a steal, at R720 to R760 double. ***Note:*** You'll need to book early to snag one.

Each wilderness camp features four two-bed units (R760 double) with their own fully equipped (gas-powered) kitchen and bathroom with a shower; linen and towels are provided, but you should stock up on food, bottled water, and firewood, none of which are available on-site. Closest are **Urikaruus** ★ and **Kieliekrankie** ★, 2 hours and 90 minutes, respectively, from Twee Rivieren. Urikaruus's timber units, built on stilts, are situated on the banks of the Auob River and overlook a busy waterhole. Kieliekrankie, built with fixed structures, feels as though it's in the middle of nowhere, and is approached via a tunnel dug into the red Kalahari dunes. From either of the wilderness camps, you can follow the course of the dry Auob River—which offers excellent game-viewing opportunities—to **Mata Mata,** which lies 120km (74 miles; 2½ hr.), and on to the nearby **Kalahari Tented Camp** ★★. Mata Mata is a great deal more rustic than Twee Rivieren, but not by any means as remote as the wilderness camps; we suggest you simply fill up here (it has a shop stocked with basic supplies and a fuel station) and press on to Kalahari Tented Camp, which lies about 3km (1¾ miles) away. Here you overnight at one of 15 en-suite desert "tents" (sandbag and canvas constructions on wooden floors, with such amenities as kitchenettes, bathrooms, and ceiling fans; R790 double), or book early for the pick of them all, the honeymoon unit (R885 double).

Alternatively, head north to the three most remote wilderness camps: **Bitterpan** ★, a stilted camp overlooking a waterhole, is accessible only by 4WD via Nossob, which is about 3 hours from Bitterpan. **Grootkolk** ★ and **Gharagab** ★ are equally popular, despite the vast distances you have to travel to reach them (some 6 hr. from Twee Rivieren); at Gharagab, you have the added benefit of showering beneath the stars. Gloriously remote and silent, it's accessible only by 4WD vehicle.

7 Undiscovered Wilderness: The Eastern Cape

The country's second-largest province has a sun-drenched coastline that stretches for 800km (496 miles), from the lush Garden Route to subtropical KwaZulu-Natal, rolling past green hills and small seaside towns. Deeper in the hinterland lie vast scrubland plains where the Big 5 again wander. A decade ago, the Eastern Cape was rarely included in international travel itineraries; most of its attractions, such as the Wild Coast and pretty Graaff-Reinet, are well off the beaten track. But the large-scale and ongoing rehabilitation of vast tracts of fallow farmland into game sanctuaries has transformed the region into a must-see destination, not least because these reserves enjoy the additional advantages of being malaria free and are easily accessible—a mere 45 to 90 minutes by car from the capital city of Port Elizabeth.

Besides the Greater Addo Elephant Park (now pushing beyond the 240,000-hectare/593,000-acre mark, along with a 120,000-hectare/297,000-acre marine reserve), there are private game reserves of between 6,000 and 25,000 hectares (14,800–61,800 acres), with accommodations as luxuriously appointed as those of their Kruger counterparts, and excellent game rangers on hand to unravel the mysteries of the bush. If you've planned a Cape Town–Garden Route itinerary, these reserves are definitely worth exploring, but bear in mind that the terrain—most of which is prickly, low-lying scrubland—is not the classic picture-postcard landscape of Africa. However, the sparseness of the vegetation means you never feel hemmed in: The vistas are huge, and the opportunities to see game are numerous. The area has its own strange beauty: You'll treasure such sights as a moonlit euphorbia forest, looking more like props from a sci-fi moonscape, or an entire hillside ablaze in orange aloe blossoms.

The Eastern Cape is also steeped in history: This is the birthplace of some of the country's most powerful political figures, the most famous of whom are Steve Biko and Nelson Mandela. And Port Elizabeth was a crucial center of the anti-apartheid movement, with a notoriously deadly security police in close attendance. Today a number of good operators offer excellent township tours that provide an insight into Port Elizabeth's role in South African history, as well as an authentic introduction into traditional Xhosa rites and ceremonies.

English-settler towns like Grahamstown also have fine examples of colonial-era architecture. Moving north into the thirstlands of the Karoo, you will find vast, uninhabited plains with such atmospheric names as the Valley of Desolation, near Graaff-Reinet, the Eastern Cape's oldest settlement. If you like unpopulated spaces, small towns, and picturesque architecture, this is a highly recommended detour, possibly on a self-drive tour between the Garden Route and Gauteng. Alternatively, opt to explore the coastal attractions, from surfing the perfect wave in Jeffrey's Bay to exploring the aptly named Wild Coast, where you'll find the country's most unspoiled beaches.

1 PORT ELIZABETH

763km (473 miles) E of Cape Town; 1,050km (651 miles) SW of Johannesburg

The approach to Port Elizabeth, referred to by locals as P.E. and now part of the Nelson Mandela Metropolitan Municipality, is somewhat depressing. Factories alternate with brown brick houses on the freeway into town, the ocean breeze is colored by the stench of smokestacks, and a network of elevated highways has effectively cut the center of the city off from the sea.

For most, Port Elizabeth is simply an entry or departure point—usually for a trip up or down the Garden Route, or to visit one of the nearby malaria-free game reserves. Thanks to a growing number of quality accommodation options and restaurants, plus some seriously appealing beaches, it can make a relaxed and unexpectedly stylish pit stop for a night or so. If you have a day to kill, take a township tour that covers some of the capital's political history, hang out on Humewood Beach, or amble along the Donkin Heritage Trail to take in P.E.'s settler history. If you're not spending the night in a game reserve, you can still take a number of good day trips (see below), though none are as satisfying as spending a few nights in the bush under a star-spangled sky.

ESSENTIALS

VISITOR INFORMATION Port Elizabeth tourism has been renamed **Nelson Mandela Bay Tourism** (✆ **041/585-8884;** Mon–Fri 8am–4:30pm, Sat–Sun 9:30am–3:30pm), but it's still in the Donkin Lighthouse Building, Donkin Reserve, central P.E; the satellite office (✆ **041/583-2030**) is at The Boardwalk, Marine Drive, in Summerstrand. The website www.nmbt.co.za is comprehensive and a good augmentation to the information here; the staff is also well informed.

The 1820 Settlers: Deceit, Despair & Courage

The Industrial Revolution and the end of the Napoleonic wars created a massive unemployment problem in Britain. With their underpopulated colony in southern Africa under threat by the indigenous tribes, the British authorities came up with the perfect solution: Lured by the promise of free land and a new life, 4,000 men, women, and children landed at Algoa Bay in 1820, more than doubling the colony's English-speaking population. Many were tradesmen and teachers with no knowledge of farming, and they were given no prior warning of their real function: to create a human barrier along the Fish River, marking the eastern border of the Cape Colony. On the other side of the river were the Xhosa (easiest to pronounce as "*kho*-sa"). The settlers were provided with tents, seeds, and a few bits of equipment, and given pockets of land too small for livestock and too poor for crops. Pestilence, flash floods, and constant attacks by the Xhosa laid waste their attempts to settle the land, and most of them slowly trickled into the towns to establish themselves in more secure trades. Thanks in no small measure to their stoic determination, Port Elizabeth is today the biggest coastal city between Cape Town and Durban, and the industrial hub of the Eastern Cape, with road, rail, and air links to every other major city in South Africa.

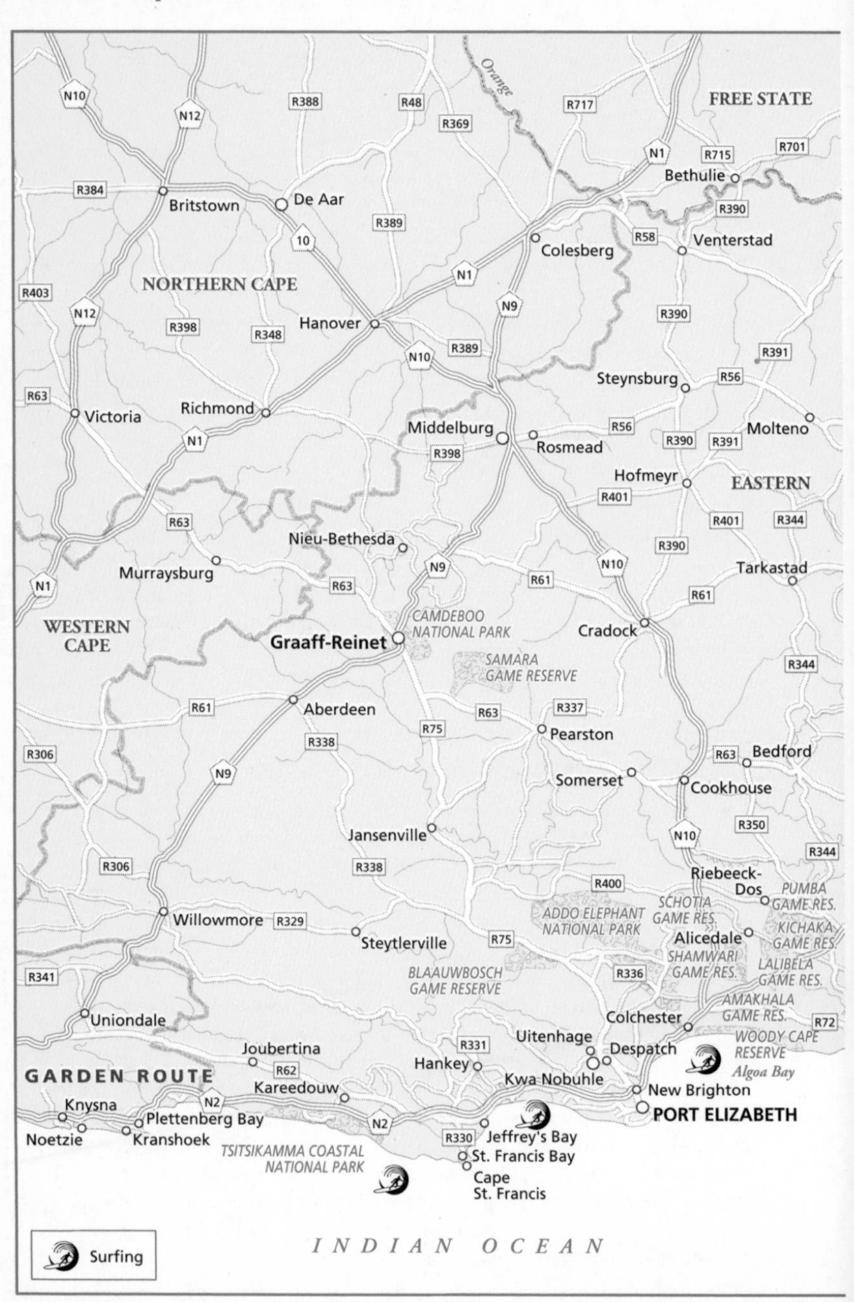
FREE STATE
NORTHERN CAPE
EASTERN
WESTERN CAPE
GARDEN ROUTE
INDIAN OCEAN
Orange
Bethulie
Britstown
De Aar
Colesberg
Venterstad
Hanover
Steynsburg
Victoria
Richmond
Middelburg
Rosmead
Molteno
Hofmeyr
Nieu-Bethesda
Murraysburg
Tarkastad
Cradock
Graaff-Reinet
CAMDEBOO NATIONAL PARK
SAMARA GAME RESERVE
Aberdeen
Pearston
Bedford
Somerset
Cookhouse
Jansenville
Riebeeck-Dos
PUMBA GAME RES.
SCHOTIA GAME RES.
ADDO ELEPHANT NATIONAL PARK
KICHAKA GAME RES.
Willowmore
Steytlerville
Alicedale
SHAMWARI GAME RES.
LALIBELA GAME RES.
BLAAUWBOSCH GAME RESERVE
AMAKHALA GAME RES.
Uniondale
Colchester
WOODY CAPE RESERVE
Algoa Bay
Uitenhage
Despatch
Joubertina
Hankey
Kwa Nobuhle
Kareedouw
New Brighton
PORT ELIZABETH
Knysna
Plettenberg Bay
Noetzie
Kranshoek
Jeffrey's Bay
St. Francis Bay
Cape St. Francis
TSITSIKAMMA COASTAL NATIONAL PARK
Surfing
N1
N2
N9
N10
N12
10
R384
R388
R48
R369
R717
R715
R701
R390
R389
R58
R403
R398
R348
R391
R63
R56
R401
R344
R61
R337
R75
R338
R306
R350
R400
R329
R336
R341
R72
R331
R62
R330

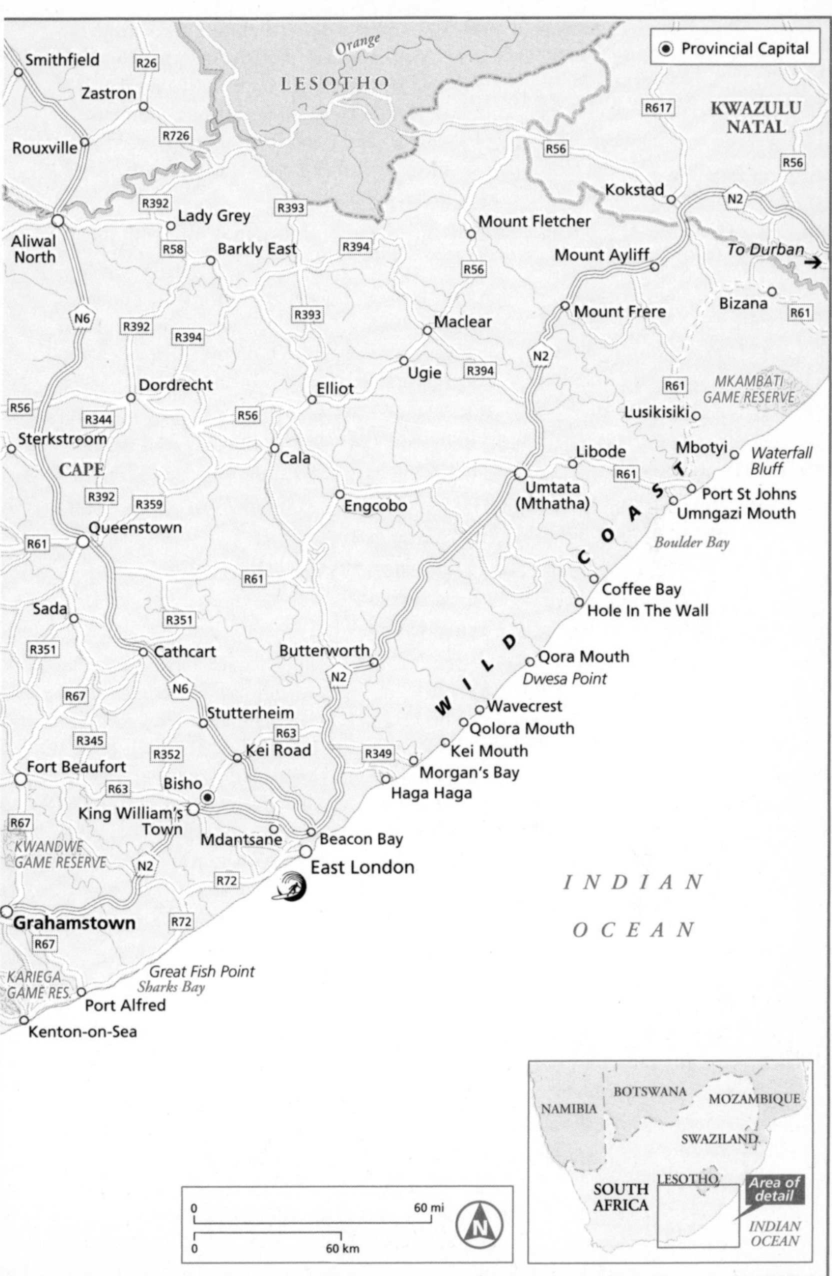

Provincial Capital
LESOTHO
Orange
KWAZULU NATAL
CAPE
Smithfield
Zastron
Rouxville
Aliwal North
Lady Grey
Barkly East
Mount Fletcher
Kokstad
Mount Ayliff
To Durban
Mount Frere
Bizana
Maclear
Ugie
Elliot
Dordrecht
Sterkstroom
Cala
Engcobo
Umtata (Mthatha)
Libode
MKAMBATI GAME RESERVE
Lusikisiki
Mbotyi
Waterfall Bluff
Port St Johns
Umngazi Mouth
Boulder Bay
Queenstown
WILD COAST
Coffee Bay
Hole In The Wall
Sada
Cathcart
Butterworth
Qora Mouth
Dwesa Point
Stutterheim
Wavecrest
Qolora Mouth
Kei Road
Kei Mouth
Morgan's Bay
Haga Haga
Fort Beaufort
Bisho
King William's Town
Mdantsane
Beacon Bay
East London
KWANDWE GAME RESERVE
Grahamstown
INDIAN OCEAN
Great Fish Point
Sharks Bay
KARIEGA GAME RES.
Port Alfred
Kenton-on-Sea
0
60 mi
0
60 km
N
NAMIBIA
BOTSWANA
MOZAMBIQUE
SWAZILAND
LESOTHO
SOUTH AFRICA
Area of detail
INDIAN OCEAN

GETTING THERE **By Car** P.E. is on the N2, which runs between Cape Town (7 hr. away; through the Garden Route) and Durban.

By Air **Port Elizabeth Airport** (✆ **041/507-7319**) is 4km (about 2½ miles) from the city center. **SAA** (✆ **041/507-1111;** www.flysaa.com) and **British Airways Domestic** (www.britishairways.com) fly between P.E. and Johannesburg, Cape Town, and Durban (✆ **041/508-8000**), as does budget airline **Kulula.com.** Budget airline **1Time.co.za** (www.1time.aero) connects P.E. with Johannesburg and Cape Town. There is an ATM in the passage connecting the terminals, and there are metered taxis outside the terminals, or call **Hurters Cabs** (✆ **041/585-7344**) for an airport transfer.

By Bus **Greyhound, Intercape, Baz Bus,** and **Translux** all connect P.E. with Johannesburg, Cape Town, and Durban. (See chapter 3 for more.)

By Train The national mainline train runs between Johannesburg and Port Elizabeth; for details, call Shosholoza Mail (✆ **086/000-8888**). Shosholoza has just introduced a **Premier Classe** train (✆ **021/449-2252;** www.premierclasse.co.za) from Cape Town to Port Elizabeth, which leaves every Friday at 3pm. (See chapter 3 for more.)

GETTING AROUND **By Car** The best way to explore the Eastern Cape is with your own wheels. **Avis** (✆ **041/501-7200**), **Budget** (✆ **041/581-4242**), **Imperial** (✆ **041/581-4391**), and **Tempest** (✆ **041/581-1256**) all have desks at the airport.

By Taxi **Hurters Taxi Cabs** (✆ **041/585-7344**) has a 24-hour taxi service. **Molo Tours** (✆ **082/970-4037**) offers direct safari transfers to reserves.

By Air Contact **John Huddlestone** (✆ **041/507-7343** or 083/653-4294) for a helicopter trip to any of the reserves or an aerial tour of P.E.

GUIDED TOURS OF PORT ELIZABETH & BEYOND Besides the highly recommended township tours (see "What to See & Do," below), orient yourself with a 90-minute **Friendly City Tour** (✆ **041/585-1801**) or book a full-day big-game private excursion with **Pembury Tours** (✆ **041/581-2581;** www.pemburytours.com). The **Eastern Cape Adventure and Hiking Association** (✆ **041/368-3761**) has a regular program of hikes; visitors are welcome to join these, and it's a good way to meet locals. If you would like to have your own historian and botanist onboard, book a tour that takes in the Eastern Cape game reserves with **Brian Aldridge** (✆ **082/801-7721;** www.capetowntours.com)—then tool down the Garden Route and back to Cape Town with him. Brian is Cape Town based (your tour could start there), but he knows the area well; he takes on only one booking at a time, so you have his undivided and very intelligent attention.

Fast Facts Port Elizabeth

Area Code Port Elizabeth's area code is **041.**

Auto Repair Call **AA Breakdown** (✆ **083/843-22** or 011/799-1500).

Emergencies For an **ambulance,** call ✆ 10177; **National Sea Rescue Institute (NSRI),** call ✆ 041/585-6011; **Police Flying Squad,** call ✆ 10111; or **police,** call ✆ 041/394-6740. The best private hospital is **Greenacres** (✆ 041/390-7000).

WHAT TO SEE & DO

TAKING A TOWNSHIP TOUR ★★★ To gain real insight into the city, the following tours are highly recommended: If you're prepared to make a night of it, **Mzolifi Quza,** of **Molo Tours** (✆ **082/970-4037;** molotours@gmail.com), offers one of the best township tours in the country. After visiting an initiation camp (see "Rights of Passage," below), he will lead you on a tour through the Walmer township, visiting a youth center, new housing projects, schools, and a local *shebeen* (informal drinking house) along the way. You can also book dinner with a Xhosa family. **Calabash Tours** (✆ **041/585-6162**) offers an excellent morning tour: The 3- to 4-hour Real City Tour starts in the city center and looks at Port Elizabeth's history and the forced removal of residents out of the city to coloured and black townships.

A WALK THROUGH SETTLER HISTORY If you're interested in P.E'.s early history, take the 5km (3-mile) **Donkin Heritage Trail,** a self-guided walk marked with a blue staggered line that takes you past 47 places of historical interest in the old Hill area of central P.E. You can pick up a map from the tourism office in the Donkin Lighthouse Building, which is in the **Donkin Reserve,** located below Belmont Terrace and Donkin Street—a quaint row of Victorian houses collectively declared a national monument. The reserve was proclaimed an open space in perpetuity by Sir Rufane Donkin, the Cape's acting governor in 1820. Take a stroll to the large stone pyramid monument the governor erected to his late wife, Elizabeth, after whom he also named the city—look for the touching inscription. From here, you might want to visit the **No. 7 Castle Hill Museum** ★ (✆ **041/582-2515;** Mon–Fri 10am–1pm and 2–4:30pm [4pm on Fri]; admission R9 adults, R5 children), one of the oldest settler cottages in the city, dating back to 1825.

At the bottom of the hill, you can either turn right to browse the **Wezandla African Art and Craft Gallery** (✆ **041/585-1185**) or turn left to view the pretty **City Hall** and the **City Library,** both on Govan Mbeki Avenue (recently renamed after the father of former president Thabo Mbeki). It's worth entering the library, a Gothic-Revival building from 1902, to take a look at the stained-glass dome on the second floor.

THE RED LOCATION MUSEUM ★★★ This fascinating museum shares its name with the township that surrounds it—Red Location was named after the color of rusted corrugated iron and was home to many famous anti-apartheid activists. The museum (which has won much praise in architecture circles) is made up of 12 unmarked, rusted "memory boxes" within a larger exhibition space; each is home to a collection of memories or stories—the spaces between are for reflection. Exhibitions focus on local heroes of the struggle against apartheid, music and jazz, trade unions, sport, cultural life, and much more; some of the exhibits have a strong oral narrative component. Find it on the corner of Olof Palme and Singaphi streets, New Brighton (✆ **041/408-8400;** Mon–Fri 9am–4pm, Sat 9am–3pm). Admission is R12 per adult.

Fun Facts Rites of Passage

It is not unusual to pass young men covered in white clay on the road—in rural as well as urban areas of the Eastern and Western Cape. These are Xhosa initiates, teenage boys who are about to learn the customs of their clan, culminating in the ancient but controversial practice of removing the foreskin (without anesthetic) to mark their transition to manhood.

The Crushing of Black Consciousness

Take a detour from the Heritage Trail and visit the sixth floor of the otherwise charmless building located on 44 Strand St.: This is where Steve Biko—the charismatic black-consciousness leader of the 1970s—died while being interrogated by the security police. This, combined with the Soweto uprising, led to the imposition of the arms embargo by the U.N. Security Council. Until the recent Truth and Reconciliation Commission hearings, the official version of events was that Biko slipped and fell, and no one was ever arrested. You can visit the room in which Biko was interrogated; it houses items relating to the man and his past.

EXPLORING THE BEACHFRONT Enjoying an average of 7½ hours of sunshine a day, and lapped by relatively warm waters, Port Elizabeth beaches see a lot of action. The first crescent is **King's Beach.** A safe swimming beach, it has good family facilities, including the **McArthur Baths Swimming Pool Complex** (© **041/582-2282**), which stretches south to **Humewood Beach,** the best swimming beach, and is proud of its Blue Flag status. Opposite you will find **Bay World Museum Complex** (© **041/584-0650;** daily 9am–4:30pm; R45), which houses the **Oceanarium,** a snake park and a museum featuring fossils, scale reconstructions of shipwrecks, and a display on the Xhosa. A little farther along is the beachfront entrance to the **Boardwalk Casino and Entertainment World,** with a number of restaurants, a cinema, shops, and, of course, a casino. Additional attractions at Humewood include a scenic day trip on the **Apple Express** (© **041/583-4480;** R160 adult, children under 11 R80), a restored narrow-gauge steam train.

To escape the crowds, keep traveling the beachfront road until it becomes Marine Drive, and then take Sardinia Bay Road to visit the big dunes of **Sardinia Bay**—this is a great picnic spot and walking beach, with warm waters. Declared a marine reserve, it's the start of the **Sacramento Trail** ★, an 8km (5-mile) coastal walk.

BIG-GAME DAY TRIPS The nearest and biggest Big 5 game reserve (a mere 45 min. from the center of town), and the only one in which you can self-drive (though guided trips are also available), is **Addo Elephant National Park** ★★ (© **042/233-0556;** www.addoelephantpark.com; daily 7am–7pm). It costs only R130 to enter. Over the past 10 years, the park has grown phenomenally (edging toward the 500,000-hectare/1,240,000-acre mark) and currently extends from Darlington Dam in the Karoo all the way to Woody Cape on the coast, including the island groups of St Croix and Bird Island, home to the largest gannet-breeding colony in the world. Be aware that fences between various areas are still up, and the full Big 5 are to be found in a relatively concentrated area linked to the main rest camp and central areas—ask exactly what animals are in the section you are planning to visit. Addo has the densest concentration of elephants in Africa; they are in evidence year-round, but the most attractive time of the year to visit is spring, when the harsh Eastern Cape bushveld is softened with flowers and herds can be seen standing in carpets of yellow daisies. Other animals to look for are the black rhino, buffalo, lion, hyena, zebra, red hartebeest, eland, kudu, bushbuck, warthog, and—on a guided trip—a few endemic species such as the flightless dung beetle, found almost exclusively in Addo. To ensure the best sightings, head for the watering holes (pick up a map at the entrance), or take a private tour to get off the beaten (and, unfortunately, now tarred) track. Three-hour guided game drives in open-topped vehicles are also provided by the park; these are not as good as heading out with a private operator (see "Essentials," above), but they're cheap; just make sure it's in one of the smaller vehicles (R190–R270). Game drives take place at sunrise, midafternoon, at sundown, or at night—the only time to view the nocturnal activities of such carnivores as the black-backed jackal and bat-eared fox.

The most famous of the private game reserves, the 25,000-hectare (61,780-acre) Shamwari reserve no longer accepts day-trippers. Two good alternatives (though less than a third of Shamwari's size) are Amakhala and Pumba, both on the road to Grahamstown. First up is the turnoff to **Amakhala** ★ (© **046/636-2750;** www.amakhala.co.za), the nearest private Big 5 reserve, offering day trips for R980. The 7,000-hectare (17,300-acre) reserve is only 45 minutes from the city center. Safaris leave from Reed Valley at 11am in winter and noon in summer; they include game drives, a lunch buffet, and a river cruise. Farther along, only 15 minutes from Grahamstown (about 70 min. from P.E.), you'll see the Alicedale/Pumba turnoff: Park your car at the Day Safari Arrivals Centre for **Pumba** ★★ (© **046/603-2000;** www.pumbagamereserve.co.za), or call from P.E. and arrange a transfer. Pumba is a 6,500-hectare (14,820-acre) reserve but boasts the additional attractions of white lions (a genetic mutation) and cheetahs. The day safari comprises a 2-hour game drive to the bush restaurant, where you will be served a meal before embarking on another 90-minute game drive back to the Arrival Centre. Day safaris depart at 7am and 4pm in summer and 10am and 3pm in winter, and cost R850 for adults and R550 for children (over 8 only).

Schotia (© **042/235-1436;** www.schotia.com), a small (1,700-hectare/4,199-acre) reserve east of Addo, offers a 6-hour experience in which you're likely to see one of the reserve's lions on the prowl, as well as rhinos, giraffes, and hippos. The drive costs R600 and includes supper around the fire. For R1,200, you can include a morning game drive through Addo to view buffaloes and elephants (neither of which occurs in Schotia), as well as transfers from P.E. and lunch.

Elephant lovers should look into booking an **Addo Elephant Back Safari** (www.addoelephantbacksafaris.co.za), a 3-hour experience that includes walking with elephants that were saved from hunting by the Knysna Elephant Park, getting to know them and their handlers, and taking a short ride to the watering hole. The cost is R875 per person. Wear trousers and comfortable walking shoes.

WHERE TO STAY & DINE

Note that the city options are only a 5-minute drive from the airport. Lodges and camps provide a tranquil alternative to staying in the city, yet are only 45 minutes (Addo) to 90 minutes (Kwandwe) from check-in.

Port Elizabeth

While the establishments reviewed below are the most stylish options in Port Elizabeth, if you're about to blow your budget on a luxury reserve, you might want to consider the comfortable B&B **Carslogie House** (© **041/583-5251;** www.carslogie.co.za); rooms are situated around a large pool and go for as little as R900 for a double (plus it's in Summerstrand, the neighborhood of choice in P.E.). Another bargain is the family-run **Chapman Hotel** (© **041/584-0678;** www.chapman.co.za). It's not manor house accommodation, as the website suggests, but all rooms have sea views, as does the pool, and at R785 for a double, it's arguably the best deal in town. It also houses a reputable seafood restaurant called **Blackbeards** (© **041/584-0623;** 6pm–late): Try one of the "brodino" dishes—your choice of fish, combined with mussels and calamari; cooked in a tomato, white-wine, and garlic sauce (herbs are secret); and served in a cast-iron pot.

Better still, head for the Boardwalk Casino and Entertainment Complex, which has a clutch of recommended eateries, of which **Kyoto** remains a personal favorite, serving up excellent teppanyaki and sushi (© **041/583-1160**). If you're not in the mood for Japanese, head straight for **34° South** (© **041/583-1085**), sibling to the popular Knysna restaurant/deli. At **Nosh,** 1 Cooper St., Richmond Hill (© **041/582-2444**), P.E.'s fashionable set like to see and be seen over ostrich filet with chocolate chili sauce or roast duck drizzled with honey and oyster sauce. They're also drawn to Summerstrand's **Ginger** (© **041/583-1220;** www.ginger-restaurant.co.za). Look out for the seared scallops on leek and sherry risotto; the line fish is also popular.

Others in search of fine dining can book a table at **Shamwari Townhouse** (see below); be sure to order the Ramsay-inspired chef's crayfish and tiger prawn cake served with a seafood bisque (R125). But if all you want to see is the twinkling ocean, **Mauro's,** Shop 1 McArthur Baths Leisure Centre, Beach Road (© **041/582-2700**), offers lovely views along with a predictable but good Italian menu.

A consistently good city favorite is nearby **De Kelders** (© **041/583-2750**). The space is old-fashioned, intimate, and comes scattered with rose petals, while the menu offers a diverse, hearty selection of steaks, poultry, vegetables dishes, and fish—owner Michelle says they "fight for" the freshest catch at the harbor. Finally, if you're in the mood for something really laid-back, follow the locals to **Natti's Thai Kitchen** (© **041/373-2763;** dinner Mon–Sat only), where Natti (assisted by her surfer husband, Mark) has been warming palates with her Thai cuisine for over a decade.

Hacklewood Hill Country House ★★★ It's almost worth making a special detour to P.E. to stay at what is rather presumptuously called a country house—4 minutes from the airport. Hacklewood is *very* much in the heart of the city, and home to any VIPs visiting P.E. Built in 1898, the gracious Victorian house has been artfully converted, with none of the generous spaces of the original home compromised. If you have a thing for bathrooms, these are world class. Each is bigger than most hotel rooms and is furnished with the same care as the bedrooms: Victorian bathtubs are set in the center of the room, with comfortable seating provided in deep armchairs, should you wish to converse in comfort. The entire house is furnished with beautiful period pieces, with colors and fabrics evincing exquisite taste, and the staff is eager to please. The four-course dinners (R225), with which P.E. romantics choose to celebrate special occasions, are presided over by Cordon Bleu–trained Chef Bernice Viviere.

152 Prospect Rd., Walmer 6065. © **041/581-1300.** Fax 041/581-4155. www.hacklewood.co.za. 8 units. High season R3,250 double; low season R2,340 double. Rate includes breakfast. AE, DC, MC, V. Children 8 and over accepted. **Amenities:** Dining room; bar; airport transfers by arrangement; pool (saltwater); room service; tennis; wine cellar. *In room:* A/C, TV, hair dryer, minibar, free Wi-Fi.

Radisson Blu Hotel ★★ Opening in 2009 and conveniently located just across the road from Summerstrand's Pollock beach, this five-star hotel offers clean-lined, well-appointed rooms, with up-to-the-minute modern conveniences and sea views. The standard rooms are not particularly large (only about 28 sq. m/301 sq. ft.), so if you need additional space, consider a suite (these were yet to be completed at press time). The hotel's many amenities and the on-site restaurant, Filini, make this an easy and convenient option, plus the Boardwalk complex and other attractions are just a stroll away. This is a large, modern hotel (for a more intimate atmosphere, you're better off at Shamwari Townhouse), but the world-class service and comfort levels make it a tempting choice.

Corner of Marine Dr. and Ninth Ave., Summerstrand, Port Elizabeth. © **041/509-5000.** Fax 041/509-5001. www.port.elizabeth.radissonsas.com. 173 units. R1,400–R1,800 standard room; R2,600 junior suite; R3,700 1-bed suite. AE, DC, MC, V. **Amenities:** Restaurant; lounge; bar; gym; pool; spa and wellness center. *In room:* A/C, TV/DVD, hair dyer, minibar, free Wi-Fi.

Shamwari Townhouse ★★★ Easily the plushest, most superior accommodations option in the urban Eastern Cape, this Art Deco–style boutique hotel, with its spot-on service, has raised the bar dramatically since it opened in 2008. Ubermodern and distinctive, yet with a business-friendly air, the seven suites are a wonderland of original South African art, sumptuous period-inspired decor, and fine fittings; all have a private balcony or small garden for those balmy summer evenings, while some even have his-and-hers TVs. To tempt you out, there's an impressive spa, fine dining in the Jazz Room, a pianist tickling the ivories in the Piano Lounge, and the striking Salon Privé, with its Fornasetti wallpaper and the second-largest collection of single malts in the country. The in-house cinema was modeled on one belonging to England's Prince Charles. Are you getting the picture? No expense has been spared to create this polished, sophisticated hotel.

5 Brighton Dr., Summerstrand, Port Elizabeth. Reservations © **041/407-1000;** hotel 041/502-6000. Fax 041/502-6001. www.shamwaritownhouse.com. 7 units. From R3,400–R4,125 per suite; presidential suite from R3,900. Rates include breakfast. AE, DC, MC, V. **Amenities:** Restaurant; bar; gym; library; pool; spa; theater; wine cellar (w/private dining facilities for 16). *In room:* A/C, TV/DVD, hair dryer, minibar, free Wi-Fi.

Singa Lodge ★★ Opulent Singa, in laid-back Summerstrand and close to lovely Pollock Beach, has 11 rooms dripping with an unusual mix of Eastern and African decor that should appeal to younger travelers: The colorful, individually decorated and privately situated suites are rich with screens, mosaics, and hand-stenciled wallpapers. They differ in size and atmosphere, but no. 1 is a beauty with green-washed concrete floors, a massive mosaic studded shower, a fireplace, and vast amounts of bright, warm space; while no. 4 has an oriental feel, with embroidered blinds and screens to separate the bathroom area from the bedroom. It's not cheap, but there are plenty of modern conveniences, good dining, lovely gardens, and a reading room with a respectable collection of single malts and cigars. It's a stylish way to spend a couple of days.

Corner of 10th Ave. and Scarbourough Dr., Summerstrand, Port Elizabeth. Reservations © **086/111-2485;** hotel 041/583-3927. Fax 041/583-3927. www.singalodge.com. 11 units. R1,990–R3,300 double. Rates include breakfast. AE, DC, MC, V. Children by arrangement. **Amenities:** Bar; lounge and dining areas; gym; library; pool. *In room:* A/C, TV/DVD, hair dryer, minibar, MP3 docking station, free Wi-Fi.

The Windermere Hotel ★★ Conveniently located one road back from King's Beach and a stone's throw from McArthur Pools, this was the first guesthouse in P.E. to embrace the modern boutique-hotel aesthetic, with customized fittings and furniture throughout, much of it designed by Haldane Martin, local *Elle Décor* Designer of the Year. Luxury rooms are huge enough to be termed suites, and furnished with all the modern conveniences needed for a comfortable stay. Book one of the upstairs rooms for views—particularly room no. 9, which has a great sea vista from its balcony. Breakfast is served in the dining room, on the veranda, or in your room. The Boardwalk complex, with its many restaurant choices, is not far away—and it's just 5 minutes' drive to the Humewood Golf Course.

35 Humewood Rd., Humewood, Port Elizabeth 6001. © **041/582-2245.** Fax 041/582-2246. www.thewindermere.co.za. 9 units. R1,900–R2,940 double. Rates include breakfast. AE, DC, MC, V. **Amenities:** Breakfast room; lounge; plunge pool. *In room:* A/C, TV/DVD, hair dryer, minibar, free Wi-Fi.

Addo was the first national park to offer **concessions** to private operators, thereby ensuring that the park had a few luxury alternatives to the more basic and crowded rest camp. If you're prepared to splurge, it's a bit of a toss-up between the 11-unit **Gorah Camp** ★★★ (see below) and **Nguni River Lodge** ★★★ (✆ **042/235-1022;** www.ngunilodges.co.za; R9,520 double, R20,020 for the King suite, ask about specials). Some prefer Nguni for its eight secluded thatched suites, each with its own viewing deck and private plunge pool. With a more intimate atmosphere, the gracious, homely **RiverBend Lodge** (✆ **042/233-8000;** www.riverbendlodge.co.za.com; from R3,600–R5,900 double, includes meals and activities), which, like Nguni, is situated within the 17,000-hectare (41,990-acre) private Nyathi concession, offers eight luxury rooms in a farmhouse-style atmosphere, superb cuisine, and personal attention. There is additional accommodation in the new and very charming **Long Hope Villa**, a three-bed 1940s farmhouse with a private chef, 500m (1,640 ft.) away (R8,000–R14,000 for 1–4 guests). Both options are very child friendly, although this is a destination for families that want to spend time together rather than pack the kids off on their own game drives.

If these prices give you pause, you can stay **outside the park** and either take a tour or drive yourself. In this case, **Elephant House** (see below) is probably the best option in the region; it's also the closest to Addo's main entrance. An extremely reasonable B&B for those on a budget is **Halstead Farm** (✆ **042/233-0114;** from R900 double); the three adjoining reed ceiling rooms are individually decorated with a colonial character (rooms 1 and 3 are more spacious; no. 1 even has a piano) and they open onto lovely gardens—but it's high-end luxury. Farther into the Sundays River Valley, off the Kirkwood Road, is **Hitgeheim Country Lodge** (✆ **042/234-0778;** www.hitgeheim-addo.co.za; R2,500–R3,100 double; closed June). It's surrounded by a minireserve with some game, and with its spectacular views, luxurious chalets, fine food and wine, and amenable hosts (they also arrange reserve tours), it is a very good, if fairly pricey, option.

Addo Park Rest Camp ★ **Value** This is a great budget option, with cabins (sleeping two, shared ablutions) for as little as R450. Better still are the comfortable self-catering cottages and rondawels with bush views—often with elephants wandering through. All units (except for some of the forest cabins) are en suite, though you need to specify whether you want a semi- or fully-equipped kitchen or shared cooking facilities. Unit nos. 1 to 6 (two-bed with communal kitchens) have views of the waterhole, as do unit nos. 7 and 8 (six-bed guesthouses with kitchens and TV); while unit nos. 17 to 24 and 29 to 32 have good park views. A restaurant serves basic, filling meals—chicken, fish, steaks (including kudu and ostrich), and a few traditional dishes like *umcabosi,* a mix of spinach and pap (maize porridge). Best of all, if you're keen on dawn drives, you can be in the game-viewing area within minutes of dragging yourself out of bed. ***Note:*** **Camp Matyholweni** (✆ **041/468-0916**), a new rest camp with comfortable cottages, is now open at the Southern entrance to the park, much closer to the beach. But you will have to drive to the main viewing section to see the Big 5—though elephants and other animals are expected to be released in the area by late 2009.

Bookings ✆ **012/428-9111.** Direct ✆ **042/233-8600.** www.addoelephantpark.com or www.sanparks.org. 66 units: 6-bed guesthouse, 2- and 4-bed chalets, 4-bed forest cabins, 2-bed rondawels, and 2-bed safari tents. R375–R810 double; R2,315 guesthouse for 4. Daily conservation fee R130 for adults, R65 for children. AE, DC, MC, V. **Amenities:** Restaurant; fuel station; pool; tennis; underground animal viewing hide. *In room:* A/C (in some units).

Elephant House ★★ Located just a few minutes' drive from the entrance to Addo, the quality of accommodations and public areas in this seven-roomed luxury lodge help make up for the fact that you're not actually in a reserve. Rooms smell of thatch and are dotted with Persian carpets, old prints, and heirlooms, while lounges and verandas are filled with soft, cozy sofas to relax on. With a gin and tonic in hand, you should get that colonial safari feeling in no time. There are two pools to wallow in and (in high season) complimentary massage treatments—when you're not touring the nearby reserves (the lodge offers a wide variety of safaris and tours if you're not keen on driving). ***Note:*** There are now six good-value B&B cottages (from R1,100 double) in a field next door to the lodge, plus a new restaurant and wine bar blessed with massive log fireplaces and chandeliers.

Off the R335, 8km (4.9 miles) from the main entrance to Addo. ✆ **042/233-2462.** Fax 042/233-0393. www.elephanthouse.co.za. 7 units, plus 6 Stable cottages. High season R2,900 double; low season R1,500 double; cottages form R1,100 double. Rates include breakfast. AE, DC, MC, V. **Amenities:** Restaurant; dining area; game drives and tours; lounges; TV/DVD library; 2 pools; room service; free Wi-Fi. *In room:* A/C, hair dryer, mosquito nets.

Gorah ★★★ Grasslands, game, and big skies stretch out before you in delicious, deep silence at Gorah, punctuated only by animal grunts and the sounds of grass being chewed (clearly audible through the canvas walls of the 11 elegant thatched tents at 2am). Small wonder that this is one of my top three safari destinations in the Eastern Cape (the others being Kwandwe and Samara). The lack of electricity at Gorah (it is solar powered and has strong green credentials) adds to the experience: The camp comes into its own at night, when winking lanterns and candles illuminate the colonial-style lodge but are no match for the dazzle of stars overhead. A waterhole a stone's throw from the lodge veranda provides down-time game-viewing of exceptional quality; drives will top up any sightings you may have missed. This is a true retreat, and the care and attention to detail brought to every aspect of your experience, combined with the exceptional surroundings, make it hard to beat.

Turn right off the R335 just after passing Addo town and follow the dirt road for 10km (6¼ miles) to Gorah's gate. Bookings ✆ **042/233-2462;** lodge 042/235-1123. Fax 042/235-1124. www.gorah.com. 11 units. High season R11,980 double; low season R7,190 double. Rates include meals and game drives. AE, DC, MC, V. No children under 8. **Amenities:** Dining areas; lounges; boma; horseback rides; library; pool; free Wi-Fi. *In room:* Fans.

Private Reserves

The reserves below are given full reviews because they offer exceptionally high standards with Big 5 viewing, but there are a number of options that might better suit your pocket. The 9,000-hectare (22,240-acre) **Kariega Private Game Reserve** (✆ **046/636-7904;** www.kariega.co.za) is in the Kariega River Valley, an 80-minute drive from the city, and near the beaches of Kenton-on-Sea. Of the four lodges, **River Lodge** (R5,400–R7,600 double all-inclusive) is the most luxurious: The thatched suites, some of which are grouped in a double-story block, ramble along the Bushman's River—units 8, 9, and 10 are farthest from the main building and thus more private. Besides the normal game drives, this lodge also offers river trips and fishing. **Ukhozi Lodge** (R5,000–R7,000 double, all-inclusive) has a wonderful relaxed and rustic feel, and the 10 suites all have private plunge pools, but **Kariega Main Lodge** (R4,200–R6,000 double, including meals and game drives) offers better value for families, with 21 spacious timber chalets, each with its own viewing decks. Some come with plunge pools at no extra cost, so make sure to book these in advance. The final option is **The Homestead,** a private sole-use

Tips A Little Golf with Your Game?

Bushman Sands (© **042/231-8000;** www.bushmansands.com; R1,700–R1,850 luxury double, including breakfast; standard rooms are less), a golfing estate and 4,000-hectare (9,880-acre) reserve in Alicedale, 90 minutes from P.E., is another successful attempt by visionary businessman Adrian Gardiner (owner of Shamwari) to develop sustainable tourism initiatives. Once a thriving railway town, Alicedale was faced with high unemployment when Spoornet moved; Gardiner provided a lifeline. The hotel now has new owners, but it still offers affordable accommodations. Be aware that the hotel is not in a game reserve as such, so this is not a typical safari experience. The reserve has elephant, rhino, and buffalo, but no big cats—you'll have to do a day safari at Pumba for those—but you do have a Gary Player–designed course (some say it's not the same standard as Garden Route courses such as Pezula, but that the last 9 holes are challenging). Game drives are extra, at R300 per adult for a 2-hour drive.

house with five rooms, its own chef and ranger, and a secluded position in a remote part of the reserve for extra privacy and those who want a more flexible schedule. It's all yours from R15,000 to R20,000 per night.

Growing in popularity is the 7,000-hectare (17,300-acre) **Amakhala Game Reserve** (© **042/235-1608;** www.amakhala.co.za), a mere 45 minutes from P.E and with excellent game-viewing. Amakhala has six separately owned and privately managed accommodations options; the top end includes the intimate **Safari Lodge** ★ (R5,160–R7,560 double, all-inclusive; rates depend on season), with accommodations in 11 thatched and luxuriously appointed safari huts, and the new **Bush Lodge** at Reed Valley (same rate). A tented safari camp with a very comfortable, if not unique, main lodge tucked away in the bush, it has a pleasant wooden deck where a campfire crackles at night. The voluminous tents have individual plunge pools plus double outdoor showers and heaters in winter; the only drawback is that you have to drive to the main game-viewing area. If you're on a budget, you can't beat Amakhala's **Carnavon Dale** (R2,600–R3,780 double), a historic Edwardian-style settler farmhouse from 1857.

There are a host of new lodges popping up in the area, many sharing game-viewing on some more established reserves. **Kichaka** ★ (© **046/622-6024;** www.kichaka.co.za; R5,500–R7,900 double, depending on season; all-inclusive) is tucked away on the northeastern side of Lalibela (see below). The lodge, nestled among trees, has a wonderful position overlooking a waterhole, and the 10 rooms are ultraluxurious. Each has a wooden deck with a plunge pool to help beat the heat, and romantic extras abound, such as the rose-petal-strewn, steaming bath that awaits as you return from your game drive. Food is good—even the hot breakfast is beautifully plated. You have a fair chance of seeing most of the Big 5, time allowing, but some of the game-viewing areas are unfortunately close to the highway and the reserve also has a problem with invasive alien trees. And, yes, it's pricey, especially in high season—which may make **Idwala Lodge** (© **046/622-2163;** www.idwalalodge.com; R3,800–R6,500 double) more attractive. This time on the western border of Lalibela, it's less luxurious but tiny and intimate (four secluded rooms); low-season specials are good.

Pumba ★ (✆ **046/603-2000;** www.pumbagamereserve.co.za; R7,600–R9,940 for standard chalets; up to R12,320 for a suite) is another smaller reserve (16,060 hectares/6,500 acres) that has been getting good feedback. Here, your best choice is probably **Water Lodge** ★★—the 12 thatched chalets with decks and private plunge pools are much the same quality as those at **Msenge Bush Lodge,** but it's the position over Lake Kariega that really gives it the edge (Msenge is also where day visitors dine, although the facilities are separate from the lodge). Of the Water Lodge chalets, the gemsbok and kudu suites are larger and, of course, more expensive. You'll be well fed, although food is probably not the main reason to visit Pumba. Besides the Big 5, you'll have the chance to look out for cheetah and rare white lions in a separate game area.

Blaauwbosch Private Game Reserve ★★ Finds The reason most guests love this reserve is the sense of being in some remote outpost; it's a mere 80-minute drive from P.E., but it's farther north, closer to the Karoo desert than the other Eastern Cape reserves (excluding Samara). Equally important is the rate: Given the standards of accommodations and facilities, this is one of the best-value Big 5 lodges in the Eastern Cape (compared to the big-name Shamwari, Samara, and Kwandwe), particularly in winter, when rates drop. Though it's unlikely to make inroads in international magazine selections, the lodge is tasteful enough and very comfortable, and although its new owners do not live on the property, manager Warrick Barnard will make you feel very much at home. Comprising seven thatched suites (large, with private veranda; views from bathtub) in a heavenly landscape, the experience is both rejuvenating and relaxing. The new, exclusive Kaai's Camp has a gorgeous mountain setting with four suites offering extra luxuries and outdoor showers. Besides tracking the Big 5 on game drives through the 5,000-hectare (12,350-acre) reserve, a highlight is the "walk and stalk" safaris, in which you track cheetahs, arguably the most intriguing of the big cats.

Off the R75 from P.E. to Graaff-Reinet. ✆ **049/835-9099** or -9098. Fax 049/581-5266. www.blaauwbosch.co.za. 11 units. High season R6,600–R7,600 double; low season R3,500–R4,000 double. Rates include meals and game activities. AE, DC, MC, V. **Amenities:** Dining area; bar; lounge; babysitting; game drives and foot tracking; pool; free Wi-Fi. *In room:* A/C, hair dryer.

Kwandwe ★★★ Operated by the hugely successful &Beyond group (previously CC Africa), Kwandwe is my top choice of the Eastern Cape reserves. Covering 20,000 hectares (49,400 acres), the reserve has two lodges, Great Fish River Lodge and Ecca, as well as Uplands, a gracious 1905 farmhouse that can accommodate six, and Melton Manor, a single-unit house full of quirky, homely luxuries accommodating eight. A Relais & Châteaux member, it has the added benefit of 30km (19 miles) of Great Fish River frontage—a big contrast to the slightly arid Eastern Cape environment. Located on the banks of the river, Great Fish River Lodge looks as though it had been furnished for Karen Blixen: Persian rugs, antiques, hand-stitched damask linen, cut-glass decanters, African spears, and old-style hunting prints—all very *Out of Africa.* The nine suites have fabulous views (even from the Victorian tub), thatched viewing decks, and private plunge pools. **Ecca Lodge,** with its contemporary corrugated iron and stone gabion architecture set on rolling slopes, is unusual and surprising. I love how it blurs the lines between indoors and outside, and the modern suites are enormous and airy, but it won't work for everyone. Kwandwe is 2 hours' drive from the P.E. airport.

Bookings through &Beyond: ✆ **011/809-4300.** Fax 011/809-4511. www.andbeyondafrica.com. 17 units. High season R13,210; low season R7,040. Rates include all meals, local beverages, game activities, and laundry. Uplands R15,750–R26,435; Melton Manor R20,990–R35,245. AE, DC, MC, V. **Amenities:** Dining area; bar; lounge; boma; bush walks; game drives; room service; free Wi-Fi. *In room:* A/C, hair dryer, minibar, plunge pool.

Lalibela ★ (Kids) Although it's not in the same category as Kwandwe, Samara, or Shamwari, this private reserve near Grahamstown is a great choice for beleaguered parents with young children. Mark's Camp leaves parents free to pursue their own game drives or relax at the pool while children are entertained by a specific program developed for kids 8 and under. From dawn, when the kids are taken to breakfast by their own full-time nanny (included in the price), they are kept busy with conservation projects, mini game drives (in their own special game vehicle, and kept well away from potentially dangerous encounters), and visits to the playroom area. Family time runs from 11am to 4pm. After high tea, the children's activities are again resumed, and they enjoy an early meal, followed up by arts and craft activities. Families can also sit in front of the campfire roasting marshmallows and listening to African bush safari stories before bedtime. For those who don't want to be disturbed by children, there are two additional camps, of which **Treetops**—featuring five spacious safari tented–style accommodations—is the most exciting.

Bookings: ✆ **041/581-8170.** Fax 041/581-2332. www.lalibela.co.za. R6,600 double, all-inclusive; R1,650 per child under 12. For specials, check when booking. Rates include all meals, drinks, and game drives. AE, DC, MC, V. **Amenities:** Dining room; bar; dance performances; game drives; 2 pools (Mark's Camp). *In room:* A/C, hair dryer.

Samara Private Game Reserve ★★★ (Kids) Okay, this is not a Big 5 reserve, but after Kwandwe, it's my top pick. Impeccable accommodations, good service, and the huge skies and horizons of the landscape make it stand out from the pack. When it opened in 2006, it quickly hit the "world's best" lists in *Tatler, Travel + Leisure,* and *Condé Nast Traveler.* Almost 3 hours from P.E., the location deep in the Karoo is distinct from the more vegetated coastal areas. This 28,300-hectare (70,000-acre) wilderness covers four of the country's seven biomes, home to more than 60 mammal species. But lions, buffaloes, and elephants are not among them. The focus here is on cheetahs. In 2003, Sibella, a rehabilitated female cheetah, was released along with two males. Six years later, Sibella has survived the wilds and successfully reared 18 cubs (2% of the wild cheetah population in S.A.). You can get up close and personal with Sibella or forgo the game drive to inspect ancient KhoiSan rock paintings or fossil sites, book a massage, or curl up with a book. You have a choice of two sumptuous lodges: the serenely colonial **Karoo Lodge** (featuring children's activities, including the reconstruction of a giraffe skeleton) or the newly built exclusive-use **Manor House,** with its more modern, Afro-chic look and feel.

P.O. Box 649, Graaff-Reinet. Reservations ✆ **049/891-0558;** lodge **049/891-0880.** Fax 049/892-4339. www.samara.co.za. 7 units. Karoo Lodge R7,200–R9,000 double; Manor House R30,000 (8 people max). Rates include all meals, game activities, and local beverages. Credit card transactions cannot be processed without signed authorization faxed to Samara Private Game Reserve. **Amenities:** Dining room; bar; lounge; airport transfers; pool; free Wi-Fi. *In room:* Hair dryer, spa treatments (by appt.).

Shamwari Private Game Reserve ★★ The first big Eastern Cape reserve to be restocked with game, Shamwari has hosted a string of famous guests—including Tiger Woods, who popped the question here. It's a little commercial in comparison to Kwandwe and Samara, but the quality of the game-viewing and the rangers' knowledge at this 25,000-hectare (61,776-acre) reserve is certainly among the best. The reserve has a choice of seven accommodations options: Aimed at the top-end market are **Eagles Cragg** ★★★, comprising nine junior suites in a forested gorge, and **Lobengula Lodge,** with six suites. Eagles Cragg suites all have private viewing decks with plunge pools (as

The Home of the Perfect Wave

Situated 75km (47 miles) west of Port Elizabeth, Jeffrey's Bay is an easy detour on the way to or from the Garden Route, particularly if you feel like stopping for lunch on the beach: Follow the signs to Marina Martinique and you'll find the rustic **Walskipper** ★ (✆ **042/292-0005** or 082/800-9478); order a plate of prawns, calamari, mussels, scallops, and crab sticks (about R110), but don't expect finesse—meals come on enamel plates, with chunks of freshly baked bread, and waiters are, more often than not, barefoot.

Considered one of the top three surfing spots in the world, J-Bay (as it's affectionately known to locals) shot to international fame in the 1960s cult movie *Endless Summer,* which featured the break at Supertubes, the fastest and best-formed break on the South African coast, as well as Bruce's Beauties, a rare right-point break you'll find a little farther west, at the quiet coastal hamlet of Cape St Francis. For lessons, call **Andrew** at **the Wave Crest Surf School** (✆ **073/509-0400;** R200 for 2 hr., includes board and wetsuit). For more activities in and around J-Bay, contact **Ed** from **J-Bay Sandboarding** (✆ **042/296-2974** or 072/294-8207). The best place to stay in J-Bay is **Diaz 15** (✆ **042/293-1779;** www.diaz15.co.za; high season R2,200–R3,700 double; low season from R1,870 double), comprising two- and three-bedroom apartments, a three-bed penthouse, and a superior suite, located right on the beach; nos. 2, 3, 5, and 10 have the best sea views. You'll want to be right on the sea, because J-Bay is architecturally a fright; you'll find much classier lodgings in **St Francis Bay** ★★, a small coastal town a 20-minute drive west of J-Bay. The best options there are **The Sands @ St Francis** (✆ **042/294-1888;** www.thesands.co.za; R3,200–R3,430 double) and **Beach House** (✆ **042/294-1225;** www.stfrancisbay.co.za; high season R2,400–R3,990 double; closed May–Aug), each offering 180-degree ocean views, beach access, and thatched luxurious accommodations, including breakfast. Travelers on a budget could consider the laid-back **Sandals** (✆ **042/294-0551;** www.sandalsguesthouse.co.za; R1,200–R1,685 for a standard double); it has good facilities, chilled Afro-Caribbean style, and 10 comfortable rooms with private decks or patios—and is just a couple of block's walk to the beach. For more information, contact the **J-Bay Tourism Office** (✆ **042/293-2923;** www.jeffreysbaytourism.org).

do two of Lobengula's junior suites—make sure you bag one of these). These thatched lodges offer the most authentic African-safari experience in the reserve, with huge suites luxuriously furnished in ethnic-chic decor, and great food. With only four rooms, **Bushmans River Lodge** (an original 1860 settler farmstead) is the most intimate; as a result, it's extremely popular, so book ahead. Personally, I still think **Bayethe** ★★★, the luxury tented camp with 12 en-suite tents (3 are superiors with such extras as TV, fireplaces, and hammocks) offers better value—at least in the summer, when you can lounge around your private deck and plunge pool. If a tent doesn't appeal, you'll have to settle for the fairly modest **Riverdene,** a farmhouse with nine moderately sized rooms—all child friendly and safely fenced. Parents seeking more luxury can opt for **Sarili,** a brand-new thatched villa that overlooks the Bushmans River; it is more exclusive and has an appealing contemporary air, but not all rooms have views. Popular with older clientele is **Long Lee Manor,** a pink Edwardian manor built in 1910, accommodating 36 guests in a more overtly colonial style. It, too, is beautifully furnished and well staffed, but is most like a hotel.

Reservations: ✆ **041/407-1000.** Reserve: ✆ 042/203-1111. Fax 041/407-1001. www.shamwari.com. Peak season: Lobengula and Eagles Cragg from R14,320 double; remaining 5 lodges from R12,200 double. Low season: Lobengula and Eagles Cragg from R14,060 double; others from R7,700 double. Some lodges close for low season—check when booking. Rates include all meals, selected beverages, and game drives. AE, DC, MC, V. **Amenities:** Dining room; bar; lounge; airport transfers; babysitting; binoculars; bush walks; cultural village; game drives; pool; Wi-Fi. *In room:* A/C, TV (some), hair dryer.

2 GRAHAMSTOWN

127km (79 miles) east from Port Elizabeth; 180km (111 miles) west from East London

Grahamstown, a medium-sized town that shrinks dramatically whenever the local university closes for vacation, is probably not an essential stop; most visitors will simply pass through on their way to their game reserve of choice. It's a bit crowded and run-down in patches (keep a firm hold on your belongings when walking in town), but it does have a lot to offer those interested in 1820 settler history and the long, bitter battle for land that took place here during the 19th century. The town was born in 1812 as a military outpost and grew as beleaguered settler families from Britain gave up trying to farm the hopelessly inadequate 40-hectare (100-acre) plots the government had given them in the hopes that farmers would secure the volatile frontier (see the box "The 1820 Settlers: Deceit, Despair & Courage"). The best way to get acquainted with this history is by taking a **Spirits of the Past** tour (✆ **046/622-2843** or 082/825-2685; www.spiritsofthepast.co.za) with highly respected guide Alan Weyer. A former pineapple farmer, Alan was named Tour Guide of the Year in 2005 and has done much to ignite interest in this fascinating period of South African history. On the R900 half-day tour, Alan takes you into the hills around town to explain—eloquently and humorously—what was at stake for the various cultures caught up in the conflict. It's a good option for those with limited time. The full-day tour (R1,250) also examines the cultures and people who influenced the region, but includes visits to forts, historic sites, and a pub, where you will have lunch. Tours that visit the Great Fish River Valley are also available.

If you don't have time for a tour, other attractions include the **Observatory Museum,** 10 Bathurst St. (✆ **046/622-2312;** Mon–Fri 9:30am–1pm and 2–5pm, Sat 9am–1pm; R8), which, in a small tower, has the only Victorian Camera Obscura in the Southern Hemisphere. The system of revolving lenses and mirrors projects a surprisingly detailed miniature moving image of the town on a flat viewing surface (the room is darkened). Music devotees can't miss the **International Library of African Music** (✆ **046/603-8557**), with its collection of over 200 African musical instruments (they are used for demonstrations or recordings), a massive music library, and a fascinating collection of photographs. For more information on the town's accommodations and attractions, stop by the comprehensive **Makana Tourism,** 63 High St. (✆ **046/622-3241;** www.grahamstown.co.za; Mon–Fri 8:30am–5pm, Sat 9am–1pm), for detailed information—Willem Makkink is particularly helpful.

Fun Facts **The Largest Pineapple in the World**

One of the tallest buildings in tiny frontier town Bathurst (15km/9¼ miles from Port Alfred) is a 17m (55 ft) fiberglass pineapple. The ground floor of **The Big Pineapple** (© **046/625-0515;** daily from 9am) sells pineapple souvenirs, jams, and chutneys; the first floor boasts an educational exhibit about the fruit; and on the top floor is a video all about the industry. The observation deck, with sweeping views across the farmlands to the sea, makes it all worthwhile.

WHERE TO STAY & DINE

Grahamstown is jampacked with character buildings, including original 1820 settlers cottages. **High Corner** (© **046/622-8284;** www.highcorner.co.za; from R750 double) incorporates the oldest cottage in Grahamstown, plus the original Gentlemen's Club, and has six character-filled, if compact, rooms (just note that the stairs to those on the first floor are extremely steep). Right in the center of town, it's a good budget option. The **Cock House** (© **046/636-1287;** www.cockhouse.co.za) is another historic landmark that dates back to the 1820s. Unfortunately, the accommodations are looking a bit shabby, but the on-site restaurant, **Norden's,** may be worth a visit; they bake their own bread and cook using fresh herbs from the garden—dishes include line fish, ostrich carpaccio, and roast pork belly. Overall, Grahamstown is woefully short on fine food. The buffet at **Bella Vita,** 131 High St. (© **046/622-3007**), isn't bad: there's always a chicken curry and oxtail on offer, plus a variety of salads, vegetable dishes, and desserts. But really, the best place to both stay and eat in town is 7 Worcester Street.

7 Worcester Street ★★ This grand Victorian stone manor house offers first-class service and accommodations in a town that's not known for luxury, and it has strong links with Alan Weyer's Spirits of the Past tours (see above). Rooms are voluminous, filled with light, and tastefully furnished. It's hard to believe that a few years ago, this was a run-down digs for university students. The house was meticulously restored after it was bought by U.S. entrepreneur Carl Di Santis (the man behind Kwandwe Game Reserve). Ask for a suite on the first floor with a balcony—these have views across town; rooms 8 to 10 are located in the old stables overlooking the pool and are smaller but still sumptuous. Meals are prepared by a Cordon Bleu chef and have an African flavor; remember to book dinner in advance. The lounge area is full of inviting couches and absorbing books—plus, the house is adorned with art and photographs.

7 Worcester St., Grahamstown. © **046/622-2843.** Fax 046/622-2846. www.worcesterstreet.co.za. 10 units. From R2,150 double, including breakfast and dinner; B&B only from R1,790 double; with a half-day Sprits of the Past tour from R3,940 double. AE, DC, MC, V. **Amenities:** Dining room; lounge; massage; pool; room service. *In room:* Fans, TV, hair dryer, minibar, free Wi-Fi.

SIDE TRIP TO PORT ALFRED & KENTON-ON-SEA

These two beach holiday towns are popular with locals during the summer season and an easy drive on the R72 from either Port Elizabeth or Grahamstown. They offer a host of outdoor activities, including golf, horseback-riding, and water sports, but the main attraction for visitors is the game reserves and resorts in the area. **Kariega Private Game Reserve** (see "Private Reserves," earlier in this chapter) has four lodges close to Kenton-on-Sea; prices suit both those seeking luxury and budget-beating families. An affordable wilderness experience can also be found at **Sibuya Game Reserve** ★ (© **046/648-1040;**

www.sibuya.co.za; R4,990 double all-inclusive), a reserve that is home to the full Big 5—lions were released in mid-2009—and is accessible only by river (the trip takes about 30 min; expect to see a host of birds, and possibly dolphins or turtles at the river mouth). There are two luxurious, eco-friendly tented camps in the riverine forest; River Camp is smaller and welcomes children. Day visits are also possible; these 6-hour excursions include a river cruise, a 3-hour game drive, and a three-course lunch, and cost R695 per adult and R345 for children 6 to 12.

Oceana ★★★ It is out of the way, but this Mantis Collection establishment, owned by Texan Rip Miller, is worth traveling for. The position is out of this world: A central thatch and stone lodge floats over coastal forest and a golden, deserted beach that stretches as far as you can see. Four private, luxurious ocean suites linked by wooden boardwalks enjoy the same outlook, as do rooms in the main lodge (the sole-use three-bed private house also has magnificent views). Staff here go out of their way to personalize this part safari lodge, part Afro-chic beach house experience. While Oceana is a reserve with a wide variety of antelope and even rhino, there's no 5am wakeup call: Arrange to go on game drives, walks, relax in the spa, or visit the magnificent beach, just as you please. This no-rules approach also applies to dining: Enjoy formal meals in the lovely dining room, or arrange for a barbecue or picnic. A real retreat, 1 night won't be enough.

Right off the R72, 7km (4¼ miles) east of Port Alfred. ✆ **083/616-0605.** Fax 086/602-3767. www.oceanareserve.com. 8 units. Ocean suites R11,800–R13,600 double; lodge suites R9,800–R11,000. Rates include meals, local beverages, and activities. MC, V. **Amenities:** Bar; dining room; bush walks; game drives; game room; gym; pool; room service; spa. *In room:* A/C, TV, hair dryer, minibar, no phone, free Wi-Fi.

3 GRAAFF-REINET

254km (158 miles) N/NW of Port Elizabeth

Graaff-Reinet, South Africa's fourth-oldest town, is 837km (519 miles) south of Johannesburg—a good stopover if you're driving down to the Garden Route. Try to stay at least 2 days. Spend a morning admiring some of the 220 national monuments, and then take one of the worthwhile side trips into the Karoo. This is one of the few towns surrounded by a nature reserve, and you'll find one of the world's best examples of outsider art in the nearby hamlet of Nieu Bethesda.

ESSENTIALS

VISITOR INFORMATION The helpful **Graaff-Reinet Publicity Association** (✆ **049/892-4248;** www.graaffreinet.co.za; Mon–Fri 8am–5pm, Sat 9am–noon) is housed in 13A Church St.

GETTING THERE **By Car** From Johannesburg, travel south on the N1, then take the N9 south at Colesberg to Graaff-Reinet. From Port Elizabeth, take the R75 north, a 3-hour drive. (If by chance you find yourself traveling on the N10 from Cookhouse to Craddock—a much longer trip—make sure to stop at the Daggaboer farm stall, a haven of hospitality, homemade ginger beer, pickles, and venison pie.)

By Bus **Translux** and **Intercape** buses pull in daily from Cape Town, the Garden Route, and Port Elizabeth. See chapter 3 for phone numbers.

GETTING AROUND The easiest and best way to explore the town is on foot or by bicycle. For guided tours of the town and surrounds and bicycle rentals, contact **Karoo Connections Tours** ★ (✆ **049/892-3978;** www.karooconnections.co.za). They provide town and township tours; trips to the Valley of Desolation, Bushman Rock Art, and the Owl House; and game-viewing drives in the Camdeboo National Park. They also can help with information about horseback-riding and hiking tours.

WHAT TO SEE & DO

With more national monuments than any other South African town, the streets of Graaff-Reinet are a pleasure to stroll. Incorporate an informal walking tour with a visit to at least one of the four buildings that comprise the **Graaff-Reinet Museum** (✆ **049/892-3801;** Mon–Fri 8am–5pm, Sat 9am–3pm, Sun 9am–4pm; admission R25). Of these, **Reinet House,** a stately Cape Dutch home facing Parsonage Street, is by far the most interesting. Built in 1812 as the Dutch Reformed Church parsonage, its large, airy rooms display period furniture, a collection of antique dolls, and various household objects. Within walking distance, the **Old Library Museum,** on the corner of Church and Somerset streets, houses a collection of fossilized Karoo reptiles that inhabited the area more than 200 million years ago. Also worth a look is the slightly scrappy but still evocative exhibition on the life of Robert Sobukwe, the founder of the Pan Africanist Congress, which broke away from the ANC in 1958. Sobukwe spent years on Robben Island and was buried in Graaff-Reinet, his hometown. Other buildings worth noting are the stately **Dutch Reformed Church,** 1 block up from the Old Library Museum, which dates back to 1886, and the delightful **Graaff-Reinet pharmacy,** a typical Victorian chemist that still operates at 24 Caledon St. Do also stop by the **Pierneef Museum,** Middle Street (✆ **049/892-6107;** Mon–Fri 9am–12:30pm and 2–5pm, Sat and Sun 9am–noon), where the artist's impressive Johannesburg Station Panels are now on display. Viewed with suspicion for years because of perceived ties to Afrikaner nationalism, Pierneef's characteristic, stylized landscapes are garnering renewed appreciation lately—and you may recognize some key South African landmarks (such as the Valley of Desolation or Knysna Heads) from your travels. Lastly, see another side of Graaff-Reinet on a walking tour of **uMasizakhe Township:** Xolile Speelman (✆ **082/844-2890;** irhafutours@yahoo.com) will share its history and introduce you to locals; if possible, he will also arrange a visit to a wedding, an initiation school, a church service, or a clinic. From R100 for 1½ hours.

GREAT SIDE TRIPS

Graaff-Reinet lies in the center of the 19,000-hectare (46,950-acre) **Camdeboo National Park** (✆ **049/892-3453;** www.sanparks.org; daily 6am–7:30pm; R56 adult), the highlight of which is the **Valley of Desolation** ★★★, 14km (8½ miles) from Graaff-Reinet. Sunset is the best time to visit, when the dolomite towers that rise some 800m (2,624 ft.) from the valley below turn a deep red, and the pink light softens the Camdeboo plains. The short, 1.5km (.9-mile) Crag Lizard walking trail that starts at the parking lot is a good introduction to the landscape. On your return, keep an eye out for the endangered mountain zebra—this is one of its last remaining habitats. All in all, the park hosts 43 mammal species; the entrance to the game-viewing area is off the same road as the Valley of Desolation, the R63.

Another highly recommended excursion is to **Nieu Bethesda,** 50km (31 miles) northeast of Graaff-Reinet. This typical Karoo *dorp* (small rural town) is charming; such modern-day luxuries as electricity are relatively recent phenomena, and donkey carts are still a main source of transport, but the main attraction is the **Owl House and Camel Yard ★★★**, on New Street (✆ **049/841-1603;** www.owlhouse.co.za). In her late 40s, after the deaths of her parents, Helen Martins became obsessed with transforming her house into a world of her own making, a project that was to absorb her for the next 30 years. She was obsessed with light: The interior features large reflecting mirrors to maximize this, and every conceivable surface is covered with finely crushed glass, with colors creating large patterns, including a favored sunbeam motif. In the candlelight, the interior glitters like a jewel. Martins's inner vision spread into her backyard, enveloping her in a mystical world of glittering peacocks, camels, mermaids, stars, shepherds, sphinxes, towers, and serpents. Immortalized in the award-winning play and movie *Road to Mecca* (starring Kathy Bates), the house is one of the world's most inspiring examples of Outsider Art. Tours are held from 9am to 5pm daily; admission is R35.

Tea and light meals are available daily at the **Village Inn** (✆ **049/841-1635**), on the corner diagonally opposite the Owl House. There is no official tourism bureau, but owner Idil can assist with just about anything. Or head for the **Two Goats Deli** (✆ **049/841-1602;** daily from 10am—book ahead if possible), which makes its own goat's cheeses and serves a delectable range of bread, cheese, salamis, and preserves for lunch—plus, it shares premises with the Sneeuberg brewery, which means ales are on tap and plentiful.

WHERE TO STAY & DINE

A reasonable B&B with a lovely garden is **Buiten Verwagten** (✆ **049/892-4504;** www.buitenverwagten.co.za; R640–R700 double); choose the Victoria room with its lovely brass bed, or the honeymoon room with its cedar floors and easy access to the pool. There's also a spa for those in need of pampering. Lunch at the **Windmill Junction** (✆ **049/892-4504**), which also sells antiques and Karoo products such as mohair blankets, or, just across the road, at the **Coral Tree** (✆ **049/892-5947**)—the latter is also open for dinner from Monday to Saturday and is surrounded by craft shops and a gallery. Other dining options include **Coldstream** (✆ **049/891-1181**) and the amiable **Kliphuis** (✆ **049/892-2345**), a stone cottage with tables indoors and out, a fine collection of hats, and a wide-ranging menu with plenty of venison and lamb (they serve a rack of roast lamb with strawberry and mint sauce).

Andries Stockenström Guest House ★ The main reason to stay in this listed house built in 1819 is the still the food—guarantee a table by booking overnight (choose one of the minisuites for more space and a bathtub). Former owner Beatrice has moved on, and Gordon now has creative control of the kitchen—his wife, Rose, makes sure comfort levels are high. Dinner, a four-course affair, is the focal point of the evening and is meant to be lingered over: Expect dishes with a Karoo focus served in either the dining room or the covered courtyard outside. Gordon hunts his own venison, grows his own vegetables, and goes fishing to supply his table with the freshest (occasionally unusual) fare—a recent summer dinner opened with a choice of bream (fish) *samoosas* with a fresh mango pickle or sweet potato and chili soup, followed by tender lamb or venison (mountain rheebok). There are cozy lounges to digest in once you're finished eating.

100 Cradock St., Graaff-Reinet 6280. ✆/fax **049/892-4575.** www.asghouse.co.za. 10 units. R1,080–R1,400 double. Rates include breakfast. Dinner from R250; book in advance. AE, DC, MC, V. Children by arrangement only. **Amenities:** Dining room; bar; room service. *In room:* A/C, hair dryer.

Mount Camdeboo ★★ Value If you absolutely have to experience the breathtaking Camdeboo plains and Sneeuberg mountains, but lovely Samara (see "Private Reserves," earlier in this chapter) is just too expensive, this private reserve with luxurious accommodation options is an excellent alternative. It's right next door to Samara, which means it's a good hour's drive from Graaff-Reinet, but once you've settled in your delicious lodge, you're not going to want to go anywhere except in search of wildlife. **Camdeboo Manor** is a stylish converted farmhouse with just four rooms—plus a tiny, romantic stone honeymoon cottage tucked away in the gardens that in another era was an old police gatehouse. There are also two other sole-use farmsteads for larger groups. This is not Big 5 territory (although there are cheetah, rhino, and buffalo), but besides game drives, you can enjoy guided walks, rock art, visits to historic battles sites, and stargazing. Prices are bound to jump, so visit soon.

Take the R75 from Graaff-Reinet, then the R63 turnoff left to Pearston, then left onto Petersberg Rd. Follow signs. ✆ **049/891-0570.** Fax 049/892-3362. www.mountcamdeboo.com. 12 units. From R3,000 double (2009 rates). Includes game drives and meals. MC, V. **Amenities:** Dining room; lounge; cheetah tracking; game drives; helicopter transfers; high-speed Internet; pool; safaris (walking). *In room:* A/C, TV, hair dryer, minibar.

4 THE WILD COAST ★★

The northernmost section of the Eastern Cape stretches 280km (174 miles) from the Kei River in the south to the mouth of the Mtamvuna River, bordering KwaZulu-Natal. The coast is lush and sparsely populated, with innumerable rivers spilling into large estuaries; waterfalls plunging directly into the ocean; coastal, dune, and mangrove forests; long, sandy beaches; rocky coves; and a number of shipwrecks, all of which have earned it the name Wild Coast. This region was part of the former *bantustan* (homeland) Transkei, where any Xhosa that weren't of economic use to the Republic were dumped, and as such it has suffered from overgrazing and underdevelopment and is one of the poorest areas in South Africa. Despite this, the people are incredibly hospitable, and exploring this region will provide you with one of the most unaffected cultural experiences available to visitors in South Africa. Note, however, that much of the coastline is difficult to access—dirt roads are pitted with deep potholes, there is virtually no public transportation, and accommodations options are limited. The exceptions to this are the coast south of Qhorha Mouth (also known as Qora Mouth) and the coastal towns of **Coffee Bay** and **Port St Johns** ★.

The only way to reach these coastal towns is via the N2, which cuts through the middle of the hinterland, passing through unfenced green valleys dotted with traditional Xhosa huts and the old Transkei capital of Umtata, now called Mthatha. The top attraction here is the **Nelson Mandela Museum** ★★ (✆ **047/532-5110;** www.mandelamuseum.org.za; Mon–Fri 9am–4pm, Sat 9am–noon; free admission). Madiba, the clan name by which Mandela is affectionately known, was born near Qunu, where he still returns for holidays (this is also where he and Oprah Winfrey distributed thousands of Christmas gifts to an overexcited crowd in 2002). The museum is situated in the Bhunga Building, a gracious colonial structure that once housed municipal offices, and comprises several rooms that have been filled with Mandela memorabilia, among them gifts from respectful statesmen, adoring children, and various other admirers. Excellent displays, including posters, videos, and photographs, record the life and works of Africa's greatest statesman.

ESSENTIALS

VISITOR INFORMATION The **Eastern Cape Tourism** office in Umtata/Mthatha can give you information on the Wild Coast. Call ✆ **047/531-5290** or visit www.ectourism.co.za (office hours are Mon–Fri 8am–4pm). Alternatively, contact **Wild Coast Holiday Reservations** (✆ **043/743-6181;** www.wildcoastholidays.co.za; meross@iafrica.com) in East London, or Ukhenketho **Tourism Port St Johns** (✆/fax **047/564-1187**). For information on Wild Coast nature reserves (of which Mkambati—also spelt Mkhambathi—is recommended; don't miss the Horseshoe Falls), contact central bookings at ✆ **043/742-4451.**

GETTING THERE & AROUND **By Car** The N2 runs the length of what used to be called the Transkei, with roads to the coast leading southeast off it. Most roads to the coast are untarred, some are badly marked, and all are time-consuming. Look out for livestock on the road, and don't travel at night. You can also charter a flight from Durban to **Umngazi River Bungalows,** the Wild Coast's best lodging.

By Bus The **Baz Bus** (see chapter 3 for regional numbers) travels from Port Elizabeth to Durban, with stops at Coffee Bay and Port St Johns.

On Foot **Wild Coast Meander** ★ (✆ **043/743-6181;** www.wildcoastholidays.co.za) offers a 6-day hike that covers 55km (34 miles), from Qhorha Mouth to Morgan Bay, accompanied by a member of the local community. Hikers ford rivers and traverse isolated beaches, but each night is spent in a hotel. Six days, including accommodations, meals, and transfers from the East London airport, costs R4,820 per person for a group of four, R6,120 per person for just two people. Prices decrease for larger groups.

On Horseback The 3-to-6-day **Amadiba Trails** (✆ **039/305-6455;** fax 039/305-6538) is a camping trip completed on foot or on horseback and canoe. You will be accompanied by a local guide, and meals may be enjoyed with members of the local community. Trails (R1,120–R1,650 for 4–6 days by foot, or R2,240–R3,300 for 4–6 days on horseback) start at the Wild Coast Casino, on the border between the Eastern Cape and KwaZulu-Natal.

WHERE TO STAY & DINE

Sadly, quality accommodations on the Wild Coast remain thin on the ground (or often take the form of sprawling resorts geared at families)—but the breathtaking natural surroundings can be worth a dip in luxury levels. At **Qhorha Mouth,** a river carves its way through forested hills to the sea; here you will find **Kob Inn** (✆ **047/499-0011;** www.kobinn.co.za), a child's paradise with trampolines, a pool, volleyball, and canoes—plus mountain bikes and a 6km (3¾-mile) trail along the coast for older nature lovers. The 45 simple rooms are in thatched blocks; request the honeymoon suite or cottage for maximum comfort. Rates reach R730 for sea-facing rooms and R770 for the honeymoon suite in peak season but include all meals; ask about specials.

Another option worth highlighting, much farther up the coast (best approached from the KwaZulu-Natal side), is **Mbotyi River Lodge** ★ (✆ **039/253-7200;** www.mbotyi.co.za; high season sea-facing units R1,860 double, upgraded units R2,080 double, low season from R1,230 double; all meals included), which has basic thatch bungalows or timber cabins with balconies or patios (ask for a sea or lagoon view; "upgraded" rooms also have air-conditioning and TVs, and specify if you want a bathtub). Don't expect too much in terms of luxury or decor, but the surroundings are exquisite—activities include walks, bird-watching, horseback-riding, fishing, mountain biking (bikes can be rented),

Moments The Serengeti of the Seas

Every year, from around mid-June to July, South Africa is host to what has been touted as "the greatest dive show in the world" by *National Geographic,* when the sea along the wild coast appears to "boil" as some three billion sardines, accompanied by migrating humpback whales and hundreds of predators (dolphins, sharks, seals, cormorants, and gannets), move from the cold Atlantic waters to the warm, subtropical Indian ocean. It's a migration to rival that of the Serengeti and a must on every serious diver's do-before-I-die list. Most packages run for 8 days, with divers based at Mbotyi River Lodge, on the Wild Coast (best accessed from Durban; see p. 302). Alternatively, simply catch one of the daily charters from Shelly Beach in KwaZulu-Natal and witness the migration from the boat. Contact www.oceansafrica.com or www.sardinerun.net.

and, of course, spending time lapping up sunshine on the pristine beaches and exploring the tidal estuary and surrounding waterfalls. Children are welcome and babysitting services are available. Those who really want to stretch their muscles can consider the **Wild Coast Pondo Walk** ★, which is run from Mbotyi, by the same people who run the Wild Coast Meander (see "Getting There & Around," above): You'll go on four different guided, 1-day trails ranging from 13 to 26km (8–16.1 miles)—two along the coast and two inland—over 4 days. You'll land back at Mbotyi every night, so no camping required. Visit www.wildcoastholidays.co.za for more information.

Umngazi River Bungalows ★★ Kids If you want to sample the subtropical pleasures of this untamed stretch of coast without roughing it much, this is the Wild Coast's finest resort. Umngazi is in its own nature reserve, overlooking an estuary and beach, and flanked by dense coastal vegetation. With a safe lagoon, boats for hire, river trips, waterskiing, spa treatments, snooker, a host of babysitters, and a separate toddlers' dining room, it offers the perfect family holiday, yet the honeymoon bungalows are private enough for lovers to remain blissfully unaware of the pitter-patter of little feet. (This is, incidentally, where Nelson Mandela chose to spend his first Christmas with wife Graca.) The en-suite bungalows are basic, with outdoor showers from which you can watch the dolphins—it's definitely worth requesting a sea-facing bungalow (unit nos. 41–43 are choice) or the most luxurious accommodations: the new Ntabeni units, on the hillside, with wonderful river and sea views. Meals are buffets and/or table d'hôte featuring salads; fish, meat, and chicken; homemade breads; and cheese. Service is generally good, though with English very much a second language, patience is, as always, a virtue.

P.O. Box 75, Port St Johns 5120. ✆/fax **047/564-1115.** www.umngazi.co.za. 66 units. R1,420–R1,860 double bungalows and honeymoon cottages; Ntabeni suite R2,300-R2,800 double. Charter flights available from Durban. Rates include all meals. AE, DC, MC, V. **Amenities:** Bird-watching; boating; guided walks; mountain biking; pool (saltwater); spa; tennis. *In room:* Fans.

8

Africa's Big Apple: Jo'burg

For many, Johannesburg, with its heady blend of First and Third worlds, is the most exhilarating city in Africa. Sprawling outward from the center of Gauteng, South Africa's smallest and most densely populated province, it is the ideal springboard from which to explore the animal-rich nature reserves that lie beyond its business-driven borders. And while its reputation as a crime hub is justified, there's no denying that the city itself is a drawing card: A nexus of social change, Jo'burg is the economic heart of Africa, where the continent's major financial deals are struck; a throbbing urban metropolis that is home to a socially vibrant, steadily growing, sassy African elite, and—with up to 1,000 people moving to the city every day—to millions more hoping to find their own elusive fortune.

Traditionally a migrant city, Gauteng was literally built on gold—its name, translated from Sotho, means "Place of Gold"—and it remains a heavily industrialized region, producing almost 40% of the country's GDP. But the city has some tourist draws, too: You can step back thousands of years by visiting the Cradle of Humankind, a World Heritage Site where paleoanthropologists are unearthing clues to humankind's origins, followed by a visit to the Origins Centre, where you can track your own ancestors with DNA testing. Visitors interested in more recent history should include a visit to the striking Apartheid Museum—which provides poignant insight into what it was like to live under one of the world's most iniquitous systems of discrimination—and take a tour of Soweto, South Africa's largest "township," a city within a city, inhabited by as many as five million people, almost all of whom are black—an enduring legacy of the country's separatist history.

Still, most leisure travelers simply use Johannesburg as a gateway to the attractions in neighboring provinces and countries. Of these, Kruger National Park and its surrounding reserves are the best known, but closer still are the malaria-free Madikwe and Waterberg reserves—both within easy driving distance, with a new generation of good-value lodges that will whip you straight from the airport into the serenity of the bush. For more, see the following chapter.

1 JOHANNESBURG & ENVIRONS

Johannesburg is 1,402km (869 miles) NE of Cape Town; Tshwane is 58km (36 miles) N of Johannesburg

Johannesburg, Jo'burg, Jozi . . . ever evolving, this vibrant city throbs to a heady, relentless beat, fueled by the paradox of its reputation as a crime hub and the tremendous sociability of its inhabitants. Jozi's diverse population is a considerably better reflection of South Africa's burgeoning hegemonic spirit than you'll encounter anywhere else in the country, with a new black aristocracy creating their own cultural stew in the clubs, bars, and restaurants in this city's more cosmopolitan areas.

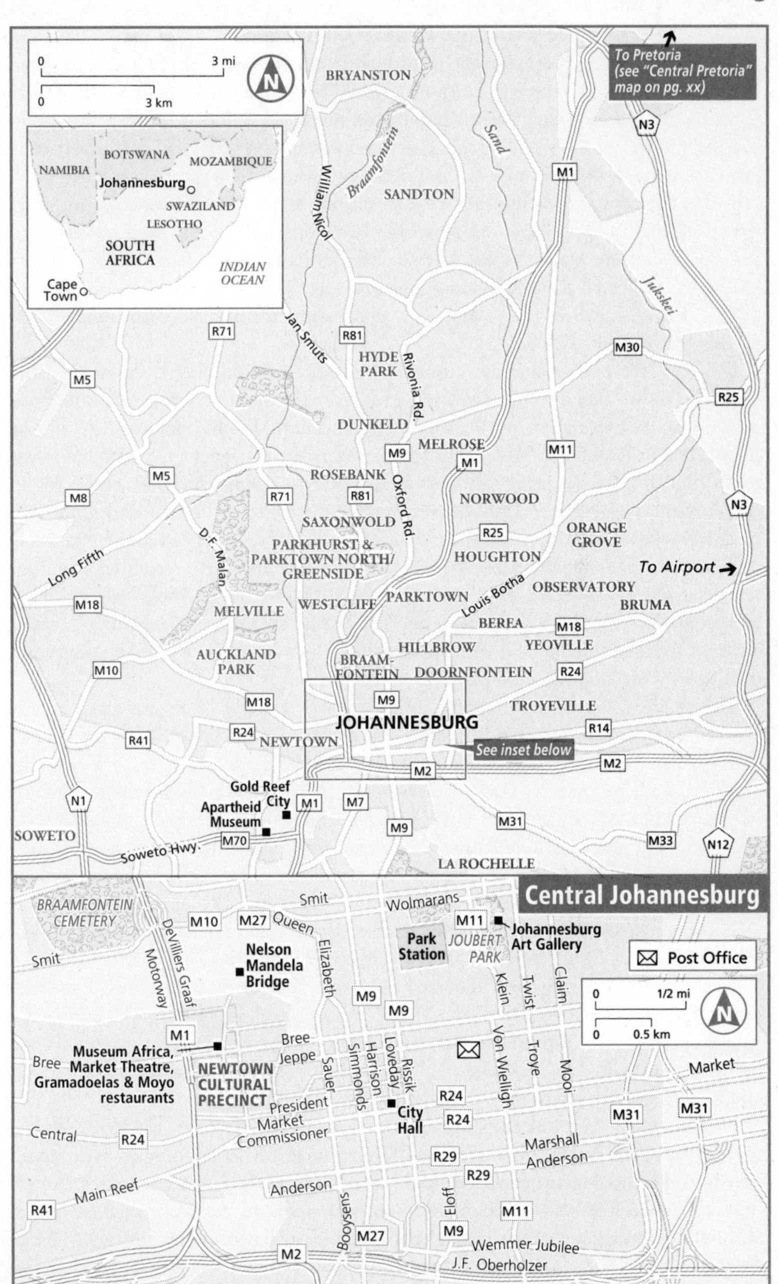

To Pretoria (see "Central Pretoria" map on pg. xx)
BRYANSTON
SANDTON
NAMIBIA
BOTSWANA
MOZAMBIQUE
Johannesburg
SWAZILAND
LESOTHO
SOUTH AFRICA
INDIAN OCEAN
Cape Town
HYDE PARK
DUNKELD
MELROSE
ROSEBANK
NORWOOD
SAXONWOLD
PARKHURST & PARKTOWN NORTH/ GREENSIDE
HOUGHTON
ORANGE GROVE
To Airport
OBSERVATORY
BRUMA
MELVILLE
WESTCLIFF
PARKTOWN
BEREA
HILLBROW
YEOVILLE
AUCKLAND PARK
BRAAM-FONTEIN
DOORNFONTEIN
TROYEVILLE
JOHANNESBURG
NEWTOWN
See inset below
Gold Reef City
Apartheid Museum
SOWETO
Soweto Hwy.
LA ROCHELLE
Central Johannesburg
BRAAMFONTEIN CEMETERY
Nelson Mandela Bridge
Park Station
JOUBERT PARK
Johannesburg Art Gallery
Post Office
Museum Africa, Market Theatre, Gramadoelas & Moyo restaurants
NEWTOWN CULTURAL PRECINCT
City Hall

But it wasn't always like this. Once rolling bushveld, the "gold capital of the world" was born when a prospector named George Harrison stumbled upon what was to become the richest gold reef in the world in 1886. Within 3 years, these nondescript highveld plains had grown into the third-biggest city in South Africa, and soon Johannesburg, or eGoli, as it came to be known, would become the largest city south of Cairo. It took only a decade for Jo'burg's population to exceed 100,000, and by 1897 it was producing 27% of the world's gold. The speed at which it grew was due in part to the power and greed of such men as Cecil Rhodes—whose diamond mines in Kimberley provided the capital to exploit the rich gold-bearing reefs of the Witwatersrand—and to the availability of cheap labor. Along with other "randlords," as the most powerful consortium of mining magnates was known, Rhodes founded the Chamber of Mines in 1889, which created policies regarding recruitment, wages, and working conditions. In 1893, it institutionalized the "colour bar," which ensured that black men could aspire to no more than manual labor.

By 1895, the ever-expanding mining settlement far outnumbered the original Boer settlers, who had fled here from what they felt to be the oppressive policies of the British in the Cape. Disgruntled by this secondary "invasion," Botha, president of the then South African Republic (ZAR), denied these *uitlanders* (foreigners) the vote and refused to develop an infrastructure to support mining activities. Four years later, the ZAR and Britain went to war, and in 1902 Britain annexed the republic. The British Empire relinquished its hold in 1910, when the Union of South Africa was proclaimed, but for the millions of black migrant laborers who toiled below the earth, working conditions remained relentlessly harsh. By 1946, more than 400,000 black people were residing in and around Jo'burg; in August that year, 70,000 African Mineworkers Union members went on strike over living and working conditions—to no avail, despite the death of 12 men and injuries to over a thousand.

During the 1950s, Johannesburg's uniquely black urban culture was given a name. "Kwela" had its own jazzy sounds, heard in the *shebeens* (drinking houses) of Sophiatown, and a slick, sophisticated style, as evidenced in the pages of *Drum* magazine. But this was also the decade of forced removals, when thousands were dumped into the new suburbs of Soweto, and, consequently, a growth phase for the African National Congress (ANC), which in 1955 proclaimed its Freedom Charter—the basis of the current constitution—in what is now known as Freedom Square.

But it would be another 2 decades before the black majority revolted. On June 16, 1976, police opened fire on a peaceful student demonstration in Soweto and sparked a nationwide riot—South Africa's black youth had declared war on apartheid. Student activism escalated during the 1980s and came to a head during the early 1990s, when political parties jostled for power after Nelson Mandela's release from prison. Some townships were reduced to utter chaos, with a mysterious "third force" (later proven to be state funded) pouring fuel on the flames. Political peace finally came with the 1994 elections, and Jo'burgers returned to their primary pursuit: making money.

For many, however, this remains an elusive goal. Unemployment has spawned crime that, in turn, has bred a culture of fear. Walled neighborhoods, burglar bars, security guards, and guard dogs are common sights, particularly in the northern suburbs. But take time (and a sensible, well-versed guide) to drive through the city, and you'll see remarkable signs of entrepreneurship, starting at virtually every traffic intersection across greater

 Staying Safe

Crime—much of it violent and senseless—forms the mainstay of conversation among Jozi's privileged and poor. While the government insists that crime statistics are improving, the city is a hothouse for those who have realized that the easiest way to make it is to take it, as is evidenced in the plethora of private security companies and fortresslike barricading of homes and businesses. Johannesburg continues to have some of the highest incidences of crime in the world, and visitors are strongly urged to keep on their toes. Carjackings are less common now, but keep your car doors locked while traveling and windows up. Don't get suckered into stopping your vehicle for strangers; scams involving mock accidents and breakdowns are designed to lure unsuspecting Samaritans. If you sense a potential threat, keep in mind that crossing against a red light—carefully, of course—is allowed. Don't leave valuables in plain sight in the car, even when you're in it, and it's a good idea to be alert at traffic lights; pay attention to what's going on around you.

Generally speaking, inconspicuous consumption is the order of the day: People who have nothing worth stealing are less likely to attract criminals. Don't carry or wear anything of obvious value (though some say it's worth carrying a small sum of cash to satisfy a demand), and don't look lost. Hillbrow, Berea, and Yeoville are no-go areas unless you're accompanied by a guide who is totally familiar with the area and prepared to walk tall. If you are ever mugged, don't protest—hand over the goods or money and walk away.

If this sort of talk makes you nervous, it may be wise to tour in a group with a guide (see "Guided Tours," below). Alternatively, you can book one of the lodging options recommended below—situated in Jo'burg's safest areas—and spend your time like the locals, sampling the city's many fine restaurants and shopping.

Jo'burg, where you'll be offered anything from coat hangers to animals made of beads; others will remove waste from your vehicle for a donation.

As Cape Town and Durban prepare to host the 2010 Soccer World Cup, Jozi, too, is demonstrating its capacity for renewal. Besides burgeoning property development in the CBD, the multibillion-rand Metro—known as the Gautrain—is due for completion at press time. This rapid-rail transport system will connect Johannesburg with the capital, Tshwane, as well as provide much-needed connections between the airport, inner city, and select neighborhoods. And while Jozi's infrastructure is getting a much-needed jolt, its social structures are already remarkably altered; the emergence of a sophisticated, wealthy black middle class has had an incredible impact on the character of a city that for so long was a bastion of white power and control. People who would have been forced to leave the suburbs at night during apartheid now come out to play, spend, and mingle. For every person living in fear, there are a dozen more enjoying the most happening city in South Africa—given a few days, you could be one of them.

Arriving

BY PLANE Most flights to South Africa arrive at Johannesburg International Airport, now known as **O.R. Tambo International Airport** (✆ **011/921-6262,** or 086/727-7888 for flight inquiries), Africa's busiest hub, and now extensively expanded and upgraded in preparation for the 2010 FIFA World Cup Soccer tournament. (Note that even if your baggage has been checked through to another South African destination, you must pick up your luggage and clear Customs continuing to your connecting flight.) The **Gauteng Tourism Authority** has a branch in the airport's International Arrivals hall (✆ **011/390-3614;** daily 6am–10pm). Foreign exchange is available 24 hours and there are many credit-card-friendly ATMs.

The **Gautrain,** South Africa's first-ever rapid rail system, linking the airport to Sandton Station, is due to be completed by the end of 2009 or early 2010; the airport link will be similar to that offered by other major international airports, and the price of a trip is estimated at press time to be around R80.

If you prefer a door-to-door service from the airport, prebook a shuttle for the 30- to 40-minute drive to the northern suburbs. Taxi lines queue up directly outside the exit, and drivers will approach you as you walk through Customs; at the risk of sounding paranoid, I'd avoid getting into a vehicle with a stranger in this city. Either shell out for the rates charged by your hotel or host (prices are included in reviews) or prebook. If you're on a budget, the best deal in the city is a prebooked **Monane's Shuttle** (✆ **012/323-7706,** after hours 072/251-5156 or 083/770-5757; monashuttle@yahoo.com): Transfers to Sandton/Rosebank area cost R230/250, every additional passenger R50. You will be met by a driver with your name on a board at Arrivals; if you'd like assistance withdrawing foreign currency from an ATM on arrival, ask the driver. Alternatively, big outfit **Ulysses** (www.ulysses.co.za) offers reliable and efficient transfers to Sandton for R300 (R320 for two); again, they meet-and-greet at Arrivals.

BY TRAIN If you have to recover from jet lag (or simply have a penchant for being rocked to sleep), I can think of nothing better than trundling to Cape Town by train, particularly on the legendary **Blue Train** ★★ or the even more luxurious **Rovos Rail** ★★★. Alternatively, choose to arrive in Gauteng this way. Both roll in to **Tshwane** (Pretoria) from Cape Town (taking around 28 hr.). Rovos also operates other luxury trips throughout the country and as far afield as Dar es Salaam; see chapter 3 for more details on both. If you like the romance of rail but can't face the steep fares, a good option is to book the **Premier Classe** coupe from Cape Town, Durban, and Port Elizabeth on **Shozoloza Meyl,** South Africa's main-line passenger services (✆ **086/000-8888;** www.spoornet.co.za); for departure times and rates, see chapter 3. ***Warning:*** Because Johannesburg's **Park Station** is a major center for people arriving from all over Africa, the consequent rich pickings for criminals have made it a hot area, so watch your belongings when you alight, and prebook a transfer to your host/hotel or with **Monane's Shuttle** (see "By Plane," above).

BY CAR Traveling by car in Johannesburg is nerve-wracking, and because the city is almost entirely flat, there are very few landmarks, so getting lost is virtually guaranteed. It's best to fly or train into the city, then use taxis, tour guides, and/or hotel transfers for the duration of your stay.

Visitor Information

Besides the office in the airport, the **Gauteng Tourism Authority** has its **head office** opposite the Market Theatre in Newtown (1 Central Place, corner of Jeppe and Henry Nxumalo sts.; ✆ **011/832-2780** or 011/639-1600; www.gauteng.net)—part of the regeneration of downtown Jozi.

GETTING AROUND

BY CAR Besides the completion of the long-awaited **Gautrain** (the rapid rail service that will ultimately link the airport to the city and Tshwane), public transport remains sketchy and, after hours, nonexistent. Getting around Johannesburg is best done by car, but self-driving is not a good idea: Jo'burg drivers are notoriously impatient, as the myriad skid marks on the roads will attest, and you will need an excellent map and innate sense of direction. If you're comfortable with self-driving, all the major car hire companies are represented here. Those heading off on an independent safari might want to look at **Britz Africa** (✆ **011/396-1860;** www.britz.co.za). They specialize in fully equipped four-wheel-drives (with tents on the roof and cooking equipment) and camper vans, and will pick you up at the airport. **Hire a Land Rover** (contact Neil Kemp, ✆ **011/608-3442** or 082/929-9237; www.hirealandrover.co.za) rents a wide range of "Landies" in good condition.

BY TAXI Taxis generally don't cruise the streets, so you'll have to call for one. Try **Rose Taxi** (✆ **011/403-9625**) and **Maxi Taxi** (✆ **011/648-1212**). In Tshwane, call **Rixi Mini Cabs** (✆ **012/325-8072**) or **SA Taxi** (✆ **012/320-2075**). Charges are around R9 to R10 per kilometer.

GUIDED TOURS

Cradle Of Humankind Tours ★★★ Finds **Palaeo-Tours** (✆ **011/726-8788;** www.palaeotours.com; by arrangement only) offers fascinating trips to some of the key sites in what has become known as the Cradle of Humankind, declared a World Heritage Site in 1999 for the significant paleoanthropological discoveries made in the area since 1966. The Cradle again made headlines in 2003 when a new dating technique (called burial cosmogenic dating) revealed that the Little Foot skeleton, found in 1997, is 4.17 million years old—one of the oldest in the world. Since the discovery, scientists have been hard at work excavating the full Little Foot skeleton. More recent developments have been banal: an "improved" visitor center and an unremarkable underground "museum." However, with Palaeo-Tours, your guides are paleoanthropology scientists or Ph.D. students who explain the history of evolution while taking you to working excavation sites. Tours cover our origins, as well as some of the philosophical aspects of the appearance of humans. The area is some 20 minutes from the city, and both half- and full-day tours include a short game drive on the way to the fossil site at the Rhino and Lion Park.

Township Tours ★★★ Popular with foreign visitors keen to experience "real" urban life, "township" tourism originated in Soweto (see the box later in this chapter). Township tours offer a fascinating insight into daily life in the segregated black neighborhoods constructed during the apartheid years and the remaining ubiquitous economic contrasts found in the City of Gold, like **Alexandra,** where an estimated 600,000 people live in abject poverty in a 19-sq.-km (7½-sq.-mile) enclave, just across the highway from glitzy Sandton, the suburb with some of the highest real estate tags. Among the sights on Alex's

Heritage Trail tour is the house Mandela lived in when he first came to Johannesburg and the headquarters of the Msomi gang, who terrorized the community in the late 1950s. To arrange a tour, contact the **Alexandra Tourism Association** (✆ **011/882-3406** or 011/882-0673).

Incidentally, the word *township*—used to denote poor black suburbs—dates back to 1912. While commonly used, it should perhaps be replaced; it's something you may want to discuss with your guide.

Fast Facts Johannesburg & Tshwane

Airport See "Arriving," earlier in this chapter.

American Express The most convenient office is in Rosebank on the ground floor at The Zone (✆ **011/880-8382**). Hours are Monday to Friday from 8:30am to 4:30pm and Saturday from 9am to 12:30pm. There is also an office in Sandton City shopping center, upper level (✆ **011/883-9009**). For lost or stolen cards, call ✆ **011/710-4747** and ask for the card division.

Area Code Johannesburg's area code is **011.** Tshwane's code is **012.**

Climate Days are usually sunny, with averages of 70°F (20°C). Even winter days are generally mild (May–Aug), though frost often occurs at night.

Drugstores Drugstores are known as chemists or pharmacies in South Africa. Ask your host or concierge for the closest pharmacy. Hospital drugstores tend to keep the longest hours; if you're in Rosebank, visit the pharmacy in the **Netcare Rosebank Hospital** (✆ **011/328-0500**); if you're based in Melville, visit the **Netcare Milpark Hospital** (✆ **011/480-5600**); both are open daily from 8am to 7pm.

Embassies & Consulates Note that all embassies (www.embassiesabroad.com) are in Tshwane: **Australia,** 292 Orient St., Arcadia (✆ 012/342-3740); **Canada,** 1103 Arcadia St., Hatfield (✆ 012/422-3000); **Ireland,** Tulbagh Park, 1234 Church St., Colbyn (✆ 012/342-5062); **United Kingdom,** 255 Hill St., Arcadia (✆ 012/483-1200); **United States,** 877 Pretorius St., Arcadia (✆ 012/431-4000); **Zambia,** 1159 Ziervogel St., Arcadia (✆ 012/326-1847 or -54); **Zimbabwe,** 798 Merton St., Arcadia (✆ 012/342-5125).

Emergencies Dial ✆ **10111** for flying-squad police, ✆ **999** for an ambulance, or ✆ **082-911** for emergency medical assistance. Call ✆ **011/3755-911** for the City of Johannesburg's Emergency Connect line, 24-hour emergency services relating to all life-threatening situations, including ambulances, fire engines, and metro police.

Hospitals Find the closest **Netcare Hospital,** South Africa's biggest private hospital group, with 31 in Gauteng alone. The staff, medical practitioners, trauma unit, and equipment at these hospitals are equal to the best in the world. If you're in Rosebank, contact **Netcare Rosebank Hospital** (✆ **011/328-0500**); in **Melville,** call ✆ **011/480-5600.** To find a particular specialist or the nearest hospital, call ✆ **08606382273** or visit www.netcare.com.

Post Office Post Office service is generally poor; ask your hotel or guesthouse to deal with any postal items. To post large items, contact FedEx (✆ **011/899-8888**) or DHL (✆ **011/921-3666**).

WHERE TO STAY

Options reviewed below are in areas where you'll be perfectly safe and a short distance from some of the city's best restaurants and shops. Johannesburg is not a popular leisure destination, but it is extremely busy for business, so don't leave this booking for the last moment or expect a bargain due to the credit crunch. Those most suited to the leisure market (though with excellent business facilities) are reviewed below—note that many of them offer much better rates on Friday and Saturday nights, so do try to coincide your visit with a weekend.

We've divided the options broadly into the Northern suburbs and Northwestern suburbs.

Northern Suburbs

Very Expensive

Fairlawns Boutique Hotel & Spa ★★ Located in a peaceful suburb a few minutes' drive from Sandton central, this certainly sequesters you from the buzz of Jozi life, with lovely lawns overlooked by a smart dining terrace. The real reason most choose to stay here are the palatial-size and luxuriously styled rooms. Each suite has its own theme and very unique personality; premier suites have two TVs, a DVD player, Jacuzzi tub, and library. Created by John and the creative Anna Thacker, the hotel feels more like a sprawling mansion, with such generous touches as complimentary tea trays (delivered to your room on request), transfers to Sandton, sherry in the room, and shoe shines. The biggest drawback is feeling totally cut off from the city lights (though, in good traffic, Sandton shopping mall is under 10 min. away); then again, with a plush spa and wonderful gardens, feeling well out of the city may be just the thing.

Alma Rd., Morningside Manor, Sandton 2052. ✆ **011/804-2540.** Fax 011/802-7261. www.fairlawns.co.za. 19 units. Courtyard wing R3,630 double; Premier wing R5,160 double; Presidential suite R19,800. Rates include breakfast. AE, DC, MC, V. **Amenities:** Restaurant; bar; airport transfers (R525); gym; library; pool; room service; spa. *In room:* TV, hair dryer, minibar, Wi-Fi (R100/unlimited).

The Grace in Rosebank ★★★ Devised as a more intimate and gracious alternative to the large city hotel, the Grace is within walking distance of Rosebank's boutiques, galleries, and art cinemas, and retains a gracious London gentleman's club atmosphere, a stark contrast to the over-the-top opulence of Fairlawns. Wood paneling, generously sized sofas, gold-framed paintings, and well-thumbed books create a serene, comfortable, and warm atmosphere in the lobby, while standard rooms are equally comforting. Staff are excellent and will do their utmost to ensure your stay is a success (although it's worth noting that rooms don't sufficiently block outside noise). Business travelers who need to be close to the action use the Grace as a base, but for all its refinement, it also attracts its fair share of package tourist groups.

54 Bath Ave., Rosebank 2196. ✆ **011/280-7200.** Fax 011/280-7474. www.thegrace.co.za. 73 units. R5,430 double; Fri–Sat R3,050 double; R6,580–R7,720 suite; Fri–Sat R4,050–R,5050 suite. Rates include breakfast. Children stay free in parent's suite. AE, DC, MC, V. **Amenities:** Restaurant; bar; airport transfers (R495); babysitting; rooftop croquet lawn; currency exchange; gym access; library; heated lap pool; room service; spa. *In room:* A/C, TV, CD/DVD player on request, hair dryer, minibar, free Wi-Fi.

Expensive

Melrose Arch ★ Jozi's self-proclaimed "hip hotel" is something of a knockoff of the Philippe Starck–Ian Schrager model, and that look is now a little tired. That said, it's useful for an overnighter, as you walk out the door and you're in a secure environment, with a host of restaurants to choose from (don't miss Orient, opposite, reviewed below); and the decor does have a quirky, playful edge that differentiates from the bland chains, while giving you the anonymity of a large hotel. I'd still opt for the ultrastylish Peech Hotel up the road, considerably less expensive and far more intimate, or the stylish new Radisson, an excellent value (see below for both).

1 Melrose Sq., Melrose Arch, Johannesburg 2196. ✆ **011/214-6666.** Fax 011/214-6600. www.africanpridehotels.com/melrosearchhotel. 118 units. Standard room R2,275–R3,970 double; price fluctuates depending on availability. Superior room costs R300 more; Executive room costs R500 more. AE, DC, MC, V. **Amenities:** Restaurant; bar; airport transfers (R420); DVD library; discounted gym access; library; pool; room service; surround-sound music and TV room. *In room:* A/C, TV/DVD, hair dryer, minibar, free Wi-Fi.

Ten Bompas ★★ This is one of the first boutique hotels to open in Gauteng, and was featured in *Design Hotels*. Proprietors Christoff van Staden and Peter Aucamp asked 10 interior designers to design a suite (each with a separate lounge and bedroom, a fireplace, guest toilet, steam bath, and plenty of natural light, with access to the outdoors via a ground-floor patio or a balcony). The results are a mixed bag and they look a little dated; personal taste will determine your affection for a particular suite, but all are extremely comfortable. Despite its relative proximity to a great deal of action (Rosebank Mall, Melville, Parkhurst, and the CBD), Bompas' small size means it offers more tranquillity than Fairlawns (though, personally, I prefer Fairlawns' decor). That said, the place is a popular dining venue (called Sides), so the vibe picks up around mealtimes. Given the suite size, all the add-ins (such as complimentary minibar and laundry), and generally good service, this is very good value. (Incidentally, Christoff and Peter also own **Honeyguide Mantobeni,** one of our favorite tented camps [see chapter 9] and can put together a smooth package.)

10 Bompas Rd., Dunkeld West, P.O. Box 786064, Sandton 2146. ✆ **011/341-0282.** Fax 011/447-4326. www.tenbompas.com. 10 units. R3,100 double. Rate includes breakfast, tea and coffee, and minibar. AE, DC, MC, V. **Amenities:** Restaurant; bar; airport transfers (R450); pool; room service. *In room:* A/C, TV, CD/hi-fi system, fax (on request), hair dryer, free minibar, free Wi-Fi.

Moderate

Clico Guest House ★★ Located in Rosebank's tree-lined residential quarter, this 60-year-old Cape Dutch–style house offers comfortable accommodations in nine luxurious rooms, a pool set in a lovely garden, and all-round good style. Finished in warm natural tones, it's a discreet, cozy place to come home to after a busy day of shopping in the nearby mall or weekend craft market, both within walking distance from the guest house (a taxi at night is advisable). Six of the rooms have balconies, while the seventh opens onto the garden; one is also wheelchair accessible. It's a real refuge, almost on par with the slightly edgier Peech.

27 Sturdee Ave., Rosebank ✆ **011/252-3300.** Fax 086/636-8770. www.clicoguesthouse.com. 9 units Double R1,970 Sun–Thurs; R1,470 Fri–Sat and public holidays. Breakfast included. AE, DC, MC, V. **Amenities:** Dining room; lounge w/honor bar; airport transfers (R380–R455); pool. *In room:* A/C, TV, DVD/VCR player, hair dryer, minibar, stereo, free Wi-Fi.

The Parkwood ★★ Value With a great location, close to the dining districts of Greenside and Parkhurst and 10 minutes' walk from Rosebank's shopping (a pleasant enough walk through the suburbs, with just one major intersection crossing), this beautiful boutique-style guesthouse was an overnight success. With a natural eye for detail, owner-designer Sarah Shonfeld has created a great integration of indoor and outdoor spaces, marrying natural design materials—stone, wood, metal, and glass—with chic

African elements, bright artworks, and playful organic displays. You can lounge on Moroccan daybeds on the patio overlooking a skinny lap pool, set in a pristine garden, or browse through your in-room selection of CDs. There's no restaurant, but there is a fine selection of wines to kick off an evening on the town.

72 Worcester Rd., Parkwood. ✆ **011/880-1748** or 082/442-7605. Fax 011/788-7896. www.theparkwood.com. 11 units. Standard double R1,550 double; luxury double R1,750; executive double R1,950. Rates include breakfast. AE, DC, MC, V. **Amenities:** Dining room; lounge areas; airport transfers (R310); doctor on call; gym; library; pool. *In room:* A/C, TV, DVD/VCR, hair dryer, minibar, stereo, Wi-Fi (signal can be unreliable).

The Peech Hotel ★★ (Value This fabulous little hotel, set in a tree-filled, upscale neighborhood, is swish and sexy, and the ideal hangout for trendy travelers who appreciate good value. The emphasis is on in-room comfort (king-size beds, soft white linen, ultracomfortable mattresses, large bathrooms with rain-shower shower heads). The eight garden units are excellent value, each with either a small terrace or direct access to the lawn; the suite above the lobby is a good deal if you value a larger space.

61 North St., Melrose. ✆ **011/537-9797.** Fax 011/537-9798. www.thepeech.co.za. 10 units. R1,850 double; R2,250 suite. Rate includes breakfast. AE, DC, MC, V. **Amenities:** Restaurant; bar; airport transfers (R420); discounted gym access; iPod sound dock; library; pool. *In room:* TV, hair dryer, iPod station, free Wi-Fi.

Radisson Blu ★★ This modern, clean-cut hotel, which opened at the beginning of 2009, is situated on the upper floors of the Sandton Isle development. Although principally a business hotel, it has stylish rooms, an excellent restaurant, spa and fitness facilities, and great proximity to the center of Sandton, with its wealth of shopping and dining options. The decor of the public areas has a playful feel, with a nod to sci-fi—neon lighting, padded reception desks, and colorful stylized furniture (both more discreet and successful than that of Melrose Arch). In contrast, the rooms are decorated in sophisticated, muted tones and provide a peaceful haven. If you're traveling with two, it's worth taking a business room, which is slightly larger and includes free pay-channel TV and the excellent breakfast, with panoramic views stretching as far as downtown. Breakfast is an additional R165 per person in a standard room; if you're on a budget, head across the road to breakfast at one of the many Village Walk options.

Corner of Rivonia Rd. and Daisy St., Sandton 2010. ✆ **011/245-8000.** Fax 011/245-8099. www.johannesburg.radissonsas.com. 290 units. Standard room R1,650–1,950 double; Fri–Sat R1,650 double; R2,100–2,350 business double; R2,100 Fri–Sat business double; inquire directly for suite rates. AE, DC, MC, V. **Amenities:** Restaurant; bar; airport transfers (R700); gym with indoor/outdoor jogging track; room service; spa. *In room*: A/C, TV, hair dryer, minibar, free Wi-Fi.

Northwestern Suburbs

Very Expensive

The Westcliff ★★★ This is our favorite Johannesburg leisure hotel, a pink "village" clinging to the steep incline of Westcliff ridge (you park at reception and are shuttled up along winding cobbled lanes). Hanging on the lip of the large infinity pool, the green suburbs of northern Johannesburg spread out before you; as dusk approaches, watch the sky turn pink over the spectacle of the endless forested canopy, forever changing your perception of this sprawling city. Guest rooms vary considerably—each is uniquely positioned and sized, but understated elegance is the order of the day, and the palatial marble bathrooms are a real treat. Do insist on a room with a view.

67 Jan Smuts Ave., Westcliff 2193. ✆ **800/237-1236** in the U.S., or 011/481-6000. Fax 011/646-3500. www.westcliff.co.za. 115 units. R3,830–R4,660 double; R5,480–R17,300 suite. Children 12–18 pay 50%. AE, DC, MC, V. **Amenities:** 2 restaurants; bar; lounge; airport transfers (R490); babysitting; golf club privileges; gym; 4 pools (2 heated swimming, 2 plunge); room service; spa; tennis court. *In room:* A/C, TV/VCR, fax, hair dryer, minibar, Wi-Fi (R50/15 min, R100/hr.; R225/day) and ADSL.

Moderate

A Room With A View & A Hundred Angels ★★ Part baroque fantasy, part neoclassical brick mansion, this over-the-top faux-Tuscan manor offers exactly what the name suggests: good views, mostly toward the Melville Koppies, and plenty of cherub statues. It's sounds garish, but somehow it works, with tall picture windows, in-room columns and archways, plush linens, conservatories, and fireplaces (and great showers). Book on the upper floor—these have the loveliest views—and in winter ask for a fireplace. The largest rooms are nos. 21, 32, and 33; nos. 22 and 23 have gorgeous views. Melville offers an array of restaurants, live music venues, and shops within walking distance: Host Lise Wallis is happy to make dining recommendations and will also chat about local art and recent developments in the city. They will also arrange transfers for a night on the town.

1 Tolip St., corner of 4th Ave., Melville. ✆ **011/482-5435** or 011/726-8589. www.aroomwithaview.co.za. 14 units. R880–R1,320 double. Rates include breakfast. Children under 10 discouraged. AE, DC, MC, V. **Amenities:** 4 dining/lounge areas w/fireplaces; night porter; pool; secure parking. *In room:* TV, hair dryer, minibar, free Wi-Fi.

A Night In the Cradle of Humankind ★★★

You can avoid Jozi completely by heading directly from the airport to the Cradle of Humankind (60–90 min. away) and checking into the decadent and stylish **Forum Homini ★★★** (✆ **011/668-7000;** www.forumhomini.co.za; R3,500 double). This is a "Find" not so much because it's unknown, but—if you're willing to forgo Jozi's attractions—because you really need look no further. A 600-hectare (1,483-acre) private game farm, the mod lodge-style boutique hotel bears an architectural resemblance to architecture from *The Jetsons,* with sleek, flat-roofed retro structures with packed stone walls and large glass doors that open directly onto the bush; all 14 suites (or "caves") are gorgeous, each featuring private outdoor courtyards and wonderful lounge areas with quirky designer furniture, stalactite-inspired light fittings, flatscreen TVs, DVD players, fireplaces, and under-floor heating. Bathrooms are another highlight, with massive his-'n'-her showers and sunken tubs (from which you can watch waterbucks grazing outside your window), and you can order spa treatments to your room. The main building, with plenty of comfortable indoor and outdoor lounging areas overlooking a small pond, is where decadent meals are served at **Roots ★★★**, one of the very best restaurants in Gauteng. Self-styled chef patron Philippe Wagenfuhrer combines his French culinary roots with African and Asian influences. It's worth overnighting here simply for the pleasure of enjoying the excellent "wine teaser," a six-course meal coupled with a different vintage and varietal. Staff will help arrange tours of the ongoing paleontological excavations around the Sterkfontein area and visit to Maropeng Visitor Centre, the new tourist-friendly heart of the Cradle, declared a World Heritage Site in 1999; there are also various adventure experiences in nearby Magaliesberg, including hot-air ballooning. The main benefit here is that you're not too far from the city, but you feel as if you're far from the rat race. The option of a fairly tame bush walk (with 20 possible mammal species to see) adds to the value of cleaner air and peaceful surrounds.

WHERE TO DINE

Johannesburg offers a thoroughly eclectic mix of dining possibilities: Just about every national cuisine is represented, so if you have a particular craving, simply ask your concierge or host to point you in the right direction. Alternatively, take your pick from the listings below, all located a reasonable distance from the above accommodations. ***Note:*** Foodies currently rate **Roots,** at Forum Homini, Johannesburg's best restaurant, but it's a schlep to get there. If you want to dine there, plan to stay overnight—a great idea in any case (see "A Night in the Cradle of Humankind," above).

If you like cafe society and browsing through menus and venues before deciding where to dine, head for one of the following restaurant-dense neighborhoods.

MELVILLE & AUCKLAND PARK Bohemian Melville is quixotic; blink and you'll discover a favorite restaurant along 7th Street replaced by another. You'll also find the mix of down-at-heel and sophisticated eateries a little confusing at times, because Melville's arty crowd will happily put up with outrageously poor service and crude decor once they've committed to a preferred venue. Also keep in mind that 7th Street is aimed at attracting the city's party crowd rather than serious foodies, and that the popularity of 7th Street means that it inevitably suffers from congestion as well as some shady characters; increasingly, restaurant owners here are selling up and reopening in Parkhurst, while nearby 44 Stanley Avenue is where the growing action is. That said, a few perennial favorites remain: **Soulsa** ★★, 16 7th Street (✆ **011/482-5572;** Tues–Sun; main courses R45–R125), a decent distance down from Melville's frenetic bar action and Melville's best restaurant, offering such tasty food as tuna wrapped in noi with a bit of wasabi, served with braised cabbage and noodles; follow this with their signature hot fig pudding with homemade vanilla ice cream. Good wine recommendations are standard. If you're in the mood for Asian cuisine, **Soi,** on the corner of 7th Avenue and 3rd Street (✆ **011/726-5775**), is still popular, serving up spicy chicken basil and angry duck along with pre- and post-dinner neck massages; while nearby, the quaint, atmospheric, ant-size **Ant** still serves up pizzas at rickety wooden tables to a loyal clientele. ***Note:*** Stick to busy 7th Street; do not venture up the intersecting avenues alone.

If you are in the area during the day, pull into the **Service Station** ★★, Bamboo Centre, corner of Rustenberg and 9th streets (✆ **011/726-1701;** daily 8am–4:30pm). This is an unpretentious vibey deli-style restaurant, where you help yourself to a buffet of great-looking salads, Mediterranean mezze, and delicious quiches, all paid for by weight (an extremely good value); alternatively, order from their predominantly sandwich menu, which includes light meals such as grilled chicken served with light curried mayo and greens. Browse for vino next door at **winesense** (www.winesense.co.za), one of the city's finest wine boutiques; ask for a wine "credit card" so you can taste from a wide selection of excellent South African vintages before making your purchase.

If you'd like to combine your meal with some *great* shopping, in far more salubrious surrounds than Melville's 7th Avenue, head over to the *très* trendy **44 Stanley Avenue** complex, headquarters of the burgeoning Milpark loft district. This is a great outdoor/indoor shopping destination experience, with a mix of carefully selected stores (see "Shopping—Flea Markets to High-End Crafts," below) that are individual. Equally so are the dining options; grab one of the city's best espresso's at **Boat,** a popular courtyard cafe (✆ **011/482-7793**) that also serves up delicious Portuguese pastries (try the custard tartlet), but keep space for lunch at **Salvation Café** ★★ **(011/482-7795;** www.44stanley.co.za), a funky bistro with a menu filled with items culled by yachting chef Claudia Giannoccaro's travels around the world. Food is organic wherever possible, and all of the meats are free-range and free of hormones; the wine list also boasts organic and biodynamic products. Open for breakfast and lunch Tuesday to Sunday 8am to 4pm.

Mammas Tavern and Shebeen ★★ SOUTH AFRICAN In urbane Greenside, this lively, vibey township-themed restaurant—more down-home than Lekgotla, where the food is more sophisticated—belts music out of the sound system, and it's filled with colorful, whimsical design details and bits of art and kitsch. The menu includes typical South African items such as wors, *skilpadjies* (minced liver patties wrapped in caul), marrow bones, impala and ostrich stew, and the very highly regarded Chief's chicken curry. Generous cuts of well-aged beef are apparently ethically sourced from a Gauteng farm; look no further than The Pirates (of Orlando) rump. All main courses come with vegetables and a choice of pap, samp, or rice. It's definitely the most vibrant option in the 'burbs, and if you stay for the late-night carousing that sometimes sets in, you'll have more than a memorable meal to take home.

18 Gleneagles Dr., Greenside. ✆ **011/646-7302.** Main courses R65–R89. DC, MC, V. Mon–Sun 11:30am–late.

PARKHURST & PARKTOWN NORTH ★★★ These two adjoining neighborhoods represent the city's most relaxed restaurant nexus, with great cuisine, popular with the chic set who combine lazy weekend lunches with the chic set who combine it with browsing: Locals flock to 4th Avenue not only for its sidewalk restaurants, but also for its quaint specialty stores—selling anything from Belgian chocolate to African art or English antiques—a far better atmosphere than the dime-a-dozen malls. Recommended restaurants are **Cilantro** ★, 24E 4th Ave., Parkhurst (✆ **011/327-4558**), which serves up an eclectic European–Asian menu, from Belgian-style moules et frites (with homemade mayo) to Greek kleftiko and sublime calamari. The folks who brought (and sold) **The Loft** to Melville have now opened **The Attic** ★ (✆ **011/880-6102**) next door, featuring a menu of Asian and French cuisine created by the London-trained chefs, though some diners have complained of less than stellar service. **Espresso** ★, 23A 4th Ave., Parkhurst (✆ **011/447-8700**), must rate as one of the most popular Italian restaurant groups in the city, serving pizzas with some fabulous combinations—try, for instance, the pear and blue cheese pizza. Note that credit cards are not accepted. But for the best dining, head to Parktown North's 4th Avenue to **Fino Bar and Restaurant** and, right next door, **La Cucina di Ciro,** both reviewed below.

Fino Bar and Restaurant ★★★ Value SPANISH/MEDITERRANEAN TAPAS Who can resist a venue that specializes in tapas and cocktails, and delivers both with aplomb? Fino is a bar/restaurant in the sun-kissed Mediterranean mold, teaming casual soft-white decor with the sensual, spicy, and citrus flavors of Spain. Choose from delicious chicken livers cooked with sherry, orange zest, and chili, or sticks of zucchini battered, then deep fried, and sprinkled with parmigiano; or, from the mains, lamb filet spiced with chili and black peppercorns and drizzled with a red wine sauce. Then order a glass of bone-dry fino sherry from the extensive wine list, or a pitch-perfect mojito.

Corner of 4th and 7th sts., Parktown North. ✆ **011/447-4608.** www.finojhb.co.za. Bookings recommended. Main courses R55–R115. AE, DC, MC, V. Mon 6–10:30pm; Tues–Sat noon–3pm and 6–10:30pm; Sun noon–3pm.

La Cucina di Ciro ★★ Value Finds ITALIAN Ciro Molinaro's three-star Michelin experience in France's Loire region simply rekindled his talent for home-cooked Italian fare, which he has been dishing up to his loyal patrons for years. It's a totally unpretentious delilike venue (and small, so book), where the focus is firmly on the food: The menu changes regularly, depending on what's in season or looks good in the market, but the focus is firmly on pasta, and mostly vegetarian. In summer, be sure to book a table on the pavement and enjoy the balmy highveld temperatures. ***Note:*** Another great Italian joint, ideal if you're based in a Sandton hotel or guest house, is **Assaggi** ★★, Post Office Centre, Rudd Road, Illovo (✆ **011/268-1370**), where locals congregate not only for the primo pasta, but also to take home jars of tangy sauce from the in-house deli.

17 4th Ave., Parktown North. ✆ **011/442-5346.** Reservations essential. Main courses R55–R95. AE, DC, MC, V. Mon–Sat 9am–3:30pm and 6:30–9:30pm.

Northern Suburbs (Melrose, Sandton)

Auberge Michel ★★★ CONTEMPORARY FRENCH Lyon-born gourmand Michel Morand fell in love with South Africa and moved here over 2 decades ago. Teaming up with local Vusi Sithole, he has created what many consider the city's top restaurant. Morand knows Jo'burg's major players, and some of the country's biggest (and wealthiest) names come to his classy Sandton restaurant to indulge in out-of-the-ordinary French dishes. Formal and gracious, with high-back chairs and stiff napkins, Auberge Michel prides itself on the fact that once the menu changes, no dish is *ever* repeated; the emphasis is on producing high-quality, highly original cuisine that evolves out of specially sought-out ingredients.

122 Pretoria Ave., Sandown, Sandton. ✆ **011/883-7013.** www.aubergemichel.co.za. Main dishes R130–R300. AE, DC, MC, V. Tues–Fri noon–2:30pm; Mon–Sat 6:30–9:30pm. Closed Dec 15–Jan 7.

Lekgotla ★★★ AFRICAN For a sophisticated take on African cuisine, head to this chic restaurant (meaning "The Meeting Place"), at Sandton City's Nelson Mandela Square. The range of dishes, some with exotic names, suggests the impressive array of culinary influences on the African continent, and all are generally very good: oxtail tangine braised with red wine and beer, barley-braised kudu with mascarpone, or a rack of springbok cooked in red wine and thyme. Whatever your choice, make space for a side order of classic, authentic mielie *pap* or, better still, samp and beans with tangy chakalaka—a South African staple. End with traditional, sickeningly sweet Afrikaner *koeksisters* or milk tart. Set menus offer good value.

5 Nelson Mandela Sq., Sandton City, Sandton. ✆ **011/884-9555.** www.lekgotla.com. Reservations highly recommended. Main courses R80–R185. AE, DC, MC, V. Daily noon–10:30pm.

Moyo Zoo Lake ★★ (Kids) MODERN PAN-AFRICAN Moyo, with three branches in Jo'burg, is touristy but good. This branch in the leafy park at Zoo Lake is one of the best daytime venues, a lovely place to spend the afternoon with kids (there are often activities arranged for them). The setting is peaceful, with a deck furnished with deep sofas overlooking the lake, a veritable gallery of African artworks and artifacts, and a garden space to explore. Most menu and buffet items are reworked to suit a Western palate (unlike at Gramadoelas, where authenticity is favored), and food is nothing to write home about. More than a restaurant, Moyo is an experience, particularly at night, when music, dance, and other entertainment are on the menu; there's even a boutique selling local wines, CDs, artworks, and toys.

Zoo Lake Park, 1 Prince of Wales Dr., Parkview. ✆ **011/646-0058.** www.moyo.co.za. Reservations essential. Main courses around R95. AE, MC, V. Daily 8am–11pm.

Orient ★★★ ASIAN With its super-slick interior, world-class dim sum, and security-conscious location, Orient is an absolute must for foodies who love Asian and find themselves in Johannesburg. Among a wide-ranging menu that includes all the usual

Moments Touring the City Within a City

Dispossessed of their land during the 1800s and further reduced to virtual slavery by taxation, thousands of black men were forced to find work in the minefields of eGoli. As more and more settled in inner-city slums, the segregationist government's concerns about the proximity of blacks to white suburbs grew until, in 1930, a solution was found. A farm 18km (11 miles) to the southwest of Johannesburg was designated as the new township, and blacks living in and around the city were served with eviction papers. It would now take 3 hours to get to work. There were as yet no roads, no shops, no parks, no electricity, no running water. Public transport and policing were hopelessly inadequate. Not surprisingly, most people refused to move, but in 1933 the government declared the Slums Clearance Act and forcibly evicted blacks from the inner cities. Defeated, these new homeless moved in, and Soweto, acronym for the South Western Township, was born. In 1944, James Mpanza led a mass occupation of open land near Orlando, the original heart of Soweto, and within 2 years, this, the country's first unofficial squatter camp, housed 40,000 people.

Today rural poverty means that Soweto remains a magnet for millions searching for a better standard of living, and South Africa's densest city-within-a-city is home to soccer heroes and politicos, record producers and shebeen queens, multimillionaires and the unemployed, murderers and Nobel Peace Prize winners. As the country prepares to host the 2010 FIFA Soccer World Cup, nowhere is development more essential than in Soweto, widely considered the emotional heart of Jozi. Local government has promised to stop pumping money into developments in the north and give focus to the upgrade of facilities and transport for the estimated 3.5 million people of Soweto (although those in the know say it's closer to 5 million). Here, **Soccer City,** a massive new stadium where the opening game of the tournament is to be held, is under construction, while an ugly power station that's been standing defunct since the 1980s will be converted into a museum fashioned on London's Tate Gallery; apparently, visitors will be able to bungee-jump from the massive cooling towers. More good news is that while 16,000 trees were planted here in 2006, another 300,000 are scheduled for planting in time for the World Cup. And as Soweto's earning capacity grows, so do its spending channels; September 2007 saw the opening of **Maponya Mall** (named after the developer Richard Maponya, Soweto's first millionaire and highly respected businessman), where a whole new generation of glam-setters can fork out their hard-earned cash on global brands and Westernized fast food. While shack dwellers are steadily

favorites (including satays; spring rolls; spicy soups; red, yellow, and green curries; and pad Thai), interesting alternatives abound—Hong Kong Pears, Chi Chee Gao, Bang Bang Duck, and Grilled Banana Fish, to name a few. And if that's not enough to tempt you, they also make great sushi.

Melrose Arch, Sandton. ✆ **011/684-1616.** Reservations recommended. Main courses R44–168. AE, DC, MC, V. Daily noon–10:30pm.

being relocated to more substantial brick abodes, properties in upmarket Diepkloof Extension 1 (colloquially known as Diepkloof "Exclusive" or "Expensive") include mansions worth R3.5 million; as you drive through the neighborhoods admiring the kitsch side of Soweto chic (plenty of face-brick topped by unwieldy satellite dishes, not to mention a mélange of pink, orange, and salmon-colored structures), you'll notice perfectly manicured gardens and the occasional BMW. Although many houses are now protected by security companies, it's tough community justice that seems to keep crime at bay; so terrifying is the prospect of being punished by community vigilantism that petty burglars have been known to turn themselves over to official police.

Despite all the healthy reports, very few white South Africans venture here for pleasure, despite the warm welcome Sowetans are famous for and the fact that the few *umlungu* (whitey) inhabitants of Soweto say they feel safer here than in the suburbs. That's not to say crime is not still a potential threat; for safety and real insight, Soweto is best visited accompanied by a knowledgeable guide, who will not only give a real sense of its history, but help you understand its ongoing evolution. Most operators cover similar ground: the **Mandela Museum,** where Madiba once lived; a stop at the **Hector Pieterson Memorial** (reviewed above); a drive down **Vilakazi Street,** the only street in the world to have housed two Nobel Prize winners; **Freedom Square,** where the ANC's Freedom Charter was proclaimed to thousands in 1956; and the **Regina Mundi Church,** the "Parliament of Soweto," where the bullet-marked walls are witness to ex-security-police brutality. The best tour I've had was with Bongani Ndlovu of **Soweto.co.za** ★★★ (also their website address, where you can book your full-day tour; ✆ **011/326-1700**); intelligent, highly knowledgeable, and great fun to tour with, Ndlovu should be requested specifically. A full-day tour, with a pickup in Rosebank, costs R660 and includes lunch at Wandie's, a drink at a shebeen, and all museum charges. If you're up for a party, ask about nighttime shebeen tours, usually limited to weekends. (Note that this operator is highly involved in community projects, so your ticket fee will help change lives.) Another operator offering personalized experiences in half-day format is **Imbizo Tours** (✆ **011/838-2667** or 083/700-9098; www.imbizotours.co.za). ***Caveat:*** The downside of driving around in a bus armed with a camera is the sense that you are treating people like animals in a reserve. For this reason, you are encouraged to get out of the vehicle and talk to the people on the street. It is, after all, a sense of community that distinguishes Soweto life from that in Jo'burg or Tshwane.

City Center

Gramadoelas ★★ AFRICAN For 40 years, Eduan Naude and Brian Shalkoff have entertained royals, rock stars, presidents, and audiences from all over Africa (including a loyal local following) in their marvelously cluttered restaurant in the Market theatre in Newtown's Cultural Precinct—a far more interesting area than the bland northern suburbs

Tshwane's Architectural Draws: Then and Now

In 1938, the secretive Afrikaner *Broederbond* (brotherhood) organized a symbolic reenactment of the Great Trek and sent a team of ox wagons from Cape Town to Pretoria (now Tshwane) to celebrate its centenary. By the time the wagons reached Pretoria, more than 200,000 Afrikaners had joined, all of whom camped at Monument Hill, where the foundation stones for a monument were laid. Ten years later, the **Voortrekker Monument**★★ (✆ **012/325-7885;** www.voortrekkermon.org.za; daily 8am–5pm; R32 adults, R10 children, R13 per vehicle) was completed, and the Afrikaner Nationalist Party swept to power. This massive granite structure, sometimes compared irreverently to a large Art Deco toaster, is quite something and dominates the skyline at the southern entrance to Tshwane. Commemorating the Great Trek, particularly the Battle of Blood River, fought on December 16, 1838, the monument remains hallowed ground for many Afrikaners. Every year on that date, exactly at noon, a ray of sunlight lights up a central plaque that reads WE FOR YOU SOUTH AFRICA. The *we* refers, of course, to Afrikaners—in the marble frieze surrounding the lower hall depicting the Trek and Battle, you will find no carvings of the many black slaves who aided the Boers in their victory. The museum below has memorabilia relating to the Great Trek. Most interesting is the "female" version of the monument frieze—huge tapestries depicting a romanticized version of the Great Trek's social events; they are the perfect foil to the Afrikaner men: ladies plaiting threads while the men wrest with stone in the monument. With the best views of South Africa's administrative and diplomatic capital, the more classical **Union Buildings**★★, Meintjieskop Ridge, Arcadia (✆ **012/325-2000**), are probably the best-known creation of prolific British Imperial architect Sir Herbert Baker. The buildings—the administrative headquarters of the South African government, and office of the president since 1913—are generally considered his finest achievement. The office-block wings are said to represent the British and Afrikaner people, linked in reconciliation by the curved amphitheater. Again, African "natives" were not represented, nor allowed to enter the buildings (except to clean). So the visitor can just image the scenes of huge emotional jubilation in the gardens and buildings on 1994 as South Africans witnessed the inauguration of Mandela, and African praise-singers in traditional garb exorcised the ghosts of the past. Visitors can walk along Government Avenue, the road that traverses the facade, but only those on official business may enter.

and one that has thoroughly regenerated itself, with Gramadoelas offering a great starting point to a night out on the town (it's certainly a great deal more authentic and satisfying than nearby Moyo). The menu sometimes sacrifices excellence in favor of authenticity, but Sen. Hillary Clinton apparently loved the mopani worms *(masonja),* and the *umnqusho,* a mixture of braised beef shins, beans, and maize, is Mandela's favorite dish. For the more timid, there are huge prawns, mild Cape Malay vegetarian and meat curries (babotie, the delicately spiced mince curry, is excellent), ostrich filet, and an aromatic *snoek* (local fish) pie. Although a half-kilo of king-size Mozambican prawns will dent your wallet, most dishes are around R80, and there are regular buffets showcasing an array of African dishes.

Market Theatre Complex, Bree St., Newtown. ✆ **011/838-6960.** www.gramadoelas.co.za. Main courses R60–R200. Mandatory 10% service charge. AE, DC, MC, V. Tues–Sat noon–3pm; Mon–Sat 6:30–11pm.

WHAT TO SEE & DO

The Top Attractions

Apartheid Museum ★★★ Moments Many visitors passing through this world-class museum find themselves emotionally unsettled by its meticulous chronicling of apartheid history. Your journey through the modernist concrete structure begins when you are given an entry pass labeling you as either white or nonwhite; you wander through galleries of massive identification cards emphasizing the dehumanizing aspect of racial profiling. A life-size photograph of an all-white race classification board greets you, as do newspaper reports about the board's ridiculous methods (such as sports preferences). It's an emotionally taxing start to a journey that grows in intensity as the history of South African racial segregation and resulting political turmoil is played out in vivid photographs, well-researched textual displays, and gut-wrenching video footage. Besides paying tribute to the triumphs of black political leaders and white liberals who contributed to democracy, several installations and spaces evoke the dreadful horrors of apartheid rule, like the bleak hangman's nooses symbolizing the number of political prisoners executed during apartheid rule until as late as 1989. You can also lock yourself in one of three tiny solitary confinement cells that would have serviced prisoners facing lengthy periods of detention without trial.

Northern Pkwy. and Gold Reef Rd., Ormonde. 6km (3¾ miles) south of city center; take a taxi or you'll get lost! ✆ **011/309-4700.** www.apartheidmuseum.org. Admission R40 adults, R25 children. Tues–Sun 10am–5pm.

Constitution Hill ★★ On a hill overlooking the inner city, this is Jo'burg's answer to Cape Town's popular Robben Island attraction, and is billed as a living tribute to the country's enshrined freedoms and human rights, housing South Africa's architecturally provocative **Constitutional Court,** where you can view artworks or—in the spirit of transparency—even attend court hearings. Like Robben Island, this is the site of a prison—the notorious 19th-century **Old Fort,** where brutalities of the worst kind were perpetrated on innocents in the name of apartheid; both Nelson Mandela and Mahatma Gandhi were detained here. The guided tour includes **Number Four,** the scene of much human torture and now replaced by an exhibition that attempts to unearth the notion of criminality. A work in progress, Constitution Hill centers on **Constitution Square,** a central piazza, where you'll find two stairwells that belonged to the original "Awaiting Trial Block" of the prison; a wall here is filled with a range of comments made by South Africans as the country attained freedom. Tours (90 min.) depart every hour, but I recommend the private tour (R40).

Constitution Hill, Braamfontein. ✆ **011/274-5300.** Tours R22 adults, R15 students and teens, R10 children under 12; night tours (beginning at 6pm) R75. Mon–Fri 9am–5pm; Sat 10am–3pm.

Hector Pieterson Memorial & Museum ★★ Erected in memory of the 1976 student protest, when police opened fire on hundreds of Sowetan schoolchildren who were peacefully demonstrating against the use of Afrikaans as a medium of instruction in their schools. The concourse leading to the entrance is marked by olive trees symbolizing peace and beautiful columns, with each piece of slate meant to represent a student who died needlessly. Inside the immaculate, modern space are emotionally compelling displays: Video footage of the event and numerous breathtaking photographs taken by such brave and talented photographers as Peter Mangubane and Sam Nzima. Included is the infamous shot of Hector Pieterson—one of the young boys who died in a hail of police bullets—being carried by a young man whose face is contorted in disbelief and pain. Hector's sister runs alongside, her mouth a silent wail of grief. The police reported 59 dead; the actual toll was thought to be closer to 500. Children turned on their parents, something hitherto unheard of in traditional society and destroyed everything they could that belonged to municipal authority—schools, post offices, and the ubiquitous beer halls. The police retaliated with brutal assaults, arrests, and killings. These photographs offer a window on the anger, fear, aggression, and grief of these times, after which Soweto and South Africa were never the same.

Hector Pieterson Sq., corner of Khumalo and Pela sts., Orlando West, Soweto. No phone. Admission R25. Tues–Sat 9am–5pm.

Johannesburg Art Gallery ★★ Predictably, the city's first gallery was financed with the sale of a diamond. In 1904, Lady Phillips, wife of the first chairman of the Rand Mines Company, sold her 21-carat ring to purchase three paintings by Wilson Steer. Over the next 5 years, she wrangled money from her wealthy connections to purchase more artwork and commissioned Sir Edwin Lutyens to design the elegant building that now houses her collection. The rather dull Flemish and Dutch collections are made up for by the Brenthurst Collection of African Art, comprising curios plundered by European explorers in the 19th century, and later collections of traditional southern African artworks. Happily, despite ignoring black talent during the apartheid years, the gallery now also has a good selection of South Africa's most renowned, including sculptures by Venda artist Jackson Hlungwani and paintings by Helen Sebidi, Alfred Toba, and Gerard Sekoto. For more representation of contemporary artists, you'd do well to try galleries such as **The Premises** (at the Civic Theatre) or the **Goodman Gallery** (in Parkwood); the latter is a commercial gallery—for more recommended galleries, see "Shopping—Flea Markets to High-End Crafts."

Klein St., Joubert Park. ✆ **011/725-3130.** Free admission. Tues–Sun 9am–5pm.

Origins Centre ★★ This museum has evolved out of the University of Witwatersrand's Rock Art Institute, and the focus is (a little zealously) on showing that racial and cultural differences between various groups of people are largely superficial, as we are all unified by a genetic thread that traces humankind back to a common ancestor in—you guessed it—Africa. It also posits that human beings are united by their unique ability to engage in symbolic thought and cultural exchange. Much of the investigation around this human cultural proclivity is dealt with through the center's extensive focus on the San tribe, whose supposedly primitive way of life is examined in a range of fascinating films, handsome displays, and quality commentary. Of particular interest are details of the mystical San spirit world, typically entered by means of shamanic trance dances. You'll need at least 90 minutes to tour the center, with the aid of the audio guide provided; afterward, you can browse for excellent but pricey African crafts in the gift store or settle for cappuccino at **Fino,** the in-house cafe, while you decide whether to apply for a DNA test to trace your ancestral origins: R800 for women (who don't have the Y chromosome, so can be tested only for maternal genetic ancestry) and R1,200 for men; the test is done at the nearby National Health Laboratory Services, also in Braamfontein, at the corner of Joubert and De Kotze (✆ **011/489-9237**).

1 Yale Rd., Braamfontein. ✆ **011/717-4700.** www.origins.org.za. Admission R60 adults, R35 children under 12; includes audio guide. V. Open daily 9am–5pm but sometimes close for functions; call ahead.

SHOPPING—FLEA MARKETS TO HIGH-END CRAFTS

Johannesburg attracts people from all over the continent with one sole purpose: to shop till they drop. To that end, the city has more than 20 malls to choose from, but the best atmosphere by far is found in the suburb of **Rosebank,** which has plenty of outdoor areas to break the monotony of the various interlinked malls, as well as a good selection of essentials such as travel agents; music, book, fashion, and craft shops (see below); and a great arts cinema (www.cinemanouveau.co.za). The rooftop at **Rosebank Mall,** which is open every Sunday and public holidays from 9:30am to 5pm, hosts the city's best market. If you're not here on Sunday, consider the worthwhile **African Craft Market** (✆ **011/ 880-2906;** daily 9am–5pm winter, 9am–6pm summer), where you can shop for artifacts and artworks from across the continent.

AUCKLAND PARK Finds Milpark's **44 Stanley Avenue** complex ★★★ (✆ **11/482-4444;** www.44stanley.co.za) is great for browsing and delightfully free of crowds and hassle; the line-up—selected for the unique stock they carry—will keep you engrossed for a few hours, and there are some lovely laid-back places to eat. You'll find whimsical and fantastic garments at **Just** ★★ (✆ **011/072-384-9969**), showcasing the work of 30 local designers: handmade toys and collectibles from all over Africa (ethically sourced, of course) at **African Toyshop** ★★ (✆ **011-4826223**); great gear in natural fabrics at **Lunar** (✆ **011/726-5558**); and a highly reputable gallery, **Art on Paper** (✆ **011/726-2234**), showcasing contemporary art by both established and young, promising South African artists.

PARKHURST This is another blissfully relaxed place to browse for everything from antiques to Afro-chic housewares; definitely visit **amoeba** ★, Shop 2, corner of 4th Avenue and 7th Street (✆ **011/447-5025;** www.amoebaconcepts.co.za), for an eclectic range of stylish contemporary local art, decor, and jewelry; look for covetable collectibles by Mark Splendid and Sarah Lovejoy. A few steps away is the other Joburg outlet for the **African Toyshop** ★★, on the corner of 4th Avenue and 6th Street (✆ **011/4422643**), with great gifts from 14 countries around the continent.

ROSEBANK Fashion divas looking for distinctive "where did you get that?" designer items need to head straight for the **Zone@Rosebank.** Start by browsing **The Space** ★, lower level (✆ **011/327-3640**); next door is **Sun Goddess** ★★ (✆ **011/447-8395;** www.sungoddess.co.za), the queen of pre-colonial African fashion, a small boutique for real African goddesses—all the local celebrities have at least one of her head-turning outfits. If you simply want a few smartish T-shirts emblazoned with retro-style South African icons (such as Mandela) or examples of silly local humor, pop into nearby **Big Blue** (✆ **011/880-3994**), a clothes-shop-cum-novelty-store that's ideal for gifts. Upstairs at **Stoned Cherrie** ★★, opposite Primi Piatti restaurant (✆ **011/447-9629**), you'll find more of the best Afro-chic threads in town. Nearby, at **Sowearto** ★ (✆ **011/447-7004;** www.sowearto.co.za), you can browse through some innovative and funky Afro-chic garments and limited accessories from the studios of happening local designers; the range is funky, while the store branding (it's now a small chain) is based on the eye-catching stripes on the packaging of Chappies bubble gum. Also upstairs at the Zone is **Ma Gents** ★★ (✆ **011/447-0996;** www.magents.co.za), which you'll recognize by the adjacent advertising for Y-FM, the country's hippest black urban radio station. It's where you'll find funky street wear worn by Jozi's trendiest young hipsters. Right next door is **Musica**

 Megastore (✆ **011/788-1087**), where staff can point you to the African music section. Don't blindly trust their suggestions, however; ask to listen to a few selections before you swipe your credit card.

JOHANNESBURG AFTER DARK

The Performing Arts

The **Market Theatre,** 56 Margaret Mcingana St., Newtown (✆ **011/832-1641;** www.markettheatre.co.za), is famous for having spawned a generation of protest theater and is likely to have a good selection of local talent. The **Johannesburg Civic Theatre,** Loveday Street, Braamfontein (✆ **011/877-6800;** www.showbusiness.co.za), is one of the largest and most technologically advanced theaters in the country; this is where large-scale musicals, operas, dance, and orchestral music are performed. The **Wits Theatre Complex,** corner of Jorissen and Station streets, Braamfontein (✆ **011/717-1372**), attracts a wide variety of local and international theater talent, including good dance productions; quality varies, so be informed. For current listings for all these venues and more, check out the daily "Tonight" section in *The Star* and the weekly *Mail & Guardian* (www.mg.co.za). Tickets can usually be booked and bought by phone; call **Computicket** (✆ **083/915-8000,** 083/131, or 011/340-8000; www.computicket.com; Mon–Sat 8am–8pm).

The Club, Bar & Music Scene

In a city where work is everything, social interaction is an important distraction. You'll discover a seemingly endless selection and variety of bars, pubs, clubs, and downright sleazy drinking holes. If you like to club- or bar-hop, several areas have a concentration of options—in fact, cruising from venue to venue is a popular pastime after dark, spawning the label "Jo'burg Joller" (Johannesburg party animal), signifying unofficial membership to the city's heavyweight party clique. Many of the larger clubs are in otherwise missable neighborhoods and require some driving to reach. To experience Jo'burg's broad social mix almost entirely on foot, consider spending the night out in **Melville's** 7th Avenue, close to central Johannesburg. It's becoming increasingly hard-core, so don't come if you're nervous, as mentioned elsewhere. Stick to where there are plenty of people, such as 7th Street (or head for nearby Roka, in laid-back Milpark; see below). Replacing Melville for many, **Newtown** (www.newtown.co.za), home of the Market Theatre Precinct, is now the destination for those in search of a good time, whether they hail from the suburbs or the townships; the best are reviewed below. For up-to-the minute news of what's hot and what's happening, navigate to **www.jhblive.com**, an excellent site with reviews of most of Jozi's entertainment spots and information on upcoming events.

If you're a **jazz** aficionado, some names to watch for are Gloria Bosman, African Jazz Pioneers, Feya Faku, the Sheer All Stars, Andile Yenana, Sipho Mabuse, Lulu Gontsana, Bheki Mbatha, Khaya Mahlangu, Barney Rachabane, Oscar Rachabane, Octavia Rachabane, Herbie Tsoaeli, McCoy Mrubata, Zim Ngqawana, Louis Mhlanga, Linda Kekana, Moses Khumalo, and Pops Mohamed. **Kwaito** acts to look for are Brothers of Peace (BOP), Mandoza, Mafikizolo, Zola, M'Du, Mzekezeke, Kabelo, Mapaputsi, Bongo Maffin, and Mzambiya.

Northern Suburbs

The Blues Room ★★ In the heart of Sandton, this upmarket nightclub, voted the best jazz and blues venue in Johannesburg for 4 years in a row, serves up live blues, jazz, fusion, comedy, and even rock 'n' roll for an older, mostly white crowd, but it's slick, safe, and well run. Village Walk Mall, corner of Rivonia and Maude sts., Sandown, Sandton. ✆ **011/784-5527.** www.bluesroom.co.za. Cover usually R60–R70.

Café Vogue ★★★ A trendy crowd flocks to this Rivonia joint on Thursday (R&B and hip-hop), which some say is the best night; Friday (fusion); and Saturday (disco and French house). The music is fine and the cocktails are cool. Corner of 9th St. and Wessels Rd., Rivonia. ✆ **011/234-9515.** Cover varies.

The Crazy 88 ★ There's more than enough posing and pretense going on at this slightly schizophrenic white suburban nightclub, but while drinks ain't cheap and the fairly young crowd likes to dress up, you can catch some highly regarded South African contemporary music (Cape Town's wonderful electronic outfit Goldfish is a regular) and hot international DJs (including those from Ministry of Sound). 114 William Rd., Norwood. ✆ **011/728-8417.** www.88.co.za. Cover varies.

Moloko Bar Lounge ★★★ Discerning yet welcoming (provided you meet the door policy: dress for success and certainly no under-25s), with Jozi's most gorgeous locals draped around the contemporary lounge-bar decor (it's hidden in Rosebank's self-proclaimed Design District). This is an intimate venue where you get to meet a mixed, upmarket slice of Jo'burg society. The music is laid back and groovy (R&B, hip-hop, gentle house, and a few Latino rhythms), and it's open Thursday to Saturday only. 160 Jan Smuts Ave., Rosebank. ✆ **082/458-0675.** www.molokojoburg.com. Cover varies.

Milpark

Roka ★ Friday's DJ club nights and themed party evenings on Saturday get the dedicated crowd swinging at this popular hangout, which draws a very mixed and cosmopolitan crowd: Creative types, students, journalists, and professionals all come here to get friendly. DJs tend to experiment with old-school funk and deep house that continues into the wee hours; there's jazz every Wednesday, live bands on Sunday, and Thursday is meant to be a showcase of Jozi music talent. 44 Stanley Ave., Milpark, Auckland Park. ✆ **011/482-2038.** www.rokalounge.com. Cover varies.

Newtown/City Central

Besides the club options reviewed below, look for events (from ripping DJ-hosted parties to arty exhibitions that evolve into late-night grooving) hosted at **Lemon8,** 38 Roger St., Selby (✆ **011/493-4887;** www.lemon8.co.za), a sleek venue in the city. **Go Go Bar,** at the corner of Henry Nxumalo Street and Bree Street (✆ **071/183-8777**), is currently closed for refurbishment but worth a strut, playing a great mix of funk, afrobeat, experimental beats, dance, and live music (strictly no house music). **Kippies International,** the city's oldest jazz club, is allegedly moving back to its laid-back downtown venue in the Market Theatre complex; it's a worthwhile pilgrimage for jazz lovers, though Bassline has basically stolen its thunder (see below).

Bassline ★★★ This popular live-music venue is still a regular hangout for Jo'burg's multiracial intelligentsia. Attracting a rich assortment of top local acts and low-key legends from farther afield, the lineup ranges from jazz, blues, and rock bands to hip-hop and world artists. Many a groovy evening features spectacular talents from around Africa; look for appearances by South African sensation Freshly Ground. 10 Henry Nxumalo St. ✆ **011/838-9145.** www.bassline.co.za. Cover varies.

Carfax ★★ In an old warehouse, this super-cool venue once set the bar; you'll still find a wide mix of parties featuring local and international musicians and DJs, playing everything from performance art to deep house parties, hip-hop events, and the odd trance evening; its perennial popularity means it can get mainstream, with long queues. 39 Pim St., Newtown. ✆ **011/834-9187.** www.carfax.co.za. Cover varies.

The Woods ★ Laid-back and buzzing, this fairly recent addition to the Jo'burg nightclub scene draws a crowd that's a blend of alternative, arty, and sophisticated. Punters lounge about on mattresses-turned-couches listening to varied tunes by DJs trying their best to keep it original. Corner of Quinn and Carr sts., Newtown. ✆ **011/838-9277.** Cover varies.

Soweto

The Rock ★★★ **Moments** Prepare to forget any and all assumptions about so-called "township life" in Soweto: The Rock is hip, stylish, and popular. It also draws a crowd from across the city, all here to drink and party furiously to kwaito and house beats, with occasional jazz. You might consider using a specialist Soweto tour operator to get you here and home safely, as Soweto is some distance out of Johannesburg and not easily navigated. To arrange this outing, contact www.soweto.co.za or visit it as part of their Soweto Shebeen Tour. 1987 Vundla St., Rockville, Soweto. ✆ **011/986-8182.**

9

Big-Game Country: Kruger National Park and Private Reserves & Concessions

Watching wild animals, dangerous and untamed, in their natural, untouched habitat brings about a deeply satisfying communion with nature. It's why we South Africans crave the bush. Much of this has to do with sheer size. South Africa has some of the largest tracts of wilderness on the continent, and as political relations in the region have stabilized, this rich heritage has expanded even farther, with fences between South Africa and parks in neighboring Mozambique and Zimbabwe falling away to create one of the largest conservation areas in the world, unfettered by the constraints of human borders. This is where you will find an unprecedented number of lodges offering unparalleled wildlife experiences in some of the most perfect (and ever more luxurious) settings known to man—particularly those able to pay top dollar.

The areas richest in big game (and luxury lodges) are the landlocked provinces of Limpopo and its southern neighbor, Mpumalanga, which together form the northeastern corner of South Africa and share one of the continent's most famous game reserves, Kruger National Park. Most people come to this region seeking the romance of untamed Africa, a place where vast plains of bush savanna and thicket teem with game, rivers are swollen with lumbering hippos and lurking crocodiles, dense indigenous jungles shroud twittering birds, horizons shimmer with heat, and the nights are lit only by stars and crackling campfires. This you will find—and more. Here lies the Escarpment, carpeted in a mosaic of indigenous and plantation forest and offering breathtaking drives and views; the spectacular Blyde River Canyon, largest in South Africa; the lush subtropical gardens of the legendary Rain Queen; Stone Age sites that recall the rich indigenous precolonial cultures; and boomtowns that tell of Mpumalanga's short but turbulent gold rush.

But the primary destination in the region remains Kruger National Park, one of Africa's greatest wildlife sanctuaries, and the private game reserves that surround it. Kruger's budget facilities and well-maintained roads make this the most affordable safari experience in Africa, accessible to independent travelers on even extremely limited budgets. By contrast, the exclusive private game reserves that run along the park's western unfenced border, as well as the selection of recently created private concessions within the Kruger, are reputed to hold the most luxurious safari lodges and camps on the continent, and it's true. Aside from the chi-chi accommodation, cuisine, and service standards, the game-viewing—in open-topped vehicles that are driven off-road by knowledgeable guides—is superlative. Spend a few nights at any one of them, and you are virtually guaranteed truly close-up encounters with the Big 5, an experience that comes highly recommended, despite the steep price tag.

Kruger National Park and its surrounding reserves are the best internationally known destinations, but visitors should also be aware of the Big 5 game reserves that lie north of Johannesburg, and enjoy the additional benefit of being malaria free: The Waterberg Mountain region and Madikwe are both within easy driving distance of Jo'burg yet are more off the beaten track than their more famous cousins in the east. Madikwe, in particular, has a wonderfully varied terrain that supports what has been dubbed the Magnificent 7: In addition to sightings of the Big 5, you stand an excellent chance of seeing cheetahs and wild dogs, Africa's most endangered predator; and most of the privately owned and managed lodges and camps here offer rates that are a far better value than those surrounding Kruger, making this arguably the best-value luxury safari destination in South Africa.

(***Note:*** For a comparative overview of these reserves, as well as those in Kwazulu-Natal, and Eastern, Western and Northern Cape, see chapter 3.)

1 STAYING ACTIVE

Principal among the activities on offer within the game reserves are game drives; these safaris typically last 3 to 4 hours and take place in the early morning and evening. If you are staying at a private safari lodge, game drives and bush walks are included in the price; fishing may also be on offer. A few lodges also offer such activities as hot-air ballooning and even helicopter rides, but always at an extra cost.

Most of the activities listed below are offered outside the game reserves themselves. If you're looking for a one-stop advice and booking shop, contact **Big 5 Country** (✆ **013/737-8191;** www.big5country.com), an agent for the largest selection of adventure operators in the Sabie, Graskop, and Hazyview areas, as well as a booking and information agent. Another high-energy outfit offering a range of adventure activities (including mountain biking, river rafting, quad biking, kloofing, and abseiling) is **Induna Adventures** (✆ **013/737-8308;** www.indunaadventures.com).

ABSEILING, SWINGING & SLIDING Choose between an abseil (rappel) down the Sabie waterfall (R150) or zipline off a granite outcrop (R140) before heading into Kruger; bookings are through **Golden Monkey** (✆ **013/737-8191;** www.big5country.com). **Big Swing** (✆ **013/767-1621;** www.bigswing.co.za) offers the world's highest free-falling swing, as well as a slide across a canyon for R300.

BALLOONING Take off at sunrise and float over the foothills of the Escarpment, possibly sighting some game, then alight for a glass of bubbly and breakfast at a nearby lodge. Based 10km (6¼ miles) from Hazyview, **Balloons Over Africa** (✆ **013/737-6950;** www.balloonsoverafrica.co.za; R2,400) prides itself on its expertise—the company's chief pilot, Kevin Roberson, is a multiple winner of the South Africa Hot Air Balloon Championships.

BIRD-WATCHING Along with KwaZulu-Natal, this is the prime bird-watching destination in South Africa, providing enormously varied habitats. For expert advice and tailor-made tours to these areas, as well as to other top birding destinations in southern Africa, contact **Lawson's Birding and Wildlife Tours** ★★★ (✆ **013/741-2458;** www.lawsons.co.za).

ELEPHANT RIDING **Kapama** (✆ **012/368-0600;** www.kapama.co.za) offers **elephant-back safaris** ★★★ in its Big 5 reserve located near Hoedspruit; either overnight

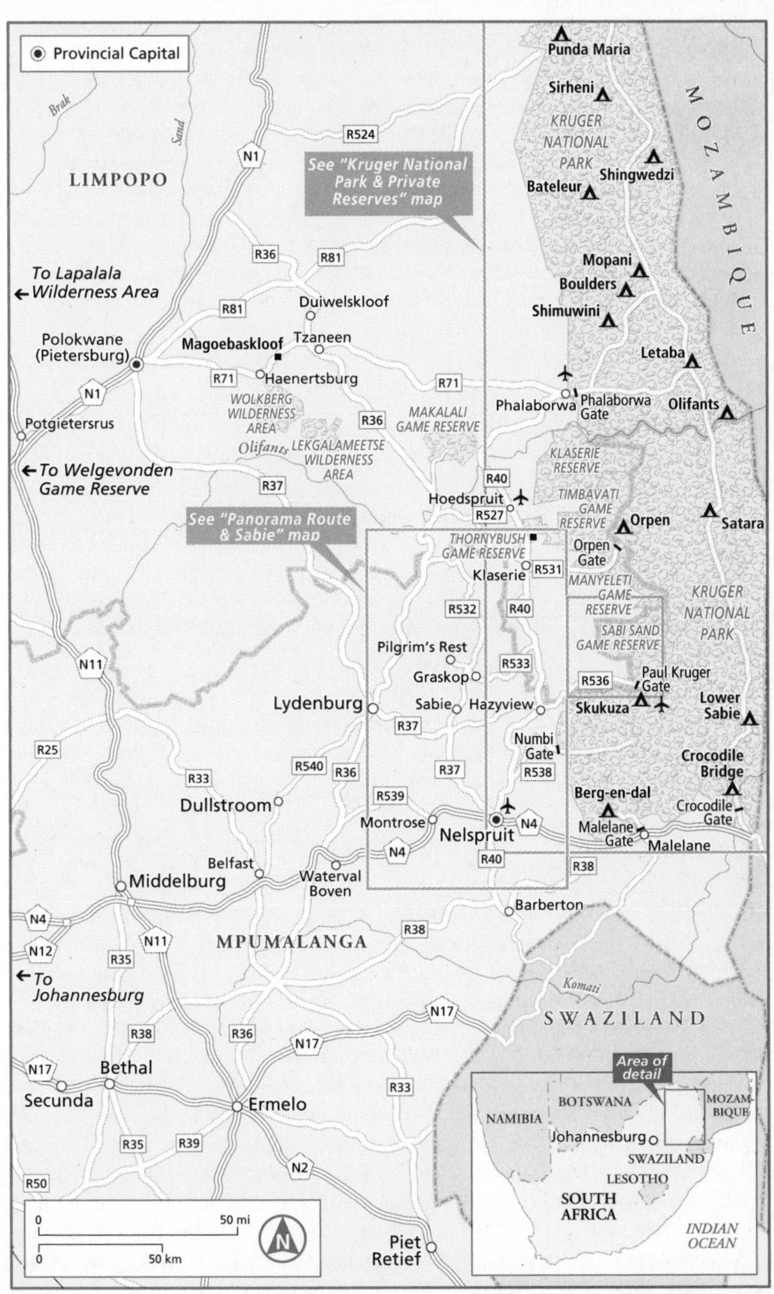

Provincial Capital
LIMPOPO
To Lapalala Wilderness Area
To Welgevonden Game Reserve
See "Kruger National Park & Private Reserves" map
See "Panorama Route & Sabie" map
Polokwane (Pietersburg)
Magoebaskloof
Duiwelskloof
Tzaneen
Haenertsburg
Potgietersrus
WOLKBERG WILDERNESS AREA
LEKGALAMEETSE WILDERNESS AREA
MAKALALI GAME RESERVE
Phalaborwa
Phalaborwa Gate
Hoedspruit
THORNYBUSH GAME RESERVE
Klaserie
Pilgrim's Rest
Graskop
Sabie
Hazyview
Lydenburg
Dullstroom
Montrose
Nelspruit
Belfast
Waterval Boven
Middelburg
Barberton
MPUMALANGA
To Johannesburg
Bethal
Secunda
Ermelo
Piet Retief
Punda Maria
Sirheni
KRUGER NATIONAL PARK
Shingwedzi
Bateleur
Mopani
Boulders
Shimuwini
Letaba
Olifants
MOZAMBIQUE
KLASERIE RESERVE
TIMBAVATI GAME RESERVE
Orpen
Orpen Gate
Satara
MANYELETI GAME RESERVE
SABI SAND GAME RESERVE
Paul Kruger Gate
Skukuza
Lower Sabie
Numbi Gate
Crocodile Bridge
Berg-en-dal
Crocodile Gate
Malelane Gate
Malelane
SWAZILAND
Komati
Area of detail
NAMIBIA
BOTSWANA
MOZAMBIQUE
Johannesburg
SWAZILAND
LESOTHO
SOUTH AFRICA
INDIAN OCEAN
50 mi
50 km

Tips Golfing in the Wild

Golfing in big-game country is not to be taken lightly—a golfer at Hans Merensky was trampled to death by an elephant that had broken through the fence from neighboring Kruger because she tried to confront it. Golfers at the clubs that are also home to wild animals should heed the warning signs posted at water hazards and elsewhere. Should you encounter a large mammal or predator, remain still, then back away quietly—under no circumstances should you run. If the thought of meeting a large pachyderm or leopard in the rough puts you right off course, you can choose a safer scenic route: The 9-hole **Pilgrim's Rest course** (✆ **013/764-1177;** www.pilgrims-rest.co.za) and the more challenging 18-hole championship course at **White River Country Club** (✆ **013/751-3781;** www.whiterivercountryclub.co.za) are both popular.

at its luxury tented flagship, Camp Jabulani (www.campjabulani.com; see review later in chapter), or come for a day trip and book a 90-minute ride for R1,350.

FLY-FISHING **Trout fishing** ★★★ on the highland Escarpment is well established, with an infrastructure of self-catering cottages, guesthouses, and lodges situated on well-stocked lakes and streams. **Dullstroom** is the unofficial capital of the trout-fishing areas, and rod rental, fees, and accommodations can be arranged through the helpful **Dullstroom Reservations** (✆ **013/254-0254;** www.dullstroom.biz). For information on trout fishing in the Letaba area, contact **Magoebaskloof-Byadladi Tourist Association** (✆ **015/276-4972** or 015/276-5047; www.magoebaskloof.com).

GOLFING This region is famous for combining golf with wildlife. The 9-hole course at **Skukuza** (✆ **013/735-5543;** www.sanparks.org/parks/kruger/tourism/activities/golf_course.php; R160, add R40 for club hire) is quite possibly the most dangerous course in the world—it is unfenced, and wild animals wander the greens at will. More wild golfing experiences await at the exclusive 18-hole course at **Leopard Creek Country Club** ★★★ (✆ **013/791-2000;** www.leopardcreek.co.za), co-owned by Jack Nicklaus and Gary Player. Besides the resident leopard, crocs and hippos lurk in the aptly named water hazards, and the clubhouse is considered the best on the continent. To play here, you'll have to book into the nearby **Buhala Game Lodge** (✆ **013/792-4372;** www.buhala.co.za). Private game lodges that can also arrange access are Jock Safari Lodge, Lukimbi, Singita, Sabi Sabi, MalaMala, Lion Sands, Leopard Hills, Ngala, and Londolozi. A good (and far less pricey) alternative is the 18-hole **Hans Merensky** ★★ (✆ **015/781-3931**), which borders Kruger and is often visited by its wildlife (see box below). You can either book into the **Hans Merensky Hotel & Estate** (www.hansmerensky.com) or combine with a safari and book into luxurious **Makalali** (also reviewed later in this chapter), a private game lodge that lies just under an hour away.

HELICOPTER TRIPS & SCENIC FLIGHTS If you fancy flying through cavernous gorges and across verdant valleys, consider getting a bird's-eye view of the region with **Mpumalanga Helicopter Co.** ★★ (✆ **084/505-2052;** www.mhelicopter.co.za). Rates for two passengers start at R5,775 for the 45-minute scenic Cascades trip; golf packages and fly-in safaris are also available. If you prefer small, single-propeller planes, Dave Gunn of **Airventures** (✆ **082/600-5388**) offers flights out of Dullstroom.

HIKING/SAFARIS ON FOOT The region's myriad **hiking trails** offer excellent scenic opportunities. Lodges and camps in and around Kruger all offer **bush walks,** but dedicated hikers should look no further than **Plains Camp at Rhino Walking Safari** (Southern Kruger). Sharing a border with MalaMala Game Reserve, this massive 12,000-hectare (29,640-acre) "restricted wilderness" concession allows no off-road game drives. The focus at the four-unit tented Plains Camp is then firmly on walking, and guests are also given the opportunity to overnight at the camp's "sleep-out digs," deep in the bush (70 min. on foot from Plains Camp), where tents have been erected on decks high up on stilts at a watering hole (www.isibindi.co.za; R4,730–5,440 double/day). Kruger National Park has excellent-value 3-day walking trails (R2,710 per person for the duration) in various locations throughout the reserve, as well as a backpack hike (all described in the "Kruger" section), while Ngala, a tented camp in the Timbavati reserve, offers walking safaris for the well-heeled (see "Where to Stay & Dine" under "Private Game Reserves," later in this chapter). If you're traveling here via the Panorama Route, note that the region has a number of excellent day trails, most of which are near the Escarpment towns of Sabie and Graskop, and either are free or charge a nominal fee—the 14km (8.75-mile) **Loerie Trail** takes you through some of the region's most attractive surrounds. If you're not that active, stroll the pretty 3km (1.75-mile) **Forest Falls Walk.** If you're traveling through the Letaba area, the 11km (6.75-mile) circular **Rooikat Trail** ★ (✆ **015/307-4310**), which follows a stream through the forests of Agatha, is highly recommended.

The top overnight hike on the Escarpment is the 3-day **Blyderivierspoort Hiking Trail** (R30 per person per night), a 33km (20-mile) walk that follows the Blyde River Canyon from the panoramic heights of God's Window to the lower-lying Bourke's Luck Potholes. Hikers' huts are basic: Bunk beds, flush toilets, *braai* (barbecue) sites, pots, and firewood are provided; all else must be carried in (don't forget toilet paper!). The views and vegetation make this one of the most popular trails in South Africa, so book in advance (✆ **013/759-5432**).

South African Forestry (SAFCOL, marketed as Komatiland Ecotourism) has created hiking trails with overnight facilities through some incredibly scenic areas in the Limpopo Province, including the relatively tough 2-, 3-, and 5-day **Magoebaskloof Trails** (highly recommended), and the 2-, 3-, and 5-day **Fanie Botha Trails** (both R75 per person per night). For details and bookings, contact ✆ **013/754-2724** or go to www.komatiecotourism.co.za.

HORSEBACK RIDING A selection of horseback and pony trails for beginner, intermediate, and experienced riders can be booked through Big 5 Country (see contact details above), ranging from 15 minutes to 3 hours in duration, and including night rides in the African bush. Pony rides start at R55 per person for 15 minutes, while bush trails are in the range of R365 to R750.

HUNTING Hunting season usually runs from April to September, though some farms enjoy year-round concessions. For more information on procedures and bookings, contact the **Mpumalanga Parks Board** (✆ **013/759-5300;** www.mpumalangaparksboard.com); for information on professional hunters and outfitters, contact the **Lowveld Hunting Association** (www.lowveldhunters.co.za).

MOUNTAIN BIKING Within Kruger Park, **Olifants rest camp** (discussed later in this chapter) offers 3- to 4-hour mountain biking trails, with the added excitement of spotting wildlife en route. Sabie is a fabulous area to explore by bike; ask about the Ceylon Trails. If you're traveling in the Letaba area, the exhilarating 19km (12-mile) **Debengeni**

 Downhill ★, a forestry road that starts at the top of the Magoebaskloof Pass and plummets down to the Debengeni Falls, is highly recommended for adrenaline junkies.

QUAD BIKING **BacTrac Adventure Trails** (✆ **082/808-0866**) offers excursions on "quad bikes" (four-wheel motorcycles) through the Magoebaskloof forests; unless you really want the T-shirt and a visit to a crocodile farm, the best-value option is the half-day trip.

RIVER RAFTING **Sabie River Adventures** (✆ **013/737-8266;** www.sabieriveradventures.co.za) offers a white-water-tubing excursion on the scenic upper reaches of the Sabie river. The excursion includes a bit of canyoning (leaping into pools, that is), so wear a bathing suit (you can hire a wet suit for R38 during the winter months). If this sounds too adventurous, the company also offers more sedate rafting excursions on the lower Sabie section. Both trips cost R290 and last about 3 to 4 hours. When water levels are high (in summer, usually Sept–May), rafting trips take place on the more exhilarating **Blyde River,** which covers a few Grade IV rapids.

2 EN ROUTE TO BIG-GAME COUNTRY

The journey between Gauteng and Kruger—a comfortable 5-hour drive with no major detours—includes some of South Africa's most dramatically beautiful drives, and the surrounds become scenic within 2 hours of leaving Johannesburg. The three routes described below take you from the highveld plateau before dropping, usually quite spectacularly, to the lowveld, much of which is taken up by Kruger National Park and the surrounding private game reserves. The best way to savor the journey is to stay at one of the many places that lie between 2 and 4 hours away from Gauteng and make the most of the Escarpment's dramatic scenery before setting off for big-game country.

The first, most popular route takes you via the Escarpment towns of Sabie and Graskop (**Pilgrim's Rest** ★ is an optional but recommended side trip) before traversing the Escarpment rim along what is called the **Panorama Route** ★★★—a spectacular half-day drive. This journey will definitely warrant an overnight stay, preferably two; you are then ideally positioned to enter one of Kruger's southern or central gates. The second approach is via Machadodorp on the N4, the main artery connecting Gauteng with Nelspruit, the capital of Mpumalanga—this is ideal if you need to enter one of Kruger's southern gates and don't have time to do much sightseeing or overnight along the way.

A lesser-known way to get to central Kruger, but in parts even more scenic, particularly from June to August, is to follow in the footsteps of the Voortrekkers on the Great North Road (N1) as far as Polokwane (ex-Pietersburg), then branch off eastward via the **Letaba/Magoebaskloof area** ★, a lush mountainous area also known as "land of the silver mist" and "garden of the Rain Queen." This route will necessitate an overnight stay; the most luxurious option is to reserve a room at the **Coach House** ★ (✆ **015/306-8000;** www.coachhouse.co.za), which lies on a 560-hectare (1,383-acre) working fruit-and-nut farm and offers old-fashioned decor, excellent amenities (including a full spa), and a great location with superb views; it's situated in Agatha, just outside Tzaneen. Rates, including a generous breakfast, are R2,000 double, R2,200 suite. Even better views are to be had from the friendly **Magoebaskloof Hotel,** off the R71, Magoebaskloof Pass (✆ **015/276-5400;** www.magoebaskloof.co.za), which reopened after a devastating fire in 2004; it has been rebuilt with fewer rooms and a slightly more contemporary look, but retains its good value at R1,040 double, including breakfast. If you'd prefer to forgo

a hotel stay for a more up-close immersion in the wild, bo
cabins at **Kurisa Moya Nature Lodge** (✆ **015/276-1131**
dinner to be delivered to your deck.

3 THE ESCARPMENT & PANO

This is the most popular route to big-game country, with ro
pine and eucalyptus plantations, interspersed with pockets of ... jungle, plunging waterfalls, and breathtaking views of the subtropical plains. A 4-hour drive from Gauteng, it's an easy escape for Johannesburg's ever-harassed city dwellers, desperate to breathe fresh air and drive around with unlocked doors. Unfortunately, the air is not always that fresh; Mpumalanga's industrial activities are responsible for one of the highest acid rainfalls in the world. This is compounded during the dry winter months, when veld fires are rife, coloring the air with a hazy smog that obscures the views. While this is one reason to consider traveling via the Letaba/Magoebaskloof area, which is generally a great deal greener in the winter, nothing matches the magnificent view of the lowveld plains from the aptly named God's Window, or watching the Blyde River snake through the floor of the eponymous canyon 700m (2,296 ft.) below. In addition, the region's popularity makes for a plethora of great accommodations; with the exception of Pilgrim's Rest, overnighting in any of the Escarpment towns (as opposed to the outlying areas) would be a mistake—the surrounding forests and farms offer a lot more in the way of views and setting.

In short, the route is as follows: After driving through **Dullstroom,** the highest town on the Escarpment, you drop down the eastern slopes via the scenic **Long Tom Pass** to the forestry towns of **Sabie** and **Graskop.** (Pilgrim's Rest, a restored gold-mining village, lies another mountain pass away and warrants a separate visit of at least a half-day, excluding travel time.) Graskop is the gateway to the **Panorama Route,** a drive that curls along the rim of the Escarpment, with lookout points along the way that provide relatively easy access to some of the most panoramic views in Africa (see "Driving the Panorama Route," later in this chapter). Once past the canyon lookouts, the final descent to the lowveld follows the Abel Erasmus Pass to **Hoedspruit,** which offers easy access to Kruger via the centrally located Orpen Gate, and also lies very close to the private Timbavati, Thornybush, Kapama, and Manyeleti game reserves. From Hoedspruit, you can also head south to **Hazyview** for access to the Paul Kruger, Phabeni, and Numbi entrance gates to Kruger Park, or to Sabi Sands Reserve, or to complete a loop returning to Sabie or Graskop.

ESSENTIALS

GETTING THERE **By Car** If you're traveling from Johannesburg, take the N12, which joins up with the N4, the main artery between Pretoria and Nelspruit, capital of Mpumalanga. When you reach the cool heights of Belfast, turn north onto the R540 to Dullstroom and Lydenburg, then take the R37 east to Sabie. From here the R532 runs north through Graskop along the Panorama route.

By Plane From **Cape Town: SA Express** flies daily to Hoedspruit's Eastgate Airport—this is the best airport to fly to if you want to do the Panorama Route as a day trip. From **Johannesburg: SA Express** flies daily to Hoedspruit's Eastgate Airport. Note that you can also fly from Cape Town, Johannesburg, and Durban to the relatively nearby Kruger–Mpumalanga International Airport, outside Nelspruit

MATION **Big 5 Country** (✆ **013/737-8191**) is one of the few cen-
es of information on the Sabie, Graskop, and Hazyview areas. To book
dations in **Dullstroom,** speak to Les Adams, at **Dullstroom Reservations,**
Street (✆ **013/254-0254;** www.dullstroom.biz; Mon–Fri 8am–5pm, Sat 9am–
m, Sun 9am–2pm); she'll also help you with reliable (and up-to-the-minute) information on what the town has to offer and where to dine. In **Sabie,** contact **Panorama Information,** at Sabie Market Square (✆ **013/767-1377;** www.panoramainfo.co.za; Mon–Fri 8am–5pm, Sat–Sun 9am–1pm). A better service, **Graskop Information,** is offered at Graskop, located in the Spar Centre, Pilgrim's Way (✆ **013/767-1833;** www.blyderiversafaris.co.za; Mon–Sat 8:30am–5pm). For **Pilgrim's Rest,** see "Visitor Information" under "Pilgrim's Rest," later in this chapter.

GETTING AROUND Most lodges supply transfers from the airport; otherwise, contact **Eastgate Safaris** (✆ **015/793-3678;** www.eastgatesafaris.co.za). For the ultimate glam transfer, contact **Mpumalanga Helicopter Co.** (✆ **084/505-2052;** www.mhelicopter.co.za). For car rentals, **Avis** and **Budget** have desks at all three airports in the Kruger region; see chapter 3 for contact details.

Unless you're heading directly (and only) to the lodges in a private game reserve, this region is best explored in your own car, at your own pace. Roads are relatively empty, signposted, and well maintained. Because Kruger officials have introduced game drives and walks, using an outside operator to explore the park also seems pretty futile. However, if you don't want to think about where to go, eat, or sleep, **Thompsons Indaba Tours** (✆ **013/737-7115;** www.indabasafaris.co.za) offers a range of overnight and day tours: Open-vehicle safaris with an experienced game ranger to Kruger cost around R920 per person for a full day (5 or 6am to 5:30pm), or R720 for a morning; prices exclude meals. Walking safaris in Kruger (weather dependent) will run you R645. Thompson's also offers night safaris, which take place in Kapama and can include an afternoon visit to the Hoedspruit Research & Breeding Centre (R1,345; dinner included). The Panorama Route tour, with a stop for lunch at Pilgrim's Rest or Graskop, costs R750 per person.

DULLSTROOM

Many travelers compare a visit to Dullstroom with a stint in the Scottish Highlands; the promise of landing a 6- to 7-pounder in the well-stocked dams and streams of the highveld's best trout-fishing region makes it a popular weekend getaway for urban South Africans. At 2,012m (6,599 ft.) above sea level, this is the highest town on the Escarpment—expect bitterly cold evenings in the winter, and don't be surprised to find fires lit even in midsummer. The town, some 230km (143 miles) northeast of Johannesburg, dates back to the 1880s, when a committee under the chairmanship of Wolterus Dull collected money in Holland to assist Boers who had suffered losses in the First Anglo-Boer War. The town was razed to the ground by the British in the Second Anglo-Boer War, but despite perennial mist and low temperatures, the townsfolk simply rebuilt it. Its popularity with tourists has created a huge rise in development in recent years, meaning that there is a greater selection of adventure activities available in the vicinity.

Where to Stay

Walkersons ★★ Set amid green, misty surrounds with trout-filled dams and weirs winding their way through the 600-hectare (1,482-acre) estate, Walkersons' grounds are pure Scottish highlands. Inside, the decor only adds to the illusion. From issues of *Majesty* to framed photographs of the Duke and Duchess of Windsor, the Walkersons have

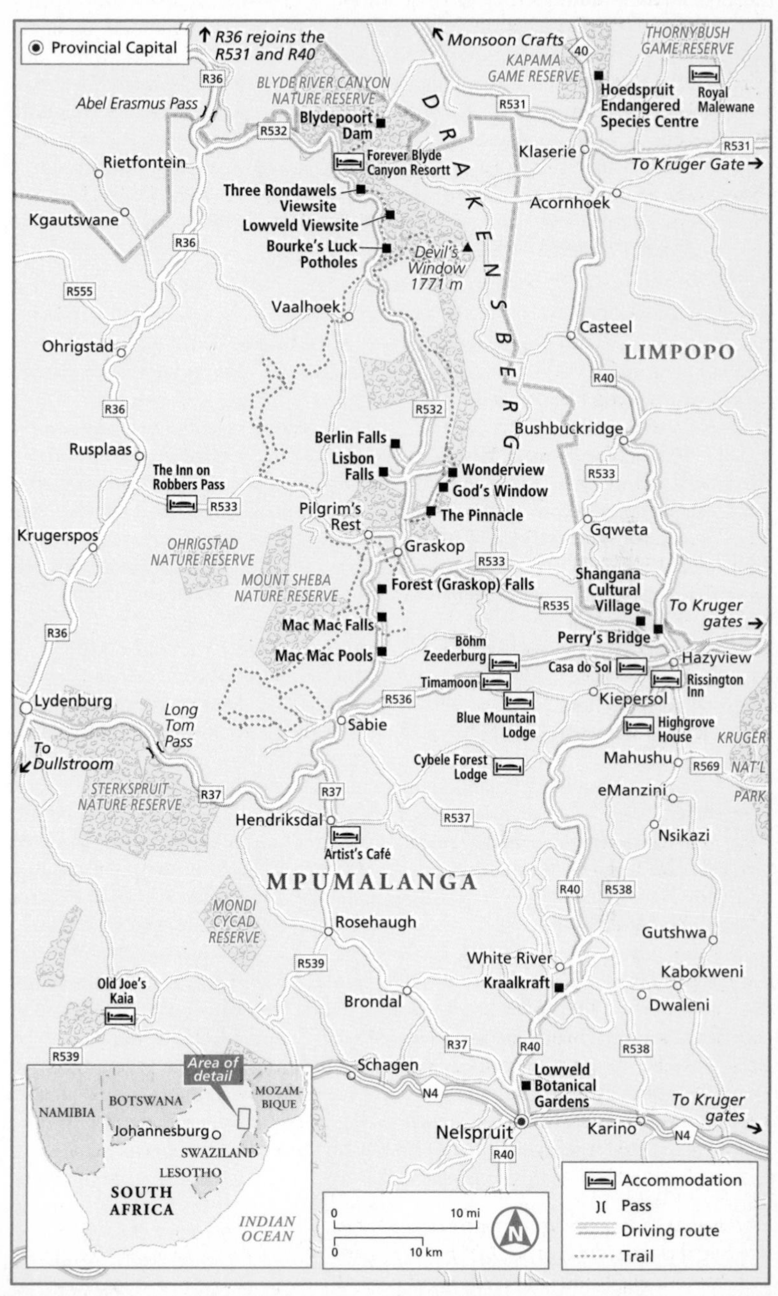
Provincial Capital
R36 rejoins the R531 and R40
Monsoon Crafts
THORNYBUSH GAME RESERVE
KAPAMA GAME RESERVE
BLYDE RIVER CANYON NATURE RESERVE
Abel Erasmus Pass
Blydepoort Dam
DRAKENSBERG
Hoedspruit Endangered Species Centre
Royal Malewane
Klaserie
To Kruger Gate
Rietfontein
Forever Blyde Canyon Resortt
Three Rondawels Viewsite
Acornhoek
Kgautswane
Lowveld Viewsite
Bourke's Luck Potholes
Devil's Window 1771 m
Vaalhoek
Ohrigstad
Casteel
LIMPOPO
Bushbuckridge
Rusplaas
Berlin Falls
Lisbon Falls
Wonderview
God's Window
The Pinnacle
The Inn on Robbers Pass
Pilgrim's Rest
Gqweta
Krugerspos
Graskop
OHRIGSTAD NATURE RESERVE
MOUNT SHEBA NATURE RESERVE
Forest (Graskop) Falls
Shangana Cultural Village
To Kruger gates
Mac Mac Falls
Perry's Bridge
Mac Mac Pools
Böhm Zeederburg
Casa do Sol
Hazyview
Timamoon
Rissington Inn
Lydenburg
Kiepersol
Long Tom Pass
Sabie
Blue Mountain Lodge
Highgrove House
KRUGER NAT'L PARK
To Dullstroom
Mahushu
Cybele Forest Lodge
STERKSPRUIT NATURE RESERVE
eManzini
Hendriksdal
Nsikazi
Artist's Café
MPUMALANGA
MONDI CYCAD RESERVE
Rosehaugh
Gutshwa
White River
Kabokweni
Kraalkraft
Old Joe's Kaia
Brondal
Dwaleni
Schagen
Lowveld Botanical Gardens
To Kruger gates
Nelspruit
Karino
R36
R531
R532
R555
R533
R535
R536
R37
R537
R40
R538
R539
R569
R541
N4
40
Area of detail
NAMIBIA
BOTSWANA
MOZAMBIQUE
Johannesburg
SWAZILAND
LESOTHO
SOUTH AFRICA
INDIAN OCEAN
0 10 mi
0 10 km
N
Accommodation
Pass
Driving route
Trail

striven to create a home reminiscent of English aristocracy. Walls are covered in tapestries and Victorian oil paintings (purchased at Sotheby's, of course), windows are draped in heavy fabrics, floors are carpeted with sisal, upon which Persian rugs add color, and rooms have individual antique pieces and fireplaces. Each bedroom is huge, with a king-size bed, a writing desk, and two comfortable chairs facing the fire (lit before you arrive). The lodge offers a full selection of fly-fishing tackle. One of the first to open, and still the best option in Dullstroom.

10km (6¼ miles) north of Dullstroom, off R540. ✆ **013/253-7000.** Fax 013/253-7230. www.walkersons.co.za. 25 units. R2,600-3,200. Rates include dinner and breakfast. Check website or call ahead for specials. AE, DC, MC, V. Children 12 and over welcome. **Amenities:** Restaurant; pub; bird of prey center; fly-fishing; helipad; hiking trails; horseback riding; room service; runway; spa; Wi-Fi (R20 for 512MB). *In room:* A/C, TV, hair dryer, minibar.

Where to Dine

The three best restaurants in town are **Fibs, Mrs. Simpsons,** and **Pickles and Things. Fibs** (✆ **082/556-0383**) is located on Lesedi Street in an old general dealer's store; try the red-wine braised lamb shank or whole trout grilled with chive yogurt. It's open Wednesday to Sunday for lunch and Wednesday to Saturday for dinner. Named for the famous Wallace, the intimate **Mrs. Simpson's** (✆ **013/254-0088**), open Thursday to Monday, is owned by culinary duo Bryan and Stephen, who like to experiment with an ever-changing menu, incorporating elements of continental, African, and Asian cuisines. **Pickles and Things** (✆ **013/254-0115;** Sun–Thurs 7am–5pm; Fri–Sat 7am–9pm) is owner-run by Thomas and Yvette; the menu is varied (from wraps to filet), but it's the trout dishes that have regulars coming back for more.

LYDENBURG & LONG TOM PASS

Lydenburg, or "Place of Suffering," was founded by a party of depressed Voortrekkers who, having lost a number of loved ones to a malaria epidemic in nearby Ohrigstad, retreated to its mosquito-free heights in 1849. Happily, *Lydenburg* proved to be a misnomer, and today the town has a substantial center, though there's little to see beyond some really interesting examples of pioneer architecture. The town is also known for a famed archaeological find: the **Lydenburg Heads,** seven ceramic masks that date back to the 5th century and were discovered in the late 1950s. You can see replicas of the heads (the originals now reside in the South African Museum in Cape Town) at the **Lydenburg Museum** (✆ **013/235-2213;** www.lydenburgmuseum.org.za), situated in the **Gustav Klingbiel Nature Reserve,** 3km (1¾ miles) out of town on the R37. Guided tours are by appointment only; call ahead. Hours are Monday through Friday from 8am to 4pm, Saturday and Sunday from 8am to 5pm; free admission. One of the most authentic pit stops in the region is here: **Vroutjies** (meaning "Little Women") **Coffee Shop** (✆ **013/235 3016**) is on the main road and does a mean apple tart and baked cheesecake.

From Lydenburg, the R37 east takes you down the **Long Tom Pass** ★★—at 2,150m (7,052 ft.), the second-highest mountain pass in South Africa. It was named after the Creusot siege guns that the Boers lugged up the pass to try to repel the British forces during the Second Anglo-Boer War (1899–1902). These guns, or cannons, were known as Long Toms because of their extended necks, which could spit a shell 9.5km (6 miles). Near the summit of the pass, at the **Devil's Knuckles,** a Long Tom replica commemorates the 4-day battle that was fought on this mountainside in 1900—the original cannons were destroyed by the Boers to prevent them from falling into British hands. You can still see the holes blasted by the cannons as the Boers retreated down the **Staircase,** a series of hairpin bends that zigzag down the pass. If you're feeling hungry or just want an excuse to enjoy the view, **Misty Mountain** (✆ **013/764-3377**) serves a reasonable plate of food.

Continuing east along the R37, passing the turnoff south for Hendriksdal, you come to the small forestry town of Sabie.

SABIE & SURROUNDS

Sabie (pronounced "*sah*-bee") dates to 1871, when a few friends, picnicking at the Lower Sabie Falls, were showing off their marksmanship skills. Bullets chipped the rocks behind the mock targets, revealing a glint of gold, and prospectors promptly followed. The initial boom was short lived, though the mining industry was still to transform Sabie. The first commercial trees, intended for mine props, were planted in 1876 and today form the heart of what are claimed to be the largest man-made forests in the world. To date, more than a million acres have been planted with pine and eucalyptus, and many of these are destined to prop up shafts in the mines that run deep below Gauteng's surface; tree-huggers can find out more at the **Forestry Museum** (✆ **013/764-1058;** Mon–Fri 8am–4:30pm, Sat 8am–noon; R10 adults, R5 children).

The area surrounding Sabie and Graskop is also renowned for its waterfalls. But if your idea of a waterfall worth detouring is Victoria Falls, give these a miss and head straight for Pilgrim's Rest and/or the Panorama Route. If you visit only one waterfall, consider **Lone Creek Falls,** reached by traveling 10km (6¼ miles) on the Old Lydenburg Road, northwest from Sabie. You will pass turnoffs for both the **Bridal Veil** (R5 per car) and **Horseshoe Falls** (R5 per car) before reaching the **Lone Creek** gate (R5 per person). The single cascade plunges 68m (223 ft.) into an attractive pool and is framed by the lush green foliage of a small damp rainforest.

A little farther along the R532, you will see the sign for **Forest Falls** (permit obtainable from Forestry Museum for a nominal fee); this is an easy 3km (1.75-mile) walk and well worth tackling, time allowing. To view the Lisbon and Berlin waterfalls, take the Panorama Route following the rim of the Escarpment. Note that Sabie town is only 55km from the nearest Kruger gate.

Where to Stay

The establishments reviewed below are located amid lush plantations, subtropical farms, or indigenous forest, and most feature superb views and very luxurious suites—all of which come at a price. If you're saving up to splurge on a private game lodge, try the excellent **Numbela Exclusive Riverside Accommodation** ★★ (✆ **013/751-3356;** www.numbela.co.za; R900–R950 double, including breakfast), with just three charming cottages on a rambling 200-acre estate with a river running through it. River Cottage is right on the river, with whitewashed walls and high thatched ceilings, and artifacts collected by the original owners from travels through Africa. Yellow Wood is slightly bigger (sleeps four) and elevated, but also has its own sandy river beach and comes with outdoor shower. Owner-host Tracey Nepten lives on the adjoining property and will ensure you find your way to the waterfalls and utilize the trails. Alternatively, the **Graskop Hotel** (✆ **013/767-1244;** www.graskophotel.co.za; R700 double, including breakfast), a more urban option (it's in the center of Graskop town) that offers a chance to shop and interesting decor: The interiors of 22 rooms in the main block have all been designed by up-and-coming South African artists. Finally, there is the **Sabie Townhouse** (✆ **013/764-2292;** www.sabietownhouse.co.za; R600 double B&B), walking distance from Sabie town but situated overlooking the forested Sabie Gorge, where Murray and Irene offer a very warm and personal environment.

Near Sabie

Blue Mountain Lodge ★★★ Located in eight separate cottages set below ponds, palms, a pool, a dining terrace, and a grand staircase that sweeps down to more immaculately manicured lawns, Blue Mountain is one of the most romantic, luxurious, and expensive accommodations options on the Escarpment. Over and above the Victorian Suites are the decadent Manor Houses—luxury villas that come with their own staff—and the Quadrant Rooms (the latter are very average, so don't book these). Food is another reason the Lodge has such a great reputation, with the chef preparing a new menu daily, delivered to your room along with canapés and an invitation for predinner drinks. It's all very luxe and comfortable, but don't expect service standards you'll get in the city (or would expect for this price tag).

P.O. Box 101, Kiepersol 1241. Take the Kiepersol turnoff, 28km (17 miles) east of Sabie on the R536, and follow for 4km (2½ miles) before turnoff. ✆ **013/737-8446.** Fax 013/737-6917. www.bluemountainlodge.co.za. 13 units; 2 manor houses. Victorian Suites R3,290 double; Quadrant Rooms R2,310 double. Call for rates for Manor Houses. Rates include dinner and breakfast. AE, DC, MC, V. No children under 12. **Amenities:** Restaurant; bar; large pool; room service; free Wi-Fi in reception area. *In room:* A/C, hair dryer, minibar.

Timamoon ★★★ It's hard to beat the peace and privacy afforded by these six thatched "lodges," each located a few minutes' drive from one another. Kruger lies but 40 minutes away, but you'll be hard-pressed to leave your well-appointed, secluded, and spacious lodge, furnished with artifacts that the owners have collected from years of travel throughout Africa. Each features an en-suite bedroom (one has two bedrooms) with four-poster king-size beds draped in mosquito netting, and decks with private plunge pools, overlooking a forested gorge through which the Sabie River cascades. Luxurious bathrooms and outdoor showers enjoy similar views. Moon River is the honeymoon suite and enjoys a spectacular location on the lip of the gorge, but as all the lodges have lovely views, it's not necessarily worth the extra money. One drawback here is that there's no phone or room service, and you have to drive to reach the restaurant—a charming candlelit stilted room that serves four-course set menus.

P.O. Box 292, Hazyview 1242. 24km (15 miles) east of Sabie, turn off from R536; follow signs for 3km (1¾ miles). ✆ **013/767-1740.** Fax 013/767-1889. www.timamoonlodge.co.za. 6 units. R3,200–R4,400 lodge. Rates include breakfast and dinner: AE, DC, MC, V. No children under 16. **Amenities:** Restaurant; cigar lounge; private plunge pool (in lodges). *In room:* Hair dryer, high-speed Internet, minibar (on request).

Near Hazyview

Casa do Sol ★ Kids A charming Mediterranean-style village, complete with cobbled streets, white stucco walls, and terra-cotta roof tiles, set in award-winning tropical gardens behind which stretch 500 hectares (1,235 acres) of indigenous bush, Casa do Sol

Tips — Stock Up on the Way to Kruger

If you're traveling on the Sabie–Hazyview road, stop at **The Windmill Wine Shop** (✆ **013/737-8175;** Mon–Sat 9am–5pm) to snack on a tapas platter or stock up on deli fare (cold meats and cheeses, pickles and olives, bread) and wine—a picnic to enjoy on your veranda in a Kruger Park rest camp.

was established in 1968 and still retains a vaguely 1970s feel, despite recent renovations following its integration into the local Relais & Châteaux group. The luxury and executive suites are ideal for families—the executive suites are upstairs and feature views of the valley and estate from the private patio. This is an all-around excellent hotel, with a good ambience, though it doesn't offer the well-bred intimacy of lodges such as Blue Mountain or Cybele, or the privacy of Timamoon.

P.O. Box 57, Hazyview 1242. Off the R536, 39km (24 miles) east of Sabie and 5km (3 miles) west of Hazyview. ✆ **013/737-8111.** Fax 013/737-8166. www.relaishotels.com. 54 units. Casa R1,720 double; Villa R1,970; luxury suite R2,350; executive suite R4,130. All rates include breakfast and dinner. Children under 12 R275; children 12 and over R325. AE, DC, MC, V. **Amenities:** Restaurant; bar; babysitting; bass fishing; horseback riding; 2 pools; room service; safaris arranged with recommended operators; tennis court (all-weather); free Wi-Fi in bar area; wildlife trails to view antelope. *In room:* A/C, TV, hair dryer, minibar (in villas and suites).

Cybele Forest Lodge & Health Spa ★★★ Long before crime encouraged Jo'burgers to take regular long-weekend getaways, Cybele ("sigh-*bee*-lee") was booked solid months in advance, and even Capetonians would travel north to relax in the subtropical surrounds and sample the legendary cuisine served by this Yellow Shield member of Relais & Châteaux. Owners Rupert and Barbara Jeffries have since added several free-standing suites, with everything from espresso machines and private heated pools to fireplaces in the bathrooms. A pool has replaced the farm dam, and there's a wonderful spa (one of the best in the province, with a beautiful forest location), but the standard of the food and the beauty of the 120-hectare (296-acre) grounds remain unchanged. If you expect jump-on-demand service, you are likely to be disappointed; this is a mellow retreat that moves at a rural pace—again, something that may irk, given the rather steep price tag.

P.O. Box 346, White River 1240. Take the Kiepersol turnoff, 28km (17 miles) east of Sabie on the R536; follow for 10km (6¼ miles) before taking a road to the left marked WHITEWATERS and following Cybele signs. Alternatively, follow signs off the R40 btw. Hazyview and White River. ✆ **013/764-9500.** Fax 013/764-9510. www.cybele.co.za. 12 units. R3,390–3,950 double; R4,570–5,980 suite; R7,480 Forest suite. Rates include breakfast and dinner. Ask about winter rates. AE, DC, MC, V. No children under 10. **Amenities:** Restaurant; bar; gym; hiking trails; horseback riding; free high-speed Internet; pool; spa; trout fishing (tackle provided). *In room:* A/C, fans, TV/VCR, fireplace, hair dryer, minibar, private pool (in suites), stereo.

Highgrove House ★★ Follow the grand tree-lined driveway, and at the end of the cul-de-sac, you'll find an elegant, old-fashioned country retreat where guests are treated like royalty. "English-country" style is a constant theme in South African decor, but here it is particularly well done: The eight garden suites are decorated in pale, earthy colors and feature separate sitting rooms with log fireplaces and double doors that lead onto verandas with marvelous views over the forest or valley. The slightly pricier Orchard Suites (Orchard 1 is a personal favorite) have private pools and saunas, as well as their own garden. The restaurant has been awarded the Chaîne des Rôtisseurs blazon for its beautifully presented gourmet dinners. The candlelit atmosphere is very romantic but may be a bit stuffy or old-fashioned for some vacationers—no jeans, shorts, or sneakers allowed.

Off R40, 17km (11 miles) south of Hazyview. P.O. Box 46, Kiepersol 1241. ✆ **013/764-1844.** Fax 013/764-1855. www.highgrove.co.za. 8 units. R3,120 double; R3,740 Orchard Suite. Rates include dinner and breakfast. AE, DC, MC, V. No children under 14. **Amenities:** Restaurant; bar; pool; room service; free Wi-Fi in reception area. *In room:* Hair dryer.

Perry's Bidge Hollow (Value) (Finds) This sensibly priced hotel lies in well-wooded grounds on the outskirts of Hazyview, immediately behind Perry's Bridge Trading Post, a low-rise mock Victorian arcade that also houses several craft shops, boutiques, and restaurants. The colonial-style accommodation is quiet, stylish, and comfortable; the

Driving the Panorama Route

This drive takes you past the Blyde River Canyon, the largest canyon in the country, as well as the sheer 1,600m (5,248-ft.) drop from the Escarpment to the warm lowveld plains shimmering below. Hot air rising over this wall generates the heavy mists and high rainfall that, in turn, create the unique montane grasslands and riverine forests of the Blyde River Canyon Nature Reserve, which starts just north of Graskop before broadening out to include the Blydepoort Dam, 60km (37 miles) north. To complete the Panorama Route as a circular trip (approx. 160km/99 miles), stopping for most of the view points and returning to either Sabie or Graskop, set aside a day.

As you follow the tour below, refer to the "Panorama Route & Sabie" map earlier in this chapter for more information.

To drive this route, take the R532 north out of Graskop before turning right on the R534. The first stop is the **Pinnacle**—a thin, tree-topped, 30m-tall (98-ft.) quartzite rock that juts below the view point. **God's Window** ★★, 4km (2½ miles) farther, which offers the first view of the open lowveld plains, is more impressive. (Wonderview is a variation of this and can be skipped if you're pressed for time.) The looping R534 now rejoins the R532. Turn left and look for the sign if you want to visit **Lisbon Falls,** which drops 37m (121 ft.). To continue on to Blyde River Canyon, turn right onto the R532, taking in the 48m (157-ft.) **Berlin Falls** on the way.

Back on the R532, head north for **Bourke's Luck Potholes** (✆ **013/761-6019**). Here gold-digger Bourke predicted that he would strike it lucky, but he found nothing in these large scooped formations, carved by the movement of pebbles and water in the swirling whirlpools created by the confluence of the Blyde and Treur rivers. Bourke was not the last person to be disappointed by the Potholes—it's a long walk to look at them, and they reveal very little. Nor does the visitor center, which, in addition to some dry displays on the geology of the area, features a few dusty stuffed animals that look close to decomposing. The lichen trail is very easy and good for children. Gates open from 7am to 5pm; admission is R25.

Some 20km (12 miles) north is the lookout for the **Three Rondawels** ★★★, by far the most impressive stop of the entire trip. The name—which refers to the three circular hut-shaped outcrops that are more or less opposite the lookout—does nothing to describe the humbling size of what beckons. A sheer drop threatens to pull you off the precipice; thousands of feet below, the Blyde River snakes its way through the canyon to the tranquil Blyde Dam, embraced by green mountains. Beyond, the great lowveld plains shimmer in the distance.

Tip: If you're feeling thirsty, drop into the **Forever Blyde Canyon Resort** (the turnoff is a couple of miles north past the Three Rondawels and clearly sign-

spacious bathrooms have indoor and outdoor showers; it's conveniently located for day trips to Kruger via Phabeni Gate; and there's a good selection of informal outdoor eateries and pubs right on your doorstep. All in all, great value.

posted; ✆ **013/769-8005**), which offers another angle on the Three Rondawels from its terrace; however, much beyond a toasted sandwich is not recommended. (To take a look at its budget self-catering lodging, go to www.foreverblydecanyon.co.za—and ask for a cottage with a view.)

From here, you will descend the **Abel Erasmus Pass** before passing through the J. G. Strijdom Tunnel. Approximately 20km (12 miles) from here is the turnoff for **Monsoon Gallery** (✆ **015/795-5114**), off the R527. Monsoon carries a fine selection of African crafts, but stock is often limited; you can also enjoy a light meal at the adjacent **Mad Dogz Café** (✆ **015/795-5425**).

At this point, you can stay on the R527, heading east for Hoedspruit, if you wish to enter the Timbavati private game reserve, or head for the airport. If not, take the R531 southeast to Klaserie—look for the turnoff to the **Forever Swadini Resort** (✆ **015/795-5961;** www.foreverswadini.co.za). From here, you can take a 90-minute boat trip on the Blyde Dam to see the mouth of the canyon and look up at the Escarpment towering above (R85 per adult, R50 children under 8). The R531 takes you to Kruger to enter via Orpen Gate (the closest to the Satara Rest Camp), or to travel to the Manyeleti or northern Sabi Sand reserves via Gowry Gate. Turn north on the R40 to Kapama, a fenced private reserve and site of the popular **Hoedspruit Endangered Species Centre** ★★ (✆ **015/793-1633;** www.wildlifecentre.co.za), also known as the "Cheetah Project." This is also the pickup point for Kapama's exciting **elephant-back safaris** ★★★. The latter is well worth considering. For R1,350, you get to be transported through big-game country on the back of one of these lumbering giants and learn more about this most intelligent of species. The Cheetah Project is equally educational but less exhilarating. Guided tours (daily every hour 8am–3pm; R120 adults, R50 children under 12) kick off with a video presentation, after which you are driven through the center by a ranger, sighting cheetahs, wild dogs, rhinos, and various bird species. At 90 minutes, the tour is a tad long, and although several of the cheetahs raised here have been successfully released into the wild, it still feels a little like a large, comfortable zoo. However, it is the one place where you can see the so-called king cheetah, a rare variant whose striking semistriped coat is associated with an unusual recessive gene.

To return to Graskop, take the R40 south from Klaserie, then follow the R533 from Bosbokrand, climbing Kowyn's Pass to Graskop. (***Note:*** The R40, between Hazyview and Acorn Hoek, is unsafe to travel at night, when animals wander at will, and a few travelers have been ambushed. During daylight, you're more likely to be pulled over for speeding, so take it easy.)

R40, Hazyview. P.O. Box 2304, Hazyview, 1242. ✆ **013/737-6784.** Fax 013/737-6784. www.perrysbridgehollow.co.za. 34 units. R1,130–1,560 double. Rates include breakfast. AE, DC, MC, V. **Amenities:** Restaurants; bar; pool; Wi-Fi (R15 per 15 min.). *In room:* A/C, fan, satellite TV, fridge, hair dryer.

Rissington Inn ★ (Value) (Kids) Rissington still offers unbeatable value, and with Kruger's Phabeni Gate just 10 minutes away, it makes an extremely comfortable base from which to explore Kruger and the Escarpment surrounds. What it lacks in style (the honeymoon suite has a false thatch roof jutting over the bed), the inn makes up for in sincere warmth, comfort, and great food. Of the 14 rooms, Euphorbia (sunset-facing, with a sitting room and a super-king-size bed) and Ivory (a garden view, a deep veranda with built-in day bed, and a super-king-size bed) are recommended. Camelfoot and Sycamore, both spacious and furnished with two queen-size beds, are good family choices. Recent additions are the hillside suites Pumalanga and Shonalanga, each of which has two bedrooms with en-suite bathrooms and an outdoor shower, a spacious sitting room, sun terrace, and shared usage of a private swimming pool.

1km (½ mile) south of Hazyview. Follow signposts off R40. P.O. Box 650, Hazyview 1242. ✆ **013/737-7700.** Fax 013/737-7112. www.rissington.co.za. 16 units. R940–R1,320 double; R1,580–1,700 suite. Rates include breakfast. Dinner R170 per person. Children sharing parent's room R170. AE, DC, MC, V. **Amenities:** Restaurant; bar; library; pool; room service; Wi-Fi in restaurant/bar (R1 per minute). *In room:* TV (in hillside suites only), hair dryer.

Where to Dine

You will dine well at all the lodges described above (note that nonresidents are welcome at all of them, space allowing). **Blue Mountain Lodge** is perhaps the top choice for a special romantic occasion (make sure to get here before dark to enjoy a drink on the deep verandas overlooking the lush, manicured gardens of this 200-hectare/494-acre estate), with close runner-up the Relais & Châteaux **Cybele Forest Lodge.** Here, the vegetables are home grown, the house salad is picked fresh daily, and the pasta is homemade. For a really laid-back atmosphere, with no pretensions and really good food, head for **Rissington Inn.** Most of the dinner entrees, such as tarragon trout, cost R70 to R80, making it the best value for quality home-cooked fare on the Escarpment. It seats only 30 and is often packed with locals, so book in advance.

A "trattoria" in the middle of nowhere, **Artists Café** (signposted off R37; ✆ **013/764-2309** or 082/565-3345) draws a steady stream of Sabie regulars, with its warm rural ambience. Owners Leon and Hetta have created a wonderful hideaway. A kitchen garden ensures that most of the vegetables are picked daily; in keeping with the simple food, the atmosphere in the restaurant is casual—chairs are mismatched, dishcloths serve as napkins, and walls are covered with local arts and crafts. Because it's a little out of the way, it opens only when it has bookings, so reservations are essential.

Founded in the 1980s by Harry, the owner of the Graskop Hotel, **Harrie's Pancakes** (✆ **013/767-1273;** daily 7:30am–5:30pm) serves up a recipe that has proven such a huge hit that you'll now find Harrie's as far away as the Cape Town Waterfront. His trademark thick crepes are filled with interesting combinations, such as trout mousse and horseradish, for example, or butternut with cumin and blue cheese sauce, or green fig preserve with pecan nuts and cream.

If you're interested in sampling traditional African fare accompanied by some superb singing and dancing by local Shangaan people, book a Lunch Tour or Evening Festival at the nearby **Shangana Cultural Village** (✆ **013/737-7000;** R353 near Hazyview; open daily, depending on tour bookings). It's touristy but worth it if you haven't experienced African dancing or mopani worms elsewhere.

Finally, if you're traveling anywhere near White River (or interested in looking at the local arts and crafts), stop at Bagdad Centre (nothing to do with the Iraqi capital), a few kilometers north of White River on the R40 to Hazyview; the Centre has a sushi bar as well as a good restaurant, **Salt** (✆ **013/751-1555**). Opposite is Casterbridge, a mixed-use village-style development that has grown along with the flow of new expats and Jo'burg and Maputo businessmen who prefer to commute to their respective cities while their families enjoy a more rural environment. Casterbridge is spread around a series of interlinked, shady courtyards with some 50 shops (up from 10 just under a decade ago), including a few galleries, a theater, restaurants, coffee bars, a local history and car museum, and an art house cinema.

PILGRIM'S REST

The village of Pilgrim's Rest was established in 1873 after Alex "Wheelbarrow" Patterson discovered gold in the stream that flows past what was to become the first gold-rush town in South Africa. Having struck out on his own to escape the crush at Mac Mac, he must have been horrified when within the year he was joined by 1,500 diggers, all frantically panning to make their fortunes. A fair number did, with the largest nugget weighing in at 11kg (24 lb.), but by 1881, the best of the pickings had been found, and the diggings were bought by the Transvaal Gold Mining Estates (TGME). A century later, the village still looked much the same, and the entire settlement was declared a national monument. The Works Department and Museum Services took charge of restoring and preserving this living museum.

If you're looking for historical accuracy, then you'll find Pilgrim's Rest overcommercialized; the town's streets are probably a great deal prettier than they were at the turn of the 20th century, and the overall effect, from the gleaming vintage fuel pumps to the flower baskets, is a sanitized, glamorized picture of life in a gold-rush town. As theme parks go, however, Pilgrim's Rest is a pleasant experience. Most of the buildings line a single main street, and the architecture is Victorian, prevalent in so many of colonial Africa's rural towns. Walls are corrugated iron with deep sash windows, and corrugated-iron roofs extend over large shaded *stoeps* (verandas).

Essentials

GETTING THERE Travel north from Sabie on R532. The R532 meets with the R533 in a T-junction; head northwest on R533 for 15km (9¼ miles). Pilgrim's Rest is 35km (22 miles) north of Sabie and about 360km (223 miles) northeast of Johannesburg.

VISITOR INFORMATION Contact the **Tourist Information Centre** (✆ **013/768-1060;** www.pilgrimsrest.org.za; daily 9am–4:30pm) and, if possible, ask for the information officer. The center is clearly marked on the main street; staff will supply free town maps as well as tickets to the museums, and will book tours for you.

GETTING AROUND Pilgrim's Rest has no street numbers; it's literally a one-horse town, with buildings stretched along a main road. Uptown, or Top Town, is literally the higher (and older) part of the main road, while Downtown stretches below the turnoff into town. Most of the tourist sights are situated in Uptown, as is the tourist office. For guided tours, contact John Pringle, the town's former information officer (✆ **083/522-6441;** about R350 per person for a full-day tour).

What to See & Do

St. Mary's Anglican Church, seen overlooking the main street as you enter town, is where sinners' souls were salvaged. Higher up the hill, the evocative **Pilgrim's Rest Cemetery** ★★ is definitely worth a visit. Besides the headstone inscribed ROBBERS GRAVE—the only tomb that lies in a north–south direction—the many children's graves are moving testimony to how hard times really were, and the many nationalities reflect the cosmopolitan character of the original gold-rush village.

The three museums in town, the **Dredzen Shop and House Museum,** the **News Printing Museum,** and the **House Museum,** can all be visited with the ticket sold at the Tourist Information Centre (R10). None of these house museums feels particularly authentic; furnishings and objects are often propped haphazardly and look much the worse for wear.

The **Alanglade Museum** ★★ (no phone; admission R20), which used to house the TGME's mine manager and his family, is more interesting. Although the furnishings, which date from 1900 to 1930, are not original, they have been selected to represent the era and are maintained with more care than those in the house museums. It is set in a forested grove 1.5km (about 1 mile) north of town. Tours run at 11am and 2pm Monday through Saturday, and must be booked half an hour in advance from the Pilgrim's Rest Tourist Information Centre.

Don't leave town without popping in to the Royal Hotel's **Church Bar** ★ (the tiny building used to be a church in Mozambique before it was relocated here, thereby answering the prayers of the thirsty Pilgrims of Mpumalanga).

Where to Stay

District Six Miners' Cottages Value The District Six cottages date back to the early 1920s. Set high up on the hill overlooking the town, these spartan accommodations have lovely views from their verandas and are serviced daily. Each has two bedrooms, a living room, a bathroom, and a fully equipped kitchen. Not surprisingly, these cheap, charming cottages are popular during school holidays—so make sure to book ahead. Keys are collected at the Royal Hotel.

Public Works Private X516, Pilgrim's Rest 1290. Book in advance; there is no on-site office. ✆ **072/314-5359.** Fax 013/768-1113. 6 units. R480 for 4-bed cottage. No credit cards.

The Royal Hotel ★ The Royal first opened its doors in 1873, and more than a century later, it's still going strong. It's one of the most charming places to overnight on the Escarpment. Besides the 11 original hotel rooms, which are arranged around a small courtyard behind the reception area, the hotel has grown to include 39 rooms located in buildings adjacent to the hotel, all dating back to the turn of the 20th century and impeccably restored and furnished in the Victorian style. The relatively small bedrooms feature brass beds (many of them four-poster), wooden ceiling fans, marble-and-oak washstands, and ball-and-claw bathtubs. This is not a luxurious experience, however—the mattresses are a little monastic, and corrugated-iron houses can become bitterly cold in winter. The honeymoon suite, situated in the Bank House, is the only room with a fireplace, and during June and July, when temperatures drop close to freezing, it's worth booking well in advance.

Main Rd., Uptown, Pilgrim's Rest 1290. ✆ **013/768-1100.** Fax 013/768-1188. www.royal-hotel.co.za. 50 units. R940 double. Rate includes breakfast. Ask about winter specials. AE, DC, MC, V. **Amenities:** Restaurant; bar; babysitting; golf; horseback riding; tennis; trout fishing can be arranged. *In room:* Hair dryer.

Where to Dine

You'll find a number of places to eat and drink all along the main road, and the Royal Hotel serves fairly innocuous grub. For lovely elevated views, head up the R533 to **Inn on Robber's Pass,** 15km (9¼ miles) from Pilgrim's Rest (✆ **013/768-1491**). The food isn't as amazing as the view, but you won't go wrong with the steak.

4 KRUGER NATIONAL PARK ★★★

Southern (Malelane) gate 428km (265 miles) NE of Johannesburg; northern (Pafuri) gate 581km (360 miles) NE of Johannesburg

Proclaimed by South African president Paul Kruger in 1898, this jewel in the South African National Parks crown stretches 381km (236 miles) from the banks of the Crocodile River in the south to the Limpopo River in the north, and covers almost 2.5 million hectares (6.2 million acres).

Even more impressive than its size, however, is the diversity of life the Kruger sustains: Sixteen eco-zones (each with its own geology, rainfall, altitude, and landscape) are home to more than 500 bird species and 147 mammal species, including an estimated 1,500 to 2,000 lions, 1,000 leopards, 6,200 white and 350 black rhinos, 12,500 elephants, and 25,000 buffaloes. Cheetah, African wild dog, spotted hyena, zebra, giraffe, hippo, crocodile, warthog, and some 21 antelope species also roam Kruger's open plains and waterways. The rich flora varies from tropical to subtropical; almost 2,000 plant species have been identified, including some 450 tree and shrub species and 235 grasses. The opportunity to see wildlife is superb—many people report seeing four of the Big 5 (the most elusive being the leopard) in a day, and some are lucky enough to see them all. Don't count on this; rather, set out to enjoy the open roads, undulating landscape, and countless species you will encounter along the way.

Kruger also has a number of archaeological sites, the most interesting being the Thulamela Heritage Site, a 16th-century stone-walled village overlooking the Luvuvhu River in the north. Others include the Stone Age village at Masorini, and more than 170 documented prehistoric rock painting sites, the most accessible being found at the Crocodile Bridge hippo pool, in the private concession leased to Jock Safari Camp, and along the Bushman and Wolhuter trails. Historical sites relating to early European explorers and Kruger's beginnings are also dotted throughout the park.

In 2002, eco-diplomacy reached new heights with the signing of a treaty in Xai-Xai, Mozambique, and the removal of some 30km (18½ miles) of fences between the Kruger and Zimbabwe's Gonarezhou National Park and Mozambique's Limpopo National Park—the first step in the creation of the new 37.5-million-hectare (92.5-million-acre) **Great Limpopo Transfrontier Park,** or **GLTP,** the biggest conservation area on the continent. Almost 4,000 animals of various species have been translocated from the KNP to the LNP since 2002, and others have made their own way there (the last count revealed that Limpopo National Park now boasts 630 elephants).

Excitement over the Kruger's incorporation into transfrontier conservation initiatives has to some extent been tempered by concerns over the current disputes before the country's Land Claims Commission, charged with returning land appropriated from its original owners under apartheid governance. Thus far, two of these claims have been settled in a manner that has had all-round benefits. The first land claim to be awarded was that of the Makuleke clan, which received ownership of the Pafuri area, now known as Makuleke Contractual Park. Two lodges have been built on the property, The Outpost and the Pafuri Tented Camp, as well as a wilderness school called Eco Training. The second land claim, in which a stretch of land to the south of Numbi Gate has been awarded to the Mdluli clan, has also become a win-win situation. It now operates as a concession called Mdluli Game Reserve, and is the site of a tented camp and field guide training academy run by a safari company called Untamed Africa (www.untamed.co.

Kruger National Park & Private Reserves

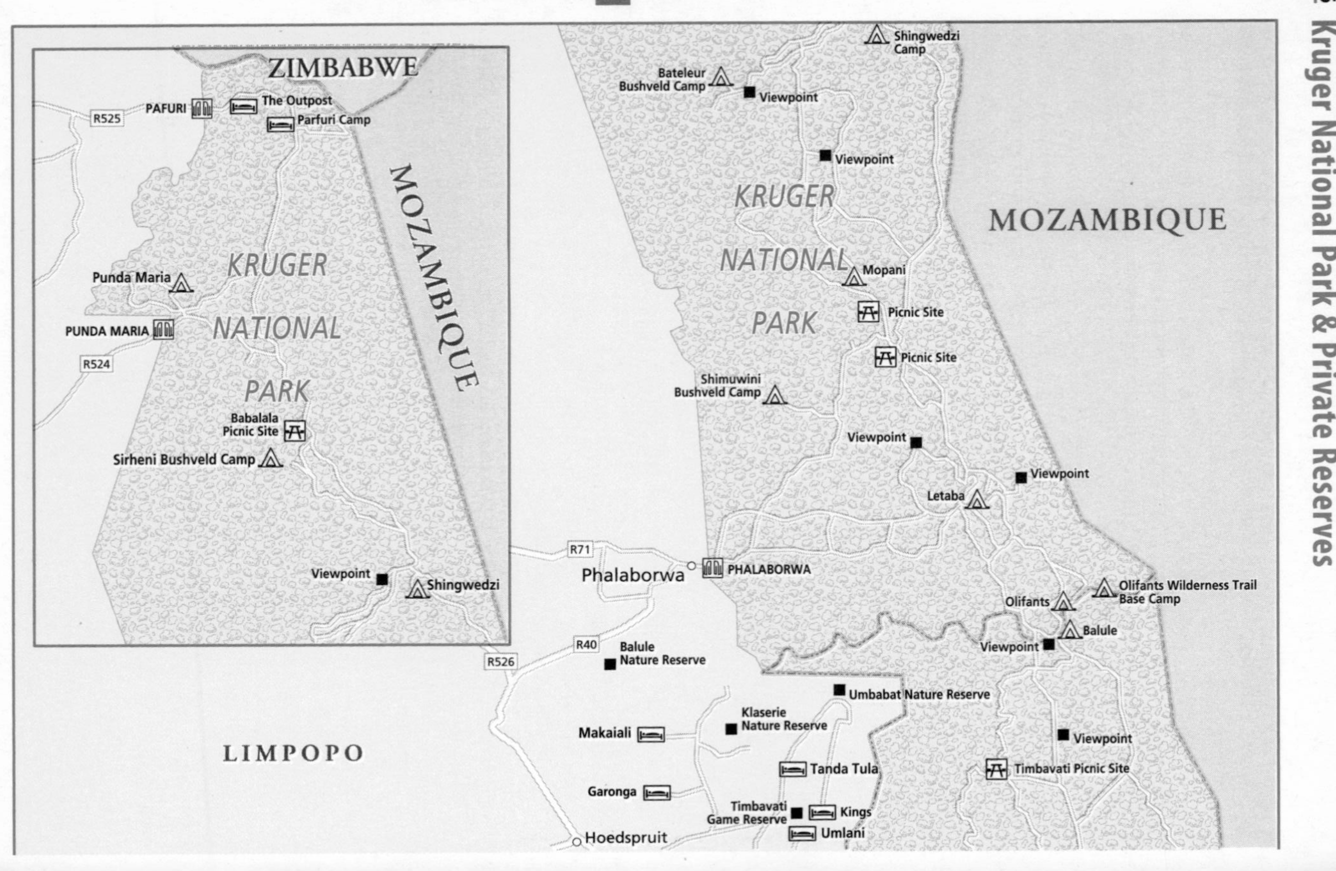

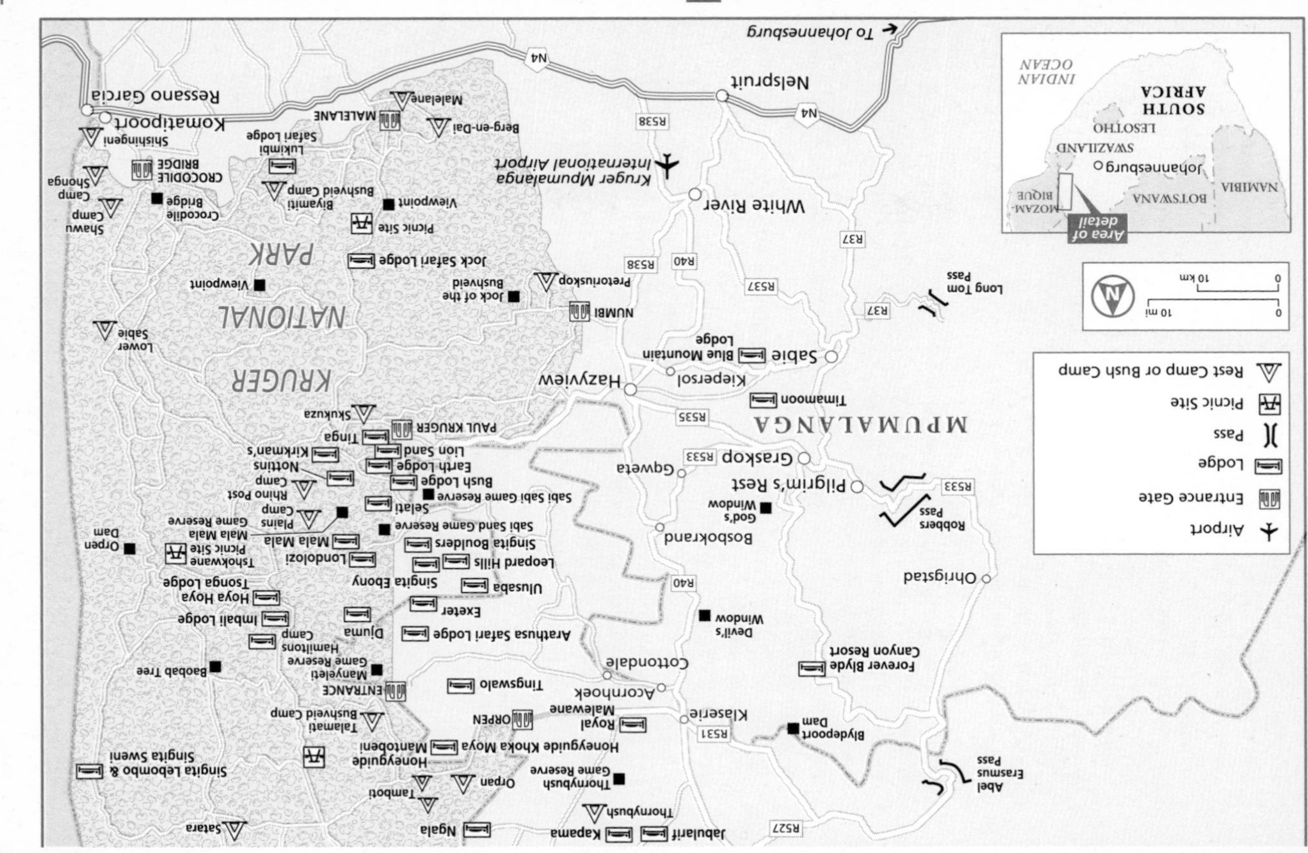
Airport
Entrance Gate
Lodge
Pass
Picnic Site
Rest Camp or Bush Camp
0 10 mi
0 10 km
Area of detail
NAMIBIA
BOTSWANA
Johannesburg
SWAZILAND
LESOTHO
SOUTH AFRICA
MOZAM-BIQUE
INDIAN OCEAN
To Johannesburg
KRUGER NATIONAL PARK
MPUMALANGA
Abel Erasmus Pass
R527
Jabularif
Kapama
Thornybush
Ngala
Satara
Thornybush Game Reserve
Orpan
Tamboti
Honeyguide Mantobeni
Honeyguide Khoka Moya
Singita Lebombo & Singita Sweni
Talamati Bushveid Camp
Blydepoort Dam
R531
Klaserie
Royal Malewane
ORPEN
Acornhoek
Tingswalo
ENTRANCE
Manyeleti Game Reserve
Baobab Tree
Forever Blyde Canyon Resort
Cottondale
Hamiltons Camp
Arathusa Safari Lodge
Djuma
Imbali Lodge
Devil's Window
Exeter
Hoya Hoya Tsonga Lodge
Ohrigstad
R40
Ulusaba
Singita Ebony
Leopard Hills
Londolozi
Tshokwane Picnic Site
Orpen Dam
Bosbokrand
Singita Boulders
Mala Mala
Mala Mala Game Reserve
Robbers Pass
God's Window
Sabi Sand Game Reserve
Plains Camp
R533
Pilgrim's Rest
Gqweta
Sabi Sabi Game Reserve
Selati
Rhino Post Camp
Bush Lodge
Nottins
Graskop
R533
Earth Lodge
Lion Sand
Kirkman's
Tinga
PAUL KRUGER
R535
Skukuza
Timamoon
Hazyview
Kiepersol
Lower Sabie
Sabie
Blue Mountain Lodge
R37
NUMBI
Long Tom Pass
Jock of the Bushveid
Viewpoint
R537
Pretoriuskop
R40
R538
Jock Safari Lodge
Picnic Site
R37
Shawu Camp
White River
Viewpoint
Crocodile Bridge
Camp Shonga
Biyamiti Bushveid Camp
Kruger Mpumalanga International Airport
CROCODILE BRIDGE
Lukimbi Safari Lodge
Shishingeni
R538
Berg-en-Dai
MALELANE
Komatipoort
N4
Malelane
Nelspruit
Ressano Garcia
N4

za)—again proving that sustainable land development can benefit both local communities and nature conservation.

ESSENTIALS

Arriving

BY PLANE There are three main airports in the Kruger vicinity. The busiest by far is Kruger–Mpumalanga International Airport (still often referred to as Nelspruit Airport), near White River and Hazyview (the gates to southern Kruger). The other options are Eastgate Airport (Hoedspruit, southern/central Kruger) and Kruger Park Gateway Airport (Phalaborwa, central Kruger). Your best bet is **SA Airlink** (www.flyairlink.com), which operates daily flights to all three from **Cape Town, Johannesburg,** and **Durban.** Alternatively, **SA Express** (www.flysax.co.za) also flies in daily from Johannesburg, and **Expressions of Africa** (✆ **011/978-3552**), a division of SA Express, puts together promotional flight and accommodations packages to safari destinations throughout southern Africa. Skukuza Airport, situated within Kruger Park near Skukuza Rest Camp, is no longer licensed for commercial flights, but this may change in the future, and it is used by charter flights such as those operated by Federal Air (www.fedair.com).

BY CAR The park has 10 entrance gates, most a comfortable 5- to 6-hour drive from Johannesburg or Pretoria. The closest gate, Malelane, is 428km (265 miles) from Johannesburg, while Pafuri (the farthest) lies around 580km (360 miles) northeast. The southern gates are **Malelane, Crocodile Bridge, Numbi, Phabeni,** and **Paul Kruger.** The central gates: **Orpen** and **Phalaborwa.** The northern gates: **Punda Maria, Giriyondo** (from Mozambique), and **Pafuri.** Allow enough time to reach the park; entrance-gate hours (see "Fast Facts: Kruger National Park," below) are strictly enforced. For safety and easy access, officials recommend the newest gate, **Phabeni.**

VISITOR INFORMATION All inquiries and applications should be made to **South African National Parks (SANParks),** P.O. Box 787, 643 Leyds St., Muckleneuk, Tshwane (Pretoria; ✆ **012/426-5000;** fax 012/426-5500; www.sanparks.org; Mon–Fri 7:30am–4pm, Sat 9am–noon). You can also phone the park directly at ✆ **013/735-4000** or 013/735-4246. Accommodation and campsites at all public rest camps within the park can also be booked by e-mail or telephone, but it's far easier and more efficient to use the very user-friendly and almost instantaneous online booking service on the SANParks website listed above. The park's headquarters is situated at Skukuza Rest Camp, located in the southern section, on the banks of the Sabie River (see later in this chapter).

GETTING AROUND **By Car** **Avis** (www.avis.co.za) has a desk at the Eastgate Airport (✆ **015/793-2014**), at the Kruger–Mpumalanga International airport (✆ **013/750-1015**), at Phalaborwa's Kruger airport (✆ **015/781-3169**), as well as at Skukuza, main camp in the Kruger (✆ **013/735-5651**). **Budget** (www.budget.co.za) operates from the Kruger–Mpumalanga airport (✆ **013/751-1774**) and Phalaborwa's Kruger airport (✆ **015/781-5404**). It's exciting to explore the park at your own pace in a rental car, but at least one guided game drive in an open-topped vehicle is recommended (see "Guided Game Drives & Walks," below). Note also that the park has opened 4- to 5-hour **4x4 Adventure Trails** that take you right off the beaten track into areas previously off-limits, but you will have to hire a 4WD vehicle to complete these. Sign up for these from Pretoriuskop, Satara, Phalaborwa Gate, Punda Maria, and Shingwedzi. The Planning trails are weather-sensitive, so they must be booked on the same day.

WHEN TO GO

Each season has advantages. Between October and March, when summer rains (often in the form of dramatic thunderstorms) have transformed the dry landscape into a flowering paradise, the park is alive with young buck and migratory birds, but at the same time, temperatures can soar above 105°F (40°C), dropping to 68°F (20°C) in the balmy evenings. The dense, junglelike foliage hides game, and the malaria risk is at its highest. In the winter, when water is scarce and the plant life recedes, animals are easier to spot, especially at water holes and riverbeds. Because this is the most popular season, however, be prepared to share your sightings with other motorists. The days are warm, but temperatures can drop close to freezing at night, and units are not heated. Try to avoid going during the school holidays, particularly in winter, when the park is packed to capacity.

Fast Facts Kruger National Park

Admission Hours **For the Park** Entrance gates open from January to February from 5:30am to 6:30pm, March from 5:30am to 6pm, April from 6am to 6pm, May to July 6am to 5:30pm, August to September 6am to 6pm, October from 5:30am to 6pm, and November to December from 5:30am to 6:30pm.

For the Rest Camps Camps are fenced off to protect residents from predators. The gates to these follow the same hours, except in the summer months (Nov–Jan), when they open an hour earlier (4:30am). If you're changing rest camps, try not to travel more than 200km (124 miles), to ensure you get to your new camp before gates close. Operating hours for camp receptions are 7am until half an hour after gate closing time; shops are typically from 8am to a half-hour after camp gates close, though they are shorter at some smaller camps; restaurants 7 to 10am, noon to 2:30pm, and 6 to 10pm.

Bank & ATM Networks There is a bank and ATM at Skukuza; it's a good idea to get cash here if you haven't already done so outside the park. (While you can pay by card for most anything, cash for a drink at a picnic site shop is useful, and all fuel must be paid for in cash.) There is also a proper ATM at Letaba. Some of the shops in other camps have mini-ATMs, but these don't always have cash, so don't wait until your wallet is empty before trying one of them.

Driving Rules Unlike private game reserves, where rangers are free to drive off road, everyone at Kruger drives on roads; the public drives on approved roads only. The speed limit is 50kmph (31 mph) on paved roads, 40kmph (25 mph) on gravel roads, and 20kmph (12 mph) in rest camps. If photographs of fatally maimed animals don't help ensure that these speeds are adhered to, speed traps do. Stay in your vehicle unless you're at a designated picnic site.

Fees SANParks charges a **daily conservation fee** for each person entering the park; 2010 fees are R160 per adult and R80 per child per day. If you plan to spend more than 6 nights in Kruger or visit other national parks in South Africa, look into purchasing a **Wild Card** (valid for 1 year), which provides free access to all national parks. At press time, a Wild Card cost R940 for an individual, R1,640 for a couple, and R2,210 for a family.

Fuel Every main rest camp has a fuel/petrol station. You must pay in cash or with a local petrol card—no credit or debit cards are accepted. (Note that bush camps don't have petrol.)

Internet & Phone The only camps with Internet cafes are Skukuza, Lower Sabie, and Berg-en-Dal, so there is no public Internet access north of Skukuza. Most of the main camps have cellphone reception, but the bushveld camps and roads don't.

Malaria While certain areas of Kruger are soon to be removed from the list of malarial areas, the risk of infection remains, and it is a disease you really want to avoid. The highest risk is between October and May, during which time a course of prescription antimalaria drugs is advised (for more information, see chapter 3).

Medical Emergencies There is a doctor in Skukuza (✆ **013/735-5638** or 082/557-9210). If you need help during the night, drive to the camp gate and beep your horn. The closest hospitals are in Nelspruit, Hoedspruit, and Phalaborwa. Of these, I'd head for Nelspruit Medi-Clinic, a 260-bed multidisciplinary private hospital and part of one of the largest, most respected private hospitals groups in Africa (✆ **013/759-0500**).

Money/Traveler's Checks/Credit Cards South African rands, traveler's checks, Visa, MasterCard, Diners Club, and American Express are accepted. Foreign currency can be exchanged at all rest camps.

Reservations The easiest way to book rest camp accommodations is on the user-friendly website www.sanparks.org. However, preference for choice units is given to written applications (this includes e-mail) received 13 months in advance. Pay your deposit as soon as possible to ensure the booking—this can be done over the telephone or Internet with a credit card.

Rules Park rules are printed on the entrance permit—read it. Park officials do not have a sense of humor when it comes to breaking the rules.

Safety Don't let the tarred road fool you—once you've left the safety of your fenced-off rest camp, you really are in the wild. *Under no circumstances* should you leave your vehicle unless you're at a designated site (see "Designated Pit Stops & Picnic Sites," below, or get a map from a rest camp shop). One ranger who left his game drive to "relieve" himself didn't survive to do up his zipper, so make sure to take care of any bathroom business before leaving camp. When in camp, try not to be frightened by spiders and other small insects you may encounter; unlike mosquitoes, they can do you no harm. Snakes are a rare occurrence in camps; if you do spot one, alert reception. (See chapter 3 for more safety tips on safaris.)

EXPLORING THE PARK

SANParks officials make no bones about the fact that their main concern is wildlife; *Homo sapiens* are a necessary nuisance. Although an effort is made to service visitors' needs, such as providing escorted game drives (highly recommended unless you're going on to a private game reserve), and the facilities and park infrastructure are undergoing a massive upgrade following a R32-million cash injection, the rules (such as gate-opening times) are inflexible, the staff can be bureaucratic, and, because services are geared toward the South African self-catering market, you're pretty much expected to toe the line. Here's how.

The Lay of the Land

Despite its many defined eco-zones, to the untrained eye, much of the park looks the same. A major portion is covered with a large shrublike tree called mopane. You'll find the most variation in the south and far north of the park—old bush hands, in fact, divide the park into three distinct regions: The south they call the "circus"; the central area, the "zoo"; and the north, the "wilderness." These are apt descriptions, particularly in the winter months, when the human and animal population soars in the water-rich south, while the less-accessible north remains a calm oasis.

Southern Kruger supports some of the richest game concentrations in Africa, which, in turn, attracts the most people. The busiest—and often very rewarding—road linking Skukuza to Lower Sabie Rest Camp is often referred to as **Piccadilly Highway,** and motorists have been known to virtually jostle each other to get a better view of lions and even create traffic jams around great sightings. It's the best part of the park for spotting rhinos (very common btw. Lower Sabie and Crocodile Bridge), leopard, and spotted hyena, and also hosts good concentrations of lion, elephant, and buffalo.

The **central area** still features a wide variety of species, particularly around Satara Rest Camp, where open plains frequently reward with good sightings and cheetah. A little more laid-back, with fewer camps, but with a reputation for the highest concentration of lions, this area continues to attract its fair share of tourists.

Most of the 13,000-odd resident elephants are found north of Olifants rest camp, but mile after mile of dense mopane scrubland makes even these huge animals difficult to see. The **northern part** of the park is probably not the best destination for a first-time visitor, unless you're a bird-watcher or it's combined with a sojourn in the south, but this remote wilderness area has definite advantages for real bush lovers, not least because there are fewer people. As you travel farther north, the mopane is broken by the lush riverine vegetation of the Shingwedzi, the baobab-dotted sandveld, fever-tree forests, and, finally, the tropical flood plains that lie between the Luvuvhu and Limpopo rivers. This northernmost part of the park is, in fact, at the crossroads of nine of Africa's major ecosystems, and the countryside is full of contrasts and the most prolific birdlife in the park: This region is Birdlife S.A.'s top destination. Spend at least 5 days in the Kruger—ideally, longer—if you include the north in your itinerary.

Designated Pit Stops & Picnic Sites

The designated sites dotted throughout the park are the only places visitors are allowed to get out of their vehicles. Maps, available at the entry gates and all rest camp shops, will indicate where these are located, as well as the types of facilities each has. (These may include restrooms, boiling water, barbecue grills, seating, shade, telephones, educational displays, and shops manned by attendants who sell wood, hot refreshments, and cold drinks.) The best-equipped and most popular sites are **Nkulu** (on the Sabie River btw. Skukuza and Lower Sabie), **Afsaal** (under a giant jackalberry tree on the main road btw. Skukuza and Malelane), and **Tshokwane** (near the three-way junction of the road connecting Skukuza and Lower Sabie to Satara, and named after an elephant bull that used to frequent the area). The shops here sell everything from scones to brandy. Less busy, with good game- and bird-viewing opportunities, are **Orpen Dam,** an elevated picnic spot overlooking the water, east of Tshokwane; and **Pafuri,** the best picnic site in the park, but located in the far north.

Better Wildlife-Viewing for the Self-Guide Safari

1. **Purchase a detailed map** that indicates all rivers, dams, dirt roads, and lookout and picnic points. These are available at all rest camp shops and entrance gates. The comprehensive *Prime Origins Guide to Exploring Kruger* is highly recommended to those who want to take a self-drive safari; you will also find plenty of inexpensive introductory booklets for sale at all the park shops.
2. Between picnic spots there are no restrooms, fuel stops, or shops, so **plan your journey along the way** and make sure you have something to drink and eat in the car, should you wish to stay with a sighting for some time.
3. **Be there at the right time.** The best times to view wildlife are in the early morning and late afternoon; animals don't move much in the heat of the day. Set off as soon as camp gates open (4:30–6:30am, depending on the season).
4. You're bound to bump into something if you **follow a river.** Always stop on bridges when crossing (traffic allowing) and look for crocodiles, herons, water monitors (lizards that can grow up to 3m/10ft.), hippos, and so on. Certain bridges, particularly those over the Letaba and Olifants rivers, allow you to get out of your vehicle—but please *exercise caution.* In winter, you're almost always assured of seeing animals at a water hole or dam; just park your car and wait.
5. **Spot a spotter.** A stationary car with binoculars pointed in a certain direction is an obvious clue. It is not considered bad form to ask what they have spotted (but you're unlikely to get a polite answer if you obscure their view).

Guided Game Drives & Walks

Even if you're self-driving, a guided game drive in an open-topped vehicle is a good way to get oriented, as experienced guides identify animals so you don't have to look them up in a book. During peak season, the major rest camps (Skukuza, Lower Sabie, Satara, Berg-en-Dal) provide these in large 23-seat vehicles; the only way to avoid potential noise and obstructed views is to book one of the less popular main camps (such as Mopani) out of season or stay at one of the recommended bush camps, where drives take place in open-topped 10-seaters (See "Where to Stay & Dine," below).

The best option, offered almost everywhere, is a **sunrise drive** ★★★ (R140 per person at rest camps, R176 at bush camps), which departs any time from 4 to 6am (30 min. before gates open). The 3-hour **sunset drives** (R140 per person at rest camps and gate entrances; bush camps R176), departing 2 hours before the gates close, are as popular as the sunrise drives ★★. You can also book these at the entrance gates, meaning you don't have to overnight here to experience this, and you'll be accommodated on a 10- or 23-seater, depending on numbers. However, the 2-hour **night drive** ★★★ (R120–R176), departing 2 hours after the gates close, is the one to make sure you're on; outside the concession areas, this is the only way to see the Kruger at night, giving visitors an opportunity to view the nocturnal activities of such animals as bushbabies, porcupines, civets, hyenas, honey badgers, and aardvarks. Be warned, however, that nocturnal animals

6. **Appreciate the rare.** Most first-time visitors want to tick off the Big 5, but it's worth finding out more about other species. Sighting a wild dog becomes that much more exciting when you know there are fewer than 400 left in the park.
7. **Bring a good pair of binoculars** and drum up some enthusiasm for the vegetation—that tree you stop to admire may reveal a leopard.
8. **Drive slowly**—sharing the shadow of the tree you just whizzed past could be a pride of lions. (The recommended speed for viewing is 25kmph/16 mph.)
9. Dirt roads give a great sense of adventure, but **don't shun the tar roads:** Besides being quieter, less dust makes for tastier grass verges.
10. **Consult the animal-sightings board** at your rest camp reception area—many animals are territorial and don't cover huge distances. Some experts advise that you concentrate on a smallish area, getting to know the movements of the animals, rather than driving all over the park.
11. Animals have the right-of-way on the roads. If a group of elephants is crossing, **keep a respectful distance,** switch the car off, and wait. If you're lucky enough to spot a black rhino (which has a hooked lip rather than the wide, square lip of the white rhino), be *very* wary.
12. **Never feed the baboons and monkeys** that hang out at picnic sites; this is tantamount to signing their death warrant, as they then become increasingly aggressive and have to be shot.
13. Most important, **be patient.** The only way you'll ever witness a kill, or any interesting animal interaction, is by watching a situation unfurl.

are shy, and on a bad night, sightings can be frustratingly rare. You can book any of these drives when making your accommodations booking—particularly advisable for early-morning and night drives, and essential during school holidays (every province has different dates, but they tend to fall in June–July, Sept, Dec–Jan, and Apr).

To appreciate one of the country's more authentic culinary experiences, you may enjoy a **bush braai,** offered by the Kruger's main camps. These barbecues under the stars are a sociable way to conclude late-afternoon game drives. **Bush "breakfasts,"** where you break for a sandwich-type meal in the bush, are less agreeable. Cost for either is about R475 per person, but confirm availability and price when booking.

If sitting in a vehicle undermines your experience of the bush, consider **morning walks** ★★★ (R270 per person), which usually last 3 to 4 hours with a maximum of eight people, offered at most rest camps and bushveld camps. If you don't mind the heat, **afternoon walks** ★ (R210) are another option.

Big Game on Foot: Wilderness Trails ★★★

These 3-night, 4-day trails (R2,710 per person for the duration), catering to a maximum of eight people, offer an opportunity to experience the real essence of the African bush in Kruger at an extremely affordable rate. Although you are unlikely to see quite as much big game on foot (and you may spend a lot of time hoping you don't), and you won't get as close to most animals as you can in a vehicle (animals don't associate the smell of gasoline with humans), you will be introduced to the trees, insects, and animals that make up the surrounding bush under the protection of an armed and experienced guide. The emphasis is on reconnecting with the wilderness in some elemental way rather than ticking off species, but guides are armed for a reason.

As yet, there has never been a human fatality on any of the Kruger trails, and considering the caliber of the guides on hand, it is unlikely to ever occur, but do follow their instructions—given at the start of each trail—closely.

The locations of the base camps—comprising thatched A-framed two-bed huts with reed-walled, solar-heated showers and a shared flushing toilet—have been selected for their natural beauty. Note that, unlike the trails offered in KwaZulu-Natal's Hluhluwe-Umfolozi reserve, you'll return to the same base camp every night. Besides bedding, towels, cutlery, and food, the park supplies rucksacks and water bottles. Drinks (which you must supply) are kept cold in gas fridges. Age limits are 12 to 60 years, and a reasonable degree of fitness is required—you will be covering from 8 to 15km (5–9¼ miles) a day.

You have seven trails to choose from: The **Napi, Bushman,** and **Wolhuter** are all situated in the southwestern section, known for white rhino, granite hills, and Bushman rock paintings. The **Metsi-Metsi,** which overlooks a small waterhole, and the **Sweni,** which overlooks the marula and knobthorn savanna, are in the central area, known for its lions. **Olifants Trail** ★, which overlooks the perennial Olifants River, west of its confluence with the Letaba, is particularly scenic and one of the most popular. **Nyalaland,** situated in the pristine northern wilderness among the sandveld's fever tree and baobab forests, is a favorite of birders. But even if you're not a birder, the vegetation and views more than make up for the relative lack of game. Reservations often need to be made well in advance; you can check availability for all trails departing up to a year ahead (and make bookings) at **www.sanparks.org**.

Hard-core wilderness enthusiasts who are very fit and want to experience a "hard" hike rather than the relaxing standard wilderness trails should sign up for the new 3-night **Olifants Back Pack Trail.** It departs from Olifants main rest camp and is fairly grueling—you walk to a new overnight spot every night, set up camp unaided, and carry all provisions in (and out), including your own tent. Olifants is also the camp to book into if you want to tackle a **Mountain Bike Trail** in the park. A relatively recent innovation, these half- or full-day guided mountain bike trails depart from Olifants Rest Camp. Places are limited to six participants per trail (reservations should be made well in advance) and are led by two qualified and armed field guides; bikes are provided. Three routes are available, graded according to difficulty and technicality (the Hardekool Draai trail is recommended for beginners).

Lastly, bear in mind that early-morning and evening guided walks for a maximum of eight persons is offered at most camps for those keen to walk, but not particularly far.

WHERE TO STAY & DINE

There are four broad options when it comes to accommodation in and around Kruger. The most affordable, and most suitable for self-drive safaris, is the network of rest camps operated by SANParks. These offer comfortable and reasonably priced self-catering accommodation, and in most cases they also have campsites, swimming pools, well-stocked grocery and gift shops, and adequate restaurants, but the emphasis is squarely on functionality rather than chic design or luxurious facilities. The other, far costlier option within the park boundaries is to stay at one of the newer and super-luxurious lodges that operate within nine exclusive concessions that were awarded to select private operators circa 2000. Costlier still, offering a universally high standard of accommodation and service, and arguably the finest close-up Big 5 experience in Africa, are the exclusive luxury lodges in Sabi Sands, MalaMala, Timbavati, and other private reserves that share an unfenced border with the western Kruger.

If you're not prepared to shell out for the luxury lodges in the Kruger concessions and private reserves, but you want a level of pampering absent from the Kruger rest camps, then the final option is to stay in one of the hotels or guesthouses situated on Kruger's periphery and enter the park daily. Only 10 minutes from the Phabeni Gate, Rissington Inn is a recommended option (see "The Escarpment & Panorama Route: Sabie & Surrounds: Where to Stay: Near Hazyview," earlier in this chapter), as is **Buhala Country House,** 10 minutes from the Malelane Gate, with excellent views overlooking the banks of the Crocodile River. With only 10 bedrooms and 2 garden suites (and no children under 10 allowed), this thatched homestead is a tranquil option; rooms are elegant and cool, and dining is superior to anything you'll find in the rest camps. Like Rissington, Buhala will organize tours of the Escarpment as well as safaris into the park; in addition, Buhala can arrange for you to play at Leopard's Creek, arguably the most exclusive golf course in South Africa (✆ **013/792-4372;** www.buhala.co.za; from R1,870 double, including breakfast). And for something completely different, take a look at www.serenitylodge.co.za: **Serenity Luxury Forest Lodge** (✆ **013/790-2000;** from R3,420 double) is everything it appears to be. The lodge's lovely treehouse-style suites are linked by timber boardwalks and located in the midst of a lush indigenous forest, with an almost tropical atmosphere more associated with a KwaZulu-Natal lodge; it's hard to believe that the more arid and relatively hostile Kruger landscape is less than 30 minutes away.

Park Rest Camps

The SANParks rest camps, though somewhat institutional in atmosphere, are difficult to fault when it comes to their primary objective of providing comfortable and affordable bases from which to explore one of Africa's truly great wildlife sanctuaries. And while many South Africans share a certain nostalgia in coming back year after year to find the same impala-lily and bird fabric on every curtain, cushion, and bed; *Custos Naturae* stamped on every sheet; and the kudu crest embossed on every soap; it's fair to say that these rest camps display little in the way of architectural or decorative flair. That said, the (mostly en-suite) accommodations—situated in camps scattered throughout the park—are scrupulously clean, relatively comfortable, and, for the most part, very cheap; in fact, they offer astonishingly good value when compared to parks anywhere else in Africa. They are also remarkably varied, with four or five accommodations types located in various options, including rest camps, satellite camps, bushveld camps, and bush lodges (the latter suitable only for groups). Of these, the **bushveld camps** are highly recommended—with only 7 to 15 units in each, they offer more privacy than the large rest camps (Skukuza, the largest, has more than 200 units, as well as a landing strip, a 9-hole golf course, a bank, and two restaurants, to mention just a few of the camp's facilities). You will have to do your own cooking, however, when the camp gates are locked at night—only the main rest camps have restaurants. But if you don't mind self-catering (get a bush barbecue going), you'll be treated to fewer crowds in the bush, as game drives in the bushveld camps are always in smaller 10-seat vehicles

For budget travelers, the most popular accommodations in Kruger are the **main rest camps,** which offer a variety of cottages, bungalows, huts, and safari tents; of these, Skukuza, Lower Sabie, Satara, and Olifants are the most popular. All units are sparely furnished and semiserviced: Beds are made and floors are swept; you're not really supposed to leave the dishes, but staff will wash up—do please leave a tip (around R10–R15 per day should do). Water is scarce, so "en suite" usually means flushing toilet, sink (often in the bedroom), and shower, though the upcoming upgrade will probably mean the basin will become part of the bathroom. The bigger camps are like small suburbs and are designed to encourage interaction among guests (units are close together and often emulate the old Voortrekker *laager,* a circle, facing inward), so there is little privacy. Try to book a river-facing unit (assuming there is one) or check to see whether you can book a perimeter unit; these face into the bush, albeit through a fence.

The three- to six-bedroom guesthouses represent the top accommodations option in each rest camp. It's well worth investigating these if you're traveling with friends, as they are usually situated in the best location in the camp and offer the most privacy and small luxuries (such as a bathtub).

It's really best to plan at least one barbecue, cooked in front of your bungalow, which is what most local visitors do. This doesn't require much advance organization, as all accommodation units have their own fridge and barbecue, and the main rest camps all have shops selling basics such as milk, bread, butter, cheese, spreads, dishwashing liquid, tea, tinned products, cereal, cold drinks, firelighters, and wood, along with a selection of fresh or frozen meats and a variable range of fresh vegetables. That said, epicureans are advised to shop at a supermarket in one of the Escarpment or Lowveld towns before entering Kruger. The wine selection in the camp shops is surprisingly good—if you don't know what you're looking for and just want an everyday drinking wine, choose one of the Nederburgs, an old standby.

If you can't be bothered to self-cater, all the larger camps also have dining facilities in the form of a Tree Restaurant and/or Wooden Banana Café. Although the food served at these chainlike eateries is not going to win any culinary awards, it's good value, filling, and caters to a great array of tastes and needs, including vegetarians and diabetics—and standards and service have greatly improved since management was outsourced a few years ago. Hours and prices at the Tree Restaurants vary slightly from one camp to the next, but breakfast typically costs R49 per person, a la carte lunches cost R60 to 90, and three-course dinners are around R140 to 180. The cheaper Wooden Banana Snack Bars are open from 7am to 9pm and serve a variety of salads, pasta dishes, burgers, toasted sandwiches, and other dishes in the R30-to-R40 range.

Note: If you're traveling during peak summer, especially with kids, think twice before booking into a camp without a swimming pool. Facilities for travelers with disabilities are available at Crocodile Bridge, Berg-en-Dal, Lower Sabie, Skukuza, Satara, Olifants, Letaba, Mopani, Shingwedzi, Pretoriuskop, and Tamboti.

The following camps accept Visa, MasterCard, Diners Club, and American Express.

Berg-en-Dal ★★ SOUTH Modern facilities and proximity to Malelane Gate make Berg-en-Dal (like Skukuza) ideal for first-night orientation before heading deeper into the park. It's quite a new rest camp, built in the 1980s, and rather different than its older counterparts, offering accommodation in prosaic brick bungalows set amid attractive indigenous gardens. Besides being ideal habitat for leopards and rhinos, the granite hills around Berg-en-Dal are the only place in Kruger where gray rhebok and mountain reedbuck occur, and the terrain offers some relief from the mostly flat bushveld elsewhere in the park. Try to book a perimeter unit (code BA3U on the website) for the opportunity to spot wildlife through the fence, or one of the spacious family cottages or exclusive guesthouses (particularly no. 26). Each unit has an enclosed patio and braai area, offering

Fun Facts Chewing Up the Scenery

An elephant consumes up to 200kg (480 lb.) of vegetation daily; a herd thus has a huge, potentially destructive impact on the landscape. This is why elephant numbers need to be controlled, by either culling or translocation. Elephants are extremely sensitive animals, however, and actively mourn the death of a family member, performing intricate burial ceremonies. When clans reunite, they make a great show of affection, "kissing" (probing each other's mouths with their trunks) and trumpeting their joy. To find out more about this amazing species, book a 90-minute **elephant safari** or stay at **Camp Jabulani** (see "Private Game Reserves Flanking Kruger").

a sense of privacy lacking in most other camps. A walking trail within the camp leaves the river and follows a narrow path through dense bush, where Braille signs are set out to guide the visually impaired past plants and animal skulls on display. The dam sees much wildlife activity, although you may have to sit on one of the benches and wait for it: Crocodiles lurk—and hunt—in its waters, and water birds are always around.

Enter through Malelane Gate, southern Kruger. © **013/735-6106/7.** Fax 013/735-6104. 88 units. Bungalows R580–635 double; family cottages R1,075 for 4 people; guesthouses R2,020 for 4 people. **Amenities:** Restaurant; auditorium; bush braais; bush walks; camping; fuel; game drives; Internet; pool.

Letaba ★ CENTRAL This rest camp is set in elephant and buffalo country, just where the mopane terrain starts to become monotonous. The location, along a large bend of the Letaba River, sees plenty of activity, particularly in the winter. The nearby Engelhardt and Mingerhout dams are also excellent game sites, and the gravel road that follows the Letaba River is worth exploring. Always a favorite with Kruger aficionados, Letaba recently gained a swimming pool and upgraded visitor facilities. Unfortunately, very few of the units have views, but the restaurant has one of the best; it's worth planning a visit to eat lunch here while watching various plains animals wandering down for a drink. Accommodations are in thatched units set in gardens grazed by resident bushbuck and shaded by well-established apple leaf trees, acacias, mopane, and lala palms that support a prolific birdlife. Bungalows on the perimeter fence (booking code BG2U or BG3U) are the pick. Better still, the pricier Fish Eagle and Melville guesthouses have good views and plenty of space. Furnished safari tents are a budget alternative but the bathrooms and kitchen facilities are shared.

Enter through Phalaborwa Gate, central Kruger. © **013/735-6636.** Fax 013/735-6662. 125 units. Safari tents R295 double (shared ablutions); bungalows en suite R575 double (shared kitchen) or R640 (with kitchen); cottages R1,095 for 4 people; guesthouses R2,020 for 4 people. **Amenities:** Restaurant; bar; bush braais and breakfasts; elephant hall; fuel; game drives and walks; pool; shop.

Lower Sabie ★★★ SOUTH Overlooking the Sabie River, with large lawns and mature trees, this newly renovated camp is among the most pleasant in Kruger, particularly if you bag a waterfront bungalow (booking code BD2U, BD3U, or BD3UZ). There are also 24 good-value East African–style safari tents, all with twin beds, en-suite shower and toilet, and an outdoor "kitchen" (hot plate, fridge, barbecue)—but, again, book one with a riverside view (booking code LST2UZ), a real bargain. Every unit has a braai, but unless you have a kitchen, you will have to rent cutlery and crockery, available for a small fee from reception. Once again, there is no privacy, as most units share walls. Stroll along

Tracker Tips

Of course, you can't expect to know in a few days what professional trackers have gleaned in many years of tracking animals or growing up in the bush, but nature does provide myriad clues for the amateur tracker.

1. **Look for "hippo highways."** Hippos don't pick up their feet when they move; they drag them. So if you see a trail of trampled grass leading to a water hole, it's likely a hippo has been going back and forth from the water (where it stays during the heat of the day) to the grass it feeds on. Don't tarry on a hippo highway; once they set off on their well-trodden paths, very little will stop them.
2. **Use your nose.** Elephant urine has a very strong scent; waterbucks have a distinctive musky smell.
3. **Train your vision.** Vultures wheeling above may indicate the presence of predators, as may fixed stares from a herd of zebras or giraffes. A cloud of dust usually hovers over a large herd of moving buffalo. And, of course, paw prints provide vital information, not only to what has passed by (you should purchase a wildlife guidebook to recognize the differing imprints), but how recently it was there. This latter skill takes years of experience to hone.
4. **Examine trees.** Bark and branches sheared off trees or trees rubbed raw are evidence that elephants have passed by—they eat the bark and use trees as scratching posts. And certain trees attract specific species—giraffes, for example, love to browse the mopane.
5. **Listen to the sounds of the bush.** The lead lioness makes a guttural grunt to alert her pride. Baboons, monkeys, squirrels, and birds give raucous alarm calls in the presence of predators. Kudus bark when frightened.
6. **Look for droppings and dung.** Elephant dung is hard to miss—extralarge clumps full of grass and bark—while a trail full of fresh black, pancakelike dung marks the passing of a herd of buffaloes. A good wildlife guidebook will have illustrations of many species' dung.
7. **Watch bird behavior.** Follow the flight of oxpeckers and you're likely to locate a herd of Cape buffalo; oxpeckers survive off the ticks and other insects that cling to the buffalo hide. Cattle egrets dine on the insects and earthworms kicked up by grazing herbivores.

the paved walkway that overlooks the Sabie River at night with a torch: The red eyes you light up probably belong to hyenas, lured by the smell of braaiing meat. Just about every animal has been spotted drinking along the riverbanks, and at night you'll fall asleep to the grunting of hippos. Lower Sabie has a plum location for game-viewing, at the junction of three of the park's most consistently rewarding roads: the H4-2 to Crocodile Bridge (excellent for rhinos), the H4-1 to Skukuza (bird-rich riparian forest that's also prime elephant, buffalo, and leopard territory), and the H10 to Satara (elephant, rhino, lion, and cheetah regulars). With two dams nearby, Lower Sabie also provides an excellent base for observing wetland birds.

Enter through Crocodile Bridge or Paul Kruger Gate, southern Kruger. ✆ **013/735-6056.** Fax 013/735-6062. 119 units. Safari tents R460–R495 double (latter with river view); bungalows R575–R610 double; guest cottages R2,020 for 4 people. **Amenities:** Restaurant; fuel; game drives and walks; Internet; pool.

Olifants ★★★ CENTRAL On a clifftop 100m (328 ft.) above the banks of the Olifants River, with views of the vast African plains that stretch beyond to the hazy Escarpment, this smallish camp is a favorite, and you'd be well advised to book as soon as you read this. The bungalows along the camp's southwest perimeter (booking codes BBD2V, BD2V, and NGU2; the latter with no kitchen) are the most private and have spectacular views of the river and the animals that drink there, watched by basking crocodiles, while eagles wheel above, searching for prey—it's almost worth rearranging your trip around their availability. One feels less caged in here than at Kruger's other camps; the sudden drop below Olifants' bungalows means that no perimeter fence is required, and the expansive views are totally uninterrupted. Like many of the Kruger units, the veranda incorporates both kitchen and dining area. (***Tip:*** Do not leave food out here; groceries must be kept under lock and key from thieving baboons, hence the lock on the fridge.) Families note that there are two-bedroom bungalows with river views, and this camp has the best guesthouses in the park, with 270-degree views. This is also currently the only camp offering mountain biking as an alternative bush experience.

Enter through Phalaborwa Gate, central Kruger. ✆ **013/735-6606.** Fax 013/735-6609. 109 units. 2-bed bungalows R530–705 double; 4-bedded bungalows R745–R795 for 4; 8-bed guesthouses R2,020. **Amenities:** Restaurant; bush braai; fuel; game drives and walks; trails (hiking and mountain biking).

Punda Maria ★★ Finds NORTH Very few people have the time to travel this far north, just one of the reasons why Punda Maria—near the Zimbabwean border—is the number-one choice for wilderness lovers. Built in the 1930s, this small thatched and whitewashed camp retains a real sense of what it must have been like to visit Kruger half a century ago, with communal kitchen facilities and old-style architecture. In 2004, the camp added seven fully equipped safari tents in a great location (well worth booking) and a much-needed pool. The area does not support large concentrations of game, but it lies in the sandveld, where several springs occur, and borders the lush alluvial plains, making it a real must for birders. A nature trail winds through the camp, and the surrounding area is scenically splendid. Make sure you head north to the Luvuvhu River, the only real tropical region of the park, and one of the top birding destinations in southern Africa. Overlooking the Luvuvhu, **Thulamela Heritage Site** protects the remains of a large stone city built in the 16th century after Great Zimbabwe was abandoned. A little farther east along the river is the most beautiful picnic site in Kruger, **Pafuri,** which lies under massive thorn, leadwood, and jackalberry trees, where the colorful Narina trogon is resident and water is constantly on the boil for tea. The camp offers guided morning expeditions to both these sites.

Enter through Punda Maria Gate, northern Kruger. ✆ **013/735-6873.** Fax 013/735-6894. 31 units. Safari tents R540 double; bungalows R485–575 double; family bungalow R1,095 for 4 people. **Amenities:** Restaurant; bird hide; bush braais; fuel; game drives and walks; pool; shop; trails (4WD).

Satara ★ CENTRAL The second-biggest and one of the four most popular camps in Kruger (the others being Skukuza, Olifants, and Lower Sabie), Satara is located in one of the finest game-viewing areas in the park. The rich basaltic soils support sweet grasses that attract some of the largest numbers of grazers, including buffalo, wildebeest, zebra, kudu, impala, and elephant. These, in turn, provide rich pickings for the park's densest lion and cheetah populations—spend 2 to 3 days here, and you are almost certain to see both. Just as well the game-viewing is so good, because the setting and housing at Satara are rather disappointing: five massive *laagers,* each 25-rondawel strong, with verandas all facing inward. The best options are the perimeter units (booking code BD2V), though the view to the bush is through an electrified fence. That said, the camp now has a pool and a new day visitor center (convenient for those who stop here for lunch); it's also one of only two camps that offer the luxury of a deli. ***Tip:*** The H7 to Orpen Gate is especially good for cheetahs and lion; the loop to Gudzani Dam and Nwanetsi Picnic Site via the S100 and H6 is famously beautiful, with wonderful river views in summer, and plentiful game in winter; while the Tshokwane area south of Satara is said to have the highest concentrations of lions in southern Africa.

Enter through Orpen Gate, central Kruger. ✆ **013/735-6306.** Fax 013/735-6304. 166 units. Bungalows R575–R640 double; luxury bungalow R875 double; cottages R1,105 for 4 people; guesthouses R2,020 for 4 people. **Amenities:** Restaurant; bush braais; deli; fuel; game drives and walks; pool; trails (4x4).

Skukuza ★★ SOUTH Just east of the Paul Kruger Gate, you will find Skukuza, so-called capital of Kruger. Skukuza (or "He Who Sweeps Clean") refers to Kruger's first warden, Stevenson-Hamilton, who set up his base camp here. Today Skukuza accommodates some 1,000 people in prime game-viewing turf—top roads include the H1-3 north to Satara and the loop to Lower Sabie via the H4-1 and S30/128. This is an ideal spot for first-time visitors, though it would be a pity if this were your only experience of the park, because it really is like a small town, with two restaurants, a bank, a post office, a doctor's office, a deli, an Internet cafe, and three pools. Besides the people and cars, there is the noise of the occasional plane landing, though this doesn't seem to distract the many visitors strolling along the wide walkway that follows the course of the Sabie River. Accommodations are in a range of thatched en-suite units, the best of which are the luxury riverside bungalows (booking codes LR2E and LR2W), which were rebuilt after the 2000 floods and offer great river views, as well as luxuries such as a double bed, fully fitted kitchen, and satellite TV. All other units have fridges on their small verandas, some with hot plates and cooking equipment. Furnished East African–style tents are available for the budget-conscious, but you have to share bathrooms and kitchen facilities with the hordes of campers and RV drivers who descend on the camp, particularly in June/July and December/January.

Enter through Paul Kruger or Phabani Gate, southern Kruger. ✆ **013/735-4152.** Fax 013/735-4054. 238 units. Safari tents R285 double or for 4; ordinary bungalows R580–620 double; luxury riverside bungalows R1,095 double; guest cottages R1,075 for 4 people; guesthouses R2,020 for 4 people. **Amenities:** 2 restaurants; bar; deli (w/Internet cafe); airport; bank w/ATM; braai; doctor; fuel; game drives and walks; 9-hole golf; library; 3 pools; post office; shop.

Other Camps

Among the other main camps, **Mopani ★** (✆ **013/735-6535/6;** from R575 for a double bungalow) is the most modern in Kruger, with a lovely setting on the Pioneer dam, untamed bush gardens, and relatively large bungalows. Try to book one of the popular units with dam views (nos. 9–12, 43, 45, 47–54, and 101–102), but even if this fails, there are plenty of decks and the bar from which to enjoy the sunset. The one drawback with Mopane is that game-viewing in the surrounding mopane woodland is somewhat hit and miss, but the camp still makes a good stopover en route between the central Kruger and the far north. The other option in northern Kruger is **Shingwedzi** (✆ **013/735-6806;** double-bed bungalows go for R270 with shared shower and kitchen, or R575 en-suite double), a medium-size rest camp with accommodations that have benefited from a much-needed upgrade. Shingwedzi is quieter than most comparably sized camps, due its remote location in prime elephant territory. But game-viewing along the Shingwedzi River can be superb, and the riparian forest between the camp and Kanniedood Dam ranks among the best areas in the park for birding.

Farther south, **Orpen** (✆ **013/735-6355;** from R600 double for a bungalow), one of the Kruger's smallest camps, with only 15 units, has benefited from a much-needed upgrade. The area also enjoys a reputation for fine sightings—lions, cheetahs, and wild dogs are regularly seen in the area. It's far better to book its satellite camp, **Tamboti** ★★, which is Kruger's answer to the East African safari tent, and one of the park's unsung gems. Tamboti comprises 40 tents, each with two to three beds, tucked away among apple leaf, jackalberry, and sycamore fig trees on the banks of the Timbavati River (R675 fully equipped double; R295 double with communal ablutions and kitchens). Book well in advance, though, as the camp is very popular, mostly because of its location and the privacy of the tents, every one of which has a view; animals, particularly elephants, are attracted by the promise of water. Do bear in mind that, as a satellite camp, it has no restaurant or any staff.

Another low-key gem, ideal for true bush aficionados, is the tiny camp of **Balule** ★ (✆ **013/735-6606**), set near the banks of the Olifants River between Olifants and Satara rest camps. There are just six three-bed huts here, at the bargain price of R205 a double using common shower blocks. The rusticity of Balule is underscored by the lack of electricity (paraffin lamps light it up by night), and the nearest shop, restaurant, and filling station are at Olifants, which is also where you need to check in, so stock up on food and firewood while you are there.

Note: Two camps aren't worth considering: **Crocodile Bridge** (✆ **013/735-6012**) is much too close to civilization, across the river from the farms that neighbor Kruger, where you might as well be, with a better view looking back at the park. **Pretoriuskop** (✆ **013/735-5128**), Kruger's oldest camp, is popular but only 8km (5 miles) from the Numbi Gate. Most people press on to Berg-en-Dal, deeper in the bush.

Bushveld Camps

The five bushveld camps are much smaller than the major rest camps and provide a greater sense of being in the bush. They have no restaurants or shops, however, so you must do your own cooking, and any last-minute shopping will have to be done at the nearest rest camp. On the plus side, most of the en-suite units are more spacious than rest-camp options and feature well-equipped kitchens with braai (barbecue) spots. Only residents are allowed to travel the access road, which makes these an excellent place to get away from it all. Best of all, the game drives are in vehicles that accommodate 8 to 10 people. You pay a little more for the seclusion—rates range from R695 to R1,275 for two to four persons—but it's still good value.

The centrally located **Talamati** ★★★, close to the Orpen Gate (✆ **013/735-6343**), and southern **Biyamiti** ★★★, close to the Malelane Gate (✆ **013/735-6171**), are the most popular, located as they are in Kruger's game-rich areas, and easily accessed. Shimuwini, Bateleur, and Sirheni are all in the northern section of the park. **Shimuwini** ★★, which is reached via the Phalaborwa Gate (✆ **013/735-6683**), and **Sirheni** ★★, halfway between Shingwedzi and Punda Maria (✆ **013/735-6860**), both have scenic waterside settings that attract a variety of game and birds, and offer night drives. **Bateleur** ★★ (✆ **031/735-6843**) is the oldest bushveld camp and the most intimate, with only 7 thatched units rather than the usual 15. The closest gate to Bateleur is Phalaborwa. ***Tip:*** If you are traveling in a large group or as a family with teenage kids, or you just want assured privacy, it is worth asking about the two bush lodges: **Roodewal**

Moments Sleepover Hides

An exciting new innovation is the introduction of two new **sleepover hides** ★★ in 2006: **Shipandane,** situated 3km (2 miles) south of Mopani camp, on the Tsendze River, and **Sable Dam** hide, near Phalaborwa Gate. Bird hides by day, they are transformed into primitive dwellings 30 minutes before the gates close. Each comprises a boma with barbecue, a sleeping area (minimum 2 persons; maximum 6; R325 for the first 2 people and R160 per additional person), and a chemical toilet. With the presence of water comes game: Large buffalo herds and elephant bulls frequent these areas, often meters from where you sleep, and this is the closest you'll get (outside a few select private lodges such as Umlani) to wild, dangerous animals without the presence of an armed ranger. It's a highly recommended experience if you like your nature untainted by noise and the presence of other people, but it's not for the fainthearted. There is no electricity (you are supplied with a chargeable lamp) or running water, you will have to make your own bed (pick up bedding and keys from Mopani camp and Phalaborwa Gate, respectively), and you will have to bring your own food, wood, and water (cutlery and crockery supplied). The perimeter is fenced, and under no circumstances—unless you have a masochistic suicidal streak—should you leave the enclosure at night.

(44km/28 miles north of Satara) and **Boulders** (25km/15 miles south of Mopani) comprise separate sleeping units connected via boardwalks to communal living areas. Booking one of these lodges (Roodewal enjoys the better setting) will give you the ultimate in 21st-century luxury: peace and privacy at a fraction of the cost of renting an entire lodge in the private reserves that abut the Kruger. The rate is R1,900 and R2,020 for the first four persons, respectively; each additional person costs R370. The lodges sleep a maximum of 19 and 12 persons, respectively.

For more information on all of the above, contact Kruger reservations (see "Visitor Information," earlier in this chapter).

Camping

Billed as a "rustic campsite," **Tzendse,** on the banks of the eponymous river, is the latest place to pitch your tent. Opened in late 2006, it is also the only "pure" campsite. With no built accommodations or reception area, it is by far the most serene and scenic campsite in the park, with open-air communal showers. Reception is at Mopani. Campsites are also available at **Balule, Berg-en-Dal, Crocodile Bridge, Letaba, Malelane, Maroela, Lower Sabie, Pretoriuskop, Punda Maria, Satara, Shingwedzi,** and **Skukuza.** Campers share bathrooms (shower/toilet blocks) and kitchens, and have access to all rest-camp facilities. Every site has a braai (barbecue), and many also have electricity; you will need to bring in all your own equipment, however, including a tent. Camping costs R120 to R150 per site for the first two people, and another R40 to R50 for every additional person, to a maximum of six per site. (If you want to camp without having to pitch a tent or lug bedding across the world, a number of camps have furnished and equipped safari tents. Most are reviewed above—the best option is Tamboti, a satellite of Orpen.)

Private Concessions Within Kruger

Modeled on the successful government program in Botswana, the Kruger concessions were awarded to various safari companies for a 20-year period, starting in the year 2000, on the condition that camps should in no way disturb the environment. This is why most camps are raised off the ground. Competition for these tenders was understandably stiff, and the operators chosen all come with experience, utilizing the best in the business to establish these camps. The standard of accommodation at most concession lodges is comparable to their luxurious counterparts in Sabi Sands and other top private reserves adjoining the national park (see "Private Game Reserves," later in this chapter), and the lodges are run in a similar manner, offering game drives in open vehicles and, in some cases, guided walks within the concession.

In keeping with the service offered by the private reserves, guides within most of these concessions can theoretically drive off-road to track or view animals from a close-up perspective, but the strict procedures imposed by Kruger authorities severely limit the number of sightings where this is permitted. Also, the animals are not always as acclimatized to vehicles as those in the private reserves. As a result, the Kruger concessions tend to offer rather erratic game-viewing and do not promise the almost guaranteed full house of Big 5 sightings associated with Sabi Sands, which makes them less suitable to the typical first-time safarigoer. On the plus side, the Kruger concessions tend to have more of a wilderness feel, and game drives are less frantically oriented toward chasing the Big 5. Guides tend to concentrate on whatever animals they might chance upon, rather than following radio alerts to other vehicles' sightings. As such, the ideal combination, budget permitting, would be to follow a few days of intensive Big 5 game-viewing in Sabi Sands (or another private reserve) with a more chilled sojourn at one of the Kruger concessions.

Which concession? Broadly, the best in terms of overall lodge/wildlife experience is (unsurprisingly) Singita, but it is priced accordingly. Your experience could be compromised by the rains, which means you can't go off-road or, in some cases, even use internal game-viewing roads. We rate Rhino highly for the general experience (though it's more foot orientated) and Shishangani/Shawu/Shonga (SSS), Lukimbi, and Imbali for wildlife. SSS is especially good for rhino, Lukimbi for lion, Imbali for lion and cheetah. In addition to the top concessions reviewed below, another option is the upscale **Tinga Private Game Lodge** (✆ **013/735-8400** or 0861/505-050; www.africanpridehotels.com/tinga), which operates two luxury lodges: Narina and Legends, both in the vicinity of Skukuza. Grand without being overly decadent, it aims high with colonial styling; each has a private lounge, a large bathroom with double showers, and its own heated plunge pool. It's pricey (from R8,000 double), but good deals are frequently found on the Internet. The most singular of the Kruger concessions, set in the far north, is **Makuleke Contractual Park,** which comprises the 23,600-hectare (58,292-acre) wedge of land between the Luvuvhu and Limpopo River. This area was incorporated into Kruger in 1969, when its 1,500 Makuleke residents were forcibly evicted at the hands of the apartheid government. In 1998, the Makulele people won the first land claim in Kruger, but instead of resettling the land that was returned to them, they opted to develop it for tourism and contract game management to the national park. Today two private lodges (Pafuri Camp and The Outpost; see below) lie within the concession, and local people contribute to the daily running of both, a landmark exercise in sustainable development. Also known as the Pafuri Triangle, Makulele has the highest biodiversity of any part in the Kruger, with more than 75% of the park's species occurring in just 1% of its surface area, it's the one part of the park with a truly tropical ecology. The area is legendary among South

African birdwatchers for the presence of several rarities, including Pel's fishing owl, racket-tailed roller, crested guinea-fowl, and triple-banded courser. It is also noted for several nonwildlife landmarks, notably the lush yellow fever forest running toward Crooks Corner near the confluence of the two rivers, the spectacular Lanner Gorge, and the 16th-century Thulamela Heritage Site. However, general game-viewing in Makulele can be rather slow and large predators are scarce, making it more attractive to dedicated wilderness enthusiasts and birdwatchers than to safari neophytes.

Hamiltons 1880 Tented Camp ★★ This traditional luxury tent camp has a rather Edwardian feel, but the comfort level is a far cry from the days of Hemingway and Blixen. All units contain bedside lamps, king-size four-poster beds, crisp white linen, flushing toilets, outdoor showers, and slipper tubs with hot and cold running water, yet they still offer a sense of authenticity and close communion with the bush. It is the most upscale of three camps in the 10,000-hectare (24,700) Imbali concession, which lies in the game-rich acacia woodland between Skukuza and Satara, an area renowned for its dense populations of lions and other large predators. Set in lush riparian woodland along the seasonal Nwatsitsonto River, it comprises six luxury en-suite tents, all set on stilts with wooden floors, private viewing decks, and an outside shower with river view. Tents are privately situated and linked via raised timber walkways to the open tented lounge and dining room and pool. Hamilton's size makes it an ideal camp for anyone wanting to escape the rat race. The nearest gate for access to Hamilton's is Orpen, 50km (31 miles) away.

Booking office in U.S.: ✆ **858/350-1354.** In S.A.: ✆ **0861/000-333** or 013/735-8915/7 direct. www.threecities.co.za. 6 units. R7,980–10,820 double, including meals and activities. AE, DC, MC, V. No children under 8. **Amenities:** Dining/bar area; boma; bush walks; butler/room service; game drives; pool. *In room:* A/C, fans.

Imbali Safari Camp ★★ The largest of the three camps on the eponymous concession, Imbali consists of 12 large thatched cottages lining a seasonal watercourse that attracts plenty of mammals and birdlife. The accommodation has a more permanent feel and is less overtly "bush" than most safari camps—indeed, when the curtains are drawn at night, you could be in a plush city hotel—making it a good option for nervous first-time safari-goers. All rooms have king-size beds with walk-in netting, a wooden game-viewing deck with a built-in Jacuzzi, and comfortable sitting areas whose old-fashioned decor seems pitched to those with relatively conservative tastes. Whatever else, Imbali is one of the top concessions in terms of pure game-viewing, offering a better chance than most of seeing all the Big 5 over the course of 2 to 3 days, and a good reputation for cheetah and wild dog sightings. The nearest gate is Orpen, 50km (31 miles) away.

Booking office in U.S.: ✆ **858/350-1354.** In S.A.: ✆ **0861/000-333** or 013/735-8915/7 direct. www.threecities.co.za. 12 units. R6,980–9,460 double, including meals and activities. AE, DC, MC, V. **Amenities:** Dining/bar area; bush walks; game drives; pool. *In room:* A/C, fans.

Jock Safari Lodge ★★ The first private lodge to open within the national park (Dec 2001), this lodge has carved a name for itself as a warm, convivial camp, elegant and tasteful, yet without pretensions of grandeur. The large thatched bungalows, situated for maximum privacy, each feature great bushveld views, tasteful furnishings, and large bathrooms with tubs and indoor as well as outdoor showers; each unit has its own *sala* (shaded outdoor pavilion) overlooking the river, and there are fireplaces for winter. The lodge is in the south, at the confluence of the Mitomeni and Biyamiti rivers, where herds of antelope and elephant gather to cool off or quench their thirst. At 6,000 hectares (14,820 acres), this is Kruger's smallest concession, but given the density of game, you don't need to travel far to start ticking off species. If you're looking for a more secluded experience, book one of the new suites at Little Jock Lodge; it's a mere kilometer (half a mile) away, but with only three suites, it's a great deal more exclusive. Honeymooners should book room no. 1; families opt for room nos. 2 and 3, which are right next to each other. Little Jock shares a communal pool and has its own staff, including chef and ranger; the only reason to go to the main camp would be for the Internet or spa treatments.

P.O. Box 781, Malelane 1320 ✆ **041/407-1000.** Fax 041/407-1001. www.jocksafarilodge.com. 12 units. R7,000–9,0000 double. Rate is all-inclusive except for imported wines and spirits. Children under 12, accommodated by prior arrangement only, pay 50%. AE, DC, MC, V. **Amenities:** Dining area; bar; babysitting; boma; bush walks; game drives; Internet; pool; room service; shop; valet (on request); wellness center. *In room:* A/C, hair dryer, minibar.

Lukimbi Safari Lodge ★★ Situated in the far south of the park, this stylish lodge, 25km (16 miles) from Malelane Gate, has an attractive location overlooking a permanent pool on the seasonal Lwakhale River. It enjoys exclusive traversing rights across a 15,000-hectare (37,050-acre) area that supports good populations of lion, elephant, black and white rhino, and the occasional wild dog. The terrain is more suited to off-road driving than most concessions. The superb split-level dining and sitting area is decorated in African style and overlooks the riverbed and animals that come to drink there. The spacious and earthily decorated rooms are spread widely along the riverbed for privacy and reached via a raised wooden walkway where the wildlife can pass under unimpeded. Despite the excellent game-viewing, Lukimbi doesn't feel as exclusive as comparably priced concession lodges, and thus seems a little overpriced.

P.O. Box 2617, Northcliff, 2115. ✆ **011/431-1120** or 013/635-8000 direct. www.lukimbi.com. 16 units. R8,300–10,300 double, all-inclusive. Discounted rate for children under 12. AE, DC, MC, V. **Amenities:** Dining room; bar; bush walks; DVD library; game drives; free Internet; library; pool; satellite TV; wine cellar. *In room:* A/C, minibar.

The Outpost ★★★ The Outpost is a superlative ultramodern designer lodge set atop a hill in the Makuleke Contractual Park, the most untouched region of northern Kruger, a good 120km (74 miles) from the nearest town. Cantilevered out of a rocky mountainside, it weds chic minimalist design with unimpeded nature. The 12 en-suite guest "spaces" ("rooms" would be misleading), designed by Italian-born architect Enrico Daffonchio, are constructed of steel, canvas, and aluminum, and are completely open to the elements except for the rock face they appear to grow out of. The unparalleled views of the Luvuvhu floodplain—a richly textured terrain of ancient baobabs, thorny acacias, and lush palms—are spectacular. For the ultimate view, reserve "space 12." The only drawback is the relative remoteness of the lodge, as well as the fact that, despite the amazing biodiversity, certain species (leopard) are less easily spotted than in the more crowded southern Kruger. The Outpost may also strike some as a little cold or too trendy for a bush experience; if you prefer a more old-fashioned approach to the safari experience, nearby Pafuri Camp is a better bet.

P.O. Box 786064, Sandton 2146. ✆ **011/245-5704.** www.theoutpost.co.za. 12 units. R5,600-8,000 double, all-inclusive. Check website for special offers. No children under 10. AE, DC, MC, V. **Amenities:** Dining room; bar; bush walks; game drives; library; pool; wine cellar. *In room:* A/C, minibar.

Pafuri Camp ★★ Value Managed by Wilderness Safaris, southern Africa's most influential safari operator, this archetypal bush camp has an unpretentious atmosphere and a magnificent location on the forested banks of the Luvuvhu River. Accommodation is in luxury standing tents with secluded river views, connected by a 2km-long (11.4-mile)

Rhinos in the Greater Kruger

Over recent decades, Kruger Park has emerged as one of the world's most important rhino sanctuaries. Ironically, however, these lumbering beasts had been hunted to extinction within the park by 1945. The present-day populations descend from animals reintroduced from Hluhluwe-Imfolozi Game Reserve, and as recently as the early 1980s, the rhino was probably the most elusive of the Big 5 in Kruger.

The first 100 white rhinos were reintroduced to southern Kruger in the late 1960s. For many years, the slowly growing population stayed rooted in the south, particularly around Crocodile Bridge. As numbers increased, however, the rhinos gradually colonized the central and northern parts of the park, as well as the adjacent private reserve, and today the greater Kruger is estimated to hold between 6,000 and 8,000 white rhino, or some 35% to 40% of the global total. The Kruger has thus been instrumental in the white rhino's IUCN Red List status rising from Endangered to Near-threatened over the past 2 decades.

Kruger also supports a population of around 300 black rhinos, descendents of the fewer than 100 individuals reintroduced between 1971 and 1998. This represents between 5% and 10% of the global black rhino population, but even so, sightings are rather scarce, with the area around Pretoriuskop and Crocodile Bridge offering the best chance of a glimpse of this thicket-loving creature. Scientists believe the park could accommodate a further 2,500 black rhino, so there is plenty of room for this endangered species to emulate the population growth of its white cousin in decades to come.

The situation with Kruger's rhinos isn't all rosy, however, as highlighted by reports that the number of rhinos poached within the park increased from 10 individuals in 2007 to 37 in 2008. Given the rapid population growth of the park's rhinos in recent years, this is scarcely cause for major alarm; nevertheless, it represents the most significant bout of rhino poaching in South Africa since the 1980s. Police believe the poaching to be the work of one single cartel that sells rhino horns to Asia (where they're valued as an aphrodisiac) for around $2,000 apiece. It remains to be seen whether the March 2009 arrest of 11 suspects—including 5 Mozambicans, 3 Chinese, and 2 South Africans—will put an end to the poaching.

raised wooden boardwalk that affords great birding opportunities and allows game—especially the lovely nyala antelope—to wander through unimpeded. It is the only other camp, besides The Outpost, in the vast Makuleke Contractual Park, so you feel—and are—surrounded by a vast tract of wilderness. It is a little off the beaten track, but it ranks among the most affordable concession lodges in the Kruger and makes a good add-on to a Wilderness itinerary to Namibia or Botswana, where this company dominates.

P.O. Box 5219, Rivonia, 2128, South Africa. ✆ **011/257-5111.** www.pafuri.com. 20 units. R5,700 double, all-inclusive. AE, DC, MC, V. **Amenities:** Dining room; bar; bush walks; game drives; library; 2 pools; river safaris; wine cellar.

Rhino Walking Safaris ★★ Value This award-winning private concession shares a border with MalaMala Game Reserve, renowned for its lush vegetation and the density of its game, particularly leopard. Although the area is a massive 12,000 hectares (29,640 acres), it is a restricted wilderness concession, meaning that off-road game drives are not allowed. Instead, the focus is on game walks and luxury sleep-outs, which are a welcome break from the monotony of most other safari lodge schedules. There are two small lodges: **Rhino Post,** which plans to give visitors a choice between game walks and drives as of late 2009, and the exclusive four-unit tented **Plains Camp,** where you'd better be prepared for a cumulative 4 to 5 hours of bush walking per day. Guests also have the opportunity to overnight at the camp's "sleep-out digs" deep in the bush (70 min. on foot from Plains Camp), where tents have been erected on decks high up on stilts at a watering hole. You need carry only a few clothes and toiletries; all other necessities are provided. Back at Rhino Post, accommodations are neat and functional. Set on raised wooden decks with private terraces overlooking the Mutlemuve River, the thatched guest rooms have canvas walls that allow the sounds of the bush to penetrate at night; bathrooms feature tubs, double basins, and an outdoor shower. Public areas are elegant and simple, with wood and packed-stone walls, and an inviting glass-walled wine cellar.

Reservations: P.O. Box 1881, Jukskei Park 2153. ✆ **011/467-1886.** www.isibindi.co.za. Rhino Post 8 units. R4,380–5,180 double. Plains Camp 4 units. R4,730–5,440 double. Packages and online specials available. AE, DC, MC, V. No children under 12 at Plains Camp or on bush walks. Children under 12 pay 50% if sharing. **Amenities:** Dining area; bar; bush walks; curio shop; game drives; gym; library; pool; wine cellar. *In room:* Hair dryer, minibar.

Shawu Camp ★★ Value Finds Set in the extreme southeast of Kruger, bordering Mozambique and the Crocodile River, Shishangani is the largest of three lodges set in a 15,000-hectare (37,500-acre) concession in prime game-viewing territory. The main lodge caters mostly to groups and was looking slightly rundown in 2009, but it's likely to change following a recent management takeover by the well-organized Three Cities hotel chain. In our estimation, the relatively low rates and superb game-viewing more than compensate. There's no better place in Kruger for rhino sightings, and lion, elephant, and buffalo are all regular, while leopard and cheetah are rather less so. Far nicer than the main lodge and not significantly more expensive, Camp Shawu and Camp Shonga are both intimate luxury tented camps (five units apiece) that share the same concession. **Camp Shonga** has an attractive location below the Lebombo Mountains, but **Shawu** has arguably the best setting of any lodge in the Kruger concessions, on the shore of a dam that supports a resident pod of hippos and prolific birdlife, regularly visited by rhinos, lions, and elephants.

Booking office in U.S.: ✆ **858/350-1354.** In S.A.: ✆ **0861/000-333** or 013/735-3300 direct. www.threecities.co.za. 22 units at Shishangani; 5 each at Camp Shawu and Shonga. R4,900-6,160 double, including meals and activities. AE, DC, MC, V. **Amenities:** Dining/bar area; bush walks; game drives; Internet (fee); pool. *In room:* A/C, fans.

Singita Lebombo & Sweni ★★★ When Lebombo opened in 2003, it immediately became the last word in designer safari experiences, chalking up numerous awards while gracing its way into the pages of chic magazines and coffee-table tomes. A year later, Lebombo received a smaller neighbor: **Sweni,** named for the beautiful river over which its six fabulous suites look. Both lodges feature the best in modern design: Dramatic wraparound glass walls and massive glass sliding doors open onto outdoor showers and private balconies where you can sleep out in summer. Constructed of saligna wood, raised on stilts, and laid out in a tasteful open plan, with enormous room-dividing curtains and sapling ceilings, this is the most stylish camp in Africa, featuring home-grown modern designs created by local craftspeople working in concert with funky young designers—and infused with retro-modernity. The whole effect is more Afro-Euro chic boutique hotel than game lodge, and there's an emphasis on fun and relaxation. Rooms are stocked with board games and treats to occupy you between meals (which are superb, and accompanied by a top-notch selection of Cape wines). Lebombo is lighter, brighter, and quite dramatic in its proportions, while Sweni is more intimate and has a more homey atmosphere and additional touches that improve on Lebombo's original design (Sweni's suite no. 5 is a personal favorite, while at Lebombo you should ask for a suite close to the river, for maximum privacy). Between Lebombo and Sweni is Singita's unique "Village," comprising a spa, a state-of-the-art gymnasium, wine-tasting facilities, and some great shopping. Yet despite the experimental design and unashamedly urban overtures, the bush is always close at hand: Situated in a 15,000-hectare (37,050-acre) concession bordered by Mozambique, the camp is elevated on a sheer cliff, with views of the Lebombo Mountains and surrounding bushveld plains. Game-viewing is possibly the best of any of the Kruger concessions, with the added bonus that off-road driving is seldom a problem.

P.O. Box 23367, Claremont 7735. ✆ **021/683-3424** or 013/735-5500 direct. Fax 021/671-6776. www.singita.co.za. Sweni 6 units. Lebombo 15 units. R19,900 double all-inclusive (except French champagne and spa treatments). No seasonal discounts. AE, DC, MC, V. Children over 10 only. **Amenities:** Each lodge has dining areas; bar; lounges; boma; bush walks; game drives; Internet; library; pool; room service; wine cellar. (The Village: art gallery; craft and gift stores; gym; spa; wine-tasting venue.) *In room:* A/C, hair dryer, minibar.

5 PRIVATE GAME RESERVES FLANKING KRUGER

Flanking the western section of Kruger Park and covering over 150,000 hectares (370,500 acres) are South Africa's most famous private game reserves, owned by groups of freehold landowners and concession-holders with traversing rights. Because most of the fences that separated the private reserves from Kruger have been taken down, animals are, to some extent, able to follow natural migratory routes, and you will find as many species in these reserves as you will in Kruger. Unless you're staying at a luxury lodge in a private concession, that is where the similarity ends.

The difference between a visit to a Kruger Park rest camp and a private lodge is so big as to be almost incomparable. Not only do the luxurious accommodations afford supreme privacy and luxury, with unfenced accommodations that make the most of the bushveld surrounds, but visitors are taken in open-topped and elevated Land Rovers to within spitting distance of animals by Shangaan trackers and armed rangers, who give a running commentary on anything from the mating habits of giraffe to the family history of a particular lion. Animals in these reserves, particularly Sabi Sand, are so used to being approached by vehicles that they almost totally ignore them. You can trail a leopard at a few feet without it so much as glancing backward. Two-way radios between rangers, many of whom are allowed to traverse on each other's land, ensure good sightings, although these can be somewhat marred when three or sometimes four vehicles (the maximum lodges allow) converge on the same spot.

Warning! Wish You Were Here

It's 5am. The phone rings. It's the lodge manager. He politely asks how you slept, then requests that you not leave your room as planned. There has been a leopard kill meters from your chalet. He apologizes for the inconvenience and informs you that an armed ranger will be along shortly to escort you to the dining room for coffee before you depart on your early-morning game drive. This seldom happens, but every so often it does. Lodges in private reserves are not fenced off from predators, so you are advised to exercise extreme caution—under no circumstances are guests of any age to walk about unaccompanied after dark.

The 2- to 4-hour game drives take place in the morning and again in the late afternoon and evening, with stops in the bush for a hot drink and snack in the morning (particularly in winter) and cocktails in the evening. It can be bitterly cold in the winter, and you may want to opt instead for an escorted walk after breakfast—another service included in the rate.

In addition to pursuing animals off-road through the African bush, these private reserves offer unfenced accommodations of luxuriously high standards. Equally high-end is the cuisine. As all meals are included in the rate, this is certainly not the time to go on a diet. Breakfasts feature a selection of cereals and fresh fruit, yogurt, and freshly baked bread and muffins. Hot breakfasts are cooked to order and usually comprise eggs, sausage, bacon, and tomato, or omelets. A few lodges offer such variations as eggs Benedict or eggs Florentine. Lunch is the lightest meal, usually a buffet with interesting salads and predictable cold meats. Breakfasts are served late (after the morning game drive, which usually ends btw. 9 and 10am), so some lodges prefer to skip lunch altogether and serve a high tea at 3pm, with quiches, sandwiches, and cakes. From there, you depart on a 3- to 4-hour evening game drive, traveling with a spotlight once it's dark, tracking nocturnal creatures on the move. You will more than likely be expected to dine with your game-drive companions (if this is a problem, alert the staff in advance, and alternative arrangements will be made). Dinners feature grilled or roasted meat, giving visitors an opportunity to taste at least one species spotted earlier that day—kudu, springbok, impala, and warthog are particularly popular. Lodges cater to dietary requirements but require advance warning, as supplies take time to arrive in the bush. If you're a vegetarian or keep kosher, notify the lodges prior to your arrival. Almost every lodge rotates dinners from their dining room to the ever-popular open-air *boma* (an open-air enclosure lit with a large fire), and some even offer surprise bush dinners, with a game drive concluding at a serene spot where tables have been set up under trees or in a riverbed.

The drawback to all this? A hefty price tag. If you've come to South Africa 0to see big game, however, it's definitely worth delving a little deeper into your savings and spending at least 2 nights in a private game reserve, preferably 3. Prices (which are often quoted in U.S. dollars and include all meals, game drives, bush walks, and most of your bar bill) do vary considerably (from season to season, for example), and it is possible to find more affordable options, the best of which are described below. Alternatively, some of the private concessions within Kruger—notably Rhino Walking Safaris and Shishangani—offer a near-comparable wildlife experience at a far lower price (see "Private Concessions Within Kruger," above).

Note: If you're self-driving, you'll pay an admission fee at the entrance gates of some of the private reserves. Not all accept credit cards, so carry cash. The fee at Timbavati, for example, is R80 per car and R100 per adult entering the reserve; Sabi Sand is R80 per vehicle. You may also have to pay a small fee at the lodge.

GETTING THERE

The closest international airport is in Johannesburg, from where it's a 5- to 7-hour drive to this region, depending on which route you choose (see the Panorama, Lowveld, and Letaba routes, earlier in this chapter). Alternatively, you can fly directly from Johannesburg, Cape Town, or Durban—see "Essentials" under "Kruger National Park," earlier in this chapter. All camps and lodges will organize pickups from any of these airports, as well as arrange transfers by air or land to or from competitors.

WHERE TO STAY & DINE

Increasingly, visitors to Africa's safari meccas are placing a premium on sophisticated luxury and designer bush experiences that enhance the traditional game-viewing phenomenon; you can expect to find some of the finest lodges in the world in the private lodges within and abutting Kruger. Because lodges and camps need adequate warning to stock up on fresh produce (remember, all meals are included in the rates below), transfers need to be prearranged; special dietary requirements also need to be sorted well in advance. And because many are extremely popular, booking ahead is essential. Although winter is the best time to view game, many lodges experience a seasonal drop-off and reduce prices from May to August—some by as much as 50%.

In Sabi Sand

Arathusa Safari Lodge (Value) The closest thing to a genuine budget bargain in Sabi Sands, this little-known 20-person lodge opened in 2006 in the far north of the reserve, bordering Djuma and accessed via the same Gowrie Gate. As might be expected, it's an unpretentious set-up offering accommodation in thatched double or twin bungalows with en-suite bathrooms and outdoor showers, and a veranda with a view over a lake that attracts plenty of wildlife, especially in the dry season. The buffet meals are hearty and down-to-earth in what the hands-on owners describe as *ma se kombuis* ("mother's kitchen") style. It may be relatively inexpensive, but the game-viewing is typical of Sabi Sands, and the odds of spotting all the Big 5—and much more besides—over the course of a 2- to 3-day stay is excellent.

P.O. Box 8034 White River 1240. ✆ **011/431-3852** or 013/735-5363 direct. www.arathusa.co.za. 10 units. R3,800–R4,200 double, depending on season. Rates include all meals and game drives/bush walks. AE, DC, MC, V. **Amenities:** Dining room; bar/lounge area; boma; bush walks; game drives; high-speed Internet; pool. *In room:* A/C, minibar.

Djuma ★★ (Value) Like many of the lodges in Sabi Sand, Djuma actually comprises three separate camps: **Galago,** a self-catering single-unit lodge; **Bush Lodge;** and **Vuyatela,** the flagship. Pricier than its good-value counterparts, Vuyatela is also the youngest of the properties, comprising eight thatched chalets, each with a generous bedroom, dressing room and bathroom, separate lounge, and large private deck with small plunge pool and shower. Djuma has access to more than 9,000 hectares (22,230 acres), 7,000 (17,290) of which it owns, making it one of the largest landowners in the Sabi Sand Reserve. As Djuma can be accessed only via the northerly Gowrie Gate, reached via 55km (34 miles) of harrowing dirt road, you should definitely consider flying in on the Djuma Shuttle, a fly-in package arranged through the lodge. Family-managed until late

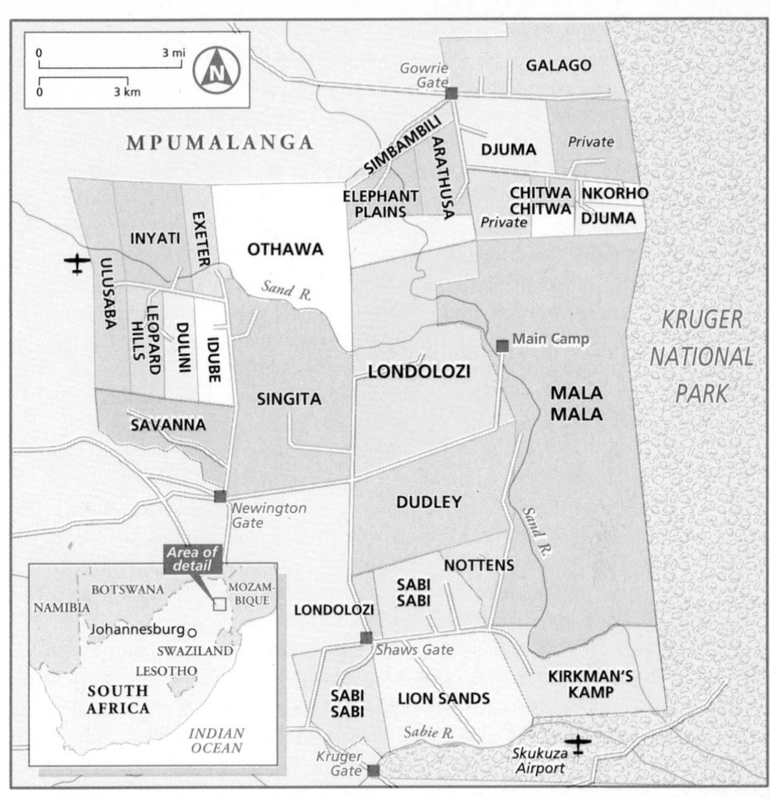

2008, Djuma is proudly Fair Trade accredited. Management has since been taken over by Seasons in Africa (which also operates Leopard Hills), and extensive renovations are underway at the time of writing.

P.O. Box 8034 White River 1240. ✆ **013/750-2358.** Fax 013/750-2364. www.djuma.co.za. Vuyatela 8 units. Bush Lodge 8 units. Galago 5 units. High season Vuyatela R10,000 double; Bush Lodge R6,600 double. Rates include all meals and drinks, and game drives/bush walks. Galago R8,000 for entire camp sleeping up to 10, including game drives but not meals. Children under 12 pay 50%. AE, DC, MC, V. **Amenities:** Dining room; bar/lounge area; aquarium; boma; bush walks; game drives; gym; high-speed Internet; massage (in Vuyatela); pool; room service. *In room:* A/C, hair dryer, minibar (in Vuyatela).

Exeter ★★ Argentine owner Stephen Saad transformed the three lodges in the Exeter stable (**River Lodge ★**, **Dulini ★**, and **Leadwood Lodge ★★**) into high-end, design-conscious, Afro-chic hideaways, then handed over management to the very capable &Beyond (formerly CC Africa), one of the top safari outfits in Africa. River Lodge offers eight suites and is the closest to a bush experience, but this does not mean you'll have to forgo private plunge pools, inside and outside showers, and luxurious living quarters. Large glass walls and huge screened doors look out onto views of the river. Shades of ocher and clay, taupe, and teak bring a slick, sophisticated look to the huge double-volume

Tips Choosing Your Private Reserve

Besides the new concessions within the Kruger, you'll need to consider the three major private reserves that border one another and Kruger's southern and central section. They are, from south to north, **Sabi Sand, Manyeleti,** and **Timbavati.** None of these reserves is fenced off from the others or Kruger, which allows a seamless migration of animals through an area roughly the size of Massachusetts—and growing bigger every year. Each of these three reserves features the **Big 5 (lions, leopards, elephants, rhinos, and buffaloes),** as does **Thornybush,** a relatively small reserve almost surrounded by Timbavati, but currently still fenced. Another private reserve in the region worth considering is **Makalali,** a large buffalo-free reserve that lies within striking distance of Kruger's central Phalaborwa Gate. For more private reserves and lodges, see chapters 6, 7, 8, 9, 10, 11, and 12. To make an informed decision about which reserve to visit, read the brief summaries on each of the reserves below, and see chapter 3.

Each private reserve usually has a number of luxury lodges or camps that share traversing rights on land, thereby increasing the range of their vehicles. Many also report major sightings to the other reserves. In fact, with a cumulative 6 hours of every day spent tracking game, you will almost certainly see four of the Big 5 (except leopards) during a 3-night stay. Bear in mind that you will enjoy yourself a great deal more (and irritate your ranger less) if you spread your focus to include an interest in the myriad species that make up life in the bush.

Sabi Sand ★★★, a 66,000-hectare (163,020-acre) reserve that encompasses the southern lowveld, is the most game-rich area in the country, and most guests leave having sighted all of the Big 5. It's hardly surprising, then, that this has become known as the continent's most exclusive reserve, with the largest number of luxury camps, including such legendary properties as MalaMala, Londolozi, and Singita. Not only does Singita offer top-notch game-viewing, but it is also regularly voted Best Destination/Hotel in the World/Africa, a distinction it has earned every year since opening. Singita's standards of service and sophisticated accommodations are incomparable, and your guides will be attentive and knowledgeable.

During the apartheid era, when black people were not allowed to vacation in Kruger, **Manyeleti** ★—the region just north of Sabi Sand—was considered "their" reserve, and a visit to the original Manyeleti Rest Camp makes the most basic Kruger camp look like a luxury option. Officially, it's actually still a poorly run 23,000-hectare (56,810-acre) public reserve (administered by the Limpopo provincial government), within which private companies operate a few key concessions. Its border with Kruger Park is unfenced, so animals can roam freely between the reserves. While other lodges—such as the luxurious **Tintswalo** ★ (✆ **011/464-1208** or 015/793-9013; www.tintswalo.co.za)—have opened their doors in the Manyeleti, the rates are comparable to Sabi Sands. Hence, the good-value **Honeyguide** (reviewed below) remains the recommended choice, particularly if you're keen on a more authentic bush experience. (Note that operators in Manyeleti are restricted in the areas in which they may drive off-road in pursuit of game.)

Timbavati ★★, the 65,000-hectare (160,500-acre) reserve alongside Kruger's central section, offers a comparable game experience to the much-vaunted Sabi Sand, but the vegetation is less arresting, and rhinos are relatively scarce. Animals are almost as habituated to vehicles here as at Sabi Sand, and you can get within a few feet of large predators. The main reason to choose Timbavati over Sabi Sand is that it has far fewer camps and fewer people, and the rates are generally friendlier—particularly at Umlani, one of the most authentic bush experiences in the area.

Bordered in the north and west by Timbavati, the 14,000-hectare (34,580-acre) **Thornybush** ★★ game reserve is currently still a fenced reserve, thereby curtailing animal migration. It boasts a high percentage of lions, but the thicket-type vegetation is not always as conducive to sightings of varied species. The best reason to choose this reserve is **Royal Malewane,** a lodge that offers unbelievably luxurious accommodations and superb style; suites are on par with Singita, but at a slightly reduced price.

Kapama is an "island" Big 5 reserve. As such, it's entirely fenced and included predominantly for those interested in an elephant-back safari. The growth in this kind of safari has not been without controversy, as human-habituated elephants require extensive feeding and sensitive care, and should not be sourced just to feed the tourist interest in riding them. That's why we recommend Kapama's **Camp Jabulani,** a winner in the Leading Eco Retreat category in 2008. In addition to Jabulani, an orphaned elephant calf that owner Lente Roode nursed back to health, there are 12 Zimbabwean elephants that were tagged for their meat by war veterans before Roode came to their rescue.

If you're not hung up on the Big 5, consider the **Makalali** ★ conservancy. Farther north, cut off from Kruger, it extends over 10,000 hectares (24,700 acres) and has lions, leopards, rhinos, and elephants. For some, the absence of buffaloes (due to foot-and-mouth regulations) is not a great loss—they provide as much viewing excitement as a herd of cows. The area is also of geological interest, with quartz rock crystals strewn throughout the area.

Note: Visitors with limited time or those unwilling to risk malaria may want to consider the 40,000-hectare (98,800-acre) **Welgevonden** ★★ and 35,382-hectare (87,394-acre) **Lapalala** reserves, only a 3-hour drive north of Johannesburg (see chapter 8). If you are planning a second visit to South Africa or are keen on combining a visit to one of the above reserves with one that has a totally contrasting biome, the other Big 5 private reserves worth considering are **Madikwe** ★★★, which covers more biomes than Kruger, with a greater variety of species, and **Tswalu Kalahari Reserve** ★★, a beautiful desert reserve and the largest private reserve in southern Africa (see chapter 8). KwaZulu-Natal's Big 5 reserves include **Phinda** ★ and **Mkuze Falls** ★, with subtropical vegetation and abundant birdlife (see chapter 9). Don't miss the reserves in Botswana's **Okavango Delta** ★★★—the "original Eden" (see chapter 12).

Tips Kidding Around

Bear in mind that many camps and lodges do not welcome children; over and above a concern for other guests' peace is the belief that the bush holds too many inherent dangers, not least of which is the ever-present threat of malaria (see "Fast Facts: Kruger National Park," earlier in this chapter). Even if they are allowed, young children may not go on game drives or dine in the outdoor boma, and you will have to sign an additional indemnity form. Two private Kruger lodgings that actively encourage children, with separate child-friendly programs, are **Londolozi** and Makalali (see later in this chapter).

lounges. Dining areas are huge, magnificent open-sided rooms with views of the nearby Sand River—a beautiful place to drink and dine. A more romantic option is Dulini, which has only six guest suites. But for the most exclusive privacy—at the same rate—book one of the four huge Leadwood suites, in stone "cottages" with fireplaces. Each lodge has its own staff complement and public spaces.

&Beyond, Private Bag X27, Benmore 2010. ✆ **011/809-4300.** Fax 011/809-4400. www.andbeyondafrica.com. 18 units. High season R12,660 double; low season R8,400 double. Rates include all meals, game drives, and bush walks. AE, DC, MC, V. **Amenities:** Dining room; bar; boma; bush walks; game drives; gym; pool; wine cellar (in Leadwood). *In room:* A/C, hair dryer, minibar.

Idube Camp *(Value)* Set in the western Sabi Sands, where it shares traversing rights with the more prestigious likes of Ulusaba and Leopard Hill, Idube stands out mainly for offering good value and friendly service rather than state-of-the-art interior decor and haute cuisine. The lushly wooded grounds, inhabited by semitame families of warthog and nyala, are more notable than the accommodation, which is in functional but comfortable brick-face cottages with private decks, en-suite bathrooms, and outdoor showers. There's a welcoming swimming pool tucked into the rocks, and a wooden boardwalk leads across a seasonal river to a well-positioned photographic hide on a large dam that attracts loads of wildlife. Game-viewing is to the usual high standards, and the buffet lunches and boma dinners are tasty and filling.

P.O. Box 2617, Northcliff, 2115. ✆ **011/431-1120.** www.idube.com. 10 units. R5,000–7,000 double, including meals and activities. Discounted rate for children under 12. AE, DC, MC, V. **Amenities:** Dining area; bar; lounge; boma; bush walks; game drives; photographic hide; pool; satellite TV. *In room:* A/C, hair dryer.

Kirkman's Camp ★ This was always my favorite MalaMala camp; now that &Beyond (formerly CC Africa) has taken over the management, it's all the more delightful. Originally established in the 1920s, it retains a strong colonial flavor—very different from the majority of rather modern luxurious safari lodges in the vicinity. It's not the most intimate choice (18 cottages), but the entire camp was renovated and refurbished in 2006; if you're into nostalgia, then this graceful homage to an early South African lowveld homestead is for you. Each of the cottages has a private veranda and is furnished in the same colonial style as the original homestead (now home to the lounge bar and dining areas), with interesting pieces and sumptuous yet understated fabrics. The large sitting room, dressed in a 1920s ambience, leads through double French doors onto rolling lawns that provide a velvety contrast to the wild and tumbling bush surrounding the lodge. Breakfast and lunch are served on shady verandas, and dinners are shared in the boma or in a lantern-lit bush setting.

&Beyond, Private Bag X27, Benmore 2010. ✆ **011/809-4300.** Fax 011/809-4400. www.andbeyondafrica.com. 18 units. R7,200–R9,810 double, including all meals and game activities. AE, DC, MC, V. Children allowed with prior arrangement. **Amenities:** Dining area; bar; boma; bush walks; game drives; high-speed Internet; lounge; pool; room service; spa treatments. *In room:* A/C, hair dryer.

Leopard Hills ★★ Like Exeter and Ulusaba (Virgin billionaire Richard Branson's neighboring lodge), Leopard Hills traverses the Western sector of the Sabi Sand, with excellent game-viewing. It's one of the classiest joints in the region, and one of the area's most elevated lodges, set on a ridge with views of the African bush savanna that go on forever. You can enjoy these views from the public areas as well as from five of the well-proportioned suites (specify an elevated suite with savanna views), which are tasteful and generous, with wraparound glass frontages opening onto private sun decks, each with its own plunge pool. The muted cream, white, tan, and brown African-themed decor is executed with a mixture of rough untreated timber, bamboo, concrete, sisal, and leopard-print fabric, used sparingly. A fully stocked wine cellar, fine cuisine, and very well-maintained library with a cozy fireplace and more fabulous views complete the picture. Leopard Hills has access to around 10,000 hectares (24,700 acres), which it shares with several other lodges; as a result, this sector sees a fair amount of traffic, but sightings are limited to a maximum of three vehicles. There is also a spa *sala,* where you can relish the view while receiving treatments.

P.O. Box 612, Hazyview 1242. ✆ **013/737-6626.** Fax 013/737-6628. www.leopardhills.com. 8 units. R14,400 double. AE, DC, MC, V. Children stay on request. **Amenities:** Dining area; bar; lounge; boma; bush walks; game drives; gym; high-speed Internet; library w/TV and DVD/VCR/CD players; pool; room service; spa treatments. *In room:* A/C, hair dryer, minibar.

Lion Sands Ivory Lodge ★★ With only 3,500 hectares (8,645 acres) of prime game country to itself, you might expect Lion Sands to be slim on sightings. But given the fact that no fences separate it from neighboring Kruger (the Skukuza airstrip is just 20 min. away) and accommodations overlook the Sabi River, **Ivory Lodge**—listed third best hotel in the world by *Tatler* Magazine in 2006—turns out to be an ideal place to watch animals while you cool off in your very own rim-flow plunge pool or have a closer look with the telescope on your private terrace. The ultrachic guest suites, housed in thatched chalets, are decorated according to a strict ebony-and-ivory theme. An extensive bathroom, with an egg-shaped stone tub and an outdoor shower in its own garden, adds to the sense of luxury. Privacy is key; morning tea is delivered through a service hatch, and spa treatments are taken in-room. In fact, you need never leave your suite at all, even at mealtimes (reserve the Peregrine suite for ultimate privacy). Such exclusivity comes at a price, of course. ***Note:*** Lion Sands' **River Lodge** is far less exclusive, with 18 small, hotel-like rooms, and rates (R9,350–R10,600) that are easily matched by far superior establishments in this price range.

P.O. Box 30, White River 1240. ✆ **013/735-5000.** Fax 013/735-5330. Reservations: P.O. Box 2667, Houghton 2041. ✆ **011/484-9911.** www.lionsands.com. 6 units. R14,700–17,000 double. AE, DC, MC, V. No children under 12. **Amenities:** Dining area; bar; lounge; boma; board room; bush walks; clay pigeon shooting; curio shop; game drives; lectures (nature and stargazing); library; pool; spa treatments; Wi-Fi; wine cellar. *In room:* A/C, CD player, fireplace, hair dryer, minibar, plunge pool, telescope.

Londolozi ★★★ (Kids) Londolozi started life as a small hunting lodge in the 1920s but turned to conservation after it was inherited by the Varty brothers in the 1970s. It has since become one of the most famous camps in Africa; indeed, having set the standard for accommodations, cuisine, and game-viewing activities, it became the model for all subsequent luxury lodges in southern Africa. In 2006, the Varty family resumed management of the lodge (which was for many years the flagship camp for the safari outfit &Beyond) and brought several changes, such as the Lion Cubs Den, a program aimed at fostering bush knowledge among children ages 2 to 10. Following extensive renovations and rebuilding, five separate camps now stand alongside the Sand River, within walking distance but out of sight of one another. These are **Pioneer, Founder, Varty,** and **Tree Camps,** and the new ultraluxurious **Private Granite Suites,** which consist of only three suites. The two right on the river are arguably the best rooms in the entire greater Kruger area, with private plunge pools that drop onto the boulders that form the Sand River banks, close enough to the river that you can hear it running while lying in bed. Today the rejuvenated Londolozi remains one of the top lodges in southern Africa, offering spacious accommodation in stylish classic safari style, fine food attested to by its Relais & Châteaux membership, and shared access (with Singita) to more than 15,000 hectares (37,050 acres) of prime game-viewing land, where the famed Londolozi leopards are relaxed enough to leave even the most amateur photographer satisfied.

P.O. Box 41864, Hyde Park 2024. ✆ **011/280-6640,** or 011/280-6655 for reservations. Fax 031/735-5100. www.londolozi.co.za. Varty Camp 10 units. Founder's Camp 5 units. Pioneer Camp 3 units. Tree Camp 6 units. Granite Suites 3 units. Varty R11,000–R13,600; Founder's R11,000; Pioneer R14,960; Tree R16,400; Granite R17,000. All double rates include all meals and game activities, and most drinks. No children at Tree Camp. Special rates for children apply **Amenities:** Each camp offers its own dining area; bar; babysitting; boma; bush walks; game drives; pool; room service; Wi-Fi (in Varty Camp only). *In room:* A/C, hair dryer, minibar, plunge pool (at Varty, Tree, and Granite only).

MalaMala ★★★ This legendary reserve pioneered the Sabi Sands–style photographic safari back in the 1960s, when everyone who was anyone came to have their photograph taken in a MalaMala Land Rover. For chic interior decorating, the original camp has since been trumped by the likes of Singita and Londolozi, but MalaMala remains *the* top destination in the greater Kruger for those whose priority is superlative game-viewing. It's the largest single private reserve in the region—extending over 13,300 hectares, it shares a 19km (12-mile) unfenced border with Kruger and boasts 20km (13 miles) of frontage either side of the perennial Sand River. Traversing rights are reserved for the guests (up to 60) accommodated across its three camps, which make for a very low vehicle density and far more relaxed atmosphere for game-viewing than elsewhere in Sabi Sands. The Big 5 were recorded on all but 9 days in 2008, with an average of four separate leopard sightings per day—an incredible record. The veteran **Main Camp** is a determinedly unpretentious and trend-resistant setup: Accommodation is in large, simply decorated cottages with two en-suite bathrooms, each and balconies with river or marsh views; and there are no restrictions on game drive hours—you can stay out all day, if you so choose. **Sable Lodge** is part of Main Camp, using the same rooms but with a smaller and more exclusive common area aimed at small groups. **Rattray's on MalaMala** ★★★, built in 2005, is the one to book: eight classically styled cottage-sized suites, each with a timber deck with plunge pool, an outside shower, and a private garden overlooking the Sand River. The staff ensures you don't have to lift a finger—there's a golf cart if you simply can't face walking back to your room—and the exclusivity of accommodation is matched on game drives, with a maximum of four persons per vehicle.

P.O. Box 55514, Northlands 2116 ✆ **011/442-2267.** Fax 011/442 2318. www.malamala.com. Main/Sable Camp 28 units. Rattray's 8 units. Main camp $1,150 double, $1,350 suite, special rates for children; Sable $1,550 double, no children under 12; Rattray's $1,750 double, no children under 16. Rates include all meals and activities. AE, DC, MC, V. **Amenities:** Dining area; bar; boma; bush walks; game drives; high-speed Internet; library; massage room; pool; room service. *In room:* A/C, hair dryer, minibar, plunge pool (in Rattray's only), Wi-Fi (in Rattray's only).

Sabi Sabi ★★ With more than 3 decades in the safari business, Sabi Sabi hardly needs to impress anybody, but clearly covetous of the attention and accolades showered upon Singita's contemporary aesthetic, the owners commissioned **Earth Lodge,** with an intent to build a thoroughly modern lodge for the new millennium. To this end, the entire lodge looks as if it has been built into the earth, with one of the most spectacular open-air entrance foyers in Africa. Even though they photograph well, the rooms are less impressive (certainly when compared with those at Singita or Royal Malewane), with dark interiors, tiny plunge pools, and hard edges. The original (and far larger) **Bush Lodge** is furnished in plush colonial style; you feel as if you're in a hotel, though, and units are too close together for privacy. You'd be better off booking into the exclusive but reasonably priced **Little Bush Camp** (formerly Londolozi's Safari Lodge), which offers six luxury rooms on a dry river bed. Alternatively, the elegant eight-unit **Selati Lodge** is a pleasantly refurbished former hunting lodge, named after the famed turn-of-the-20th-century railway line that ran through the area, and decorated with vintage railway memorabilia, antiques, and old sepia-tone photographs. As for the game-viewing, Sabi Sabi matches any other property in Sabi Sands when it comes to the Big 5, and like MalaMala, its lodges enjoy exclusive traversing rights, but over a far smaller area catering to almost twice the bed capacity, so it doesn't feel quite so untrammeled.

P.O. Box 52665, Saxonwold 2132. ✆ **011/447-7172.** Fax 011/442-0728. www.sabisabi.com. Bush Lodge 25 units. Selati Lodge 8 units. Earth Lodge 13 units. Bush Lodge R11,200 double; R15,000 suite. Little Bush R8,400 double; R36,000 exclusive usage for up to 12 people. Selati R11,600 double; R12,800–15,000 suite. Earth Lodge R15,000 double; R30,000 suite. Low season discounts May–July. Rates include all meals, local beverages, game drives, and bush walks. AE, DC, MC, V. No children under 13 at Selati or Earth. Special rates for children apply. **Amenities:** Dining area; bar; boma; bush walks; game drives; high-speed Internet (Bush and Earth); pool; room service. (Earth and Bush Lodges also offer spa, small gym, IT center, and wine cellar.) *In room:* A/C, hair dryer, minibar. (Presidential suites come with a Land Rover and ranger; at Earth, they'll throw in a butler.)

Singita Ebony & Boulders ★★★ Frommer's has rated this lodge as the best in the country since it first opened. Awards and accolades for Luke Bailes's sumptuous lodge keep flooding in—the most recent being Best Hotel in Africa, the Middle East & Indian Ocean in both the U.S. and U.K.'s *Condé Nast Traveler* Gold List 2009. While you might find it difficult to leave your room at Londolozi, here it is virtually impossible. But move you must, for the quality of the game-viewing is superlative; Singita enjoys semiexclusive traversing rights to more than 18,000 hectares (44,460 acres), and the best rangers in the business will look after you. Sabi Sands Singita comprises two totally separate lodges, **Boulders** and **Ebony,** both built on the Sand River, but each so different you'll feel like you're in an entirely new lodge. Suites in the contemporary-style Boulders Lodge are the size of a small house; Ebony Lodge features the same standard of luxury, service, and privacy, but the decor has an African colonial theme. A Relais & Châteaux lodge, Singita offers superb dining at all meals; wine tastings (largely South African wines) in Boulders' handsome wine cellar are popular ongoing events. The Singita staff is one of the friendliest around, and the vibe is happy, free of snootiness. For families with children under 10, there are now two new family units at both Boulders and Ebony.

P.O. Box 23367, Claremont 7735. ✆ **021/683-3424** or 013/735-5456 direct. Fax 021/683-3502. www.singita.co.za. Ebony Lodge 12 units. Boulders Lodge 12 units. R19,800 double, all-inclusive (except French champagne). No seasonal discounts. AE, DC, MC, V. Children over 10 only. **Amenities:** Dining room; bar; lounge; bush walks; game drives; gym; high-speed Internet; library; room service; home and curio shop; spa; 12,000-bottle wine cellar. *In room:* A/C, hair dryer, minibar, private pool.

Ulusaba ★ Ulusaba, owned by Sir Richard Branson since 1999, lies in the far west of Sabi Sands, where its aura of exclusivity is undermined somewhat by the fact that it shares traversing rights with half-a-dozen other properties. Hilltop Rock Lodge stands out for its exceptional facilities, including a sumptuous hilltop swimming pool, and for its panoramic views across the acacia-studded plains running eastward to Kruger. The less elevated Safari Lodge has a more conventional setting in riparian forest running along a seasonal watercourse. It makes ample used of organic material and stilted walkways that evoke Tarzan's jungle. It attracts many American and British travelers, including plenty of celebrities, politicians, and the like, drawn by the prospect of staying as a kind of house guest in a rakish billionaire's lodge.

P.O. Box 71, Skukuza 1350, South Africa. ✆ **011/325-4405.** www.ulusaba.virgin.com. Safari Lodge 10 units. Rock Lodge 6 units. R9,200–18,200 double all-inclusive, depending on room type. AE, DC, MC, V. Children welcome. **Amenities:** Dining area; bar; lounges; boma; bush walks; children's room w/TV, DVDs, computer, and board games; game drives; gym; high-speed Internet; library; pool; room service; star observatory; wine cellar. *In room:* A/C, hair dryer, minibar, Wi-Fi (in 2 suites).

In Manyeleti

Honeyguide Tented Safari Camps ★★ Value Honeyguide's tented camps offer some of the best value-for-money game experiences in the country and tend to attract a young, occasionally raucous crowd. Relaxed safari chic comes close to describing the informal minimalism of **Mantobeni Tented Camp,** with its Morris chairs, leather couches, cotton sheets, old-style lanterns, and damask linen evoking *Out of Africa.* Guests are accommodated in East African–style tents, set on raised wooden decks with lovely concrete bathrooms featuring double showers and partially sunken tubs. Set in a riverine forest, most of the 12 tents overlook a riverbed (usually dry) or the water hole; it's a good idea, however, to reserve tent no.1, which enjoys more privacy and is likely to be farther away from loud neighbors. The central lounge/dining and lazing area is sparsely furnished, and tents can become hot in summer, when guests head for the narrow, elegant pool. Early-morning drums alert you to the dawning game drive, and tea is brought to your tent—a luxury even the most upmarket camps don't always offer. Five minutes away, the 12 en-suite tents at Honeyguide's **Khoka Moya Tented Camp** offer almost exactly the same experience, but the tents (this time set on concrete slabs) are slightly more spacious, and the somewhat more elegant bathrooms don't have tubs. Khoka Moya's more contemporary furnishings include large plush ottomans and beanbags around the fire. Most important, Khoka Moya allows children, making it great for families, while Mantobeni is more suitable for romance.

P.O. Box 786064, Sandton 2146. ✆ **011/341-0282.** Fax 011/341-0281. www.honeyguidecamp.com. Mantobeni 12 units. Khoka Moya 12 units. R6,700 double. No children under 12 at Mantobeni; children under 10 pay 50% at Khoka Moya. AE, DC, MC, V. **Amenities:** Dining room; bar; lounge; boma; bush walks; game drives; pool; Wi-Fi. *In room:* Standing fan.

In Kapama

Camp Jabulani ★★★ Moments This is the top lodge in Kapama—a fenced "island" private reserve near Hoedspruit that harbors all the Big 5 but is best known for its elephant-back safaris, an activity that offers a unique giraffe's-eye view over the African bush and its inhabitants. Founded in 2003, the camp itself is a stunner, with an opulent dining area and lounge overlooking a pretty waterhole, delicious Relais & Châteaux cuisine, and accommodation in six spacious and beautifully decorated wood, stone, and thatch cottages, all with private deck and plunge pool, carved into a patch of riparian forest alive with monkeys and birds. Game drives, bush walks, and visits to the associated Hoedspruit Endangered Species Center are all on offer, but the stars of the show are the elephants, which consist of the young male Jabulani, who was hand-reared after being orphaned at the age of 4 months, and a herd of 12 adolescents rescued from Zimbabwe in 2002. The nighttime elephant-back trips below a glittering African night sky are wondrous.

R40, 5km (3 miles) south of Hoedspruit. P.O. Box 25745, Monument Park, 0105. ✆ **015/793-1265.** www.campjabulani.com. 6 units. R8,600 double, including meals, game drives, and guided bush walks. R14,000 double, including meals, drinks, transfers from Hoedspruit Airport, and all activities (including elephant-back safaris). No children under 12 unless the entire camp is reserved. AE, DC, MC, V. **Amenities:** Dining room; bar; lounge; bush walks; clay pigeon shooting (by request); elephant activities (safaris and stable visits); game drives; hot-air ballooning (by request); high-speed Internet; library; massage. *In room:* A/C, fan, hair dryer, minibar, plunge pool.

In Timbavati

Gomo Gomo Game Lodge (www.gomogomo.co.za) is not going to be featured in the pages of a glossy design mag anytime soon, but it's worth a mention for the good-value rate alone: R2,960 double during the winter months and R3,400 during the summer—excellent, given that this includes all game activities (two drives and a bush walk daily) and all your meals. The game-viewing is excellent—there's every chance you'll see the same amount of game as someone staying at Royal Malewane, at a fraction of the price. The lodge comprises nine units; make sure to book one of the four safari tents rather than the thatched rondawels, and ask for one that is river-facing. Decor is functional, but you're here for the bush experience, which is exceptional.

Kings Camp ★★ This is an ideal place to find yourself if your idea of "roughing it" is letting the butler have the afternoon off. While Tanda Tula (reviewed below) provides a more authentic bush experience, accommodations at Kings Camp are pure luxury (better value than &Beyond's main Ngala camp, reviewed below; it's also exceptional value by comparison to lodges of a similar standard in Sabi Sands). Actually, it's hardly a "camp" at all; the large, private thatched chalets are arranged at the edges of a well-tailored lawn with a pool and various cozy and comfortable lounge-cum-viewing-areas, and the slightly old-fashioned decor is being addressed by a program of modernizing renovations over the course of 2009. On your personal terrace, you can sip martinis or lounge on a hammock just meters from the animal-rich Timbavati bush, while in your suite you're cocooned in traditional luxury. Rooms are air-conditioned and spacious; bathrooms are large, with his-and-hers outdoor showers. Upon returning from a grueling early evening of tracking leopard, lion, and buffalo, your room will be filled with an herbal scent and your bath drawn piping hot.

Seasons in Africa, P.O. Box 19516, Nelspruit 1218. ✆ **013/755-4408.** Fax 013/752-5842. www.kingscamp.com. 10 units. R8,400 double; R7,000 in winter. Rates include meals, wildlife activities, tea, and coffee. Children under 12 pay 50% if sharing with 2 adults. AE, DC, MC, V. **Amenities:** Dining room; bar; lounge/viewing deck; babysitting; bush walks; doctor; game drives; gym; library; pool; room service; shop; therapy tent; TV. *In room:* A/C, hair dryer, minibar.

Ngala Tented Safari Camp ★★★ Kids &Beyond (formerly CC Africa) is one of southern Africa's premier safari operators, with a variety of camps and lodges working to varying standards. They have two operations in the Timbavati, one of which is this highly recommended camp, comprising six deluxe en-suite tents on the banks of the Timbavati River. It delivers a superb bush experience, with operating rights within 14,000 hectares (34,580 acres) of land providing one of the best game-viewing experiences outside of Sabi Sand. (It's a little cheaper, but don't be tempted by **Ngala Main Camp,** with its thatched cottages that are cramped and too stacked on top of one another to provide a relaxing experience or any sense of privacy; it's more like a small hotel than a safari.) ***Note:*** Ngala also offers a highly recommended 3-day walking safari for R1,500 per person per night.

Private Bag X27, Benmore 2010. ✆ **011/809-4300.** Fax 011/809-4315. www.andbeyondafrica.com. Main Camp 21 units. Tented Camp 6 units. Tented Camp R7,700–R12,900 double. Main Camp R5,760–R8,560 double. All rates include meals, game drives, and bush walks. Children under 11 pay 50%. AE, DC, MC, V. **Amenities:** Restaurant; boma; bar; lounge; babysitting; game activities; pool. *In room:* Hair dryer.

Tanda Tula ★★ One of the very first luxury tented camps in the Kruger area, Tanda Tula gives a real sense of being in the heart of the bush. The 12 tents are all privately situated, each with its own furnished *stoep* (veranda); try to reserve tent no. 1 for the best view (or no. 10 as an alternative). Because the surrounding bush is dense and rooms are not as luxurious as its competitors', you're more likely to spend time in the elegant and comfortably furnished open-sided lounge and dining area, which leads out onto the lawns and pool. This is where drinks and lunch are served, and at night a huge fire blazes, although dinner is served in the adjacent boma. Weather permitting, breakfasts are served in the bush, and braais (barbecues) take place regularly on the riverbed. Tanda Tula means "To Love the Quiet," and the team does everything possible to ensure that you can do just that. Game drives cover a potential 20,000 hectares (49,400 acres), providing Tanda Tula with access to the largest area in Timbavati, and you'll likely spot at least three of the Big 5 in 1 day.

P.O. Box 32, Constantia 7848. ✆ **021/794-6500.** Fax 021/794-7605. www.tandatula.co.za. 12 units. High season (Dec–Mar) R8,500 double; low season discount Apr–Nov. Rates are all-inclusive. AE, DC, MC, V. No children under 12. **Amenities:** Dining area; bar; lounge; boma; riverbed braais; bush breakfasts; bush walks; game drives; pool. *In room:* Fan, hair dryer.

Umlani Bushcamp ★ (Value) (Kids) Offering one of the most authentic bush experiences in Africa, Umlani ("Place of Rest") is not luxurious (accommodations are in thatched, reed-wall en-suite rondawels) but remains a personal favorite. It's relatively affordable, but such key features as the absence of electricity make the experience more authentic. It has no formal gardens and very few staff, the en-suite huts are relatively basic, and at night the camp is lit only by firelight and paraffin lamps. Umlani is a really relaxed camp, the kind of place where you sit with your toes in the sand listening to the sounds of the bush (rather than the hum of the pool filter) or swing in the hammock hoping a predator won't come padding down the dry Nshlaralumi riverbed. Hosts are laid-back, and every effort has been made to retain a sense of what it's like to camp in the middle of the bush; there's even a stilted treehouse overlooking a water hole, where you can spend the night with only the sounds of nocturnal animals—highly recommended. Umlani is small, but with traversing rights to parts of Tanda Tula, it covers 10,000 hectares (24,700 acres) and regularly has good sightings.

P.O. Box 11604, Maroelana 0161. ✆ **012/785-5547.** Fax 0866/968518. www.umlani.com. 8 units. R5,500 double; 3-night special R14,060 double; winter (May–June) R4,950 double. Rates include all meals, drinks, game drives, and bush walks. Children under 12 pay 50%. AE, DC, MC, V. **Amenities:** Dining room; bar; boma; bush breakfasts; bush walks; game drives; library; microlighting and ballooning by arrangement; pool; shop.

In Thornybush

Royal Malewane ★★★ It's difficult to imagine that anything would be too much trouble for the gracious staff at Liz Biden's much-lauded luxury lodge, and for all its superlative luxury, it's a remarkably unpretentious lodge and puts up a very strong fight with Singita as *the* ultimate luxury safari destination in Africa. Elevated walkways are the only link between the wonderfully private units, set on stilts right in the midst of the bush, each with a huge open-plan bedroom/sitting room with fireplace and equally enormous bathroom. Whether you're lying draped in Ralph Lauren linen in the antique canopied king-size bed or luxuriating in the elegant claw-foot bathtub or huge open shower, floor-to-ceiling windows provide wonderfully unobscured views of your private outdoor terrace, with outside shower and gazebo and, beyond that, the bush. Chef John Jackson conjures up remarkable meals, including a sumptuous Bedouin-themed affair served in the bush, but don't be surprised if, immediately after dessert, you're whisked away on an impromptu game drive, prompted by roaring lions. For the ultimate honeymoon or getaway destination, you won't find better than the palatial Royal and Malewane Suites, where up to four guests can enjoy the same unfettered luxuries visited upon regulars Elton John and Bono, including the personal attentions of a private butler, private chef, and masseur. With traversing rights on 11,500 hectares (28,405 acres) and some of South Africa's top trackers, the lodge also offers excellent game-viewing opportunities—elephant and lion are easily seen within the hour.

P.O. Box 1542, Hoedspruit 1380. ✆ **015/793-0150.** Fax 015/793-2879. www.royalmalewane.com. 6 units. R17,700 double; Royal and Malewane Suites R47,500 for 4 people. Rates include all meals, local beverages, game drives, and bush walks. AE, DC, MC, V. **Amenities:** Dining room; lounge/bar; aromatherapy; boma; bush and theme dinners; bush walks; game drives; gift shop; gym; library; massage; room service; spa w/heated lap pool; Wi-Fi. *In room:* A/C, hair dryer, minibar, plunge pool. (Royal and Malewane Suites include TV, CD/DVD player; full kitchen; private chef and butler; masseuse; Royal Suite includes laptop, fax/printer; Wi-Fi [rooms 1 and 8].)

In Makalali

Makalali Game Lodge ★★ Kids Makalali means "Place of Rest" in the local Shangaan language, and you can expect plenty of it in what *Tatler* magazine once voted the Most Innovatively Designed Hotel in the World. Aiming for a sensual bush experience with something seemingly inspired by Antoni Gaudí, architect Silvio Rech has combined architectural styles from all over Africa—shaggy East African roof thatching adorns mud and stone walls, while rugged North African–inspired turrets create a mythical village palace sensibility. Makalali consists of four camps—each with its own swimming pool, boma, and lounge and dining area—situated on various points of the Makhutswi River, which flows for approximately 8 months of the year. Rooms are huge and totally private; each features a fireplace as well as a *sala,* joined to your hut via a boardwalk, where you can arrange to have a romantic dinner. Try to book a room in the uniquely situated camp 4, where the rooms are most dispersed and you reach your public areas via a swing-bridge—*very* romantic. Don't get stuck with room no. 3 in camp 4 (adjacent the staff village) or room no. 4 in Camp 1; the latter is too close to the kitchen. Makalali offer a 3-day "wildlife mini-rangers" course for kids ages 6 and older. While you relax by the pool, they spend a couple of hours a day learning basic bush survival skills, including field exercises with a qualified ranger.

P.O. Box 809, Hoedspruit 1380. ✆ **015/793-9300.** www.makalali.co.za. 4 camps, each with 6 units. R7,700. See website for special offers. Rate includes meals, game drives, and laundry. Children under 12 pay 25%. AE, DC, MC, V. **Amenities:** Each camp includes dining area; bar; lounge; boma; babysitting; bush walks; game drives; free high-speed Internet; pool; room service. *In room:* A/C, fans, hair dryer, phones (in Camps 1–3).

Garonga ★ Value Garonga's approach to the bush experience is more "soul safari" than big game. The lodge abuts Makalali (reviewed above) and both have access to four of the Big 5, but the emphasis is on "re-earthing" the senses rather than tracking animals. This is the perfect place to end a frenetic vacation, with no scheduled game drives imposed on you—an easel, pencils, and small Zen garden are placed in your room, and an aromatherapist is on standby to further help de-stress you. Situated on raised platforms along a dry riverbed, the six standard units have low adobe walls, topped by a vast tent of cream canvas. King-size beds are swaddled in white muslin, and a large hammock swings above every deck. For those who'd love a soak in the wilds, the staff will set up a private bush bath with candles and bath salts; there is also a sleeping platform on stilts 20 minutes from camp for the more adventurous.

P.O. Box 737, Hoedspruit 1380 ✆ **087/806-2080.** Fax 011/447-0993. www.garonga.com. 7 units. R4,000–R5,900 double, depending on season; Hambledon suite R7,000–R8,200. Rates include all meals, drinks, game drives, and bush walks. AE, MC, V. No children under 12. **Amenities:** Dining area; bar; boma; aromatherapy; bush walks; curio shop; game drives; library; pool; reflexology; free Wi-Fi. *In room:* Hair dryer. Hambledon suite: A/C, minibar, plunge pool.

6 THE WATERBERG & WELGEVONDEN RESERVE

Approximately 350km (217 miles) N of Johannesburg

The Waterberg, a 150km-long (93-mile) mountain ridge that rises quite dramatically from the bushveld plains to 2,085m (6,839 ft.) above sea level, is substantially less populated than the big-game country that lies to the east of the Escarpment, in and around Kruger. With no major roads and only one town (Vaalwater) within a 15,000-sq.-km (5,850-sq.-mile) area, the region is almost totally devoid of humans. With no forestry or industry contributing to pollution, it's one of the most pristine wilderness areas in the country. It also offers a more varied terrain within a smaller area, with majestic mountainscapes and rocky ravines, grassed valleys, and lush riverines. Besides its proximity (a

Moments Close Encounter on Horseback

Tired of watching animals while confined to a Jeep listening to the ramblings of your fellow safari enthusiasts? Saddle up and head out for a totally intoxicating wildlife adventure—you can get remarkably close to game on horseback. Besides **Ant's Hill & Nest** (see review below), there is **Horizon Horseback Adventures & Safaris** ★★ (✆ **014/755-4003;** www.ridinginafrica.com; R1,599–R1,968 per person per day; due to popular demand, three rooms have no single supplement), which offers various riding experiences. Besides venturing across the outback in search of three of the Big 5, you can saddle up for a game of polocrosse (a fusion of polo and lacrosse) or muster cattle at the Triple B Ranch. Guests are hosted in a lodge on the edge of a cliff overlooking a beautiful lake with the plains beyond. But for the best equestrian experience ever, with Big 5 sightings, book 4 days in Botswana's Delta with **Okavango Horse Safari** ★★★ (www.okavangohorse.com).

2½-hr. drive) to Johannesburg, the reserve is also malaria free, which makes it ideal for those with children or an aversion to medication. Add to this the mountainous landscape and lack of congestion when compared with some of the private game reserves around Kruger, and the relatively good-value rates charged by some of the lodges, and it becomes a very appealing choice indeed.

Waterberg has three major players. The **Welgevonden Reserve,** a magnificent 40,000-hectare (98,800-acre) wilderness, is the most accessible to visitors. It has for some time been managed and restocked by a consortium of wealthy concession holders, all of whom have had to develop their camps along very strict guidelines, ensuring a very tightly run operation with high levels of professionalism and respect for the environment. Vehicles are not allowed off-road, for example, which can be a major drawback if you spot a lion lying 100m (328 ft.) away, and it makes leopard sightings extremely rare. But the relatively high density of animals ensures good sightings, and the intimacy of the small lodges is most conducive to relaxing.

ESSENTIALS

Welgevonden Reserve has four landing strips. Your lodge will arrange the 1-hour charter from Johannesburg airport, or make the 2½-hour journey by car to the Welgevonden's main entrance (if you are self-driving, park at the entrance gate and wait for your lodge to collect you; ask for the lodge to fax or e-mail a map).

WHERE TO STAY & DINE

Besides the following options, look into possible specials from **Clearwater Lodges,** P.O. Box 365, Stellenbosch 7599 (✆ **021/889-2034;** www.clearwaterlodges.co.za). It is comprised of two totally separate camps. Of the two, **Kudu Lodge** ★★ is the better: Set in the middle of a large, open, short-grass savanna, it's surrounded by grazing antelope, zebra, and rhino. Each generously sized chalet has a deck from which you can enjoy the passing parade at the nearby watering hole. At R4,580 double, all-inclusive, the rate during winter (May–Oct) is an excellent value (summer: R8,780).

Ant's Nest & Ant Hill ★★ (Finds) Very personally owned and run by Ant and Tessa Baber, these two "bush homes" are in Waterberg reserves that have over 40 species of game (but no lion or elephant). They are great family destinations, particularly those who want to ride horseback, which allows you to get very close to game. It also has impeccable green credentials. These model eco-lodges received four stars in the 2009 Eco Hotels of the World awards for waste disposal, water recycling, locally sourced food, and energy management. Ant's Nest is a renovated ranch house; Ant's Hill, built overlooking a gorge and waterhole, was purpose-built a few years later. It's very much a home-away-from-home experience, so it will suit families or groups traveling together, but it's also open to individuals. Besides the usual game activities, they offer horse safaris with a choice of 60 horses (see box above); inexperienced riders are provided with lessons. Ant's Hill accommodates 12 persons in four chalets (the family unit sleeps six, with master bedroom and two twins). Ant's Nest has six luxurious en-suite bedrooms that accommodate a maximum of 12 guests. The highlight here is the huge swimming pool, heated all year, and the big shaded sofa beds.

P.O. Box 441, Vaalwater, Waterberg 0530. ✆ **014/755-3584.** Fax 086/509-8239. www.waterberg.net. 5 units. Sep–Apr R7,200 double; May–Aug R5,600 double. Rates include all meals, drinks, game drives, safari walks, and horseback riding. Group discounts. **Amenities:** Dining room; bar; boma; bush walks; game drives; horseback riding; pool. *In room:* Hair dryer.

Makweti Safari Lodge ★★★ This intimate stone-and-thatch lodge is architecturally one of the most attractive options in Welgevonden. Beyond the low-key and tasteful use of African artworks and artifacts, the layout of the boutique-style lodge emphasizes privacy, and the setting is fabulous, on a rocky ravine at the edge of a verdant valley. Warthogs, zebras, and other herbivores graze and play around a watering hole adjacent to one viewing terrace, while you can enjoy fantastic views of the bush from the main lounge areas. Accommodations are in generously proportioned chalets, most with king-size beds, small verandas on stilts, and spectacular bathrooms. The beautifully presented meals are accompanied by fine South African wines from less commercial estates and, weather allowing, are served in the boma.

P.O. Box 310, Vaalwater, Waterberg 0530. ✆ **011/837-6776.** Fax 011/837-4771. www.makweti.com. 5 units. Sept–Apr R8,500 double; winter R5,720 double. Rates include all meals, game drives, walking safaris, tea, and coffee. No children under 12 unless entire lodge is rented out. **Amenities:** Dining area; boma; bar; *sala;* African art boutique; bush walks; game drives; plunge pool. *In room:* Fan, hair dryer.

Mhondoro Lodge ★★ Value Guests at this small, intimate lodge—offering excellent value—are made to feel well and truly at home. And what a lovely, unassuming home: Like Makweti, it was built to blend harmoniously with the landscape; you almost don't notice the handful of stone and thatch structures until you're right on top of them. The decor is classic safari: all muted earth tones and natural fibers, and selectively chosen African artworks. The main living space consists of a cozy lounge (with a fantastic fire in winter), impressively stocked bar and dining area, and comfortably furnished deck overlooking a small, very active watering hole. The four guest chalets (one sleeps four) are all free-standing and private; furnishing is understated plush. The real highlights are watching the sunrise from your private terrace and dancing in the moonlight in your outdoor shower. Staff are laid-back and extremely good-natured, encouraging guests to relax and do as they please; guides have unusually sharp eyes, casually spotting well-hidden game; and kids under 8, while not allowed on game drives, will be spoiled rotten by the fabulous babysitters.

P.O. Box 1120, Rivonia, 2128. ✆ 073/819-4233. Fax 016/364-2470. www.mhondoro.com. 4 units. Summer (Sept–Apr) R6,600 double; winter (May–July) R5,000 double. Rates include all meals, game drives, bush walks, and beverages. Children 2–9 pay 60%. Children under 8 not permitted on game drives. **Amenities:** Dining area; bar; boma; babysitting; bush walks; doctor; game drives; gym; Jacuzzi; library; plunge pool; room service; sauna; steam room. *In room:* Fan, hair dryer.

7 MADIKWE GAME RESERVE ★★★

With an even more varied and beautiful terrain than Waterberg, right near on the Botswana border, this is prime game-viewing turf. And, like the Waterberg, it's malaria free. It's not quite in the same league as the Sabi Sands in terms of game densities, riverine forests, and pristine vegetation, but it's catching up: At the end of the 1980s, this 75,000-hectare (185,250-acre) area was overgrazed farmland, but in a financially astute decision, it was proclaimed the Madikwe Game Reserve in 1991, transforming it into South Africa's fourth-largest reserve. Within 6 years, 10,000 animals were once again roaming the Madikwe plains in what was dubbed Operation Phoenix, the largest game-translocation exercise in the world. The decision to do this here was based on the area's highly diverse eco-zones—bordered by the Dwarsberg Mountains in the south and the Marico River in the east, the reserve's rocky hills, perennial rivers, seasonal wetlands, acacia bushveld, savanna grassland, and Kalahari's desertlike sandveld allow it to support an unusual range of animal species. Today it has the second-largest elephant population in the country, and visitors are virtually assured of sighting what they term the Magnificent 7 on a 2-night stay. This includes the Big 5 as well as cheetahs (very rare in the reserves around Kruger) and wild dogs, Southern Africa's most endangered predator. Commercial expansion over the last few years has been rapid, seeing construction of a host of new-generation lodges, yet Madikwe remains large enough to satisfy visitors craving solitude and exclusivity—something the more popular reserves adjoining Kruger can't always deliver.

MADIKWE ESSENTIALS

Madikwe is some 280km (174 miles) northwest of Johannesburg. There are daily flights to the reserve from Johannesburg (occasionally two flights); your lodge will arrange air transfers (it's a 45-min. flight). If you have the time, however, a road journey is definitely recommended. With no one else on the road, and surrounded by bush and classic big African skies, the journey alone is a holiday. It's an easy road trip, particularly if you follow the main roads to Zeerust and then head for the Abjaterskop Gate, which means you won't hit dirt roads until you're inside the reserve itself. To get to Makanyane, you will spend some time on some pretty unnerving dirt roads, but this last stretch will surely add to the sense of getting away from it all. The journey by car should take between 3 and 4 hours from Johannesburg; most lodges will arrange the road transfer, meeting you off the flight at the airport (bank on around R3,000 per car). If your time is limited, fly. Note that it gets very hot in summer and, surprisingly, cold in winter. The best times to visit are at the beginning (Nov) or the end (Apr) of the season, when temperatures are more temperate. Visiting during the winter months (May–Oct) represents substantial savings, however; simply pack a few ultrawarm layers. ***Note:*** There is a R50 reserve entrance fee, as well as a new government levy of about R25 for the upliftment of the previously disadvantaged local communities. Make sure these are included in the rate or bring along some cash.

Where to Stay & Dine

Besides the following options, the small and imaginatively designed **Jaci's Tree Lodge** ★ (✆ **083/700-2071** or 014/778-9900; www.madikwe.com) is worth serious consideration, as is **Jaci's Safari Lodge** (the latter is particularly good for families). Comprising just eight air-conditioned treehouses built around giant tambotie and leadwood trees, the Tree Lodge setting is more magical than neighboring Jaci's Safari Lodge's, but the latter is one of the most family-friendly lodges in Southern Africa. Both lodges cost R6,790 to R9,590 double, including all meals and game activities; each child sharing is R1,495 to R2,195 per night.

Most of the lodges reviewed below are in the eastern part of Madikwe; more centrally located is **Mateya Safari Lodge** ★★★ (P.O. Box 439, Molatedi 2838; ✆ **014/778-9200;** www.mateyasafari.com), with only five superluxurious suites, offering a great sense of privacy and excellent service standards. An incentive for basing yourself here is the highly rated wellness center: The spa team offers everything from hot-stone therapy to African head massages. That said, a major drawback is the Sabie-Sands level tariff: R15,000 double (R11,000 during Aug–Sep low season), and that does not include the spa treatments.

With just 10 elevated glass-fronted luxury chalets overlooking a natural spring and fantastic views, **Impodimo Lodge** ★★★ is also highly rated, not only for its game-viewing. It's an excellent-value lodge (www.impodimo.com; ✆ **018/350 940;** Oct–Apr

Tips More for Your Money

Madikwe is proudly home to the first wholly owned community safari lodges to be developed in South Africa: **Buffalo Ridge,** an elevated eight-unit lodge that affords grand views of the thornveld plains of Madikwe while making the most of its breezes, is owned and run by the Balete community; its sister lodge on the eastern edge of Madikwe, **Thakadu River Camp,** is managed and owned by the Molatedi people. Both communities have enlisted the aid of the Madikwe Collection to help with promotions and safari logistics. Of the two, I slightly prefer **Thakadu** (✆ **011/805-9995** or 082-926-7373; www.thakadurivercamp.com or www.madikwecollection.com; R6,700 double). The camp is also more child friendly, with special programs for kids. Set within the riverine forest that lines the banks of the Marico River, each of the 12 tented suites has a viewing deck and views of the Marico River. It's a lovely camp, and the game-viewing is as good as anywhere else in Madikwe. It's nice knowing that you're helping a community that has taken the initiative to create employment opportunities and negotiate a substantial stake in the profits. (Incidentally, the Madikwe Collection is also partnering with De Hoop Nature Reserve [see Western Cape chapter], South Africa's most beautiful coastal reserve, so it's worth inquiring into packages that combine a trip here, too.)

R6,700, May–Sept R5,000 double; rates all-inclusive). Rates are a quarter of those for Mateya (and half those for Makanyane), but you'll want for nothing, from the minute you are met at the airport to the moment you stop in front of your first lion sighting. For seriously good value, you can't beat Mosetlha.

Mosetlha Bush Camp Value Moments Finds If you're looking for a no-nonsense eco-camp with minimal impact on its environment—one that will make you feel okay to get your feet in the dust, sitting around campfires while warming your coffee—this is it. Warmly owner-managed by retired civil engineer Chris Lucas, wife June, and daughter Caroline, Mosetlha is perhaps the most authentic bush camps left in Big 5 territory: a breath of fresh air, given that virtually every other concession holder's dream is to re-create an urban sanctuary in the bush (and charge for the privilege). Here accommodation is very basic: raised, partly open-sided wooden cabins, built around a central campfire, sharing three private toilet/shower complexes situated among the cabins. There is no electricity, and water is heated through a donkey boiler; home-style cuisine, prepared in the traditional bush style on the open fire, is as no-nonsense as the decor. Family owned and run, this is a rustic no-frills experience, but essentially you get to see the same amount of game (there are four excellent ranger-trackers), and many who combine a few days here with a five-star experience at a nearby lodge (a rather good idea) say that Mosetlha was by far the more memorable of the two. Note that they cannot process credit cards, so bring cash for tips and drinks (which are, like everything else, very reasonably priced).

P.O. Box 78690, Sandton, 2146 South Africa. ✆/fax **011/444-9345.** www.thebushcamp.com. 9 units. R3,370 double. Rate includes all meals, game activities, and emergency evacuation insurance. No children under 8. AE, DC, MC, V (processed post your visit in Johanessburg). **Amenities:** Dining area; lounge/bar area; boma; game drives and walks.

Madikwe Safari Lodge ★★★ High on style and low on pretense, this lodge has drawn inspiration from the turreted anthills that dot the Madikwe landscape, with packed earth, stone, huge leadwood branches, and thatch to fashion a series of organic living spaces. Interiors are filled with clever details, including many interesting artifacts from around Africa, to give the spaces a quirky tongue-in-cheek edge. It's the type of safari lodge that makes you want to explore the property as much as the wildlife, which often appears right out front. If you're traveling with children, you'll probably be stationed in West or South Camp, where guest rooms are larger and have sleeper couches. East Camp is the largest in terms of capacity (seven rooms); North Camp, with only four guest rooms, is the one for romance. No matter where you're stationed, you'll enjoy a great sense of privacy: Separated from each other by fat stone walls, the rooms open onto expansive views of the bush, which begins at the edge of your wooden deck (with private plunge pool, outdoor shower, and lounge chairs). Game drives are professional, as you'd expect from &Beyond, as is the cuisine, served in a variety of eye-catching spaces, including one of three bomas. This doesn't have the same level of exclusivity as Morukuru, however.

Private Bag X27, Benmore 2010. ✆ **011/809-4300.** Fax 011/809-4315. www.andbeyond.com. 20 units total. R5,750–R7,900. Rates include all meals, beverages, game drives, and laundry. AE, DC, MC, V. **Amenities:** 3 of the camps each have their own dining area, bar, lounge, boma; babysitting; currency exchange; doctor on call; game drives; library; massage. *In room:* A/C, hair dryer, minibar, plunge pool.

Makanyane Safari Lodge ★★ Each suite at this private game reserve along Madikwe's eastern border has huge wraparound glass walls that not only allow you to feel immersed in the bush, but afford picturesque views of the river where animals come to drink in early morning. You can spend your entire day lazing on your bed, watching the comings and goings of thirsty wildlife from your private lounge-deck or enjoying an in-room massage. Of course, then you'd miss out on the excellent game drives; game is plentiful and the lodge is frequently visited by all sorts of animals: Don't investigate if you hear a snuffling outside your door at night. ("Lion," the ranger sniffed indifferently, looking at the paw imprint). At the main lodge, pachyderms also cross the river to try to drink from the infinity pool at the edge of the large, stilted terrace, partially canopied by thorn trees that grow straight through the wooden deck.

Krokodildrift 87KP, Madikwe Game Reserve. P.O. Box 9, Derdepoort 2876. ✆ **014/778-9600.** Fax 014/778-9611. www.makanyane.com. High season (Sept–Apr) R10,800 double. Low season (May–Oct) R8,900 double. Rates include all meals, most beverages, game drives, and walks. Visit the website for package rates. AE, DC, MC, V. **Amenities:** Multiple dining areas; wine cellar; bar; lounge; sala; bush walks; curio shop; doctor on call; game drives; gym; Internet facility; library; pool; spa; free Wi-Fi in main lodge. *In room:* A/C, hair dryer, minibar.

Morukuru ★★★ Kids It has a magnificent setting, fabulous service, and wonderful game drives, but exclusivity and privacy make this a great retreat. Occupying a private game reserve that abuts Madikwe, Morukuru has thousands of hectares of additional private game-viewing territory that can be traversed in addition to the entire Madikwe. Perched on one bank of the Groot Marico River, it comprises two well-appointed "bush villas" (referred to as Main Lodge and the Owner's House) each with its own lounge, kitchen, indoor and outdoor dining areas, and infinity pool hanging over the river. Large multilevel decks invite you to chill out while enjoying the river and lush forest canopy, and there are never any other guests besides you and those you choose to accompany you (4–10 guests), all with your own chef, own butler, nanny (if needed), and a private safari guide and tracker. Quintin, your personal game ranger, works with Tom, a gifted Shangaan tracker; together they're a sharp team. While Quintin's love of the bush is infectious, Tom is also brilliant with kids, making the whole wildlife experience interactive and fascinating; be sure to include a bush walk during your stay. Unlike almost every other lodge in Africa, here there is no schedule and absolutely no pressure (a real gripe if you've traveled to many); you can do whatever you want and pretty much set your own itinerary. The small staff complement is permanently at your beck and call, but you can also ask to help yourself if you'd prefer to be alone. Unless you're exceptionally gregarious, this is pure, unadulterated bliss. (If you like the sound of this but not the price tag, Ant's Hill or Ant's Nest in the Waterberg, reviewed above, is where you should be looking.)

Reservations (in the Netherlands): ✆ **31/229/29-9555.** Fax 31/229/23-4139. info@morukuru.com. www.morukuru.com. Main lodge with 3 bedrooms, Owner's House with 2 bedrooms. Main lodge R20,000–R22,000 for 4 guests; additional person R5,250; child R2,625. Owner's House R30,000 for 4 guests. Rates include all meals, beverages (except wine cellar stock), game drives, walks, laundry, and meet-and-greet personal airport transfers. MC, V. **Amenities:** Multiple dining areas; bar; lounge; boma; kitchen; babysitting; bush walks; bush dinners; butler; dancing (traditional, on request); doctor on call; game drives; golf (on request); library (book, CD, and DVD); pool; spa and gym visits (on request); free Wi-Fi; wine cellar. *In room:* A/C, hair dryer.

Kingdom of the Zulu: KwaZulu-Natal

Demarcated in the west by the soaring Drakensberg Mountains, its eastern borders lapped by the warm Indian Ocean, the densely vegetated KwaZulu-Natal is often described as the country's most "African" province. Its subtropical latitude translates into long, hot summers—at times oppressively humid—and balmy moderate winters, while the warm Mozambique current ensures that the ocean is never more than 2° to 3° F cooler than the air. These sultry conditions have not gone unnoticed by the region's landlocked neighbors, making it the most popular local seaside destination in the country, resulting in a tide of condominiums, timeshares, and gated resort communities, ruining, at least for nature lovers, the coastal belt south of the Tugela River. In the center of this development is Durban, the busiest and largest natural port in Africa. Durban is enjoying a revival as a tourism hub for locals in search of affordable beach-based holidays and international travelers looking for good-value Big 5 safaris and the best wilderness trails in the country.

Durban itself has a unique energy that continues to spawn some of the continent's most creative trendsetters, but most international travelers come for the region north of the Tugela River, known as Zululand—where the amaZulu rose to power during the early 19th century under the legendary ruler Shaka. Traditional ethnic ways and rituals still play a major role in contemporary life here, and visitors can witness authentic ceremonies such as *sangoma* initiation rites and the annual reed dance, attended by thousands of Zulu virgins and their king. Zululand is also home to the majority of the KwaZulu-Natal game reserves, some of Africa's oldest and most famous wildlife sanctuaries. Given the difference in landscape, flora, and fauna, they make a worthwhile addition to a safari in Kruger or Botswana. Less than 3 hours' drive north of Durban, you can see the Big 5 at Hluhluwe-iMfolozi Game Reserve or at one of the nearby private reserves. This is one of the few places in the world where you can track a pride of lions or walk with black rhino in the morning, then spend the afternoon cruising for hippos and crocs along the lush waterways of the Greater St Lucia Wetland (a World Heritage Site), or diving the rich coral reefs off Sodwana Bay. If you have time, and it's well worth making it, join the privileged few who have explored the rich marine life and pristine coastline that lies even farther north, diving or snorkeling off beautiful Mabibi or Rocktail Bay. More intrepid nature lovers should head to Kosi Bay in the far northern corner of the province, where the swamp and Rafia Palm forests afford great birding, as do the inland reserves of Mkhuze and Ndumo, considered the country's premier bird-watching reserves. To the west are the historically important battle sites of the many wars fought among the Zulu, British, and Boers in the 19th century.

The Natal Midlands, with its fine country establishments and arts and crafts route, leads up into what is surely the pride of place for those who enjoy walking: the soaring Drakensberg Mountains, or uKhahlamba, "Barrier of Spears," as the amaZulu called them. The site of more than 35,000 ancient San rock paintings—thought to be the most densely concentrated on the African continent (including the famous Game Pass Shelter, the "Rosetta Stone" of Bushmen Paintings)—the Drakensberg was declared a World Heritage Site in 2000, garnering attention for southern Africa's most majestic mountainscape.

KwaZulu-Natal's growing popularity is assured, given its warm subtropical climate and its vast geographic and historic diversity, with most of the region's top sights within a 3-hour drive from Durban on excellent roads.

1 STAYING ACTIVE

BIRD-WATCHING Three of South Africa's best bird-watching destinations—St Lucia/iSimangaliso, and the Mkhuze and Ndumo reserves—are located here. The ever popular Zululand Birding Route has recently celebrated 10 years, and you can't beat the local residents' passionate knowledge of all the best places. For local guides and info, contact ✆ **035/753-5644** or www.zbr.co.za. Alternatively, contact Peter at **Lawson's Birding and Wildlife Tours** ★★★ (✆ **013/741-2458;** www.lawsons.co.za), which operates throughout southern Africa but invariably includes the KZN reserves in its fully catered and tailored bird-watching safaris. A 4-hour drive north from Durban, the Mkhuze Game Reserve, with more than 420 bird species on record, has chalets and en-suite tents with limited facilities (a small restaurant, the Rhino Diner serves simple pub-grub-style dishes; a shop stocking curios, clothing, basic food supplies and liquid refreshments; and a swimming pool, which is essential during the hot summer months). Ensure that your itinerary includes **Ndumo Game Reserve,** on the border between KwaZulu-Natal and Mozambique. With some 430 species, this KZN Parks Board camp is in an exquisite area, often compared with the Okavango Delta in Botswana, with numerous pans and yellow fever tree forests, wetlands, and reedbeds teeming with more than 60% of South Africa's birdlife. Situated near the Tembe Elephant Park on the Mozambique border, it has seven twin-bed chalets situated in a parkland setting under spreading marula trees. A camp cook provides excellent meals from the food provided by the guests. The camp is served by a kitchen and ablution block with hot and cold water. It's equipped with air-conditioning, a fridge, and a communal pool.

HIKING ★★★ Within the 66,000-hectare (163,020-acre) **Hluhluwe-iMfolozi Reserve,** between the White and Black iMfolozi rivers, is a 25,000-hectare (308,750-acre) wilderness untouched by human beings. Uncharted by roads, it's accessible only on foot. The five wilderness trails here are considered the country's best, superior even to those in Kruger. They offer the best opportunity to appreciate the silence and solitude of the wilderness, refreshing visitors physically, mentally, and spiritually. Most popular is the 3-night **Base Camp Trail,** based in the tented Mndindini Trails Camp. Trialists share showers and toilets with piped water. There's a fridge for BYO drinks, and you carry only daypacks with your personal effects, water, and lunch. Cost is R3,080 per person, excluding the R90 per day conservation levy. The cheaper 2-night (with option to extend to 3) **Short Wilderness Trail** is based around a more basic satellite camp; showers are buckets, and toilets consist of a spade, match, and paper; cost is R1,870 per person, excluding levy. Hard-core nature lovers or those ready for a life-changing experience should opt for the 3- or 4-day **Primitive Trail,** a return to the original pioneering tradition, in which you walk to a new campsite every night, carry your gear, and sleep under the stars (note that a fair degree of fitness is required for this trail); cost is R2,300–R4,600 per person.

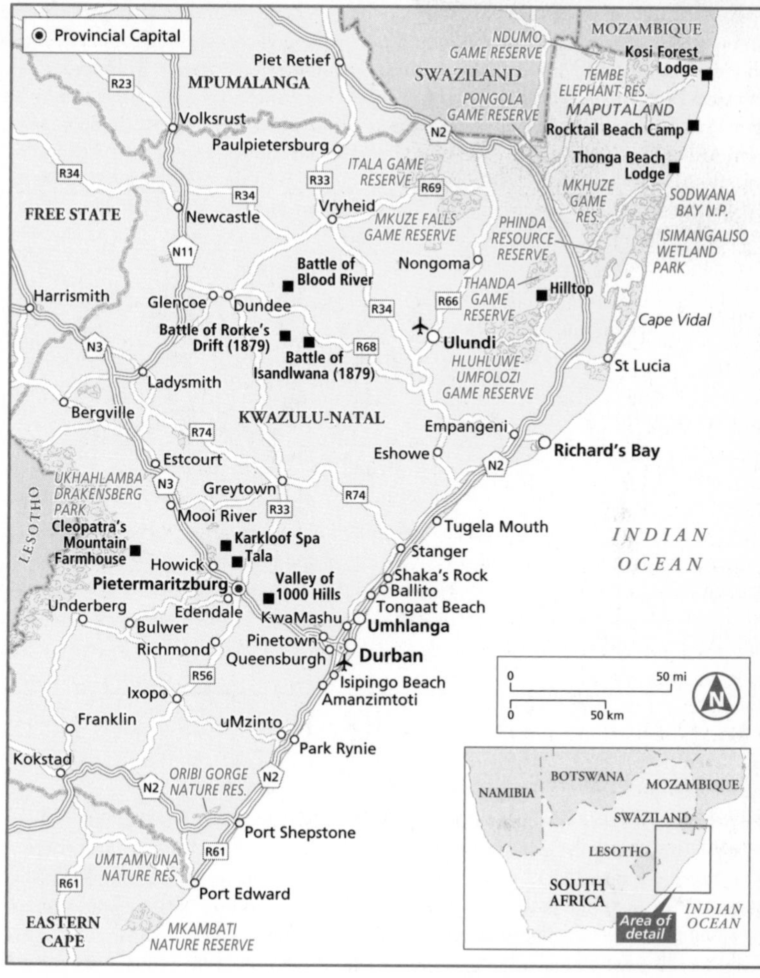

All trails mostly run from mid-February to mid-November (to avoid the worst of the heat) and are fully catered (including all equipment, bedding, food); they do, however, require a minimum number of four individuals to go out on the trail as scheduled. If this quota isn't booked, the trail will be cancelled and payments refunded. Participants have the option, however, to pay the minimum charge for four people, to ensure the trail takes place. For more information, call © **035/550-8478** or visit www.kznwildlife.com; for bookings, call © **033/845-1000** or e-mail trails@kznwildlife.com. KZN Wildlife also manages bookings for a second popular wilderness hiking destination: **Giant's Cup Hiking Trail** ★★, located in the Cobham area. Of the many trails traversing the Drakensberg, we highly recommend this 3- to 5-day self-guided, clearly marked hike that takes you past caves with San paintings, crystal-clear rivers, pools, and deep grass valleys.

Alternatively, if you have only a day, try the **Sentinel Trail,** connecting the Royal Natal and Cathedral Peak Parks.

Back in Zululand, the 3km (1.75-mile) circular guided **Mkhuze Fig Forest Walk,** through one of the area's rarest and most attractive woodlands, is also recommended; to arrange this, call © **035/573-9004.** At press time, some of the trails in Greater St Lucia Wetland Park (or iSimangaliso Wetland Park, as it's now known) had been suspended (temporarily, we hope). For up-to-the-minute information, contact **iSimangaliso Wetland Authority** (© **035/590-1633** or © 035/590-1162), or e-mail info@iSimangaliso.com (www.shakabarker.com). If it is operational, don't miss the **Mziki Trail** ★★ (in the Mfabeni area), comprising three 1-day loops of 10km to 18km (6¼–11 miles). Accompanied by an armed field ranger, you explore the park's estuary shore, dune forests, and coastline, with the chance to see elephants, buffaloes, hippos, and crocodiles.

SURFING To rent a surfboard and arrange lessons, contact Ira at **Blind Sunrise Surf Tours and Accommodation** (© **0798136718;** blindsunrise@live.com). **Safari Surf Shop** is another reputable Durban surf institution that will supply gear and lessons. They are located at 6 Milne St. (© **031/337-4231;** info@safarisurfco.co.za). In addition, lessons and gear for most watersports are available at **uShaka Marine World**. Good surf spots around the city are North Beach and the adjacent Bay of Plenty. Check out Green Point, Scottburgh, the Spot, Warner Beach, and Cave Rock; the latter has an excellent right reef break but is a little farther out of town; trips can be arranged by Blind Sunrise.

WHITE-WATER RAFTING **Umko** offers full- and half-day trips (R495/R395) on the Umkomaas/Mkomazi River, which boasts some of the best rapids in South Africa (the Section from Hella Hella to Number 8 is regarded as the longest stretch of traversable white water south of the Zambezi). These excursions can be extended into 2-day trips; call Clyde at © **082/561-5660.**

2 DURBAN

1,753km (1,087 miles) NE of Cape Town; 588km (365 miles) SE of Johannesburg

The Union Jack was first planted in Durban's fertile soil in 1824, a year after George Farewell fortuitously happened upon its harbor. It was only after the fledgling settlement was formally annexed in 1844, however, that the dense coastal vegetation was gradually consumed by buildings with broad verandas and civilized with English traditions such as morning papers, afternoon tea, and weekend horse racing.

Sugar was this region's "white gold," yielding fortunes for the so-called sugar barons. The most famous was Sir Marshall Campbell; today his home, housing the Campbell Collection, is one of Durban's star attractions, and one can still travel along the tacky beachfront in the two-wheeled "rickshaws" he introduced to the city in 1893. The world's voracious appetite for sugar was responsible for the strong Indian strain in Durban's architecture, cuisine, and customs—during the 19th century, thousands of indentured laborers were shipped in from India to work the sugar plantations, and today Durban is said to house the largest Indian population outside of India.

South Africa's third-largest city, Durban attracts the lion's share of South Africa's domestic tourists and offers a completely unique atmosphere. On the surface is the creeping sense of decay typical of tropical places, in which the constant presence of humidity brings about a kind of torpor. Yet beneath the surface, the city pulsates with promise—and not only among real estate agents exhilarated by the property boom that has followed

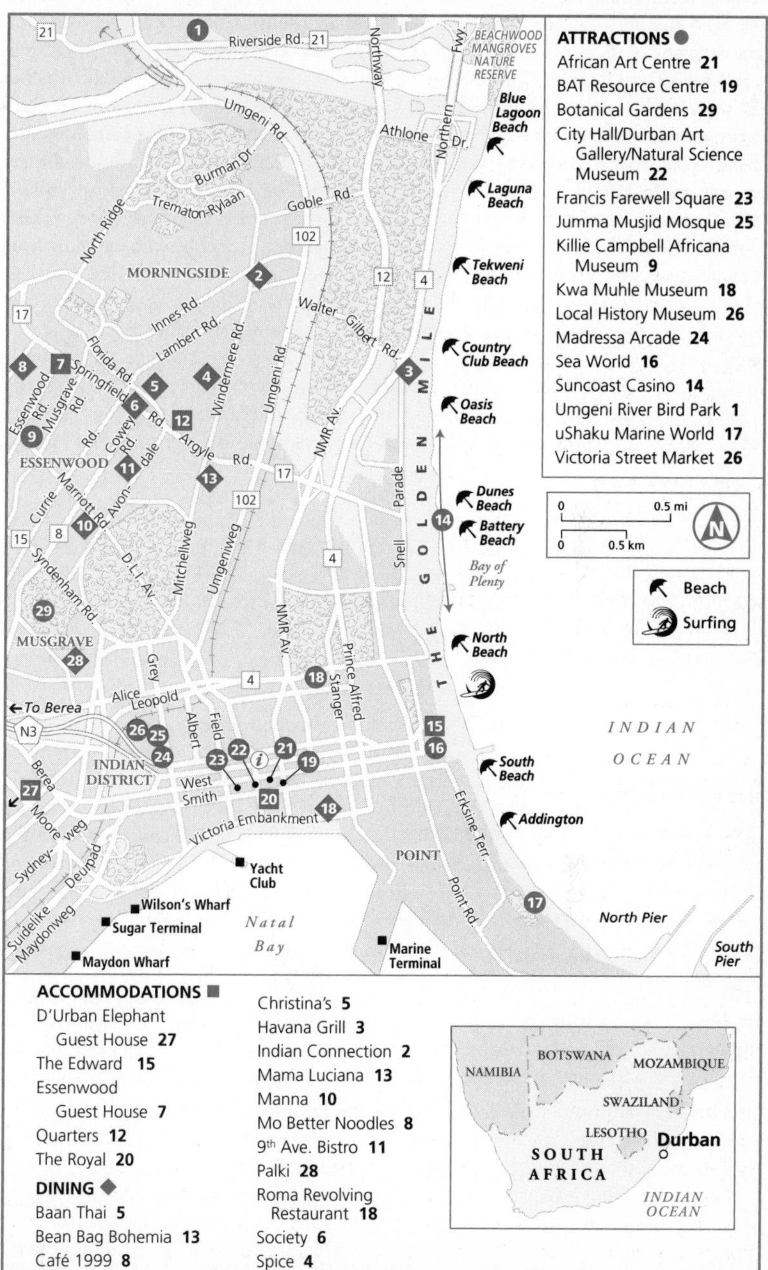
ATTRACTIONS
African Art Centre 21
BAT Resource Centre 19
Botanical Gardens 29
City Hall/Durban Art Gallery/Natural Science Museum 22
Francis Farewell Square 23
Jumma Musjid Mosque 25
Killie Campbell Africana Museum 9
Kwa Muhle Museum 18
Local History Museum 26
Madressa Arcade 24
Sea World 16
Suncoast Casino 14
Umgeni River Bird Park 1
uShaku Marine World 17
Victoria Street Market 26
ACCOMMODATIONS
D'Urban Elephant Guest House 27
The Edward 15
Essenwood Guest House 7
Quarters 12
The Royal 20
DINING
Baan Thai 5
Bean Bag Bohemia 13
Café 1999 8
Christina's 5
Havana Grill 3
Indian Connection 2
Mama Luciana 13
Manna 10
Mo Better Noodles 8
9th Ave. Bistro 11
Palki 28
Roma Revolving Restaurant 18
Society 6
Spice 4
0 0.5 mi
0 0.5 km
N
Beach
Surfing
Riverside Rd.
Northway
Fwy.
BEACHWOOD MANGROVES NATURE RESERVE
Blue Lagoon Beach
Umgeni Rd.
Athlone Dr.
Northern
Burman Dr.
Trematon-Rylaan
Goble Rd.
North Ridge
Laguna Beach
MORNINGSIDE
Tekweni Beach
Innes Rd.
Walter Gilbert Rd.
Lambert Rd.
Windermere Rd.
Umgeni Rd.
Florida Rd.
Springfield Rd.
Country Club Beach
Essenwood Rd.
Musgrave Rd.
Cowey Rd.
Argyle Rd.
NMR Av.
Oasis Beach
ESSENWOOD
Avondale
Currie Rd.
Marriott Rd.
THE GOLDEN MILE
Snell Parade
Dunes Beach
Battery Beach
Bay of Plenty
Syndenham Rd.
D.L.I. Av.
Mitchellweg
Umgeniweg
MUSGRAVE
Grey
NMR Av.
Prince Alfred
Stanger
North Beach
Alice
Leopold
Albert
Field
To Berea
INDIAN DISTRICT
Berea
West
Smith
Victoria Embankment
South Beach
Erksine Terr.
Addington
INDIAN OCEAN
Moore
Sydney
Deurpad
POINT
Yacht Club
Point Rd.
Wilson's Wharf
Sugar Terminal
Suidelike
Maydonweg
Natal Bay
Maydon Wharf
Marine Terminal
North Pier
South Pier
NAMIBIA
BOTSWANA
MOZAMBIQUE
SWAZILAND
LESOTHO
Durban
SOUTH AFRICA
INDIAN OCEAN

 urban beachfront rejuvenation projects such as the R21.5-million ($3.2-million) Wilson's Wharf, the R750-million ($112-million) uShaka Marine World theme park, and the R1.5-billion ($224-million) Suncoast Casino. There's a general sense of pride in Durban's ability to consistently birth some of the country's greatest creative talents, producing traditional pottery and beadwork as well as cutting-edge fashion and interior design. Durban cooks, and it's certainly worth scheduling a night here. If you're interested in the region's arts and crafts, make it a priority to visit the Durban Art Museum, the KwaZulu-Natal Society of the Arts (NSA) Gallery, and the BAT Centre. But to experience the essence of South Africa's most multicultural city, take a guided walking tour of the Indian District, where Indian dealers trade in everything from spices and sari fabrics to fresh fish and meat, while Zulu street hawkers ply passersby with anything from haircuts to *muti*—baboon skulls, bits of bark, bone, and dried herbs—used to heal wounds, improve spirits, ward off evil, or cast spells. Or just take a stroll along Battery Beach, where the Shembe may be conducting a baptism while surfers look for the perfect wave, or a group of Hindus may be lighting clay votive lamps while a Zulu *sangoma* tosses in an offering to the ancestors. It is a bizarre and wonderful city, a truly African city, undergoing its own little renaissance. And with the new international airport at La Mercy taking shape, Durban may eventually give Eurocentric Cape Town a run for its money.

ESSENTIALS

VISITOR INFORMATION You can make all your travel arrangements at the Tourist Junction, where **Durban Africa Tourism** (© **031/304-4934;** www.durbanexperience.co.za; Mon–Fri 8am–4:30pm, Sat 9am–2pm) is located, as is a branch of **eZemvelo KwaZulu-Natal Wildlife (KZN Wildlife)** and **Tourism KwaZulu-Natal.** The Tourist Junction is in the Old Station Building, 160 Pine St. ***Note:*** If you plan to travel north to the Zululand reserves and beyond, consider **Camera Africa,** a recommended agent that specializes in the Zululand area (© **031/266-4172;** www.camera-africa.com).

GETTING THERE **By Plane** At press time, **Durban International Airport** was located a few minutes south of the city center, but by mid-2010, the new international airport, renamed King Shaka International Airport, and located on the north coast at La Mercy (about 35 min. north of the center), is due to open. This northern location is far more convenient for those wishing to visit the game reserves in Zululand, with transfers arranged direct from the airport, though it would be a pity to leave Durban entirely off the itinerary. For arrival and departure information, call © **031/451-6666.** For 24-hour taxi service, call **Super Shuttle** (© **0860/333-4444** or 031/275-3836).

By Train The **Trans-Natal** from Johannesburg pulls into Durban Station (© **086/000-8888**), on NMR Avenue, above the bus service terminal.

By Bus Country-wide operators **Greyhound, Intercape,** and **Translux** (see chapter 2 for contact information) all arrive and depart at the station complex. The **Baz Bus** has an office at Tourist Junction and does drop-offs at hostels.

By Car The N2 from Cape Town runs parallel to the coast as far as Zululand; the N3 to Johannesburg meets the N2 at Durban.

WHEN TO GO The best time to visit is from February to mid-May, when it's not too humid. Temperatures range from 61°F to 73°F (16°C–25°C) in winter (May–Aug) and 73°F to 91°F (23°C–33°C) in summer (Sept–Apr).

GETTING AROUND **By Car** The city center is relatively small, but to explore farther afield, your best bet is to rent a car. A number of companies have desks at the airport,

Moments Sangomas at Dawn

The Durban beachfront and its warm and inviting ocean is a mecca for all walks of life: Stroll along a Durban beach at dawn, and you may see a group of Zulu *sangomas* (traditional healers), their beads and buckskin adornments covered in brightly colored cloth, wading into the ocean to collect seawater to be used in *muti* (traditional medicines) to protect crops. An estimated two-thirds of South Africans regularly consult *sangomas,* and recently even large pharmaceutical companies have been tapping into their knowledge of the medicinal properties of plants.

including **Avis** and **Budget**—the latter usually offers a slightly better rate. For a cheaper deal, call **Windermere Car Hire** (✆ **031/312-0339** or 082/454-1625) or **Comfort Car Rentals** (✆ **031/368-6563**).

By Bus The city center, beachfront, and Berea are serviced by **Mynah** buses (✆ **031/309-5942**); trips cost from R3.20. You can catch the **Umhlanga Express** (✆ **082/268-0651**) to Umhlanga Rocks.

By Taxi **Mozzies Taxicabs** (✆ **086/066-9943**) and **Eagle Taxis** (✆ **031/337-8333**) are both reputable cab companies. **Super Shuttle** (✆ **0860/333-4444** or 082/903-0971) offers a personalized transfer service to any destination in KwaZulu-Natal.

GUIDED TOURS **On Foot** **Historical Walkabout** and **Oriental Walkabout** ★★ walking tours (both R100) can be arranged through **Durban Africa** (✆ **031/304-4934**). Book the day before.

By Bus The most authentic city tour is offered by **Tekweni Ecotour** ★ (✆ **031/3320575;** 082/3039112; www.tekweniecotours.co.za). The full-day tour takes in the multicultural sights of the city and the harbor before moving on to the township of Cato Manor, where a local guide takes you on a short walking tour that ends at a *shebeen* (informal bar), where you enjoy a meal with members of the community; the cost is R380, including transport and drinks, but excluding dinner. Best of all, a percentage of the money is reinvested in the community.

By Boat Board the luxury charter yacht ***African Queen*** (✆ **083/262-6099**) for a cruise, and set sail for the north coast. Trips last 2½ hours and cost R200 per person. Less romantic is the engine-powered **Sarie Marais Pleasure Cruisers** (✆ **031/305-4022**), a ferryboat that does 30-minute harbor cruises and 90-minute "deep-sea" cruises (R50 and R60, respectively, every 30 minutes). **Adventure Ocean Safaris** (✆ **082/960-7682**) is the only licensed boat-based whale-watcher in the Durban area. For more boating options, contact the **Durban Charter Boat Association** (✆ **031/301-1115**).

By Air **Nac Helicopters** (✆ **031/571-8320**) offers a variety of trips, from a 30-minute flight around greater Durban and a 1-hour trip along the coast and the Valley of a Thousand Hills, to golf trips, Drakensberg tours, and game tours.

CITY LAYOUT The **city center** encompasses the buildings and memorials surrounding Francis Farewell Square, as well as the Indian District—the latter is now very seedy and best explored with a guide (see above)—and **Golden Mile,** the beachfront that forms the eastern arm of the city. Running south from Blue Lagoon Beach, it terminates in Durban Point, where uShaka Marine World leads the regeneration of this previously underutilized harbor area. Stretching eastward from here is the **Victoria Embankment** (or Esplanade); running at more or less 90 degrees to the Golden Mile along the harbor's edge, it creates the city's southern border. This is where you will find the BAT Centre (overlooking the Small Craft Harbour) and, a little farther along, Wilson's Wharf. On the western outskirts of the city lies **the Ridge,** as Durbanites refer to the wealthy colonial-era suburbs, like **Berea,** with elevated views of the city and harbor. Most of the city's best guesthouses and most centralized restaurant and nightlife areas are here, so it's a good place to base yourself. If you'd prefer to be on the ocean, **Umhlanga** or even Umdloti ("Oom-shlow-tea")—once separate seaside villages but now both northern suburbs of the city—are the areas to be.

Fast Facts Durban

American Express Located in "The Vibe" East Coast Radio House, Umhlanga Rocks Drive (✆ **031/566-8650;** Mon–Fri 8am–5pm, Sat 8:30–11am).

Area Code Durban's area code is **031.**

Emergencies For an **ambulance,** call ✆ 10177 and ask to be taken to the casualty unit at **Entabeni Private Hospital** (✆ 031/204-1300). Staff will also treat non-emergencies. Another good option is **St Augustine's Hospital,** 107 Chelmsford Rd., Glenwood (✆ 031/268-5000). **Police:** ✆ 031/325-4111; **Flying Squad:** ✆ 10111; **SAP Tourist Protection Unit:** ✆ 031/368-4453; **Fire Brigade:** ✆ 031/361-0000; **NSRI** (sea rescue): ✆ 031/361-8567; **Rape Crisis:** ✆ 031/312-2323.

Pharmacy Late-night chemists include **Medicine Chest** (✆ **031/305-6151**), 155 Berea Rd., and **Day-Night Pharmacy** (✆ **031/368-3666**), 9A Nedbank Circle, corner of Point and West (the latter has free delivery).

Safety Malaria has not been reported in Durban for more than 50 years, but if you plan to travel into northern Zululand, a course of antimalarial drugs is necessary (see chapter 2). Like any large city where a large percentage of the population is poor, Durban is troubled by street crime. The display of wealth is unwise anywhere in the city or beachfront, and visitors are advised to do their explorations of these areas during the day.

Weather For a weather report, call ✆ **082/231-1603.**

EXPLORING THE CITY

CITY CENTER If you're interested in taking a look at the city's Indian District, it's best (certainly safest) to call and book an **Oriental Walkabout** through **Durban Africa** (✆ **031/304-4934**). Walking tours start at the Tourist Junction (see "Visitor Information," above), where you can take a look at the African Art Centre. Also on offer is the **Historical Tour;** alternatively, head for nearby Francis Farewell Square, to **City Hall** (1910), a stone-for-stone replica of City Hall in Belfast, Ireland. City Hall's first floor houses the **Natural Science Museum** (✆ **031/311-2256**). The usual array of very dead-looking animals is useful as a crash course in wildlife identification if you're traveling north, and kids will also appreciate the gross-out qualities of the Kwanunu section, where the insect displays include some large, truly revolting roaches. One floor up, you'll find the excellent **Durban Art Gallery** ★★ (✆ **031/311-2264;** Mon–Sat 8:30am–4pm,

Sun 11am–4pm; free admission). Back in the 1970s, this was the first national gallery to recognize African crafts as art, and today it has arguably the most representative and exciting collection of traditional and contemporary South "Africana" art in the country (see "Discovering Zulu History," p. 406). East of the City Hall, facing Aliwal Road, is the **Old Court House,** home of Durban's local-history museum (✆ **031/311-2229;** Mon–Sat 8:30am–4pm, Sun 11am–4pm; free admission). The first public building erected in Durban (1866), this is a lovely example of the Natal Verandah style and today houses a rather dry collection of exhibits that focus on 19th-century history. Wander past the costumes worn by the disparate groups that made up Durban society for over 200 years (look for the beadwork items). A few of Gandhi's artifacts are also housed here (see "The Making of Mahatma: Gandhi's Turning Point," p. 398).

THE GOLDEN MILE BEACHFRONT The Portuguese explorers who first laid eyes on Durban's beachfront must have been a poetic lot, and their description—"sands of gold"—has stuck long after the high-rises and concrete promenades dwarfed the beaches. Central and South beaches are clean and less frequented, but swimmers and surfers (and a host of others) still head for Bay of Plenty **Battery and North Beach,** the latter now overlooked by the new **Suncoast Casino & Entertainment World**—which, aside from the casino, contains cinemas and restaurants, including the popular **Havana Grill and Winebar,** which has a deck area a stone's throw away from the sea. Located in the far north of the Golden Mile, at the estuary mouth, is **Blue Lagoon,** a great place to spend a romantic early evening. Nearby is **Umgeni River Bird Park** (✆ **031/579-4600**), good for kids, with more than 300 species from around the world housed in large aviaries, and planted with palms, cycads, and other tropical plants.

THE POINT & VICTORIA EMBANKMENT (Kids) The star attraction here (particularly for families) is **uShaka Marine World** ★★ (✆ **031/328-8000;** www.ushakamarineworld.co.za), located at The Point. Set over 16 hectares (40 acres), this waterfront theme park incorporates sea and fresh water, a recreation of a 1920 cargo ship, lush indigenous vegetation, and a spanking-new aquarium, Sea World (daily 9am–6pm, some activities closed Mon–Tues; R104 adult and R70 children)—one of the world's biggest and featuring the largest collection of sharks in the Southern Hemisphere. There are also dolphin and seal stadiums, a shark cage, a snorkel lagoon, and a "Wet 'n Wild" world—slides and rides to keep the kids happy for the entire day. And uShaka is justifiably proud of the fact that every drop of water pumped into its system returns cleaner than when it came in.

At the Small Craft Harbour, you can shop for crafts or have a sundowner and listen to jazz on the BAT Deck at the **BAT Centre** (✆ **031/332-0451**) and have a meal at the **Yacht Mole;** for even more impressive harbor views, head a little farther to **Wilson's Wharf,** Durban's mini waterfront complex, replete with bars and restaurants overlooking the very active harbor. This is an alternative to Suncoast on North Beach, and a good place to sink into a beer when the sun starts to go down.

BEREA This gracious old suburb is home to the **Campbell Collections** ★★, arguably Durban's top attraction. Housed in Muckleneuk, the neo–Cape Dutch home that sugar baron Sir Marshall Campbell built for his family in 1914, it gives one a great sense of what it must have been like to live in colonial splendor high up on the Ridge, with sweeping views from the upstairs rooms of the harbor below. Tours take in the gracious gardens and the Cape Dutch furniture and artwork collected by Campbell's son (whose private hunting farm became what is today the private game reserve MalaMala), as well as the extensive Africana library and ethnological artifacts collected by his daughter, "Killie" Campbell. Killie was a voracious collector of traditional utensils, ornaments, art, musical

Fun Facts **The Making of Mahatma: Gandhi's Turning Point**

On June 7, 1893, a young lawyer named Mohandas Gandhi, recently arrived in Durban, found himself stranded at the nearby Pietermaritzburg Station after being ejected from a whites-only first-class carriage. He spent the night mulling the incident over in the waiting room, and, according to the great man himself, "[his] active nonviolence started from that day." Mohandas (later to become Mahatma) was to spend the next 21 years peacefully fighting the South African laws that discriminated against Indians before leaving to liberate India from English rule. If for some reason you find yourself in Pietermaritzburg, you can visit the platform where Gandhi was unceremoniously tossed (at the seedy end of Church St.), the **Gandhi statue** (near the City Hall end of Church St.), or the **Natal Museum,** 237 Loop St. (www.nmsa.org.za), with exhibits on Gandhi.

instruments, sticks, and various items of beaded clothing (don't miss the necklace of British redcoat buttons worn by Zulu warriors as a sign of bravery). Today her collection, known as the **Mashu Museum of Ethnology,** at the corner of Marriott and Essenwood roads, is considered one of the country's finest groupings of African artifacts. Tours of the Campbell Collections and the Mashu Museum of Ethnology are by appointment only; contact the Senior Museum Officer (✆ **031/207-3432;** HadebeM@ukzn.ac.za.w).

UMHLANGA & NORTH The most popular seaside suburb on the North Coast, **Umhlanga Rocks** (pronounced "*oom*-shlung-ga") is a 20- to 30-minute drive north of the city center. Originally part of Marshall Campbell's sugar estate, it is now simply an extension of Durban, with well-developed facilities, safe bathing areas, and plenty of accommodations options. It also has its own visitor center: **Umhlanga Tourism Association** (✆ **031/561-4257;** www.umhlanga-rocks.com; Mon–Fri 8:30am–5pm, Sat 9am–1pm), on Chartwell Drive. Besides the beach, the one noteworthy place worth visiting in Umhlanga is the office of the **Natal Sharks Board** (✆ **031/566-0400;** www.shark.co.za). One of the most prestigious centers for shark research in the world, the board offers informative audiovisual presentations about these awesome predators—up to 14 species swim off this coast. Get there for the first showing at 9am, or at 2pm, and you can watch one of the sharks—who are regularly caught in the shark nets—being dissected. Currently the most viable protection for swimmers, these controversial nets are responsible for the deaths of hundreds of sharks, as well as numerous rays, dolphins, and endangered turtles. You can also catch a ride on a **Sharks Board** boat to observe firsthand how the meshing crews go about servicing the shark nets; trips are 2 hours and need to be prebooked (✆ **082/403-9206**).

Sibaya, the casino just beyond Umhlanga (✆ **031/580-5002**), is Zulu-ethnic on a palatial scale, with a re-created Zulu village offering insight into how Zulu communities lived many decades ago—and still do in remote corners of the country. You can see it all as either a kind of "living museum" or simply rather tacky.

If you're looking for uncrowded beaches, head farther north, beyond Ballito to **Zimbali Lodge** (see "Where to Stay" below), the North Coast's premier resort. Even farther north, **Blythedale** (roughly 25km/16 miles north of Ballito and 70km/43 miles north of Durban) has a lovely beach; some 13km (8 miles) farther, the tiny hamlet of **Zinkwasi,** the least developed beach resort on the North Coast, marks the end of the Holiday Coast. If you plan to spend time in this area, contact the **Dolphin Coast Tourist Information** (© **032/946-1997;** fax 032/946-3515) in Ballito.

SHOPPING FOR AFRICAN CRAFTS & DESIGN

The **African Art Centre** ★★★, opposite Quarters Hotel, at 94 Florida Rd. (© **031/312-3804;** www.afriart.org.za; Mon–Fri 8:30am–5pm, Sat 9am–3pm, Sun 10am–3pm), is the best place to browse for woodcarvings, ceramics, beadwork, baskets, tapestries, rugs, fine art, and fabrics sourced from craftsmen and artists located throughout the province. This nonprofit organization has a staff that is extremely helpful and knowledgeable about the products and their creators. Proceeds are reinvested in the development of local talent. If this whets your appetite, a visit to the **KwaZulu-Natal Society of the Arts (NSA) Gallery** ★★★, 166 Bulwer Rd., Glenwood (© **031/202-3686;** Tues–Fri 9am–5pm, Sat 9am–4pm, Sun 10am–3pm), is a must. The excellent exhibitions feature artists from different cultural and ethnic backgrounds and include paintings, mosaics, beadwork, and embroidery. The adjacent shop has a wide variety of visual arts, including works by master craftspeople, and the area has become a dining hub (including the NSA's alfresco Arts Café), so time your visit to coincide with lunch. If you're here on a Saturday, you could also explore the **Essenwood Flea Market,** held in nearby Berea Park

It can't really compete in terms of variety, but the **BAT shop** (© **031/332-9951;** Mon–Fri 9am–4:30pm, Sat–Sun 10am–4pm) in the **BAT Resource Centre,** Small Craft Harbour, 45 Maritime Place (© **031/332-0451;** www.batcentre.co.za), offers relatively good prices and a harborside setting. Established in 1995, this innovative community arts center is a pleasant place to shop, with several art studios where you can watch artists at work.

WHERE TO STAY

Hotels line the city center's beachfront, but with the exception of **The Edward** (© **031/337-3681;** www.proteahotels.com; sea-facing double (R2,060), the faded grande dame of Durban's city center beachfront, most are pretty tacky; if you're looking for character and value, you're better off in a great guesthouse on what is known as "The Ridge," with views overlooking the city and harbor—here **D'Urban Elephant Guest House** and **Essenwood** are our top picks, reviewed below. Businesspeople prefer **The Royal** (© **031/333-6000;** www.theroyal.co.za; from R3,040 double), which has exceptional service (it's a member of Leading Hotels of the World), or the **Hilton** (© **031/336-8100;** from R2,730 double), which neighbors the city's conference center; both are in the center of town. If you want to be closer to the heart of Durban's nightlife but you're on a budget, try the slightly shabby **La Bordello** (© **031/309- 6019;** R600 double), centrally located off Windermere Road. It's right next to Bean Bag Bohemia, so it's a good choice if you want immediate access to a bit of nightlife (© **031/309-6019;** www.beanbagbohemia.co.za). But with the relocation of Durban's airport north of the city, and Zululand's reserves and coastline beckoning, the Beverly Hills Hotel, Temerok Marine, and Zimbali are the most popular places to stay.

Durban

Beverly Hills Hotel ★★ In the northern suburb of Umhlanga (useful for the new airport location), this is also the best leisure hotel in the Durban environs, with a great beachside location; cool, breezy public spaces; and bland, standard-issue room decor. It is home to one of the city's best restaurants (**The Sugar Club** is a member of Chaine de Rotisseurs and Moët et Chandon Restaurant Circle), has good facilities, and affords great sea views from every room and public area, and such personal touches as your own lounger on the beach (it's one of the few hotels on the entire coastline to offer this obvious service). **Gateway,** the best shopping center in Durban, is within walking distance. ***Note:*** If the price strikes you as a tad steep, or you prefer real opulence in a more intimate atmosphere, take a look at nearby **Teremok Marine** ★★★ (✆ **031/561-5848;** www.teremok.co.za; R2,500 double), a plush guesthouse with excellent facilities shared by just eight gorgeous suites.

Lighthouse Rd., Umhlanga Rocks 4320. ✆ **031/561-2211.** www.southernsun.com. 89 units. From R3,800 double. Deluxe rooms R5,000–R7,500. Rate includes breakfast. AE, DC, MC, V. **Amenities:** 2 restaurants; Internet cafe; airport transfers (R650); babysitting; concierge; gym; pool; room service. *In room:* A/C, TV, hair dryer, minibar, free Wi-Fi.

D'Urban Elephant Guest House ★ Value Finds With panoramic views of the harbor, bluff, and Indian Ocean, this grand old Edwardian property, set in lush tropical gardens (often visited by monkeys), offers the best-value stay in Durban. Public spaces (including a lounge with library and a large collection of African history books) are by no means slickly decorated, having more the atmosphere of a peaceful commune (there are often long-stay academic or NGO guests), but each bedroom has its own outside entrance leading out either into the garden or onto its own patio/veranda. The neighborhood has many good restaurants and a great art gallery (NSA), and three shopping centers are within walking distance. The nature reserve, Pigeon Valley, is also a 5-minute walk away.

330 Cato Rd., Glenwood, Durban 4001. ✆/fax **031/205-6926**. www.durbanelephant.co.za. 6 units. R700 double. Rate includes breakfast. AE, DC, MC, V. **Amenities:** Pool. *In room:* A/C, TV, hair dryer (on request), free Wi-Fi.

Essenwood Guest House ★★ Value If you don't enjoy the anonymity of a hotel and would like to experience firsthand what it's like to live in the most sought-after residential area in Durban, then Essenwood Guest House is ideal. A rose-tinted colonial homestead built in 1924 in a large tropical garden with a pool, this was originally the family home of one of Durban's sugar barons. Paddy and John, themselves former sugarcane farmers, have restored the house, furnished it with tasteful antiques and artworks, and—thankfully—opened it to guests. The spacious suites have views of the city and distant ocean; request one of the four with private, broad verandas. Breakfasts are great; dinners can be served by prior arrangement, but the city center and Morningside's restaurants are a mere 5-minute drive away.

630 Essenwood Rd., Berea 4001. ✆/fax **031/207-4547.** www.essenwoodhouse.co.za. 7 units. R795–R995 double. Rate includes breakfast. AE, DC, MC, V. No children under 12. **Amenities:** Pool. *In room:* A/C, TV, hair dryer (on request), minibar, Wi-Fi (R1/minute).

Quarters ★★ Comprising four Victorian houses set on fashionable Florida Road, Quarters is a corporate, boutique-style guest lodge whose intersection location is at once convenient and noisy. All rooms are relatively spacious, have queen-size sleigh beds, and are double-glazed to eliminate the constant neighborhood noise, though this is scant protection from the sound of the person above flushing the toilet—ask for a room on one of the top floors. Bathrooms are big and well designed; specify shower or bathtub.

The **Brasserie** has a small but highly rated menu, attracting locals as well as in-house patrons; alternatively, some 20 restaurants lie within a 5km (3-mile) radius, many within walking distance. The new addition, Quarters on Avondale, farther up Argyle Road, is a more luxurious affair, with executive suites, yet rooms still have the same bland decor and ever-present road noise. Single R1,610, double R2,400.

101 Florida Rd., Durban 4001. ✆ **031/303-5246.** Fax 031/303-5269. www.quarters.co.za. 23 units. R1,720 standard double; R1,780 superior double. Rates include breakfast. AE, DC, MC, V. Children accepted by prior arrangement only. **Amenities:** Restaurant; bar; room service. *In room:* A/C, TV, hair dryer, Wi-Fi (R30/30 min.).

Zimbali Lodge ★★★ Surrounded by secluded indigenous coastal forest, with a private-access beach and golf course, Zimbali is inspired by the architecture of tropical climates, with local influences including the nearby sugar baron estates and Indian temples. The opulent interior (decorated by the same team responsible for the Palace of the Lost City) is a fine example of Afro-colonial-chic style, with many of the objects custom made for the resort. Set on a bluff, the buildings (including the rooms, which are situated in the gardens surrounding the lodge) overlook a natural lake, surrounded by forested hillsides and, beyond, the ocean. A large number of activities are on offer, including the Tom Weiskopf–designed 18-hole championship golf course, with a new golf course planned for completion in 2009. A selection of villas offering two- to six-bed luxury self-catering accommodations are scattered around the estate. The Forest Suites comprises 10 luxury suites located near the Country Club and has its own private pool and concierge. Also watch for the opening of the new Fairmont Resort Hotel on the beach at Zimbali Estate.

P.O. Box 404, Umhlali 4390 (off M4 just before Ballito). ✆ **032/538-1007.** Fax 032/538-1019. www.fairmont.co.za. 76 units. R4,565 double; R9,385 suite; Forest Suites R7,400 per suite. For villa rentals, contact 032/538-1984. Ask about winter specials; children's rates by arrangement. AE, DC, MC, V. **Amenities:** Restaurant; bar; babysitting; beach; bicycles; golf; horseback riding; pool; room service; spa; tennis. *In room:* A/C, TV, hair dryer, minibar, free Wi-Fi.

West of Durban

An hour west of Durban, just beyond Pietermaritizberg, is the start of the Midlands Meander, an area of undulating green hills, numerous arts and crafts stops, and some of the best accommodation destinations in the province; it's a great way to take to the Drakensberg or Battlefields (see "A Brief History of the Battlefields").

WHERE TO DINE

Combine weather so benign you can dine outdoors year-round; panoramic sea views; a rich Victorian, Art Deco, and Indian architectural heritage; and a melting pot of cultural flavors, and you can see why Durban's dining scene is so interesting. It's also quite easy to navigate, with much of it concentrated in the Glenwood–Berea–Morningside residential belt (the best are highlighted below). Florida and Windermere roads in Morningside are still the hot spots, but newcomer Davenport Road, in Glenwood, is one to watch.

WINDERMERE ROAD At the bottom end of Windermere, you'll find **Bean Bag Bohemia,** no. 18 (✆ **031/309-6019**). Located in an elegant old Durban building, this is home away from home for Durban's arty set, who, like BBB, never seem to sleep. On the ground floor, a buzzy bar and cafe-style eatery serves pizzas, sandwiches, and spoonfuls of tasty tidbits ranging from olives to won tons. Come here for a drink, then move on to **Mama Luciana's,** no. 45 (✆ **031/303-8350**), where Mama Luciana offers a family-style welcome. Better still, around the corner at 40 Marriot Rd., **Manna** serves tasty, healthy, clever food in a quiet, off-road, shaded courtyard.

FLORIDA ROAD Midway up Florida Road, at no. 178, is **Society** (✆ **031/312-3213**), a stylish restaurant and bar sprawling over two floors in one of the finest examples of early Durban architecture. The small, contemporary fusion menu features sushi and Asian-style tapas. Practically next door is **Spiga D'Ore** ★★ (✆ **031/303-9511**), a popular family-owned Italian eatery. Food is good and cheap, but you might have to wait for a table. If you're in the mood for light Asian, head straight to the **Mo Better Noodles** ★★, Shop 5, 275 Florida Rd. (✆ **031/312-4193**), an airy noodle bar serving consistently fine Thai-style food. The menu is small, but a long list of daily specials keeps regulars loyal.

DAVENPORT ROAD Packed cheek to jowl, this new dining district in Glenwood has become a serious challenge to Florida Road's culinary dominance. **Olive and Oil,** on the corner of Bulwer and Davenport roads (✆ **031/201-6146**), serves a somewhat conservative menu of Mediterranean food that relies on rich but satisfying sauces. Or trundle on to **Pizzetta,** no 139 (✆ **031/201-1019**), a casual but stylish eatery serving gourmet pizza combinations such as smoked salmon, capers, and mascarpone cheese. A few doors away, **Hemingways,** no. 131 (✆ **031/202-4906**), offers contemporary cafe food, light lunches, breakfasts, seriously good coffee, and both indoor and alfresco dining. Across the road is Dawn Glenny's **Euforia,** no. 134 (✆ **031/202-8951**), a vegetarian joint, where the food is fresh, healthy, and organic. Middle Eastern **Yossi's,** at no. 127 (✆ **031/201-0090**), is hugely popular, but, truth be told, it's really the warm vibe, open terrace, and chance to smoke a hookah that keep people coming back for more. (Don't miss the live jazz on Wed and Sun evenings.) Around the corner on Bulwer Road is the **Arts Cafe** (✆ **031/201-9969**), where you can eat from a light, cafe-style menu while sitting under spreading trees. A supervised play area allows kids to run around. Good coffee, too.

FOR FOODIES Perhaps it's the year-round balmy weather, perhaps it's the casual laid-back atmosphere, but Durban has fewer fine-dining outlets than other cities. Undoubtedly the best, **9th Avenue Bistro** ★★★, in the Avonmore Centre, not far from the buzz of Florida Road (✆ **031/312-9134**), is where award-winning chef/owner Carly Goncalves serves up modern bistro fare. The menu is small and changes seasonally, but expect the likes of pear and Gorgonzola salad with candied pecans; seared tuna carpaccio; or seafood sausages served with seared scallops, basil mash, saffron emulsion, and tomato relish. Loin of venison is a popular perennial. **Green Mango** (✆ **031/312-7054**), in the same center, serves superb and authentic Thai dishes, sushi, and sashimi—their spicy, crispy duck is the stuff of culinary fantasies.

The other top option is **Cafe 1999** ★★★, high up on the Berea in the Silvervause Centre (✆ **031/202-3406**), where Chef Marcelle Labuschagne and her partner, Sean Roberts, who handles the front of house, continue to pack them in with a modern Mediterranean menu, including their signature boned loin of lamb, grilled with lemon and rosemary, served with wilted bok choy, smashed baby potatoes, olive tapenade, and feta, and drizzled with red wine jus. Best of all, menu items are offered in "tidbit" or "bigbit" portions, so you can taste to your stomach's capacity. The only downside is the noise levels. If you're looking for a quiet tête-à-tête, pop next door to **The Store** (✆ **031/202-6182**). Owners Monique and Sherwin have garnered a devoted following for such dishes as duck breast flavored with star anise and cayenne and sweetened with honey, and a roasted sweet potato and leek stack. Finally, if you're in Umhlanga, top picks are **The Sugar Club** (see below) and **Ile Maurice** ★★, 9 McCausland Crescent (✆ **031/561-7609**), where the Mauvis family has been offering a mix of traditional French and Mauritian cuisine and excellent seafood for decades.

TABLE WITH A SEA VIEW, PLEASE Perched over the small-crafts harbor, with water lapping at its foundation and moored yachts just a touch away, **Yacht Mole** (✆ **031/305-5062**) specializes in seafood. A good wine list will keep discerning wine drinkers happy. For a range of dining options with a view, head farther along the Embankment to **Wilson's Wharf,** at the southern end of Durban's bay, where you can choose among several restaurants, including a good sushi and oyster bar and a Thai restaurant, all with decks overlooking the harbor. Suncoast Casino, overlooking Durban's North Beach, is a casino and family-entertainment center rolled into one; the best option here is **Havana Grill and Wine Bar** (✆ **031/337-1305**), which offers top-quality steaks as well as a few interesting seafood and vegetarian options. In Umhlanga, head for **The Sugar Club** ★★ (✆ **031/561-2211**), in the Beverly Hills Hotel, offering contemporary fine dining right next to the ocean. Downstairs, overlooking the sea and large swimming pool, is **Elements** (✆ **031/561-2211**), with an appealing all-white decor and a light, contemporary cafe menu.

Just 20 minutes north of Durban city centre, in Umdloti (the beach town just north of Umhlanga), is **Bean Bag Bahia,** Beach Cafe & Deli (32 North Beach Rd., Umdloti; ✆ **031/568-2229**). Floor-to-ceiling windows overlook the beach and provide a light-filled space with the freshness of salty sea air. The menu promises "flavours and tastes from South American and modern Portuguese influences," and they're reasonably priced from R70 to R120. But locals have all been lining up for a sea-facing table at **Bel Punto** ★ (Umdloti Centre, 1 South Beach Rd.; ✆ **031/5682407**), a family-run Italian restaurant: Try Mamma's homemade gnocchi and tiramisu.

But if you'd like to combine your seaview table with a dip, the best seaview dining to be had lies a little farther north, in Salt Rock (approximately 30 min. north of Durban city center), at the Salt Rock Hotel (✆ **032/525-5025;** www.saltrockbeach.co.za). It's by no means fancy food, but this old, laidback beach hotel is an institution: Amid tropical grounds, waiters serve up a number of fresh curries all day on the terrace (try the crab and prawn curries, after a round of fresh oysters). It's an easy stroll down to the beach and the tidal pool (great for kids), and for a fee you can wash off afterward in the hotel pool.

KINGS OF CURRY Currently, the hot option in town is new **Spice** ★★, at 362 Windermere Rd., in a comfortable old Edwardian home set back from the road (✆ **031-3036375;** Tues–Sun noon–3pm, Tues–Sat 6pm–late), where owners Linda Govender-Burger and Russell Burger have a different take on spice. In a marriage of East and West, oxtail is tweaked with cinnamon, a pear and leek soup fringed with cumin, and trout spiced with fennel. Farther down the drag, at 20 Windermere Rd., **Vintage** (✆ **031/309-1328**), another popular Indian restaurant in an old Berea home, serves up a selection of more traditional north and south Indian food. Also in Windermere, the **Indian Connection** (✆ **031/312-1440**) serves mainly north Indian, but with a comprehensive vegetarian selection. **Palki,** on Musgrave Road (✆ **031/201-0019**), serves north and south Indian foods in a cheerful, spacious first-floor room. If you're in Umhlanga, or looking for a grand and elegant dining experience befitting Indian royalty, head for the imposing **Gateway to India,** Gateway Theatre of Shopping, Umhlanga (✆ **031/566-5711**), where a team of chefs from India prepares north Indian dishes.

3 ZULULAND

Cross the Tugela River (88km/55 miles north of Durban), traditionally the southern frontier of Zululand, and it soon feels as if you've entered a new country. Passing a largely rural population through KwaZulu-Natal's Big 5 reserves and coastal wetlands, you are now traveling the ancestral lands of the Zulu, and the designated Zulu "homeland" prior to 1994.

Most visitors to Zululand spend at least 2 days in or near Hluhluwe-iMfolozi, the province's largest game reserve. Run by eZemvelo KwaZulu-Natal Wildlife, it is home to the Big 5 and has the most sought-after wilderness trails in the country. In addition, its proximity to Durban (less than a 3-hr. drive on good roads) makes it one of South Africa's most accessible Big 5 game reserves, and its prolific game, varied vegetation, and top-value accommodations make for an experience to rival Kruger National Park.

If, however, your idea of the "wild life" is pausing in your pursuit of lions with a drink poured by your personal ranger, there are also a number of private reserves to cater to your every need. Lying north of Hluhluwe and close to (in the case of Phinda, part of) iSimangaliso Wetland Park, these luxurious private game reserves are close enough to the coast to add diving with dolphins, sharks, and a magical array of tropical fish to your Big 5 experience—the combination of big game, lagoon, and beach is, in fact, one of the major benefits of choosing a safari in KwaZulu-Natal.

The first area in South Africa to be declared a World Heritage Site, iSimangaliso Wetland Park (previously, Greater St Lucia Wetland Park, for which you may still see signage) is a top destination for South Africa's divers, fishermen, and birders, as well as the rare loggerhead and leatherback turtles that have been returning to these beaches to breed every summer for thousands of years. Encompassing the foothills of the Lebombo Mountains, wetlands, forests, lakes, and the coastal coral reefs, the park is quite literally a paradise, but its proximity to Durban—and, indeed, Johannesburg—means you may have to share it with many others who similarly appreciate its natural bounty. If you're looking for a more exclusive experience, you're best off traveling farther north to Mabibi, Rocktail, and Kosi Bay—the real highlight of the KwaZulu-Natal coast, where a handful of guests find themselves alone on a stretch of pristine beach and coastal forest that stretches for hundreds of miles.

ESSENTIALS

VISITOR INFORMATION The best regional office to visit en route from Durban is **Eshowe Publicity** (✆ **035/473-3474;** Mon–Thurs 7:30am–4pm, Fri till 3pm), on Hutchinson Street. For information on the Hluhluwe region, call the **Hluhluwe Information Office** (✆ **035/562-0353**). For information on the **iSimangaliso Wetland Park,** call ✆ **035/590-1633** (www.iSimangaliso.com), or the **St Lucia Publicity Association** (✆ **035/550-4059**). For specific information and reservations on the other provincial game reserves, contact **eZemvelo KwaZulu-Natal Wildlife** (✆ **033/845-1000;** www.kznwildlife.com).

GETTING THERE & AROUND The quickest way to get to Zululand is to fly to Richard's Bay Airport, but it is more practical to fly to Durban and hire a car, as there is virtually no public transport in Zululand. If so, you'll have to contact a tour operator, rent a car, or arrange a transfer with **Thompsons Hluhluwe Shuttle** (✆ **035/562-3002**). (Private reserves such as Thanda, Phinda, and iSibindi Lodges all supply their own transfers from Richard's Bay or Durban airport.)

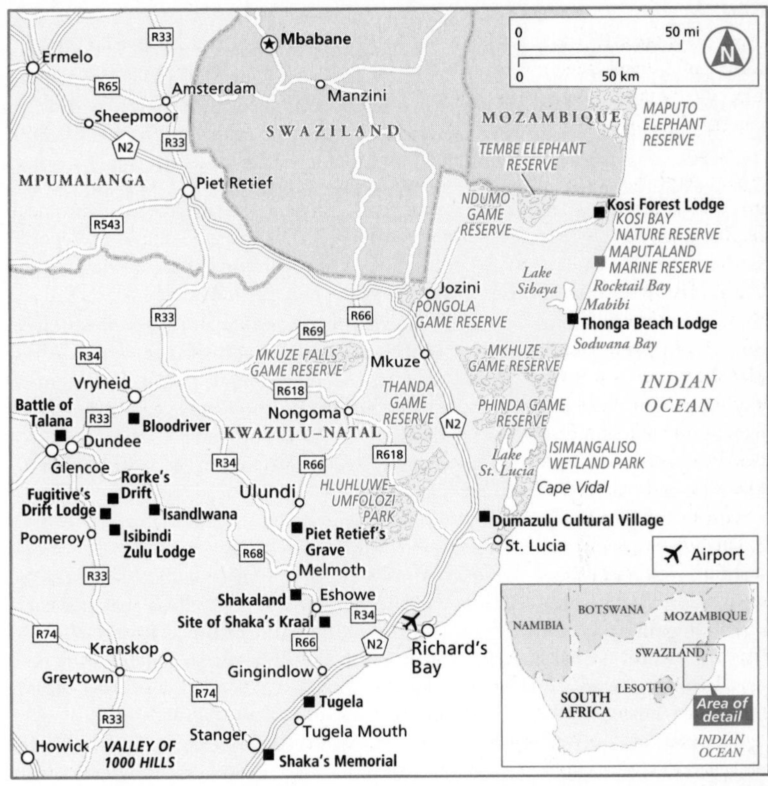

The N2 toll road leading north out of Durban traverses the Zululand hinterland; east lie the Greater St Lucia Wetland Park, Phinda private game reserve, and the birding reserves (Ndumo and Mkuzi); west lies Hluhluwe and most of the Zulu museums and cultural villages.

SAFETY Northern Zululand is a high-risk malarial area in the rainy summer season, and there is a medium-to-low risk in iSimangaliso Wetland Park, depending on the time of the year. For the most up-to-date advice, contact your doctor (also see chapter 3). There were reports of carjackings in the far north several years ago, but these have altogether ceased; still, it's best to use caution when traveling outside of reserves and highly trafficked areas.

GUIDED TOURS Ex-mayor of Eshowe (and proprietor of local Eshowe hangout the George Hotel), **Graham Chennells** ★★★ offers the most authentic and exhilarating opportunities to see contemporary Zulu life in Africa. *National Geographic* has commissioned no less than three film shoots of his tours. Guests are provided with a Zulu guide, who introduces them to friends in the broader community. On most weekends, Graham can arrange attendance at either a Zulu wedding, a coming-of-age celebration, *sangomas'* healing rituals, or traditional church services, where guests are treated as part of the extended family. For more information, go to www.eshowe.com, or call the George Hotel, 36 Main St., Eshowe (✆ **035/474-4919** or 082/492-6918; www.wheretostay.co.za/georgehotel).

SPECIAL EVENTS On February 23, Sangoma Khekheke's **Annual Snake Dance,** attended by 1,000 people, is held. September also sees **King Shaka Day Celebrations** and the **Zulu King's Reed Dance**—here some 15,000 maidens congregate to dance for King Goodwill Zweliteni. Most of October is taken up with the **Prophet Shembe's celebrations;** on Sundays some 30,000 people participate in prayer dancing. During the first week in December, the King's first **"Fruit Ceremony"** must be held before the reaping of crops can begin. To arrange attendance at any of these, contact Graham Chennells (see "Guided Tours," above).

DISCOVERING ZULU HISTORY

The proud amaZulu have fascinated Westerners ever since the first party of British settlers gained permission to trade from the great Zulu king Shaka, known as "Africa's Napoleon" for his military genius. As king, he was to unite the amaZulu into the mightiest army in the Southern Hemisphere and develop new and lethal fighting implements and tactics, including the highly successful "horns of the bull" maneuver to outflank the enemy. In 1828, Shaka was murdered by his half-brothers Mhlangana and Dingaan, and Dingaan was crowned king.

Distrustful of the large number of "white wizards" settling in the region, Dingaan ordered the massacre of the Trekker party, led by Piet Retief, whom he had invited—unarmed—to a celebratory banquet at his royal *kraal* uMgungundlovu. (A kraal is a series of thatched beehive-shaped huts encircling a central, smaller kraal, or cattle enclosure.) Dingaan paid heavily for this treachery at the **Battle of Blood River** (see p. 416, "A Brief History of the Battlefields"), in which the Zulu nation suffered such heavy casualties that it was to split the state for a generation. In 1840, Dingaan was killed by his brother Mpande, who succeeded him as king.

The amaZulu were reunited again under Mpande's eldest, Cetshwayo, who became king in 1873 after murdering a number of his siblings, and built a new royal kraal at Ulundi. Though by all accounts a reasonable man, Cetshwayo could not negotiate with the uncompromising English, who now wanted total control of southern Africa, with no pesky savages to destroy their imperialist advance on the goldfields. In 1878, the British ordered Cetshwayo to disband his army within 30 days, give up Zululand's independence, and place himself under the supervision of an English commissioner. This totally unreasonable ultimatum, designed to ignite a war, resulted in the **Battle of Islandwana** and England's most crushing defeat (see "A Brief History of the Battlefields," below). Nine months later, on July 4, 1879, 5,000 British redcoats under a vengeful Lord Chelmsford advanced on Ulundi and razed it to the ground. A captured King Cetshwayo was exiled to Cape Town and later England; he was reinstated as a puppet in 1883. This was to be the last Anglo-Zulu battle; the might of the Zulu empire had finally been broken.

The area known today as Emakhosini, "Valley of the Kings," has applied for status as a World Heritage Site, an indication of its value and general interest, even to travelers who aren't South African history buffs; you can visit Dingaan's homestead at **uMgungundlovu** (or "Secret Place of the Great Elephant"), part of which has been reconstructed and features 200-year-old artifacts; there is also a memorial to Piet Retief and his 100-strong delegation (✆ **035/450-2254;** daily 9am–4pm). You can also visit a reconstruction of the royal kraal at **Ondini,** near Ulundi. To get here, take the R68 off the N2 to Eshowe, stopping to visit the **Zulu Historical Museum** and the **Vukani Collection** first (see reviews below), or to meet Graham Chennells at the George Hotel for his highly recommended tours of the region (see "Guided Tours," above). To reach uMgungundlovu, take the R34 to Vryheid and look for the turnoff on your left.

While Westerners head for the many cultural villages dotted throughout Zululand, many urban Zulu parents bring their children to the **Vukani Collection,** housed at the **Fort Nongqayi Heritage Village** ★★ (**© 035/474-5274;** www.eshowemuseums.org.za; R30; daily 9am–4pm), in eShowe, to gain insight into the rituals, codes, and crafts of the past. This is the finest collection of Zulu traditional arts and crafts anywhere, and a visit here is essential for anyone interested in collecting or understanding Zulu art, particularly traditional basketware (not least to browse the handpicked selection of art and basketware in the museum shop). Another highlight of the collection are the pots made by master potter Nesta Nala (her work is sold in international galleries throughout the world; since her recent death, her pots have sold for increasingly vast sums). Nesta walked for miles to find just the right clay before grinding and mixing, then sunbaking her paper-thin shapes and firing them in a hole in the ground. Pots are finally rubbed with fat and ashes, applied with a river stone. Keep an eye out for another award-winner, Allina Ndebele, whose tapestries are inspired by Zulu myths and legends as told to her by her grandmother.

Besides the collection, there is the **Zulu History Museum** housed in the 1883 **Fort Nongqayi,** where the Natal "Native" Police were garrisoned. This museum traces the history of the fort and the virtual enslavement of the Zulu as a result of a poll tax; it also houses a good beadwork collection, dating back to the 1920s, and a collection of John Dunn's furniture. The son of settlers, Dunn became King Cetshwayo's political advisor and was the only white man to become a true Zulu chief, embracing Zulu polygamy by taking 49 wives. (***Note:*** Book ahead so that a guide can be arranged.)

TRACKING DOWN THE BIG 5 AND MORE IN ZULULAND

Run by eZemvelo KZN Wildlife, **Hluhluwe-iMfolozi** (previously Hluhluwe-Umfolozi) is, at 96,453 hectares (238,824 acres), by far the province's largest Big 5 reserve and offers excellent value. It is open to daytime visitors as well as overnight guests, which gives you the flexibility to base yourself in the **iSimangaliso Wetland Park,** where you are closer to both the ocean and the estuary, and to visit Hluhluwe as a day-tripper. Twenty kilometers (12 miles) north of Hluhluwe lies the new 5,000-hectare (12,350-acre) **Thanda Private Game Reserve.** Modeled on the luxury lodges surrounding Kruger, the reserve—if you opt for the tiny tented camp—provides one of the most exclusive bush experiences in southern Africa. There's more laid-on luxury (with a touch of kitsch) to be had at **Mkhuze Falls Private Game Reserve**—a private reserve that comprises more than 17,000 hectares (41,990 acres) and is one of the best-value Big 5 reserves in the country—and nearby Amakhosi Lodge, in the 10,000-hectare (24,700-acre) **AmaZulu Private Game Reserve. Phinda Private Game Reserve**'s camps—particularly Forest and Vlei—afford the most stylish bush accommodations in the province, but note that, for this kind of money, you could be staying in a top-notch lodge around Kruger. Finally, there are the beautiful coastal marine reserves, where you can stay at **Thonga Beach Lodge** or **Rocktail Bay,** both of which offer a chance to explore the coastal dune forest, laze away the days snorkeling and scuba-diving in tropical waters, and perhaps witness one of nature's most primeval miracles. From October to February, the large leatherback turtle (weighing in at 600kg/1,320 lb.) and its smaller relative, the loggerhead turtle, travel thousands of miles, using ancient navigational techniques to return to the precise beach on which they were born, heaving themselves ashore to produce the next generation—a cycle some believe dates back more than 6,000 years. **Kosi Forest Lodge,** sister lodge of Thonga Beach Lodge, is the ideal base for exploring the Kosi Bay estuarine system, another Maputaland jewel. This intricate hub of wonder comprises swamp, dune, coastal, mangrove, and sand forests, including an extraordinary collection of tropical plants, animals, and birds, including the rare Palm Nut Vulture.

Hluhluwe-iMfolozi Game Reserve ★★

Established in 1895, Hluhluwe-iMfolozi (the first part pronounced "shloe-shloe-whee") is one of the oldest wildlife sanctuaries in Africa and birthplace of the Wilderness Trail concept (see box). Once separate reserves, Mluhluwe and iMfolozi were united in 1989 and now encompass 96,453 hectares (238,239 acres). The provinces' premier wildlife destination, it's the second-most-popular park after Kruger. Though it's a mere 20th the size of its Mpumalanga counterpart, the reserve is home to a large variety of wildlife, including the Big 5, cheetahs, hyenas, wild dogs, wildebeests, giraffes, hippos, zebras, and a large variety of antelopes. Certainly, this is the best place in the world to spot rhino, particularly the white (from the Afrikaans-Dutch "wijd" or square-lipped) variety. Many consider its unique combination of forest, woodland, savanna, and grasslands, and its hot, humid, wet summers, the "real" Africa—well worth visiting as an alternative or addition to Kruger.

Treks along the **Wilderness Trails** ★★★ are conducted by rangers from March to November in the 25,000-hectare (61,750-acre) iMfolozi wilderness, once the royal hunting grounds of King Shaka. Access to this area has only ever been permitted to those on foot, making this one of the most pristine reserves in the world. Book them well in advance through **KZN Wildlife** (for more information, see "Hiking" under "Staying Active," earlier in this chapter).

VISITOR INFORMATION Open daily March through October from 6am to 6pm, and November through February from 5am to 7pm. Admission is R90 per adult, R45 per child. Guided 2-hour (R180 per person, no kids) and 3-hour game drives (R180) take place in the early morning and late afternoon through early evening, when it is cooler and the animals are prepared to move about more; these are open to residents only. For more information, call **Hilltop Camp** (✆ **035/562-0848**) or **iMfolozi Camp** (✆ **035/550-8477**).

GETTING THERE The reserve is about 280km (174 miles) north of Durban, with two entrances leading off the N2. The quickest way to get to Hilltop Camp is via Memorial Gate, 50km (31 miles) north of Mtubatuba (Hilltop is approximately 30 min. from here), but if you want to enter the park sooner, enter via Nyalazi Gate (turn off on the R618 at Mtubatuba). Adhering to the 40kmph (25-mph) speed limit, it's about a 50-minute drive to the camp. The third entrance, Cengeni Gate, is approached from the west, 30km (19 miles) from Ulundi. To drive from Cengeni to Hilltop, allow 3 hours.

Where to Stay & Dine

Of the two public rest camps in Hluhluwe-iMfolozi, **Mpila**—an unfenced camp in iMfolozi—is the best choice for an authentic, self-catering bush stayover. Accommodations are mostly basic, with shared kitchen facilities and baths. You may want to ask about one of the two-bedroom cottages or tents (en suite and electrified, but with shared kitchen). There is no restaurant; Mpila camp shop provides basic provisions. At the other end of the spectrum, **Hilltop,** in the Hluhluwe section, is rated one of the best public camps in the country; it's a good base not just for the reserve, but also for day forays to Mkuzi or Lake St Lucia (2 hr. from Hilltop).

Tips Shopping for Zulu Africa

Established some 30 years ago to revitalize the age-old Zulu traditions, **Ilala Weavers** today helps more than 2,000 Zulu men and women who practice traditional basket-weaving and beadwork techniques passed down through generations. The stunning works of art they produce are sought after the world over. The Ilala Centre combines a museum featuring the unique and interesting Zulu weaving techniques, along with a fantastic shop that has a huge array of woven, beaded, and carved goods for purchase. The intricate nature of some of the pieces is incredible and certainly worth stopping in to see. To get there, take the Hluhluwe off-ramp off the N2. Just past Hluhluwe Town and the airfield, turn left. Travel northward for approximately 3km (1 3/4 miles), and the road ends and becomes gravel (the tar road curves sharply to the right at this point). Travel along the gravel road for approximately 500m (1,640 ft), and Ilala Weavers/The Orchard Farm Cottages is clearly signposted on the left side (✆ **035/562-0630;** www.ilala.co.za).

Note: Also available are a number of houses, which KZN Wildlife calls **lodges,** situated in secluded areas picked for their natural beauty. These are unfenced, necessitating the protection of an armed ranger for bush walks; most also have a resident cook (though you may have to provide ingredients; check beforehand), or you may choose self-catering. These lodges (sleeping six to eight) are available only for single bookings, making this option suitable for a group or family, or a couple prepared to pay a little extra for total privacy. For more information on these, take a look at the Yellowwood and Red Ivory collections under www.kznwildlife.com; write to bookings@kznwildlife.com, or call ✆ **033/845-1000.**

Hilltop Camp ★★ Value Appropriately named, this KZN Wildlife camp commands lovely views of the surrounding hills and valleys, and offers a variety of accommodations options. The best are the two-bed en-suite chalets (all feature minifridges, tea- and coffee-making facilities, and an equipped kitchenette) and the four-bed chalets (all with equipped kitchens). For some of the best locations, request nos. 10 to 14, 28 to 33, or 44 to 49. The shop sells basic provisions (frozen meat, fire lighters, liquor, camera film), but it's worth stocking up in Durban or dining at the restaurant. If *nyala* steak is on the menu, order it; the meat of this shy, pretty antelope is delicious and hard to find. Hilltop also has a fully catered and hosted lodge, suitable for a group or family, and two bush lodges where a cook is available on request.

KN NCS, P.O. Box 13053, Cascades 3202. Reservations ✆ **033/845-1000;** direct inquiries ✆ **035/562-0255.** Fax 035/562-0113. www.kznwildlife.com. 70 units, consisting of 2-bed huts (no bathroom), 2-bed rondawels, 2- and 4-bed chalets, and a 9-bed lodge. From R550 double; R1,100 for 2- or 4-bed fully equipped chalet. AE, DC, M, V. **Amenities:** Restaurant; bar/lounge; babysitting; fax; fuel station; high-speed Internet (R10/15 min., when operational); pool.

iSimangaliso Wetland Park ★★★

From the Mfolozi swamps in the south, this RAMSAR and World Heritage Site stretches 220km (136 miles) northward to Mozambique, incorporating the **St Lucia Game and Marine Reserves, False Bay Park, Cape Vidal, Sodwana Bay,** and **Mkhuze Game Reserve.** Covering 254,500 hectares (628,615 acres), it encompasses five distinct ecosystems, including one of the three most important wetlands in Africa, mangrove forests, the dry savanna and thornveld of the western shores and the vegetated sand dunes of the eastern shores, the Mkhuze swamps (home to more than 400 bird species, including the rare Pel's fishing owl and Palm Nut Vulture), and the great estuary and offshore coral reefs.

The most easily accessed aspect is Lake St Lucia. A 38,882-hectare (96,039-acre) expanse of water dotted with islands, it supports an abundance of wildlife, including Nile crocodiles, hippos, rhinos, elephants, buffaloes, and giraffes, as well as a host of waterbirds, including pelican, flamingos, herons, fish eagles, kingfishers, geese, ducks, and storks. The lake is flanked on the west by typical bushveld terrain and on the east by the highest forested dunes in the world. These, incidentally, contain large deposits of titanium and zirconium, and conservationists waged and won a long-running war with mining consortia over their fate.

The easiest way to explore the lake is to catch a ride on the 85-seat ***Santa Lucia*** ★★ (bookings advisable; ✆ **035/590-1340**). The 90-minute guided tours depart four times a day and cost R120. If you're here on a Friday or Saturday, take the 4pm sundowner cruise with a fully licensed bar onboard. The launch point is clearly marked off the R618 east, which leads to St Lucia Village at the mouth of the St Lucia Estuary. The top attraction here is the informative **Crocodile Centre** ★★, McKenzie Street (✆ **035/590-1387;** daily 7:30am–4:30pm; R40, depending on the day). Of the literally hundreds of crocodile parks throughout the country, this is by far the best—and the only recognized crocodile research facility in South Africa. Arrive at 2pm on a Saturday for a snake presentation, followed by feeding time for the crocs at 3pm. The center houses all of the African species of crocodile—though you'll certainly spot at least one of the estimated 2,000 Nile crocs that lurk in the lake if you take a cruise on the *Santa Lucia.* Swimming in the lake, understandably, is strictly prohibited.

There are three guided hiking options in St. Lucia. We recommend the St Lucia Nature trail, which winds through coastal grassland and floodplains, with excellent forest bird sightings and small antelopes. The 8km (5-mile) route starts at the Crocodile Center and lasts 3 hours. The beach hike from Mission Rocks to Bat Cave and back (5km/3 miles) are is also worthwhile.

The only other reason to find yourself in St Lucia Village is because you're on your way to **Cape Vidal** ★ (✆ **035/590-9012;** KZN Reservations ✆ **033/845-1000**), a

Tips How to Avoid Becoming Dinner

Always keep a distance of about 3m (9¾ ft.) from the water's edge. Remember that crocodiles can remain underwater for up to 2 hours in just a foot of water, so don't assume you're safe just because there's no sign of 'em. If you see a V-shape on the surface of the water moving toward shore, get away fast; if the critter actually gets hold of you, try to locate its eyes and stick your thumbs in as deep as they'll go. Better looking but equally dangerous, hippos are more widespread and said to be the animal responsible for the greatest number of deaths in Africa. This is largely because hippos travel great distances at night for grazing, creating paths oft-used by humans to reach riverbanks. Hippos don't like anyone getting in their way, however, and they are particularly unpredictable when accompanied by their young.

Value Self-Serve Savings

The best budget option—ideal for families or small groups—is to hire a **self-catering unit** within the reserve from **eZemvelo KwaZulu-Natal Wildlife.** I particularly recommend **Bhangazi Bush Lodge ★★**, an eight-sleeper private lodge with a private cook and deck overlooking Lake Bhangazi; it's an easy 10-minute drive to the ocean at **Cape Vidal.** For reservations, call ✆ **033/845-1000;** for inquiries, call ✆ **033/845-1002** or log onto www.kznwildlife.com.

2-hour trip north to the coast. Besides the Umvubu Forest and Imboma trails, which take you over the tallest vegetated dunes in the world, the offshore reef at Cape Vidal makes the sea safe for swimming and ideal for snorkeling, and a whale-watching tower provides an excellent view of passing marine mammals (including 18m/59-ft. whale sharks). Day-visitor numbers to Cape Vidal are restricted to 120 vehicles, so it's worth considering an overnight at the camp. Comprising 18 five-bed and 11 eight-bed log cabins (from R444 double), all well equipped for self-catering (stop for provisions in St Lucia Village) and situated for relative privacy, this is one of the best-value options in the area. The rustic log cabins are shaded under the large forest of casuarinas a stone's throw from the beach and the warm Indian ocean (with an easily accessible tidal pool).

Birders must include a visit to **Mkhuze Game Reserve ★** (✆ **035/573-9004;** 5am–7pm; R35/vehicle, R35/person), which is connected to the coastal plain via the Mkhuze River. Reached via the N2 (take the Mkhuze Village turnoff; the Emshopi Gate entrance is 28km/17 miles farther), this reserve has 430 species of bird on record and a variety of game, which is indicative of the astonishingly varied vegetation and landscape. Maps are issued at the reception office; don't miss the three bird hides at Nsumo and Nhlonhlela Pans, where you can picnic and watch the changing spectacle on the waterway. This is also the start of the 3km (1.75-mile) circular guided (R100 adults, R50 kids) **Mkhuze Fig Forest Walk,** one of the area's rarest and most attractive woodlands. This can be booked directly through the Mantuma Camp office (✆ **035/573-9004**).

Last but not least of the Greater St Lucia Wetland Park attractions is **Sodwana Bay ★**, South Africa's diving mecca. Here the warm Agulhus current brings in some 1,200 varieties of fish, second in number only to Australia's Great Barrier Reef. This is the best place in the country to become a qualified diver, but if you just want to snorkel and bob around in the warm Indian Ocean, head for Jesser Point.

Where to Stay & Dine

St Lucia Village has a few B&B and small hotel and lodge options, none of them very inspiring (call **St Lucia Tourism,** an informal bureau run by volunteers, at ✆ **035/590-1247** or 035/562-0353, or see for yourself by visiting www.kzn.org.za). A far better option is to stay in one of the privately owned lodges on the western shore, immersed in natural surrounds. The best of these is the exclusive **Makakatana Bay Lodge ★★** (✆ **035/550-4189;** www.makakatana.co.za), in the heart of the St Lucia Wetland Reserve and comprising six privately located suites overlooking the lake. Activities include canoe safaris through the wetlands, snorkeling, full-day safaris in nearby Hluhluwe-iMfolozi, and Zulu dancing at Dumazulu. The all-inclusive rate (all meals and game activities) is R5,360 to R6,000 double. With 12 thatched chalets, **Hluhluwe River Lodge** (✆ **035/562-0246;** www.hluhluwe.co.za) offers similar activities for less money (from R3,880 in high season double, including all meals and activities; R3,200 double, including breakfast). If even this price strikes you as steep, it's worth considering **Falaza Game Park,** a tented camp on the western dunes of False Bay (✆ **035/562-2319;** www.falaza.co.za; from R1,300 double with breakfast; R1,950 double all-inclusive with game drive).

Phinda Private Game Reserve

Bordering the iSimangaliso Wetland Park and adjoining Mkhuze Game Reserve in the south, Phinda is home to the Big 5 and comprises 23,000 hectares (57,000 acres) encompassing seven distinct habitats, including sand forests, mountains, wetlands, and river valleys. Wildlife numbers are not as abundant as in, say, Sabie Sands adjoining Kruger (see p. 345), but most visitors are here for the exceptional range of experiences available, though guests have to stay overnight to gain access. Referred to as **Phinda Adventures,** these include diving expeditions to the coral reefs at nearby Mabibi and Sodwana, flights over the surrounding Maputaland wilderness (including to Lake Sibaya, the largest freshwater lake in Africa), deep-sea fishing, black-rhino trailing in Mkuzi, turtle-tracking, and canoeing and cruising the Mzinene River. Phinda also offers, without a doubt, the most stylish bush accommodations in KwaZulu-Natal.

Phinda Lodges ★★★ (Kids When CC Africa launched **Forest Camp** in 1993, these 16 Zen-like hand-built, glass-encased suites were lauded as the most stylish bedrooms in Africa. Each is privately located within a torchwood tree sand forest and constructed with minimal impact on the environment. Look out for the Cecil Skotnes and Lucky Sibiya woodprints. The 25 air-conditioned suites have en-suite bathrooms. The oldest, **Mountain Camp,** underwent an overhaul in 2008; each suite now has a private sitting room, personal bar and veranda, private plunge pool, and a romantic al fresco shower. The complex has a hotel-like atmosphere, but it's the most family friendly, with excellent views of the distant Lebombo Mountains and surrounding plains. The pick of the bunch are the modern glass boxes at **Vlei Camp** (pronounced "flay"): six glass-fronted timber dwellings on stilts located a discreet distance from one another, each with a private plunge pool overlooking marsh and woodland. Equally exclusive, but a bit more hippie, **Rock Camp** consists of six adobelike chalets built into the mountainside, with private plunge pools overlooking a watering hole. The latest additions are **Phinda Zuka Lodge,** a private lodge in the savannah south of the conservancy comprising four chalets, with dedicated use of your own pool, ranger and tracker, chef, and other staff; it's perfect for family gatherings and special-occasion safaris. Pricing is seasonal, from R25, 775 to R35, 575 per night. The drop-dead-gorgeous and modern **Phinda Getty House,** a plush four-bedroom mansion, will set you back R44,000 for a night.

Private Bag X27, Benmore 2010. ✆ **011/809-4300** or 021/532-5800. Fax 011/809-4524. www.andbeyond.com or www.phinda.com. Rock and Vlei 6 units each. Forest 16 units. Mountain 20 units. Rock and Vlei R7,700–R13,050 double all-inclusive; Forest and Mountain R6,600–R11,000 double. Rates include all meals and activities within the reserve. AE, DC, MC, V. **Amenities:** Dining room; bar; airport transfers by vehicle R3,282, by air R4,550 double; babysitting (Mountain and Forest only); game drives; guided bush walks and the Phinda Adventures (see above); pool; room service; free Wi-Fi (unreliable in main lodges). *In room:* A/C, minibar.

Thanda Private Game Reserve

Just 23km (14 miles) north of Hluhluwe, Thanda (which means "love" in Zulu) is another rehabilitated tract of land—this one the work of Swedish entrepreneur and philanthropist Dan Olofsson. In addition to the usual KZN reserve activities, Thanda provides a broad view of the local culture; guests receive a Zulu bedtime story on their pillow at night, and they can attend a Zulu *impi* dance performance at Vula Zulu, a traditional Zulu homestead. A shared community project with the backing of King Goodwill Zwelithini, Thanda employs local residents and pays a percentage of proceeds directly to the community.

Thanda Bush Villas & Tented Camp ★★ Value Thanda has been reeling in the awards since it opened late 2004, including the Africa's Leading Luxury Lodge prize at both the 2007 and 2008 World Travel Awards. The tented camp affords luxury you'd never associate with camping. It's a good value, but if money is no object, indulge in the huge and sumptuous villas, which are right up there with Phinda Vlei Lodge. In a nod to Singita, decor is African modern (chandeliers made from high-gloss dried seeds, curtains from wire threaded with tiny stones, stone fireplaces). Each villa has a large four-poster bed with the de-rigueur private plunge pool and huge viewing deck with thatched *sala* and circular daybed from which to enjoy the sublime views. Service is discreet (some would say too much so), and the wellness spa is very good. During low season (May–Sept), which happens to be best for game-viewing, the tents, in particular, are a very good value. In high season, however, the general level of service and game-viewing do not warrant the high prices—for this money, you could be in the game-rich Kruger or Okavango Delta.

P.O. Box 652585, Benmore, 2010. ✆ **011/465-0765** or direct 035/573-1899. Fax 011/465-3477. www.thanda.co.za. Villas 9 units. Tented camp 4 units. High season (Oct–Apr) villas R11,000 double; tented camp from R5,010; low season (May–Sept) villas R9,900 double, tents R4,510 double. Rates include meals, local drinks, game drives, and bush walks. AE, DC, MC, V. **Amenities:** Restaurant; bar; lounge; air and road transfers; game drives and walks; gym; room service. *In room:* Private deck w/plunge pool.

Maputaland Coastal & Marine Reserves: Mabibi, Rocktail & Kosi Bay

Home of the Tonga, Tembe, and Mabudu peoples, KwaZulu-Natal northeastern seaboard, marketed as the "Elephant Coast," is the most remote part of the province. Large tracts are accessible only on foot, horseback, canoe, or four-wheel-drive, and much of it is off the electrical mainframe. This inaccessibility has protected it from development, and the coastline is absolutely pristine. The entire coastline stretching from Mapelane in the south to Kosi Bay (on the Mozambique border) and extending 5km (3 miles) into the ocean is divided into 2 marine reserves protecting the coastal dune forest and hinterland, beaches, aquatic life, and coral reefs. A minimum 3-day stay is necessary to validate the effort it takes to get here and take advantage of all there is to do: sunbathing, snorkeling, fishing, bird-watching (60% of the birds in South Africa have been recorded here, including the Raffia Palm Nut vulture, one of the rarest birds in the country), canoeing the lakes (avoiding hippos and crocs), sampling *ilala* palm wine, and getting to know the region's 7,000 species of flora.

South Africa's largest freshwater lake, Lake Sibaya, lies only 10km (6¼ miles) north of Sodwana; but if you're headed for Rocktail or Kosi Bay, this is a major detour by road, and there's nothing much to do here but bird-watch or canoe. This in itself may be a major benefit—besides, on the west side of Sibaya is **Mabibi,** one of the most remote and beautiful stretches of beach in Africa.

The **Kosi Reserve** is about 15km (9¼ miles) northeast of Kwangwanase via a dirt road. You will, however, need a four-wheel-drive vehicle (and guide) to get to the mouth (some 5km/3 miles from the camp), where one of the most impressive views in the country overlooks Kosi Bay (in reality, an estuary, comprising four lakes linked by a network of channels), which is laced with intricate Tonga fish traps—a sight unchanged for 7 centuries. Turning back, you can see each of Kosi's four lakes, extending inland for some 20km (12 miles). Nowhere is Zululand's transition between tropical and subtropical more apparent than here. If you have the time and the will to visit, this true wilderness area will not fail to deliver.

Where to Stay & Dine

The coast's most romantic destination was closed at press time: **Thonga Beach Lodge** ★★★ (✆ **035/474-7100;** www.isibindiafrica.co.za; R4,090–R4,490) is set amid the coastal milkwood forest with sweeping views over the secluded coral-sand beaches of Mabibi. The luxury thatched-bush suites provide total privacy and were carefully constructed to ensure minimal impact on the environment. The lodge offers luxurious accommodation, mouth-watering meals, and one of the best dive sites in South Africa. Managers Kevin and Bev and their friendly local Thonga staff are enthusiastic and incredibly knowledgeable about the area. They can arrange memorable snorkeling and diving excursions, guided beach or forest walks, sundowner trips on Lake Sibaya, dolphin-encounter boat trips, turtle-tracking, and sea-spa treatments. The lodge will arrange transfers from anywhere in Zululand or the Richard's Bay airport.

An alternative to Thonga is **Rocktail Beach Camp,** run by respected outfit Wilderness Safaris. Although the beach is a 15-minute walk from the camp and only a few of the rooms have sea views, set back in and shaded by the lush Coastal Sand Forest, the Maputaland Marine Reserve is just offshore and, there is world-class diving and snorkeling to be enjoyed. The camp is simple and unfussy but comfortable, consisting of 12 rooms (including 3 family units), a dining room, bar, and lounge with a wraparound veranda and swimming pool. All have en-suite bathrooms with an indoor shower and overhead fans (✆ **011/257-5111;** www.safariadventurecompany.com; from R2,700 double; rates include breakfast and dinner).

A highly recommended add-on to **Thonga** is a sojourn at sister establishment **Kosi Forest Lodge,** the only private lodge in the Kosi Bay Nature Reserve—part of Isimangaliso Wetland Park and an easy 1½-hour drive north of Thonga. This little gem is tucked away amid the coastal dune forest alongside the Siyadla River, which feeds into the Kosi Lake system, one of the world's most pristine estuarine systems. There are eight luxury tented rooms; one is a family room (unit 6), and all have romantic outdoor showers and baths, reminding you that you are really deep in the coastal forest reserve and in one of South Africa's best ecotourist destinations. Kosi Forest Lodge caters to a host of estuarine, beach, and wilderness activities, including guided canoe and boat trips, raffia forest walks, or day excursions to nearby coastal beaches and reserves such as Tembe Elephant Park, with the aptly named Blessing, who has been with the lodge since its inception and hails from the area. His knowledge of local flora and fauna is exceptional, and it is a treat spending time with him in this magical wilderness arena.

4 THE BATTLEFIELDS

Ladysmith 251km (156 miles) NW of Durban; Dundee 320km (198 miles) N of Durban

Most of the battles fought on South African soil took place in the northwestern corner of KwaZulu-Natal, where the rolling grasslands were regularly soaked with blood as battles for territorial supremacy would, in turn, pit Zulu against Boer (Afrikaner), Brit against Zulu, and Afrikaner against Brit. The official Battlefields Route covers 4 wars, 15 towns, and more than 50 battlefields, and includes numerous museums and memorials to the dead and victorious. Few would argue that the heroic Anglo-Zulu battles that took place on January 22, 1879, at Isandlwana and Rorke's Drift—immortalized in the movie *Zulu,* starring Michael Caine—are the most compelling, and their battlefields are the best for those with limited time to see.

Another site worth investigating is that of the Battle of Blood River (near Dundee), which took place 41 years earlier, this time between the Trekkers and the Zulus. This victory was to validate Afrikaner arrogance and religious self-righteousness. Visitors should also visit Ladysmith to immerse themselves in the siege that jumpstarted the Second Anglo-Boer War. It would take the world's mightiest nation 3 years and thousands of pounds to defeat one of the world's smallest, embroiling some of the century's most powerful leaders, such as Winston Churchill and Gandhi, in the battle.

This is one area where a guide is almost essential, and top of the line are those trained by the late David Rattray (see below). If, however, you are eager to tackle a self-guided tour but are unfamiliar with the historical background of the wars, consider the brief chronological account supplied below.

Tip: It is important to understand that the Battlefields—while seemingly out of the way from the usual tourist attractions—are in many ways the historical core of the modern South African nation. If understanding this people and their history is important to you, then a visit here is essential. It is advisable to pass through here from Zululand en route to the uKhahlamba Drakensberg region, or up from the Midlands Meander. You'll gain a strong sense of historical narrative while contextualizing the great tribal population movements of that time. Those who are not interested in walking around battlefields, no matter how vivid or moving the storytelling, can take pleasure in the fact that this is one of most scenic and, ironically, tranquil parts of the country, with beautiful lodges and a range of activities, including horse riding, guided walks, rock art, mountain biking, and strolls through the bushveld.

ESSENTIALS

VISITOR INFORMATION Contact **Dundee Tourism** (✆ **034/2122121**), which is the area's central hub, at Rorke's Drift and Isandlwana. The **Ladysmith Tourism Information Bureau,** site of the Second Anglo-Boer War (✆ **036/637-2992;** www.ladysmith.kzn.org.za) is also very helpful.

GETTING THERE **By Car** It takes around 3½ hours by car from Durban to get to the battlefields, 4½ hours from Jo'burg. You have a choice of a number of routes, but the N3 toll road is the safest. If you're interested in Zulu culture, travel to or from Durban via Eshowe.

By Bus **Greyhound** and **Translux** (see chapter 3 for regional phone numbers) both travel through Ladysmith daily.

GUIDED TOUR Exploring with a recommended guide is highly advised; unless you are an African history guru, it would be remiss to attempt a tour of the area without one. David Rattray, the late legendary storyteller whose family still runs **Fugitive's Drift** (✆ **034/642-1843** or 034/271-8051; also see "Where to Stay & Dine," below), has left behind a more than capable team of handpicked staff members well versed and rehearsed in the inimitable Rattray style. Their detailed research on the individuals who fought on both sides of the Anglo-Zulu War humanizes the battles, and even those who find history rather dry will find themselves enthralled. Space allowing, nonresidents may join these tours for a fee starting at R410 for Rorkes Drift and Isandlwana, depending on the tour and season.

A Brief History of the Battlefields

The first major battle in this area took place some 48km (30 miles) east of Dundee, at what came to be known as **Blood River.** Following the treacherous murder of Retief and his men (see p. 406, "Discovering Zulu History") and Dingaan's ruthless persecution of white settlers, Trekker leader Andries Pretorius moved an Afrikaner commando of 464 men to a strategic spot on the banks of the ironically named Ncome (Peace) River. There he created an impenetrable *laager* (a circular encampment of wagons, with oxen in the center), with 64 ox-wagons, and prayed for victory. On behalf of the Afrikaner nation, Pretorius made a solemn vow to God that, should they survive, Afrikaners would hold the day sacred in perpetuity. On December 16, 1838, the Zulus attacked. Three times they were driven off by fire before Pretorius led a mounted charge. Eventually, the Zulus fled, leaving 3,000 dead and the river dark with blood. Not one Boer died, giving rise to the nationalistic Afrikaner myth that their Old Testament God had protected them against invincible odds, proving that they were indeed the chosen race. Today, December 16 remains a national holiday (though renamed Day of Reconciliation), and visitors can view the eerie spectacle of a replica laager, 64 life-size ox-wagons cast in bronze, at the original site of **Blood River Battlefield.** The site is off the R33 and is open daily from 8am to 5pm.

Zulu might rose again under Cetshwayo. This clearly did not fit in with British imperialist plans, and, having delivered a totally unreasonable ultimatum, three British columns under an overconfident Chelmsford marched into Zululand in January 1879. On January 21, Chelmsford set up temporary camp at **Isandlwana Hill** and, believing that the Zulu army was elsewhere, took a large detachment to support a reconnaissance force, leaving the camp defenseless. Six kilometers (3¾ miles) away, 24,000 Zulu soldiers sat in the long grass, waiting silently for a signal. At about 11:30am the following day, a British patrol inadvertently stumbled upon them, and the Zulu warriors quickly surrounded the patrol, chanting their famed rallying cry, *"uSuthu"* (oo-*soo*-too).

Two hours later, 1,329 of the 1,700 British soldiers were dead. Survivors fled across **Fugitive's Drift,** where more died. Two men made it to the nearby mission station called **Rorke's Drift,** where a contingent of 139 men (35 of them seriously ill) were waiting with provisions for Chelmsford's return. With seconds to spare, the men barricaded themselves behind a makeshift wall of army biscuit boxes, tinned meat, and bags of maize meal, and warded off the

For the Battle of Spioenkop of the Anglo Boer War (see below), stay at **Three Tree Hill Lodge,** which continues the Rattray tradition of enthralling tours and wonderful hospitality (© **036/448-1171** or 082/379-1864; www.threetreehill.co.za).

Other guides worth mentioning are Mike Nel, who is based in Dundee (© **082/366-2639** or 034/212-2601). **Prince Sibusiso Shibe,** the local historian working with Thompson's Tours (© **031/275-3500** or 083/967-6347); **Rob Gerrard,** resident historian and Fellow of the Royal Geographical Society, based at Isandlwana Lodge (see

4,000-strong Zulu onslaught. The battle raged until dawn, when the Zulus finally withdrew. Despite incredible odds, only 17 British soldiers died at Rorke's Drift, and 11 Victoria Crosses were awarded—more than at any other battle in British history. Six months later, on July 4, 1879, the Zulus suffered their final defeat at Ondini.

A year later, the British would begin a new brawl, this time with the Afrikaners. Although a peace treaty was signed in March 1881, it sowed the seeds for the Second Anglo-Boer War, a 3-year battle that captured the world's attention and introduced the concept of guerrilla warfare. On October 20, 1899, the first battle was pitched on **Talana Hill,** when 14,000 Afrikaners attacked 4,000 British troops. The Brits managed to repel the attackers, but, on November 2, the little town of Ladysmith was besieged by the Afrikaners for 118 days. Thousands died of disease, trapped without access to clean water, and more fell as the British tried to break through the Afrikaner defenses. (Winston Churchill, covering the war for the *London Morning Post,* narrowly escaped death when Boer forces blew up the train he was traveling on some 40km/25 miles south of Ladysmith.)

The most ignominious and famous of all battles between the British and the Boers took place on **Spioenkop** (literally, "Spies Hill"), when Boers and Brits battled for this strategic position until both sides believed they had lost. The British were the first to withdraw, leaving the astonished but triumphant Boer in force on this strategic hill (off the R600). On that hill were Louis Botha (the first Prime Minister of the Union of South Africa); Winston Churchill, then a reporter; and Mohandas Ghandi (the future Mahatma), then a stretcher bearer. Two years later, following the scorched-earth policy of the British—when hundreds of acres of farmland were burned and Afrikaner women and children were placed in concentration camps, where they perished from malnourishment and disease—the Boers conceded defeat.

Tip: Look out for David Rattray's audio CDs, *Day of the Dead Moon: The Story of the Anglo-Zulu War of 1879,* a series of five audio CDs by David Rattray. Also seek out Andrew Ardington's *Spioenkop to Versailles—A Story of the Anglo-Boer War*, which covers the conflict between the British and the Boers in Southern Africa, from the Great Trek through their two wars. Spioenkop forms the major focus of the story, which continues through to South Africa's involvement in the Great War, inspired by Louis Botha and Jan Smuts.

"Where to Stay & Dine," below); and natural scientist **John Turner** (© **035/835-0062**), who combines battlefield tours with trips to nearby reserves, such as Hluhluwe-iMfolozi, where he puts his degree in animal behavior to excellent use.

EXPLORING THE BATTLEFIELDS

Isandlwana Battlefield ★★ Other than the rather beautiful "Zulu-necklace" monument and the many white painted rocks, there is not much here to evoke the 1879 battle of Isandlwana. With a good guide, you may be able to hear the sound of 20,000 Zulu warriors chanting *"zee, zee, zee,"* like angry bees amassing, before attacking with the Zulu deep-throated war cry *"uSuthu, uSuthu, uSuthu,"* ultimately delivering the most crushing defeat the mighty British Empire was to suffer in Africa at the hands of "savages armed with sticks." The white cairns mark the places where British soldiers fell and were buried. The British were horrified to find their men disemboweled—proof, they thought, of the savagery of the Zulu. In fact, the Zulus were honoring the men by setting their spirits free.

Off the R68, btw. Nqutu and Babanango. ✆ **034/271-8165.** Admission R15 adults. Mon–Fri 8am–4pm; Sat–Sun 9am–4pm.

Ladysmith Siege Museum ★★ If your interest lies in the battle between the Boers and the British, this is an essential stop. Displays and photographs vividly depict the wars that so greatly affected 20th-century South Africa, as well as the appalling conditions at the end of the siege, when 28 to 30 people died daily. Farther up Murchison Street, next to the Town Hall, is the **Cultural Centre and Museum** (Mon–Fri 9am–4pm; admission R11), where you can listen to the sounds of **Ladysmith Black Mambazo,** the a cappella group that shot to fame with the record *Homeless.*

Murchison St. (the main road running through Ladysmith), next to the Town Hall. ✆ **036/637-2992.** Admission R11. Mon–Fri 9am–4pm; Sat 9am–1pm.

Rorke's Drift ★★ Located in the reconstructed hospital where 100 men holed up for 12 hours and successfully warded off 4,000 Zulus led by Cetshwayo's brother Dabulamanzi, this is the most evocative interpretation center on the route. Realistic scenes are augmented by battle sounds and electronic diagrams. An added bonus is the adjoining **ELC Craft Centre** (✆ **034/642-1627**), where you can browse for textiles, carpets, tapestries, and pottery.

Off the R68, 42km (26 miles) from Dundee on the road to Nqutu. ✆ **034/642-1687.** www.centrerorkesdrift.com. Admission R20. Mon–Fri 8am–4pm; Sat–Sun 9am–4pm.

Spioenkop Battlefields The Battle of Spioenkop is a focal point in the history of the 2nd Anglo-Boer War (1899–1902). Scenically situated on top of a hill with 360-degree views of the 'berg, the tour tells of the bloodiest day of the war, played out by a cast seldom challenged (see box above).

At the end of a clearly signposted short gravel road from the R616 to Bergville. The R616 is easily accessible from the N3 at the Bergville/Ladysmith off-ramps, exit 230. Call Ladysmith Tourism at ✆ **036/637-2992** or visit www.ladysmith.kzn.org.za.

WHERE TO STAY & DINE

Fugitive's Drift Lodge ★★, situated within a 2,500-hectare (6,175-acre) nature reserve in the heart of battlefield country, is undoubtedly the highlight of the area. Led by the finest guides in South Africa, these famously thought-provoking and often emotionally charged tours are conducted daily to Isandlwana and Rorke's Drift. Walks and horseback rides take visitors through the reserve to view abundant game and birdlife and to fish the 20km frontage on the Buffalo River (where Lts. Melvill and Coghill died on its banks defending the Queens Colour). The reserve offers a choice of accommodation in either the Lodge or the Guest House, both owned by the Rattrays, whose love of South Africa, its people, and its unique history is evident in every corner. Spacious, luxury en-suite cottages with a tasteful blend of Anglo-Zulu memorabilia and country comfort each have private verandas and broad views over the plains flanking the Buffalo River Gorge. The

Lodge and Guest House both have large swimming pools, set in well-established indigenous gardens home to innumerable bird species. The hospitality is superb. (© **034/642-1843** or 034/271-8051; www.fugitives-drift-lodge.com; from R3,640 double in low season [May–July] to R5,180 double in high season; rates include all meals and tourism levy.) Tours are from R660 in low season to R880 per person, in addition to the accommodation rate.

If you'd like to stay in more obviously "African"-style accommodations—very exclusive, but at a more reasonable rate—take a look at neighboring **Isibindi Zulu Lodge.** "Rooms" take a traditional Zulu beehive hut as their departure point and must rate as one of the most successful blends of Western and African architecture in Zululand. It is also situated within the 1,600-hectare (4,000-acre) Isibindi Eco-Reserve, offering diverse habitats ranging from montane grassland and valley thornveld to riverine forests. The lodge runs morning and evening game drives, and the bird-watching is excellent. (© **035/474-1473;** fax 035/474-1490; www.isibindi.co.za; high season [Sept–Apr] R2,700 double, low season [May–Aug] R2,300; includes all meals and a game drive). The lodge is a stone's throw away from the historically momentous Anglo-Zulu battlefields of Rorke's Drift and Isandlwana.

For a more hotel-like experience, there's **Isandlwana Lodge** (© **034/271-8301,** -04, -05 for reservations; www.isandlwana.co.za; R3,600–R3,970 double, including meals; battlefield tours are R450): An elegant Afro-colonial lodge that enjoys a great location overlooking the historic battlefield, it offers a host of activities, including a Zulu Village "Safari," in which a licensed Zulu guide takes visitors to a local church, home, clinic, and *sangoma.*

The above are great places to stay when viewing Isandlwana and Rorke's Drift. If you've moved on to visit Spioenkop in the Ladysmith area, **Three Tree Hill Lodge** is the place to stay. Brainchild of world-renowned Anglo-Zulu War historian David Rattray, his intent here was again to bring to vivid life the struggle between one of the largest empires in history and one of the smallest nations in the world, this time the Afrikaner. Proprietors Simon and Cheryl Blackburn (previously of Singita and Kwando) have continued Rattray's vision and more—both are highly experienced safari guides and combine guided tours of Spioenkop and surrounds with a variety of activities, all conducted with their signature hospitality in this beautiful family-run lodge. From R1,990 double to R 4,630 (high season) for the Family Suite, which sleeps two adults and two kids (© **036/448-1171** or 082/379-1864; www.threetreehill.co.za).

5 UKHAHLAMBA DRAKENSBERG MOUNTAINS

The Drakensberg extends from just north of Hoedspruit in the Northern Province 1,000km (620 miles) south to the mountain kingdom of Lesotho, where a series of spectacular peaks some 240km (149 miles) long creates the western border of KwaZulu-Natal. It is this border most people refer to when they speak of the Drakensberg. Known as **uKhahlamba** (Barrier of Spears) to the Zulus, they were renamed "Dragon Mountains" by the Trekkers seeking to cross them. Both are apt descriptions of South Africa's premier mountain wilderness—the second-largest range in Africa, venerated for centuries by the ancient San people, who have made it the world's largest open-air gallery, with more than 35,000 images painted at 600 sites.

Meandering through the Midlands: SA's Creative Countryside

One of the prettiest parts of the country, the Midlands is an area of gently rolling green hills interspersed with rivers and indigenous and commercial forests, just an hour or two beyond Durban on the N3 (less than 5 hr. from Johannesburg), stretching west to the majestic Drakensberg. With its cooler, drier climate, these hillsides are carpeted in flowers in spring, while crisp cold autumns turn the Midlands palette burnt orange and yellow. Its beauty has attracted creative types since the early 1800s, and it remains home to artisans and slow-food proponents, who live among small country inns between dairy farms. The **Midlands Meander** (© **033/330-5305** or 082/803-2327; www.midlandsmeander.co.za) is South Africa's first, largest, and most popular art-and-crafts route (and probably the easiest to follow, given the excellent signage). Weavers, potters, woodcrafters, leather workers, artists, metalworkers, box makers, herb growers, cheese makers, and beer brewers line the route. There are well over a hundred stops on four varying but converging routes, extending over some 80km (50 miles). It's a great way to shop (don't miss **Ardmore Ceramics** in Caversham © **033/234-4869**). Prices stay low because there's no middleman. The spectrum of nearby dining and lodging options runs from luxurious to rustic and from full-service to self-catering; many establishments are converted from old farmhouses or outbuildings. Outdoor activities include trout fishing, hiking, mountain biking, hot-air ballooning, and "canopy hopping." This 3-hour "slide" through the Karkloof Nature Reserve with **Karkloof Canopy Tours** (© **033/300-3415;** www.karkloofcanopytour.co.za) is the most exhilarating way to explore the province's largest mist-belt forest, with towering yellowwoods harboring endemic Butler butterflies and Marshall eagles.

The main range falls within **uKhahlamba-Drakensberg Park,** a 243,000-hectare (600,210-acre) semicircle that forms the western boundary of the province. Of this, the northern and central sections are the most spectacular, with majestic peaks surrounding grassed valleys fed by crystal-clear streams and pools—a hiker's paradise. The lower slopes of the Drakensberg are also breathtaking yet allow for a gentler, easier hike. The entire region is home to some 290 species of birds and 48 species of mammals. You don't have to be a particularly fit walker to appreciate the San rock paintings, to spot rare raptors, or to simply enjoy the chance to breathe the air in the aptly named Champagne Valley or Cathedral Peak. To enjoy the benefits of this World Heritage Site, all you need is a couple of days, a car, and the following information.

ESSENTIALS

VISITOR INFORMATION Much of the Berg falls under the protection of eZemvelo **KwaZulu-Natal Wildlife** (© **033/845-1000;** www.kznwildlife.com). If you're traveling to Cathedral Peak, take time to visit the informal bureau at **Thokozisa Centre,** off the R600, 13km (8 miles) from Winterton (© **036/488-1207;** www.cdic.co.za), where you can grab a bite to eat and browse for local crafts.

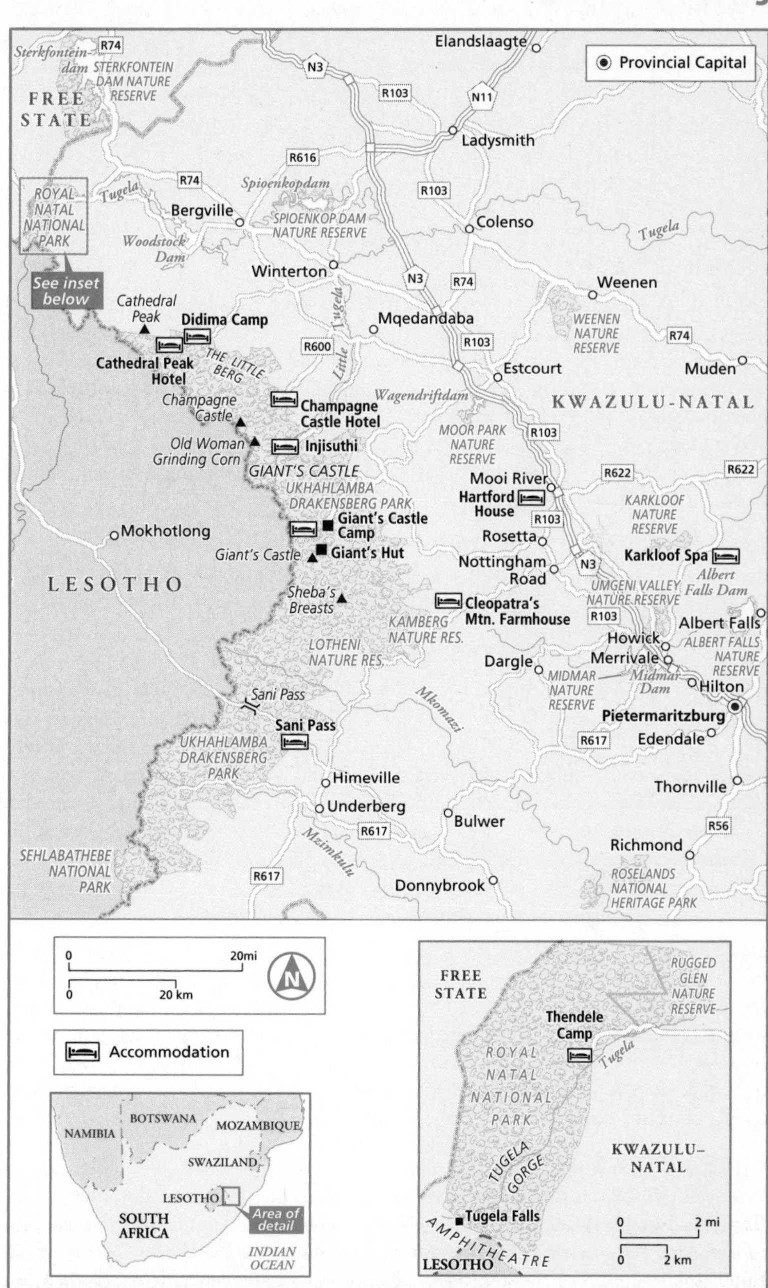
Provincial Capital
Elandslaagte
Ladysmith
Sterkfontein-dam
STERKFONTEIN DAM NATURE RESERVE
FREE STATE
ROYAL NATAL NATIONAL PARK
See inset below
Bergville
Spioenkopdam
SPIOENKOP DAM NATURE RESERVE
Woodstock Dam
Winterton
Colenso
Tugela
Weenen
WEENEN NATURE RESERVE
Muden
Mqedandaba
Estcourt
KWAZULU-NATAL
Cathedral Peak
Didima Camp
Cathedral Peak Hotel
THE LITTLE BERG
Champagne Castle
Champagne Castle Hotel
Wagendriftdam
Old Woman Grinding Corn
Injisuthi
GIANT'S CASTLE
UKHAHLAMBA DRAKENSBERG PARK
MOOR PARK NATURE RESERVE
Mooi River
Hartford House
KARKLOOF NATURE RESERVE
Mokhotlong
Giant's Castle Camp
Giant's Castle
Giant's Hut
Rosetta
Nottingham Road
Karkloof Spa
Albert Falls Dam
LESOTHO
Sheba's Breasts
Cleopatra's Mtn. Farmhouse
UMGENI VALLEY NATURE RESERVE
KAMBERG NATURE RES.
LOTHENI NATURE RES.
Albert Falls
Howick
ALBERT FALLS NATURE RESERVE
Merrivale
Dargle
MIDMAR NATURE RESERVE
Midmar Dam
Hilton
Pietermaritzburg
Edendale
Sani Pass
Mkomazi
UKHAHLAMBA DRAKENSBERG PARK
Himeville
Underberg
Bulwer
Thornville
Mzimkulu
Richmond
SEHLABATHEBE NATIONAL PARK
Donnybrook
ROSELANDS NATIONAL HERITAGE PARK
R74
N3
R103
N11
R616
R600
R622
R617
R56
0 20mi
0 20 km
N
Accommodation
NAMIBIA
BOTSWANA
MOZAMBIQUE
SWAZILAND
LESOTHO
SOUTH AFRICA
Area of detail
INDIAN OCEAN
FREE STATE
RUGGED GLEN NATURE RESERVE
Thendele Camp
ROYAL NATAL NATIONAL PARK
TUGELA GORGE
KWAZULU-NATAL
Tugela Falls
AMPHITHEATRE
LESOTHO
0 2 mi
0 2 km

GETTING THERE The only way to get to the Berg is by road (or by helicopter). To get to the **KwaZulu-Natal Wildlife** properties, you will need to self-drive from Durban or Johannesburg. The excellent N3 toll road is the main artery off which a number of tributaries feed, depending on which area you are visiting. Signposting is clear and the roads are good, but look out for thick mist and summer thunderstorms.

GETTING AROUND Due to the geography of the area, there are no connecting road systems, making long, circuitous routes necessary to move from one part of the Berg to the next. Depending on where you are coming from, it's best to base yourself in one or two areas: I recommend a night at Royal Natal (possibly hiking to Cathedral Peak), followed by a night at Giant's Castle. If you're traveling with young kids, spend a few days at Cathedral Peak hotel.

On Foot Walks range from a few hours to several days. Detailed maps are available at Parks Board camps, the departure point for all of the best hikes. The most popular books are David Bristow's *Best Walks of the Drakensberg* and *Drakensberg Walks: 120 Graded Hikes and Trails in the Berg* (Struik), which are light enough to carry and available from most bookshops, on the Internet, and at the Parks Board shops. Because winter snows and summer rainfalls can put a damper on hiking expeditions, the best times to explore the Berg, as locals call it, are spring and autumn. (For more information, see "Hiking" under "Staying Active," earlier in this chapter.)

WHERE TO STAY & DINE

Cleopatra's Mountain Farmhouse ★★★ Just 2 hours from Durban on good roads, this restaurant/inn is a restful refuge after walking the uKhahlamba Drakensberg ranges. It's also close enough to Giant's Castle to make it a suitable base from which to see the San paintings. Most gourmands, however, need no ulterior motives to head straight here. Every year brings a new slew of awards, and 2008 was no exception; Cleopatra's was listed in the Top 10 Diners Club Dine Awards Deluxe Category and awarded an American Express Platinum Fine Dining Restaurant Award. Surrounded by mountains and the burbling of crystal clear streams and waterfalls, the setting is as memorable as the meals, and service is professional yet understated. If you can afford it, book cottages nos. 10 and 11; given the views and privacy, they're worth the extra R500. ***Warning:*** In winter, night temperatures can drop to below 32°F (0°C).

P.O. Box 17, Balgowan 3275, South Africa. ✆ **033/267-7243.** www.cleomountain.co.za. R2,790–R2,390 double, including breakfast and dinner; check for frequent specials. No children.

Hartford House ★★ Another award-wining five-star fine-dining country establishment, **Hartford House** offers authentic colonial opulence on a racehorse stud farm that was established almost a century ago. It's also a plum spot for trout and bass fishing; Wildfly, one of the premier fly-fishing outfits in South Africa, offers master-class tuition here.

P.O. Box 31, Mooi River 3300, South Africa. ✆ **033/263-2713.** www.hartford.co.za. From R1,500 double. No children.

Karkloof Spa ★★★ If you're celebrating a special occasion or dealing with any sense of loss or challenge, take refuge at **Karkloof Spa.** A relative newcomer to the area, it has taken the local media by storm and reenergized interest in the midlands. South Africa's most holistic luxury retreat, Karkloof offers 16 luxurious villas and an expansive world-class spa, surrounded by 3,500 hectares (8,645 acres). Essentially a destination spa, the focus is on holistic well-being, with counseling therapists on call, as well as game-viewing to soothe and reconnect (game includes black and white rhino, giraffe, buffalo, zebra, and wildebeest). Hikes on walkways, paths, and trails follow the Karkloof River; there's a heated pool and library, but it's the well-being treatments that make this one of the most rejuvenating destinations in the province (and a member of the "healing hotels of the world").

P.O. Box 647, Msunduzi, 3231, South Africa. ✆ **033/5691321.** www.karkloofspa.com. From R7,980 double.

EXPLORING THE UKHAHLAMBA DRAKENSBERG PARK

The Northern Drakensberg is dominated by the Amphitheatre, a dramatic wall of rock that is some 8km (5 miles) long, flanked by the Sentinel (3,165m/10,381 ft.) and Eastern Buttress (3,047m/9,994 ft.). Falling within the 8,000-hectare (19,760-acre) **Royal Natal National Park,** it's the most awesome rock formation in the Drakensberg and the most photographed. This is where you'll find Mont-aux-Sources, so named by the French missionaries who visited the region in 1836. The highest point itself is an uninteresting peak that attains an altitude of 3,282m (10,765 ft.) 7km (4¼ miles) from the Drakensberg escarpment. The mountain acts as a watershed and is the source for three major rivers (hence the name Mont-aux-Sources), the Tugela, Vaal River, and Orange River. The Orange River flows into the Atlantic Ocean on the west coast of Southern Africa, while the Tugela flows into the Indian Ocean on the east coast of the subcontinent. Seven kilometers (4¼ miles) from the source, the Tugela plunges 948m (3,109 ft.) in a series of falls, the second-highest series of falls in the world. The 6-hour Tugela Gorge Walk, in the Royal Natal Drakensberg Park, will take you past the base of these falls, which afford marvelous views of the Amphitheatre. Royal Natal National Park is ideal for hiking, with a superb network of graded walks catering to all levels of fitness and agility. One of the most memorable views is from the summit of Mont-aux-Sources, which can be reached by walking from the summit plateau and scaling a 100-rung chain ladder. Entrance to the Royal Natal (✆ **036/438-6303**) costs R25; open 6am to 6pm in winter (Apr–Sept), 5am to 7pm in summer (Oct–Mar). Gates close at 10pm if you are staying at **Thendele** (✆ **036/438-6411**).

The Central Drakensberg comprises three distinct areas: the beautiful (3,004m/9,853-ft.) **Cathedral Peak** in the north, which has the easiest mountain to climb (a 9-hr. round-trip) and the best hotel in the Drakensberg at its feet; the relatively populated **Champagne Valley,** where most of the Berg resorts are based, and the Giant's Castle area, a magnet for both hikers and those interested in San rock art. Situated in the northern section of Giant's Castle, **Injisuthi** camp is cradled between the Injasuti (or "Little Tugela") and Delmhlwazini rivers at the head of the Injasuti Valley. This is a truly isolated wilderness, ideal for hikers, with breathtaking walks dominated by Cathkin Peak, Monk's Cowl, Champagne Castle, and Battle Cave. The **Giant's Castle** camp, famous for its relatively easy access to San rock art, is a short walk away in the main caves museum, situated on a gassy plateau among the deep valleys running down from the face of the High Drakensberg. The Injisuthi and (relatively luxurious) Giant's Castle camps serve as the departure point for numerous trails, serviced by an extensive network of overnight huts and caves. Within the reserve, Ndedema Gorge contains almost 4,000 paintings at 17 sites, including Sebaayeni Cave, which has 1,146 paintings. The reserve is open daily April through September from 6am to 6pm, and October through March from 5am to 7pm; admission to Giant's Castle is R25 per adult and R13 per child, and to Injisuthi is R20 per person. Initially established to protect the eland, Africa's largest antelope, the Giant's Castle reserve is today one of the few places where you'll see the rare

 lammergeyer, or "bearded vulture," particularly in winter; when rangers feed the vultures in what is known as the "vulture restaurant."

WHERE TO STAY & DINE IN THE UKHAHLAMBA DRAKENSBERG PARK

Hikers who want to stay overnight in the mountains must book their huts and caves through the eZemvelo KwaZulu-Natal Wildlife office closest to the trail (✆ **033/8451000;** www.kznwildlife.com); the camps below are the best bases for walking—hikes start literally from your front door. ***Note:*** Have your entry fee ready: R25 per adult and R13 per child for all the parks.

Cathedral Peak has a comfortable good-value alternative; KZN Wildlife developed **Didima Camp** ★, the most "modern" of the official parks camps, in 2002, with each of the 63 comfortably outfitted two-bed chalets vaguely shaped to resemble a cave (from R840 double for two adults, depending on chalet type). There are also two self-catering four-bed chalets and a three-bedroom lodge; all units are equipped with satellite TV and fireplaces. There is also a restaurant, bar, and lounge, as well as a San Art Interpretive Centre.

If you decide to visit the Ardmore Studio (on the R600, which leads to Champagne Castle), stop at **Thokozisa Restaurant, Deli & Information Centre,** 13km (8 miles) from Winterton (✆ **036/488-1827**), for a light meal made with organic produce. A little farther is the oldest of all the Berg resorts, **The Nest** (✆ **036/468-1068**), where filling food (roasts, cottage pie) is served in a rather fusty atmosphere. For overnight stays in Champagne Valley, the old-fashioned **Champagne Castle Hotel** (✆ **036/468-1063;** www.champagnecastlehotel.co.za; also off the R600; R660–R990, depending on the room type and season) is closest to the mountains and enjoys the best views, though it's nowhere as remote or charming as Cathedral Peak.

Cathedral Peak ★★ **Kids** This is without a doubt the best hotel option in the Drakensberg. The only one situated in its own valley, at the base of the mountains within the Natal Parks' protected area, it offers great alpine views, comfortable rooms, super-friendly staff, and a very relaxed atmosphere. Even getting here is a good experience, on a road that provides charming vignettes of rural bliss. Book a luxury room; they cost a bit more but are more spacious, with French doors opening onto the gardens and some excellent views of the mountains. The varied facilities also make this one of the best family resorts in the country. Trails start from the hotel, which provides maps. The 11km (6¾-mile) Rainbow Gorge round-trip is recommended. Meals are huge buffets, with something for everyone, including finicky kids.

P.O. Winterton, KwaZulu-Natal 3340. ✆ **036/488-1888.** Fax 036/488-1889. www.cathedralpeak.co.za. 96 units. R1,440–R1,850 double. All rates include dinner and breakfast, and midmorning and afternoon tea. Children under 10 sharing a unit R320–R475. AE, DC, MC, V. All routes clearly signposted from Winterton. **Amenities:** Dining room; bar; babysitting; bowling; 9-hole golf course; helicopter trips; hiking; horseback; pool; tennis; squash; volleyball; Wi-Fi (R50/12 hr., R100/24 hr.). *In room:* TV, Wi-Fi (in some).

Giant's Castle ★★ KZN Wildlife's flagship Berg camp is exceptionally well maintained and close to some of the best, most accessible examples of San cave art in the country. Today it comprises 37 comfortable two-bed self-catering cottages (equipped with cutlery, crockery, bedding, and fireplaces); a private, upmarket six-person lodge (chef included); four larger two-bedroom chalets; and four three-bedroom chalets; as well as the three-bedroom Rock Lodge, which has a truly exceptional and private setting. All units are well equipped for self-catering, but a fully licensed restaurant and bar with viewing deck make it unnecessary. A shop offers basic provisions, but visitors planning to self-cater should stock up before arriving.

Bookings through eZemvelo KwaZulu-Natal Wildlife (see "Visitor Information," above). Direct ✆ **036/353-3718** or 033/845-1000. 44 units, consisting of 2- and 4-bed chalets, 6-bed cottages, and a 6-bed lodge. R720–R1,600 double; from 1,560 lodge. AE, MC, V. **Amenities:** Restaurant; bar; filling station; San paintings; shop.

Thendele Hutted Camp ★★ Value Deep within the Royal Natal National Park in one of the most picturesque settings in the country, with a view of the world-famous amphitheater from every chalet, these units enjoy the best location of all the KwaZulu-Natal Wildlife camps. The camp is overlooked by the brooding sandstone cliffs of Dooley, among yellowwood forests and protea savanna, where visitors can often hear the rumble of boulders in the Thukela River below after a fierce summer thunderstorm. However, the fact that the camp has no restaurant could be a drawback. There's a shop with basic provisions, but for fresh supplies, stock up in Bergville. Another option is the restaurant at the Orion Mount-aux-Sources hotel, about 15 minutes away; but you must get back to camp before 10pm, when the gates close. Upper camp has slightly more modern units, but for totally unobstructed views of the Amphitheatre, book cottages no. 1 or 2, or the wonderfully situated three-bed lodge.

Reservations through KwaZulu-Natal Wildlife (see "Visitor Information," above). Direct ✆ **036/438-6411.** 29 units, consisting of 2- and 4-bed bungalows, 2- and 4-bed cottages, and a 6-bed lodge. R360–R420 per adult double. AE, MC, V.

11

Thundering World Wonder: Victoria Falls & Vicinity

When explorer David Livingstone became the first white man to set eyes on the falls, he described the crashing waters as exuding such power that they must have been "gazed upon by angels in their flight," and promptly named them for his queen. A century and a half later, the might of the British crown has waned, but the Zambezi River still pounds the Batoka Gorge, drawing travelers to witness the spectacle as the falls plummet 100m (328 ft.), twice the height of Niagara.

Straddling the western border between the beautiful but poverty-stricken state of Zimbabwe and hot new safari destination Zambia, Victoria Falls is justifiably called one of the Wonders of the Natural World, and spans almost 2km (1¼ miles), making it the largest show of its kind on Earth. The sight of more than 9 million liters of water crashing down into the Batoka Gorge is one not easily forgotten; on a clear day, the veil of roaring spray can be seen from up to 80km (50 miles) away, and provides perpetual moisture to nourish the rainforest that clings to the cliffs opposite Victoria Falls. It is this phenomenon that gave the falls its local name: *Mosi-Oa-Tunya*—literally, "The Smoke That Thunders."

People come here not only to immerse themselves in the spectacle of the falls, but also to partake in the varied adventure activities, from bungee jumping off the bridge between Zimbabwe and Zambia to surfing the world's most challenging commercially run rapids. Not for nothing has this area been dubbed the adrenaline capital of southern Africa.

If, however, your idea of the ideal Vic Falls trip is to soak in the Thundering Wonder, then return to your lodge and kick back with a gin and tonic, admiring the savanna, or watching hippos patrol the great Zambezi, rest easy: Lodgings on both sides of the falls will provide this opportunity—and more.

1 ORIENTATION

VISITOR INFORMATION & TOUR COMPANIES

IN ZAMBIA With tourism to this country growing as fast as it is declining in Zimbabwe, the **Zambia National Tourism Board** is maintaining an up-to-date website (www.zambiatourism.com). For more background information on the destination, with useful (but not necessarily current) trip-planning advice, visit the ***Getaway*** website (www.getawaytoafrica.com) for features on Zambia. As *Getaway* is predominantly aimed at the local South African market, you can put together a trip that will halve costs. Then again, you'll spare yourself some hassle and ensure a smooth trip by dealing directly with www.wilderness-safaris.com and www.kerdowney.com, the two most established Zambian

 **Country Codes**

This chapter contains phone numbers for three countries. Phone numbers starting with **263** are in Zimbabwe, those starting with **260** are in Zambia, and those beginning with **27** are in South Africa. The Zimbabwean telephone exchange is temperamental. At certain times of the day, it is impossible to get through to any number.

operators, each with a great lodging near Vic Falls, as well as upmarket camps in the big Zambian national parks.

The largest Victoria Falls operator, specializing in the full spectrum of adventure activities, budget accommodations, and transfers on both sides of the falls, is **Safari Par Excellence** (**© 44/845/293-0512;** this U.K. number is for an agent, available 24/7; you can also contact them at res@saf-par.co.za or visit www.safpar.com). The Zambia office is at Zambezi Waterfront Lodge, off Mosi-Oa-Tunya Road, halfway between Livingstone and the Vic Falls bridge; if you're traveling from South Africa, contact the local representative at **Maplanga Africa** (**© 27/11/794-1446;** www.maplanga.co.za).

Safari Par Excellence serves as booking agents for the widest number of activities on and near the falls, and specializes predominantly in accommodating groups of overland travelers. If you're in the U.K. and looking for more personal, discriminatory assistance or considering a more substantial safari adventure into Zambia (which is highly recommended, given that the country is still relatively undiscovered and the bush is wild), contact the London-based **Zambia Safari & Travel Company** ★★★ (**© 44/800/840-1377;** www.zambezi.com), a small, independent family-owned safari company serving adventurous spirits from all corners of the globe. U.S. travelers should look no further than **Mashinda** ★★★ (info@mashinda.com), headed by Judy Udwin, who visits every lodging she recommends across the budget spectrum and has a great eye.

IN ZIMBABWE To plan your trip on the Zimbabwean side, start by browsing **www.gotovictoriafalls.com**; it's an excellent site, cohosted by all the tourist stakeholders in Victoria Falls. Low tourism numbers in the village mean that hotel staff, private operators, and other tourist stakeholders will bend over backward to assist you; this website is their initiative and their passion for the village and falls shows.

For more essential information on Vic Falls, including getting there, travel documents, health, and more, see chapter 3.

GETTING THERE

By Plane

FROM JOHANNESBURG The majority of visitors are more likely to arrive on the Zambian side of the falls, at nearby **Livingstone International Airport:** BA Comair and SAA fly here daily. You might want to compare prices with the daily flights to **Victoria Falls International Airport** (even if you're heading for the Zambian side, it's relatively easy to arrange a transfer, visas are not expensive, and it's only an hour to Livingstone; see "Visas," under "Fast Facts: Victoria Falls & Livingstone," below). Both SAA and BA fly once daily; Air Zimbabwe offers the same route and was recently given a clean bill of health (but I'd still stick with the big carriers). See chapter 3.

Most hotels offer a complimentary shuttle from the airport; arrange this in advance. Departure taxes are now included in the price of your air ticket.

By Train

If you fancy chugging to the falls in style, consider the **Shongololo Express** Southern Cross Adventure, a 16-day journey that travels leisurely between Victoria Falls and Johannesburg, making calls at destinations in Mozambique, Swaziland, Botswana, Zambia, Zimbabwe, and South Africa. (✆ **27/11/483-0657,** -58, -59; www.shongololo.com; R38,850–R58,000, depending on carriage.)

GETTING AROUND

The most convenient way to get around is to have your hotel or lodge arrange transfers, or book a hotel within walking distance of the falls (there are a number of options in Vic Falls Village on the Zimbabwean side, and the Royal Livingstone and Zambian Sun are within ambling distance on the Zambian side). **Safari Par Excellence** (see "Visitor Information & Tour Companies," above) offers prearranged transfers anywhere, as well as a shuttle service from both airports and Victoria Falls Village to its Waterfront Lodge (on the Zambian side), where many of the adventure activities take place. **Hemingways** offers tours and transfers in vehicles that are also wheelchair accessible (www.hemingways zambia.com); they also hire specialist safari vehicles and will help plan itineraries for those who wish to explore Zambia further.

Victoria Falls Village is a very small town; most attractions (including the falls) are within walking distance or, at worst, a short taxi ride. Taxis are relatively cheap (make sure you negotiate the price up front), but almost all of the hotels and lodges offer a shuttle service to the falls and around town; many of them are complimentary.

Getting Beyond: Sefofane Zambia (www.sefofane.com) recently announced a new flying schedule to collaborate with the photographic safari season. Commencing on May 1, it will operate three times a week, including Tuesday, Thursday, and Saturday. Travelers fly in air-conditioned C208 Cessna Caravans. The route will start in Livingstone, continuing onto Kafue National Park, Lusaka, and back to Livingstone.

By Boat

A number of companies run breakfast, lunch, bird-watching, and sunset river cruises. All cruises take place on the calmer, game-rich waters of the Upper Zambezi (the area above the falls) and are usually in large, twin-deck boats. It's a wonderful way to enjoy wildlife such as hippos, elephants, and aquatic birds, though you'll probably also see plenty of other tourists. One of the oldest operators is **Dabula Safaris,** represented by the South African–based **African Adrenalin** safari company (✆ **27/11/888-4037;** www.african adrenalin.com). If you're averse to crowds, it's worth inquiring about the cruises on smaller (maximum eight people), shallower, propeller-free **jet boats;** they're a bit more expensive ($95 per person) but quieter, and can explore places larger boats can't access. (Also see "Canoe Safaris," later in this chapter.)

By Train

Board a beautifully restored steam train—a 1954 Dlass 14A steam locomotive, dining cars, and first-class coaches operated by **Victoria Falls Steam Train Company** (✆ **263/13/42912,** 263/11/203688, or 27/82/294-4684; www.steamtraincompany.com)—and leave Zimbabwe's Victoria Falls to cross the mighty Zambezi via the Victoria Falls Bridge to Livingstone, Zambia (or vice versa). You can do the bridge run at sunset, voted as one of the World's 15 Most Spectacular Sundowner Spots, or opt for "royal tea" ($120 per person) or the Moonlight Dinner Run ($168 per person). Reservations are essential, with a 20% nonrefundable deposit payable on reservation. Bring your passport, and be aware that rates don't cover visas (see "Visas" under "Fast Facts," below).

Fast Facts Victoria Falls & Livingstone

Banks In Zimbabwe, you will need foreign currency (see "Money Matters in Zimbabwe"). On the Zambian side, you can buy ***kwacha*** (Zambian currency) at hotels, or use the ATM at The Falls casino and entertainment center, near the border. Most prices are quoted in U.S. dollars, but getting change on large notes is hard, so carry some local currency or small dollar denominations.

Business Hours Shops are generally open Monday through Saturday from 8am to 5pm. Activity centers and markets are open daily 6am to 6pm; many close only when the last traveler leaves.

Climate See "The Best Times to Come," above.

Crime Despite the political crisis that has almost crippled Zimbabwe, the falls remain largely unaffected and relatively quiet and safe. Hoteliers in Victoria Falls are mindful of the vulnerability of their guests in a place where people are starving, so there's tight security as well as a Tourism Police service (look out for the yellow jackets), with guards patrolling a broad area on foot, horseback, quadbike, and bicycle from 7am to 9pm daily. Avoid petty crime by not flashing valuables, and stay in groups, particularly at night; also stay clear of deserted areas, including the banks of the Zambezi. Bear in mind that Livingstone is a much larger town than Victoria Falls, and many people live here to cash in on tourists; be alert and don't walk around alone.

Currency See "Money," in chapter 3, and "Money Matters in Zimbabwe," above.

Doctors **In Livingstone:** Contact Dr. Shafik, 1115 Kateti Rd. (✆ **260/213/32-1130**). **In Victoria Falls:** Contact Dr. Nyoni at **Victoria Falls Surgery,** West Drive, off Park Way (✆ **263/13/43356;** Mon–Fri 9:30am–5pm, Sat 9:30am–5pm, Sun 9:30–5pm; after hours ✆ **263/13/40529**).

Drugstores Drugstores are called chemists or pharmacies. **In Livingstone: LF Moore Chemist** is the establishment store on Akapelwa Street (✆ **260/213/32-1640**). **In Victoria Falls: Victoria Falls Pharmacy** is located in Phumula Centre, Park Way (✆ **263/13/44403;** Mon–Fri 8am–6pm, Sat–Sun 8am–noon). A drugstore in the Kingdom Hotel is open daily.

Electricity Electricity in southern Africa runs on 220/230V, 50Hz AC, and sockets in Zimbabwe and Zambia take flat-pinned plugs. Bring an adapter/voltage converter; note that some bush camps have no electricity.

Embassies & Consulates All offices are in the capital cities of Harare (Zimbabwe) and Lusaka (Zambia); if you have diplomatic problems, speak to your hotel manager and ask him to contact your country's local representative.

Emergencies Your hotel or lodge is your best bet for the safest medical and emergency care. Alternatively, contact **Medical Air Rescue Service,** a 24-hour emergency evacuation service (✆ **263/13/44764**). For an **ambulance,** call

✆ **44210;** for the **police,** call ✆ **44206;** to report a **fire,** call ✆ **44400;** for **general emergencies,** call ✆ **112** or 44206.

Health **Malaria** Before leaving, ask your physician about starting a course of antimalarial prophylactics. If you suspect you have malaria, get to a doctor immediately for a test. For more information, see "Health," in chapter 3.

Language English is spoken in the tourist regions of Zimbabwe and Zambia.

Telephone Phone numbers in this chapter use codes for three countries. See "Country Codes," above. For tips on making international and local calls, see chapter 3.

Time Zone Both Zimbabwe and Zambia are 5 hours ahead of GMT and 7 hours ahead of Eastern Standard Time.

Tipping For a meal, leave 10%; for small services such as hotel porters carrying your bags, tip $1 to $3, or the equivalent.

Visas **Zambia:** Thankfully, the Zambian government has slashed visa fees, and single entry now costs $50 (double entry is $80); a daytripper visa costs $20. **Zimbabwe:** Visa fees depend on nationality. For British nationals, a single entry costs $55 ($70 for double entry). U.S. nationals must pay $45 (this is automatically a double-entry visa). Canadians pay $75. Australians, New Zealanders, and Americans can purchase one for $30 (double entry $45). Do double-check these figures (they tend to change pretty regularly), if you intend to purchase a visa on arrival (see www.zambiaimmigration.gov.zm).

Water Tap water is generally considered safe, but it's worth asking first. You're often better off drinking the bottled water provided in your hotel room, because local water is less processed and may be richer in mineral content than your stomach is used to. The recent cholera outbreaks in Zimbabwe did not affect Victoria Falls, and the area remains cholera free.

Wildlife Keep your eye out for elephants and hippos when you're out walking, cycling, or canoeing. Do not block their routes—it's best not to turn around, but back away slowly. When driving on highways that are part of national parkland, never speed, and keep a watchful eye out for animals emerging from the bush to cross the road. Baboons are a nuisance on both sides of the falls. Keep food out of sight and remember that—like all wild animals—they are unpredictable and potentially dangerous.

2 WHAT TO SEE & DO

The area is famous for its myriad adventure activities and excellent wildlife-viewing opportunities, but when all is said and done, the falls are the star of the show.

SOAKING UP THE FALLS

There are two great vantage points, each in a national park and affording a different angle; it's worth covering both, which will take at least half a day. Break up your return journey by stopping for high tea at the colonial-era Victoria Falls Hotel (or the Royal Livingstone, if you've opted to stay on the Zambian side), and drink in more views.

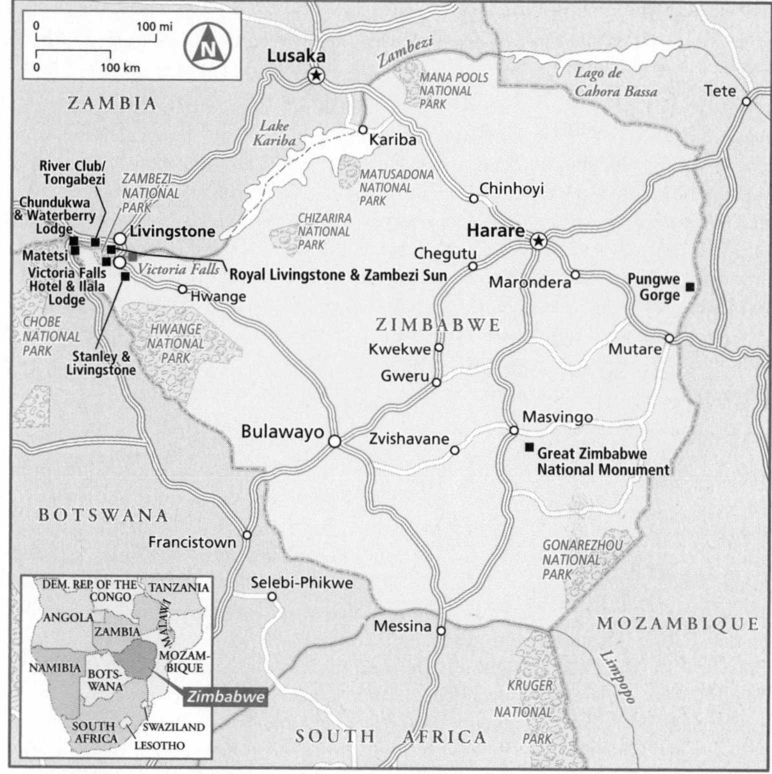

Victoria Falls National Park ★★★ (Moments Victoria Falls National Park—which some say affords the best vantage point of the falls—is a 2,340-hectare (5,780-acre) narrow strip that runs along the southern bank of the Zambezi River and protects the sensitive rainforest around the falls. You will almost certainly get drenched by the permanent spray, so rent a raincoat or umbrella at the entrance (or just relish the experience and take a change of clothes). Remember to put your camera in a waterproof bag. A clearly marked trail runs through the lush rainforest (look out for the aptly named flame lilies), with side trails leading to good viewing points of the falls. Head down the steep stairs to **Cataract View** for views of **Devil's Cataract** ★★; this is also where you'll find the unremarkable statue of David Livingstone. The final view point, nearest the falls bridge, is called **Danger Point**—here you can perch right on the edge of a cliff and peer down into the abyss. When the moon is full, the park stays open later so that visitors can witness the lunar rainbow formed by the spray. Not only is it a beautiful sight, but the experience is untarnished by the sounds of helicopters and microlights, which can be something of a nuisance during the day.

You don't need a guide to visit the falls. Many unofficial guides stand near the entrances, but unless you want to learn more about the rainforests (in which case, hire a guide from a reputable company), chances are that they won't be able to show you anything other than the direction of the path. Livingstone Way leads from the Victoria Falls Village directly to the entrance.

No phone. Admission $20. Daily 6am–6pm, later during full-moon nights, when entry is $30 (includes guide).

Mosi-Oa-Tunya ★★★ **Moments** The Zambian side offers a more spectacular vantage point than its Zimbabwean counterpart during high water (Apr/May–June), when the view is less obscured by spray. After a long, dry winter, however, when water on this side can be reduced to a trickle, the views can be dire (around Oct). The focus of a tour here is on seeing the main gorge and Eastern Cataract; you can also walk (or scramble, rather) across to a vantage called Knife Edge, where you will stand suspended above the churning waters of Boiling Pot—a vicious rapid most rafters get to know a little too intimately. ***Warning:*** There are no fences on this side of the river, and every year, one or two people slip on the wet rocks attempting to get that extra-special shot or glimpse. If you don't recover your footing, the chance of survival is nil.

Entrance off Livingstone Rd. No phone. Admission $5–$20. Year-round daily 6am–6pm.

VIEWING WILDLIFE

Despite the commercialism of Vic Falls Village, the falls remain surrounded by dense bush, and you can start your African safari right here. Venture a few miles upstream from the river along Zambezi Drive for a look at the **Big Tree,** a 1,500-year-old baobab (if you're lucky, you'll see elephants, too), or take a guided **Zambezi River walk** (see "Bush Walks" under "Staying Active," below) to view species like hippo and crocodile. A number of tour operators will arrange morning, afternoon, and night drives to Zambezi National Park, Mosi-Oa-Tunya Park, and Hwange, as well as full days in Chobe, Botswana; the three biggest operators are Shearwater (www.shearwateradventures.com), Wild Horizons (www.wildhorizons.co.za), and, of course, Safari Par Excellence (www.safpar.com). For safaris by canoe, plane, helicopter, and horse- or elephant-back, see "Staying Active," below.

3 STAYING ACTIVE

All hotels will arrange reservations and give advice on activities, most at no additional charge. If you want to check that this is the case (as well as view the very latest on activities), visit **Safari Par Excellence's** comprehensive website (www.safpar.com; see "Visitor Information," above).

ABSEILING, GORGE SWING & FLYING FOX ★★★ Rappel down a 50m (164-ft.) drop into the Batoka Gorge, then tackle the gorge swing or traverse the Flying Fox. Attached to the world's highest commercial high wire, the gorge swing allows you to experience free-fall for 70m (230 ft.), then swing over the Zambezi, churning 120m (394 ft.) below. The Flying Fox is one of the world's longest cable slide lines, whereupon you more or less fly, fully harnessed to the cable, above the Zambezi rapids at speeds of up to 105kmph (65 mph). For the Flying Fox alone, the cost is $75, or you can do any activity as often as you want for $95 for a half-day, $115 for the full day.

BUNGEE JUMPING ★★ The checklists of most adventure-sportsmen aren't complete until they've done the heart-stopping 111m (364-ft.) bungee off the Vic Falls

Bridge, stopping about 10m (33 ft.) from the boiling waters in the Batoka Gorge. Jumps take place daily (9am–1pm and 2–5pm); the first jump costs $105 ($145 for tandem). Jumps may be delayed during the months of heavy spray (Mar–June).

BUSH WALKS Operators like **www.natureways.com** (© **263/47/44159**) or **www.cansaf.com** (© **263/13/43352**) will accompany you on a variety of expeditions, from 2-hour bush walks to 2-night walking safaris, as well as canoe safaris. A 3-hour birding or game-viewing walk costs around $65. "Walking with lion cubs," an activity now available on both sides of the falls, is understandably tempting, but it remains highly criticized in conservation circles, who see no benefit whatsoever to the lions. Some suspect the cubs are released into private reserves where they become targets in "canned" hunts. If you're still keen, book in advance through Safari Par Excellence ($115).

CANOE SAFARIS ★★ Canoe safaris offer a more sedate option than rafting, with the added bonus of seeing hippos, elephants, and crocodiles while you paddle the broad expanse of the Upper Zambezi. There are no (or very small) rapids on this trip, so you won't get your hair wet, though be aware that hippos do occasionally upend canoes (in which case, your guide will whisk you aboard almost immediately). **Sunset cruises** are particularly recommended ($45), or opt for a full-day overnight canoe safari ★★★ ($155–$200, depending on the side of the falls). Contact Robin Brown at Cansaf (© **27/83/278-5770** or 263/011/60-5063) or book through an adventure outfit.

ELEPHANT-BACK SAFARIS Four major companies now offer elephant-back safaris, and it is suspected that some 50 elephants are held captive in the area. The growth of the activity has raised many controversial questions. The industry is under-regulated and, apart from the obvious animal welfare issues relating to concerns over the captive methods (in 2006, Shearwater Adventures captured 12 wild elephants from Hwange National Park), the training methods used, and the environmental impact of keeping these animals captive, there is no obligation for commercial operators to provide for the life-time care of these emotionally sensitive animals. Ascertain where the elephants have come from, how they are trained, where they are kept, and what the company's long-term plans are before you saddle up ($90–$150).

FLYING ★★★ (Moments To get a real idea of the size of the falls, take to the skies on a microlight or ultralight flight—both are quieter than helicopter or fixed-wing flights, and you'll be sailing a great deal closer to nature. **Batoka Sky** (book through any of the adventure-activity operators above; flights leave from Livingstone) operates tricycle-style microlight flights from Zambia and charges $120 for 15 minutes. You can't take a camera (if you drop it, it may stop the engine below), so Batoka has a camera attached to the wheels; your pilot will take a photograph of you flying past the falls. Ultralights, marginally safer than microlights, cost about $110 for 15 minutes.

For helicopter trips, book through an adventure center or direct with the **Zambezi Helicopter Company** (© **263/13/44513;** $130 for 15 min.); for fixed-wing flights, try **Ngwazi Air Charter** (© **260/096/665-7001**) or **United Air Charter** (© **260/3/32-3095** or 263/11/40-7573; www.uaczam.com).

GOLFING The 6,786-yard **Elephant Hills Intercontinental** (© **263/13/44793**) course is at times just a stroke from the roaring Zambezi River, and the constant presence of the falls—not to mention wildlife—makes this Gary Player–designed course one of the most interesting in Africa.

HORSEBACK SAFARIS ★ **Zambezi Horse Trails** (© **263/13/44611**) provides riders with an opportunity to get closer to game than they can on foot or in a car. Led by an experienced guide with an extensive knowledge of the flora and fauna of the area, rides take place on 30,000 hectares (74,100 acres) of the Matetsi River Ranch, which borders Zambezi National Park. Experienced riders can choose among half-, full-, or multiday riding safaris; a full day will cost around $95, excluding park fees ($10). Novices are taken on a 2-hour ride ($45) into areas where such potentially dangerous animals as elephants are avoided. Alternatively, if you stay at **Chundukwa** (see below), you can hire the owner's horses for guided game-viewing trips along the river. E-mail info@rideafrica.com for reservations and prices.

SKYDIVING ★★ If you think bungee jumping is for babies, a tandem skydive—accelerating toward Victoria Falls before enjoying a restful 5-minute parachute ride—is for you. The folks at **Sky Dive Vic Falls** (**© 260/977/33-7153;** www.skydivevicfalls.com) are the ones to contact; weather permitting, you'll be whisked up to 2,700m (9,000 ft.), ready for the most exciting outlook on the falls.

WHITE-WATER RAFTING ★★★ Moments This is the most exhilarating ride you'll ever have. Operators pride themselves on offering the best commercially run rapids in the world. You need to be reasonably fit (not only to deal with the Class III to Class V rapids, but also for the 230m/754-ft. climb out of the gorge at the end of a tiring day). You should also be a competent swimmer. Don't worry if you haven't done anything like it before—organizers offer dry-ground preparation before launching onto the water, and the safety and guiding standards are excellent (note that this does not prevent unforeseen disasters). The best time for rafting is when the water is low and the rapids impressive, from July to January; September and October are particularly good months. (From Apr through May, when the water is particularly high, some rafting companies close altogether.) You should be aware that there *is* a certain level of danger and that the rapids claim a few lives every year. The safest option is to get on a boat that has an oarsman who guides you along the safest path. The alternative, where everyone in the group has his or her own paddle, is much more fun, despite the fact that—or in large part because of it—you'll definitely end up in the water. River-boarding is the most hair-raising way to brave the rapids—alone, on a boogie board, you literally surf the waves created by a selection of Class III to Class V rapids. Most river-rafting companies offer an optional half-day rafting, half-day boarding experience. The kings of the river are **Raft Extreme** (**© 260/3/32-3929;** www.raftextreme.com) and **Safari Par Excellence** (see above). Both offer trips from both the Zimbabwean and the Zambian side—Zambia has the added advantage of including a few extra rapids, and they also begin right beneath the falls; the benefit of being on the Zimbabwe side are the multirafting trips ★★★—after a full day rafting, overnighting on a sandy beach in the gorge is bliss—sure to be the highlight of your trip. This costs only $165 per person, meals included. Alternatively, expect to pay $110 to $145 for a full day (depending on which side you start at). Prices include lunch, drinks, and all equipment.

4 WHERE TO STAY & DINE

The instability of the Zimbabwean economy and political unease have resulted in a downturn in international tourism business on the Zimbabwean side of the falls, but there are many more visitors from Africa taking advantage of the lower prices and safe environment. For years, I have advised visitors to stay on the Zambian side, but given the bargain prices and the great effort that the various tourist stakeholders have made to secure visitors' safety, I'd personally opt to stay on the Zimbabwean side. For most visitors flying to the falls, though, it's still the norm to stay in Zambia.

IN ZAMBIA

The most convenient option is **Royal Livingstone** and sister hotel **Zambezi Sun,** which are right next to the falls. If you don't like large, impersonal hotels, upstream from here are a number of lovely options, all overlooking the Zambezi River (which sees hippo and elephant action), the best of which are reviewed below. If you're watching your budget, your best bet is **Chundukwa River Lodge** ★ (www.chundukwariverlodge.com; $460 double; includes full board, sunset river cruise, and falls tour): a tiny lodge with only five rooms on stilts (one of them ideal for a family of four), located right on the river, 25km (16 miles) upstream from the falls. In addition to assisting with the usual falls activities, the lodge specializes in horseback safaris. Neighboring **Waterberry Lodge** (www.waterberrylodge.com; $500 double; includes full board and airport transfers) is a slightly tamer, intimate option that will suit those with an eye on their budget, with seven bungalows on the grassed river banks.

The River Club ★★★ A neighbor to Tongabezi (see below), with even better views, this romantic retreat on the banks of the Zambezi is the most overtly colonial of the Zambian lodges, and a top choice. Set amid lovely lawns, the main house is filled with period pieces that evoke a distinctly Edwardian atmosphere. Meals are elegant affairs, particularly dinners, after which you may choose to take a drink in the library, partake of a game of moonlit croquet, or flop into your huge bed, romantically swathed in mosquito nets. During the day, enjoy a rejuvenating riverside massage treatment, or laze around in the gorgeous pool, located on the high bank of the river. The open-sided split-level bungalows are built overlooking the Zambezi; Victorian bathrooms, almost touching distance of the river, are a real highlight (for best views, request the Edward suite). ***Note:*** If the price strikes you as a tad steep, take a look at the other Wilderness-Safari option, **Toka Leya** ★★★, which enjoys an equally good location on the river banks, about 10km (6¼ miles) upstream from the falls. It's not the colonial luxury of River Club, but it's a gorgeous-looking camp, with great staff. Given that certain activities are included in the rate ($950 double, year-round), it's an excellent value.

Bookings through S.A.: ✆ **27/11/807-1800.** Lodge: 263/11/40-6563. Fax 27/11/883-0911. www.wilderness-safaris.com. 10 units. High season (June–Nov) $1,300 double; low season (Dec–May) $1,020. Rates are all-inclusive except for premium-brand alcohol imports. Ask which activities are included. MC, V. **Amenities:** Dining room; lounge; *pétanque*; bush golf; canoeing; croquet; sunset cruises; day trips (to Mosi-Oa-Tunya National Park, Livingstone and Railway Museum, croc farm); fishing; free high-speed Internet; library; pool. *In room:* Hair dryer, fans.

Royal Livingstone & Zambezi Sun ★★ Kids Within spitting distance of the border, on the banks of the Zambezi, is the massive Sun International hotel and entertainment complex, incorporating the two hotels as well as **The Activity Centre,** an adult playground with a small casino, shops, eateries, offices, and banking facilities. The single biggest reason to book into this flashy resort is its proximity to the falls—the park entrance is within easy walking distance (100m/328 ft. from the Zambezi Sun), so you can visit as often as you want. The downside is that the Sun is often filled to capacity with tour groups, who share access to all facilities, so there's little chance for privacy other than in your room—all the more reason to book at the more exclusive and very luxurious Royal Livingstone, where all accommodations overlook the river (book the second floor for better views). Service levels at Livingstone are also excellent—even if you arrive in a dilapidated taxi from Kasane, looking as if you've lived in the bush for a week, you'll be treated like royalty. (But for a less hotel-like experience, book The River Club or Tongabezi, or look at the Zim options.) Guests get a 10% discount on all adventure bookings done through the hotel.

Mosi-Oa-Tunya Rd., P.O. Box 60151, Livingstone, Zambia. ✆ **260/3/32-1122.** www.suninternational.com. Zambezi Sun (212 units): From $551 double, excluding breakfast; Royal Livingstone (173 units): High season (Dec 19–Jan 3; Feb–Oct) $925 double; low season $878. Suite $1,673–$2,637, depending on size and season. Rates include breakfast. AC, DC, MC, V. **Amenities:** 2 restaurants; activity center (see above); sunset deck; 2 pools; airport transfers. *In room:* A/C, TV, hair dryer, minibar (Livingstone only).

Tongabezi ★★★ Situated 20km (12 miles) upstream from the falls, overlooking a broad expanse of the Zambezi, Tongabezi Lodge is set in a grove of African ebony trees. Each of the thatched River Cottages has a private veranda overlooking the river. Ideally, you should try to reserve one of the huge "houses"—particularly the **Tree House,** which is carved out of the rock and completely open to the elements, with the mighty Zambezi River just meters from your bedroom and a sumptuous bathroom, where the tub is low enough to make you feel as if you're almost part of the river. The new Nut House is the epitome of African luxury; choose to have the folding doors completely closed or open them out onto your private infinity plunge pool. For the ultimate in romance, ask for a "sampan dinner" (included in the rate), a private candlelit meal on a raft delivered by waiters in canoes. For those with a taste for adventure, a night at the satellite **Sindabezi Island Camp** ★★★ is a must. Located on its own island 3km (1¾ miles) downstream, the five chalets are elevated into the trees with en-suite bathrooms (hot water on demand) and wonderful views of the river and its banks. Dinner is served on raised decks and lit by candle and paraffin lamp—a truly romantic and restorative experience.

From July to March, Tongabezi organizes lavish picnics on **Livingstone Island** ★★★, on the edge of the falls. They can also arrange an overnight here—an unbelievable privilege, especially during full moon when there's a lunar rainbow.

Lastly, groups traveling together should inquire into renting the gorgeous **Tangala House** (sleeps eight), completely serviced and offering excellent value.

Private Bag 31, Livingstone. ✆ **260/213/32-7450** or 260/213/32-4450. Fax 260/213/32-7484. www.tongabezi.com. Tongabezi 12 units. Sindabezi 5 units. Tongabezi river cottages $900–$1,080 double; Tongabezi houses $1,100–$1,480 double. Sindabezi $830–$1,080 double. Rates are fully inclusive (excluding premium wines, champagne, and liqueurs). MC, V. No children under 7 at Tongabezi; no children under 14 at Sindabezi. **Amenities:** Dining areas; bar; bird walks; bush/gorge walks; canoeing; fishing; game drives; library; pool; sunrise and sunset boat cruises; village tours visit to Zambian side of falls.

IN ZIMBABWE

Ilala Lodge ★ Value Kids This pleasant thatched hotel offers midrange comfortable accommodations and eager, professional service; it's an easy 10-minute walk from the falls and close to the craft markets. The lodge has an African theme, with thatched roofs, colonial-era paintings, cane furniture, and views of the lawn and thick bush of the national park. The hotel is not completely fenced in, so don't be surprised if you hear the sounds of elephants feeding outdoors at night. Their on-site sister-company, Zambezi Wildlife Safaris, will arrange all activities, tours, and transfers.

411 Livingstone Way, Box 18, Victoria Falls. ✆ **263/13/44737,** 38, 39. Fax 263/13/44740. www.ilalalodge.com. 32 units. $340–$488 double, including breakfast. Children under 12 pay $72 if sharing with parents. DC, MC, V. **Amenities:** Restaurant; bar; high-speed Internet ($2/30 min.); pool; room service. *In room:* TV, hair dryer.

Matetsi Water Lodge ★★★ Value Kids Located 40km (25 miles) upstream from the falls (30 min. by complimentary daily shuttle), on a 73,500-hectare (181,545-acre) reserve with access to the adjacent Zambezi National Park, this highly recommended lodge comprises three small, separate camps (each with only six suites), built right on the Zambezi River. A stay here combines a safari experience with a visit to the falls, so plan to spend 2 nights. Previously a hunting concession area, Matetsi is now home to herds of buffalo, elephant, and sable antelope, as well as such predators as lion, hyena, and leopard. Each privately located and luxurious suite—with teak fittings, canopied king-size beds, and enormous bathrooms—has its own plunge pool and deck overlooking the river (similar accommodations in South Africa and Botswana would cost much more).

Reservations through &Beyond: Private Bag x27, Benmore 2010, S.A. ✆ **27/11/809-4300.** Fax 27/11/809-4315. www.andbeyond.com. 18 units. High season $870 double; low season $510 double. Rates include all meals, all game activities, boating, fishing, shuttle, and laundry. MC, V. **Amenities:** Dining room; bar; babysitting; boat cruises; guided bush walks; canoeing; fishing; game drives; limited free high-speed Internet. *In room:* A/C, hair dryer, minibar.

Stanley & Livingstone ★★★ Value Tranquil, luxurious, and elegant, the Stanley & Livingstone offers the most expensive and exclusive accommodations in Zimbabwe, at an unbelievably good rate. Each of the 16 luxurious suites opens onto an elegantly furnished private veranda; decor consists of elegant period furnishings and colonial-style fittings such as ball-and-claw bathtubs. Ten minutes from the falls (complimentary shuttle) and 2 minutes from the Zambezi National Park entrance, it's in its own 2,400-hectare (5,928-acre) private reserve bordering the national park (the restaurant and bar overlook a water hole that attracts a variety of species), with a choice of game drives, bush walks, or fishing as part of the package. Service and dining are excellent.

Reservations: Rani Africa, Box 2682, Witkoppen 2068. ✆ **27/11/467-1277.** Fax 27/11/465-8764. www.raniresorts.com. 16 units. Bed and breakfast $400–$548 double. AE, MC, DC, V. Children under 12 by arrangement only and pay 50% if sharing with parents. **Amenities:** Dining room; bar; airport transfers; bush walks; canoeing; fishing; elephant-back safari; game drives; pool; room service; walking w/lion experience. *In room:* A/C, TV, minibar.

Victoria Falls Hotel ★★ Kids This Edwardian colonial-era hotel (built in 1904) is the most genteel accommodations option in the village. It's also in a prime spot: within Victoria Falls National Park, overlooking the equally gracious Victoria Falls Bridge, and within walking distance of the falls. A member of Leading Hotels of the World, it was built for Cecil Rhodes's Cape-to-Cairo railway; today it's a reminder of the overstated opulence of a bygone age, with columns, arched loggias, broad verandas, and decorous chandeliers. The deluxe rooms (with views of the spray and bridge) and suites are definitely worth it; standard rooms are tiny. Enjoy drinks and high tea served on a generous, sweeping terrace with excellent views—a must even if you're not staying here. A path through the gardens leads to the falls, and a 30-minute trail descends into the gorge to the river. David Livingstone enthusiasts should inquire about the excellent talks given by Russell Gammon. Service is well meaning but slow, and power failures are not unheard of. (Golfers can play the Gary Player–designed course at nearby The Elephant Hills.)

Mallet Dr., Box 10, Victoria Falls. ✆ **263/13/44751.** Fax 263/13/42354. www.victoriafallshotel.com. 161 units. High season (July–Dec) standard room $444 double, deluxe room $535 double, suite $660–$1,602; low season (Jan–June) standard room $410 double; deluxe room $494 double, suite $615–$1,482. Rates include breakfast. AE, DC, MC, V. **Amenities:** 3 restaurants; 2 bars; various lounges; babysitting; chapel; high-speed Internet in business center ($5/15 min.); library w/faxed international newspapers; playground; pool; room service; spa; tennis. *In room:* A/C, TV, hair dryer.

12 Original Eden: Botswana

Botswana is home to one of the world's great natural phenomena: the tranquil Okavango Delta, a 15,000-sq.-km (5,850-sq.-mile) inland flood plain that fans out in the northwestern corner of the country, creating a paradise of palms, papyrus, and crystal-clear channels and deep lagoons. Set in a massive sea of desert sand, this fragile wonderland of waterways, islands, and forests is an oasis for wildlife drawn to its life-giving waters from the surrounding thirstlands. Here, the evening air is filled with the sounds of birds calling, frogs trilling, and antelope rustling in the reeds. Wildebeest, hartebeest, buffalo, and zebra roam the islands; elephants wade across channels guarded by hippos and crocs; and predators rule the night.

But it is not only animals and birds that are attracted to this huge, verdant oasis. Because the area is so sensitive, the Botswana government operates a policy of low-volume, high-income tourism, making southern Africa's premier wilderness destination a pricey destination—but this doesn't stop people from flocking to the limited beds in one of the world's most game-rich and unspoiled wilderness areas. To service these visitors, a number of safari companies have been established in and around the delta, particularly in the Moremi Game Reserve, in the northeastern sector. Because it is both expensive and complicated to travel independently in Botswana (huge distances are involved, and the road network is poor) and almost impossible in the delta itself, visitors are advised to contact one of these companies to arrange their trip. Most offer full-package holidays that cover the delta and surrounds and will organize everything for you, including flights, transfers, accommodations, and game-viewing.

Bear in mind that if you do a whistlestop visit, flying in one night and out the next day, you will be disappointed. The delta has its own unique moods and rhythms and a varying landscape: To experience these, you should plan to spend 3 nights here, preferably 4.

But there is more to Botswana than the delta. To the northeast lies **Chobe National Park,** a 12,000-sq.-km (4,680-sq.-mile) home to some 100,000 elephants. To the southeast is the **Kalahari Desert** and its spectacular Makgadikgadi and Nxai pans, where the space is so vast that, it is said, you can hear the stars sing. Most safari companies include the Chobe area on their itineraries, and some venture south into the endless horizons of the Kalahari pans.

Like so many of Africa's wilderness areas, the delta is under threat. A shortage of good grazing on adjacent lands makes the lush grass in the delta a standing temptation to stock farmers, especially in times of drought. The demands of Botswana's diamond-mining industry and the ever-expanding town of Maun (principal jumping-off point for the delta), both thirsty for water, pose an ongoing threat to the delta's precious liquid reserves, as does the proposed dam at Popa Falls, Namibia. So if you want to experience the untamed Africa of our ancestors, unadulterated by development, make a trip to Botswana a high priority.

1 ORIENTATION

VISITOR INFORMATION

Botswana's **Department of Tourism** has a website (www.botswanatourism.co.bw) listing its international representatives; in the U.S., you can contact **Leslee Hall** (info@botswanatourism.us), and in the U.K., **Dawn Parr** (dparr@govbw.bw). (Botswana does not yet have representatives in Canada or Australia.) Alternatively, contact one of the specialist safari operators listed later in the chapter directly, or read some of the useful features published in ***Getaway*** (www.getawaytoafrica.com; search using keyword "features"), Africa's largest-circulation travel magazine. This is primarily aimed at the local South African market (that is, those traveling on a tighter budget and usually not that discriminatory) but features great accounts of journalists on safari in Botswana. If you are considering a self-drive safari, you will need to contact the **Parks & Reservations Office,** P.O. Box 20364, Boseja, Maun (✆ **267/686-1265** or 267/686-0368) for permits.

For essential information on Botswana, including getting there, travel documents, health, and more, see chapter 3.

GETTING THERE

BY PLANE **Air Botswana** (www.airbotswana.co.bw; see chapter 3 for more contact details) flies directly from Johannesburg to **Maun,** which is the jumping-off point for most destinations in the Okavango Delta. Prices can vary greatly depending on the month you fly, but you're not going to get much change from R3,900 for a return ticket from Johannesburg. Most operators will arrange for you to fly into Maun and then transfer you to your Delta camp by charter flight; make sure this is part of the package. To reach Chobe National Park and surrounds, fly to **Kasane,** from where you can transfer by road (Vic Falls is incidentally only a 9-min. drive away); again, your operator or lodge should arrange this pickup. Note that you must bring your onward international airline ticket with you on safari, or you may be refused reentry into South Africa.

GETTING AROUND

BY PLANE The region's large wilderness areas are mostly inaccessible by car, so flying is the most sensible way to get around. From Maun, visitors usually join overland safari operators or fly in light aircrafts into their camps. Many charter companies operate out of Maun: **Sefofane** (✆ **267/686-0778;** www.sefofane.com) is the biggest; others are **Mack Air** (✆ **267/686-0675;** www.mackair.co.bw) and **Delta Air** (✆ **267/686-0044;** www.okavango.bw). Unless you're claustrophobic, this is an exciting way to travel: Views of the delta and Botswana's untamed wilderness are spectacular. The plane (which may be anything from a 6- to a 12-seater) often has to buzz the airstrip to clear herds of grazing animals, and the "departure/arrivals" lounge may be a bench under a tree.

BY CAR Traveling under your own steam at your own pace could be the adventure of a lifetime, but it will certainly impact your time. You will need permits and a fully equipped four-wheel-drive and camping vehicle (R1,070 a day gets you a 4x4 rental outfitted with a tent on the roof, tables, chairs, cutlery, gas lamp, extra fuel, bedding, and torch). For details, log on to **Maun Self Drive 4x4** (http://maunselfdrive4x4.webs.com). You can also hire a four-wheel-drive vehicle from **Avis,** Mathiba I Road (✆ **267/686-0039;** www.avis.com), or **Budget,** Mathiba I Road (✆ **267/686-3728;** www.budget.com), both located near Maun Airport. Note that, to rent a car, you must be 25 or older;

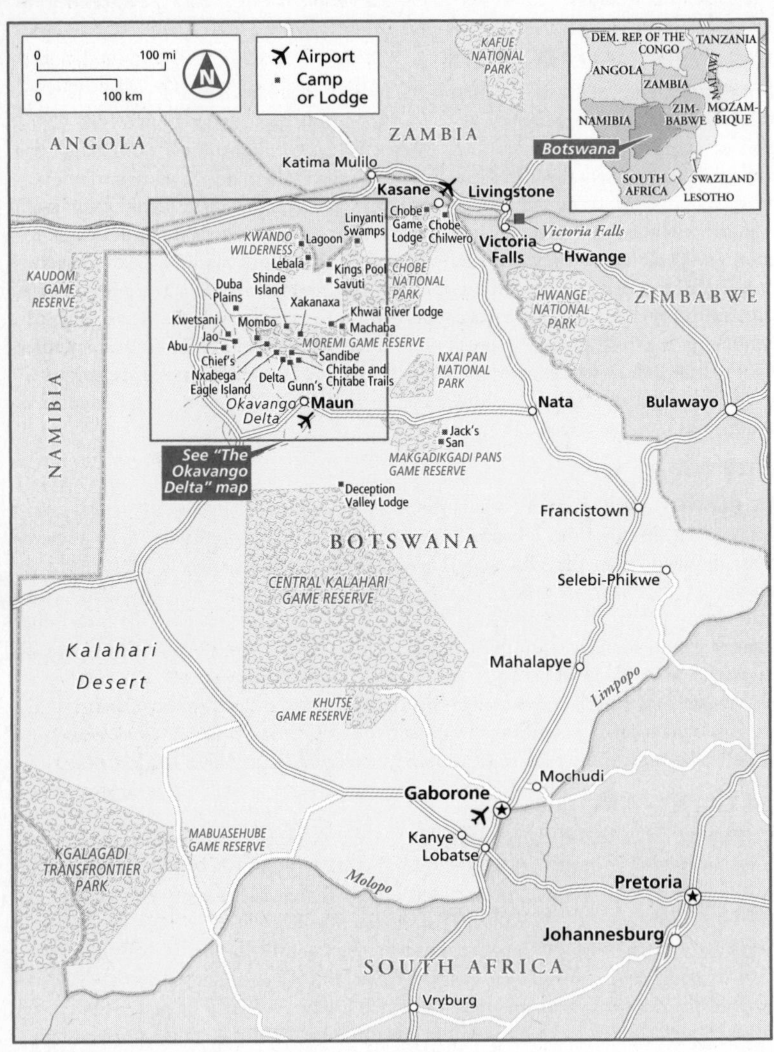

your home driving license is good for 6 months, provided it's in English. If you rent your own safari vehicle, you will also need to hire camping and cooking gear from **Kalahari Canvas** in Maun, Mathiba I Road (© **267/686-0568**), also near the airport. The delta is huge, but because of variable water levels and private concessions, there are only four "regular" campsites available in the Moremi Wildlife Reserve; there are more in and around Chobe. Facilities are simple, providing drinkable water, showers (equipped with boilers), and rudimentary toilets. Both Maun and Kasane (612km/380 miles away) have large, well-stocked supermarkets.

WITH A PACKAGE TOUR In Botswana, it really is worth using an established operator to make your bookings. At the very least, you should compare package prices before booking. Going it alone can be as expensive as buying a car from spare parts. Packages include, among other things, transport to the lodge or base camp; accommodations; food, soft drinks, and, in many cases, all alcoholic drinks except for imported liquors; game-viewing, fishing, and photographic expeditions; professional guides; boat hire; and *mokoro* trips (sometimes you pay extra for park entry fees). See recommended operators under "Specialist Safaris & Operators," below.

WHEN TO GO Much of the **Delta**'s high season is during winter (June–Oct). Temperatures are cool enough that you'll have to pack in warm layers for the night, but game can be less concentrated because of the floods. October is an ideal month because game centers on water. During low season (Nov, Apr, and May), temperatures are sweltering. Surprisingly healthy game populations move through the **Kalahari** year-round, but the desert comes to life with the summer rainfall (Dec–Apr), and thousands of plains game, such as springbok, gemsbok, and wildebeest, converge to feed on the grasses, with predators in close attendance.

Fast Facts Botswana

Airport See "Getting There" in this chapter and in chapter 3.

Banks **In Maun: Standard Chartered** and **Barclays** are both open Monday through Friday from 8:30am to 5pm, and Saturday from 8:15am to 10:45pm.

Directory Inquiries Dial ✆ **192.** You can also download **Kasane Phone Directory** (www.kasaneonline.com) or **Maun's Phone Directory** (www.jacanaent.com).

Doctor If you need a doctor or dentist in Maun, the **Delta Medical Centre** is on the Tsheko–Tsheko road, which runs through the center of town (✆ **267/686-1411**). Should you experience a medical emergency in the bush, the operators and camps recommended below will take appropriate and immediate action.

Documents See "Entry Requirements" and "Customs" in chapter 3.

Drugstore **Okavango Pharmacy** (✆ **267/686-0043**) is on Maun's main street, in the Lewis Building opposite Riley's garage complex.

Electricity As in the rest of southern Africa, you'll need an adapter/voltage converter. Botswana uses 220/240V 15/13-amp plug sockets. Plugs are two- and three-pin, round and flat. Remember that many bush camps do not have electricity but run on generators.

Embassies & Consulates **U.S. Embassy** (✆ **267/395-3982;** the after-hours emergency telephone number is ✆ **267/395-7111**); the **British High Commission** (✆ **267/395-2841**); the **Canadian Consulate** (✆ **267/390-4411**); the **Irish Honorary Consul** (✆ **267/390-5807**). Note that the Australian and New Zealand offices are in Pretoria, South Africa.

Language English is the official language and is widely spoken; Setswana is the national language, spoken by the Batswana people, who make up 50% of the population.

Safety Before you depart, consult your physician (or a travel-health specialist) about starting a course of antimalarial prophylactics. For more on malaria and safety in the bush, see "Health" and "Safety" in chapter 3.

Taxes Sales tax is 10%, included in all prices quoted in this chapter, unless otherwise indicated.

Telephone & Internet Most camps communicate with Maun and each other via satellite radio and will transmit only emergency messages this way, rendering you unreachable for the duration of your stay. With the exception of &Beyond (free) and Orient Express camps (first 45 min. free), no Botswana camps offer Internet access (and even &Beyond and Orient Express cannot guarantee the quality of the line), so let everyone know and enjoy being marooned. ***Note:*** This chapter lists numbers for Botswana and South Africa, indicated by their country codes. Remember, Botswana has no regional or town codes.

To call southern Africa from another country: Dial the international access code (United States or Canada 011, United Kingdom or New Zealand 00, Australia 0011), plus the country code (**27** for South Africa, **263** for Zimbabwe, **267** for Botswana, and **260** for Zambia), plus the local number minus the 0 at the beginning of the city/area code. **To make an international call:** Dial 00, wait for a dial tone, then dial the country code (United States or Canada **1,** United Kingdom **44,** Australia **61,** New Zealand **64**), the area code, and the local number. **To make calls within Botswana:** Drop the 267 country code; there are no area codes. **To charge international calls:** The toll-free international access code for **Sprint** is ✆ **0800/180-280.** At press time, there was no international access code for AT&T and MCI.

Time Zone Botswana is 2 hours ahead of GMT, or 7 hours ahead of Eastern Standard Time.

Tipping Tipping at bush and delta camps is at guests' discretion, but a general rule of thumb is $10 to $20 a day, to be shared among the staff. If you are delighted by the services of your guide, you can tip him in addition to this.

Water Water in camp is drinkable, but most camps/lodges do supply plenty of bottled mineral water. There is some disagreement about the safety of water in the smaller towns, so to be on the safe side, drink bottled water or bring along a purification system.

2 SPECIALIST SAFARIS & OPERATORS

You'll have no trouble finding safari operators or packages. They run the gamut to suit a range of interests and pockets, from fly-in safaris to luxurious lodges, to all-hands-on-deck-type trips with nights spent under canvas.

MOBILE VS. FLY-IN SAFARIS

Certainly, the only way to appreciate the broad changes of scenery in Botswana is to plan a trip that encompasses the Delta (in which you should try to visit both a "wet" and "dry" camp, or one that combines these terrains), the greater Chobe Area, and the Kalahari; Victoria Falls (see chapter 11) is an easy add-on. To cover this, you'll need to stay a minimum of 7 nights and to opt for a fly-in safari. (If you don't have enough time or don't like to move around that much, combine a 3-night Delta stay with 2 nights in the Kalahari for greatest contrast.)

Most people with limited time opt for fly-in safaris, moving between camps to experience different landscapes within an hour, and usually with the same operator to ensure smooth transfers between camps (the exception being the Kalahari region, which many operators in the north do not cover; if you wish to add on a visit to this area, either choose an operator that covers it, or book a recommended operator in the north and then with Uncharted Africa, the best Kalahari outfit). Depending on your budget and what you want out of your trip, however, mobile safaris—the more traditional safari, in which you ride, walk, or canoe to your next camp—range from basic participation tours, during which you may be expected to erect your own tent, to the ultraluxurious expeditions that require you to lift a finger only to summon another cold drink. Participants are transported in a suitably modified open-topped vehicle (or a mokoro/canoe), and they camp or lodge overnight at predetermined destinations. Usually the camps will be without electricity or the comforts of plumbing, but the experience of an authentic back-to-nature safari in this prime wilderness is unforgettably thrilling.

The following operators (websites above), mostly local to southern Africa (that is, they will be used by international agents, who may add a commission), are all highly recommended; for separate reviews of their top camps, see "Where to Stay & Dine," later in this chapter.

Tip: Another way to shop is with two excellent Web-based agents, www.expertafrica.com and www.africatravelresource.com. Their agents travel regularly and provide honest information on just about every lodge and camp in Botswana (expertafrica.com also has traveler reviews), and will create an itinerary to suit your budget.

African Bushcamps ★★★ Value A small portfolio of owner-run semipermanent tented camps, as well as mobile tented camp expeditions, this is for the luxury camping seeker who is looking for the real deal: a simple, understated tented safari experience, similar to the original explorations of Africa, hosted by a couple who are passionate about the bush and guest experience. Great value for your money.

&Beyond ★★★ &Beyond (previously CC Africa, but now with an international portfolio) are known for the great design ethos of their camps; every new camp they open—such as the latest, Xudum and Xaranna—is destined to feature in top decor magazines. And the exclusivity, privacy, and space of their suites are hard to beat. Service at their top camps is also top notch, including private butlers. With four camps, their penetration in the Delta has improved, and they also have the best selection of luxury camps in South Africa.

Bush Ways Safaris ★ Value This operator offers small and custom participation tours, themed around certain animals and best suited for more adventurous travelers who want an authentic experience. Guests stay in small dome tents and travel overland in an open Land Rover. Several itineraries are available, taking in all parts of Botswana, including Chobe, Moremi, the delta, Makgadikgadi, and the Kalahari.

Footsteps in Africa ★★ Value Finds This relatively new company is a breath of fresh air in this seriously expensive region. Footsteps specializes in Botswana (Kruger is the only other destination), and they probably offer the most affordable way to experience the country's key destinations. You'll stay in moderate budget camps, such as Oddballs, Delta Camp, and Mapula Lodge, but fly in with Delta Air, which they own. It's an unpretentious outfit, offering much more for your money than most.

Ker & Downey ★★★ Along with their five Botswana camps, this well-known top-end operator has a superb hand-picked property portfolio across southern Africa. With the best walking program (Footsteps) and mokoro trails (from their Kanana camp) in the Delta, Ker & Downey expeditions are an excellent value for those who want an authentic safari experience (camping in comfort). Agents will customize a very personal itinerary, depending on interest and budget; given their spread throughout southern Africa, you could do a grand journey across five countries, including semiurban and city destinations. (Wilderness Safaris, with an even greater spread in southern Africa, is concentrated solely in wilderness areas.)

Kwando ★★★ Value This small, very professional outfit is a relatively good value, with some of the best camps in Botswana (Kwara, Little Kwara, and Lebala, in particular). It's more expensive than Footsteps, which is where you should look if you are watching your budget (or consider Zambia), but the Kwando camps are in a class of their own and well worth the extra cost if you can afford it.

Mike Penman's Wild Lifestyles ★★★ Voted one of the top 15 safari guides in the world by *Condé Nast Traveler,* Penman—who has produced and facilitated a number of wildlife documentaries—offers private, custom-made luxury tented safaris aimed particularly at people with an interest in photography or filmmaking. Tents usually house no more than four guests. For contact information, see "Photography & Film Safaris," below.

Orient Express Safaris ★★★ Orient Express is another operator that needs no introduction. The well-heeled international globetrotter has a choice of three camps in Botswana: two in the delta and one in Chobe. In classic Orient Express style, it offers top-of-the-range, unabashed luxury. &Beyond has the edge in terms of camp design and knowledge of the bush, but the staff training at Orient Express shines through.

Penduka Safaris ★★ Though it's based in Namibia, this trusted, reliable operator is one of the most established mobile safari companies in Botswana, offering fully catered and serviced camping trips in campsites throughout most of southern Africa.

Sanctuary Lodges & Camps ★★ This top-end operator, a division of the otherwise increasingly second-rate Abercrombie & Kent, offers a similar experience (at a similar price) as Wilderness Safaris. With just four lovely camps in northern Botswana (Baines', Stanley's, Chief's, and Chobe Chilwero, all reviewed below), they don't penetrate Southern Africa like Wilderness Safaris does, but they can set up an itinerary that includes visits to one or more of their five new camps in Zambia.

Uncharted Africa Safari Co. ★★★ This is the foremost operator in Botswana's Kalahari region. Besides the luxurious HQ camp (Jack's Camp; see later in this chapter), you can ask for mobile expeditions into the desert, as well as trips north to the delta and Chobe—though that area is better serviced by Wilderness Safaris. I would urge you to include this personal favorite of mine into a Delta trip.

Wilderness Safaris ★★★ Wilderness Safaris has some of the best concessions in Botswana, and by far the most camps. Since launching the much-lauded Mombo Camp in mid-2000, the company has grown exponentially. Today they operate some 60 lodges and camps in southern Africa (21 in Botswana), producing enough revenue to conserve 2.7 million hectares of wilderness. Service and design is not quite as OTT as &Beyond's—with the exception of their pricey Premier Camps, the ethos is determinedly conservation. But this company has garnered immense respect within the industry, even among direct competitors. Given also their impeccable responsible tourism standards, it's a top choice.

MOKORO & ISLAND CAMPING EXPEDITIONS

The cheapest and one of the most adventurous ways to enjoy the delta is to join a mokoro trip through the islands, accompanied by a poler with an intimate knowledge of these waters. **Oddballs** specializes in budget mokoro camping trips and also runs one of the best-known budget camps in the delta (for more, see "Delta on a Budget," later in this chapter). A little more pricey (but still way less per night than staying at one of the Delta's permanent camps, and a very exclusive, authentic experience), is Ker & Downey's **Kanana Mokoro Trail** ★★★, in the western part of the Delta. The trail camp is on a remote island and accommodates a maximum of four people in two twin bedded tents (both with bucket shower and bush toilet); besides the luxury of being alone on an island in paradise, the camp includes the services of five staff members: a personal chef, waiter, housekeeper, and mokoro guides ($420–$540 per person per night all inclusive, depending on season). Another option is the 3-day **Xigera Mokoro Trail,** departing every 3 days from May to October (www.sunsafaris.net).

ELEPHANT-BACK SAFARIS

Abu Camp ★★★ Randall Moore's pioneering camp—the first place in the world to introduce fully fledged safaris on the back of a pachyderm—is still a great way to explore the delta from the back of an elephant. Elephants cope equally well with water and sand, and they also get very close to other game. Guests ride on comfortable, custom-made saddles. Accommodations comprise six extremely luxurious, custom-designed en-suite tents, furnished with kilim rugs and mahogany sleigh beds. The newer **Seba Camp** offers five additional en-suite tents and there is also a two-bedroom Villa, featured in *Travel + Leisure*'s list of the 50 Most Romantic Places on Earth. The main drawbacks are the price (it has the dubious distinction of being the most expensive camp in Botswana) and the western delta location (game on the eastern part of the delta tends to be better). ***Note:*** For a more sensitive elephant experience, book with Doug Groves at Stanley's Camp or Baines' Camp (see "Where to Stay & Dine," below).

© **267/686-1260.** www.abucamp.com or www.wilderness-safaris.com. Abu $5,146 double. AE, DC, MC, V. Abu camp is closed in wet season (mid-Dec to Feb). No children under 12.

HORSE SAFARIS

Limpopo Valley Horse Safaris ★★ During Limpopo Valley's 7-night wilderness safaris, guests spend each night at a different camp within the Mashatu Game Reserve, in the eastern tip of Botswana; the focus is often on riding with the vast elephant herds. Participants spend the first night at the semipermanent Two Mashatus camp, in double safari tents that include en-suite toilets and hot-water showers. The rest of the week is spent in bush camps, including 2 nights under the stars in an old tribal court called the Kgotla. Horses are professionally schooled to be responsive, athletic, and forward going. Riders must be experienced, due to the presence of game such as lion, leopard, and elephant. Visitors who don't want a mobile safari can choose the Two Mashatus Safari or the Limpopo Lodge ride.

P.O. Box 26. Lentswe Le Moriti Botswana. © **267/232-0024.** www.lvhsafaris.co.za. $450 per person per night. AE, MC, V. Rates are all-inclusive except for tips and curios. No children under 14.

Okavango Horse Safaris ★★★ These safaris are run in a private concession in the western delta bordering Moremi Game Reserve (better than Tuli for game-viewing) and take you deep into the wetlands. Expect to spend between 4 and 6 hours a day in the saddle. The minimum riding ability required is a mastery of the basics, including an ability to trot for stretches of 10 minutes at a time and—even more important—the ability to gallop out of trouble. The maximum weight limit is 90kg (200 lb.). The tack is English style, and each saddle has a seat-saver for comfort. Trail riders move from **Kujwana Camp** (spacious safari tents with shower en suite and flush toilets) to **Moklowane** (tree houses 2m/6½ ft.) off the ground with flush toilets and hot showers) to **Fly Camp** (spacious Meru tents with camp beds, bush toilets, and bucket showers). A maximum of eight riders can participate, and the safaris last between 5 and 10 days. Besides horse rides, guests are treated to game drives, bush walks, and mokoro trips, which helps keep activities varied and interesting. The camps are closed December through February. Private Bag 23, Maun. ✆ **267/686-1671.** Fax 267/686-1672. www.okavangohorse.com. For a 5-, 7-, or 10-night safari, the high season (June–Oct) rate is £420 per person per night; low season (Mar–May and Nov) £380 per person per night. Rates are all-inclusive. Air transfers are £210 per person return from Maun. There is a 50% single supplement for people unwilling to share. No credit card facilities. Children are accepted if they are strong, confident riders.

CYCLING SAFARIS

Mashatu ★★ Radio-linked groups of cyclists set out at dawn and again at dusk on mountain bikes in search of animals; visits to the ruins of 600-year-old settlements on the reserve are included. The program is entirely flexible and can be adapted to the needs and skills of the particular cyclists; game drives can also be included. These safaris run March through October. You can base yourself at Main Camp or Mashatu Tented Camp, but for a real adventure, head out to the wilderness and camp out in basic tents with a guide and minimal staff; budget around $1,500 per person per trip. For more information, call ✆ **27/11/442-2267** or 0861-SAFARI (723274; www.cyclemashatu.com).

WALKING SAFARIS

Footsteps Across the Delta ★★★ Value Moments It doesn't get more authentic than at this camp, the best for walking safaris in the Delta. Every day a small group of guests (up to six) make their way by foot and mokoro to the next campsite. There's no electricity or flush toilets, but the experience is in many ways the ultimate in luxury for the right kind of person. The emphasis is on enjoying the slow pace of the delta—the maximum distance each day is about 6km (3¾ miles), and you can travel light; while you cover the distance, the camp staff transports baggage and camp essentials. Accommodations are in three twin-bedded en-suite tents; cuisine is exceptional, given the remoteness of the location. Minimum age is 12. For contact details, see Ker & Downey in "At a Glance: Safari Operators Specializing in Botswana," earlier in this chapter; rate is $420 to $570 per person per night (all inclusive), depending on the season. To explore a different ecosystem—the highly rated Linyanti concession—look into **Linyanti Walking Safaris** ★★★ (www.africanbushcamps.com); see accommodation review below.

PHOTOGRAPHY & FILM SAFARIS

Mike Penman's Wild Lifestyles ★★★ These highly adventurous yet luxury tented safaris focus on learning about wildlife while affording you the best opportunities to capture the experience on film. Penman has been involved in conservation, photography, and filmmaking in Botswana for 18 years, producing his own documentaries and helping independent filmmakers and major TV networks. He personally conducts safaris into Moremi, the delta, Kalahari, Makgadikgadi, Nxai Pans, and Drotsky's Caves. Penman is known for his bold approach to lions and his ability to get right into the mix of things, placing you in a great position from which to capture the moment. Other, tamer photographic and birding safaris with professional guides are offered by Wilderness Safaris (see "Specialist Safaris & Operators," earlier in this chapter).

P.O. Box 250059, Maun, Botswana. ✆ **267/686-3664.** Fax 267/686-1045. www.wildlifestyles.com. Mobile safaris $550–$650 per person per day, depending on the season.

CULTURAL SAFARIS

If you're interested in Bushman (or "San") culture, make sure you spend a few nights with **Uncharted Africa Safari Co.** in the Kalahari (see Jack's Camp, San Camp, and Planet Baobab, later in this chapter); one of the most exciting trips held once a year, personally led by Ralph Bousfield, is an 8-night initiation hunt, a rapidly disappearing Bushmen ritual. Uncharted will also, along with such operators as **Moremi Safaris & Tours,** organize a visit to the **Tsodilo Hills** (in the northwest, near the panhandle), where you can view some 3,000 rock paintings. The paintings are known for their fine clarity and wide variety, and trips can be made by air or four-wheel drive. There is also a traditional village in the foothills. For contact details, see "Specialist Safaris & Operators," earlier in this chapter.

3 THE OKAVANGO DELTA & MOREMI GAME RESERVE

For most, the highlight of a trip to southern Africa is a sojourn in the world's largest inland delta. Originating in Angola, the Okavango River flows southward for 1,300km (806 miles), finally spilling into the northwestern corner of Botswana and turning it into an aquatic paradise. Thanks to the same geological activity that caused the Great African Rift Valley, the delta is more or less contained by fault lines between which the crust has sunk and filled up with sediment. It is into this bowl that the Okavango River seeps and finally evaporates into the Kalahari Desert, rather than making its rightful way to the sea. The annual southward flow of water is precipitated by the rainy season in the north, which begins in the Angolan uplands between January and March, and usually arrives at its southernmost point—the delta—around June or July, when the water spreads out to form innumerable pools, channels, and lagoons, and the temperatures are ideal.

Where to Stay & Dine

The northeastern segment of the delta has been set aside as the **Moremi Game Reserve,** an 1,800-sq.-km (702-sq.-mile) expanse of wilderness extending across both wetland and dry terrain covering an estimated 20% of the Delta. This, the most popular national park in Botswana, is both scenically exquisite and dense with exciting game (it's sometimes referred to as the Predator Capital of Africa), most of them quite habituated to humans. But being a National Park, it also attracts its fair share of tourists, some of them on self-drive safaris from neighboring countries. So although you're paying top dollar, you may not feel as removed from civilization as you will in one of the private concessions that surround Moremi Game Reserve. These are southern Africa's most sought-after private reserves or concessions; most contain only a couple of small, private safari camps and offer a greater variety of safari activities than the park: Only camps outside the Moremi Game Reserve are allowed to have night game drives and walking safaris, or drive off designated roads to follow game. Concessions located in the south and east tend to have a greater density and variety of game sightings (worth noting if your time is limited, but not a deal breaker). Rates are almost always quoted in dollars and usually include transfers from Maun, but please check up front to be sure. Book as early as possible: These camps embody Botswana's prevailing tourism ethos of high-end and low volume, so in peak season, beds in sought-after camps are soon filled.

In Moremi Game Park

Chief's Camp ★★★ This is one of the most luxurious camps in the heart of the delta, in the exclusive Mombo Concession (on the western side of Chief's Island), with 52 different lions identified in a 9km (5½-mile) radius and almost daily leopard sightings; both white and black rhinos are also regular visitors to the area. One of the other reasons the camp is so popular is that it offers the experience of both a wet and dry camp: From June to October, when the floodwaters arrive, mokoro activities are available; this is also the time to book soothing spa treatments in the *sala* (pavilion) alongside the pool. Tents are very comfortable; each is furnished with large twin beds and comfortable armchairs, and features spacious, well-equipped bathrooms and private viewing decks sheltered by jackalberry and sausage trees.

Reservations: Sanctuary Lodges & Camps. ✆ **27/11/438-4650.** Fax 27/11/787-7658. www.sanctuarylodges.com. (see "Specialist Safaris & Operators," earlier in this chapter). 12 units. High season (June 15–Oct) $2,900; low season (Nov–June 14) $1,800. MC, V. No children under 9. **Amenities:** Dining area; bar; lounge; game drives; library; seasonal mokoro trips; pool; spa treatments in high season; free Wi-Fi. *In room:* Ceiling fan, hair dryer, emergency telephone.

Mombo and Little Mombo ★★★ Located in the no. 1 game-viewing area in the delta, Mombo has been host to numerous *National Geographic* and BBC shoots, and it is not unheard of to see as many as 12 mammal species without leaving your veranda. The camps are on an island at the northwestern tip of Chief's Island, deep within the Moremi Game Reserve in an area where dense concentrations of plains game congregate. Tents are the size of small houses and use all-natural materials; suites are connected by a long walkway more than 1.8m (6 ft.) off the ground; this allows game to wander freely through the camp. Public areas are wonderful and make the most of the gorgeous views. You certainly pay for the privilege of being here, and while the camps are pretty luxurious by Wilderness Safaris standards, this is not &Beyond. Some believe that Duba Plains (also Wilderness Safaris; see below) offers equally good game-viewing for less.

Book through Wilderness Safaris (see "Specialist Safaris & Operators," earlier in this chapter). Mombo 9 units. Little Mombo 3 units. High season (June–Nov) $3,540; low season $2,940 double. Rates are all-inclusive. MC, V. No children under 8; July 1–Oct 31 age limit increases to 12. **Amenities:** Dining room; bar; lounge areas; game drives; 2 pools. *In room:* Hair dryer.

Xakanaxa Camp ★★ (Value) One of three camps located on the large Xakanaxa lagoon, Xakanaxa (pronounced "ka-*ka*-na-ka") is the best here, offering year-round boating trips and extensive nature drives into great game country; bird-watching is equally good. Tents are a tad too close (you may have to put up with your neighbor recounting his day), but visually they're private and gorgeous. There is no electrical lighting, so the bush experience is genuine, with candles and lanterns. It's not the most luxurious option, but it's a class act nevertheless, and by far the best-value option in the Delta. The new Owner's Cottage, a private, elevated wood and thatch cottage, offers an open-fronted

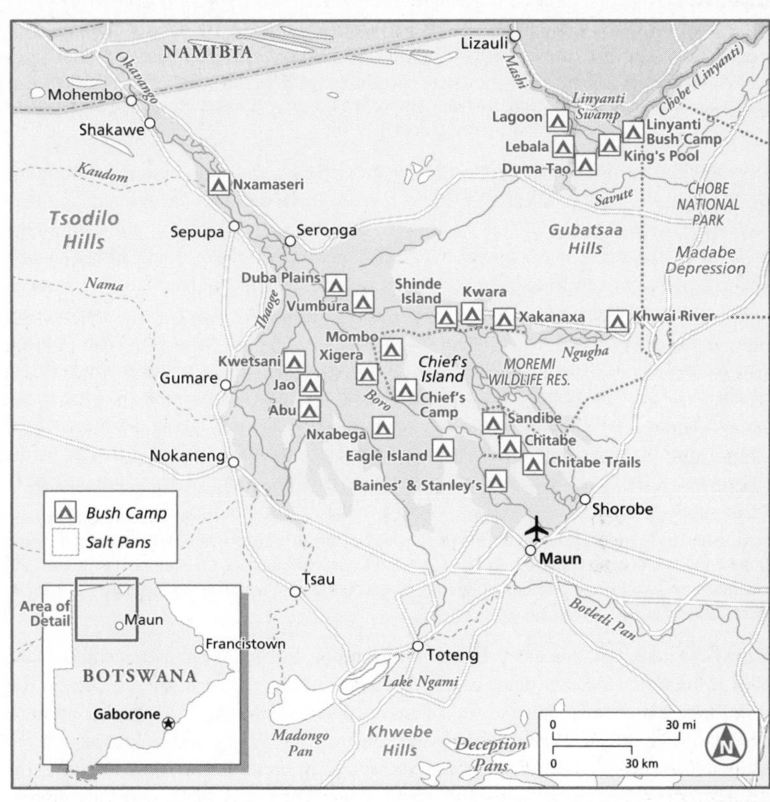

bedroom with a king-size bed, personal plunge pool, sala, fire deck, viewing deck, free-standing tub, and double shower.

Book through Moremi Safaris & Tours (see "Specialist Safaris & Operators," earlier in this chapter). 12 units. Tents: High season (July–Oct) $1,750 double; shoulder season (Apr–June, Nov) $1,840; low season (Dec–March) $1,040 double. Owners house: High season $2,100; shoulder season $1,480; low season $1,240. Specials available on website. AE, DC, MC, V. **Amenities:** 2 dining and lounge areas; boat and mokoro trips; game drives; plunge pool.

Private Concessions Bordering Moremi Game Park

Baines' Camp ★★ On a concession south of Moremi, this personal favorite has only five guest chalets, four-poster beds that can be rolled out onto your deck so you can sleep under the stars, and a lovely infinity pool. Each suite is very privately situated, with terraces that look out onto the wilderness (ask for a view of the waterway) and spacious, well-laid-out bathrooms (no tubs, though). On arrival, you find yourself in a tranquil, tastefully decorated lounge built around a massive tree and overlooking a permanent waterway where noisy hippos play and wallow; they will keep you entertained for hours. Nearby, the more established **Stanley's Camp ★** offers eight tents at cheaper rates. Both properties offer the same activities, and one great drawing card is the **Elephant**

Experience ★★★, a morning in which you spend some intimate time with three semi-habituated elephants, under the sensitive and expert guidance of Doug Groves.

Reservations: Sanctuary Lodges & Camps. ✆ **27/11/438-4650.** Fax 27/11/787-7658. www.sanctuarylodges.com. 5 units. High season (June 16–Oct) $2,060 double; low season (Nov–June 15) $1,240 double. All-inclusive, except for Elephant Experience, which costs $584–$732 per person. MC, V. Children 9–11 must share with an adult. No children under 9. **Amenities:** Dining area; bar; lounge; game drives; library; pool. *In room:* A/C, hair dryer, minibar, emergency telephone.

Chitabe Camp and Chitabe Lediba ★★ Chitabe Reserve is virtually surrounded by Moremi and is more forested, with narrow channels; as such, it offers excellent dry-land game drives, but it's not ideal for those looking for aquatic bird and animal life. That said, it's very beautiful and exclusive, with only two camps in the reserve; **Chitabe Letaba** is the most intimate, with only five en-suite tents (two suitable for families) with wooden floors and metal-framed four-poster beds under a canopy of trees. A few minutes away, in a similar setting, the **Chitabe** main camp is an eight-tented camp with tents built on wooden decks linked by raised wooden footbridges; service and guiding standards are excellent. Guests staying for a few nights have the option of doing a short walking safari: On a **Chitabe Trail,** a max of four guests walk with an armed ranger, have their food cooked over an open fire, and spend the night sleeping under the stars in one of the camp's raised timber hides, swathed in mosquito nets—a recommended authentic bush experience.

Book through Wilderness Safaris (see "Specialist Safaris & Operators," earlier in this chapter). High season (June–Nov) $1,800 double; low season $1,200. Rates are all-inclusive. MC, V. Children 8–12 permitted, but parents must book private game-drive vehicles. **Amenities:** Dining area; bar; lounge; bush walks; game drives; plunge pool. *In room:* Fans.

Duba Plains Camp ★★★ In the northernmost reaches of the delta, remote Duba used to be a find because of its superlative game-viewing yet "entry-level" pricing. It's now been discovered, though, so cough up and book early. The only camp in a 35,000-hectare (86,450-acre) private reserve, with sweeping grass plains, gin-clear fresh-water pools, and palm islands, the camp itself remains pretty rustic. Its exclusivity is the real luxury (only six tents, each with wooden floors, fine linens, and a veranda overlooking the flood plains), along with the reserve's famous lion and buffalo interactions: You'll see huge herds of buffalo (1,500–3,000), which, in turn, attract lions—sometimes up to 15 a day. Guests may choose among game drives, mokoro rides (dependent on floodwaters, best usually May–Oct), and walking safaris. Guiding standards are excellent, and rangers will go out of their way to track particular species.

Book through Wilderness Safaris (see "Specialist Safaris & Operators," earlier in this chapter). High season (June–Nov) $2,060 double; low season $1,540 double. Rates all-inclusive. MC, V. No children under 8. **Amenities:** Dining room; bar; game drives; library; pool on a raised terrace overlooking the plains. *In room:* Fan.

Eagle Island Camp ★★★ This camp, made up of 12 luxury tents, each with a private deck facing the lagoon (1 with a private plunge pool, along with private guide and boat), is at Xaxaba, an island refuge. Accommodations are pleasantly spread out for privacy, and the Fish Eagle Bar is the ideal romantic hideaway after a day of game-viewing. Besides affording you all the luxury you'd expect from the Orient Express group, this is the ideal destination for birders. Set among the flood plains, Eagle Island enjoys a high concentration of fish eagles and other bird species, including kingfishers, herons, cormorants, pelicans, darters, and storks. To augment your water-based game activities, a helicopter flight is part of the deal. Orient Express regularly transfers guests from here to **Khwai,** its semi-"dry" camp in neighboring Moremi National Park, or, for real contrast, **Savute Elephant,** its Chobe camp; both are a 25-minute flight away.

Book through Orient Express Safaris (in South Africa, call ✆ **011/481-6052**). www.orient-express-safaris.co.za. 12 units. High season (July–Oct) $2,490 double; shoulder season /(Nov–Dec/Apr—June) $1,780/$2,000 double; low season (Jan–Mar) $1,610 double. Rates are all-inclusive. AE, MC, V. No children under 12 except by prior arrangement. **Amenities:** Dining area; bar; airstrip; game drives; hiking; Internet lounge (1st 45 min. each day free); library; mokoro trips; heated pool; light-aircraft safaris. *In room:* A/C, hair dryer, intercom, minibar.

Jao Camp ★★★ Jao (rhymes with *ciao*) is one of Wilderness Safaris' top camps (joining flagship Mombo, King's Pool, and Vumbura). Located in one of the finest concessions in the delta, it covers 60,000 hectares (148,200 acres); much of the land experiences huge fluctuations in water levels, with ever-changing views and game experiences. Location aside, it is—in terms of style and luxury—one of the most gorgeous, romantic camps in the delta, designed by renowned architect Silvio Rech (of Ngorongoro Crater Lodge fame). The Zen-like simplicity and airy elegance are soothing, and the natural materials neatly blend with the great views. The eight suites are arranged along a long, raised wooden footbridge, ensuring privacy. Built on stilts alongside a lily-speckled waterway, each suite has a large private viewing deck, a *sala* for afternoon siestas, a beautiful open-air shower, and spacious living areas with open-plan en-suite bathrooms. Note, however, that at Kwetsani (see below), Jacana, and Tubu Tree Camp (all Wilderness Safaris), the same game-viewing is half the price.

Book through Wilderness Safaris (see "Specialist Safaris & Operators," earlier in this chapter). High season (June–Nov) $3,540 double; low season $2,050 double. Rates are all-inclusive. MC, V. Children 8–12 permitted, but special arrangements must be made with management for private vehicles. **Amenities:** Dining area; bar; lounge; fishing; library; 2 pools; spa. *In room:* A/C, fans, hair dryer.

Khwai River Lodge ★★★ This is one of the oldest lodges in Botswana, opened in 1968 by Harry Selby (who, incidentally, worked for Philip Percival, immortalized by Hemingway as Pop in his *Green Hills of Africa*). Today it is the Orient Express Group's most popular camp. It's gorgeous, with all the bells and whistles associated with Orient Express's luxurious approach to the bush safari. Facilities include air-conditioned tents, a heated swimming pool, and a video library (and in one suite, a private plunge pool and indoor and outdoor bathrooms). The camp comprises 15 large twin-bedded tents, each with generous bathroom and a private deck furnished with hammocks for comfortable eyeballing of the resident hippo and croc. The complex is built in the shade of indigenous leadwood and fig trees, and overlooks the Khwai River flood plain, where you are likely to see large numbers of elephants. Your chances of spotting lions, hyenas, wild dogs, and leopards are equally high. Due to popular demand, the spa has doubled in size.

Book through Orient Express Safaris (see "Specialist Safaris & Operators," earlier in this chapter). 15 units. High season (July–Oct) $1,940 double; shoulder season (Nov–Dec/Apr–June) $1,230/$1,450 double; low season (Jan–Mar) $1,060 double. Rates are all-inclusive. AE, MC, V. No children under 12 except by prior arrangement. **Amenities:** Dining room and lounge; bar; airstrip; boat and mokoro trips; game drives; heated pool; Internet lounge (1st 45 min. per day free); library; room service; VHS video and monitor. *In room:* A/C, fan, hair dryer, intercom, minibar.

Khwai Tented Camp ★★ Value This small tented camp is on the banks of the Khwai River, where the Okavango Delta stretches into its banks and provides myriad life along the Moremi Game Reserve. With only four tents, this intimate camp offers the perfect small group or family atmosphere. Excursions include walking and game drives into the Moremi, and night drives in Khwai. This is not luxury on the scale of the similarly named Orient Express camp, but it's an authentic safari, and the high levels of service and professional guidance will leave you feeling both pampered and well educated. It's a great value option.

Book through African Bush Camps. (see "Specialist Safaris & Operators," earlier in this chapter). High season (June–Oct) $1,360 double, all-inclusive; low season (Nov–May) $900 double. No credit cards. No children under 10. **Amenities:** Dining/lounge area; game drives; game walks.

Kwetsani Camp ★★★ Value Also situated in the stunning Jao Concession area (to the northwest of Moremi Game Reserve), this camp features five tree house chalets built on stilts under thatched roofs and linked by raised walkways. Designed similarly to Jao (although far less ostentatiously), Kwetsani is much smaller and enjoys an intimate, relaxed atmosphere; dedicated guides make exploration of the varied terrain memorable, and besides mokoro and boat trips, night drives are available. Built on a heavily wooded island with mangosteen and fig trees, it is particularly beautiful from May to September, when the water levels are at their highest, but the game-viewing is best from October to April, when the flood plains are drier. Guests who want a "rougher" bush experience can book a night in an animal hide at nearby Jao camp. ***Note:*** Jao Concession is so beautiful that all its camps are worth a look. Aside from Jao and Kwetsani, there are also **Jacana Camp** ★★★—comfortable, small, and in a great location overlooking the floodplains—and **Tubu Tree Camp** ★★, with equally beautiful views, stylish tents on raised stilts, plunge pool, and more; both cost the same as Kwetsani. (All camps in the Jao concession belong to Wilderness Safaris.)

Book through Wilderness Safaris (see "Specialist Safaris & Operators," earlier in this chapter). 5 units High season $1,800 double; low season $1,200 double. Rates are all-inclusive. MC, V. Children 8–12 are permitted only if they are in a group with a private vehicle. **Amenities:** Dining area; bar; lounge; boat and mokoro trips; game drives; pool. *In room:* Fan.

Little Vumbura & Vumbura Plains ★★★ East of Moremi and Duba is this superbly scenic private concession on the 52,609-hectare (130,000-acre) Vumbura Reserve (pronounced *Voom*-ber-a). With only two camps, it offers access to a great variety of habitats—from palm-fringed waterways to open savanna and deep forest. No doubt inspired by the success of the much-feted Singita in the Kruger area (not to mention the excellent quality of the game-viewing here), Wilderness Safaris revamped the Plains camp in 2005 to create a delta option that would appeal to a younger, more design-conscious market, with huge, minimalist spaces. Each of the 14 privately situated rooms, connected via elevated timber walkways, has its own lounge as well as a private plunge pool and *sala* from which to enjoy the passing parade on the flood plains beyond. Personally, I'd head straight for its more realistically priced little sister, which offers the same game-viewing experience. If you don't mind sharing a plunge pool, **Little Vumbura** remains very exclusive, with only six tents and lovely public areas, all much rejuvenated by a classy face-lift in 2007.

Book through Wilderness Safaris (see "Specialist Safaris & Operators," earlier in this chapter). High season (June–Nov) $3,540 double; low season $2,050 double. Rates are all-inclusive. MC, V. Children 8–12 permitted, but special arrangements must be made with management for private vehicles. **Amenities:** Dining area; bar; lounge area; game drives; mokoro trips; pool. *In room:* Fans.

Nxabega Okavango Tented Camp ★★ This 8,000-hectare (19,800-acre) private concession on the western border of Moremi Game Reserve is best visited when there is plenty of water (Feb–May). This concession encompasses three camps. Nxabega is by far the most luxurious; the others are Ker & Downey's Kanana and the nine-unit Pom Pom Camp. Nxabega has the feel of an elegant gentlemen's club, with burnished teak, crisp white linen, parchment lampshades, and dressing tables with leather boxes. The 10 luxury en-suite tents, on raised wooden platforms with private verandas, feature all the comforts. This is one of four Botswana properties owned by &Beyond (formerly CC Africa), renowned for luxurious camps in well-chosen settings throughout the continent, excellent food, and attentive service.

Book through &Beyond (see "Specialist Safaris & Operators," earlier in this chapter). $800–$1,890 double. Rates are all-inclusive. AE, DC, MC, V. Children welcome. **Amenities:** Dining room; lounge w/bar; airstrip; boat and mokoro trips; bush walks; game drives; interpretive center; pool. *In room:* Fan, hair dryer.

Sandibe Safari Lodge ★★ Bordering the southern edges of Chief's Island, the Santantadibe area is one of the most beautiful in the Delta, and this is without a doubt the best camp from which to experience it. &Beyond is renowned for the quality of its guides, and Sandibe offers exclusive access to 8,000 hectares (19,800 acres), an area that includes permanent land and water activities, as well as bush walks and night drives. Eight African-style chalets have great outdoor showers, slightly pedestrian but elegant fittings and furnishings, and large private decks with hammocks overlooking game-rich grassy plains. Food and guiding standards are equally good. It's not as cutting edge as their new camps, Xudum and Xaranna (see below), but then, it's not as expensive, either.

Book through &Beyond (see "Specialist Safaris & Operators," earlier in this chapter). High season $1,890 double; low season $800 double. Rates are all-inclusive. DC, MC, V. Children welcome. **Amenities:** Dining/lounge area; bar; boat and mokoro trips; bush walks; game drives; massage; pool. *In room:* Hair dryer.

Shinde Island Camp ★★ East of Vumbura (see above), on a lush palm island in the heart of the northern delta, Shinde is surrounded by waterways that teem with birds and game. From the veranda of your tent, you can watch game moving across the plains and listen to the sounds of woodpeckers tapping in the trees. Activities include game drives, powerboat excursions, guided walks, fishing (guides are all well practiced and will cook what you catch), and mokoro safaris. There are eight twin-bedded tents, but you can also hire a private section of Shinde known as **The Enclave:** Three tents are reserved for the use of a private party; the minimum stay here is 3 nights, and you get your own dining area, bar, lounge, and staff, including a top-notch guide. This is also the base headquarters for the nearby **Footsteps Across the Delta ★★★** trail camp, the best walking safari option. ***Note:*** Offering the same basic facilities in a totally different setting, Ker & Downey's **Kanana Camp ★★** (referred to as Shinde's watery sister) is situated in the southwestern part of the delta at the edge of the Xudum River; rates are slightly more affordable ($1,080 in high season), and mokoro trips are offered from here into the Delta for two to four persons; for these you camp out (with staff to look after you) on a remote island—idyllic. Their newly revamped **Okuti** (same rate) is one of the most interestingly designed camps in the Delta (see the website for details).

Book through Ker & Downey (see "Specialist Safaris & Operators," earlier in this chapter). Shinde: 8 units. High season (July–Oct) $1,700 double; shoulder season (Apr–June and Nov) $1,240 double; low season (Jan–Mar) $840. DC, MC, V. No children under 10. **Amenities:** Dining area; bar; lounge/library; boat and mokoro trips; bush walks; game drives; pool.

Xudum and Xaranna ★★★ The latest flagship camps from &Beyond, Xudum and Xaranna have both graced the pages of various international decor and gourmet magazines. Located on its own island in a private concession of some 25,000 hectares (61,800 acres) to the southeast of the Delta, Xaranna offers just 9 beautifully furnished tents, each with a great view of the shimmering water that defines a stay here, private plunge pool, bathtub, and outdoor shower. Xudum, with nine split-level suites topped with thatched roofs and rooftop lookouts, is more earthbound and has a more permanent feel, but is equally modern, with private plunge pools and al fresco showers. The public spaces provide a surreal counterpoint of urban chic against a backdrop of paradise—together these are currently the most stylish camps in the Delta, and worth every penny.

Book through &Beyond (see "Specialist Safaris & Operators," earlier in this chapter). $1,100–$2,750 double. Rates are all-inclusive. DC, MC, V. **Amenities:** Dining room/lounge; bar; boat and mokoro trips; bush walks; game drives; pool. *In room:* Hair dryer.

4 CHOBE & LINYANTI REGION ★★★

The far northern region of Botswana, comprising the Chobe National Park, Chobe Forest Reserve, Linyanti and Savuti channels, and Kwando Wilderness, is almost as popular as the delta. It is certainly vast: Chobe National Park alone covers more than 11,000 sq. km (4,290 sq. miles) of northern Botswana and affords access to a variety of wildlife, but the major drawing card here is elephants: The area harbors a large proportion—some 100,000—of Botswana's elephant population (said to be the largest in the world). In the dry season, the Chobe River is the only major source of water north of the Okavango, so game travels here from great distances, which, in turn, ensures a large lion population. The area is also alive with more than 460 species of birds. The Savuti area, in the west-central region, was once submerged beneath an enormous inland sea and connected to the Okavango and Zambezi rivers, but that was eons ago. Today it's a relatively harsh wilderness landscape, with vast swathes of open grassland. There is a fair number of permanently resident game here, including leopard, lion, and spotted hyena, but game numbers are greatly augmented at the beginning of the dry season, when large numbers of zebras and wildebeests move through the area from the west to the sweeter grasses on offer in the Mababe Depression to the south.

West of Chobe, four large reserves abut the Kwando and Linyanti rivers. **Selinda** is linked by the Okavango and Linyanti rivers. **Kwando** is a massive reserve with only two camps; one of them, Lebala, is rated as one of the best in Botswana. **Chobe Enclave**—a private concession featuring one of our favorite owner-run camps and a great walking safari—is an excellent value. The pick of the bunch is **Linyati,** comprising only three exclusive camps. Like elsewhere, the private reserves are not fenced off from national parks, so animals migrate freely between them. These camps are best during the dry season, when the perennial waters of the Kwando and Linyanti rivers attract thirsty game.

ESSENTIALS

VISITOR INFORMATION See "Visitor Information," at the start of the chapter. For information and reservations, go to "Specialist Safaris & Operators," earlier in the chapter, or one of the camp listings below.

GETTING THERE **By Plane** Access is typically by charter plane (from either Kasane or Maun), which can be arranged when booking your accommodations. **Kasane International Airport** (✆ **267/625-0133**) is 3km (1¾ miles) from the entrance to Chobe National Park. **Air Botswana** has connections from Gaborone, Maun, and Johannesburg. See "By Plane" under "Getting There & Getting Around," in chapter 3, for more information on flying into Botswana.

By Car From Victoria Falls, there's a road heading southwest to Kasane, a 40- to 45-minute drive away.

GETTING AROUND Again, it is recommended that you prearrange all transfers, including a possible trip to Vic Falls, with your lodge or safari operator.

WHERE TO STAY & DINE

Just a few minutes from Kasane International Airport, Chobe National Park's 35km (22 miles) of river frontage is conveniently close to the Zimbabwe and Zambia borders, making Victoria Falls day trips possible. As a result, it's a tourist-heavy area. With the exception of the superb Chobe Chilwero and Savute Elephant Park, reviewed below, we recommend that you opt for one of the lodges on private reserves in and around the greater Chobe region, particularly on the rivers in the Linyanti, a safari area to the north of Okavango, or Kwando Reserves. The Linyanti riverfront is similar to that of the Chobe, with open floodplains and riverine forest. Many rate it as high or higher than the Delta: A massive 500,000 hectare area, Linyanti comprises only three private concessions with a combined limit of 100 guests at a time, making for a genuine wilderness experience with less tourist traffic.

Near Kasane, Along the Chobe River

Chobe Chilwero ★★★ One of Botswana's most luxurious safari lodges, this Abercrombie & Kent–affiliated property overlooks the Chobe River and is just a few minutes from the main gates of Chobe National Park. Organized activities include game drives into the park, sunset boat cruises along the Chobe River (weather dependent), and day trips to Victoria Falls—this is the place to stay if you want to include a trip to the falls without staying overnight there. Accommodations are in spacious, high thatch-roofed private cottages with massive bathrooms that feature sunken hand-hewn tubs, and indoor and outdoor showers. A private garden and/or private balcony provides wonderful views over the Chobe River islands and flood plains as far as Namibia. A spa, opened in 2007, completes the experience.

Reservations: Sanctuary Lodges & Camps. ✆ **27/11/438-4500.** Fax 27/11/787-7658. www.sanctuarylodges.com. (see "Specialist Safaris & Operators," earlier in this chapter). 15 units. High season (June 16–Oct) $1,800 double; low season (Nov–June 15) $1,200 double. Rates are all-inclusive. MC, V. **Amenities:** Dining area; lounge; boat excursions; fishing; game drives; library; pool; spa; tours to Victoria Falls; wine cellar; free Wi-Fi. *In room:* A/C, hair dryer.

Chobe National Park

Chobe Under Canvas ★★ (Finds If you like being pampered but relish the idea of sleeping under canvas and showering in water that's been perfumed by woodsmoke, there is simply no better way to experience Chobe than to book a few nights in one of these elegant tented camps. Inspired by their Serengeti operation, this has all the hallmarks of &Beyond: elegantly styled tents and comfortable beds in carefully selected wilderness sites, excellent food, and superb service, including a private butler. With only six tents, it's an exclusive way to get really close to the wilderness. ***Note:*** &Beyond also offer Savute Under Canvas, a similar experience, also within the Park; it's a good idea to combine them.

Book through &Beyond (see "Specialist Safaris & Operators," earlier in this chapter). $700–$1,210 double. Rates are all-inclusive. DC, MC, V. **Amenities:** Dining/lounge area; bush walks; game drives.

Savute Elephant Camp ★★★ This distinguished Orient Express lodge is situated in the heart of the Chobe National Park, in the arid regions of the Kalahari sandveld. Chosen as the second-best camp in Botswana by *Travel + Leisure* in 2005, after renowned Mombo, it was completely overhauled in 2007. It's accessible only by chartered light aircraft, so a stay here allows you to experience the magnetic pull of water on wildlife, particularly elephants, in a region where water is scarce. Expect the standard Orient Express luxury: accommodations in air-conditioned tents with large private viewing decks and outside showers, plus one suite with full indoor and outdoor bathroom and plunge pool.

Book through Orient Express Safaris (see "Specialist Safaris & Operators," earlier in this chapter). 12 units. High season (July–Oct) $1,940 double; shoulder season Nov–Dec/Apr–June) $1,230/$1,450 double; low season (Jan–Mar) $1,060 double. Rates are all-inclusive. AE, MC, V. No children under 12 except by prior arrangement. **Amenities:** Dining and lounge areas; bar; airstrip; book and video library; game drives; heated pool; room service; VHS video and monitor. *In room:* A/C, fan, hair dryer, minibar.

Linyanti & Savuti Channel Area

Kings Pool Camp ★★★ This is Wilderness Safaris' premier camp in a private concession in the massive Linyanti reserve, just outside the western boundary of the Chobe National Park. Each of the nine large suites, built on raised teak decks, features the ultimate in luxury: a private plunge pool and *sala* (small pavilion) with wonderful views of the Kings Pool Lagoon. This waterway has great bird life and hippos, crocodiles, bushbucks, impalas, elephants, and sables. Game-viewing activities include drives in open 4WD vehicles, night drives, walks with a professional guide, and cruises along the Linyanti River in a double-decker boat (water levels permitting). A cheaper alternative is **Savuti Camp,** with the same game-viewing (it's also located in the sought-after Linyanti reserve) for almost half the price (see below).

Book through Wilderness Safaris (see "Specialist Safaris & Operators," earlier in this chapter). High season (June–Nov) $3,540 double; low season $2,050 double. Rates are all-inclusive. MC, V. Children 8–12 are permitted with prior arrangement. **Amenities:** Restaurant; bar; lounge; pool.

Linyanti Bush Camp ★★★ Value On the edge of the Linyati marshes, bordering the Chobe National Park, the Chobe Enclave sees huge concentrations of game in the winter months when water elsewhere is scarce. The only option within this area is this small, 12-bedded tented camp—and what an option! Personally run by owners Beks and Sophia, the tents offer understated luxury and superlative guides. Given the standard of game-viewing and accommodations (and the prices charged elsewhere), it also offers exceptional value. If you're relatively fit, you should consider a 3-night **Linyanti Walking Safari**—a rudimentary but maximally authentic bush experience (a maximum of 6 guests sleep in mobile tents). Should you require a family atmosphere in a private setting, consider the seasonal **Saile Tented Camp,** a small, 8-bedded camp on the concession that affords an exclusive and intimate experience.

Book through African Bush Camps. (see "Specialist Safaris & Operators," earlier in this chapter). High season (June–Oct) $1,450 double; low season (Nov–May) $900 double. Rates are all-inclusive. No credit cards. No children under 10. **Amenities:** Dining/lounge area; game drives; game walks.

Savuti Camp ★★ Value This tented camp, built along the Savute Channel, lies in a region known for its large number of predators, including lions. Activities include game drives, night drives, and walks. The channel has been dry for some years, but the grasslands here make great game-viewing, and the watering hole in front of the camp is very productive. Accommodations are in seven large walk-in tents. Major renovations in 2007 equipped all tents (and every seating in the restaurant) with a view of the watering hole—one of very few in the area, making it a magnet for animals.

Book through Wilderness Safaris (see "Specialist Safaris & Operators," earlier in this chapter). High season (June–Nov) $1,800; low season $1,200 double. Rates are all-inclusive. MC, V. No children under 8. **Amenities:** Dining area; bar; plunge pool.

Kwando Wilderness

Kwando Lagoon & Lebala ★★★ Kids The remote Kwando concession sprawls over more than 232,000 hectares (573,040 acres), making it one of the largest privately run wildlife areas in Africa. Noted for its large herds of elephants, especially during the winter months, the area has some 80km (50 miles) of river frontage on its eastern boundary and attracts big numbers of large cats, buffaloes, kudus, and tsessebes as well. If you want to spot Africa's rarest predator, the wild dog, this is the place to come, especially around the middle of the year, when a pack returns to den here for 2 to 3 months (they've been returning to Kwando for 8 years now); the lions here are also famous for their spectacular kills. With more than 320 species of birds recorded, this area is understandably popular with birders. Thanks to specialist guides for families, it's popular with parents as well. Kwando Safaris runs two luxury tented camps on the Kwando River: **Lagoon** ★★ and **Lebala** ★★★—although they're just 30km (19 miles) apart, the area is so wild that the trip takes 2 hours. Both camps accommodate only 16 guests, in stilted en-suite safari tents with hot running water, flush toilets, and double basins; Lebala is more luxurious and features Victorian bathtubs and open-air showers. Both camps offer morning and night drives, as well as boat cruises and fishing expeditions to catch the famed tiger fish at Lagoon. A number of the guides are keen, award-winning photographers. Kwando also has two camps in the Delta—**Kwara** ★★★ (eight rooms), on a forested island in the remote northern part; the smaller and more exclusive **Little Kwara** ★★★ (five rooms); a camp in the Kalahari, **Tau Pan** ★★; and one in Nxai Pan: **Nxai Camp** ★★ (just eight purpose-built desert rooms), which represents excellent value in the Kalahari. All camps have a pool.

Book through Kwando Safaris (see "Specialist Safaris & Operators," earlier in this chapter). Lagoon Camp 8 units. Lebala Camp 8 units. Lebala: High season (June–Oct) $1,930 double; shoulder season (Apr–May, Nov) $1,340; low season (Mar) $1,048. Lagoon: High season $1,750; shoulder season $1,240; low season $984. AE, DC, MC, V. Rates are all-inclusive. **Amenities:** Dining area; lounge; boat and mokoro trips; fishing; game drives; pool; guided walks.

5 THE DRY SOUTH: MAKGADIKGADI & NXAI PANS

The Kalahari, one of the longest unbroken stretches of sand in the world, reaches across the center of Botswana, north into Zaire, and south to the Orange River in South Africa. On its northern edge are the enormous complexes of the Makgadikgadi Pans and the relatively small but no less interesting Nxai Pans, characterized by ancient baobabs and large camelthorn trees. Game migrates between the two throughout the year: In the dry season (Apr–Nov), Makgadikgadi is best; during the rains (Nov–Mar), the animals—which include springboks, gemsboks (oryx), red hartebeests, black backed jackals, and, occasionally, cheetahs and lions—move northward to Nxai.

The Makgadikgadi Pans are a vast (12,000-sq.-km/4,680-sq.-mile) game-filled expanse of flat, seasonally inundated land. When the pans fill with water after the rains, they host countless migratory birds, most notably huge flocks of flamingos. This is the place to go to experience space at its purest: The horizons seem endless, and, at night, above the pie-crust surface of the pans, the stars shine with a vibrancy found only in vast deserts.

ESSENTIALS

VISITOR INFORMATION The best safari operator here is **Uncharted Africa**—see "At a Glance: Safari Operators Specializing in Botswana," earlier in this chapter. For campsite reservations and more information, contact the **Department of Wildlife & National Parks** (www.botswanatourism.org).

GETTING THERE **By Plane** Your best bet is to fly to Maun and arrange a transfer with a tour company that arranges tours in the area (see "Getting Around," below), or deal directly with Uncharted Africa.

By Car It is not a good idea to venture onto the pans without a guide or a 4WD vehicle. You will find both in the towns of Gweta and Nata. These towns can be reached in 2 days from South Africa in a normal two-wheel-drive vehicle, and can be a useful stopover if you're driving to Maun.

GETTING AROUND **On a Guided Tour** For custom-made tours in the pans, contact **Uncharted Africa Safari Co., Moremi Safaris & Tours, Bush Ways, Penduka,** or **Footsteps in Africa** (see "At a Glance: Safari Operators Specializing in Botswana," earlier in this chapter, for contact details), or one of the other overland operators listed.

WHERE TO STAY & DINE

Besides the following choices, **Wilderness Safaris** (see specialist operators above) has recently opened a camp situated close to Deception Valley (a 3-hr. game drive transfer from the Deception Valley Lodge airstrip): **Kalahari Plains Camps** comprises just six Meru-style en-suite tents; like Deception Valley Lodge, they're raised off the ground to catch the breeze and take in the sweeping views across the Kalahari ($960–$1,150 double per night, all-inclusive). It's not in the same league as Jack's Camp, however.

Deception Valley Lodge ★★ This small lodge—comprising a new villa plus eight thatched units with Victorian-style bathrooms, outdoor showers, and a comfortable lounge—is situated near the northern border of the Central Kalahari Reserve and offers an excellent base from which to explore this vast, arid wilderness. Accommodations, done out in the hues and tones of the desert, are raised on stilts and linked to the lodge by walkways; from the deck, you can gaze over the vastness of the Kalahari, which you can also explore on afternoon and night drives when guests are taken out in search of lion, cheetah, leopard, various desert antelope, and the occasional brown hyena. Of particular interest are the guided walks with traditional Bushmen, providing an opportunity to experience how they draw on ancient knowledge to survive the inhospitable conditions of this dry wilderness.

Private Bag 114, Ste. 58, Maun, Botswana. ✆ **44/121/286-8393** or 27/82/355-6910. www.dvl.co.za or www.footsteps-in-africa.com. 8 units. High season (July–Oct) $1,600 double; shoulder season (Mar–June) $1,050 double; low season (Dec–Apr) $840 double. Rates are all-inclusive. AE, DISC, MC, V. No children under 12. **Amenities:** Dining/lounge area; game drives; library; pool; nature walks. *In room:* Fan, hair dryer, minibar.

Jack's Camp ★★★ (Moments) Jack's Camp is the place to go to experience the Kalahari in style. Deep in the desert, at the edge of the world's largest saltpans, accommodations comprise 10 en-suite open-air safari tents, and styling is Bedouin-meets-Africa, with Persian rugs and teak furniture providing a counterpoint to the endless desert surrounds. If you grow bored of lolling about on antique rugs, you can head out for game drives, walking safaris with Bushmen trackers, or explorations of remote archaeological sites and geological features. December through April sees the spectacular migration of massive wildebeest and zebra herds, followed by hungry predators. Besides standard trips in custom 4WD vehicles, adventurous winter guests can take guided rides across the saltpans on quad bikes to **Kubu Island** ★★ and sleep for 2 nights under the stars amid the surreal desert boulders and baobabs, or experience "God's minimalism" at romantic **San Camp** ★★★. Count on outstanding staff, including qualified zoologists and biologists, Bushman trackers, and charming and well-trained local guides. All have been thoroughly trained by the very glamorous owner Ralph Bousfield (the camp is named for his father), whose 13-part Discovery Channel series has made him one of the most famous guides in Botswana. ***Note:*** The camp has no electricity (lighting is fueled by paraffin) and no pool.

Book through Uncharted Africa Safari Co. (see "Specialist Safaris & Operators," earlier in this chapter). Jack's Camp 10 units. High season (Apr 16–Oct) $2,500 double; low season (Jan–Apr 15); Nov–Dec $2,000. San/Kubu $1,960; closed Nov–Mar. Rates are all-inclusive. Only cash is accepted in camp. **Amenities:** Drinks tent; mess tent; tea tent; game drives; game/nature walks; library; museum; quad biking; cultural/historical tours.

Planet Baobab ★★ Value Kids Imagine a giant anthill with a Planet Hollywood look-alike sign, a bar with a beer-bottle chandelier, and funkily decorated mud and grass huts in a grove of eight ancient baobab trees. Planet Baobab provides a fun base for younger budget travelers to explore the fascinating Makgadikgadi Pans. Guests can take guided walks with the San through the plants and trees of this fascinating area, or ride 4WD quad bikes over the salt pans during the dry season. Although you can opt to stay in a Bushman grass hut, you'll be better off in one of the traditional Bakalanga mud huts, which have private bathrooms. Meals are available, but you can also buy or bring your own provisions and make use of the shared kitchen. Planet Baobab is accessible by road; it's off the main road to Maun, 15 minutes from Gweta, but most visitors fly in.

Book through Uncharted Africa Safari Co. (see "Specialist Safaris & Operators," earlier in this chapter). 14 units. Twin hut $155 double; family hut (sleeps 4) $227; camping $13 per person. Meals, drinks, and activities are extra. Ask about the various good-value itineraries. MC, V. **Amenities:** Dining area; bar; camping facilities; expeditions; communal kitchen; pool; quad biking; guided walks.

13

Fast Facts

AREA CODES The country code for South Africa is **27,** for Zambia **260,** for Zimbabwe **263,** for Botswana **267.** Regional codes in South Africa: Cape Town/Western Cape is **021,** Johannesburg is **011,** Pretoria is **012,** Durban/Kwa-Zulu Natal is **031,** Eastern Cape is **041.**

AUTOMOBILE ORGANIZATIONS For South African road conditions and route planning, call the **Travel Information Centre** (✆ **27/11/799-14 00;** aasa@aasa.co.za; Mon–Fri 8am–5pm). For breakdowns, dial ✆ **083-843-22.**

DRIVING See "Getting There & Getting Around," in chapter 3.

ELECTRICITY Electricity in South Africa, Botswana, and Zambia is 230 volts, alternating at 50 cycles per second. Electrical sockets in Zimbabwe usually supply between 220 and 240 volts AC.

EMBASSIES & CONSULATES **South Africa's in the U.S.:** 3051 Massachusetts Ave. NW, Washington, DC 20008 (✆ **202/232-4400;** http://usaembassy.southafrica.net). **In Canada:** 15 Sussex Dr., Ottawa, ON, K1M 1M8 (✆ **613/744-0330;** fax 613/741-1639; www.DocuWeb.ca/SouthAfrica). **In the U.K.:** South Africa House, Trafalgar Square, London WC2N 5DP (✆ **020/7451-7299;** fax 020/7451-7284; www.southafricahouse.com). **In Australia:** Corner State Circle and Rhodes Place, Yarralumla ACT 2600 (✆ **02/6273-2424,** -25, -26, -27; www.rsa.emb.gov.au).

Zambia in the U.S.: 2419 Massachusetts Ave. NW, Washington, DC (✆ **202/265-9717**). **In the U.K.:** 2 Palace Gate, Kensington, London W8 5NG (✆ **020/7589-6655;** fax 020/7581-1353).

Zimbabwe in the U.S.: 1608 New Hampshire NW, Washington, DC 20009 (✆ **202/332-7100**). **In Canada:** 332 Somerset St. West, Ottawa, ON, K2P 0J9 (✆ **613/237-4388;** fax 613/563-8269; www.DocuWeb.ca/Zimbabwe). **In the U.K.:** 429 Strand, London WC2R 0QE (✆ **020/7836-7755;** fax 020/7379-1167; http://ukinzimbabwe.fco.gov.uk/en/). **In Australia:** 11 Culgoa Circuit, O'Malley ACT 2606 (✆ **02/6286-2281;** fax 02/6290-1680).

Botswana in the U.S.: 1531–1533 New Hampshire Ave. NW, Washington, DC 20036 (✆ **202/244-4990,** -91; fax 202/244-4164). **In the U.K.:** 6 Stratford Place, London W1C 1AY (✆ **020/7499-0031;** fax 020/7495-8595). **In Australia:** 52 Culgoa Circuit, O'Malley ACT 2606 (✆ **02/6290-7500;** fax 02/6286-2566).

Embassies or Consulates in South Africa: U.S. Embassy: 877 Pretorius Street Arcadia, in Pretoria (✆ **27/12/342-1048;** fax 27/12/342-5504; http://southafrica.usembassy.gov). **Consulates:** No. 1 River St. (corner of River and Riviera roads), Killarney, Johannesburg (✆ **27/11/644-8000;** fax 27/11/646-6916); Broadway Industries Center, Heerengracht, Foreshore (✆ **27/21/421-4280;** fax 27/21/425-3014); Old Mutual Building, 31st floor, 303 West St. (✆ **27/31/305-7600;** fax 27/31/305-7691). **Canadian Embassy:** 1103 Arcadia St., Hatfield, Pretoria 0083 (✆ **27/12/422-3000;** fax 27/12/422-3052; **U.K. Embassy:** 255 Hill St., Arcadia 0002, Pretoria (✆ **27/12/483-1200;** fax 27/12/483-1302; http://ukinsouthafrica.fco.gov.uk/en/). **Australian Embassy:** 292 Orient St., Arcadia, Pretoria 0083 (✆ **27/12/342-3740;** fax 27/12/342-8442; www.australia.co.za).

EMERGENCIES **South Africa: ✆ 10177** ambulance, **✆ 10111** police and fire, **✆ 112** cellphone.

In Zambia: ✆ 999 police, **✆ 991** medical, **✆ 993** fire; **✆ 112** from mobiles.

In Zimbabwe: ✆ 999 for police, medical emergency, and fire.

GASOLINE (PETROL) See "Getting Around" in chapter 3.

HOLIDAYS Banks, government offices, post offices, and most museums are closed on the following legal national holidays: January 1 (New Year's Day); March 21 (Human Rights Day); Good Friday, Easter Sunday and Monday; April 27 (Founders/Freedom Day); May 1 (Workers Day); June 16 (Soweto/Youth Day); August 9 (Women's Day); September 24 (Heritage Day); December 16 (Day of Reconciliation); Christmas Day; and December 26 (Boxing Day). For more information on holidays, see "South Africa Calendar of Events," in chapter 3.

HOSPITALS See **www.netcare.co.za**, a collection of top private clinics throughout South Africa. See "Health" in chapter 3.

INSURANCE For information on traveler's insurance, trip cancellation insurance, and medical insurance while traveling, see www.frommers.com/planning.

INTERNET ACCESS See "Staying Connected" in chapter 3.

LEGAL AID If you are pulled over for a minor infraction (such as speeding), never attempt to pay the fine directly to a police officer; this could be construed as attempted bribery, a much more serious crime. Pay fines by mail or directly into the hands of the clerk of the court. If you're accused of a more serious offense, say and do nothing before consulting a lawyer. Once arrested, a person can make one telephone call to a party of his or her choice. International visitors should call your embassy or consulate.

MAIL You can post postcards and letters through your hotel, and they will invariably reach their destination. If you wish to post a parcel however, it is worth registering it (thereby getting a tracking number) at any local post office, or sending it with FedEx or UPS. Include zip codes when mailing items.

NEWSPAPERS & MAGAZINES The weekly ***Mail & Guardian*** (www.mg.co.za) is one of the most intelligent papers and comes out every Friday, with a comprehensive entertainment section. Local papers include the ***Star*** and the ***Sowetan,*** in Johannesburg; the ***Cape Times*** and ***Argus,*** in Cape Town; the ***Natal Mercury,*** in Durban; and the ***Eastern Province Herald,*** in Port Elizabeth. ***Business Day*** is South Africa's (very slim) version of the ***Wall Street Journal*** or ***Financial Times. Getaway*** (www.getawaytoafrica.com) is an excellent monthly travel magazine that covers destinations throughout Africa.

PASSPORTS See www.frommers.com/planning for information on how to obtain a passport.

For Residents of Australia Contact the **Australian Passport Information Service** at **✆ 131-232,** or visit the government website at www.passports.gov.au.

For Residents of Canada Contact the central **Passport Office,** Department of Foreign Affairs and International Trade, Ottawa, ON K1A 0G3 (**✆ 800/567-6868;** www.ppt.gc.ca).

For Residents of Ireland Contact the **Passport Office,** Setanta Centre, Molesworth Street, Dublin 2 (**✆ 01/671-1633;** www.irlgov.ie/iveagh).

For Residents of New Zealand Contact the **Passports Office** at **✆ 0800/225-050,** in New Zealand, or 04/474-8100; or log on to www.passports.govt.nz.

For Residents of the United Kingdom Visit your nearest passport office, major post office, or travel agency; contact the **United Kingdom Passport Service** at ✆ **0870/521-0410;** or search the website www.ukpa.gov.uk.

For Residents of the United States To find your regional passport office, either check the U.S. Department of State's website or call the **National Passport Information Center** toll-free number (✆ **877/487-2778**) for automated information.

POLICE South Africa: ✆ 10111 or ✆ 112 from mobile phones (soon also from fixed line phones).

SMOKING Smoking is not permitted in public enclosed places. Some restaurants have partitioned areas for smokers.

TAXES South Africa levies a 14% value-added tax (VAT) on most goods and services—make sure this is included in any quoted price (by law, items must be marked as clearly excluding VAT or having VAT included). Foreign visitors are not exempt for paying VAT on purchased goods. They may, however, claim back VAT paid on items taken out of the country when the total value exceeds R250. The refund may be lodged by presenting the tax invoice (make sure it has a VAT registration number on it) together with their passport to the VAT Refund Administrator's offices, which are situated at Johannesburg and Cape Town International Airports, as well as at visitor bureaus. Call ✆ **021/934-8675** to find locations and hours.

TELEPHONES See "Staying Connected" in chapter 3.

USEFUL TELEPHONE NUMBERS In South Africa, call directory assistance at ✆ **1023** for numbers in South Africa and ✆ **0903** for international numbers. **Computicket** (✆ **27/11/340-8000** in Johannesburg; ✆ **27/83/915-8000** in Cape Town and Durban) is a free national booking service that covers cinema and concert seats, as well as intercity bus tickets; payment can be made over the phone by credit card.

TIME Southern Africa is 2 hours ahead of GMT (that is, 7 hr. ahead of Eastern Standard Time).

TIPPING Add 10% to 20% to your restaurant bill, 10% to your taxi. Porters get around R5 per bag. There are no self-serve garages or gas stations; when filling up with fuel, tip the person around R2 to R5; this is also what you tip informal car guards (identified by their neon bib) who look after cars on the street. It's also worth leaving some money for the person cleaning your hotel room. Be generous if you feel the service warrants it—this is one of the best ways to alleviate the poverty you may find distressing.

VISAS See chapter 3.

VISITOR INFORMATION **South Africa** South African Tourism (www.southafrica.net or www.southafrica.info).

In the U.S. 500 Fifth Ave., 20th Floor, Ste. 2040, New York, NY 10110 (✆ **212/730-2929;** info.us@southafrica.net). Brochure line ✆ **800/593-1318.** Los Angeles office ✆ **310/407-8642.** **In Canada** 4117 Lawrence Ave. E., Ste. 2, Ontario M1E 2S2 (✆ **0416/966-4059**). **In the U.K.** 6 Alt Grove, London SW19 4DZ (✆ **020/8971-9350;** info.uk@southafrica.net). Brochure line ✆ **0870/1550044.** **In Australia** 117 York St., Ste. 301, Level 3, Sydney, NSW 2000 (✆ **02-9261-5000;** info.au@southafrica.net). Brochure line ✆ **800/238-643.**

Useful websites include **ww.southafrica.net, www.southafrica.org, www.getawaytoafrica.co.za,** and **www.mg.co.za,** the home page for the *Mail & Guardian,* South Africa's best national weekly newspaper.

WATER South African tap water is safe to drink in all cities and most rural areas. Always ask in game reserves.

WEATHER See www.weathersa.co.za or call ✆ **082-162.**

INDEX